S0-CPE-199

by

**R. M. MASON**

Produced in the United States of America by the Transcript Printing Company; phototypeset by the author.

First Edition

10 9 8 7 6 5 4 3 2 1

For information address the publisher, Schoolhouse Press, 46 Mountain View Drive, Peterborough, NH 03458.

**Library of Congress Cataloging-in-Publication Data**
Mason, R. M. (Robert Marion), 1928-
Modern methods of music analysis using computers.
Bibliography: p.
Includes index.
1. Musical analysis — Data processing. I. Title.
MT6.M3453M6 1985 781'.028'5 85-26142
ISBN 0-9615669-0-6

# Preface

This book describes a simple means of utilizing a digital computer to analyze music. It contains compact descriptions of some of the theoretical tools needed for this purpose. The text is arranged as a series of closely interrelated parts that concern an extended investigation into the basics of automated, as distinguished from automatic, musical data processing. Included are theoretical derivations, computer program descriptions, and discussions of mathematical modeling principles. Charts (some in polar form), tables, and block diagrams are presented to impart to the reader an understanding of the structure of music analysis programs and of the philosophy of their use, as well as to describe the motivations and justifications of the novel aspects of the musical theory that is implemented. Within the scope of the book, however, it is impossible to discuss all of the factors that define such a study, or even to discuss the feasibility of applying computing machinery to musical research in general.

From the point of view of source materials, there is little doubt that automated music analysis is a necessity, and yet from the point of view of computer hardware and software, there are still many questions to answer, difficult questions that will challenge talented people's imaginations for years to come. For this reason, rather than any other, this book deals primarily with computer algorithms and not with the hardware and software systems for implementing them.

The book is divided into two parts. The first part begins by recalling some elementary facts about harmonies and sonorities, which were published earlier by the author in the *Journal of Research in Music Education*. These facts are used repeatedly and extended in some of the constructions in this book. The problem of music orthography next receives some careful deliberation. The task of teaching a computer musical spelling is made easier because the twelve-tone equitempered system fixes the number of possible harmonies at 4096 and the number of sonorities at 352.

The second and main part of the book consists of seven chapters each dealing with a subject of intrinsic importance for developing the necessary computer methodology. The material presented here encompasses the broad areas of tonality, polytonality, and atonality. The mathematical theory provides a vivid unified explanation of keys, chromaticity, modulation, and other features that are paramount in the general theory of music.

This book as a whole is a suitable text for a one-semester course in music analysis by computers, or as the basis of a graduate seminar in analytic tonality. Much of it may be regarded as foundation material for work on more advanced levels. It is for this reason that exercises have been interspersed where appropriate throughout the text. Answers to the few exercises that apparently do not relate to the text usually can be obtained from the literature, by individual study, or through group discussion. Special effort has been made to develop the theory so as to bring the reader to the frontiers of the subject and to prepare him or her for conducting independent musical research using computers.

I am grateful to Kenneth Durbin for reading the manuscript and making many helpful comments.

ROBERT MARION MASON

April 1985

Peterborough, New Hampshire

# Contents

Page

PART II-Con.

CHAPTER SIX - Modulation



CHAPTER SEVEN - Modeling



CHAPTER EIGHT - Methodology



CHAPTER NINE - Mechanization

*Supposing, for instance, that the fundamental relations of pitched sounds in the science of harmony and of musical composition were susceptible of such expression and adaptations, the engine might compose elaborate and scientific pieces of music of any degree of complexity or extent.*

*ADA AUGUSTA LOVELACE, Notes to L. F. Menabra's Memoir, 1842*

PART I

# Chapter 1 Introduction

## ELECTRONIC MUSIC

Undoubtedly, the tiny yet powerful electron is shaping the world's musical future. Sound engineers in many countries are actively engaged in audio signal processing activities. Contemporary composers, primarily working in academic or industrial settings, also are using the tools commonly found in electronic music studios today. They are using them to create original music for radio and television broadcasting or for cinematic and video soundtracks. Electronic music is becoming the backbone of mixed and multimedia presentations. And, it has become fashionable in the arts of theater and dance.

Recording artists and even music theoreticians currently depend on a dizzying array of interesting and complicated electric and electronic devices. Just listing some of these devices will provide a rough idea of the increasing importance of electronics in fields of musical endeavor.

In the first category are familiar consumer items: the electric guitars, electronic organs, metronomes, and single or multichannel magnetic tape recorders. Because of their unwonted uses in experimental music, microphones, loudspeakers, phonographs, radio receivers, and television sets may be added here.

In the next category come electronic components, along with other pieces of laboratory apparatus: photocells, adders, multipliers, dividers, sound level meters, differentiators, integrators, analog-to-digital (A/D) and digital-to-analog (D/A) converters, oscilloscopes, delay units, spectrum analyzers, and above all computers. Many of these items are combined in larger systems.

In the third category are to be found music synthesizer modules: tone generators, rotary and slide potentiometers, sequencers, switches, sample and hold circuits, and voltage processors. Included as well are electrostatic, electromagnetic, and photoelectric pickups, such voltage controlled devices as filtering circuits, solid-state amplifiers, or audio frequency oscillators, and digital ring modulators. Basically, a music synthesizer combines into one system a means of sound generation, a means of sound modification or transformation, and a control.

In the fourth and final category are listed miscellaneous components: mixers, scramblers, fuzz boxes, reverberation units, envelope shapers, noise generators (white, pink, and so on), variable function generators, and vocoders.

Attention is restricted to two fundamentally different ways of composing electronic music--by **patchwork** and by **calculation.** The first way, patchwork, which might be renamed "pattern juxtaposition," developed principally from magnetic tape music. This practice originated in a school of musical thought founded by Pierre Shaeffer in Paris in 1948. In tape music, or **musique concrète**, there is a penchant for capturing and treating natural or everyday (that is, "concrete") sounds along with sounds made by conventional musical instruments [1].

Many of the sounds used are loud industrial or military noises: steam whistles, factory machinery, foundries, explosions, or the discharge of guns. Added are the serene sounds of songbirds, brooks, and campfires. Some use is made of more agitated sounds like animal cries, storms at sea, or nearby thunder. Household sounds too are used, noises of plumbing, bottles, or tin cans. A wide selection of traffic noises is employed, including sirens, horns, and motors. Finally, much effective use is made of human voices, intelligible and unintelligible, those of hawkers, soapbox orators, and revivalists. Adults and children are recorded while singing, laughing, talking, or playing.

These vocal expressions, along with the other sounds encountered in daily activity, are recorded on tape and the resulting reels labeled and filed away in a taped collection. When the time arrives to construct a sound montage, various reels are retrieved and their contents identified. Assorted snippets are cut to the required size and joined together. Great rhythmic precision can be attained during this process, as the duration of any sound event is directly proportional to the length of the corresponding tape segment. Another advantage is that the music can be viewed as a physical object rather than as a temporal one, and structured accordingly. The procedure is enhanced by invoking basic tricks of the trade, such as reversing the direction of some pieces of tape before connecting them, or speeding up and slowing down the tape motion during recording or in playback, or splicing the pieces together in unusual but thoughtful ways.

As it relies upon a mathematical formula, a graph, or a logical procedure, calculation--the second way of composing electronic music--might be termed "pattern production." This method of creativity goes beyond that of tape music because there is a preference for dealing purely with electronically generated sounds. As in much modern music, however, there is a predilection by some composers for nondescript noises also, which are layered, or stratified, or given the semblance of pitch, or of pitch scales in semitones or smaller microtones.

Repetitive patterns of sound often are used in modern music, whether electronic, or conventional, or a combination of the two. Sometimes these are generated by tape loops, or by the delay and feedback of recorded signals. Deep concentration often is required to perform such music on stage. In some musical passages the separate phrases or cyclic figures are not of the same length, so that many variations are produced by simple repetition before the separate parts arrive together under conditions identical to those at the start. This situation will occur at a distance into the composition equal to the least common multiple of the phrase lengths. Quite a pleasant effect can be achieved in the tonal relationships of the parts as the repeated figures shift slowly in and out of phase.

Although much of today's music, its impact dulled a bit by many more striking achievements of the space age, sometimes tries to compensate with programmed cacophony for what it still lacks in inspiration, once in awhile in the realm of electronic music can be heard an incipient

**NOTE:** Numbers (integers) in square brackets indicate references listed at the end of the chapter.

strength or a nascent grace that could foreshadow the rebirth of true musical majesty. A prime example is a serious commissioned work, TIME's ENCOMIUM for Synthesized & Processed Synthesized Sound (Nonesuch H 71225), a totally electronic composition by Charles Wuorinen, which in 1970 won a Pulitzer prize for music. The composition was done on the large RCA synthesizer at the Columbia-Princeton Center.

## EXERCISES

1.1 Trace the development of (a) Dutch electronic music starting with the work of composer Henk Badings, (b) German electronic music starting with the work of Herbert Eimert and his associates, (c) European music concrète beginning with the French composer Pierre Schaeffer and including the work of English composer Daphne Oram, and (d) Japanese tape and electronic music starting with the work of Toshiro Mayuzumi.

1.2 It is hard to realize that sound recording, in some form or other has been a part of everyday living for over a century. (Thomas Edison, cylinder phonograph, 1877; Emile Berliner, flat disk phonograph, 1896; Valdenar Poulsen, magnetic recording machine, 1898) Suppose that a standard instrumental solo originally recorded at a tape speed of 7.5 inches per second (ips) is replayed at 15 ips. What three things will happen? How can these same effects be achieved separately?

1.3 (a) What is magnetic tape dubbing? (b) Explain in detail how to use tape cutting and splicing to obtain at least five special musical effects. List and discuss some other classic recording studio manipulations that have been applied in editing and creating tape music.

## COMPUTER HARDWARE

Computers come in various sizes and configurations. Today, some of the smallest of these machines, having performance ratings in millions of instructions per second, are fully as powerful as the early Univac, yet they are easier to use and much less expensive. The coming of low-cost microcomputers at the lower end of the performance scale has encouraged the development of new methods for teaching. So it is no wonder that microcomputers have entered every grade school level; moreover, they are not unfamiliar to preschool children.

Computer hardware consists of three essential parts: namely, the central processing unit (CPU), some form of internal memory, and other devices linked to the CPU for input/output (I/O) and for mass storage. The CPU--essentially an arithmetic logic unit (ALU) plus its control--executes instructions in binary-coded machine language, unquestionably the lowest linguistic level, and transfers information to and from memory. Usually these functions are independently performed under the control of an operating system, which manages the computer's activities and its peripheral environment.

The computer memory holds data to be processed and instructions that the computer must execute to carry out the steps of a program. Really the computer knows how to perform only instructions written in machine language, that is, instructions built into the hardware of the machine. All problems coded in higher level languages must be translated before they can be undertaken.

Necessary information is read in from input media (cards, tapes, or disks) and then held in memory by magnetic techniques. Usual acronyms for distinguishing among common types of high-speed computer memory elements are:

RAM Random Access

ROM Read only
PROM Programmable Read Only
EPROM Erasable Programmable Read Only
EEPROM Electrically Erasable Programmable Read Only
UVEPROM Ultraviolet Erasable Programmable Read Only

Slower speed storage devices include magnetic tapes, hard disks, and magnetic drums.

RAM is both readable and writeable. It is a microprocessor chip used for temporary storage of information. RAM is classed as "volatile" because its contents are lost when machine power is turned off. Today, computer software items (programs and data) are usually stored on disk and then loaded into the internal RAM. Random access allows data to be stored arbitrarily and to be retrieved directly by specifying the address location. Once the power is disconnected, a volatile memory permanently loses all information that is stored in it.

ROM, another memory device, does not lose its information when the power supply is interrupted. It is a special kind of unerasable memory for storage of fixed sets of instructions and numerical constants comprising computer programs, called "firmware." As it is impossible to write into ROM, the instructions can never be changed. Sometimes the manufacturer provides ROMs as plug-in modules. In this manner several versions of special programs are made available.

PROM is a blank chip that is user programmable at the manufacturing site using electrical pulses from a PROM burner. Once programmed, it cannot be either erased or revised. EPROM is an improvement on PROM that can be reprogrammed after it has been erased, either electrically (EEPROM) or with ultraviolet light (UVEPROM).

A **terminal** is a unit of hardware bridging the human/computer interface. It provides for a two-way flow of information and services and can be attached to a host computer to join large networks of concurrent users. In the area of musicology, interactive terminals can be used for specialized tasks such as preparing teaching materials, retrieving bibliographic information, testing hypotheses, writing new programs, and composing and analyzing music. With the passage of time computer video display terminals (VDTs) are becoming more intelligent, as they continue to acquire additional nice features. A partial listing would include detachable upper/lower case alphanumeric keyboards with international and specialized character sets, separate numeric and cursor control keypads, reverse video, a split screen, flash, blank, underline, and half-intensity options, touch-sensitive screens that tilt and swivel, user adjustable communications, integral modems, local processing capability, full editing with insertion and deletion of characters or lines, separate function keys for nonvolatile user-programmable applications, voice recognition, several pages of RAM, monochrome or color graphics, printer ports, self-test diagnostics, one or more floppy disk drives, bar code scanning devices, and possibly hard disk files.

EXERCISES

1.4 Some background is essential for understanding how a computer controls and interacts with other devices. After consulting several standard programming textbooks, write a brief description of these basic computer elements: (a) the control section, including logic for sequencing of instructions; (b) the arithmetic section, including number representation systems and binary arithmetic; (c) the storage section, including memory addressing modes, size, cycle time, and parity checking; (d) the I/O section, including card readers, line printers, card punches, and magnetic tape units; and (e) the operator console, including job processing and diagnostic routines.

1.5 The range of existing input devices includes data files, digitizing panels, joysticks, track balls, programmable keyboards, the mouse, light pens, touch panels, and menu tablets. Describe these and tell how each might be used in a musical application.

1.6 Classes of hard-copy output devices include pen plotters, printer plotters, cathode ray tube (CRT) copiers, impact graphics printers, and camera systems. Describe these and tell how each might be used in a musical application.

1.7 There are several kinds of printers on the market, including electrostatic, impact, inkjet, laser, and thermal. Describe two. Which ones listed produce letter quality text? Which ones would be most suitable for preparing musical scores for publication?

1.8 Four properties of mass storage devices are average access time, transfer rate, capacity, and addressability. Define these terms and relate them to currently available equipment.

1.9 Illustrate how a stored program can cause its own instructions to be modified. Tell why this is important.

1.10 Three types of computer graphics display devices now rely on raster, vector, and direct view video storage tubes. Of these, the vector type is best suited for drawing geometrical figures. How many characters can be displayed on the screen of a typical alphanumeric CRT display terminal? (Hint. Give the dimensions of the display area, number of characters per line, and number of lines per display.)

## COMPUTER SOFTWARE

A "bit" is a binary digit--always either a zero, 0, or a one, 1. A "computer word" is comprised of groupings of bits representing numerical digits, upper and lower case letters of the alphabet, and other special characters. The length of these words is usually fixed at one to eight characters. Two prominent coding schemes are ASCII (American Standard Code for Information Exchange) and EBCDIC (Extended Binary-Coded Decimal Interchange Code). Both schemes can represent 256 different eight-bit characters.

A computer program or **routine** is a set of instructions for accomplishing a specific task. A **subroutine** is a sequence of related instructions that are executed when it is called by a main program.

A computer programming **language** is a standard set of symbols and rules of syntax used for communication and data retention within computer systems or networks. An assembly routine, or **assembler**, is used to read a symbolic language source program which amounts to a machine-language representation of data and instructions that is relocatable. It translates this language into binary code that can be directly understood and then executed by the computer. Assembler use is generally reserved for system development, for which binary machine-dependent operations are required that are not found in the higher-level compiler languages such as Cobol or Fortran.

A compiling program, or **compiler**, reads symbolic language source programs and converts them entirely to an equivalent machine language object program. Compiler languages like Fortran, Cobol, Algol, Pascal, PL/1, and so on, have a problem-oriented syntax and so avoid reference to machine architecture. An interpretive routine, or **interpreter**, on the other hand, converts each line of a program into machine code every time it is encountered. Programs written in some languages, Basic for example, might be either compiled or interpreted depending upon the power of the computer.

ALGOL is an influential, efficient, science-oriented algebraic language. It is designed for communicating algorithms.

APL is a terse, mathematics-oriented language, well suited for operating on data arrays. Internationally known, it provides operators for manipulating vectors and matrices. Moreover, it has been used successfully in scientific applications, text editing, information retrieval, systems programming, data processing, and hardware description.

BASIC is a general computational language, which avoids unnecessary details. Particularly adaptable to timesharing, it finds widespread applications in schools, colleges, and small businesses. Because it is simple and natural, it has become the standard microcomputer programming language. Very often used by engineers and mathematicians, the Basic system can translate formulas from mathematical language into machine language. More advanced capabilities of Basic include file or string manipulation, formatted output, functions, and matrix statements.

"C" is a portable language (that is, easy to implement on various machines), which affords an attractive alternative to Pascal.

COBOL is a well known computer programming language based on English expressions, which is used most often for I/O, data manipulation, basic mathematical functions, and report generation. Designed primarily for data processing applications, it is especially suited for file maintenance tasks and keeping financial records.

FORTH is an interactive data definition language used for data acquisition and process control. A Forth program can be developed in an interpretive mode. After it has been codechecked, it can be compiled to increase its efficiency.

FORTRAN is a universal, problem-oriented programming language useful in solving algebraic equations and evaluating special mathematical functions such as arise in various scientific, engineering, and biomedical applications. Fortran is easy enough to learn, but at the same time it is considerably more difficult than Basic. A Fortran compiler also may generate a symbolic listing of the machine-language object program it creates. Optimization algorithms often are available from the vendor for minimizing object program size and execution time.

LISP is a functional programming language, based on recursion, used extensively by artificial intelligence (AI) researchers for organizing and controlling large collections of facts and ideas (a knowledge base). Lisp executes symbolic expressions (called "S-expressions") and it has been applied to symbolic derivations in both differential and integral calculus, as well as playing games like chess, formulating electric circuit theory, and discovering and proving theorems in mathematical logic. Programs written in Lisp can be compiled or interpreted. The many existing nonstandard versions of Lisp include MacLisp, InterLisp, Zeta Lisp, Common Lisp, Franz Lisp, and MuLisp. For efficiency, the language requires a specialized host computer.

MODULA-2 is an improved successor to Pascal language. Modula-2 relies extensively on structured, modular concepts.

PASCAL, which is a quite highly structured language, is useful in business, scientific, and systems programming. Although it provides for advanced techniques such as nested recursive procedure calls, it has deficiencies, some of which were corrected in Modula-2. Commercial implementations exist for computers of all sizes.

**PL/1** is a modular, multipurpose programming language that contains substantially all of the capabilities of Algol, Cobol, and Fortran, plus provisions for string manipulation and list processing. Consequently it can be used for both scientific and mathematical calculations as well as general information processing.

**PROLOG** is a Lisp-competitive mostly nonprocedural language, which is based on first-order predicate logic. Typical applications lie in the field of artificial intelligence, especially with expert systems and knowledge database systems.

**SNOBOL** is a character string manipulating language designed to handle nonnumerical data. Snobol has been applied to research studies in the humanities and the social sciences, including fields such as library science, cryptoanalysis, linguistics, music, psychological modeling, and theorem proving, since it is well suited to rearranging strings and searching for patterns.

Three modes of computer operation are recognized. These are **real time** processing, in which the computer must be able to respond to external stimuli (events) sufficiently fast to achieve aims; **batch** processing, in which problems generally are not run immediately, but rather are queued in backlog by priority and the order of runs is chosen by the operating system according to a prescribed schedule; and **interactive** or **demand** processing in which one or more users may enter into dialog with the computer in foreground more or less concurrently with a batch run as background.

## EXERCISES

1.11 What is an operating system? How does one work? Name an example. How is it used? What are its strengths and weaknesses?

1.12 Describe certain auxiliary functions that an assembler should provide, which might be useful in the development of a program for music synthesis requiring computer control over machine storage and timing.

1.13 (a) What advantages are shared by all high-level programming languages? (b) How does a nonprocedural programming language differ from a procedural one?

1.14 In Basic, give examples of (a) statement types and command types, (b) mathematical functions and string functions, (c) integer arithmetic and floating-point arithmetic.

1.15 List some Fortran subroutines that should be included in a program library to support acoustics research. Explain why each entry is important.

1.16 As noted earlier, the list processor language Lisp has figured prominently as a vehicle of research in artificial intelligence. Applications of work in this field include expert advisor systems for drilling oil wells, medical diagnosis and prescription, financial analysis, and the deduction of chemical structures from mass-spectronomy data. Give examples of the use of Lisp in two areas of the humanities.

1.17 (a) Define the following programming terms: array, string, list, and tree. (b) Illustrate how these internal data structures model external data structures.

1.18 (a) Give an example of the concatenation of character strings. (b) In how many ways can three different strings be concatenated? (c) How are strings processed by Snobol? (d) Provide illustrations of pattern shifting, matching, and deletion.

## TIMESHARING

In a timesharing environment the work can be accomplished at some distance from the central computer site. This is a particularly convenient arrangement for music analysis by computers. The CPU processes the input from one or more remote workstations in a conversational manner. The computer timesharing monitor routine can call various processors such as the Fortran and Cobol compilers, and may include several diagnostic or help facilities and a desk-calculator mode. The terminal may be essentially a typewriter; or, it may provide a video display. Used for communicating with any commercial or university timesharing service, these devices nowadays are procurable at a reasonable expense through lease or purchase. They allow the user to dial up and connect to a remote computer by means of either a standard private telephone or a dedicated line. Usually such a system performs quite smoothly, giving perhaps several hundred simultaneous users the illusion of having their own private individual computer. One major factor in the growth of timesharing usage is the extra power to build programs made available via such conversational interaction.

Here is a short explanation of how timesharing works, viewed from the standpoint of the customer. A typical user has access to a remote terminal in his or her work area. This terminal is equipped with a keyboard like that of an ordinary office typewriter. To obtain a solution to some problem already programmed, the user switches on the terminal, picks up the telephone, and calls the computer center, using a regular voice-grade line. Often an acoustic coupler or modem (modulator/demodulator) is used to interface the terminal to the telephone line. Upon receiving a high pitched connect tone, the user then cradles the telephone handset in the indentation on top or at the side of the modem. At this point, work begins.

Before executing any program from a remote terminal, the user must provide identification to the timesharing computer by providing his or her user number and also give the correct password when interrogated. Next, it is necessary for the user to specify the subsystem or language to be used. Finally, the user has to notify the computer of the old or new problem name or some other project identification. After he or she has completed these few simple log-in procedures, which establish user identity, the required subsystem, and the right program, the user continues to converse with the timesharing system telling it how to manipulate data files or programs, and when to call forth different programs and create new files. This is accomplished by entering various system commands and task-oriented instructions necessary to process the data.

Timesharing terminals and communication networks allow individual users to share very expensive computer systems by having each user contribute to the cost. System logs, usage records, and charge accounts are kept by the central processor. Consequently, a portion of the cost of timesharing is due to overhead.

## EXERCISES

**1.19** What operational commands are required, with either Basic or Fortran, to cause a timesharing system to (a) run a program, (b) stop printing, (c) save a program for later use, (d) destroy a previously saved program, (e) erase a current program and start a new one, (f) rename a program, or (g) combine two programs.

**1.20** State and give the interpretation of twenty-four different error messages that might be encountered in a timesharing session.

**1.21** Cite difficulties that have been experienced by music researchers in bridging successive generation gaps in computer systems hardware and software.

## MICROCOMPUTERS

Desktop computers can provide an attractive alternative to common time-sharing terminals or minicomputers, especially in the home music studio environment. The first commercially available unit (the MITS "altair") was introduced in 1974 in kit form for electronics students. This event marked the beginning of the personal computer (PC) era. Over the next decade the PC evolved from a toy assembled by hobbyists to a highly valued data- and word-processing tool for dedicated professional use by managers, scientists, engineers, or educators. Over the same period the technology of small computers has advanced substantially. Prices have lowered to the point where microcomputers for individual use are becoming commonplace, as are home entertainment and educational applications for black-and-white and color CRT display terminals and monitors. Music teachers should not underestimate the value of PCs, even those that rely on just a TV speaker for sound production and are limited to three or four tone generators and a range of several octaves.

The new microprocessor technology allows the neophyte composer (as well as the established musician) to achieve, through the application of elementary computer methods, greater mastery of the tonal alphabet. Usually the cost of add-on music-synthesis hardware and software does not significantly exceed the cost of the basic small computer system, and costs seem to be coming down. Numerous other supporting products, at a price, meet various music research requirements. Among them are Winchester disks (inflexible, nonremovable platters hermetically sealed in plastic containers), diskettes (floppies), tape drives, floating-point speed enhancements, plotting and hardcopy devices, networking and communication options, such as a modem to permit direct electrical connection of a PC to standard telephone lines for either full-duplex (simultaneous two-way) or half-duplex (one-way either way) communications, and so on.

The microcomputer is a relatively new and promising analytical tool for use by musicologists. Proficiency in its use requires a blend of knowledge, intuition, and programming skill. Computer-based research can involve sifting for specific answers. Unless care is taken in defining the problem, the answer could become covered up by an avalanche of statistical output. To derive real benefits from computer use, the analyst must achieve mastery of the study and retain firm control of the computation.

Most often, alphanumeric keyboards are used for computer input and magnetic media are used to retain musical data between runs. Punched cards are still in use, but on small systems programs and data now are reloaded from disks. Special typewriters or output printers may allow many ordinary musical characters to be written. For outputs requiring a graphical format, an X,Y plotter or a high-resolution vector graphics video display device with hard copy printer should be available too, so that output material can be made ready for visual presentation for purposes of monitoring or classroom demonstration.

It is possible for a musician seated at a graphics workstation to write a score with a stylus upon a fine-wire-grid input tablet, or with a light pen on a CRT display. Afterwards, the musician can either transpose, to any key, or otherwise modify what has been written by pushing function buttons, or by causing light pen interactions with a progressively displayed, prestored menu on the video screen. Forms of electronic information transfer could include printed text, handwritten or lithographed musical scores, normal speech, and high quality, spatially distributed sound sources.

## COMPUTERS IN MUSICAL RESEARCH

As defined in the National Foundation on the Arts and the Humanities Act of 1965, the term humanities covers the study of "language, both modern and classical; linguistics; literature; history; jurisprudence; philosophy; archeology; the history, criticism, theory and practice of the arts; and those aspects of the social sciences which have humanistic content and employ humanistic methods." Judging from the growing number of college computer courses, whether survey-type or discipline-oriented, computer methods are playing an enlarging role in many of these fields. During the 1960's especially, computers gained increased usage in applications to literature, linguistics, folklore, music, and the visual arts. Quite important musical applications were discovered in the development of systems of automatic bibliographical control and thematic indexing.

This trend is due in part to a change in the attitude of scholars towards computers. With the appearance on the market of a variety of small computing machines, the cloak of mystery that has surrounded such equipment in the past is disappearing rapidly. People now are beginning to take a more realistic view and are coming to see the value of computer assistance in analyzing stylistic patterns as well as in solving large-scale bibliographic and thematic problems.

In the field of music this change of attitude has manifested itself in two ways: it has stimulated experimental research into techniques for composing, or **music synthesis**, and it has brought about a deeper understanding of what it means to talk about music, or **music analysis**. The trained music analyst can gain very useful insights concerning many of the physical and dynamic processes occurring in the live performance of a musical composition from simply examining computer outputs.

Some aspects of research problems can be formulated mathematically or logically, so these parts can be relegated to machines for solution. This relieves the music theorist of the necessity for performing routine functions and permits him or her to concentrate on those thorny analytical problems in which judgment and deduction must be based on experience and intuition as well as on purely objective factors.

At present, much of the work in this area of computer music is of a tentative and experimental nature. As a science, music analysis using computers is fairly new, and no formal approach to creating methodology has been discovered. Nevertheless, after more than a decade's experience, this development seems to be of permanent usefulness. For instance, research groups working in computerized sound production under the direction of Mathews at the Bell Telephone Laboratories have obtained good experimental results involving the determination of psychoacoustical parameters of music, which encourages the belief that this kind of computer research may help to bring about new and significant advances in the understanding of certain basic musical phenomena. This work by Mathews, culminating in the development of the **Music 5** program (**Music 11** is a recent update), was paralleled, or has been followed, by many other research efforts in sound generation. Investigators during this period of early progress included, but were not limited to, Randall, Winham, and Howe at Princeton; Tenney at Yale; and Ferretti and Slawson at MIT [2]. Even so, the pyschophysiological properties of the human ear, the resolving power of the auditory cortex, and the sensitivity of hearing to tonality and changes in key, all deserve greater attention [3].

In many respects a comprehensive understanding by theoreticians as to how music develops lags far behind the intense exploration of musical ideas that has been undertaken by composers during this half of the twentieth century. Advantages to be achieved by using computers in musical research, which may tend to reduce the time lag, include the development of improved and more sophisticated theoretical procedures for music synthesis and analysis. In combination, the advances to be brought about through intelligent computer usage may tend to reduce the number of published, informal music analyses in which the results usually are presented in an unstructured manner with little concern for specific data or for quantitative information.

Despite the excellence and broad coverage of the articles published in **CHum** [4] and in the **Computer Music Journal** [5], it is difficult for anyone today to comprehend fully just what is happening in the developing world of musical research. As a rough guess, several hundreds of this nation's foremost musicologists, folklorists, composers, and acousticians already are finding electronic equipment and computer know-how to be invaluable aids in their attempts to piece together the fascinating puzzle of sound and music. Other countries too, such as Canada [6], have exceptional centers of activity where workers are approaching a wide range of challenging problems with great zest and intelligence. In this singular period of dramatic exploration, one almost can touch the drive, enthusiasm, and creativity of the modern human spirit as it goes after the personal excitement that is attached to this new area of musical endeavor.

Still, a major breakthrough does not yet appear likely. Limitations of conventional theory have inhibited the advance on many fronts. Music theorists--who now are thoroughly schooled in the analytic methods of Schenker--must learn to utilize other research techniques in order to realize the unique potential of small computers. What is available for assessing present computer methods for musical text processing, information retrieval, stylistic analysis, and sound generation is the user's opinion or evaluation of the extent to which the current pieces of software satisfy their purpose and provide for greater accomplishment.

Specialized programming languages for musical projects at present include ALMA, CLML, DARMS, IML-MIR, MUSE, MUSICOMP, MUSIC 11, SAM, SCORE, and TEMPO, all of which require first translating music into machine-readable format. Acceptance of these practical tools requires some flexibility on the part of the user who is forced to break temporarily with some of the traditional notational habits with which he or she has become so very much at ease.

It is safe to predict that the trend toward more music-oriented computer methods will continue with growing reliance upon universal programming languages such as Lisp or APL to make them computer independent. There will be steady progress in the creation and certification of new algorithms for the solution of musicological problems, influenced by such factors as the interchange of personnel among musical research centers, accompanied by more rapid progress in direct application of existing advanced software (list processors, string manipulators, or logic-based compilers) to facilitate interactive teamwork through computer timesharing networks.

The main objective of this text is to draw attention to several critical points of methodology, to classify various tasks that the computer can do, but not to dwell on computer programming, a subject well treated elsewhere. Books by Bateman, Forte, Hiller and Isaacson, Howe, Lincoln, Mathews, and Xenakis [7-13] contain useful collateral information about computer music and can be studied profitably.

## EXERCISES

1.22 Write an informal report summarizing the background and current status of a computer project in the humanities, not necessarily in the field of music. State the objectives, resources, projects, and achievements as they might carry over to future capabilities for music analysis generally. Include if possible, some reference to the design, development, testing, or evaluation of special systems.

1.23 Name at least one musical composition by each of the following: Milton Babbitt, Lejaren Hiller, Vladimir Ussachevsky, and Iannis Xenakis based on computer technology.

1.24 Describe the system for computer acceptance and playback of common musical notation developed by W. B. Barker and D. Cantor, which displays the familiar graphic symbols of musical notation on the face of CRT oscilloscopes.

1.25 Enormous quantities of good musical texts await the graduate student anxious to produce new bibliographies, concordances, indexes, composer attributions, etc. Cite at least one published article which deals with each of these techniques of musical research: (a) information retrieval, (b) textual analysis, (c) question answering, (d) statistical analysis, (e) preparation of lists and indexes, (f) analysis of chord relations, and (g) extraction of relevant numerical data.

1.26 Discuss the recent thematic and bibliographic work of Lawrence Bernstein, Barry Brook, Harry B. Lincoln, and Jan LaRue.

1.27 How are orchestral instruments defined when using the Music V sound generation program?

## STYLISTIC ANALYSIS

It would be natural to ask whether music is really a language, just as people sometimes say. If music is indeed a language, then clearly it must be semantically isolated, because it is impossible to translate a musical text into either Mandarin Chinese or into American English, or for that matter to translate a Chinese or English language text into music. Furthermore, the knack of writing good music is not based on following any formal linguistic system for which exact rules of syntax have been given. It might be countered that the explicitness of rules for strict counterpoint is sufficient for computer routines to be prepared for both its synthesis and its analysis. But as all good music must, counterpoint soon frees itself from strict confinement and reappears in florid fullness and variety.

With any analytical procedure, it is undeniably true that the particular techniques, approximations, and level of detail used depend as much on the specific objectives of the analysis as they do on the system being analyzed. The performance of a musical work essentially is seen to be a data reconstruction process by means of which the discretely coded musical information appearing as spots of ink on the pages of musical manuscript is converted into a continuous data format, ordered in time and carried as a sound pressure wave. To a good approximation, music making may be treated as a discrete or sampled-data process, by acoustically sampling the sound pressure wave successively at a fixed time interval specified by the analyst. This approach makes it possible to work strictly with finite sequences of numbers rather than with continuous functions of time.

Every musical composition may be regarded as a piece of temporal architecture. Superimposed on the structure is the message. The composer acts as a message source that produces finite, generally meaningful, sequences of elements drawn from a standard set. Consequently each musical phrase comes from a discrete source, that is, a source that produces messages from a finite vocabulary. It remains to find out, in terms of notes and measures, what characteristic properties are represented by these messages. Moreover, it remains to examine the phrasing and to search for the meaning. The analyst must remember throughout grammatic and semantic analysis that interpretation is relative. Compositions vary in both mood and complexity. Music always must be related to a particular composer, to a particular style, to a particular purpose, to a particular culture, and to a particular epoch. It is exceedingly difficult to mechanize music analysis completely, because of the many factors that are associated with a collection of notes and measures. For this reason it is impractical at present to attempt to construct a methodology for conducting a precise, global analysis using conventional techniques.

It would be pleasant to be able to determine to what extent a composer's work is written in an individual style. Does each musical message carry the hidden signature of its source? In partial answer to this question, it is fairly obvious from the statistical tables prepared by Budge [14] and from a recent study of stylistic organization in music of Josquin Des Prez that, for a sufficiently large collection of works by a single composer, strong characteristic features can become evident. But certainly, to establish exact discriminators of musical style that would be delicate enough to determine the influence of one composer, genre, or school on another must presuppose the establishment of a firm music theoretic foundation. To proceed rationally requires, if not mastery of the rules of melody, counterpoint, tonal harmony, and polyphony, at least some familiarity with examples of them.

Probably everyone will agree that composers are usually time limited individuals. Their creative faculties constitute computing devices with unique capacities of judgment and interpretation. Yet, the true nature of the artistic process is not known with certainty and does not appear to be governed by exact laws. Rules perpetually are broken because they often severely restrict the richness of musical utterance. In composing a fugue for example, part of the creative process evolves subconsciously, often beyond the understanding of the composer [15,16]. This occasionally results in works of surprising complexity, which is a challenge to untangle. It is reasonably clear that the tones comprising a favorite musical composition must have been fitted together by a design of some sort. Otherwise, the tonal disorganization would soon disorient and tire out the listener, rather than enhance enjoyment upon repeated hearings. A well written piece of music must communicate. It must stimulate the critical listener's mind, within limitations of cultural heritage and training. Also, it must satisfy the discerning music lover that it is a valid and relevant work within professional standards. To accomplish this, it must be performed artistically, expressively, and accurately.

There can be no easy solution to this multidimensional problem. That is why it is probably not possible for a computer to act as a music critic. To proceed as if there were just one musical truth, or just one valid analytic approach to take, would be like saying that the triangle is the only instrument of percussion that the world has ever known. In short, there is no single system of music analysis that can serve all purposes. This does not say, however, that a consistent, general, descriptive approach is inevitably foredoomed.

## EXERCISES

**1.28** What various meanings are attached to the word "language" by dictionary compilers, computer specialists, linguists, logicians, and music critics. Using the results of this survey, reinterpret and resolve two questions: "Is atonality a musical language? If it is a language, has it any other than an academic future?" [17]

**1.29** What if anything is wrong with the following reasoning: "There are several times as many different styles of composition as there are (or ever have been) composers. This is because each composer's style changes as he matures, and since Beethoven's expansion of classical forms, there has been less and less tendency to unify compositions."

**1.30** (a) Discuss the relative merits of single- versus multiple-pass methods for encoding music. (b) Describe the innovations in computer-assisted stylistic analysis contributed by Allen Forte, by Stefan M. Kostka, and by Lewis Lockwood and Arthur Mendel.

**1.31** List several composers by name along with sets of associated stylistic attributes that might be applied as a means for the specific identification of their work. Design a computer program that could test a given sample musical input with the slate of attributes to determine whether or not the sample was written by a member of the group of composers listed.

**1.32** It is always very difficult to predict from present efforts the specific direction of research in any field. Analyze and project trends in computer music on the basis of recent events, ongoing research, and major accomplishments.

## OUTLINE OF METHODOLOGY

During their research, musicologists must perform various time-consuming analyses pertaining to the formal design or to the communicative effectiveness of some particular musical selection in order to obtain the necessary critical information to prove their theoretical contentions. Although these undertakings permit the musicologist to come to grips meaningfully with the score, they may require a significant amount of time to complete, even with the help of a digital computer. Accepted methods of data preparation demand extensive human editing and data keying. So, when seeking computer assistance, careful planning and close coordination are almost always necessary to ensure that the costs are not prohibitive. When considered in the light of its purpose, each piece of music normally must be treated as a self-consistent entity. Often, much can be learned from a detailed note-by-note study of a brief passage. A small research budget can be stretched a long way if the attitude of the microbiologist is adopted, who often works with a drop of water and never with the whole ocean.

It goes almost without saying that generality in analytical procedures must characterize the computer methodology in order for it to cope with changes in musical objectives, style, and performance capabilities, such as have occurred throughout the entire history of musical development. To achieve this generality it is necessary to realize that, fundamentally, just three things are of primary importance and interest in music: (a) the cumulative effect of each of the actual tones that have sounded up to any given point of time, which is the composition; (b) the time rate of change of the composition as new tones cause its reorientation, which is the tonality; and (c) the time rate of change of tonality as new key alliances are formed, which is the modulation.

Shown in Fig. 1.1 is a flowchart providing a functional overview of the proposed computer methodology. The solid boxes represent the elements of computer software to which the present study is addressed. The first section, labeled INITIALIZATION, refers collectively to all of the preliminary steps that must be taken in order to set up a problem for computer solution. The main program must be selected and read into readily accessible storage along with all of the required subroutines. The chief reason for this is simply that some of the subroutines use inputs supplied by others and most of them produce outputs required by the main program itself. Initialization concludes with the input of musical data. These data normally include pitch and duration codes. In advanced work, they also may include the time signatures, key signatures, elements of articulation, dynamic indicators, expressive markings, or text.

Figure 1.1

Functional block diagram for music analysis.

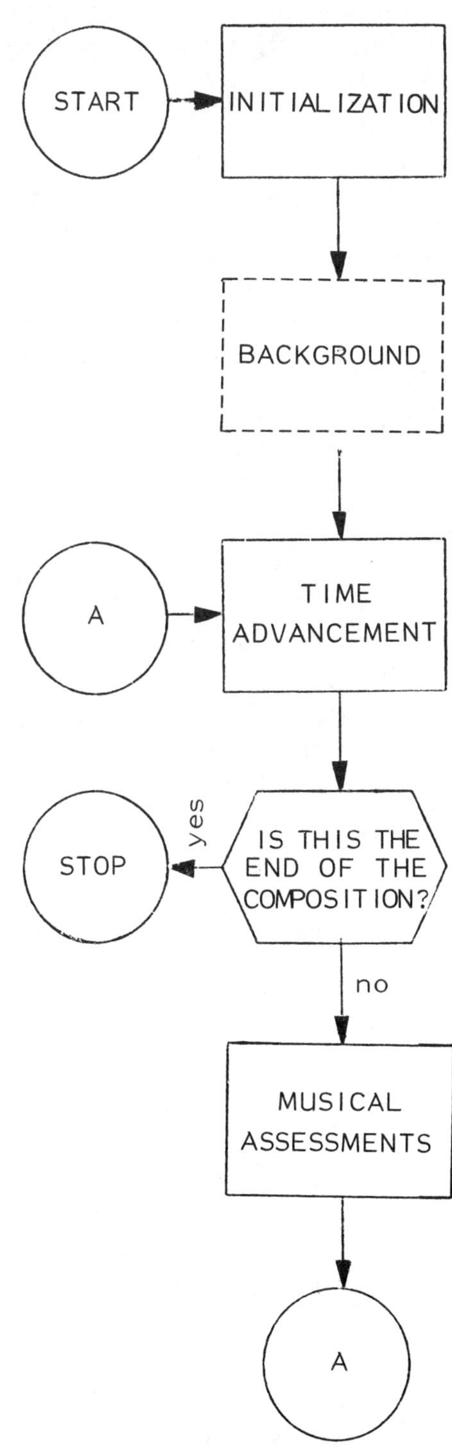


In certain types of analyses not dealt with in this book the computer would be informed of the historical setting of the subject matter. This information could be inserted in the second section represented by the block labeled BACKGROUND. Possibly, the information deemed essential to the study would be the names of the composer, lyricist, arranger, publisher, and critic; title, opus number, sources, geographical location, date of publication, date of copyright renewal, dedication, and price; the serial number, book and page, form, structure, modes, patterns, and relationships; geographical origin, location of autographed manuscript, ensemble configuration, the number of voices, instrumentation and characteristics, or range of vocal parts. Other intelligence could be inserted concerning the conditions existing when the composition was first written or performed. Occasionally a knowledge would be required of all the participants in a performance. The particular instrumentalists would be listed along with their degrees of excellence or other biographical data. To illustrate, if a singer has a phenomenal range, this fact might be important. If the work is theatrical, any preplanned stage action or gesture of dominating dramatic influence might be entered as a significant external event. In an opera, the appearance of the tenor stage left, for example, might indicate the beginning of a duet, or at least the addition of a part.

The third section is labeled TIME ADVANCEMENT, for it deals with the time parameter. Auditory impressions are fleeting and change significantly due to musical motion. Therefore, it is necessary in performance analysis to sample the acoustic pressure wave often enough to detect very quick changes. But, in manuscript analysis, the principal concern of this book, a musical score presents a complete chronology of events, so that it simplifies matters somewhat to take into consideration unequal timestep intervals, which elapse during the sounding of fixed components. This section is traversed repeatedly until the time value has advanced to reach the prespecified iteration limit, usually the end of the composition.

The fourth and final section is labeled MUSICAL ASSESSMENTS. In this section musical features are explored and factors relating to tonal interactions are interpreted. Certain false starts may be recognized and deleted. Among the many analytical processes that may be brought to bear during this part of the program are (1) the determination of intervallic content, harmonic designations, sonoral characteristics, chord specifications; and (2), the investigation of the basic properties of the musical motion--the amount of energy expended, the size and line of application of the tonal impulse, the amplitude and phase of the tonality, and so on. During the analysis, details of melodic, rhythmic, and harmonic structure are recorded. When the evaluation has been finished, the final results may be tabulated. A statistical summary might list, for instance, the number of occurrences of middle C, or the proportion of all cadences that are deceptive. It could contain frequency percentages, averages, or standard deviations of interest.

The music analysis programs, given in Chapter 9, print out summary data describing each musical passage under investigation. These data include harmonic designations and sonoral characteristics, which may be determined for each vertical structure (component chord or simultaneity) in the music under study. A small computer or programmable calculator has sufficient power to handle these tasks. An X,Y plotter will provide polar charts of tonal displacement as the musical composition advances. Instantaneous values of the tonality and tonal impulse also can be obtained using such a machine. Moreover, the tonality and modulation may be averaged over prescribed segments of the composition.

It may be worth mentioning, at this point, that the correct statement of intervallic content depends upon the musical passage being written with orthographic clarity and accuracy. Only after a chord or harmony has been rightly spelled, in or out of context, is it at all meaningful to ask if it is diatonic, or related to a given key signature. The key, which is at best an ambiguous concept, is essentially a function of mind involving the orientation or positioning of the listener's mindset. Assuming a few things about human thought processes amounting to a realization that music appreciation can involve no more than a finite memory, and quite possibly imperfect recall, it is possible to build a mathematical model with the power to deduce the key direction* from the observables in a musical passage.

---

*The customary term **key center** becomes synonymous with the term **key direction** used here, if the key centers are postulated to lie on the circumference of what geometers call the "circle at infinity."

## EXERCISES

**1.33** (a) What is meant by the term **musical incipit**? (**b**) How are encoded incipits arranged alphabetically? (**c**) What other arrangements are worth considering? (**d**) Why are incipits sometimes limited to eight notes? (**e**) How is an incipit related to a pitch contour? (**f**) How are incipit interval sequences arranged in numerical order? (**g**) How are musical properties of incipits transformed into mathematical properties of high degree polynomials.

**1.34** Using Snobol or some other string processing language, write a program to show if a sharp, flat, double sharp, or double flat occurs in a given incipit.

**1.35** Can the dynamic levels *ff*, *mf*, and *pp* be defined in isolation from any musical context?

**1.36** Devise a thorough checklist for computer-assisted music analysis that covers the significant elements of (**a**) melodic motion, and (**b**) harmonic progression. What would be required in order to extend it to treat artistic performance and musical effectiveness?

**1.37** Explain how cluster analysis can be applied in attempting to resolve questions of disputed authorship. Include, if necessary, aspects of the machine extraction of quantitative stylistic data.

**1.38** It is customary in music analysis to consider music as consisting of sequences of discrete units. Discuss the ingenious and efficient notational encoding systems (**a**) DARMS invented by Bauer-Mengelberg and Ferentz, (**b**) IML developed by Howe and Jones, and (**c**) "Plaine and Easie Code" originated by Brook and Gould from this aspect. (**d**) How are clef signs, notes, and rests represented? How are rhythmic durations indicated?

**1.39** Describe the computer analysis of Béla Bartók's Serbo-Croatian material carried out by Benjamin Suchoff.

**1.40** Explain the Bartók Z-symbol procedure for indicating the metrical structure of heterometric melodies.

**1.41** H. H. Stuckenschmidt [18] states that the extent to which new harmonic and melodic techniques were developed from the time of the romantic *Lied* of Franz Schubert to the early works of Schoenberg exceeded the achievements of the whole period between 1600 and 1800. Determine graphically whether or not there is a significant trend toward contraction in waiting time between ideas over the centuries. Consider each successive period in music history.

**1.42** Elaborate on the statement that music analysis by computers may entail sensing, feature characterization, and classification.

## REFERENCES

[1] F. C. Judd, *Electronic Music and Musique Concrete* (Neville Spearman, London, 1961).

[2] Sandra L. Tjepkema, *A Bibliography of Computer Music* (University of Iowa Press, Iowa City, 1981).

[3] Reinier Plomp, *Aspects of Tone Sensation: A Psychophysical Study* (Academic Press, London, 1976).

[4] *Computers and the Humanities* (Paradigm Press, Inc., Osprey, Florida).

[5] *Computer Music Journal* (MIT Press, Cambridge, Massachusetts).

[6] William S. Buxton, Ed., *Computer Music 1976/1977: a Directory to Current Work* (Canadian Commission for UNESCO, Ottawa, Ontario, 1977).

[7] Wayne Bateman, *Introduction to Computer Music* (John Wiley & Sons, New York, 1980).

[8] Allen Forte, *Syntax-Based Analytic Reading of Musical Scores* (Project MAC TR-39, MIT, Cambridge, Massachusetts, Apr. 1967).

[9] Lejaren Hiller and Leonard M. Isaacson, *Experimental Music: Composition with an Electronic Computer* (McGraw-Hill, New York, 1959).

[10] Hubert S. Howe, *Electronic Music Synthesis: Concepts, Facilities, Techniques* (Norton, New York, 1975).

[11] Harry B. Lincoln, Ed., *The Computer and Music* (Cornell University Press, Ithaca, New York, 1970).

[12] Max V. Mathews, et al., *The Technology of Computer Music* (MIT Press, Boston, Massachusetts, 1969).

[13] Iannis Xenakis, *Formalized Music* (Indiana University Press, Bloomington, Indiana, 1971)

[14] Helen Budge, *A Study of Chord Frequencies* (Bureau of Publications, Teachers College, Columbia University, New York, 1943).

[15] M. Sanchez and W.R. Reitman, "The Composition of a Fugue: Protocol and Composition," *CIP Working Paper No. 37*, (Carnegie Institute of Technology, 1960)

[16] Walter R. Reitman, *Cognition and Thought: An Information-Processing Approach* (John Wiley & Sons, Inc., New York, 1965) pp. 143-146, 166-180.

[17] Henry Pleasants, *The Agony of Modern Music* (Simon and Schuster, New York 1955) p. 93.

[18] H. H. Stuckenschmidt, *Twentieth Century Music* (McGraw-Hill, New York, 1970) p. 7.

PART II

# Chapter 2 Notation

*I must tell you that orthography, in the true sense of the word, is so absolutely necessary for a man of letters, or a gentleman, that one false spelling may fix ridicule upon him for the rest of his life.*

*LORD CHESTERFIELD*

## PREPARATION

Part of the author's previous study of computer methods in music consisted in searching for the most concise expressions for harmonies of the twelve-tone system. It is quite difficult to catalog such a large collection of entities until they have been encoded properly. In an earlier article [1] summarizing the outcome of this research, two new and powerful representations were proposed as a standard nomenclature for harmonies. For convenience in denomination and manipulation, the first, or "designative" form, expresses the 4096 harmonies of Western music as whole numbers from 0 to 4095 inclusive. This numerical scheme is extended in a later chapter of this book in order to apply it to a generalization of the concept of a harmony. The second one, or "characteristic" form, which is related to the first scheme by integer factorization, expresses once again the harmonic totality, but this time in terms of membership in harmonic equivalence classes or **sonorities.** The article characterized the use of these numbers as an intermediate working language and limited itself to a discussion of the encoding or digitalization process. It left for the future the reverse problem of devising a decoding algorithm and tables applicable to reconverting from designative form into preferred literal notation, or so-called "notative" form.

The quest to discover and understand the complex mechanism governing musical spelling and the attempt to develop practical rules of orthography for computer implementation entail uncovering the attributes of literal notation at two levels. First, it is necessary to find a systematic framework within which the discrete musical events that undergird music creation and esthetic appreciation can be described. This framework might best be specified in terms of a heirarchy of musical constructs whose inventory is determined by combinatorial properties of the musical system undergoing scrutiny. Second, the dependence of each construct upon its immediate context during the production of musical utterances should be examined thoroughly.

Some of these contextual dependencies come about because of semiflexible rules of grammatical construction, which control the allowed patterns of tones that can occur in a given compositional form. And since these edicts of musical grammar are reflected partly by orthographic constraints, the conventions of spelling, although apparently subject to considerable variablity, almost always carry cues concerning certain aspects of the tonal process. Encompassed in this examination, therefore, and leading toward a mathematical model of tonality and modulation, is an attempt to determine both the nature of the underlying musical constructs and their orthographic manifestations in various contexts.

The remainder of this chapter begins with a careful formulation of the central problem of music orthography, namely, the construction of an algorithm to enable a computer (or programmable calculator!) to perform musical transcription by converting numerical designations to preferred literal notations. One such decoding algorithm employs what will be called a stencil or template, to allow the appropriate letters and inflections to be printed by the computer. At the same time it excludes all irrelevant literals. Through application of the orthographic principle that is enunciated for the first time in this book, it is possible to achieve a completely consistent and unambiguous system of music orthography, a system that is at the same time practical and not cumbersome. The use of notative form simplifies the examination of context in the computer analysis of music and allows for a straightforward method of calculating the figured bass. Later on in the text it will become increasingly evident that correct notation and tonality are intimately connected.

Knowledge of a system requires the ability to speak of it in precise terms. For this reason the study of music orthography is particularly important and fundamental in learning to apply the principles of music theory to computer analysis of music. To construct a meaningful programmed analysis of a particular musical selection requires an accurate description of it in the orthodox symbolism of music. The guide to music spelling presented in this book forms the basis for such a description. Moreover, the methods developed in the following chapters offer complete flexibility since they are applicable to every tonality and chord occurring in the twelve-tone equitempered system, even in works of the twentieth century. Expressing musical material in terms of preferred notations results in a description that is both compact and elegant. Only because the underlying notational scheme is internally consistent is it suitable for use in music analysis by computers.

## EXERCISES

**2.1** Suggest ways in which computer outputs might (a) facilitate the identification of useful musical features, (b) provide a statistical basis for analytical arguments, and (c) simplify the listing of musical parameters and the preparation of formal musical descriptions.

**2.2** (a) State the differences between a tone and a note and between a note and a literal. (b) Explain how musical notation is an exceptionally clever coding system, and prepare a block diagram of the decoding process for use as a visual aid in instructing a class of beginning piano students. (c) Develop this block diagram into a computer flowchart, assuming that whatever is needed can be obtained by optical character recognition.

**2.3** (a) The English alphabet has only 26 letters with which to represent 44 elementary sounds. Give examples of (1) letters representing more than one sound, (2) letters representing no sound, and (3) letters put together to represent one sound. (b) Why are the letters c, j, q, and x said to be redundant? (c) List similar properties of the 21, 35, and ∞ literal alphabets.

## DIGITALIZATION

The first step in promoting a manual procedure to a computer procedure is to digitalize it. In the article just cited, a technique for digitalizing harmonies and sonorities was developed and explored. This encoding method can be exploited in a perfectly straightforward way to clarify the problem of finding the correct literal notation for chords and harmonies. Therefore, the main points of the digitalization process are reviewed again in brief summary in the present section.

Before examining how numerical designations work, it is necessary to recall something about the notions of chords, harmonies, and sonorities. First, a "chord" is defined as a collection of musical tones considered together or sounding together. Now from a practical point of view, a harmony is just a chord folded in upon itself so that it all will fit into a twelve-tone register within the compass of an octave. Actually, a "harmony" is best defined as a subset of the collection of those primitive twelve tones that make up the conventional equitempered system. Thus, a harmony is really a collection of enharmonic equivalence classes. Harmonies also may be thought of as sets of **literals**, or inflected letters, excluding enharmonic equivalents. The number of different tones in a particular harmony is called its "cardinality"; it can be any integer from zero to twelve, inclusive. Finally, a "sonority" is a set of harmonies related by transposition and consequently forming an **orbit** under transposition. It follows that a sonority is a harmonic equivalence class. There are 352 sonorities: 1 oudenad, 1 monad, 6 dyads, 19 triads, 43 tetrads, 66 pentads, 80 hexads, 66 heptads, 43 octads, 19 nonads, 6 decads, 1 undecad, and 1 duodecad, including the two improper sonorities. The cardinality of a sonority is induced by the cardinality of its members.

To find the correct designation for a given harmony requires only the ordinary addition of a few numbers to be read from a **weighted keyboard chart** (see Fig. 2.1). Several basic musical manipulations, including complementation, transposition, and alteration of harmonies, reduce to simple arithmetic operations when this representation is used. To find the correct characterization for a given harmony requires only consulting a table that separates each designation into two factors. These factors are joined by an asterisk, indicating multiplication **modulo** 4095. The leading factor of such a form characterizes the congruence classification or sonority of the harmony in question and tells immediately whether or not it is a major scale subharmony. The trailing factor establishes the frequency or pitch level of the given harmony. Thus,

DESIGNATION =

CHARACTERISTIC * LEVEL.

To summarize: a decimal number H, which is an integer on the range $0 \leq H \leq 4095$, designates a harmony; the values H = 0, 1, 2, ..., 4095 correspond to the various harmonies comprising the harmonic totality.

A number S, which is either zero or some positive integer less than or equal to H, designates a sonority. The number S is related to the number H by the formula

$$H = S * L$$

where the asterisk indicates that the quantity 4095 is to be subtracted from the ordinary product of S and L as many times as it is possible do so without producing a negative result, and L denotes a power of two from the set

$$\{2^i : i = 0, 1, ..., 11\}.$$

**Figure 2.1**

WEIGHTED KEYBOARD CHART

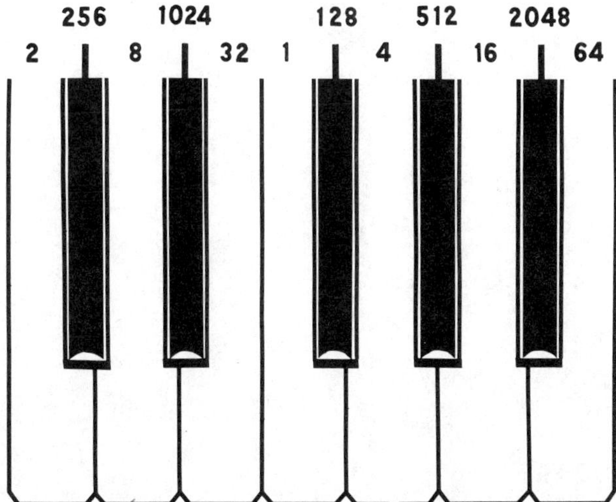

## EXERCISES

**2.4** The process of literal reconstitution can be mechanized. For the harmony formed by the tones of the pentatonic scale found on the black keys of the piano, the designation is 3968. (Verify this.) Subtracting powers of two in descending order,

| | | |
|---|---|---|
| 3968 | | |
| -2048 | implies | A♯\|B♭\|C♭♭ |
| 1920 | | |
| -1024 | implies | D♯\|E♭\|F♭♭ |
| 896 | | |
| -512 | implies | G♯\|A♭ |
| 384 | | |
| -256 | implies | Bx\|C♯\|D♭ |
| 128 | | |
| -128 | implies | Ex\|F♯\|G♭ |
| 0 | | |

Exactly how many different, although unusual, notations do these literals permit for this harmony?

**2.5** Reconstitute literal notations from the designations (a) 63, (b) 455, and (c) 819.

**2.6** Show that for the 35-literal alphabet, there are

$$\text{(a) } 3^{11}\times 2 = 354{,}294$$

notationally different ways of writing down the one-octave chromatic scale, and

$$\text{(b) } 4^{11}\times 3 = 12{,}382{,}912$$

notationally different ways of writing down all the members of the harmonic totality.

**2.7** A binary number is a grouping of zeros and ones that occupy positions weighted consecutively left-to-right by descending powers of two. For example, if the grouping 101011 is considered to be a binary number, then it would represent the decimal number 43. Thus,

$$101011_2 =$$

$$32\times1+16\times0+8\times1+4\times0+2\times1+1\times1 =$$

$$32 + 8 + 2 + 1 =$$

$$43_{10}$$

Evaluate

(a) 101.101,

(b) 111111111111,

(c) .100110011001 ...

(<u>Hint</u>. $0.1_2 = \frac{1}{2}$.) See [2].

**2.8** A positive decimal integer N is expressed in the binary number system by the polynomial

$$N = a_k 2^k + a_{k-1} 2^{k-1} + \ldots + a_0,$$

where each coefficient $a_i$ with i = 0, 1, ..., k is either 0 or 1. So,

$$N_{\text{ten}} = a_k a_{k-1} \ldots a_1 a_0 \,_{\text{two}}.$$

The "weight" of a binary integer is defined as the number of **ones** it contains. That is,

$$W = a_0 + a_1 + \ldots + a_k = \Sigma a_i.$$

(a) Apply this concept to chords. (b) When the weight of a chord equals the cardinality of its harmony, the chord is said to be "simple." Why?

**2.9** A subset of a collection of harmonies may be defined by requiring that it be fixed in one or more tones and unrestricted in all others. Following customary practice, such subsets may be termed "cylindrical sets." Appraise the serial development of three, five, seven, and nine unit pitch scales given by Joseph Schillinger in <u>Kaleidophone</u> [3]. Do these lists form cylindrical sets? Using an alternate coding scheme in which the weight given tone C is unity, say S(C,7) in the terminology of the paper cited [1], identify these lists with the odd numbers contained in the sections of Table I, reprinted on the following pages, labelled TRIADS, PENTADS, HEPTADS, and NONADS. [Permission to include Tables I and II was granted by the publishers of the **Journal of Research in Music Education.**]

**2.10** In the first of three piano pieces, Opus 11, Number 1, Arnold Schoenberg has given the direction: *"Die Tasten tonlos niederdrücken!"* ("Press the keys down silently!") above a harmony FAC♯E. Should this set be treated as the **null harmony** (that harmony which contains no tones) in analyzing this passage? Justify the answer given.

FIGURE 2.3

Table use is illustrated as follows: The designation of the F major triad is given by the sum 1 + 2 + 16 = 19 (see Figure 2.1). This value appears in column one, row four of the grouping TRIADS. Consequently the F major triad is the **characteristic harmony** of the fourth sonority having cardinality three. Its complete orbit is defined by the numbers: 19, 38, 76, 152, 304, 608, 1216, 2432, 769 (= 2 × 2432 − 4095), 1538, 3076, and 2057 (= 2 × 3076 − 4095).

## ROSTER OF HARMONIES AND SONORITIES IN THE TWELVE-TONE EQUITEMPERED SYSTEM

OUDENADS

| 0 | 1 | 2 | 3 | 4 | 5 | 6 | 7 | 8 | 9 | 10 | 11 |
|---|---|---|---|---|---|---|---|---|---|---|---|
| 0 | 0 | 0 | 0 | 0 | 0 | 0 | 0 | 0 | 0 | 0 | 0 * |

MONADS

| 0 | 1 | 2 | 3 | 4 | 5 | 6 | 7 | 8 | 9 | 10 | 11 |
|---|---|---|---|---|---|---|---|---|---|---|---|
| 1 | 2 | 4 | 8 | 16 | 32 | 64 | 128 | 256 | 512 | 1024 | 2048 |

DYADS

| 0 | 1 | 2 | 3 | 4 | 5 | 6 | 7 | 8 | 9 | 10 | 11 |
|---|---|---|---|---|---|---|---|---|---|---|---|
| 3 | 6 | 12 | 24 | 48 | 96 | 192 | 384 | 768 | 1536 | 3072 | 2049 |
| 5 | 10 | 20 | 40 | 80 | 160 | 320 | 640 | 1280 | 2560 | 1025 | 2050 |
| 9 | 18 | 36 | 72 | 144 | 288 | 576 | 1152 | 2304 | 513 | 1026 | 2052 |
| 17 | 34 | 68 | 136 | 272 | 544 | 1088 | 2176 | 257 | 514 | 1028 | 2056 |
| 33 | 66 | 132 | 264 | 528 | 1056 | 2112 | 129 | 258 | 516 | 1032 | 2064 |
| 65 | 130 | 260 | 520 | 1040 | 2080 | 65 | 130 | 260 | 520 | 1040 | 2080 * |

TRIADS

| 0 | 1 | 2 | 3 | 4 | 5 | 6 | 7 | 8 | 9 | 10 | 11 |
|---|---|---|---|---|---|---|---|---|---|---|---|
| 7 | 14 | 28 | 56 | 112 | 224 | 448 | 896 | 1792 | 3584 | 3073 | 2051 |
| 11 | 22 | 44 | 88 | 176 | 352 | 704 | 1408 | 2816 | 1537 | 3074 | 2053 |
| 13 | 26 | 52 | 104 | 208 | 416 | 832 | 1664 | 3328 | 2561 | 1027 | 2054 |
| 19 | 38 | 76 | 152 | 304 | 608 | 1216 | 2432 | 769 | 1538 | 3076 | 2057 |
| 21 | 42 | 84 | 168 | 336 | 672 | 1344 | 2688 | 1281 | 2562 | 1029 | 2058 |
| 25 | 50 | 100 | 200 | 400 | 800 | 1600 | 3200 | 2305 | 515 | 1030 | 2060 |
| 35 | 70 | 140 | 280 | 560 | 1120 | 2240 | 385 | 770 | 1540 | 3080 | 2065 |
| 37 | 74 | 148 | 296 | 592 | 1184 | 2368 | 641 | 1282 | 2564 | 1033 | 2066 |
| 41 | 82 | 164 | 328 | 656 | 1312 | 2624 | 1153 | 2306 | 517 | 1034 | 2068 |
| 49 | 98 | 196 | 392 | 784 | 1568 | 3136 | 2177 | 259 | 518 | 1036 | 2072 |
| 67 | 134 | 268 | 536 | 1072 | 2144 | 193 | 386 | 772 | 1544 | 3088 | 2081 |
| 69 | 138 | 276 | 552 | 1104 | 2208 | 321 | 642 | 1284 | 2568 | 1041 | 2082 |
| 73 | 146 | 292 | 584 | 1168 | 2336 | 577 | 1154 | 2308 | 521 | 1042 | 2084 |
| 81 | 162 | 324 | 648 | 1296 | 2592 | 1089 | 2178 | 261 | 522 | 1044 | 2088 |
| 97 | 194 | 388 | 776 | 1552 | 3104 | 2113 | 131 | 262 | 524 | 1048 | 2096 |
| 133 | 266 | 532 | 1064 | 2128 | 161 | 322 | 644 | 1288 | 2576 | 1057 | 2114 |
| 137 | 274 | 548 | 1096 | 2192 | 289 | 578 | 1156 | 2312 | 529 | 1058 | 2116 |
| 145 | 290 | 580 | 1160 | 2320 | 545 | 1090 | 2180 | 265 | 530 | 1060 | 2120 |
| 273 | 546 | 1092 | 2184 | 273 | 546 | 1092 | 2184 | 273 | 546 | 1092 | 2184 * |

TETRADS

| 0 | 1 | 2 | 3 | 4 | 5 | 6 | 7 | 8 | 9 | 10 | 11 | |
|---|---|---|---|---|---|---|---|---|---|---|---|---|
| 15 | 30 | 60 | 120 | 240 | 480 | 960 | 1920 | 3840 | 3585 | 3075 | 2055 | |
| 23 | 46 | 92 | 184 | 368 | 736 | 1472 | 2944 | 1793 | 3586 | 3077 | 2059 | |
| 27 | 54 | 108 | 216 | 432 | 864 | 1728 | 3456 | 2817 | 1539 | 3078 | 2061 | |
| 29 | 58 | 116 | 232 | 464 | 928 | 1856 | 3712 | 3329 | 2563 | 1031 | 2062 | |
| 39 | 78 | 156 | 312 | 624 | 1248 | 2496 | 897 | 1794 | 3588 | 3081 | 2067 | |
| 43 | 86 | 172 | 344 | 688 | 1376 | 2752 | 1409 | 2818 | 1541 | 3082 | 2069 | |
| 45 | 90 | 180 | 360 | 720 | 1440 | 2880 | 1665 | 3330 | 2565 | 1035 | 2070 | |
| 51 | 102 | 204 | 408 | 816 | 1632 | 3264 | 2433 | 771 | 1542 | 3084 | 2073 | |
| 53 | 106 | 212 | 424 | 848 | 1696 | 3392 | 2689 | 1283 | 2566 | 1037 | 2074 | |
| 57 | 114 | 228 | 456 | 912 | 1824 | 3648 | 3201 | 2307 | 519 | 1038 | 2076 | |
| 71 | 142 | 284 | 568 | 1136 | 2272 | 449 | 898 | 1796 | 3592 | 3089 | 2083 | |
| 75 | 150 | 300 | 600 | 1200 | 2400 | 705 | 1410 | 2820 | 1545 | 3090 | 2085 | |
| 77 | 154 | 308 | 616 | 1232 | 2464 | 833 | 1666 | 3332 | 2569 | 1043 | 2086 | |
| 83 | 166 | 332 | 664 | 1328 | 2656 | 1217 | 2434 | 773 | 1546 | 3092 | 2089 | |
| 85 | 170 | 340 | 680 | 1360 | 2720 | 1345 | 2690 | 1285 | 2570 | 1045 | 2090 | |
| 89 | 178 | 356 | 712 | 1424 | 2848 | 1601 | 3202 | 2309 | 523 | 1046 | 2092 | |
| 99 | 198 | 396 | 792 | 1584 | 3168 | 2241 | 387 | 774 | 1548 | 3096 | 2097 | |
| 101 | 202 | 404 | 808 | 1616 | 3232 | 2369 | 643 | 1286 | 2572 | 1049 | 2098 | |
| 105 | 210 | 420 | 840 | 1680 | 3360 | 2625 | 1155 | 2310 | 525 | 1050 | 2100 | |
| 113 | 226 | 452 | 904 | 1808 | 3616 | 3137 | 2179 | 263 | 526 | 1052 | 2104 | |
| 135 | 270 | 540 | 1080 | 2160 | 225 | 450 | 900 | 1800 | 3600 | 3105 | 2115 | |
| 139 | 278 | 556 | 1112 | 2224 | 353 | 706 | 1412 | 2824 | 1553 | 3106 | 2117 | |
| 141 | 282 | 564 | 1128 | 2256 | 417 | 834 | 1668 | 3336 | 2577 | 1059 | 2118 | |
| 147 | 294 | 588 | 1176 | 2352 | 609 | 1218 | 2436 | 777 | 1554 | 3108 | 2121 | |
| 149 | 298 | 596 | 1192 | 2384 | 673 | 1346 | 2692 | 1289 | 2578 | 1061 | 2122 | |
| 153 | 306 | 612 | 1224 | 2448 | 801 | 1602 | 3204 | 2313 | 531 | 1062 | 2124 | |
| 163 | 326 | 652 | 1304 | 2608 | 1121 | 2242 | 389 | 778 | 1556 | 3112 | 2129 | |
| 165 | 330 | 660 | 1320 | 2640 | 1185 | 2370 | 645 | 1290 | 2580 | 1065 | 2130 | |
| 169 | 338 | 676 | 1352 | 2704 | 1313 | 2626 | 1157 | 2314 | 533 | 1066 | 2132 | |
| 177 | 354 | 708 | 1416 | 2832 | 1569 | 3138 | 2181 | 267 | 534 | 1068 | 2136 | |
| 195 | 390 | 780 | 1560 | 3120 | 2145 | 195 | 390 | 780 | 1560 | 3120 | 2145 | * |
| 197 | 394 | 788 | 1576 | 3152 | 2209 | 323 | 646 | 1292 | 2584 | 1073 | 2146 | |
| 201 | 402 | 804 | 1608 | 3216 | 2337 | 579 | 1158 | 2316 | 537 | 1074 | 2148 | |
| 209 | 418 | 836 | 1672 | 3344 | 2593 | 1091 | 2182 | 269 | 538 | 1076 | 2152 | |
| 275 | 550 | 1100 | 2200 | 305 | 610 | 1220 | 2440 | 785 | 1570 | 3140 | 2185 | |
| 277 | 554 | 1108 | 2216 | 337 | 674 | 1348 | 2696 | 1297 | 2594 | 1093 | 2186 | |
| 281 | 562 | 1124 | 2248 | 401 | 802 | 1604 | 3208 | 2321 | 547 | 1094 | 2188 | |
| 291 | 582 | 1164 | 2328 | 561 | 1122 | 2244 | 393 | 786 | 1572 | 3144 | 2193 | |
| 293 | 586 | 1172 | 2344 | 593 | 1186 | 2372 | 649 | 1298 | 2596 | 1097 | 2194 | |
| 297 | 594 | 1188 | 2376 | 657 | 1314 | 2628 | 1161 | 2322 | 549 | 1098 | 2196 | |
| 325 | 650 | 1300 | 2600 | 1105 | 2210 | 325 | 650 | 1300 | 2600 | 1105 | 2210 | * |
| 329 | 658 | 1316 | 2632 | 1169 | 2338 | 581 | 1162 | 2324 | 553 | 1106 | 2212 | |
| 585 | 1170 | 2340 | 585 | 1170 | 2340 | 585 | 1170 | 2340 | 585 | 1170 | 2340 | * |

PENTADS

| 0 | 1 | 2 | 3 | 4 | 5 | 6 | 7 | 8 | 9 | 10 | 11 |
|---|---|---|---|---|---|---|---|---|---|---|---|
| 31 | 62 | 124 | 248 | 496 | 992 | 1984 | 3968 | 3841 | 3587 | 3079 | 2063 |
| 47 | 94 | 188 | 376 | 752 | 1504 | 3008 | 1921 | 3842 | 3589 | 3083 | 2071 |
| 55 | 110 | 220 | 440 | 880 | 1760 | 3520 | 2945 | 1795 | 3590 | 3085 | 2075 |
| 59 | 118 | 236 | 472 | 944 | 1888 | 3776 | 3457 | 2819 | 1543 | 3086 | 2077 |
| 61 | 122 | 244 | 488 | 976 | 1952 | 3904 | 3713 | 3331 | 2567 | 1039 | 2078 |
| 79 | 158 | 316 | 632 | 1264 | 2528 | 961 | 1922 | 3844 | 3593 | 3091 | 2087 |
| 87 | 174 | 348 | 696 | 1392 | 2784 | 1473 | 2946 | 1797 | 3594 | 3093 | 2091 |
| 91 | 182 | 364 | 728 | 1456 | 2912 | 1729 | 3458 | 2821 | 1547 | 3094 | 2093 |
| 93 | 186 | 372 | 744 | 1488 | 2976 | 1857 | 3714 | 3333 | 2571 | 1047 | 2094 |
| 103 | 206 | 412 | 824 | 1648 | 3296 | 2497 | 899 | 1798 | 3596 | 3097 | 2099 |
| 107 | 214 | 428 | 856 | 1712 | 3424 | 2753 | 1411 | 2822 | 1549 | 3098 | 2101 |
| 109 | 218 | 436 | 872 | 1744 | 3488 | 2881 | 1667 | 3334 | 2573 | 1051 | 2102 |
| 115 | 230 | 460 | 920 | 1840 | 3680 | 3265 | 2435 | 775 | 1550 | 3100 | 2105 |
| 117 | 234 | 468 | 936 | 1872 | 3744 | 3393 | 2691 | 1287 | 2574 | 1053 | 2106 |
| 121 | 242 | 484 | 968 | 1936 | 3872 | 3649 | 3203 | 2311 | 527 | 1054 | 2108 |
| 143 | 286 | 572 | 1144 | 2288 | 481 | 962 | 1924 | 3848 | 3601 | 3107 | 2119 |
| 151 | 302 | 604 | 1208 | 2416 | 737 | 1474 | 2948 | 1801 | 3602 | 3109 | 2123 |

| | | | | | | | | | | | |
|---|---|---|---|---|---|---|---|---|---|---|---|
| 155 | 310 | 620 | 1240 | 2480 | 865 | 1730 | 3460 | 2825 | 1555 | 3110 | 2125 |
| 157 | 314 | 628 | 1256 | 2512 | 929 | 1858 | 3716 | 3337 | 2579 | 1063 | 2126 |
| 167 | 334 | 668 | 1336 | 2672 | 1249 | 2498 | 901 | 1802 | 3604 | 3113 | 2131 |
| 171 | 342 | 684 | 1368 | 2736 | 1377 | 2754 | 1413 | 2826 | 1557 | 3114 | 2133 |
| 173 | 346 | 692 | 1384 | 2768 | 1441 | 2882 | 1669 | 3338 | 2581 | 1067 | 2134 |
| 179 | 358 | 716 | 1432 | 2864 | 1633 | 3266 | 2437 | 779 | 1558 | 3116 | 2137 |
| 181 | 362 | 724 | 1448 | 2896 | 1697 | 3394 | 2693 | 1291 | 2582 | 1069 | 2138 |
| 185 | 370 | 740 | 1480 | 2960 | 1825 | 3650 | 3205 | 2315 | 535 | 1070 | 2140 |
| 199 | 398 | 796 | 1592 | 3184 | 2273 | 451 | 902 | 1804 | 3608 | 3121 | 2147 |
| 203 | 406 | 812 | 1624 | 3248 | 2401 | 707 | 1414 | 2828 | 1561 | 3122 | 2149 |
| 205 | 410 | 820 | 1640 | 3280 | 2465 | 835 | 1670 | 3340 | 2585 | 1075 | 2150 |
| 211 | 422 | 844 | 1688 | 3376 | 2657 | 1219 | 2438 | 781 | 1562 | 3124 | 2153 |
| 213 | 426 | 852 | 1704 | 3408 | 2721 | 1347 | 2694 | 1293 | 2586 | 1077 | 2154 |
| 217 | 434 | 868 | 1736 | 3472 | 2849 | 1603 | 3206 | 2317 | 539 | 1078 | 2156 |
| 227 | 454 | 908 | 1816 | 3632 | 3169 | 2243 | 391 | 782 | 1564 | 3128 | 2161 |
| 229 | 458 | 916 | 1832 | 3664 | 3233 | 2371 | 647 | 1294 | 2588 | 1081 | 2162 |
| 233 | 466 | 932 | 1864 | 3728 | 3361 | 2627 | 1159 | 2318 | 541 | 1082 | 2164 |
| 241 | 482 | 964 | 1928 | 3856 | 3617 | 3139 | 2183 | 271 | 542 | 1084 | 2168 |
| 279 | 558 | 1116 | 2232 | 369 | 738 | 1476 | 2952 | 1809 | 3618 | 3141 | 2187 |
| 283 | 566 | 1132 | 2264 | 433 | 866 | 1732 | 3464 | 2833 | 1571 | 3142 | 2189 |
| 285 | 570 | 1140 | 2280 | 465 | 930 | 1860 | 3720 | 3345 | 2595 | 1095 | 2190 |
| 295 | 590 | 1180 | 2360 | 625 | 1250 | 2500 | 905 | 1810 | 3620 | 3145 | 2195 |
| 299 | 598 | 1196 | 2392 | 689 | 1378 | 2756 | 1417 | 2834 | 1573 | 3146 | 2197 |
| 301 | 602 | 1204 | 2408 | 721 | 1442 | 2884 | 1673 | 3346 | 2597 | 1099 | 2198 |
| 307 | 614 | 1228 | 2456 | 817 | 1634 | 3268 | 2441 | 787 | 1574 | 3148 | 2201 |
| 309 | 618 | 1236 | 2472 | 849 | 1698 | 3396 | 2697 | 1299 | 2598 | 1101 | 2202 |
| 313 | 626 | 1252 | 2504 | 913 | 1826 | 3652 | 3209 | 2323 | 551 | 1102 | 2204 |
| 327 | 654 | 1308 | 2616 | 1137 | 2274 | 453 | 906 | 1812 | 3624 | 3153 | 2211 |
| 331 | 662 | 1324 | 2648 | 1201 | 2402 | 709 | 1418 | 2836 | 1577 | 3154 | 2213 |
| 333 | 666 | 1332 | 2664 | 1233 | 2466 | 837 | 1674 | 3348 | 2601 | 1107 | 2214 |
| 339 | 678 | 1356 | 2712 | 1329 | 2658 | 1221 | 2442 | 789 | 1578 | 3156 | 2217 |
| 341 | 682 | 1364 | 2728 | 1361 | 2722 | 1349 | 2698 | 1301 | 2602 | 1109 | 2218 |
| 345 | 690 | 1380 | 2760 | 1425 | 2850 | 1605 | 3210 | 2325 | 555 | 1110 | 2220 |
| 355 | 710 | 1420 | 2840 | 1585 | 3170 | 2245 | 395 | 790 | 1580 | 3160 | 2225 |
| 357 | 714 | 1428 | 2856 | 1617 | 3234 | 2373 | 651 | 1302 | 2604 | 1113 | 2226 |
| 361 | 722 | 1444 | 2888 | 1681 | 3362 | 2629 | 1163 | 2326 | 557 | 1114 | 2228 |
| 397 | 794 | 1588 | 3176 | 2257 | 419 | 838 | 1676 | 3352 | 2609 | 1123 | 2246 |
| 403 | 806 | 1612 | 3224 | 2353 | 611 | 1222 | 2444 | 793 | 1586 | 3172 | 2249 |
| 405 | 810 | 1620 | 3240 | 2385 | 675 | 1350 | 2700 | 1305 | 2610 | 1125 | 2250 |
| 409 | 818 | 1636 | 3272 | 2449 | 803 | 1606 | 3212 | 2329 | 563 | 1126 | 2252 |
| 421 | 842 | 1684 | 3368 | 2641 | 1187 | 2374 | 653 | 1306 | 2612 | 1129 | 2258 |
| 425 | 850 | 1700 | 3400 | 2705 | 1315 | 2630 | 1165 | 2330 | 565 | 1130 | 2260 |
| 457 | 914 | 1828 | 3656 | 3217 | 2339 | 583 | 1166 | 2332 | 569 | 1138 | 2276 |
| 587 | 1174 | 2348 | 601 | 1202 | 2404 | 713 | 1426 | 2852 | 1609 | 3218 | 2341 |
| 589 | 1178 | 2356 | 617 | 1234 | 2468 | 841 | 1682 | 3364 | 2633 | 1171 | 2342 |
| 595 | 1190 | 2380 | 665 | 1330 | 2660 | 1225 | 2450 | 805 | 1610 | 3220 | 2345 |
| 597 | 1194 | 2388 | 681 | 1362 | 2724 | 1353 | 2706 | 1317 | 2634 | 1173 | 2346 |
| 613 | 1226 | 2452 | 809 | 1618 | 3236 | 2377 | 659 | 1318 | 2636 | 1177 | 2354 |
| 661 | 1322 | 2644 | 1193 | 2386 | 677 | 1354 | 2708 | 1321 | 2642 | 1189 | 2378 |

HEXADS

| 0 | 1 | 2 | 3 | 4 | 5 | 6 | 7 | 8 | 9 | 10 | 11 |
|---|---|---|---|---|---|---|---|---|---|---|---|
| 63 | 126 | 252 | 504 | 1008 | 2016 | 4032 | 3969 | 3843 | 3591 | 3087 | 2079 |
| 95 | 190 | 380 | 760 | 1520 | 3040 | 1985 | 3970 | 3845 | 3595 | 3095 | 2095 |
| 111 | 222 | 444 | 888 | 1776 | 3552 | 3009 | 1923 | 3846 | 3597 | 3099 | 2103 |
| 119 | 238 | 476 | 952 | 1904 | 3808 | 3521 | 2947 | 1799 | 3598 | 3101 | 2107 |
| 123 | 246 | 492 | 984 | 1968 | 3936 | 3777 | 3459 | 2823 | 1551 | 3102 | 2109 |
| 125 | 250 | 500 | 1000 | 2000 | 4000 | 3905 | 3715 | 3335 | 2575 | 1055 | 2110 |
| 159 | 318 | 636 | 1272 | 2544 | 993 | 1986 | 3972 | 3849 | 3603 | 3111 | 2127 |
| 175 | 350 | 700 | 1400 | 2800 | 1505 | 3010 | 1925 | 3850 | 3605 | 3115 | 2135 |
| 183 | 366 | 732 | 1464 | 2928 | 1761 | 3522 | 2949 | 1803 | 3606 | 3117 | 2139 |
| 187 | 374 | 748 | 1496 | 2992 | 1889 | 3778 | 3461 | 2827 | 1559 | 3118 | 2141 |
| 189 | 378 | 756 | 1512 | 3024 | 1953 | 3906 | 3717 | 3339 | 2583 | 1071 | 2142 |
| 207 | 414 | 828 | 1656 | 3312 | 2529 | 963 | 1926 | 3852 | 3609 | 3123 | 2151 |
| 215 | 430 | 860 | 1720 | 3440 | 2785 | 1475 | 2950 | 1805 | 3610 | 3125 | 2155 |
| 219 | 438 | 876 | 1752 | 3504 | 2913 | 1731 | 3462 | 2829 | 1563 | 3126 | 2157 |
| 221 | 442 | 884 | 1768 | 3536 | 2977 | 1859 | 3718 | 3341 | 2587 | 1079 | 2158 |
| 231 | 462 | 924 | 1848 | 3696 | 3297 | 2499 | 903 | 1806 | 3612 | 3129 | 2163 |

| | | | | | | | | | | | | |
|---|---|---|---|---|---|---|---|---|---|---|---|---|
| 235 | 470 | 940 | 1880 | 3760 | 3425 | 2755 | 1415 | 2830 | 1565 | 3130 | 2165 | |
| 237 | 474 | 948 | 1896 | 3792 | 3489 | 2883 | 1671 | 3342 | 2589 | 1083 | 2166 | |
| 243 | 486 | 972 | 1944 | 3888 | 3681 | 3267 | 2439 | 783 | 1566 | 3132 | 2169 | |
| 245 | 490 | 980 | 1960 | 3920 | 3745 | 3395 | 2695 | 1295 | 2590 | 1085 | 2170 | |
| 249 | 498 | 996 | 1992 | 3984 | 3873 | 3651 | 3207 | 2319 | 543 | 1086 | 2172 | |
| 287 | 574 | 1148 | 2296 | 497 | 994 | 1988 | 3976 | 3857 | 3619 | 3143 | 2191 | |
| 303 | 606 | 1212 | 2424 | 753 | 1506 | 3012 | 1929 | 3858 | 3621 | 3147 | 2199 | |
| 311 | 622 | 1244 | 2488 | 881 | 1762 | 3524 | 2953 | 1811 | 3622 | 3149 | 2203 | |
| 315 | 630 | 1260 | 2520 | 945 | 1890 | 3780 | 3465 | 2835 | 1575 | 3150 | 2205 | |
| 317 | 634 | 1268 | 2536 | 977 | 1954 | 3908 | 3721 | 3347 | 2599 | 1103 | 2206 | |
| 335 | 670 | 1340 | 2680 | 1265 | 2530 | 965 | 1930 | 3860 | 3625 | 3155 | 2215 | |
| 343 | 686 | 1372 | 2744 | 1393 | 2786 | 1477 | 2954 | 1813 | 3626 | 3157 | 2219 | |
| 347 | 694 | 1388 | 2776 | 1457 | 2914 | 1733 | 3466 | 2837 | 1579 | 3158 | 2221 | |
| 349 | 698 | 1396 | 2792 | 1489 | 2978 | 1861 | 3722 | 3349 | 2603 | 1111 | 2222 | |
| 359 | 718 | 1436 | 2872 | 1649 | 3298 | 2501 | 907 | 1814 | 3628 | 3161 | 2227 | |
| 363 | 726 | 1452 | 2904 | 1713 | 3426 | 2757 | 1419 | 2838 | 1581 | 3162 | 2229 | |
| 365 | 730 | 1460 | 2920 | 1745 | 3490 | 2885 | 1675 | 3350 | 2605 | 1115 | 2230 | |
| 371 | 742 | 1484 | 2968 | 1841 | 3682 | 3269 | 2443 | 791 | 1582 | 3164 | 2233 | |
| 373 | 746 | 1492 | 2984 | 1873 | 3746 | 3397 | 2699 | 1303 | 2606 | 1117 | 2234 | |
| 377 | 754 | 1508 | 3016 | 1937 | 3874 | 3653 | 3211 | 2327 | 559 | 1118 | 2236 | |
| 399 | 798 | 1596 | 3192 | 2289 | 483 | 966 | 1932 | 3864 | 3633 | 3171 | 2247 | |
| 407 | 814 | 1628 | 3256 | 2417 | 739 | 1478 | 2956 | 1817 | 3634 | 3173 | 2251 | |
| 411 | 822 | 1644 | 3288 | 2481 | 867 | 1734 | 3468 | 2841 | 1587 | 3174 | 2253 | |
| 413 | 826 | 1652 | 3304 | 2513 | 931 | 1862 | 3724 | 3353 | 2611 | 1127 | 2254 | |
| 423 | 846 | 1692 | 3384 | 2673 | 1251 | 2502 | 909 | 1818 | 3636 | 3177 | 2259 | |
| 427 | 854 | 1708 | 3416 | 2737 | 1379 | 2758 | 1421 | 2842 | 1589 | 3178 | 2261 | |
| 429 | 858 | 1716 | 3432 | 2769 | 1443 | 2886 | 1677 | 3354 | 2613 | 1131 | 2262 | |
| 435 | 870 | 1740 | 3480 | 2865 | 1635 | 3270 | 2445 | 795 | 1590 | 3180 | 2265 | |
| 437 | 874 | 1748 | 3496 | 2897 | 1699 | 3398 | 2701 | 1307 | 2614 | 1133 | 2266 | |
| 441 | 882 | 1764 | 3528 | 2961 | 1827 | 3654 | 3213 | 2331 | 567 | 1134 | 2268 | |
| 455 | 910 | 1820 | 3640 | 3185 | 2275 | 455 | 910 | 1820 | 3640 | 3185 | 2275 | * |
| 459 | 918 | 1836 | 3672 | 3249 | 2403 | 711 | 1422 | 2844 | 1593 | 3186 | 2277 | |
| 461 | 922 | 1844 | 3688 | 3281 | 2467 | 839 | 1678 | 3356 | 2617 | 1139 | 2278 | |
| 467 | 934 | 1868 | 3736 | 3377 | 2659 | 1223 | 2446 | 797 | 1594 | 3188 | 2281 | |
| 469 | 938 | 1876 | 3752 | 3409 | 2723 | 1351 | 2702 | 1309 | 2618 | 1141 | 2282 | |
| 473 | 946 | 1892 | 3784 | 3473 | 2851 | 1607 | 3214 | 2333 | 571 | 1142 | 2284 | |
| 485 | 970 | 1940 | 3880 | 3665 | 3235 | 2375 | 655 | 1310 | 2620 | 1145 | 2290 | |
| 489 | 978 | 1956 | 3912 | 3729 | 3363 | 2631 | 1167 | 2334 | 573 | 1146 | 2292 | |
| 591 | 1182 | 2364 | 633 | 1266 | 2532 | 969 | 1938 | 3876 | 3657 | 3219 | 2343 | |
| 599 | 1198 | 2396 | 697 | 1394 | 2788 | 1481 | 2962 | 1829 | 3658 | 3221 | 2347 | |
| 603 | 1206 | 2412 | 729 | 1458 | 2916 | 1737 | 3474 | 2853 | 1611 | 3222 | 2349 | |
| 605 | 1210 | 2420 | 745 | 1490 | 2980 | 1865 | 3730 | 3365 | 2635 | 1175 | 2350 | |
| 615 | 1230 | 2460 | 825 | 1650 | 3300 | 2505 | 915 | 1830 | 3660 | 3225 | 2355 | |
| 619 | 1238 | 2476 | 857 | 1714 | 3428 | 2761 | 1427 | 2854 | 1613 | 3226 | 2357 | |
| 621 | 1242 | 2484 | 873 | 1746 | 3492 | 2889 | 1683 | 3366 | 2637 | 1179 | 2358 | |
| 627 | 1254 | 2508 | 921 | 1842 | 3684 | 3273 | 2451 | 807 | 1614 | 3228 | 2361 | |
| 629 | 1258 | 2516 | 937 | 1874 | 3748 | 3401 | 2707 | 1319 | 2638 | 1181 | 2362 | |
| 663 | 1326 | 2652 | 1209 | 2418 | 741 | 1482 | 2964 | 1833 | 3666 | 3237 | 2379 | |
| 667 | 1334 | 2668 | 1241 | 2482 | 869 | 1738 | 3476 | 2857 | 1619 | 3238 | 2381 | |
| 669 | 1338 | 2676 | 1257 | 2514 | 933 | 1866 | 3732 | 3369 | 2643 | 1191 | 2382 | |
| 679 | 1358 | 2716 | 1337 | 2674 | 1253 | 2506 | 917 | 1834 | 3668 | 3241 | 2387 | |
| 683 | 1366 | 2732 | 1369 | 2738 | 1381 | 2762 | 1429 | 2858 | 1621 | 3242 | 2389 | |
| 685 | 1370 | 2740 | 1385 | 2770 | 1445 | 2890 | 1685 | 3370 | 2645 | 1195 | 2390 | |
| 691 | 1382 | 2764 | 1433 | 2866 | 1637 | 3274 | 2453 | 811 | 1622 | 3244 | 2393 | |
| 693 | 1386 | 2772 | 1449 | 2898 | 1701 | 3402 | 2709 | 1323 | 2646 | 1197 | 2394 | |
| 715 | 1430 | 2860 | 1625 | 3250 | 2405 | 715 | 1430 | 2860 | 1625 | 3250 | 2405 | * |
| 717 | 1434 | 2868 | 1641 | 3282 | 2469 | 843 | 1686 | 3372 | 2649 | 1203 | 2406 | |
| 723 | 1446 | 2892 | 1689 | 3378 | 2661 | 1227 | 2454 | 813 | 1626 | 3252 | 2409 | |
| 725 | 1450 | 2900 | 1705 | 3410 | 2725 | 1355 | 2710 | 1325 | 2650 | 1205 | 2410 | |
| 819 | 1638 | 3276 | 2457 | 819 | 1638 | 3276 | 2457 | 819 | 1638 | 3276 | 2457 | * |
| 821 | 1642 | 3284 | 2473 | 851 | 1702 | 3404 | 2713 | 1331 | 2662 | 1229 | 2458 | |
| 845 | 1690 | 3380 | 2665 | 1235 | 2470 | 845 | 1690 | 3380 | 2665 | 1235 | 2470 | * |
| 853 | 1706 | 3412 | 2729 | 1363 | 2726 | 1357 | 2714 | 1333 | 2666 | 1237 | 2474 | |
| 1365 | 2730 | 1365 | 2730 | 1365 | 2730 | 1365 | 2730 | 1365 | 2730 | 1365 | 2730 | * |

HEPTADS

| 0 | 1 | 2 | 3 | 4 | 5 | 6 | 7 | 8 | 9 | 10 | 11 |
|---|---|---|---|---|---|---|---|---|---|---|---|
| 127 | 254 | 508 | 1016 | 2032 | 4064 | 4033 | 3971 | 3847 | 3599 | 3103 | 2111 |
| 191 | 382 | 764 | 1528 | 3056 | 2017 | 4034 | 3973 | 3851 | 3607 | 3119 | 2143 |
| 223 | 446 | 892 | 1784 | 3568 | 3041 | 1987 | 3974 | 3853 | 3611 | 3127 | 2159 |
| 239 | 478 | 956 | 1912 | 3824 | 3553 | 3011 | 1927 | 3854 | 3613 | 3131 | 2167 |
| 247 | 494 | 988 | 1976 | 3952 | 3809 | 3523 | 2951 | 1807 | 3614 | 3133 | 2171 |
| 251 | 502 | 1004 | 2008 | 4016 | 3937 | 3779 | 3463 | 2831 | 1567 | 3134 | 2173 |
| 253 | 506 | 1012 | 2024 | 4048 | 4001 | 3907 | 3719 | 3343 | 2591 | 1087 | 2174 |
| 319 | 638 | 1276 | 2552 | 1009 | 2018 | 4036 | 3977 | 3859 | 3623 | 3151 | 2207 |
| 351 | 702 | 1404 | 2808 | 1521 | 3042 | 1989 | 3978 | 3861 | 3627 | 3159 | 2223 |
| 367 | 734 | 1468 | 2936 | 1777 | 3554 | 3013 | 1931 | 3862 | 3629 | 3163 | 2231 |
| 375 | 750 | 1500 | 3000 | 1905 | 3810 | 3525 | 2955 | 1815 | 3630 | 3165 | 2235 |
| 379 | 758 | 1516 | 3032 | 1969 | 3938 | 3781 | 3467 | 2839 | 1583 | 3166 | 2237 |
| 381 | 762 | 1524 | 3048 | 2001 | 4002 | 3909 | 3723 | 3351 | 2607 | 1119 | 2238 |
| 415 | 830 | 1660 | 3320 | 2545 | 995 | 1990 | 3980 | 3865 | 3635 | 3175 | 2255 |
| 431 | 862 | 1724 | 3448 | 2801 | 1507 | 3014 | 1933 | 3866 | 3637 | 3179 | 2263 |
| 439 | 878 | 1756 | 3512 | 2929 | 1763 | 3526 | 2957 | 1819 | 3638 | 3181 | 2267 |
| 443 | 886 | 1772 | 3544 | 2993 | 1891 | 3782 | 3469 | 2843 | 1591 | 3182 | 2269 |
| 445 | 890 | 1780 | 3560 | 3025 | 1955 | 3910 | 3725 | 3355 | 2615 | 1135 | 2270 |
| 463 | 926 | 1852 | 3704 | 3313 | 2531 | 967 | 1934 | 3868 | 3641 | 3187 | 2279 |
| 471 | 942 | 1884 | 3768 | 3441 | 2787 | 1479 | 2958 | 1821 | 3642 | 3189 | 2283 |
| 475 | 950 | 1900 | 3800 | 3505 | 2915 | 1735 | 3470 | 2845 | 1595 | 3190 | 2285 |
| 477 | 954 | 1908 | 3816 | 3537 | 2979 | 1863 | 3726 | 3357 | 2619 | 1143 | 2286 |
| 487 | 974 | 1948 | 3896 | 3697 | 3299 | 2503 | 911 | 1822 | 3644 | 3193 | 2291 |
| 491 | 982 | 1964 | 3928 | 3761 | 3427 | 2759 | 1423 | 2846 | 1597 | 3194 | 2293 |
| 493 | 986 | 1972 | 3944 | 3793 | 3491 | 2887 | 1679 | 3358 | 2621 | 1147 | 2294 |
| 499 | 998 | 1996 | 3992 | 3889 | 3683 | 3271 | 2447 | 799 | 1598 | 3196 | 2297 |
| 501 | 1002 | 2004 | 4008 | 3921 | 3747 | 3399 | 2703 | 1311 | 2622 | 1149 | 2298 |
| 505 | 1010 | 2020 | 4040 | 3985 | 3875 | 3655 | 3215 | 2335 | 575 | 1150 | 2300 |
| 607 | 1214 | 2428 | 761 | 1522 | 3044 | 1993 | 3986 | 3877 | 3659 | 3223 | 2351 |
| 623 | 1246 | 2492 | 889 | 1778 | 3556 | 3017 | 1939 | 3878 | 3661 | 3227 | 2359 |
| 631 | 1262 | 2524 | 953 | 1906 | 3812 | 3529 | 2963 | 1831 | 3662 | 3229 | 2363 |
| 635 | 1270 | 2540 | 985 | 1970 | 3940 | 3785 | 3475 | 2855 | 1615 | 3230 | 2365 |
| 637 | 1274 | 2548 | 1001 | 2002 | 4004 | 3913 | 3731 | 3367 | 2639 | 1183 | 2366 |
| 671 | 1342 | 2684 | 1273 | 2546 | 997 | 1994 | 3988 | 3881 | 3667 | 3239 | 2383 |
| 687 | 1374 | 2748 | 1401 | 2802 | 1509 | 3018 | 1941 | 3882 | 3669 | 3243 | 2391 |
| 695 | 1390 | 2780 | 1465 | 2930 | 1765 | 3530 | 2965 | 1835 | 3670 | 3245 | 2395 |
| 699 | 1398 | 2796 | 1497 | 2994 | 1893 | 3786 | 3477 | 2859 | 1623 | 3246 | 2397 |
| 701 | 1402 | 2804 | 1513 | 3026 | 1957 | 3914 | 3733 | 3371 | 2647 | 1199 | 2398 |
| 719 | 1438 | 2876 | 1657 | 3314 | 2533 | 971 | 1942 | 3884 | 3673 | 3251 | 2407 |
| 727 | 1454 | 2908 | 1721 | 3442 | 2789 | 1483 | 2966 | 1837 | 3674 | 3253 | 2411 |
| 731 | 1462 | 2924 | 1753 | 3506 | 2917 | 1739 | 3478 | 2861 | 1627 | 3254 | 2413 |
| 733 | 1466 | 2932 | 1769 | 3538 | 2981 | 1867 | 3734 | 3373 | 2651 | 1207 | 2414 |
| 743 | 1486 | 2972 | 1849 | 3698 | 3301 | 2507 | 919 | 1838 | 3676 | 3257 | 2419 |
| 747 | 1494 | 2988 | 1881 | 3762 | 3429 | 2763 | 1431 | 2862 | 1629 | 3258 | 2421 |
| 749 | 1498 | 2996 | 1897 | 3794 | 3493 | 2891 | 1687 | 3374 | 2653 | 1211 | 2422 |
| 755 | 1510 | 3020 | 1945 | 3890 | 3685 | 3275 | 2455 | 815 | 1630 | 3260 | 2425 |
| 757 | 1514 | 3028 | 1961 | 3922 | 3749 | 3403 | 2711 | 1327 | 2654 | 1213 | 2426 |
| 823 | 1646 | 3292 | 2489 | 883 | 1766 | 3532 | 2969 | 1843 | 3686 | 3277 | 2459 |
| 827 | 1654 | 3308 | 2521 | 947 | 1894 | 3788 | 3481 | 2867 | 1639 | 3278 | 2461 |
| 829 | 1658 | 3316 | 2537 | 979 | 1958 | 3916 | 3737 | 3379 | 2663 | 1231 | 2462 |
| 847 | 1694 | 3388 | 2681 | 1267 | 2534 | 973 | 1946 | 3892 | 3689 | 3283 | 2471 |
| 855 | 1710 | 3420 | 2745 | 1395 | 2790 | 1485 | 2970 | 1845 | 3690 | 3285 | 2475 |
| 859 | 1718 | 3436 | 2777 | 1459 | 2918 | 1741 | 3482 | 2869 | 1643 | 3286 | 2477 |
| 861 | 1722 | 3444 | 2793 | 1491 | 2982 | 1869 | 3738 | 3381 | 2667 | 1239 | 2478 |
| 871 | 1742 | 3484 | 2873 | 1651 | 3302 | 2509 | 923 | 1846 | 3692 | 3289 | 2483 |
| 875 | 1750 | 3500 | 2905 | 1715 | 3430 | 2765 | 1435 | 2870 | 1645 | 3290 | 2485 |
| 877 | 1754 | 3508 | 2921 | 1747 | 3494 | 2893 | 1691 | 3382 | 2669 | 1243 | 2486 |
| 885 | 1770 | 3540 | 2985 | 1875 | 3750 | 3405 | 2715 | 1335 | 2670 | 1245 | 2490 |
| 925 | 1850 | 3700 | 3305 | 2515 | 935 | 1870 | 3740 | 3385 | 2675 | 1255 | 2510 |
| 939 | 1878 | 3756 | 3417 | 2739 | 1383 | 2766 | 1437 | 2874 | 1653 | 3306 | 2517 |
| 941 | 1882 | 3764 | 3433 | 2771 | 1447 | 2894 | 1693 | 3386 | 2677 | 1259 | 2518 |
| 949 | 1898 | 3796 | 3497 | 2899 | 1703 | 3406 | 2717 | 1339 | 2678 | 1261 | 2522 |
| 981 | 1962 | 3924 | 3753 | 3411 | 2727 | 1359 | 2718 | 1341 | 2682 | 1269 | 2538 |
| 1367 | 2734 | 1373 | 2746 | 1397 | 2794 | 1493 | 2986 | 1877 | 3754 | 3413 | 2731 |
| 1371 | 2742 | 1389 | 2778 | 1461 | 2922 | 1749 | 3498 | 2901 | 1707 | 3414 | 2733 |
| 1387 | 2774 | 1453 | 2906 | 1717 | 3434 | 2773 | 1451 | 2902 | 1709 | 3418 | 2741 |

OCTADS

| 0 | 1 | 2 | 3 | 4 | 5 | 6 | 7 | 8 | 9 | 10 | 11 | |
|---|---|---|---|---|---|---|---|---|---|---|---|---|
| 255 | 510 | 1020 | 2040 | 4080 | 4065 | 4035 | 3975 | 3855 | 3615 | 3135 | 2175 | |
| 383 | 766 | 1532 | 3064 | 2033 | 4066 | 4037 | 3979 | 3863 | 3631 | 3167 | 2239 | |
| 447 | 894 | 1788 | 3576 | 3057 | 2019 | 4038 | 3981 | 3867 | 3639 | 3183 | 2271 | |
| 479 | 958 | 1916 | 3832 | 3569 | 3043 | 1991 | 3982 | 3869 | 3643 | 3191 | 2287 | |
| 495 | 990 | 1980 | 3960 | 3825 | 3555 | 3015 | 1935 | 3870 | 3645 | 3195 | 2295 | |
| 503 | 1006 | 2012 | 4024 | 3953 | 3811 | 3527 | 2959 | 1823 | 3646 | 3197 | 2299 | |
| 507 | 1014 | 2028 | 4056 | 4017 | 3939 | 3783 | 3471 | 2847 | 1599 | 3198 | 2301 | |
| 509 | 1018 | 2036 | 4072 | 4049 | 4003 | 3911 | 3727 | 3359 | 2623 | 1151 | 2302 | |
| 639 | 1278 | 2556 | 1017 | 2034 | 4068 | 4041 | 3987 | 3879 | 3663 | 3231 | 2367 | |
| 703 | 1406 | 2812 | 1529 | 3058 | 2021 | 4042 | 3989 | 3883 | 3671 | 3247 | 2399 | |
| 735 | 1470 | 2940 | 1785 | 3570 | 3045 | 1995 | 3990 | 3885 | 3675 | 3255 | 2415 | |
| 751 | 1502 | 3004 | 1913 | 3826 | 3557 | 3019 | 1943 | 3886 | 3677 | 3259 | 2423 | |
| 759 | 1518 | 3036 | 1977 | 3954 | 3813 | 3531 | 2967 | 1839 | 3678 | 3261 | 2427 | |
| 763 | 1526 | 3052 | 2009 | 4018 | 3941 | 3787 | 3479 | 2863 | 1631 | 3262 | 2429 | |
| 765 | 1530 | 3060 | 2025 | 4050 | 4005 | 3915 | 3735 | 3375 | 2655 | 1215 | 2430 | |
| 831 | 1662 | 3324 | 2553 | 1011 | 2022 | 4044 | 3993 | 3891 | 3687 | 3279 | 2463 | |
| 863 | 1726 | 3452 | 2809 | 1523 | 3046 | 1997 | 3994 | 3893 | 3691 | 3287 | 2479 | |
| 879 | 1758 | 3516 | 2937 | 1779 | 3558 | 3021 | 1947 | 3894 | 3693 | 3291 | 2487 | |
| 887 | 1774 | 3548 | 3001 | 1907 | 3814 | 3533 | 2971 | 1847 | 3694 | 3293 | 2491 | |
| 891 | 1782 | 3564 | 3033 | 1971 | 3942 | 3789 | 3483 | 2871 | 1647 | 3294 | 2493 | |
| 893 | 1786 | 3572 | 3049 | 2003 | 4006 | 3917 | 3739 | 3383 | 2671 | 1247 | 2494 | |
| 927 | 1854 | 3708 | 3321 | 2547 | 999 | 1998 | 3996 | 3897 | 3699 | 3303 | 2511 | |
| 943 | 1886 | 3772 | 3449 | 2803 | 1511 | 3022 | 1949 | 3898 | 3701 | 3307 | 2519 | |
| 951 | 1902 | 3804 | 3513 | 2931 | 1767 | 3534 | 2973 | 1851 | 3702 | 3309 | 2523 | |
| 955 | 1910 | 3820 | 3545 | 2995 | 1895 | 3790 | 3485 | 2875 | 1655 | 3310 | 2525 | |
| 957 | 1914 | 3828 | 3561 | 3027 | 1959 | 3918 | 3741 | 3387 | 2679 | 1263 | 2526 | |
| 975 | 1950 | 3900 | 3705 | 3315 | 2535 | 975 | 1950 | 3900 | 3705 | 3315 | 2535 | * |
| 983 | 1966 | 3932 | 3769 | 3443 | 2791 | 1487 | 2974 | 1853 | 3706 | 3317 | 2539 | |
| 987 | 1974 | 3948 | 3801 | 3507 | 2919 | 1743 | 3486 | 2877 | 1659 | 3318 | 2541 | |
| 989 | 1978 | 3956 | 3817 | 3539 | 2983 | 1871 | 3742 | 3389 | 2683 | 1271 | 2542 | |
| 1003 | 2006 | 4012 | 3929 | 3763 | 3431 | 2767 | 1439 | 2878 | 1661 | 3322 | 2549 | |
| 1005 | 2010 | 4020 | 3945 | 3795 | 3495 | 2895 | 1695 | 3390 | 2685 | 1275 | 2550 | |
| 1013 | 2026 | 4052 | 4009 | 3923 | 3751 | 3407 | 2719 | 1343 | 2686 | 1277 | 2554 | |
| 1375 | 2750 | 1405 | 2810 | 1525 | 3050 | 2005 | 4010 | 3925 | 3755 | 3415 | 2735 | |
| 1391 | 2782 | 1469 | 2938 | 1781 | 3562 | 3029 | 1963 | 3926 | 3757 | 3419 | 2743 | |
| 1399 | 2798 | 1501 | 3002 | 1909 | 3818 | 3541 | 2987 | 1879 | 3758 | 3421 | 2747 | |
| 1403 | 2806 | 1517 | 3034 | 1973 | 3946 | 3797 | 3499 | 2903 | 1711 | 3422 | 2749 | |
| 1455 | 2910 | 1725 | 3450 | 2805 | 1515 | 3030 | 1965 | 3930 | 3765 | 3435 | 2775 | |
| 1463 | 2926 | 1757 | 3514 | 2933 | 1771 | 3542 | 2989 | 1883 | 3766 | 3437 | 2779 | |
| 1467 | 2934 | 1773 | 3546 | 2997 | 1899 | 3798 | 3501 | 2907 | 1719 | 3438 | 2781 | |
| 1495 | 2990 | 1885 | 3770 | 3445 | 2795 | 1495 | 2990 | 1885 | 3770 | 3445 | 2795 | * |
| 1499 | 2998 | 1901 | 3802 | 3509 | 2923 | 1751 | 3502 | 2909 | 1723 | 3446 | 2797 | |
| 1755 | 3510 | 2925 | 1755 | 3510 | 2925 | 1755 | 3510 | 2925 | 1755 | 3510 | 2925 | * |

NONADS

| 0 | 1 | 2 | 3 | 4 | 5 | 6 | 7 | 8 | 9 | 10 | 11 | |
|---|---|---|---|---|---|---|---|---|---|---|---|---|
| 511 | 1022 | 2044 | 4088 | 4081 | 4067 | 4039 | 3983 | 3871 | 3647 | 3199 | 2303 | |
| 767 | 1534 | 3068 | 2041 | 4082 | 4069 | 4043 | 3991 | 3887 | 3679 | 3263 | 2431 | |
| 895 | 1790 | 3580 | 3065 | 2035 | 4070 | 4045 | 3995 | 3895 | 3695 | 3295 | 2495 | |
| 959 | 1918 | 3836 | 3577 | 3059 | 2023 | 4046 | 3997 | 3899 | 3703 | 3311 | 2527 | |
| 991 | 1982 | 3964 | 3833 | 3571 | 3047 | 1999 | 3998 | 3901 | 3707 | 3319 | 2543 | |
| 1007 | 2014 | 4028 | 3961 | 3827 | 3559 | 3023 | 1951 | 3902 | 3709 | 3323 | 2551 | |
| 1015 | 2030 | 4060 | 4025 | 3955 | 3815 | 3535 | 2975 | 1855 | 3710 | 3325 | 2555 | |
| 1019 | 2038 | 4076 | 4057 | 4019 | 3943 | 3791 | 3487 | 2879 | 1663 | 3326 | 2557 | |
| 1021 | 2042 | 4084 | 4073 | 4051 | 4007 | 3919 | 3743 | 3391 | 2687 | 1279 | 2558 | |
| 1407 | 2814 | 1533 | 3066 | 2037 | 4074 | 4053 | 4011 | 3927 | 3759 | 3423 | 2751 | |
| 1471 | 2942 | 1789 | 3578 | 3061 | 2027 | 4054 | 4013 | 3931 | 3767 | 3439 | 2783 | |
| 1503 | 3006 | 1917 | 3834 | 3573 | 3051 | 2007 | 4014 | 3933 | 3771 | 3447 | 2799 | |
| 1519 | 3038 | 1981 | 3962 | 3829 | 3563 | 3031 | 1967 | 3934 | 3773 | 3451 | 2807 | |
| 1527 | 3054 | 2013 | 4026 | 3957 | 3819 | 3543 | 2991 | 1887 | 3774 | 3453 | 2811 | |
| 1531 | 3062 | 2029 | 4058 | 4021 | 3947 | 3799 | 3503 | 2911 | 1727 | 3454 | 2813 | |
| 1759 | 3518 | 2941 | 1787 | 3574 | 3053 | 2011 | 4022 | 3949 | 3803 | 3511 | 2927 | |
| 1775 | 3550 | 3005 | 1915 | 3830 | 3565 | 3035 | 1975 | 3950 | 3805 | 3515 | 2935 | |
| 1783 | 3566 | 3037 | 1979 | 3958 | 3821 | 3547 | 2999 | 1903 | 3806 | 3517 | 2939 | |
| 1911 | 3822 | 3549 | 3003 | 1911 | 3822 | 3549 | 3003 | 1911 | 3822 | 3549 | 3003 | * |

DECADS

| 0 | 1 | 2 | 3 | 4 | 5 | 6 | 7 | 8 | 9 | 10 | 11 | |
|---|---|---|---|---|---|---|---|---|---|---|---|---|
| 1023 | 2046 | 4092 | 4089 | 4083 | 4071 | 4047 | 3999 | 3903 | 3711 | 3327 | 2559 | |
| 1535 | 3070 | 2045 | 4090 | 4085 | 4075 | 4055 | 4015 | 3935 | 3775 | 3455 | 2815 | |
| 1791 | 3582 | 3069 | 2043 | 4086 | 4077 | 4059 | 4023 | 3951 | 3807 | 3519 | 2943 | |
| 1919 | 3838 | 3581 | 3067 | 2039 | 4078 | 4061 | 4027 | 3959 | 3823 | 3551 | 3007 | |
| 1983 | 3966 | 3837 | 3579 | 3063 | 2031 | 4062 | 4029 | 3963 | 3831 | 3567 | 3039 | |
| 2015 | 4030 | 3965 | 3835 | 3575 | 3055 | 2015 | 4030 | 3965 | 3835 | 3575 | 3055 | * |

UNDECADS

| 0 | 1 | 2 | 3 | 4 | 5 | 6 | 7 | 8 | 9 | 10 | 11 |
|---|---|---|---|---|---|---|---|---|---|---|---|
| 2047 | 4094 | 4093 | 4091 | 4087 | 4079 | 4063 | 4031 | 3967 | 3839 | 3583 | 3071 |

DUODECADS

| 0 | 1 | 2 | 3 | 4 | 5 | 6 | 7 | 8 | 9 | 10 | 11 | |
|---|---|---|---|---|---|---|---|---|---|---|---|---|
| 4095 | 4095 | 4095 | 4095 | 4095 | 4095 | 4095 | 4095 | 4095 | 4095 | 4095 | 4095 | * |

## EXERCISES

**2.11** Two strings of beads are said to be "equivalent" or "the same" if and only if they differ only by a rotation about their centers either in the plane or about an axis in the plane. John Riordan [4] has given the enumerator for necklaces with <u>n</u> beads, each of which may have any of <u>c</u> colors, when necklace turnovers are not permitted and equivalences are produced by turns in one direction. Using this necklace counting formula, show that the arrangement of Table I above is correct. (<u>Hint.</u> Let the tones of a harmony be identified with beads of one color, the tones of its complement, another color. Find the answer to the question: How many distinct twelve-bead necklaces can be made out of an infinite supply of beads in two different colors?)

**2.12** Solve the necklace problem for the 19-tone equitempered quantization scale and prepare a computer program to calculate tables similar to Tables I (above) and II (below) for this and other microtonal scales.

**2.13** To program a computer to identify a given harmony by name is conceptually simple, even without using factored notation. The computer is instructed to consult a code directory or stored table linking the numerical designation of each given harmony with its established name, or with an indication that no such name exists. The 4096 designations provide, either directly or indirectly, the address pointing to the correct names. Alternatively, to conserve storage, the computer is caused to cyclically left shift the twelve-digit binary equivalent to find a minimum orbital value. When this value is determined, the computer relates it to a corresponding entry in a book of names associated with the 352 characteristic harmonies in order to find the one intended. After reducing the "traditional" chords listed in Appendix II of Grove's <u>Dictionary</u> [5] to characteristic form, program a computer to use this information to analyze elementary harmonic progressions.

**2.14** Show that there are exactly

$$4096^2$$

possible different harmonic progressions two units long;

$$4096^3,$$

three units long;

$$4096^n,$$

n units long; and

$$4096(4096^{n+1} - 1)/4095$$

strings of length at most n units.

FIGURE 2.4

Table look-up is exemplified as follows: In order to reduce that pentatonic scale designated by 3968 to characteristic form, first break off the right-hand digit 8 to use as a column index and then take the remaining digits 396 to use as a row index. The element of the table pointed to by these indices is 31*128. Thus harmony 3968 has characteristic 31 and level 128. As 31, 62, and 124 are each less than or equal to 127 and this inequality holds for no other orbital value, it may be seen immediately that every major scale includes three pentatonic scales as subharmonies.

<u>REDUCTION TO CHARACTERISTIC FORM</u>

| | 0 | 1 | 2 | 3 | 4 | 5 | 6 | 7 | 8 | 9 |
|---|---|---|---|---|---|---|---|---|---|---|
| 0 | 0*1 | 1*1 | 1*2 | 3*1 | 1*4 | 5*1 | 3*2 | 7*1 | 1*8 | 9*1 |
| 1 | 5*2 | 11*1 | 3*4 | 13*1 | 7*2 | 15*1 | 1*16 | 17*1 | 9*2 | 19*1 |
| 2 | 5*4 | 21*1 | 11*2 | 23*1 | 3*8 | 25*1 | 13*2 | 27*1 | 7*4 | 29*1 |
| 3 | 15*2 | 31*1 | 1*32 | 33*1 | 17*2 | 35*1 | 9*4 | 37*1 | 19*2 | 39*1 |
| 4 | 5*8 | 41*1 | 21*2 | 43*1 | 11*4 | 45*1 | 23*2 | 47*1 | 3*16 | 49*1 |
| 5 | 25*2 | 51*1 | 13*4 | 53*1 | 27*2 | 55*1 | 7*8 | 57*1 | 29*2 | 59*1 |
| 6 | 15*4 | 61*1 | 31*2 | 63*1 | 1*64 | 65*1 | 33*2 | 67*1 | 17*4 | 69*1 |
| 7 | 35*2 | 71*1 | 9*8 | 73*1 | 37*2 | 75*1 | 19*4 | 77*1 | 39*2 | 79*1 |
| 8 | 5*16 | 81*1 | 41*2 | 83*1 | 21*4 | 85*1 | 43*2 | 87*1 | 11*8 | 89*1 |
| 9 | 45*2 | 91*1 | 23*4 | 93*1 | 47*2 | 95*1 | 3*32 | 97*1 | 49*2 | 99*1 |

| | 0 | 1 | 2 | 3 | 4 | 5 | 6 | 7 | 8 | 9 |
|---|---|---|---|---|---|---|---|---|---|---|
| 10 | 25*4 | 101*1 | 51*2 | 103*1 | 13*8 | 105*1 | 53*2 | 107*1 | 27*4 | 109*1 |
| 11 | 55*2 | 111*1 | 7*16 | 113*1 | 57*2 | 115*1 | 29*4 | 117*1 | 59*2 | 119*1 |
| 12 | 15*8 | 121*1 | 61*2 | 123*1 | 31*4 | 125*1 | 63*2 | 127*1 | 1*128 | 33*128 |
| 13 | 65*2 | 97*128 | 33*4 | 133*1 | 67*2 | 135*1 | 17*8 | 137*1 | 69*2 | 139*1 |
| 14 | 35*4 | 141*1 | 71*2 | 143*1 | 9*16 | 145*1 | 73*2 | 147*1 | 37*4 | 149*1 |
| 15 | 75*2 | 151*1 | 19*8 | 153*1 | 77*2 | 155*1 | 39*4 | 157*1 | 79*2 | 159*1 |
| 16 | 5*32 | 133*32 | 81*2 | 163*1 | 41*4 | 165*1 | 83*2 | 167*1 | 21*8 | 169*1 |
| 17 | 85*2 | 171*1 | 43*4 | 173*1 | 87*2 | 175*1 | 11*16 | 177*1 | 89*2 | 179*1 |
| 18 | 45*4 | 181*1 | 91*2 | 183*1 | 23*8 | 185*1 | 93*2 | 187*1 | 47*4 | 189*1 |
| 19 | 95*2 | 191*1 | 3*64 | 67*64 | 97*2 | 195*1 | 49*4 | 197*1 | 99*2 | 199*1 |
| 20 | 25*8 | 201*1 | 101*2 | 203*1 | 51*4 | 205*1 | 103*2 | 207*1 | 13*16 | 209*1 |
| 21 | 105*2 | 211*1 | 53*4 | 213*1 | 107*2 | 215*1 | 27*8 | 217*1 | 109*2 | 219*1 |
| 22 | 55*4 | 221*1 | 111*2 | 223*1 | 7*32 | 135*32 | 113*2 | 227*1 | 57*4 | 229*1 |
| 23 | 115*2 | 231*1 | 29*8 | 233*1 | 117*2 | 235*1 | 59*4 | 237*1 | 119*2 | 239*1 |
| 24 | 15*16 | 241*1 | 121*2 | 243*1 | 61*4 | 245*1 | 123*2 | 247*1 | 31*8 | 249*1 |
| 25 | 125*2 | 251*1 | 63*4 | 253*1 | 127*2 | 255*1 | 1*256 | 17*256 | 33*256 | 49*256 |
| 26 | 65*4 | 81*256 | 97*256 | 113*256 | 33*8 | 145*256 | 133*2 | 177*256 | 67*4 | 209*256 |
| 27 | 135*2 | 241*256 | 17*16 | 273*1 | 137*2 | 275*1 | 69*4 | 277*1 | 139*2 | 279*1 |
| 28 | 35*8 | 281*1 | 141*2 | 283*1 | 71*4 | 285*1 | 143*2 | 287*1 | 9*32 | 137*32 |
| 29 | 145*2 | 291*1 | 73*4 | 293*1 | 147*2 | 295*1 | 37*8 | 297*1 | 149*2 | 299*1 |
| 30 | 75*4 | 301*1 | 151*2 | 303*1 | 19*16 | 275*16 | 153*2 | 307*1 | 77*4 | 309*1 |
| 31 | 155*2 | 311*1 | 39*8 | 313*1 | 157*2 | 315*1 | 79*4 | 317*1 | 159*2 | 319*1 |
| 32 | 5*64 | 69*64 | 133*64 | 197*64 | 81*4 | 325*1 | 163*2 | 327*1 | 41*8 | 329*1 |
| 33 | 165*2 | 331*1 | 83*4 | 333*1 | 167*2 | 335*1 | 21*16 | 277*16 | 169*2 | 339*1 |
| 34 | 85*4 | 341*1 | 171*2 | 343*1 | 43*8 | 345*1 | 173*2 | 347*1 | 87*4 | 349*1 |
| 35 | 175*2 | 351*1 | 11*32 | 139*32 | 177*2 | 355*1 | 89*4 | 357*1 | 179*2 | 359*1 |
| 36 | 45*8 | 361*1 | 181*2 | 363*1 | 91*4 | 365*1 | 183*2 | 367*1 | 23*16 | 279*16 |
| 37 | 185*2 | 371*1 | 93*4 | 373*1 | 187*2 | 375*1 | 47*8 | 377*1 | 189*2 | 379*1 |
| 38 | 95*4 | 381*1 | 191*2 | 383*1 | 3*128 | 35*128 | 67*128 | 99*128 | 97*4 | 163*128 |
| 39 | 195*2 | 227*128 | 49*8 | 291*128 | 197*2 | 355*128 | 99*4 | 397*1 | 199*2 | 399*1 |
| 40 | 25*16 | 281*16 | 201*2 | 403*1 | 101*4 | 405*1 | 203*2 | 407*1 | 51*8 | 409*1 |
| 41 | 205*2 | 411*1 | 103*4 | 413*1 | 207*2 | 415*1 | 13*32 | 141*32 | 209*2 | 397*32 |
| 42 | 105*4 | 421*1 | 211*2 | 423*1 | 53*8 | 425*1 | 213*2 | 427*1 | 107*4 | 429*1 |
| 43 | 215*2 | 431*1 | 27*16 | 283*16 | 217*2 | 435*1 | 109*4 | 437*1 | 219*2 | 439*1 |
| 44 | 55*8 | 441*1 | 221*2 | 443*1 | 111*4 | 445*1 | 223*2 | 447*1 | 7*64 | 71*64 |
| 45 | 135*64 | 199*64 | 113*4 | 327*64 | 227*2 | 455*1 | 57*8 | 457*1 | 229*2 | 459*1 |
| 46 | 115*4 | 461*1 | 231*2 | 463*1 | 29*16 | 285*16 | 233*2 | 467*1 | 117*4 | 469*1 |
| 47 | 235*2 | 471*1 | 59*8 | 473*1 | 237*2 | 475*1 | 119*4 | 477*1 | 239*2 | 479*1 |
| 48 | 15*32 | 143*32 | 241*2 | 399*32 | 121*4 | 485*1 | 243*2 | 487*1 | 61*8 | 489*1 |
| 49 | 245*2 | 491*1 | 123*4 | 493*1 | 247*2 | 495*1 | 31*16 | 287*16 | 249*2 | 499*1 |
| 50 | 125*4 | 501*1 | 251*2 | 503*1 | 63*8 | 505*1 | 253*2 | 507*1 | 127*4 | 509*1 |
| 51 | 255*2 | 511*1 | 1*512 | 9*512 | 17*512 | 25*512 | 33*512 | 41*512 | 49*512 | 57*512 |
| 52 | 65*8 | 73*512 | 81*512 | 89*512 | 97*512 | 105*512 | 113*512 | 121*512 | 33*16 | 137*512 |
| 53 | 145*512 | 153*512 | 133*4 | 169*512 | 177*512 | 185*512 | 67*8 | 201*512 | 209*512 | 217*512 |
| 54 | 135*4 | 233*512 | 241*512 | 249*512 | 17*32 | 145*32 | 273*2 | 281*512 | 137*4 | 297*512 |
| 55 | 275*2 | 313*512 | 69*8 | 329*512 | 277*2 | 345*512 | 139*4 | 361*512 | 279*2 | 377*512 |
| 56 | 35*16 | 291*16 | 281*2 | 409*512 | 141*4 | 425*512 | 283*2 | 441*512 | 71*8 | 457*512 |
| 57 | 285*2 | 473*512 | 143*4 | 489*512 | 287*2 | 505*512 | 9*64 | 73*64 | 137*64 | 201*64 |
| 58 | 145*4 | 329*64 | 291*2 | 457*64 | 73*8 | 585*1 | 293*2 | 587*1 | 147*4 | 589*1 |
| 59 | 295*2 | 591*1 | 37*16 | 293*16 | 297*2 | 595*1 | 149*4 | 597*1 | 299*2 | 599*1 |
| 60 | 75*8 | 587*8 | 301*2 | 603*1 | 151*4 | 605*1 | 303*2 | 607*1 | 19*32 | 147*32 |
| 61 | 275*32 | 403*32 | 153*4 | 613*1 | 307*2 | 615*1 | 77*8 | 589*8 | 309*2 | 619*1 |
| 62 | 155*4 | 621*1 | 311*2 | 623*1 | 39*16 | 295*16 | 313*2 | 627*1 | 157*4 | 629*1 |
| 63 | 315*2 | 631*1 | 79*8 | 591*8 | 317*2 | 635*1 | 159*4 | 637*1 | 319*2 | 639*1 |
| 64 | 5*128 | 37*128 | 69*128 | 101*128 | 133*128 | 165*128 | 197*128 | 229*128 | 81*8 | 293*128 |
| 65 | 325*2 | 357*128 | 163*4 | 421*128 | 327*2 | 485*128 | 41*16 | 297*16 | 329*2 | 613*128 |
| 66 | 165*4 | 661*1 | 331*2 | 663*1 | 83*8 | 595*8 | 333*2 | 667*1 | 167*4 | 669*1 |
| 67 | 335*2 | 671*1 | 21*32 | 149*32 | 277*32 | 405*32 | 169*4 | 661*32 | 339*2 | 679*1 |
| 68 | 85*8 | 597*8 | 341*2 | 683*1 | 171*4 | 685*1 | 343*2 | 687*1 | 43*16 | 299*16 |
| 69 | 345*2 | 691*1 | 173*4 | 693*1 | 347*2 | 695*1 | 87*8 | 599*8 | 349*2 | 699*1 |
| 70 | 175*4 | 701*1 | 351*2 | 703*1 | 11*64 | 75*64 | 139*64 | 203*64 | 177*4 | 331*64 |
| 71 | 355*2 | 459*64 | 89*8 | 587*64 | 357*2 | 715*1 | 179*4 | 717*1 | 359*2 | 719*1 |
| 72 | 45*16 | 301*16 | 361*2 | 723*1 | 181*4 | 725*1 | 363*2 | 727*1 | 91*8 | 603*8 |
| 73 | 365*2 | 731*1 | 183*4 | 733*1 | 367*2 | 735*1 | 23*32 | 151*32 | 279*32 | 407*32 |
| 74 | 185*4 | 663*32 | 371*2 | 743*1 | 93*8 | 605*8 | 373*2 | 747*1 | 187*4 | 749*1 |
| 75 | 375*2 | 751*1 | 47*16 | 303*16 | 377*2 | 755*1 | 189*4 | 757*1 | 379*2 | 759*1 |
| 76 | 95*8 | 607*8 | 381*2 | 763*1 | 191*4 | 765*1 | 383*2 | 767*1 | 3*256 | 19*256 |
| 77 | 35*256 | 51*256 | 67*256 | 83*256 | 99*256 | 115*256 | 97*8 | 147*256 | 163*256 | 179*256 |
| 78 | 195*4 | 211*256 | 227*256 | 243*256 | 49*16 | 275*256 | 291*256 | 307*256 | 197*4 | 339*256 |
| 79 | 355*256 | 371*256 | 99*8 | 403*256 | 397*2 | 435*256 | 199*4 | 467*256 | 399*2 | 499*256 |
| 80 | 25*32 | 153*32 | 281*32 | 409*32 | 201*4 | 595*256 | 403*2 | 627*256 | 101*8 | 613*8 |
| 81 | 405*2 | 691*256 | 203*4 | 723*256 | 407*2 | 755*256 | 51*16 | 307*16 | 409*2 | 819*1 |
| 82 | 205*4 | 821*1 | 411*2 | 823*1 | 103*8 | 615*8 | 413*2 | 827*1 | 207*4 | 829*1 |
| 83 | 415*2 | 831*1 | 13*64 | 77*64 | 141*64 | 205*64 | 209*4 | 333*64 | 397*64 | 461*64 |
| 84 | 105*8 | 589*64 | 421*2 | 717*64 | 211*4 | 845*1 | 423*2 | 847*1 | 53*16 | 309*16 |
| 85 | 425*2 | 821*16 | 213*4 | 853*1 | 427*2 | 855*1 | 107*8 | 619*8 | 429*2 | 859*1 |
| 86 | 215*4 | 861*1 | 431*2 | 863*1 | 27*32 | 155*32 | 283*32 | 411*32 | 217*4 | 667*32 |
| 87 | 435*2 | 871*1 | 109*8 | 621*8 | 437*2 | 875*1 | 219*4 | 877*1 | 439*2 | 879*1 |
| 88 | 55*16 | 311*16 | 441*2 | 823*16 | 221*4 | 885*1 | 443*2 | 887*1 | 111*8 | 623*8 |
| 89 | 445*2 | 891*1 | 223*4 | 893*1 | 447*2 | 895*1 | 7*128 | 39*128 | 71*128 | 103*128 |
| 90 | 135*128 | 167*128 | 199*128 | 231*128 | 113*8 | 295*128 | 327*128 | 359*128 | 227*4 | 423*128 |
| 91 | 455*2 | 487*128 | 57*16 | 313*16 | 457*2 | 615*128 | 229*4 | 679*128 | 459*2 | 743*128 |
| 92 | 115*8 | 627*8 | 461*2 | 871*128 | 231*4 | 925*1 | 463*2 | 927*1 | 29*32 | 157*32 |
| 93 | 285*32 | 413*32 | 233*4 | 669*32 | 467*2 | 925*32 | 117*8 | 629*8 | 469*2 | 939*1 |
| 94 | 235*4 | 941*1 | 471*2 | 943*1 | 59*16 | 315*16 | 473*2 | 827*16 | 237*4 | 949*1 |
| 95 | 475*2 | 951*1 | 119*8 | 631*8 | 477*2 | 955*1 | 239*4 | 957*1 | 479*2 | 959*1 |
| 96 | 15*64 | 79*64 | 143*64 | 207*64 | 241*4 | 335*64 | 399*64 | 463*64 | 121*8 | 591*64 |
| 97 | 485*2 | 719*64 | 243*4 | 847*64 | 487*2 | 975*1 | 61*16 | 317*16 | 489*2 | 829*16 |
| 98 | 245*4 | 981*1 | 491*2 | 983*1 | 123*8 | 635*8 | 493*2 | 987*1 | 247*4 | 989*1 |
| 99 | 495*2 | 991*1 | 31*32 | 159*32 | 287*32 | 415*32 | 249*4 | 671*32 | 499*2 | 927*32 |

| | 0 | 1 | 2 | 3 | 4 | 5 | 6 | 7 | 8 | 9 |
|---|---|---|---|---|---|---|---|---|---|---|
| 100 | 125*8 | 637*8 | 501*2 | 1003*1 | 251*4 | 1005*1 | 503*2 | 1007*1 | 63*16 | 319*16 |
| 101 | 505*2 | 831*16 | 253*4 | 1013*1 | 507*2 | 1015*1 | 127*8 | 639*8 | 509*2 | 1019*1 |
| 102 | 255*4 | 1021*1 | 511*2 | 1023*1 | 1*1024 | 5*1024 | 9*1024 | 13*1024 | 17*1024 | 21*1024 |
| 103 | 25*1024 | 29*1024 | 33*1024 | 37*1024 | 41*1024 | 45*1024 | 49*1024 | 53*1024 | 57*1024 | 61*1024 |
| 104 | 65*16 | 69*1024 | 73*1024 | 77*1024 | 81*1024 | 85*1024 | 89*1024 | 93*1024 | 97*1024 | 101*1024 |
| 105 | 105*1024 | 109*1024 | 113*1024 | 117*1024 | 121*1024 | 125*1024 | 33*32 | 133*1024 | 137*1024 | 141*1024 |
| 106 | 145*1024 | 149*1024 | 153*1024 | 157*1024 | 133*8 | 165*1024 | 169*1024 | 173*1024 | 177*1024 | 181*1024 |
| 107 | 185*1024 | 189*1024 | 67*16 | 197*1024 | 201*1024 | 205*1024 | 209*1024 | 213*1024 | 217*1024 | 221*1024 |
| 108 | 135*8 | 229*1024 | 233*1024 | 237*1024 | 241*1024 | 245*1024 | 249*1024 | 253*1024 | 17*64 | 81*64 |
| 109 | 145*64 | 209*64 | 273*4 | 277*1024 | 281*1024 | 285*1024 | 137*8 | 293*1024 | 297*1024 | 301*1024 |
| 110 | 275*4 | 309*1024 | 313*1024 | 317*1024 | 69*16 | 325*16 | 329*1024 | 333*1024 | 277*4 | 341*1024 |
| 111 | 345*1024 | 349*1024 | 139*8 | 357*1024 | 361*1024 | 365*1024 | 279*4 | 373*1024 | 377*1024 | 381*1024 |
| 112 | 35*32 | 163*32 | 291*32 | 397*1024 | 281*4 | 405*1024 | 409*1024 | 413*1024 | 141*8 | 421*1024 |
| 113 | 425*1024 | 429*1024 | 283*4 | 437*1024 | 441*1024 | 445*1024 | 71*16 | 327*16 | 457*1024 | 461*1024 |
| 114 | 285*4 | 469*1024 | 473*1024 | 477*1024 | 143*8 | 485*1024 | 489*1024 | 493*1024 | 287*4 | 501*1024 |
| 115 | 505*1024 | 509*1024 | 9*128 | 41*128 | 73*128 | 105*128 | 137*128 | 169*128 | 201*128 | 233*128 |
| 116 | 145*8 | 297*128 | 329*128 | 361*128 | 291*4 | 425*128 | 457*128 | 489*128 | 73*16 | 329*16 |
| 117 | 585*2 | 589*1024 | 293*4 | 597*1024 | 587*2 | 605*1024 | 147*8 | 613*1024 | 589*2 | 621*1024 |
| 118 | 295*4 | 629*1024 | 591*2 | 637*1024 | 37*32 | 165*32 | 293*32 | 421*32 | 297*4 | 661*1024 |
| 119 | 595*2 | 669*1024 | 149*8 | 661*8 | 597*2 | 685*1024 | 299*4 | 693*1024 | 599*2 | 701*1024 |
| 120 | 75*16 | 331*16 | 587*16 | 717*1024 | 301*4 | 725*1024 | 603*2 | 733*1024 | 151*8 | 663*8 |
| 121 | 605*2 | 749*1024 | 303*4 | 757*1024 | 607*2 | 765*1024 | 19*64 | 83*64 | 147*64 | 211*64 |
| 122 | 275*64 | 339*64 | 403*64 | 467*64 | 153*8 | 595*64 | 613*2 | 723*64 | 307*4 | 821*1024 |
| 123 | 615*2 | 829*1024 | 77*16 | 333*16 | 589*16 | 845*16 | 309*4 | 853*1024 | 619*2 | 861*1024 |
| 124 | 155*8 | 667*8 | 621*2 | 877*1024 | 311*4 | 885*1024 | 623*2 | 893*1024 | 39*32 | 167*32 |
| 125 | 295*32 | 423*32 | 313*4 | 679*32 | 627*2 | 925*1024 | 157*8 | 669*8 | 629*2 | 941*1024 |
| 126 | 315*4 | 949*1024 | 631*2 | 957*1024 | 79*16 | 335*16 | 591*16 | 847*16 | 317*4 | 981*1024 |
| 127 | 635*2 | 989*1024 | 159*8 | 671*8 | 637*2 | 1005*1024 | 319*4 | 1013*1024 | 639*2 | 1021*1024 |
| 128 | 5*256 | 21*256 | 37*256 | 53*256 | 69*256 | 85*256 | 101*256 | 117*256 | 133*256 | 149*256 |
| 129 | 165*256 | 181*256 | 197*256 | 213*256 | 229*256 | 245*256 | 81*16 | 277*256 | 293*256 | 309*256 |
| 130 | 325*4 | 341*256 | 357*256 | 373*256 | 163*8 | 405*256 | 421*256 | 437*256 | 327*4 | 469*256 |
| 131 | 485*256 | 501*256 | 41*32 | 169*32 | 297*32 | 425*32 | 329*4 | 597*256 | 613*256 | 629*256 |
| 132 | 165*8 | 661*256 | 661*2 | 693*256 | 331*4 | 725*256 | 663*2 | 757*256 | 83*16 | 339*16 |
| 133 | 595*16 | 821*256 | 333*4 | 853*256 | 667*2 | 885*256 | 167*8 | 679*8 | 669*2 | 949*256 |
| 134 | 335*4 | 981*256 | 671*2 | 1013*256 | 21*64 | 85*64 | 149*64 | 213*64 | 277*64 | 341*64 |
| 135 | 405*64 | 469*64 | 169*8 | 597*64 | 661*64 | 725*64 | 339*4 | 853*64 | 679*2 | 981*64 |
| 136 | 85*16 | 341*16 | 597*16 | 853*16 | 341*4 | 1365*1 | 683*2 | 1367*1 | 171*8 | 683*8 |
| 137 | 685*2 | 1371*1 | 343*4 | 1367*4 | 687*2 | 1375*1 | 43*32 | 171*32 | 299*32 | 427*32 |
| 138 | 345*4 | 683*32 | 691*2 | 939*32 | 173*8 | 685*8 | 693*2 | 1387*1 | 347*4 | 1371*4 |
| 139 | 695*2 | 1391*1 | 87*16 | 343*16 | 599*16 | 855*16 | 349*4 | 1367*16 | 699*2 | 1399*1 |
| 140 | 175*8 | 687*8 | 701*2 | 1403*1 | 351*4 | 1375*4 | 703*2 | 1407*1 | 11*128 | 43*128 |
| 141 | 75*128 | 107*128 | 139*128 | 171*128 | 203*128 | 235*128 | 177*8 | 299*128 | 331*128 | 363*128 |
| 142 | 355*4 | 427*128 | 459*128 | 491*128 | 89*16 | 345*16 | 587*128 | 619*128 | 357*4 | 683*128 |
| 143 | 715*2 | 747*128 | 179*8 | 691*8 | 717*2 | 875*128 | 359*4 | 939*128 | 719*2 | 1003*128 |
| 144 | 45*32 | 173*32 | 301*32 | 429*32 | 361*4 | 685*32 | 723*2 | 941*32 | 181*8 | 693*8 |
| 145 | 725*2 | 1387*128 | 363*4 | 1387*4 | 727*2 | 1455*1 | 91*16 | 347*16 | 603*16 | 859*16 |
| 146 | 365*4 | 1371*16 | 731*2 | 1463*1 | 183*8 | 695*8 | 733*2 | 1467*1 | 367*4 | 1391*4 |
| 147 | 735*2 | 1471*1 | 23*64 | 87*64 | 151*64 | 215*64 | 279*64 | 343*64 | 407*64 | 471*64 |
| 148 | 185*8 | 599*64 | 663*64 | 727*64 | 371*4 | 855*64 | 743*2 | 983*64 | 93*16 | 349*16 |
| 149 | 605*16 | 861*16 | 373*4 | 1367*64 | 747*2 | 1495*1 | 187*8 | 699*8 | 749*2 | 1499*1 |
| 150 | 375*4 | 1399*4 | 751*2 | 1503*1 | 47*32 | 175*32 | 303*32 | 431*32 | 377*4 | 687*32 |
| 151 | 755*2 | 943*32 | 189*8 | 701*8 | 757*2 | 1455*32 | 379*4 | 1403*4 | 759*2 | 1519*1 |
| 152 | 95*16 | 351*16 | 607*16 | 863*16 | 381*4 | 1375*16 | 763*2 | 1527*1 | 191*8 | 703*8 |
| 153 | 765*2 | 1531*1 | 383*4 | 1407*4 | 767*2 | 1535*1 | 3*512 | 11*512 | 19*512 | 27*512 |
| 154 | 35*512 | 43*512 | 51*512 | 59*512 | 67*512 | 75*512 | 83*512 | 91*512 | 99*512 | 107*512 |
| 155 | 115*512 | 123*512 | 97*16 | 139*512 | 147*512 | 155*512 | 163*512 | 171*512 | 179*512 | 187*512 |
| 156 | 195*8 | 203*512 | 211*512 | 219*512 | 227*512 | 235*512 | 243*512 | 251*512 | 49*32 | 177*32 |
| 157 | 275*512 | 283*512 | 291*512 | 299*512 | 307*512 | 315*512 | 197*8 | 331*512 | 339*512 | 347*512 |
| 158 | 355*512 | 363*512 | 371*512 | 379*512 | 99*16 | 355*16 | 403*512 | 411*512 | 397*4 | 427*512 |
| 159 | 435*512 | 443*512 | 199*8 | 459*512 | 467*512 | 475*512 | 399*4 | 491*512 | 499*512 | 507*512 |
| 160 | 25*64 | 89*64 | 153*64 | 217*64 | 281*64 | 345*64 | 409*64 | 473*64 | 201*8 | 587*512 |
| 161 | 595*512 | 603*512 | 403*4 | 619*512 | 627*512 | 635*512 | 101*16 | 357*16 | 613*16 | 667*512 |
| 162 | 405*4 | 683*512 | 691*512 | 699*512 | 203*8 | 715*8 | 723*512 | 731*512 | 407*4 | 747*512 |
| 163 | 755*512 | 763*512 | 51*32 | 179*32 | 307*32 | 435*32 | 409*4 | 691*32 | 819*2 | 827*512 |
| 164 | 205*8 | 717*8 | 821*2 | 859*512 | 411*4 | 875*512 | 823*2 | 891*512 | 103*16 | 359*16 |
| 165 | 615*16 | 871*16 | 413*4 | 939*512 | 827*2 | 955*512 | 207*8 | 719*8 | 829*2 | 987*512 |
| 166 | 415*4 | 1003*512 | 831*2 | 1019*512 | 13*128 | 45*128 | 77*128 | 109*128 | 141*128 | 173*128 |
| 167 | 205*128 | 237*128 | 209*8 | 301*128 | 333*128 | 365*128 | 397*128 | 429*128 | 461*128 | 493*128 |
| 168 | 105*16 | 361*16 | 589*128 | 621*128 | 421*4 | 685*128 | 717*128 | 749*128 | 211*8 | 723*8 |
| 169 | 845*2 | 877*128 | 423*4 | 941*128 | 847*2 | 1005*128 | 53*32 | 181*32 | 309*32 | 437*32 |
| 170 | 425*4 | 693*32 | 821*32 | 949*32 | 213*8 | 725*8 | 853*2 | 1371*512 | 427*4 | 1387*512 |
| 171 | 855*2 | 1403*512 | 107*16 | 363*16 | 619*16 | 875*16 | 429*4 | 1387*16 | 859*2 | 1467*512 |
| 172 | 215*8 | 727*8 | 861*2 | 1499*512 | 431*4 | 1455*4 | 863*2 | 1531*512 | 27*64 | 91*64 |
| 173 | 155*64 | 219*64 | 283*64 | 347*64 | 411*64 | 475*64 | 217*8 | 603*64 | 667*64 | 731*64 |
| 174 | 435*4 | 859*64 | 871*2 | 987*64 | 109*16 | 365*16 | 621*16 | 877*16 | 437*4 | 1371*64 |
| 175 | 875*2 | 1499*64 | 219*8 | 731*8 | 877*2 | 1755*1 | 439*4 | 1463*4 | 879*2 | 1759*1 |
| 176 | 55*32 | 183*32 | 311*32 | 439*32 | 441*4 | 695*32 | 823*32 | 951*32 | 221*8 | 733*8 |
| 177 | 885*2 | 1463*32 | 443*4 | 1467*4 | 887*2 | 1775*1 | 111*16 | 367*16 | 623*16 | 879*16 |
| 178 | 445*4 | 1391*16 | 891*2 | 1783*1 | 223*8 | 735*8 | 893*2 | 1759*8 | 447*4 | 1471*4 |
| 179 | 895*2 | 1791*1 | 7*256 | 23*256 | 39*256 | 55*256 | 71*256 | 87*256 | 103*256 | 119*256 |
| 180 | 135*256 | 151*256 | 167*256 | 183*256 | 199*256 | 215*256 | 231*256 | 247*256 | 113*16 | 279*256 |
| 181 | 295*256 | 311*256 | 327*256 | 343*256 | 359*256 | 375*256 | 227*8 | 407*256 | 423*256 | 439*256 |
| 182 | 455*4 | 471*256 | 487*256 | 503*256 | 57*32 | 185*32 | 313*32 | 441*32 | 457*4 | 599*256 |
| 183 | 615*256 | 631*256 | 229*8 | 663*256 | 679*256 | 695*256 | 459*4 | 727*256 | 743*256 | 759*256 |
| 184 | 115*16 | 371*16 | 627*16 | 823*256 | 461*4 | 855*256 | 871*256 | 887*256 | 231*8 | 743*8 |
| 185 | 925*2 | 951*256 | 463*4 | 983*256 | 927*2 | 1015*256 | 29*64 | 93*64 | 157*64 | 221*64 |
| 186 | 285*64 | 349*64 | 413*64 | 477*64 | 233*8 | 605*64 | 669*64 | 733*64 | 467*4 | 861*64 |
| 187 | 925*64 | 989*64 | 117*16 | 373*16 | 629*16 | 885*16 | 469*4 | 1367*256 | 939*2 | 1399*256 |
| 188 | 235*8 | 747*8 | 941*2 | 1463*256 | 471*4 | 1495*4 | 943*2 | 1527*256 | 59*32 | 187*32 |
| 189 | 315*32 | 443*32 | 473*4 | 699*32 | 827*32 | 955*32 | 237*8 | 749*8 | 949*2 | 1467*32 |

| | 0 | 1 | 2 | 3 | 4 | 5 | 6 | 7 | 8 | 9 |
|---|---|---|---|---|---|---|---|---|---|---|
| 190 | 475*4 | 1499*4 | 951*2 | 1783*256 | 119*16 | 375*16 | 631*16 | 887*16 | 477*4 | 1399*16 |
| 191 | 955*2 | 1911*1 | 239*8 | 751*8 | 957*2 | 1775*8 | 479*4 | 1503*4 | 959*2 | 1919*1 |
| 192 | 15*128 | 47*128 | 79*128 | 111*128 | 143*128 | 175*128 | 207*128 | 239*128 | 241*8 | 303*128 |
| 193 | 335*128 | 367*128 | 399*128 | 431*128 | 463*128 | 495*128 | 121*16 | 377*16 | 591*128 | 623*128 |
| 194 | 485*4 | 687*128 | 719*128 | 751*128 | 243*8 | 755*8 | 847*128 | 879*128 | 487*4 | 943*128 |
| 195 | 975*2 | 1007*128 | 61*32 | 189*32 | 317*32 | 445*32 | 489*4 | 701*32 | 829*32 | 957*32 |
| 196 | 245*8 | 757*8 | 981*2 | 1391*128 | 491*4 | 1455*128 | 983*2 | 1519*128 | 123*16 | 379*16 |
| 197 | 635*16 | 891*16 | 493*4 | 1403*16 | 987*2 | 1775*128 | 247*8 | 759*8 | 989*2 | 1783*8 |
| 198 | 495*4 | 1519*4 | 991*2 | 1983*1 | 31*64 | 95*64 | 159*64 | 223*64 | 287*64 | 351*64 |
| 199 | 415*64 | 479*64 | 249*8 | 607*64 | 671*64 | 735*64 | 499*4 | 863*64 | 927*64 | 991*64 |
| 200 | 125*16 | 381*16 | 637*16 | 893*16 | 501*4 | 1375*64 | 1003*2 | 1503*64 | 251*8 | 763*8 |
| 201 | 1005*2 | 1759*64 | 503*4 | 1527*4 | 1007*2 | 2015*1 | 63*32 | 191*32 | 319*32 | 447*32 |
| 202 | 505*4 | 703*32 | 831*32 | 959*32 | 253*8 | 765*8 | 1013*2 | 1471*32 | 507*4 | 1531*4 |
| 203 | 1015*2 | 1983*32 | 127*16 | 383*16 | 639*16 | 895*16 | 509*4 | 1407*16 | 1019*2 | 1919*16 |
| 204 | 255*8 | 767*8 | 1021*2 | 1791*8 | 511*4 | 1535*4 | 1023*2 | 2047*1 | 1*2048 | 3*2048 |
| 205 | 5*2048 | 7*2048 | 9*2048 | 11*2048 | 13*2048 | 15*2048 | 17*2048 | 19*2048 | 21*2048 | 23*2048 |
| 206 | 25*2048 | 27*2048 | 29*2048 | 31*2048 | 33*2048 | 35*2048 | 37*2048 | 39*2048 | 41*2048 | 43*2048 |
| 207 | 45*2048 | 47*2048 | 49*2048 | 51*2048 | 53*2048 | 55*2048 | 57*2048 | 59*2048 | 61*2048 | 63*2048 |
| 208 | 65*32 | 67*2048 | 69*2048 | 71*2048 | 73*2048 | 75*2048 | 77*2048 | 79*2048 | 81*2048 | 83*2048 |
| 209 | 85*2048 | 87*2048 | 89*2048 | 91*2048 | 93*2048 | 95*2048 | 97*2048 | 99*2048 | 101*2048 | 103*2048 |
| 210 | 105*2048 | 107*2048 | 109*2048 | 111*2048 | 113*2048 | 115*2048 | 117*2048 | 119*2048 | 121*2048 | 123*2048 |
| 211 | 125*2048 | 127*2048 | 33*64 | 97*64 | 133*2048 | 135*2048 | 137*2048 | 139*2048 | 141*2048 | 143*2048 |
| 212 | 145*2048 | 147*2048 | 149*2048 | 151*2048 | 153*2048 | 155*2048 | 157*2048 | 159*2048 | 133*16 | 163*2048 |
| 213 | 165*2048 | 167*2048 | 169*2048 | 171*2048 | 173*2048 | 175*2048 | 177*2048 | 179*2048 | 181*2048 | 183*2048 |
| 214 | 185*2048 | 187*2048 | 189*2048 | 191*2048 | 67*32 | 195*32 | 197*2048 | 199*2048 | 201*2048 | 203*2048 |
| 215 | 205*2048 | 207*2048 | 209*2048 | 211*2048 | 213*2048 | 215*2048 | 217*2048 | 219*2048 | 221*2048 | 223*2048 |
| 216 | 135*16 | 227*2048 | 229*2048 | 231*2048 | 233*2048 | 235*2048 | 237*2048 | 239*2048 | 241*2048 | 243*2048 |
| 217 | 245*2048 | 247*2048 | 249*2048 | 251*2048 | 253*2048 | 255*2048 | 17*128 | 49*128 | 81*128 | 113*128 |
| 218 | 145*128 | 177*128 | 209*128 | 241*128 | 273*8 | 275*2048 | 277*2048 | 279*2048 | 281*2048 | 283*2048 |
| 219 | 285*2048 | 287*2048 | 137*16 | 291*2048 | 293*2048 | 295*2048 | 297*2048 | 299*2048 | 301*2048 | 303*2048 |
| 220 | 275*8 | 307*2048 | 309*2048 | 311*2048 | 313*2048 | 315*2048 | 317*2048 | 319*2048 | 69*32 | 197*32 |
| 221 | 325*32 | 327*2048 | 329*2048 | 331*2048 | 333*2048 | 335*2048 | 277*8 | 339*2048 | 341*2048 | 343*2048 |
| 222 | 345*2048 | 347*2048 | 349*2048 | 351*2048 | 139*16 | 355*2048 | 357*2048 | 359*2048 | 361*2048 | 363*2048 |
| 223 | 365*2048 | 367*2048 | 279*8 | 371*2048 | 373*2048 | 375*2048 | 377*2048 | 379*2048 | 381*2048 | 383*2048 |
| 224 | 35*64 | 99*64 | 163*64 | 227*64 | 291*64 | 355*64 | 397*2048 | 399*2048 | 281*8 | 403*2048 |
| 225 | 405*2048 | 407*2048 | 409*2048 | 411*2048 | 413*2048 | 415*2048 | 141*16 | 397*16 | 421*2048 | 423*2048 |
| 226 | 425*2048 | 427*2048 | 429*2048 | 431*2048 | 283*8 | 435*2048 | 437*2048 | 439*2048 | 441*2048 | 443*2048 |
| 227 | 445*2048 | 447*2048 | 71*32 | 199*32 | 327*32 | 455*32 | 457*2048 | 459*2048 | 461*2048 | 463*2048 |
| 228 | 285*8 | 467*2048 | 469*2048 | 471*2048 | 473*2048 | 475*2048 | 477*2048 | 479*2048 | 143*16 | 399*16 |
| 229 | 485*2048 | 487*2048 | 489*2048 | 491*2048 | 493*2048 | 495*2048 | 287*8 | 499*2048 | 501*2048 | 503*2048 |
| 230 | 505*2048 | 507*2048 | 509*2048 | 511*2048 | 9*256 | 25*256 | 41*256 | 57*256 | 73*256 | 89*256 |
| 231 | 105*256 | 121*256 | 137*256 | 153*256 | 169*256 | 185*256 | 201*256 | 217*256 | 233*256 | 249*256 |
| 232 | 145*16 | 281*256 | 297*256 | 313*256 | 329*256 | 345*256 | 361*256 | 377*256 | 291*8 | 409*256 |
| 233 | 425*256 | 441*256 | 457*256 | 473*256 | 489*256 | 505*256 | 73*32 | 201*32 | 329*32 | 457*32 |
| 234 | 585*4 | 587*2048 | 589*2048 | 591*2048 | 293*8 | 595*2048 | 597*2048 | 599*2048 | 587*4 | 603*2048 |
| 235 | 605*2048 | 607*2048 | 147*16 | 403*16 | 613*2048 | 615*2048 | 589*4 | 619*2048 | 621*2048 | 623*2048 |
| 236 | 295*8 | 627*2048 | 629*2048 | 631*2048 | 591*4 | 635*2048 | 637*2048 | 639*2048 | 37*64 | 101*64 |
| 237 | 165*64 | 229*64 | 293*64 | 357*64 | 421*64 | 485*64 | 297*8 | 613*64 | 661*2048 | 663*2048 |
| 238 | 595*4 | 667*2048 | 669*2048 | 671*2048 | 149*16 | 405*16 | 661*16 | 679*2048 | 597*4 | 683*2048 |
| 239 | 685*2048 | 687*2048 | 299*8 | 691*2048 | 693*2048 | 695*2048 | 599*4 | 699*2048 | 701*2048 | 703*2048 |
| 240 | 75*32 | 203*32 | 331*32 | 459*32 | 587*32 | 715*32 | 717*2048 | 719*2048 | 301*8 | 723*2048 |
| 241 | 725*2048 | 727*2048 | 603*4 | 731*2048 | 733*2048 | 735*2048 | 151*16 | 407*16 | 663*16 | 743*2048 |
| 242 | 605*4 | 747*2048 | 749*2048 | 751*2048 | 303*8 | 755*2048 | 757*2048 | 759*2048 | 607*4 | 763*2048 |
| 243 | 765*2048 | 767*2048 | 19*128 | 51*128 | 83*128 | 115*128 | 147*128 | 179*128 | 211*128 | 243*128 |
| 244 | 275*128 | 307*128 | 339*128 | 371*128 | 403*128 | 435*128 | 467*128 | 499*128 | 153*16 | 409*16 |
| 245 | 595*128 | 627*128 | 613*4 | 691*128 | 723*128 | 755*128 | 307*8 | 819*8 | 821*2048 | 823*2048 |
| 246 | 615*4 | 827*2048 | 829*2048 | 831*2048 | 77*32 | 205*32 | 333*32 | 461*32 | 589*32 | 717*32 |
| 247 | 845*32 | 847*2048 | 309*8 | 821*8 | 853*2048 | 855*2048 | 619*4 | 859*2048 | 861*2048 | 863*2048 |
| 248 | 155*16 | 411*16 | 667*16 | 871*2048 | 621*4 | 875*2048 | 877*2048 | 879*2048 | 311*8 | 823*8 |
| 249 | 885*2048 | 887*2048 | 623*4 | 891*2048 | 893*2048 | 895*2048 | 39*64 | 103*64 | 167*64 | 231*64 |
| 250 | 295*64 | 359*64 | 423*64 | 487*64 | 313*8 | 615*64 | 679*64 | 743*64 | 627*4 | 871*64 |
| 251 | 925*2048 | 927*2048 | 157*16 | 413*16 | 669*16 | 925*16 | 629*4 | 939*2048 | 941*2048 | 943*2048 |
| 252 | 315*8 | 827*8 | 949*2048 | 951*2048 | 631*4 | 955*2048 | 957*2048 | 959*2048 | 79*32 | 207*32 |
| 253 | 335*32 | 463*32 | 591*32 | 719*32 | 847*32 | 975*32 | 317*8 | 829*8 | 981*2048 | 983*2048 |
| 254 | 635*4 | 987*2048 | 989*2048 | 991*2048 | 159*16 | 415*16 | 671*16 | 927*16 | 637*4 | 1003*2048 |
| 255 | 1005*2048 | 1007*2048 | 319*8 | 831*8 | 1013*2048 | 1015*2048 | 639*4 | 1019*2048 | 1021*2048 | 1023*2048 |
| 256 | 5*512 | 13*512 | 21*512 | 29*512 | 37*512 | 45*512 | 53*512 | 61*512 | 69*512 | 77*512 |
| 257 | 85*512 | 93*512 | 101*512 | 109*512 | 117*512 | 125*512 | 133*512 | 141*512 | 149*512 | 157*512 |
| 258 | 165*512 | 173*512 | 181*512 | 189*512 | 197*512 | 205*512 | 213*512 | 221*512 | 229*512 | 237*512 |
| 259 | 245*512 | 253*512 | 81*32 | 209*32 | 277*512 | 285*512 | 293*512 | 301*512 | 309*512 | 317*512 |
| 260 | 325*8 | 333*512 | 341*512 | 349*512 | 357*512 | 365*512 | 373*512 | 381*512 | 163*16 | 397*512 |
| 261 | 405*512 | 413*512 | 421*512 | 429*512 | 437*512 | 445*512 | 327*8 | 461*512 | 469*512 | 477*512 |
| 262 | 485*512 | 493*512 | 501*512 | 509*512 | 41*64 | 105*64 | 169*64 | 233*64 | 297*64 | 361*64 |
| 263 | 425*64 | 489*64 | 329*8 | 589*512 | 597*512 | 605*512 | 613*512 | 621*512 | 629*512 | 637*512 |
| 264 | 165*16 | 421*16 | 661*512 | 669*512 | 661*4 | 685*512 | 693*512 | 701*512 | 331*8 | 717*512 |
| 265 | 725*512 | 733*512 | 663*4 | 749*512 | 757*512 | 765*512 | 83*32 | 211*32 | 339*32 | 467*32 |
| 266 | 595*32 | 723*32 | 821*512 | 829*512 | 333*8 | 845*8 | 853*512 | 861*512 | 667*4 | 877*512 |
| 267 | 885*512 | 893*512 | 167*16 | 423*16 | 679*16 | 925*512 | 669*4 | 941*512 | 949*512 | 957*512 |
| 268 | 335*8 | 847*8 | 981*512 | 989*512 | 671*4 | 1005*512 | 1013*512 | 1021*512 | 21*128 | 53*128 |
| 269 | 85*128 | 117*128 | 149*128 | 181*128 | 213*128 | 245*128 | 277*128 | 309*128 | 341*128 | 373*128 |
| 270 | 405*128 | 437*128 | 469*128 | 501*128 | 169*16 | 425*16 | 597*128 | 629*128 | 661*128 | 693*128 |
| 271 | 725*128 | 757*128 | 339*8 | 821*128 | 853*128 | 885*128 | 679*4 | 949*128 | 981*128 | 1013*128 |
| 272 | 85*32 | 213*32 | 341*32 | 469*32 | 597*32 | 725*32 | 853*32 | 981*32 | 341*8 | 853*8 |
| 273 | 1365*2 | 1367*2048 | 683*4 | 1371*2048 | 1367*2 | 1375*2048 | 171*16 | 427*16 | 683*16 | 939*16 |
| 274 | 685*4 | 1387*2048 | 1371*2 | 1391*2048 | 343*8 | 855*8 | 1367*8 | 1399*2048 | 687*4 | 1403*2048 |
| 275 | 1375*2 | 1407*2048 | 43*64 | 107*64 | 171*64 | 235*64 | 299*64 | 363*64 | 427*64 | 491*64 |
| 276 | 345*8 | 619*64 | 683*64 | 747*64 | 691*4 | 875*64 | 939*64 | 1003*64 | 173*16 | 429*16 |
| 277 | 685*16 | 941*16 | 693*4 | 1387*64 | 1387*2 | 1455*2048 | 347*8 | 859*8 | 1371*8 | 1463*2048 |
| 278 | 695*4 | 1467*2048 | 1391*2 | 1471*2048 | 87*32 | 215*32 | 343*32 | 471*32 | 599*32 | 727*32 |
| 279 | 855*32 | 983*32 | 349*8 | 861*8 | 1367*32 | 1495*32 | 699*4 | 1499*2048 | 1399*2 | 1503*2048 |

| | 0 | 1 | 2 | 3 | 4 | 5 | 6 | 7 | 8 | 9 |
|---|---|---|---|---|---|---|---|---|---|---|
| 280 | 175*16 | 431*16 | 687*16 | 943*16 | 701*4 | 1455*16 | 1403*2 | 1519*2048 | 351*8 | 863*8 |
| 281 | 1375*8 | 1527*2048 | 703*4 | 1531*2048 | 1407*2 | 1535*2048 | 11*256 | 27*256 | 43*256 | 59*256 |
| 282 | 75*256 | 91*256 | 107*256 | 123*256 | 139*256 | 155*256 | 171*256 | 187*256 | 203*256 | 219*256 |
| 283 | 235*256 | 251*256 | 177*16 | 283*256 | 299*256 | 315*256 | 331*256 | 347*256 | 363*256 | 379*256 |
| 284 | 355*8 | 411*256 | 427*256 | 443*256 | 459*256 | 475*256 | 491*256 | 507*256 | 89*32 | 217*32 |
| 285 | 345*32 | 473*32 | 587*256 | 603*256 | 619*256 | 635*256 | 357*8 | 667*256 | 683*256 | 699*256 |
| 286 | 715*4 | 731*256 | 747*256 | 763*256 | 179*16 | 435*16 | 691*16 | 827*256 | 717*4 | 859*256 |
| 287 | 875*256 | 891*256 | 359*8 | 871*8 | 939*256 | 955*256 | 719*4 | 987*256 | 1003*256 | 1019*256 |
| 288 | 45*64 | 109*64 | 173*64 | 237*64 | 301*64 | 365*64 | 429*64 | 493*64 | 361*8 | 621*64 |
| 289 | 685*64 | 749*64 | 723*4 | 877*64 | 941*64 | 1005*64 | 181*16 | 437*16 | 693*16 | 949*16 |
| 290 | 725*4 | 1371*256 | 1387*256 | 1403*256 | 363*8 | 875*8 | 1387*8 | 1467*256 | 727*4 | 1499*256 |
| 291 | 1455*2 | 1531*256 | 91*32 | 219*32 | 347*32 | 475*32 | 603*32 | 731*32 | 859*32 | 987*32 |
| 292 | 365*8 | 877*8 | 1371*32 | 1499*32 | 731*4 | 1755*4 | 1463*2 | 1759*2048 | 183*16 | 439*16 |
| 293 | 695*16 | 951*16 | 733*4 | 1463*16 | 1467*2 | 1775*2048 | 367*8 | 879*8 | 1391*8 | 1783*2048 |
| 294 | 735*4 | 1759*4 | 1471*2 | 1791*2048 | 23*128 | 55*128 | 87*128 | 119*128 | 151*128 | 183*128 |
| 295 | 215*128 | 247*128 | 279*128 | 311*128 | 343*128 | 375*128 | 407*128 | 439*128 | 471*128 | 503*128 |
| 296 | 185*16 | 441*16 | 599*128 | 631*128 | 663*128 | 695*128 | 727*128 | 759*128 | 371*8 | 823*128 |
| 297 | 855*128 | 887*128 | 743*4 | 951*128 | 983*128 | 1015*128 | 93*32 | 221*32 | 349*32 | 477*32 |
| 298 | 605*32 | 733*32 | 861*32 | 989*32 | 373*8 | 885*8 | 1367*128 | 1399*128 | 747*4 | 1463*128 |
| 299 | 1495*2 | 1527*128 | 187*16 | 443*16 | 699*16 | 955*16 | 749*4 | 1467*16 | 1499*2 | 1783*128 |
| 300 | 375*8 | 887*8 | 1399*8 | 1911*8 | 751*4 | 1775*4 | 1503*2 | 1919*2048 | 47*64 | 111*64 |
| 301 | 175*64 | 239*64 | 303*64 | 367*64 | 431*64 | 495*64 | 377*8 | 623*64 | 687*64 | 751*64 |
| 302 | 755*4 | 879*64 | 943*64 | 1007*64 | 189*16 | 445*16 | 701*16 | 957*16 | 757*4 | 1391*64 |
| 303 | 1455*64 | 1519*64 | 379*8 | 891*8 | 1403*8 | 1775*64 | 759*4 | 1783*4 | 1519*2 | 1983*2048 |
| 304 | 95*32 | 223*32 | 351*32 | 479*32 | 607*32 | 735*32 | 863*32 | 991*32 | 381*8 | 893*8 |
| 305 | 1375*32 | 1503*32 | 763*4 | 1759*32 | 1527*2 | 2015*32 | 191*16 | 447*16 | 703*16 | 959*16 |
| 306 | 765*4 | 1471*16 | 1531*2 | 1983*16 | 383*8 | 895*8 | 1407*8 | 1919*8 | 767*4 | 1791*4 |
| 307 | 1535*2 | 2047*2048 | 3*1024 | 7*1024 | 11*1024 | 15*1024 | 19*1024 | 23*1024 | 27*1024 | 31*1024 |
| 308 | 35*1024 | 39*1024 | 43*1024 | 47*1024 | 51*1024 | 55*1024 | 59*1024 | 63*1024 | 67*1024 | 71*1024 |
| 309 | 75*1024 | 79*1024 | 83*1024 | 87*1024 | 91*1024 | 95*1024 | 99*1024 | 103*1024 | 107*1024 | 111*1024 |
| 310 | 115*1024 | 119*1024 | 123*1024 | 127*1024 | 97*32 | 135*1024 | 139*1024 | 143*1024 | 147*1024 | 151*1024 |
| 311 | 155*1024 | 159*1024 | 163*1024 | 167*1024 | 171*1024 | 175*1024 | 179*1024 | 183*1024 | 187*1024 | 191*1024 |
| 312 | 195*16 | 199*1024 | 203*1024 | 207*1024 | 211*1024 | 215*1024 | 219*1024 | 223*1024 | 227*1024 | 231*1024 |
| 313 | 235*1024 | 239*1024 | 243*1024 | 247*1024 | 251*1024 | 255*1024 | 49*64 | 113*64 | 177*64 | 241*64 |
| 314 | 275*1024 | 279*1024 | 283*1024 | 287*1024 | 291*1024 | 295*1024 | 299*1024 | 303*1024 | 307*1024 | 311*1024 |
| 315 | 315*1024 | 319*1024 | 197*16 | 327*1024 | 331*1024 | 335*1024 | 339*1024 | 343*1024 | 347*1024 | 351*1024 |
| 316 | 355*1024 | 359*1024 | 363*1024 | 367*1024 | 371*1024 | 375*1024 | 379*1024 | 383*1024 | 99*32 | 227*32 |
| 317 | 355*32 | 399*1024 | 403*1024 | 407*1024 | 411*1024 | 415*1024 | 397*8 | 423*1024 | 427*1024 | 431*1024 |
| 318 | 435*1024 | 439*1024 | 443*1024 | 447*1024 | 199*16 | 455*16 | 459*1024 | 463*1024 | 467*1024 | 471*1024 |
| 319 | 475*1024 | 479*1024 | 399*8 | 487*1024 | 491*1024 | 495*1024 | 499*1024 | 503*1024 | 507*1024 | 511*1024 |
| 320 | 25*128 | 57*128 | 89*128 | 121*128 | 153*128 | 185*128 | 217*128 | 249*128 | 281*128 | 313*128 |
| 321 | 345*128 | 377*128 | 409*128 | 441*128 | 473*128 | 505*128 | 201*16 | 457*16 | 587*1024 | 591*1024 |
| 322 | 595*1024 | 599*1024 | 603*1024 | 607*1024 | 403*8 | 615*1024 | 619*1024 | 623*1024 | 627*1024 | 631*1024 |
| 323 | 635*1024 | 639*1024 | 101*32 | 229*32 | 357*32 | 485*32 | 613*32 | 663*1024 | 667*1024 | 671*1024 |
| 324 | 405*8 | 679*1024 | 683*1024 | 687*1024 | 691*1024 | 695*1024 | 699*1024 | 703*1024 | 203*16 | 459*16 |
| 325 | 715*16 | 719*1024 | 723*1024 | 727*1024 | 731*1024 | 735*1024 | 407*8 | 743*1024 | 747*1024 | 751*1024 |
| 326 | 755*1024 | 759*1024 | 763*1024 | 767*1024 | 51*64 | 115*64 | 179*64 | 243*64 | 307*64 | 371*64 |
| 327 | 435*64 | 499*64 | 409*8 | 627*64 | 691*64 | 755*64 | 819*4 | 823*1024 | 827*1024 | 831*1024 |
| 328 | 205*16 | 461*16 | 717*16 | 847*1024 | 821*4 | 855*1024 | 859*1024 | 863*1024 | 411*8 | 871*1024 |
| 329 | 875*1024 | 879*1024 | 823*4 | 887*1024 | 891*1024 | 895*1024 | 103*32 | 231*32 | 359*32 | 487*32 |
| 330 | 615*32 | 743*32 | 871*32 | 927*1024 | 413*8 | 925*8 | 939*1024 | 943*1024 | 827*4 | 951*1024 |
| 331 | 955*1024 | 959*1024 | 207*16 | 463*16 | 719*16 | 975*16 | 829*4 | 983*1024 | 987*1024 | 991*1024 |
| 332 | 415*8 | 927*8 | 1003*1024 | 1007*1024 | 831*4 | 1015*1024 | 1019*1024 | 1023*1024 | 13*256 | 29*256 |
| 333 | 45*256 | 61*256 | 77*256 | 93*256 | 109*256 | 125*256 | 141*256 | 157*256 | 173*256 | 189*256 |
| 334 | 205*256 | 221*256 | 237*256 | 253*256 | 209*16 | 285*256 | 301*256 | 317*256 | 333*256 | 349*256 |
| 335 | 365*256 | 381*256 | 397*256 | 413*256 | 429*256 | 445*256 | 461*256 | 477*256 | 493*256 | 509*256 |
| 336 | 105*32 | 233*32 | 361*32 | 489*32 | 589*256 | 605*256 | 621*256 | 637*256 | 421*8 | 669*256 |
| 337 | 685*256 | 701*256 | 717*256 | 733*256 | 749*256 | 765*256 | 211*16 | 467*16 | 723*16 | 829*256 |
| 338 | 845*4 | 861*256 | 877*256 | 893*256 | 423*8 | 925*256 | 941*256 | 957*256 | 847*4 | 989*256 |
| 339 | 1005*256 | 1021*256 | 53*64 | 117*64 | 181*64 | 245*64 | 309*64 | 373*64 | 437*64 | 501*64 |
| 340 | 425*8 | 629*64 | 693*64 | 757*64 | 821*64 | 885*64 | 949*64 | 1013*64 | 213*16 | 469*16 |
| 341 | 725*16 | 981*16 | 853*4 | 1367*1024 | 1371*1024 | 1375*1024 | 427*8 | 939*8 | 1387*1024 | 1391*1024 |
| 342 | 855*4 | 1399*1024 | 1403*1024 | 1407*1024 | 107*32 | 235*32 | 363*32 | 491*32 | 619*32 | 747*32 |
| 343 | 875*32 | 1003*32 | 429*8 | 941*8 | 1387*32 | 1455*1024 | 859*4 | 1463*1024 | 1467*1024 | 1471*1024 |
| 344 | 215*16 | 471*16 | 727*16 | 983*16 | 861*4 | 1495*16 | 1499*1024 | 1503*1024 | 431*8 | 943*8 |
| 345 | 1455*8 | 1519*1024 | 863*4 | 1527*1024 | 1531*1024 | 1535*1024 | 27*128 | 59*128 | 91*128 | 123*128 |
| 346 | 155*128 | 187*128 | 219*128 | 251*128 | 283*128 | 315*128 | 347*128 | 379*128 | 411*128 | 443*128 |
| 347 | 475*128 | 507*128 | 217*16 | 473*16 | 603*128 | 635*128 | 667*128 | 699*128 | 731*128 | 763*128 |
| 348 | 435*8 | 827*128 | 859*128 | 891*128 | 871*4 | 955*128 | 987*128 | 1019*128 | 109*32 | 237*32 |
| 349 | 365*32 | 493*32 | 621*32 | 749*32 | 877*32 | 1005*32 | 437*8 | 949*8 | 1371*128 | 1403*128 |
| 350 | 875*4 | 1467*128 | 1499*128 | 1531*128 | 219*16 | 475*16 | 731*16 | 987*16 | 877*4 | 1499*16 |
| 351 | 1755*2 | 1759*1024 | 439*8 | 951*8 | 1463*8 | 1775*1024 | 879*4 | 1783*1024 | 1759*2 | 1791*1024 |
| 352 | 55*64 | 119*64 | 183*64 | 247*64 | 311*64 | 375*64 | 439*64 | 503*64 | 441*8 | 631*64 |
| 353 | 695*64 | 759*64 | 823*64 | 887*64 | 951*64 | 1015*64 | 221*16 | 477*16 | 733*16 | 989*16 |
| 354 | 885*4 | 1399*64 | 1463*64 | 1527*64 | 443*8 | 955*8 | 1467*8 | 1783*64 | 887*4 | 1911*4 |
| 355 | 1775*2 | 1919*1024 | 111*32 | 239*32 | 367*32 | 495*32 | 623*32 | 751*32 | 879*32 | 1007*32 |
| 356 | 445*8 | 957*8 | 1391*32 | 1519*32 | 891*4 | 1775*32 | 1783*2 | 1983*1024 | 223*16 | 479*16 |
| 357 | 735*16 | 991*16 | 893*4 | 1503*16 | 1759*16 | 2015*16 | 447*8 | 959*8 | 1471*8 | 1983*8 |
| 358 | 895*4 | 1919*4 | 1791*2 | 2047*1024 | 7*512 | 15*512 | 23*512 | 31*512 | 39*512 | 47*512 |
| 359 | 55*512 | 63*512 | 71*512 | 79*512 | 87*512 | 95*512 | 103*512 | 111*512 | 119*512 | 127*512 |
| 360 | 135*512 | 143*512 | 151*512 | 159*512 | 167*512 | 175*512 | 183*512 | 191*512 | 199*512 | 207*512 |
| 361 | 215*512 | 223*512 | 231*512 | 239*512 | 247*512 | 255*512 | 113*32 | 241*32 | 279*512 | 287*512 |
| 362 | 295*512 | 303*512 | 311*512 | 319*512 | 327*512 | 335*512 | 343*512 | 351*512 | 359*512 | 367*512 |
| 363 | 375*512 | 383*512 | 227*16 | 399*512 | 407*512 | 415*512 | 423*512 | 431*512 | 439*512 | 447*512 |
| 364 | 455*8 | 463*512 | 471*512 | 479*512 | 487*512 | 495*512 | 503*512 | 511*512 | 57*64 | 121*64 |
| 365 | 185*64 | 249*64 | 313*64 | 377*64 | 441*64 | 505*64 | 457*8 | 591*512 | 599*512 | 607*512 |
| 366 | 615*512 | 623*512 | 631*512 | 639*512 | 229*16 | 485*16 | 663*512 | 671*512 | 679*512 | 687*512 |
| 367 | 695*512 | 703*512 | 459*8 | 719*512 | 727*512 | 735*512 | 743*512 | 751*512 | 759*512 | 767*512 |
| 368 | 115*32 | 243*32 | 371*32 | 499*32 | 627*32 | 755*32 | 823*512 | 831*512 | 461*8 | 847*512 |
| 369 | 855*512 | 863*512 | 871*512 | 879*512 | 887*512 | 895*512 | 231*16 | 487*16 | 743*16 | 927*512 |

| | 0 | 1 | 2 | 3 | 4 | 5 | 6 | 7 | 8 | 9 |
|---|---|---|---|---|---|---|---|---|---|---|
| 370 | 925*4 | 943*512 | 951*512 | 959*512 | 463*8 | 975*8 | 983*512 | 991*512 | 927*4 | 1007*512 |
| 371 | 1015*512 | 1023*512 | 29*128 | 61*128 | 93*12( | 125*128 | 157*128 | 189*128 | 221*128 | 253*128 |
| 372 | 285*128 | 317*128 | 349*128 | 381*128 | 413*128 | 445*128 | 477*128 | 509*128 | 233*16 | 489*16 |
| 373 | 605*128 | 637*128 | 669*128 | 701*128 | 733*128 | 765*128 | 467*8 | 829*128 | 861*128 | 893*128 |
| 374 | 925*128 | 957*128 | 989*128 | 1021*128 | 117*32 | 245*32 | 373*32 | 501*32 | 629*32 | 757*32 |
| 375 | 885*32 | 1013*32 | 469*8 | 981*8 | 1367*512 | 1375*512 | 939*4 | 1391*512 | 1399*512 | 1407*512 |
| 376 | 235*16 | 491*16 | 747*16 | 1003*16 | 941*4 | 1455*512 | 1463*512 | 1471*512 | 471*8 | 983*8 |
| 377 | 1495*8 | 1503*512 | 943*4 | 1519*512 | 1527*512 | 1535*512 | 59*64 | 123*64 | 187*64 | 251*64 |
| 378 | 315*64 | 379*64 | 443*64 | 507*64 | 473*8 | 635*64 | 699*64 | 763*64 | 827*64 | 891*64 |
| 379 | 955*64 | 1019*64 | 237*16 | 493*16 | 749*16 | 1005*16 | 949*4 | 1403*64 | 1467*64 | 1531*64 |
| 380 | 475*8 | 987*8 | 1499*8 | 1759*512 | 951*4 | 1775*512 | 1783*512 | 1791*512 | 119*32 | 247*32 |
| 381 | 375*32 | 503*32 | 631*32 | 759*32 | 887*32 | 1015*32 | 477*8 | 989*8 | 1399*32 | 1527*32 |
| 382 | 955*4 | 1783*32 | 1911*2 | 1919*512 | 239*16 | 495*16 | 751*16 | 1007*16 | 957*4 | 1519*16 |
| 383 | 1775*16 | 1983*512 | 479*8 | 991*8 | 1503*8 | 2015*8 | 959*4 | 1983*4 | 1919*2 | 2047*512 |
| 384 | 15*256 | 31*256 | 47*256 | 63*256 | 79*256 | 95*256 | 111*256 | 127*256 | 143*256 | 159*256 |
| 385 | 175*256 | 191*256 | 207*256 | 223*256 | 239*256 | 255*256 | 241*16 | 287*256 | 303*256 | 319*256 |
| 386 | 335*256 | 351*256 | 367*256 | 383*256 | 399*256 | 415*256 | 431*256 | 447*256 | 463*256 | 479*256 |
| 387 | 495*256 | 511*256 | 121*32 | 249*32 | 377*32 | 505*32 | 591*256 | 607*256 | 623*256 | 639*256 |
| 388 | 485*8 | 671*256 | 687*256 | 703*256 | 719*256 | 735*256 | 751*256 | 767*256 | 243*16 | 499*16 |
| 389 | 755*16 | 831*256 | 847*256 | 863*256 | 879*256 | 895*256 | 487*8 | 927*256 | 943*256 | 959*256 |
| 390 | 975*4 | 991*256 | 1007*256 | 1023*256 | 61*64 | 125*64 | 189*64 | 253*64 | 317*64 | 381*64 |
| 391 | 445*64 | 509*64 | 489*8 | 637*64 | 701*64 | 765*64 | 829*64 | 893*64 | 957*64 | 1021*64 |
| 392 | 245*16 | 501*16 | 757*16 | 1013*16 | 981*4 | 1375*256 | 1391*256 | 1407*256 | 491*8 | 1003*8 |
| 393 | 1455*256 | 1471*256 | 983*4 | 1503*256 | 1519*256 | 1535*256 | 123*32 | 251*32 | 379*32 | 507*32 |
| 394 | 635*32 | 763*32 | 891*32 | 1019*32 | 493*8 | 1005*8 | 1403*32 | 1531*32 | 987*4 | 1759*256 |
| 395 | 1775*256 | 1791*256 | 247*16 | 503*16 | 759*16 | 1015*16 | 989*4 | 1527*16 | 1783*16 | 1919*256 |
| 396 | 495*8 | 1007*8 | 1519*8 | 1983*256 | 991*4 | 2015*4 | 1983*2 | 2047*256 | 31*128 | 63*128 |
| 397 | 95*128 | 127*128 | 159*128 | 191*128 | 223*128 | 255*128 | 287*128 | 319*128 | 351*128 | 383*128 |
| 398 | 415*128 | 447*128 | 479*128 | 511*128 | 249*16 | 505*16 | 607*128 | 639*128 | 671*128 | 703*128 |
| 399 | 735*128 | 767*128 | 499*8 | 831*128 | 863*128 | 895*128 | 927*128 | 959*128 | 991*128 | 1023*128 |
| 400 | 125*32 | 253*32 | 381*32 | 509*32 | 637*32 | 765*32 | 893*32 | 1021*32 | 501*8 | 1013*8 |
| 401 | 1375*128 | 1407*128 | 1003*4 | 1471*128 | 1503*128 | 1535*128 | 251*16 | 507*16 | 763*16 | 1019*16 |
| 402 | 1005*4 | 1531*16 | 1759*128 | 1791*128 | 503*8 | 1015*8 | 1527*8 | 1919*128 | 1007*4 | 1983*128 |
| 403 | 2015*2 | 2047*128 | 63*64 | 127*64 | 191*64 | 255*64 | 319*64 | 383*64 | 447*64 | 511*64 |
| 404 | 505*8 | 639*64 | 703*64 | 767*64 | 831*64 | 895*64 | 959*64 | 1023*64 | 253*16 | 509*16 |
| 405 | 765*16 | 1021*16 | 1013*4 | 1407*64 | 1471*64 | 1535*64 | 507*8 | 1019*8 | 1531*8 | 1791*64 |
| 406 | 1015*4 | 1919*64 | 1983*64 | 2047*64 | 127*32 | 255*32 | 383*32 | 511*32 | 639*32 | 767*32 |
| 407 | 895*32 | 1023*32 | 509*8 | 1021*8 | 1407*32 | 1535*32 | 1019*4 | 1791*32 | 1919*32 | 2047*32 |
| 408 | 255*16 | 511*16 | 767*16 | 1023*16 | 1021*4 | 1535*16 | 1791*16 | 2047*16 | 511*8 | 1023*8 |
| 409 | 1535*8 | 2047*8 | 1023*4 | 2047*4 | 2047*2 | 4095*1 | | | | |

## TRANSPOSITION

It is possible to regard ordinary transposition of chords and harmonies as either a mechanical translation or a rotation. For **translation**, define the operation of transposition as a rigid rectilinear motion or shifting of a given literal notation along the chain of perfect fifths. For **rotation**, define the operation of transposition as a rigid circular motion or revolving of a given literal notation around the circle of tempered fifths. Both formulations have certain advantages, principally the avoidance of the concept of keys or key signatures. To see this, consider the chromatic scale harmony. It has no key affiliation, at least in the usual sense. Yet it can be transposed easily through any musical interval. For example, start with

CC♯DD♯EFF♯GG♯AA♯B.

After transposition down a major third to A♭, it becomes literally

CD♭DE♭EFF♯GA♭AB♭B.

And after transposition up a major third, it becomes literally

B♯C♯C×D♯EE♯F♯F×G♯AA♯B.

These results are easy to see schematically in terms of Fig. 2.5.

In producing Fig. 2.6 the chain of perfect fifths is taken to be tempered rather than justly intoned. The chain is wrapped around a circle so that the enharmonic values are made to coincide. When this is done, the operation of translation shown in Fig. 2.5, which is a one-dimensional rigid motion, becomes a pure rotation, which is a two-dimensional rigid motion, not involving any change in size.

In trigonometry, the angle between any two intersecting lines is expressed either in degrees or in radians. Recall that the total angle about a central point contains exactly $360^{\circ}$ (or $2\pi$ radians). A right angle is one-fourth of this angle. By inspection the angular separation between the endnotes of each tempered fifth on the circumference of the circles in Fig. 2.6 is $30^{\circ}$. Less obvious, perhaps, is the fact that the angular separation between enharmonic equivalents such a A♭ and G♯ is $360^{\circ}$ and between those such as F♭♭ and D♯ is $720^{\circ}$.

Figure 2.5

Transposition as translation.

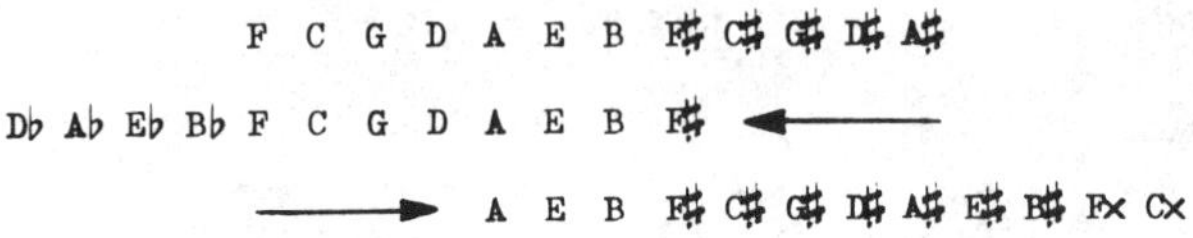

F C G D A E B F♯ C♯ G♯ D♯ A♯

D♭ A♭ E♭ B♭ F C G D A E B F♯ ←

→ A E B F♯ C♯ G♯ D♯ A♯ E♯ B♯ F× C×

Figure 2.6

Transposition as rotation.

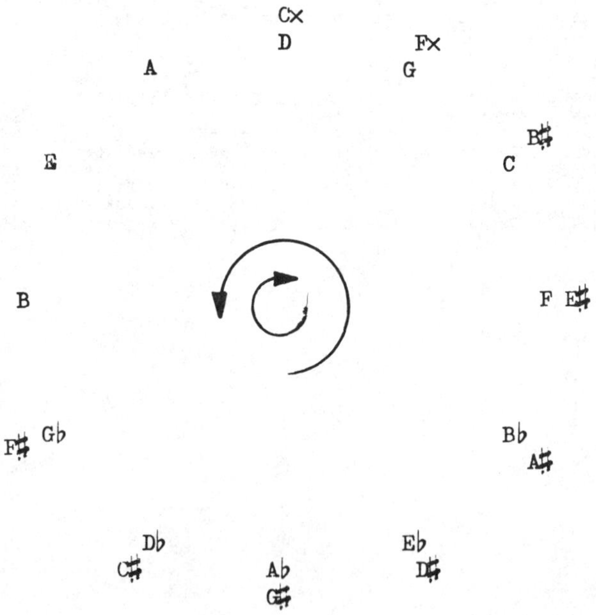

C×
D
F×
G
A
B♯
C
E
B
F E♯
F♯ G♭
B♭
A♯
D♭
C♯
A♭
G♯
E♭
D♯

A full counterclockwise revolution about an axis perpendicular to the central point or "origin" generates an angle of $360^{\circ}$ or $2\pi$, a half revolution $180^{\circ}$ or $\pi$, a quarter revolution $90^{\circ}$ or $\pi/2$, a twelfth revolution $30^{\circ}$ or $\pi/6$, and so on. A transposition, T, up a tempered perfect fifth (down a tempered perfect fourth) represents a $30^{\circ}$ rotation in the assumed positive sense, which corresponds to a counterclockwise motion (see Fig. 2.6). Thus,

T(CEG) = GBD,

$T^{2}$(CEG) = DF♯A, and

$T^{-1}$(CEG) = FAC.

## EXERCISES

**2.15** Shift the tetrad FBDG♯ along the 35-literal chain to obtain as many transposes as possible.

**2.16** Show that every major triad possesses a Tonic, Dominant, and Subdominant significance.

**2.17** List various harmonies having no key affiliation. Give reasons to support this selection.

**2.18** Given the postulate that transposition is a rigid motion along the chain of perfect fifths; prove that transposition preserves all musical interval relationships.

**2.19** Transposition corresponds to a $30^\circ k$ rotation with $k = 0, \pm 1, \pm 2, \ldots$ Explain this remark and tell why rotation in the geometrical sense is more general than rotation in the musical sense.

**2.20** Chord spellings are not invariant under rotation. Let $R(\theta)$ denote the **rotation operator** acting through an angle $\theta$ Accordingly, $R(360^\circ)$G♭ = F♯ and $R(-360^\circ)$F♯ = G♭. The same kind of mathematics leads to $R(720^\circ)$G♭ = Ex. Clearly, a shift by an integral multiple of $2\pi$ amounts to an enharmonic change of a literal. Solve this problem: set FxxAxxCxx equal to $R(\theta)$FAC and determine the value of theta. Admittedly, any notation using quadruple sharps is a representation much too cumbersome for practical utilization, except in exercises. Such outlandish notations cannot be ignored, however, without making recourse to a fundamental assumption:

Postulate 1. Enharmonic transposes generated by integer multiples $k360^\circ$ of complete $360^\circ$ rotations ($k = \ldots, -2, -1, 0, 1, 2, \ldots$) are identical in all their musical properties to a principal value that lies in a basic range such as $(180^\circ, 180^\circ]$.

The left parenthesis ( and the right bracket ] signify that the point $-180^\circ$ is not contained in the interval, but the point $180^\circ$ is. Speaking technically, such an interval is **open** on the left and **closed** on the right.

## BUSONI SCALES

Some appreciation of the power of the new computational methods--explicit descriptions of the subroutines used are presented in Chapter 9--can be gained from an understanding of the results of their specific employment in the notational treatment of Busoni scales. The basis for this discussion is Ferruccio Busoni's proposal for forming synthetic musical scales by sharping or flatting tones of the C major scale, as specified in his **Sketch of a New Esthetic of Music** [6]. Busoni apparently assumed that no tonal duplications (for example, G♯A♭) or overlappings (for example, E♯F♭) are to be permitted. James Murray Barbour showed [7] that, because of these restrictions, there are just 155 possible synthetic musical scales if modal variants (cyclic rearrangements) are not distinguished.

The purpose of this section is to give an overview of the 1254 possible Busoni scales derivable when double sharps and double flats are used. The principal results of an earlier analysis [8] are extracted:

(a) an alphabet having only three inflections is insufficient to yield a Busoni scale to represent each of the sixty-six possible harmonically distinct classes of heptatonic scales,

(b) an alphabet having five inflections, although sufficient to yield at least five representatives, nevertheless is insufficient to ensure that all twelve enharmonically distinct Busoni scales in each such class appear at least once in the list, and

(c) an extension of a table built upon five inflections to alphabets having six or more inflections is trivial.

Also, two new theorems emerged:

(1) an alphabet having six inflections is both necessary and sufficient to ensure that all twelve enharmonically distinct Busoni scales in each of the sixty-six possible harmonically distinct classes of hep-

tatonic scales appear at least once in the list, and

(2) every scale that has seven or fewer tones can be written without using any letter more than once, although to do so may require as many as six inflections.

On the basis of this information, it may be concluded that Table III, which lists the 66 different characteristic Busoni scales, can occupy a central position in the calculation of a more extensive catalogue. A few exercises are given now, which should provide a firmer grasp of the material thus far covered. The discussion alluded to earlier, concerning the notational treatment of the scales listed in Table III, will follow closely after the introduction of various aspects of the subject of musical spelling, including what is meant by the term **preferred notation.**

TABLE III CHARACTERISTIC BUSONI SCALES

| | | | | | | | | | | | | | | | |
|---|---|---|---|---|---|---|---|---|---|---|---|---|---|---|---|
| 0003 | G♭♭ | A♭♭ | B♭♭ | C♭ | D♭♭ | E♭♭ | F♭ | 0711 | G♭ | A | B | C | D♭ | E | F |
| 0034 | A♭♭ | B♭♭ | C♭ | D♭ | E♭♭ | F | G♭ | 0737 | A♭ | B | C♯ | D | E | F | G |
| 0057 | G♭♭ | A♭♭ | B♭♭ | C♭ | D♭ | E♭♭ | F♭ | 0759 | G♭ | A | B | C | D | E | F |
| 0092 | D♭ | E♭ | F | G | A | B | C | 0779 | E♭♭ | F | G | A♭ | B | C | D♭ |
| 0111 | A♭♭ | B♭♭ | C♭ | D♭ | E | F | G♭ | 0800 | B♭♭ | C | D | E | F | G♭ | A♭ |
| 0129 | G♭♭ | A♭♭ | B♭♭ | C | D♭ | E♭♭ | F♭ | 0825 | G♭ | A | B | C♯ | D | E | F |
| 0155 | B♭♭ | C♭ | D♭ | E | F | G | A♭ | 0843 | E♭♭ | F | G | A | B | C | D♭ |
| 0175 | A♭♭ | B♭♭ | C♭ | D | E | F | G♭ | 0864 | B♭♭ | C | D | E♯ | F♯ | G | A♭ |
| 0197 | B♭♭ | C♭ | D♭ | E♯ | F♯ | G | A♭ | 0875 | G♭♭ | A♭ | B | C | D♭ | E♭♭ | F♭ |
| 0209 | D♭♭ | E♭♭ | F | G♭ | A♭♭ | B♭♭ | C♭ | 0899 | G♭ | A | B♯ | C♯ | D | E | F |
| 0234 | A♭♭ | B♭♭ | C | D♭ | E♭♭ | F | G♭ | 0912 | E♭♭ | F | G♯ | A | B | C | D♭ |
| 0257 | D♭♭ | E♭♭ | F | G♭ | A♭ | B♭♭ | C♭ | 0935 | A♭ | B | C𝄪 | D𝄪 | E♯ | F♯ | G |
| 0287 | G♭ | A♭ | B | C | D | E | F | 0945 | B♭♭ | C | D𝄪 | E♯ | F♯ | G | A♭ |
| 0306 | A♭♭ | B♭♭ | C | D♭ | E | F | G♭ | 0952 | D♭♭ | E | F | G♭ | A♭♭ | B♭♭ | C♭ |
| 0325 | D♭♭ | E♭♭ | F | G | A♭ | B♭♭ | C♭ | 0972 | A♭♭ | B | C | D♭ | E♭♭ | F | G♭ |
| 0350 | B♭♭ | C♭ | D | E | F | G | A♭ | 0990 | D♭♭ | E | F | G♭ | A♭ | B♭♭ | C♭ |
| 0370 | A♭♭ | B♭♭ | C | D | E | F | G♭ | 1016 | D♭ | E♯ | F♯ | G | A | B | C |
| 0392 | B♭♭ | C♭ | D | E♯ | F♯ | G | A♭ | 1029 | A♭♭ | B | C | D♭ | E | F | G♭ |
| 0403 | G♭♭ | A♭♭ | B | C | D♭ | E♭♭ | F♭ | 1047 | D♭♭ | E | F | G | A♭ | B♭♭ | C♭ |
| 0427 | G♭ | A♭ | B♯ | C♯ | D | E | F | 1069 | B♭♭ | C♯ | D | E | F | G | A♭ |
| 0439 | A♭♭ | B♭♭ | C♯ | D | E | F | G♭ | 1086 | A♭♭ | B | C | D | E | F | G♭ |
| 0452 | F♭♭ | G♭♭ | A | B | C | D♭ | E♭♭ | 1107 | B♭♭ | C♯ | D | E♯ | F♯ | G | A♭ |
| 0473 | B♭♭ | C♭ | D𝄪 | E♯ | F♯ | G | A♭ | 1118 | G♭♭ | A | B | C | D♭ | E♭♭ | F♭ |
| 0479 | G♭♭ | A♭ | B♭♭ | C♭ | D♭♭ | E♭♭ | F♭ | 1143 | D♭ | E♯ | F𝄪 | G♯ | A | B | C |
| 0513 | D♭ | E | F | G | A♭ | B | C | 1154 | A♭♭ | B | C♯ | D | E | F | G♭ |
| 0539 | A♭ | B | C | D | E | F | G | 1178 | A♭ | B♯ | C𝄪 | D𝄪 | E♯ | F♯ | G |
| 0564 | D♭ | E | F | G | A | B | C | 1188 | B♭♭ | C♯ | D𝄪 | E♯ | F♯ | G | A♭ |
| 0590 | A♭ | B | C | D | E♯ | F♯ | G | 1195 | D♭♭ | E♯ | F♯ | G | A♭ | B♭♭ | C♭ |
| 0601 | G♭♭ | A♭ | B♭♭ | C | D♭ | E♭♭ | F♭ | 1213 | G♭ | A𝄪 | B♯ | C♯ | D | E | F |
| 0627 | B♭♭ | C | D♭ | E | F | G | A♭ | 1220 | A♭♭ | B♯ | C♯ | D | E | F | G♭ |
| 0648 | E♭♭ | F | G♭ | A | B | C | D♭ | 1239 | A♭ | B𝄪 | C𝄪 | D𝄪 | E♯ | F♯ | G |
| 0674 | A♭ | B | C | D𝄪 | E♯ | F♯ | G | 1246 | B♭♭ | C𝄪 | D𝄪 | E♯ | F♯ | G | A♭ |
| 0683 | E♭♭ | F | G | A♭ | B♭♭ | C♭ | D♭ | 1252 | G♭♭ | A𝄪 | B♯ | C♯ | D | E♭ | F♭ |

## EXERCISES

**2.21** Although the situation is not complicated, the enumeration of synthetic musical scales is an interesting combinatorial problem; the details are treated elsewhere [8]. Now following the method proposed by Barbour [9] for classifying heptatonic scales by their intervals, identify each of the characteristic Busoni scales listed in Table III.

**2.22** As once noted by Barbour, Slonimsky gives examples [10] of fewer than a third of the sixty-six possible heptatonic scale sonorities. (a) Which ones did he omit? (b) How would this question be handled using a digital computer?

**2.23** It is possible to define seven different kinds of Busoni scales by the generalized generating function

$$[u^{-12k}(u^{19}+u^{26}+u^{33}+u^{40}+\ldots)]^7$$

where k = 1 gives the first kind, and so on. Explain this statement and give examples.

**2.24** The 35-literal alphabet provides the basic elements of musical notation. Define the "span" of a literal notation to be the number of literals in the chain of perfect fifths bracketed by the notation. For example, the span of CEG is 5 and the span of B♯EA♭♭ is 24.

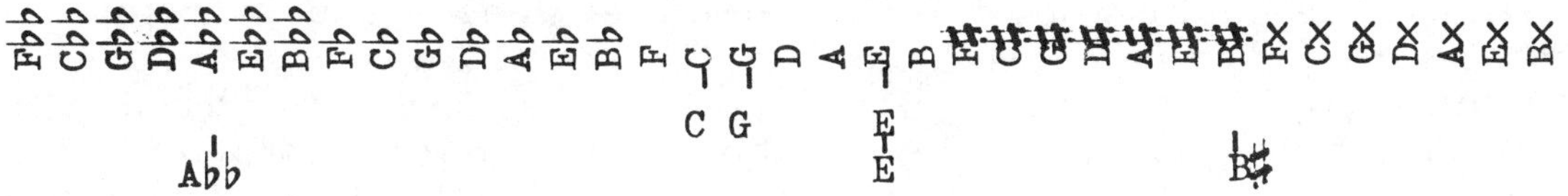

F♭♭ C♭♭ G♭♭ D♭♭ A♭♭ E♭♭ B♭♭ F♭ C♭ G♭ D♭ A♭ E♭ B♭ F C G D A E B F♯ C♯ G♯ D♯ A♯ E♯ B♯ Fx Cx Gx Dx Ax Ex Bx

C G E E

A♭♭ B♯

Determine the span of the characteristic Busoni scales listed in Table

**2.25** Define the operation of mirror inversion for literal notations. How does it differ from mirror inversion for chords?

**2.26** About what axis is the B♭ minor triad harmony symmetrically placed on the literal chain with respect to (a) the G major triad harmony and (b) the F♯ major triad harmony?

**2.27** Does reflection in an axis through the letter D of the chain of perfect fifths preserve notational complexity? Why is this the case?

**2.28** Although the 35-literal alphabet (F♭♭, C♭♭, ..., Bx) is built on the **direct product** of two most familiar symbol sets--the letters (A, B, ..., G) and the inflections (♭♭, ♭, ♮, ♯, ♯♯=x)--it is sometimes necessary to code these symbols as decimal digits, since these are used on the numerical pads of computer terminals and calculator keyboards. The following correspondence is convenient:

| | | | | | | |
|---|---|---|---|---|---|---|
| B | ♭ | ♯ | | 7 | 8 | 9 |
| D | A | E | | 4 | 5 | 6 |
| F | C | G | | 1 | 2 | 3 |
| end | | | | 0 | | |

Using this coding scheme, the chord CEF♯B♭ is written 2,6,19,78,0. A literal containing a double sharp, such as $\ell$ = Bx, is encoded 799. For practice in making numerical conversions, encode the characteristic Busoni scales in Table III, treating them as chords. Are commas necessary for unique decypherability?

**2.29** As far as it goes, the valuable listing by Otterström [11] of permutations of well-known seven-tone scales is almost identical to the set constructed by taking one scale containing either a B♯, C, or D♭♭ to represent each class of modal variants in the catalogue of Busoni scales cited earlier. Using the index to Table I given in [8], correct Otterström's list of permutations of the Harmonic Minor Scale by comparing it to the catalogue.

**2.30** Outline the steps required to expand Table III mechanically. The end product should have 1254 entries.

**2.31** (a) Making use of a **Fortran library** subroutine for carrying out ordinary matrix multiplication, prepare a digital computer program to obtain the matrices

$$P^7 \text{ and } Q^7$$

given in the paper [8] on Busoni scales. (b) Suppose that two-octave Busoni scales are defined by the condition that $\Sigma N_i = 14$, that is, as comprising fifteen degrees. Show that besides the usual two-octave scales in which the second half is a replica of the first, a large number of other scales can be produced. (Hint. Square the matrices

$$P^7 \text{ and } Q^7$$

to form

$$P^{14} \text{ and } Q^{14},$$

respectively. Explain the origin of each nonzero element in these products in terms of the italicised entries in the second and third tables of [8]. (c) Program a digital computer to compute the complete list of two-octave Busoni scales and to store it on magnetic tape or disk. Determine the number of output pages that would be required to print out this catalogue at one scale per line and sixty lines per page. Devise a means of establishing the correctness of the stored list without printing it, either by spot checking or by verifying known properties of the table.

## PRESENT USAGE

There are apparently no immutable laws governing the use of literals in scoring. The criterion usually recognized in assigning note names is conformity with standard practice. But today's standard practice unfortunately is not consistent and students are put to considerable trouble needlessly to verify that certain harmonies are identical in structure, especially when they appear at different pitch levels. A fresh viewpoint may bring clarity to this vague area. Perhaps it also will bring about a demand for musical spelling reform.

In practical situations the discovery of the correct literal notation is sometimes easy and sometimes not. If a musical passage involves only major or minor subharmonies, then the key signature provides a most convenient and straightforward solution to any spelling problem. Normally, for example, C major scale subharmonies are denoted by uninflected letters or "naturals" and subharmonies of other major scales, which all are obtainable by transposition, are denoted by letters modified by the application of the appropriate key signature. By extension, relative minor scale subharmonies are denoted by the literals belonging to the **adjunct** major scale. For that part of the harmony lying outside the key signature (the set made up of accidentals), the rule of thumb generally applied is either to resolve the question on the basis of smoothness in voice leading, or to make a haphazard assignment for ease in sightreading. As a consequence, the composer normally has no information basis (or methods) for deciding whether the notation that he or she specifies is really compatible with the intent, and the music analyst sometimes is placed in a quandary.

In actual fact, of course, many if not most of the problems encountered in the realm of music orthography involve multitonal structures, with or without accidentals, and with a prescribed signature that may be in conflict. For atonal writing, an essentially different attitude, due to Schoenberg, has secured general acceptance. In atonal works, in which the predication of a key signature is rare, it has been considered preferable to proceed from note to note following voice lines and to omit consistency in transposing from one instrument to another, treating each as though it were in the key of C.

In his well-conceived book [12] exploring the resources of the tempered scale, Hanson does not consider notational aspects to be important. He states: "This point of view has the advantage of freeing the composer from certain inhibiting preoccupations with academic symbolization as such. For the composer, the important matter is the sound of the notes, not their 'spelling.' For example, the sonority G-B-D-F sounds like a dominant seventh chord whether it is spelled G-B-D-F, G-B-D-E♯, G-B-Cx-E♯, G-C♭-Cx-F, or in some other manner." This simplifying point of view, advocating what herein will be called "phonetic musical spelling," carries with it the high cost of no longer being able to distinguish certain musical intervals, although obviously proper distinction is essential to correct figuring. In spite of the views of these great authorities, therefore, the present work recommends that the orthographic treatment of accidentals should not be arbitrary, but that instead their precise values must be determinable as strict consequences of a single unifying principle, which grows out of the mathematical theory underlying the methodology for the computer analysis of music.

## EXERCISES

**2.32** The scales and melodic patterns in Slonimsky's **Thesaurus** [10] are written in enharmonic notation. This means that accidentals are used according to convenience and double sharps and double flats are avoided entirely. Is this treatment justified by the application? Explain.

**2.33** In mathematics, a set with a relation that linearly orders it is called a "chain." What relations can serve to connect the elements of a literal alphabet into a chain?

**2.34** A naïve approach sometimes leads to a useful result. Forget for the moment the precise mathematical meaning expressed by the statement that the 35-literal alphabet forms a chain. Instead, think about a colorful paper chain, with the literals written out one by one on the loops. It takes very little imagination to visualize the links of this sort of literal chain being pinned upon a wall or bulletin board in various patterns, depending upon the placement of thumbtacks. Here are two ways in which it can be done; there are of course many others.

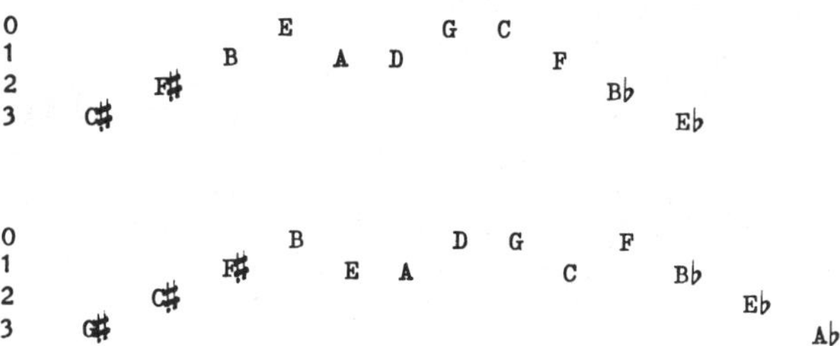


Now from the first pattern it is easy to see that the literal F♯ is at a distance of two units from the literals of the C major triad. From the second pattern, however, it appears that F♯ is at a distance of one unit from the dominant seventh chord built upon G. By definition, the **greatest lower bound** of the distances of a literal $\ell$ from the individual literals of the literal set L is called the "distance of the literal $\ell$ from the literal set L." Moreover, the greatest lower bound of the distances $|\ell_1 - \ell_2|$ of the literal $\ell_1$ of a literal set $L_1$ from a literal $\ell_2$ of a literal set $L_2$ is called the "distance between the two literal sets $L_1$ and $L_2$." Both of these distances are assumed, always. (a) What is the pattern for CEG♯, for CEA♭? (b) How far is the literal C from the literal set

B♭G♭D♭, from the literal set BDFG♯? (c) What is the distance between I and II, I and III, I and IV, I and V, I and VI, and I and VII in the key of C major? (d) How far is A♭CE♭F♯ from BD♯G♭A?

## ORTHOGRAPHIC REQUIREMENTS

Questions about spelling arise almost continually in musical scoring, so it would be extremely useful, especially when utilizing a computer, to have a complete tabulation of correct notations available. In the presence of some as-yet-to-be-determined unifying principle for enlarging the key signature to cover all cases, no spelling difficulty ever could be incurred. All spellings then would correspond to the dictates of the enlarged key signature, even at the level of detail representing full expression of the composer's probable intent (to the analyst). Before undertaking a search to find the **perfect othographic principle** that it is hoped can serve as the guiding star of musical notation, it is advisable first to list the mandatory features of an acceptable system of musical notation. These features assume that the problem of musical spelling to be settled is not as much a question of right or wrong, or correct or incorrect, as it is a question of internal consistency.

1. The unifying principle must be simple.

It is apparent that the concept of simplicity houses many ill-defined and subjective variables. Clearly, the rules of spelling must not be simple at the expense of making the rest of the theory of harmony complicated.

2. The unifying principle must be explicit.

In production of literal expressions, there may be some borderline cases, but there should be no vagueness.

3. The unifying principle must be precise.

Precision is necessary to make explicit the assumptions that underlie the spelling rules and for the latter to be evaluable for over-all economy and consistency. The formulation of these spelling rules must be precise enough to be programmable on a digital computer.

4. The unifying principle must be an extension of existing practice, but only insofar as such practice is well defined.

It is of obvious importance to pay due heed to current usage in securing an orthographic system. Standard notations must be adhered to when such things exist. The notations for the major and minor scale subharmonies must induce an extension that will provide explicit prescriptions for the values of all accidentals.

5. The unifying principle must provide a complete prescription.

Full prescription entails specification to the last literal symbol.

6. The unifying principle must yield reproducible results.

Researcher A should obtain the same answer on machine a using program $\alpha$ as researcher B on machine b using program $\beta$.

7. The unifying principle must produce readable and meaningful literal notations.

This is clear.

8. The unifying principle must guarantee closure of the set of preferred notations under the involutory operation of mirror inversion.

This is not so clear. Nevertheless it is a fundamental requirement to prevent a major triad such as CEG from inverting into a minor triad spelled FG♯C and then reinverting into a major triad spelled B♯EG, or worse.

9. The unifying principle must be derived on a logical basis.

In itself this is a strong requirement. It is, however, a weaker requirement than asking for uniqueness or single valuedness. This would be asking too much. Clearly F♯A♯C♯ and G♭B♭D♭ are equally valid notations for the same harmony, since one can be obtained from the other by a rigid motion or musical transposition. Thus, the solution is by no means unique. Moreover, there is no way to decide which of CC♯D or CD♭D is best out of context. Equally valid, these two spellings are related by mirror inversion and are not related by transposition. So, the solution to the orthographic problem is not single valued. Once these facts are really understood there is no ambiguity.

10. The unifying principle must restrict the number of inflections.

Obviously B♯F♭A♭♭ is notationally inferior to CEG.

EXERCISES

**2.35** The search for an analytic criterion for establishing enharmonically correct spellings continues in the next section. Before going on, the reader may be interested in trying to invent a method for inferring a correct decoding algorithm in accordance with these ten requirements.

**2.36** The improvement in spelling brought about by reducing the number of inflections measures less when B♯DxFx is replaced by CEG than when B♯F♭A♭♭ is replaced by CEG. Show why from several points of view.

**2.37** Give a numerical reason for preferring the spelling B♭DF to A♯DF.

ASSUMPTIONS

It is the duty of a correct theory of music orthography to provide acceptable literal notations to express both chords and harmonies, but not sonorities, since the latter are not subject to transposition. Often a fixed chord or harmony must be partly respelled in order for it to belong to a new key. And it is always true that a chord or harmony must be entirely respelled when it is transposed to a new pitch level. So, literal notations are not invariant under transposition. The property of having preferred status or acceptability, however, must be preserved under this operation. Further investigation will show that this kind of behavior can be guaranteed.

It would be reasonable to ask: what is the basic problem involved in choosing a preferred literal notation? (To prevent trivial exceptions, let it be agreed upon in the beginning that the preferred notation for silence will be a rest sign of the proper duration or else a natural sign standing alone.) To be specific, assume that the music calligrapher is confronted with a musical structure comprised of $\underline{M}$ tones, not necessarily different. Moreover, assume that the underlying harmony is made up of $\underline{n}$ primitive tones

$$T_{j_1},\ T_{j_2},\ \ldots,\ T_{j_n},$$

where $\underline{n}$ ranges from 1 through 12 and is less than or equal to $\underline{M}$. The problem is to select $\underline{n}$ literals from an alphabet

$$\pounds = L \times I = \{\langle l, i\rangle:\ l = A, B, C, D, E, F, G;\ i = \ldots, \times, \sharp, \natural, \flat, \flat\flat, \ldots\}$$

to label these tones subject to the ten mandatory requirements stated in the preceding section. The set £ is defined as the **Cartesian product** of the two sets L and I and composed of ordered pairs ⟨l, i⟩ whose first element l is a member of the set L of letters and whose second element i is a member of the set I of inflections. (If the ordered pairs are written simply as li, that is with the elements in juxtaposition rather than within angular brackets, then the alphabet is the familiar set

£={..., F♭♭, C♭♭, ...,
F♭, C♭, ..., F♯, C♯, ...,
Fx, Cx, ..., Bx, ...}

of all literals $\ell$.)

Consider the following definitions as trial conditions for acceptability.

**Definition 1. A literal notation is said to be "proper" if and only if all the equivalent enharmonic values contained in it are identical.**

This condition means that no distinct enharmonic equivalents, such as C and B♯, may be used simultaneously to spell any chord. (See [13].)

**Definition 2. A literal notation is said to be "feasible" if and only if its span is no greater than 12.**

According to this condition CEG is a feasible notation since the span of CEG is 5; by the same token, B♯EA♭♭ is an infeasible notation since its span is 24. (See Exercise 2.24.)

**Definition 3. A literal notation is said to be "minimal" if and only if its span is a minimum with respect to the spans of elements of the set containing all the variant spellings.**

By this condition CEG is a minimal notation because no other spelling of this harmony has a smaller span than 5.

As yet no optimality condition has been set, but usually the musician would like to choose the least inflected literal notation consistent with the condition imposed in Definition 3, although it will become evident later on that it is sometimes better to settle for agreement with the condition imposed in Definition 2. Rather than being precise on this point, for it would be arbitrary and therefore wrong to insist upon a formal procedure such as minimizing the sums of the squares of the numbers of inflections, for example, the assertion will be made instead that for a notation to be "optimal" a sprinkling of sharps and flats is to be tolerated; thereafter, if it is necessary to go that far, double sharps and flats can be used, but seldom, if ever should a letter be carried beyond the second level of inflection. The fundamental conclusion to which this discussion has been tending should now be obvious.

**Lemma 1. A feasible notation exists for every chord and harmony.**

This observation, the proof of which is left to the reader, provides the basis for demonstrating the following important result.

**Theorem 1 (Existence). Every chord and harmony has an optimal literal notation.**

Proof. It follows from the existence of a feasible notation that there is also a minimal notation, because the span is bounded below by zero. Furthermore, since a minimal notation always exists, it follows that there is an optimal notation too, because the number of possible inflections is again bounded below by zero.

EXERCISES

**2.38** Which of the following expressions are feasible notations for the chromatic scale?

(a) CC♯DD♯EFF♯GG♯AA♯B,

'Melodic' Chromatic: "Major" form;

(b) CC♯DE♭EFF♯GG♯AA♯B,

'Melodic' Chromatic: "Minor" form;

(c) CD♭DE♭EFF♯GA♭AB♭B,

'Harmonic' Chromatic: "Minor" form;

and (d) CD♭DE♭F♭FG♭GA♭B♭♭B♭C♭.

**2.39** Verify that the notations EFF♯ and EE♯F♯ are both feasible. If they are mirror images of each other, what is their axis of symmetry?

**2.40** (a) Prove that Condition 3 implies Condition 2, and Condition 2 implies Condition 1; (b) prove Lemma 1.

**2.41** Give two examples of chords whose literal notations are (a) proper, but not feasible; (b) feasible, but not minimal; and (c) minimal, but not optimal.

**2.42** Under what operations is span an invariant?

THEORETICAL DEVELOPMENT

For present purposes only, assume for simplicity that the spelling for a harmony will not be affected by changes made to the chord structure by replicating tones. By the binary coding technique, harmonies can be expressed as twelve-bit binary numbers, that is, by strings of ones and zeros of length twelve. For example, the harmony CEG, which has the designation 38 in decimal, has also the designation 000000100110 in binary. When listed horizontally, this bit configuration can be broken into groups of 4 binary digits each (**hexadecimal** or "base sixteen")

$$0000\ 0010\ 0110_2 = 026_{16},$$

or into groups of 3 binary digits each (**octal** or "base eight")

$$000\ 000\ 100\ 110_2 = 0046_8.$$

It is natural to assume that there is some logical relationship between certain notations that are preferable, and some yet to be discovered property of the corresponding bit configurations. Indeed this is true, but the relationship is somewhat mysterious. To obtain this condition, it is sufficient to consider a simple device called a binary shift register, which serves to redistribute the ones in any given bit configuration (see Fig. 2.8).

Figure 2.8

Schematic representation of a twelve-bit cyclic shift register.

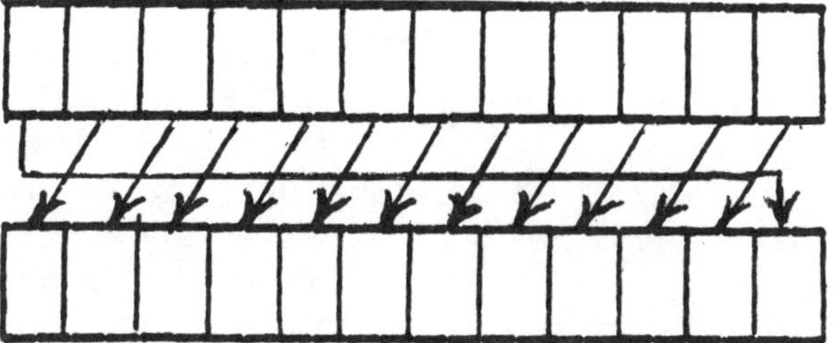

Using this device, the designation for the C major triad given above can be made to go through its orbit:

000000100110
000001001100
000010011000
000100110000
001001100000
010011000000
100110000000

Now notice the end-around operation at the next shift.

001100000001 odd
011000000010
110000000100

and again,

100000001001 odd

and for a last time,

000000010011 odd

This closes the orbit because the next shift reproduces the starting value. Note that the number of odd values occurring in any orbit is equal to the cardinality of the sonority.

By so rearranging the bit configurations via this prescribed cyclic left-shift rule (through an orbit), one or more distinct, odd, zero-one patterns may be produced. In the present example there are three, namely:

000000010011,

001100000001, and

100000001001.

The resulting binary configurations, being different, carry within them genetic clues to different literal notations. All of these notations are feasible since their spans are less than or equal to twelve, but some of them are not minimal as there are other notations with smaller span.

The first step has been to convert the harmony into its binary designative form; the next step is going to be to set up a sliding correspondence between the distinct twelve-digit zero-one patterns produced and parts of the 35-literal chain.

Afterward the bit configuration will be masked over the chosen segment of the literal alphabet, called a "stencil," and that portion of the stencil which is extracted by **logical multiplication** or "intersection" shall be identified as a feasible notation.

Consider these three examples:

| | | | | | | | | | | | | | |
|---|---|---|---|---|---|---|---|---|---|---|---|---|---|
| Stencil | E♯ | A♯ | D♯ | G♯ | C♯ | F♯ | B | E | A | D | G | C | |
| Extraction operator | | | | | | | | ∩ | | | ∩ | ∩ | |
| Mask | 0 | 0 | 0 | 0 | 0 | 0 | 0 | 1 | 0 | 0 | 1 | 1 | →EGC |

| | | | | | | | | | | | | | |
|---|---|---|---|---|---|---|---|---|---|---|---|---|---|
| Stencil | A | D | G | C | F | B♭ | E♭ | A♭ | D♭ | G♭ | C♭ | F♭ | |
| Extraction operator | | | ∩ | ∩ | | | | | | | | ∩ | |
| Mask | 0 | 0 | 1 | 1 | 0 | 0 | 0 | 0 | 0 | 0 | 0 | 1 | →GCF♭ |

and

| | | | | | | | | | | | | | |
|---|---|---|---|---|---|---|---|---|---|---|---|---|---|
| Stencil | B♯ | E♯ | A♯ | D♯ | G♯ | C♯ | F♯ | B | E | A | D | G | |
| Extraction operator | ∩ | | | | | | | | ∩ | | | ∩ | |
| Mask | 1 | 0 | 0 | 0 | 0 | 0 | 0 | 0 | 1 | 0 | 0 | 1 | →B♯EG |

It is evident that every nonzero bit in a binary configuration will produce a corresponding literal; the position of any given one-bit will dictate the specific literal to be selected. The zeros in the bit configuration being used for reference, on the other hand, will indicate with exactitude which literals of the chain are not to be extracted in deriving the particular notation. Fortunately the cyclic left-shift rule rearranges the bit configurations in such a manner that the parent sonority remains invariant. When a chord is transposed, the effect on the underlying harmony is a shifting and interchanging of the bits (zeros and ones) in its binary designation in such a way that the folded chord still lies within the range of a single octave, or more precisely, in such a way that a transposed harmony is obtained. That is, the given harmony goes through its orbit, taking on successively the guise of the various other harmonies belonging to the same sonority. By compensating for this transposition by an opposite shift of the (infinite) literal chain, in the manner just illustrated, additional ways of spelling the original harmony may be found that can be applied to the original chord, rather than to its transposes. Moreover, among these patterns there will exist a required optimal solution.

Although these odd, integer-valued, binary numbers that help to isolate the feasible notations are generated in a completely deterministic manner by cyclic left shifts, it is important to emphasize that the process just described is not transpositional in nature. If it were, then CEG would undergo a rigid motion and become either B♯D×F× or D♭♭F♭A♭♭. Moreover, it is intuitively obvious that although CF♭G and B♯EG are proper and feasible solutions, they are not optimal. This can be seen in two ways. First, their spans are ten and twelve, respectively, which are not nearly as small as that of CEG, which is five. So, CEG is the only minimal spelling. Second, the inflectional values of CF♭G and B♯EG are each one; the inflectional value of CEG is zero. Hence, among all proper and feasible notations that can be found for the harmony whose decimal designation is 38, CEG is that particular minimal notation having the least number of inflections on a sharp-flat basis. It follows that if a decoding algorithm could be based somehow on characteristic designations, this would have the obvious advantage of minimizing the span. Using the smallest designation number in an orbit to prescribe the mask can be justified only on the basis of programming convenience, however. Certainly there are no grounds for inferring that the dynamic processes involved in tonality and modulation favor the least representative. In addition, such a scheme has a severe defect, the discovery of which is left as an exercise.

Given a complete system of distinct representatives, or **residue system,** it is relatively easy to work out all of the optimal spellings for each harmony using a digital computer. With a little thought it becomes clear that every decimal number from 0 to 4095, when expressed in binary, can be used as a mask to extract a feasible notation from a finite segment of the infinite literal chain. Further, the resulting collection includes every conceivable spelling variant of span twelve or less, for each specified harmony of the twelve-tone system. There are in all $2^{12}$ = 4096 possible binary configurations that occur within the range

000000000000:silence, to

111111111111:chromatic scale harmony.

When all the possible configurations of zeros and ones that can occupy twelve empty adjacent cells

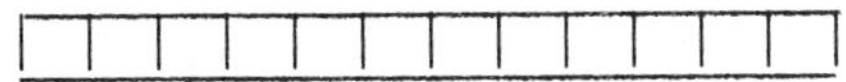

are listed in an orderly manner, the result represents a complete table of harmonies. The related sequences of literals are obtained by sliding the binary designation alongside the infinite literal chain, truncated to a convenient length, and producing a notation at each shift. The result this time will be a complete table of feasible notations.

It is preferable to work with a finite literal chain--the 35-literal alphabet is ample for most situations arising in practice. Consequently the basic range of literals lies between F♭♭ and Bx inclusive. To ensure that the notation will fall in the right bracket, the conditions and stored information must be reduced to the bare essentials, including only the alphabet, the tone marks or designation numbers serving as binary masks, and the stencil boundaries. For many chords and harmonies, only twelve literals need to be specified in the stencil. As will become evident, it so happens that in borderline cases, thirteen literals are necessary and sufficient. The "enlarged key signature" has, by definition, the same number of sharps and flats as does the stencil.

As an example consider the following case involving the chromatic semitones CC♯ and D♭D, where the slash indicates an enharmonic ambiguity arising at a key boundary.

| | | | | | | | | | | | | | |
|---|---|---|---|---|---|---|---|---|---|---|---|---|---|
| Stencil | | | | | | | | | | | | | |
| Extraction | D♭/C♯ | F♯ | B | E | A | D | G | C | F | B♭ | E♭ | A♭ | |
| operator | ∩ | | | | | ∩ | | ∩ | | | | | |
| Mask | 1 | 0 | 0 | 0 | 0 | 1 | 0 | 1 | 0 | 0 | 0 | 0 | → CC♯D & CD♭D = C(C♯/D♭)D, |

Here, the expression (C♯/D♭) expresses a **don't-care** attitude that must be adopted in a **no-way-to-decide-without-being-arbitrary** situation. In this example the enlarged key signature has two sharps and four flats.

At this point it is worth mentioning that the ultimate answer to the musical spelling question rests upon a new and revolutionary principle, which--with questionable modesty, but quite appropriately--has been christened the "perfect orthographic principle." But since the statement of this new principle requires complex arithmetic, its theoretical development and illustration will be postponed to a later chapter. The perfect orthographic principle is constructive in the sense that it tells precisely how to go about finding all of the solutions of the musical spelling problem by computer. This task is accomplished for vertical and horizontal musical structures alike, in a systematic manner, by applying a logical procedure or **decoding algorithm** to the underlying harmonies. If the structure under scrutiny is regarded in isolation from context, the resulting preferred notation is termed "true"; otherwise, it is termed "relative." The algorithm is based on a collection of literal stencils. Later chapters of this book explain carefully how these are constructed and use them in combination as a tool, called the "stencil tableau," for the derivation of preferred notations, either true or relative, under a variety of driving inputs. The computer program, for example, will enable the user to pass directly from numerical designations to true preferred notations, that is, from designative to notative form. A remarkable result of the theory is that under certain easily ascertainable conditions each feasible notation can become a relative preferred notation.

Having advanced to the point where the computer can be programmed for printing out well formed notative expressions, remaining interest centers upon deducing in a precise fashion some of the consequences that the perfect orthographic principle has in music theory. These deductions include the relationship of the enlarged key signature to the field of accidentals of a generalized key and the demarcation of roles by means of thresholds of enharmonic change.

## EXERCISES

**2.43** Devise examples to illuminate the flaw in the least representative decoding algorithm. (<u>Hint</u>. Consider mirror inversion.)

**2.44** Prove that contrary to widespread impression the statement "chromatically raised degrees belong exclusively to ascending motion and chromatically lowered degrees, to descending motion" is erroneous.

**2.45** An alternate and not so practical approach to preferred musical notation would be to provide the computer with a list of rote responses to the spelling problem. Describe such an approach and point out its major disadvantage.

## CHROMATICITY, DIATONICITY, AND INTERVALLIC CONTENT

The 35-literal alphabet centered on D is constructed out of the letters A, B, C, D, E, F, G and the inflections ♭♭, ♭, ♮, ♯, ×. Let X denote one of these seven letters. Then a given literal notation is said to be "chromatic in X" if and only if (a) X♭♭ is paired with X♭, X, X♯, X×; (b) X♭ is paired with X♭♭, X, X♯, X×; (c) X is paired with X♭♭, X♭, X♯, X×; (d) X# is paired with X♭♭, X♭, X, X×; or (e) X× is paired with X♭♭, X♭, X, X♯. In short, a literal notation will be called "chromatic" if and only if two or more letters in it agree at the same time their inflections disagree. As a consequence, it is true without exception that every literal notation will be chromatic provided only that the underlying harmony is of cardinality greater than seven. On the other hand, if there are no such conflicting literals then the literal notation is said to be "monotone." It will be seen shortly that monotonicity is a somewhat broader term than diatonicity.

The explicit orthography provided by the totality of preferred literal notations removes two barriers to automated music analysis. First, it clearly establishes the true musical intervals contained in a tonal structure; and second, it immediately relates the structure to the appropriate key families. Given a single preferred notation for some harmony in a sonority, many of the remaining preferred notations for other members of this sonority can be found by rotational transposition. The collection of preferred notations so obtained forms a kind of model of that sonority, and the recognition and development of this model is crucial to the solution of the larger problem of music analysis by computers.

Such a collection can be represented by a standardized notation growing out of a special convention that regards the rightmost (or **least significant**) bit position in the associated binary designation as bearing the label "F." The next bit to the left, depicting the next tone in the stencil, bears the label "C," and so on. This procedure gives rise to what will be called the "standard stencil." The standard stencil, namely:

|A♯ D♯ G♯ C♯ F♯ B E A D G C F|,

is helpful in defining an important property of literal notations--their "chromaticity index." For example, the literal notation FGF♯, extracted from the standard stencil by means of the mask 000010000101, is chromatic since it exhibits a conflict in the F variable, and is chromatic of degree 1, since it exhibits only one conflict. The chromaticity index is found to be unity from the chart:

CHROMATICITY INDEX

| ADGCF | INDEX | ADGCF | INDEX | ADGCF | INDEX | ADGCF | INDEX |
|---|---|---|---|---|---|---|---|
| 00000 | 0 | 01000 | 8 | 10000 | 16 | 11000 | 24 |
| 00001 | 1 | 01001 | 9 | 10001 | 17 | 11001 | 25 |
| 00010 | 2 | 01010 | 10 | 10010 | 18 | 11010 | 26 |
| 00011 | 3 | 01011 | 11 | 10011 | 19 | 11011 | 27 |
| 00100 | 4 | 01100 | 12 | 10100 | 20 | 11100 | 28 |
| 00101 | 5 | 01101 | 13 | 10101 | 21 | 11101 | 29 |
| 00110 | 6 | 01110 | 14 | 10110 | 22 | 11110 | 30 |
| 00111 | 7 | 01111 | 15 | 10111 | 23 | 11111 | 31 |

One of the principal problems of an explanatory theory of music is to account for the high stability or consonance of certain configurations of tones, for example of major triads and dominant seventh tetrads. Musicians today generally agree that the justification for the widespread use and importance of these harmonies resides in the overtone series. Chords embodying these harmonies appeal to the musical ear since frequencies of the upper partials are related in simple ways to the fundamental and happen to sound well together. Before attempting to account for the emergence and endurance of the diatonic scales, of which the C major scale C,D,E,F,G,A,B,C (the white keys of the piano) is a prime example, it might be of interest to digress momentarily in order to relate a short anecdote.

Some years ago in Vienna, a student of Schoenberg came to the mathematician Isadore Heller for help with a theoretical problem that was troubling him in connection with his study of the principles of atonality. Spurred on by friendly rivalry with his fellow composers, the student had been seeking a particular tone row, which he thought would have the greatest potential utility because it would possess certain natural symmetries. Frustrated in every attempt thus far to find this elusive tone row, he now asked Dr. Heller to determine whether it was possible that the tone row might not exist, as in that case it would be meaningless to continue his search.

The several constraints prescribed by the inventor of this problem introduced some difficulties of a combinatorial nature. And, since Dr. Heller could devote only a limited portion of each evening to the investigation, five days passed before the solution was obtained. When informed of the outcome of the investigation, the student became crestfallen. His dream of acquiring a personalized tone row surpassing all others was shattered. Dr. Heller had discovered that not just one, but something in excess of five million tone rows could be constructed satisfying the prescribed conditions. Needless to say, for a short time this *embarras des richesses* was a source of considerable disappointment to the student.

Now the word "diatonic" generally refers only to those harmonies that can be spelled using inflections of the letters A through G without repeating any letter. Clearly, no octad can be diatonic, nor can any harmony of greater cardinality, because there are only seven letters available. So, it would be natural to ask: does there exist a diatonic heptad? Or, to put the question another way: how many of the 66 different seven-tone scale families are diatonic? Actually, as Table III has shown, the 66 possible heptad harmonies can be written using inflections of the letters A through G without repeating a letter, simply by regarding them as Busoni scales. But fortunately, this time there is a neat way out of the predicament posed by an overpopulated solution space.

As stated elsewhere, all Busoni notations are **weakly** diatonic. Moreover, every harmony that can be spelled monotonically is weakly diatonic; this includes all harmonies of cardinality less than or equal to seven. Obviously this type of diatonicity is too broad in concept. The solution is simple. Decide to adopt a more restrictive definition. Therefore it is proposed that any harmony arising in the twelve-tone equitempered system be called "strongly diatonic" if, and only if, except for unisons none of its internal musical interval relationships are **firsts** when the harmony is expressed in **true preferred notation.** Adherence to this new definition drastically reduces the number of heptadiatonic scales. Moreover, it is pleasant to discover that the survivors are all old friends--the traditional diatonic scales.

Figure 2.9

Judging from the spans, there are only sixteen feasible notations among the sixty-six Busoni scales of Table III. In the remaining cases the spellings are consistent with Busoni's definition of a synthetic musical scale, but otherwise do not make much sense. This programmable calculator output was written automatically by an x,y plotter making use of the present computer methodology.

00 Cb Dbb Ebb Fb Gbb Abb Bbb 07
01 Cb Db Ebb F Gb Abb Bbb 11
02 Cb Db Ebb Fb Gbb Abb Bbb 09
03 C Db Eb F G A B 11
04 Cb Db E F Gb Abb Bbb 16
05 C Db Ebb Fb Gbb Abb Bbb 14
06 Cb Db E F G Ab Bbb 14
07 Cb D E F Gb Abb Bbb 16
08 Cb Db E# F# G Ab Bbb 21
09 Cb Dbb Ebb F Gb Abb Bbb 12
10 C Db Ebb F Gb Abb Bbb 12
11 Cb Dbb Ebb F Gb Ab Bbb 12
12 C D E F Gb Ab B 12
13 C Db E F Gb Abb Bbb 16
14 Cb Dbb Ebb F G Ab Bbb 14
15 Cb D E F G Ab Bbb 14
16 C D E F Gb Abb Bbb 16
17 Cb D E# F# G Ab Bbb 21
18 C Db Ebb Fb Gbb Abb B 19
19 C# D E F Gb Ab B# 19
20 C# D E F Gb Abb Bbb 19
21 C Db Ebb Fbb Gbb A B 21
22 Cb Dx E# F# G Ab Bbb 26
23 Cb Dbb Ebb Fb Gbb Ab Bbb 10
24 C Db E F G Ab B 11
25 C D E F G Ab B 10
26 C Db E F G A B 11
27 C D E# F# G Ab B 16
28 C Db Ebb Fb Gbb Ab Bbb 14
29 C Db E F G Ab Bbb 14
30 C Db Ebb F Gb A B 16
31 C Dx E# F# G Ab B 21
32 Cb Db Ebb F G Ab Bbb 12
33 C Db E F Gb A B 12
34 C# D E F G Ab B 12
35 C D E F Gb A B 12
36 C Db Ebb F G Ab B 16
37 C D E F Gb Ab Bbb 14
38 C# D E F Gb A B 14
39 C Db Ebb F G A B 16
40 C D E# F# G Ab Bbb 21
41 C Db Ebb Fb Gbb Ab B 19
42 C# D E F Gb A B# 19
43 C Db Ebb F G# A B 19
44 Cx Dx E# F# G Ab B 21
45 C Dx E# F# G Ab Bbb 26
46 Cb Dbb E F Gb Abb Bbb 17
47 C Db Ebb F Gb Abb B 17
48 Cb Dbb E F Gb Ab Bbb 17
49 C Db E# F# G A B 17
50 C Db E F Gb Abb B 17
51 Cb Dbb E F G Ab Bbb 17
52 C# D E F G Ab Bbb 17
53 C D E F Gb Abb B 17
54 C# D E# F# G Ab Bbb 21
55 C Db Ebb Fb Gbb A B 19
56 C Db E# Fx G# A B 19
57 C# D E F Gb Abb B 19
58 Cx Dx E# F# G Ab B# 21
59 C# Dx E# F# G Ab Bbb 26
60 Cb Dbb E# F# G Ab Bbb 24
61 C# D E F Gb Ax B# 24
62 C# D E F Gb Abb B# 24
63 Cx Dx E# F# G Ab Bx 24
64 Cx Dx E# F# G Ab Bbb 26
65 C# D Eb Fb Gbb Ax B# 31

In order to carry out this project, it is necessary to make use of some of the tools that are going to be developed throughout the remainder of this book. Pre-eminent among these is the perfect orthographic principle, which affords in the present application a decision procedure for the logical predicate "H is diatonic" with H a harmony of cardinality seven.

The first sample output from the computer is shown in Fig. 2.9. Columns 2 and 5 provide a verification that the input data are correct. Columns 3 and 6 are the machine calculated spans. The next output, in Fig. 2.10, carries the process a step further. Here are displayed the true preferred notations for the Busoni scale harmonies. Notice that in four cases (lines 08, 19, 59,

Figure 2.10

The asterisks were added afterwards to this sample-output table of heptads to distinguish strongly diatonic harmonies. The hand-drawn ellipses enclose chromatic semitones. Columns two and three contain the numerical values of the amplitude and phase for the associated tonalities. Later on in this book it will be shown that the so-called "Gypsy" scale has more than one true preferred spelling, since its amplitude (line 24, second column) is zero. As one of these preferred spellings is diatonic, it will be said that harmony 871, the **Gypsy scale harmony**, is "quasi-diatonic."

| | | | | |
|---|---|---|---|---|
| *00 | 3.732 | 090.000 | BCDEFGA | major |
| 01 | 1.932 | 135.000 | BC#DFF#GA | |
| *02 | 2.732 | 120.000 | BC#DEFGA | melodic minor |
| *03 | 1.000 | 030.000 | CDbEbFGAB | whole tone plus one |
| 04 | 2.394 | 158.794 | BC#EFF#GA | |
| 05 | 2.909 | 080.104 | CC#DEFGA | |
| 06 | 1.414 | 165.000 | BC#EFGG#A | |
| 07 | 3.235 | 122.374 | BDEFF#GA | |
| 08 | 1.506 | -155.104 | CbDbFGbAbbAbBbb BC#E#F#GG#A | |
| 09 | 2.732 | 090.000 | BCDFF#GA | |
| 10 | 1.932 | 075.000 | CC#DFF#GA | |
| 11 | 1.000 | 120.000 | BCDFF#G#A | |
| 12 | 1.000 | 150.000 | CDEFF#G#B | |
| 13 | 1.414 | 105.000 | CC#EFF#GA | |
| 14 | 2.394 | 068.794 | BCDFGAbA | |
| 15 | 2.394 | 111.206 | BDEFGG#A | |
| 16 | 3.235 | 087.626 | CDEFF#GA | |
| 17 | 1.506 | 125.104 | BDFF#GG#A | |
| 18 | 2.000 | 090.000 | CC#DEFGB | |
| 19 | 0.518 | -135.000 | DbEbbFbFGbAbC C#DEE#F#G#B# | |
| 20 | 2.236 | 123.435 | C#DEFF#GA | |
| 21 | 0.732 | 060.000 | CC#DbDEbFAB | |
| 22 | 1.880 | 157.089 | BEFF#GG#A | |
| *23 | 1.932 | 105.000 | BCDEFG#A | harmonic minor |
| 24 | 0.000 | 145.008 | CC#EFGG#B | "Gypsy" |
| *25 | 1.932 | 075.000 | CDEFGAbB | harmonic major |
| 26 | 1.932 | 105.000 | CC#EFGAB | |
| 27 | 1.000 | 060.000 | CDFF#GAbB | |
| 28 | 1.000 | 090.000 | CC#DEFG#AbA | |
| 29 | 1.000 | 060.000 | CC#DbEFGAbA | |
| 30 | 1.414 | 135.000 | CC#DFF#AB | |
| 31 | 0.518 | 135.000 | CEFF#GG#B | |
| 32 | 1.000 | 120.000 | BC#DFGG#A | |
| 33 | 1.932 | 165.000 | CC#EFF#AB | |
| 34 | 1.000 | 150.000 | C#DEFGG#B | |
| 35 | 2.732 | 120.000 | CDEFF#AB | |
| 36 | 1.000 | 030.000 | CDbDFGAbB | |
| 37 | 1.414 | 105.000 | CDEFF#G#A | |
| 38 | 2.909 | 159.896 | C#DEFF#AB | |
| 39 | 2.394 | 081.206 | CC#DFGAB | |
| 40 | 2.000 | 060.000 | CDFF#GAbA | |
| 41 | 0.518 | 165.000 | CC#DEFG#B | |
| 42 | 1.732 | 120.000 | C#DEFF#AC | |
| 43 | 0.518 | 105.000 | CC#DFG#AB | |
| 44 | 1.506 | 144.896 | DEFF#GG#B | |
| 45 | 1.239 | 083.794 | CEFF#GAbB | |
| 46 | 2.394 | 111.206 | BCEFF#GA | |
| 47 | 1.000 | 090.000 | CC#DFF#GB | |
| 48 | 1.414 | 165.000 | BCEFF#G#A | |
| 49 | 1.000 | 120.000 | CC#FF#GAB | |
| 50 | 1.000 | 150.000 | CC#EFF#GB | |
| 51 | 1.732 | 090.000 | BCEFGG#AbA | |
| 52 | 1.414 | 105.000 | C#DEFGG#A | |
| 53 | 2.394 | 098.794 | CDEFF#GB | |
| 54 | 0.518 | 135.000 | C#DFF#GG#A | |
| 55 | 2.236 | 116.565 | CC#DEFAB | |
| 56 | 0.518 | 045.000 | CDbFGAbAB | |
| 57 | 2.000 | 150.000 | C#DEFF#GB | |
| 58 | 1.506 | 065.104 | DEFF#GAbC | |
| 59 | 1.239 | -173.794 | DbFbFGbAbbAbBbb C#EE#F#GG#A | |
| 60 | 0.732 | 090.000 | BCFF#GG#AbA | |
| 61 | 1.506 | 155.104 | C#DEFF#BC | |
| 62 | 1.506 | 084.896 | C#DEFF#BC | |
| 63 | 0.732 | -180.000 | EbbFbFGbbGbAbbAbDb DEE#FF#GG#C# | |
| 64 | 1.880 | 112.911 | DEFF#GG#A | |
| 65 | 0.268 | 090.000 | C#DEbDFBC | |

and 63) two distinct spellings, differing only by a transposition, vie for recognition, so that it is only fair to record both of them. The numerical columns play an important part in the decoding process. Their meaning and derivation will be explained soon. The conclusion to be drawn from this experiment may at first seem surprising. There are exactly five strongly diatonic heptads and one quasi-diatonic heptad predicted by the mathematical model. This conclusion evidently is consistent with traditional musical theory to the extent that it recognizes every well known seven-tone structural formation. Moreover, it clearly establishes that the traditional diatonic scales (and their subharmonies, the triads and seventh chords) can be derived without recourse to the harmonic series.

In this application of the perfect orthographic principle, the Busoni scale harmonies are considered as isolated objects. A static picture results from the lack of musical movement. For this reason, attention is focussed on so-called "true" notation--notation divorced from context. Actually, as everyone must agree, the most significant musical relationships are dynamic. It is not an exaggeration to say that the problems of music analysis which involve motion can be studied adequately only through the tonal window provided by relative preferred notation.

In addition to chromaticity and diatonicity, another factor relevant to the study of literal notation is **intervallic content.** In conformity with the theory of preferred notation, attention is restricted to the intervals that can be built out of the elements of the standard stencil. Fig. 2.11 contains a square array of positive, zero, and negative integers called "I-values." As the name suggests, the integers are assigned to various musical interval relationships. To be more specific, assume that the two literals G♯ and D are taken in that order to form a musical interval whose lower endnote is G♯ and whose upper endnote is D, then the associated I-value will be the numerical entry -6 that is to be found at the intersection of the row beginning with G♯ and the column headed with D. This musical interval G♯D is expressed mathematically as the ordered pair ⟨G♯,D⟩. The name of the musical interval relationship typified by the dyad G♯D is "diminished fifth," symbolized o5th. The determination is carried out by following the diagonal line of minus sixes to the adjacent margin.

## EXERCISES

**2.46** (a) Prepare a block diagram showing the logical steps necessary to list all of the musical interval relationships making up an arbitrary feasible notation. (b) Contrast the present approach to the analysis of musical intervals with that of Hanson in **Harmonic Materials of Modern Music.** (Hint. Consider the two Cartesian products T×T and £×£, where T denotes the set of 12 primitive tones and £ denotes the set of 35 literals.) (c) Is either system too cumbersome for direct practical application? (d) Give musical evidence that in dealing with semitone distances rather than using I-values, a veil is cast over the true meaning of a harmony, and clues to its tonality and basis in just intonation are obscured.

**2.47** Preferably using a digital computer, calculate the chromaticity index for each of the 4096 feasible literal notations. (Hint. The process in full would require the following steps:

1. Use the standard stencil.
2. Generate every binary mask from 000000000000 to 111111111111.
3. Apply each mask to the standard stencil in order to extract the corresponding feasible notation.
4. Determine the associated chromaticity index from a stored chart.

As this process would be laborious, it is suggested that the work be

Figure 2.11

Musical interval relationships for the standard stencil.

| upper endnote / lower endnote | A♯ | D♯ | G♯ | C♯ | F♯ | B | E | A | D | G | C | F |
|---|---|---|---|---|---|---|---|---|---|---|---|---|
| A♯ | 0 | -1 | -2 | -3 | -4 | -5 | -6 | (-7) | -8 | -9 | -10 | -11 |
| D♯ | 1 | 0 | -1 | -2 | -3 | -4 | -5 | -6 | (-7) | -8 | -9 | -10 |
| G♯ | 2 | 1 | 0 | -1 | -2 | -3 | -4 | -5 | -6 | (-7) | -8 | -9 |
| C♯ | 3 | 2 | 1 | 0 | -1 | -2 | -3 | -4 | -5 | -6 | (-7) | -8 |
| F♯ | 4 | 3 | 2 | 1 | 0 | -1 | -2 | -3 | -4 | -5 | -6 | (-7) |
| B | 5 | 4 | 3 | 2 | 1 | 0 | -1 | -2 | -3 | -4 | -5 | -6 |
| E | 6 | 5 | 4 | 3 | 2 | 1 | 0 | -1 | -2 | -3 | -4 | -5 |
| A | (7) | 6 | 5 | 4 | 3 | 2 | 1 | 0 | -1 | -2 | -3 | -4 |
| D | 8 | (7) | 6 | 5 | 4 | 3 | 2 | 1 | 0 | -1 | -2 | -3 |
| G | 9 | 8 | (7) | 6 | 5 | 4 | 3 | 2 | 1 | 0 | -1 | -2 |
| C | 10 | 9 | 8 | (7) | 6 | 5 | 4 | 3 | 2 | 1 | 0 | -1 |
| F | 11 | 10 | 9 | 8 | (7) | 6 | 5 | 4 | 3 | 2 | 1 | 0 |

o6th o3rd o7th o4th o1st o5th m2nd m6th m3rd m7th P4th P1st

+3rd +6th +2nd +5th +1st +4th M7th M3rd M6th M2nd P5th P1st

Legend

- \+ singly augmented
- o singly diminished
- M major
- m minor
- P perfect
- ⊙ chromaticity

streamlined by omitting steps 1 and 3 and carrying out the analogous steps in binary.)

**2.48** Transpose the following theorem and its proof to fifteen keys.

**CHARLOTTE RUEGGER'S THEOREM. If the harmony GBDF is in a major key, then it must be in the major key of C only.**

Proof. This little known musical theorem can be demonstrated by the following argument based upon a knowledge of the progression of key signatures. First, the presence of the B natural has a marked effect. It excludes the harmony GBDF from the region of flat keys, since the first flat to be introduced into the key signature is B♭. Second, the presence of the F natural has a parallel effect. It excludes the harmony GBDF from the region of sharp keys, since the first sharp to be introduced into the key signature is F♯. Although this evidence is suggestive, it is not quite conclusive. What is required at this point is to make use of the hypothesis. It has been assumed that the harmony is in a major key. Therefore, GBDF must be in the major key of C only.

**2.49** Write out all the feasible notations that can be obtained for the chromatic scale harmony using the 35-literal alphabet.

**2.50** A stencil is placed in so-called "standard form" by arranging its elements so that the order of columns is the same as that of the standard stencil under enharmonic equivalence. Place the feasible chromatic scale notations found in answer to the previous exercise in standard form.

**2.51** (a) Is an equitempered whole tone one-sixth part of an octave? (b) Is a major second one-sixth part of an augmented seventh? (c) Is an augmented seventh an octave? (d) Is an equitempered whole tone a major second?

**2.52** Hexadecimal integers from 000 to fff inclusive may be said to possess "property Δ" (suggesting diatonic) if and only if they contain none of the following pairs of binary powers:

$$\langle 2^0,2^7\rangle,\ \langle 2^1,2^8\rangle,\ \langle 2^2,2^9\rangle,\ \langle 2^3,2^{10}\rangle,$$
$$\text{and } \langle 2^4,2^{11}\rangle.$$

Prove: If x is a hexadecimal integer that possesses property Δ and $2x \leq \text{fff}$, then 2x possesses property Δ. Moreover, if x does not possess property Δ and $2x \leq \text{fff}$, then 2x does not possess property Δ.

**2.53** Elaborate on the following structure for classifying literal notations by giving examples of spellings at each level of the decision pattern.

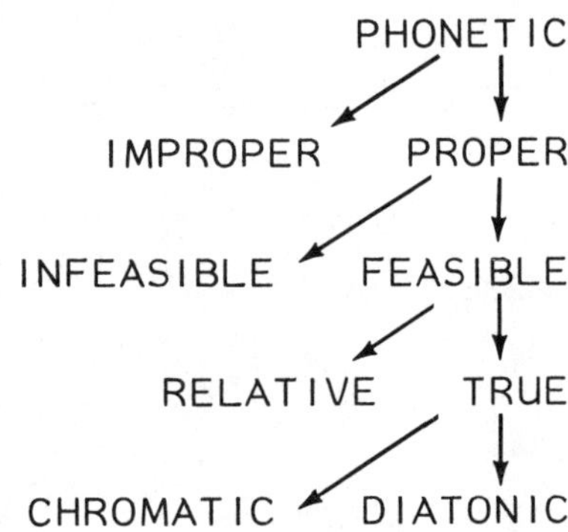


**2.54** (a) How are the five diatonic scales related under mirror inversion? (b) Construct all the fifth (triad), seventh (tetrad), and ninth (pentad) chords possible by superposition of thirds on successive scale degrees of each of the five diatonic, and one quasi-diatonic, scales.

**2.55** It is obvious that a marked reduction of spans has occurred between corresponding entries in Fig. 2.9 and Fig. 2.10. Support this observation by numerical calculations.

**2.56** Discuss the application of the nomogram and tables in Fig. 2.12 to the representation of the intervallic structure of musical themes or incipits. (Permission to include these tutorial aids, which appeared in [14], was granted by the Society for Research in Music Education of the Music Educators National Conference.)

**2.57** Prove the assertion that all harmonies of cardinality less than eight are weakly diatonic.

Figure 2.12a

Nomogram use is exemplified as follows: A straight line drawn to connect a lower note on the L-stem, say E, with an upper note on the R-stem, say F♯, will intersect the I-stem at a point bearing the correct musical interval relationship, in this case, M2nd.

## AN ALINEMENT CHART FOR CALCULATING SIMPLE INTERVAL RELATIONSHIPS

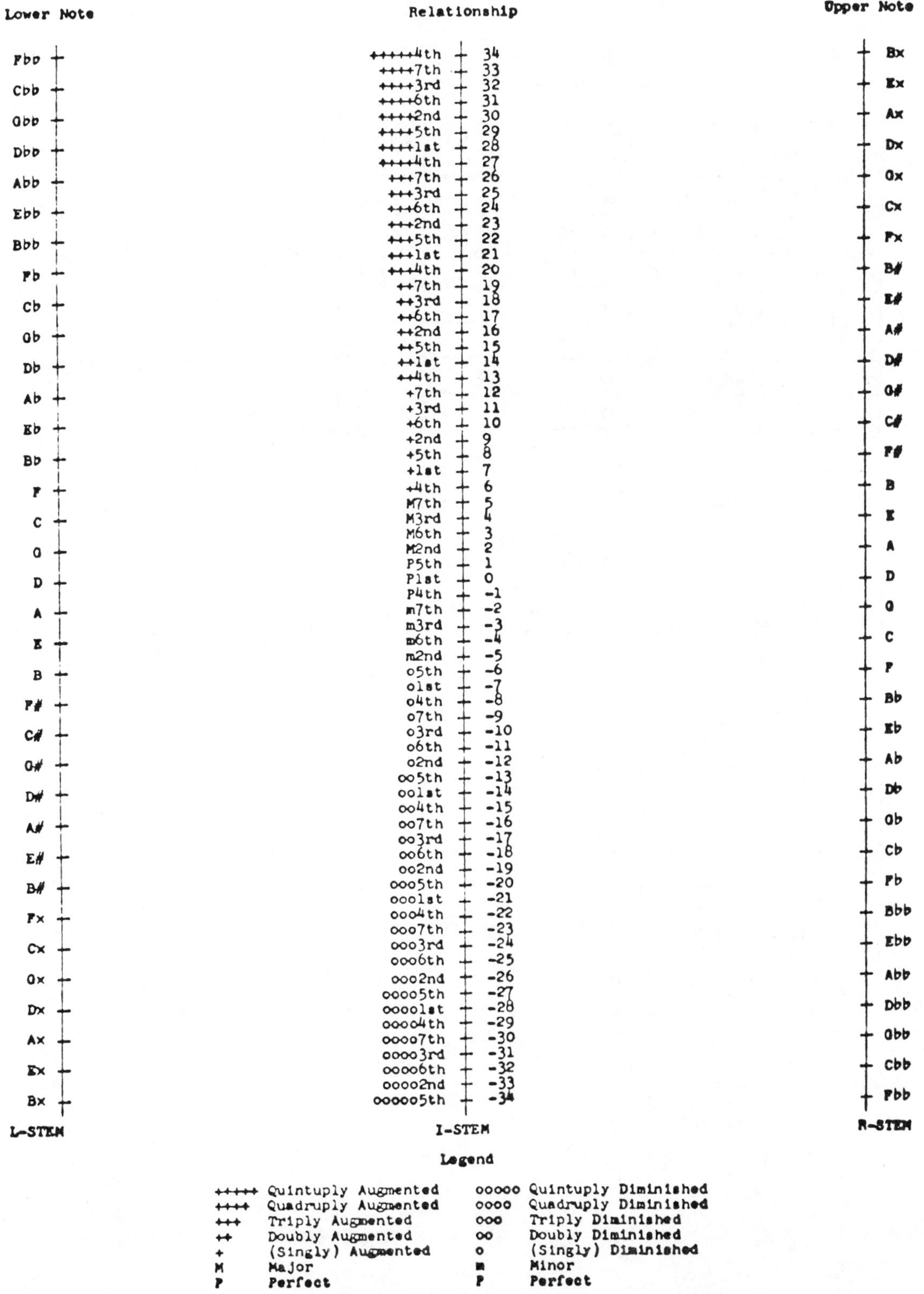

Figure 2.12b

Table use is exemplified as follows: First, k-values are read from the top array; k(E) = -2 and k(F♯) = -4. Second, the formula: I = k(L) - k(R) is applied to determine the I-value: 2 = -2 -(-4). Last, the musical interval relationship M2nd is found from the margins of the bottom array corresponding to I = 2.

k-values

| INFLECTION / LETTER | $\flat^6$ | $\flat^5$ | $\flat^4$ | $\flat^3$ | $\flat^2$ | $\flat$ | $\natural$ | $\sharp$ | $\sharp^2$ | $\sharp^3$ | $\sharp^4$ | $\sharp^5$ | $\sharp^6$ |
|---|---|---|---|---|---|---|---|---|---|---|---|---|---|
| F | 45 | 38 | 31 | 24 | 17 | 10 | 3 | -4 | -11 | -18 | -25 | -32 | -39 |
| C | 44 | 37 | 30 | 23 | 16 | 9 | 2 | -5 | -12 | -19 | -26 | -33 | -40 |
| G | 43 | 36 | 29 | 22 | 15 | 8 | 1 | -6 | -13 | -20 | -27 | -34 | -41 |
| D | 42 | 35 | 28 | 21 | 14 | 7 | 0 | -7 | -14 | -21 | -28 | -35 | -42 |
| A | 41 | 34 | 27 | 20 | 13 | 6 | -1 | -8 | -15 | -22 | -29 | -36 | -43 |
| E | 40 | 33 | 26 | 19 | 12 | 5 | -2 | -9 | -16 | -23 | -30 | -37 | -44 |
| B | 39 | 32 | 25 | 18 | 11 | 4 | -3 | -10 | -17 | -24 | -31 | -38 | -45 |

I-values

| SPECIFIC / GENERAL | $O^{10}$ | $O^9$ | $O^8$ | $O^7$ | $O^6$ | $O^5$ | $O^4$ | $O^3$ | $O^2$ | $O^1$ | *m* | *P* | *M* | $+^1$ | $+^2$ | $+^3$ | $+^4$ | $+^5$ | $+^6$ | $+^7$ | $+^8$ | $+^9$ | $+^{10}$ |
|---|---|---|---|---|---|---|---|---|---|---|---|---|---|---|---|---|---|---|---|---|---|---|---|
| Seventh | | | | | | | | | | | | | 5 | 12 | 19 | 26 | 33 | 40 | 47 | 54 | 61 | 68 | 75 |
| Third | | | | | | | | | | | | | 4 | 11 | 18 | 25 | 32 | 39 | 46 | 53 | 60 | 67 | 74 |
| Sixth | | | | | | | | | | | | | 3 | 10 | 17 | 24 | 31 | 38 | 45 | 52 | 59 | 66 | 73 |
| Second | | | | | | | | | | | | | 2 | 9 | 16 | 23 | 30 | 37 | 44 | 51 | 58 | 65 | 72 |
| Fifth | -69 | -62 | -55 | -48 | -41 | -34 | -27 | -20 | -13 | -6 | | 1 | | 8 | 15 | 22 | 29 | 36 | 43 | 50 | 57 | 64 | 71 |
| First | -70 | -63 | -56 | -49 | -42 | -35 | -28 | -21 | -14 | -7 | | 0 | | 7 | 14 | 21 | 28 | 35 | 42 | 49 | 56 | 63 | 70 |
| Fourth | -71 | -64 | -57 | -50 | -43 | -36 | -29 | -22 | -15 | -8 | | -1 | | 6 | 13 | 20 | 27 | 34 | 41 | 48 | 55 | 62 | 69 |
| Seventh | -72 | -65 | -58 | -51 | -44 | -37 | -30 | -23 | -16 | -9 | -2 | | | | | | | | | | | | |
| Third | -73 | -66 | -59 | -52 | -45 | -38 | -31 | -24 | -17 | -10 | -3 | | | | | | | | | | | | |
| Sixth | -74 | -67 | -60 | -53 | -46 | -39 | -32 | -25 | -18 | -11 | -4 | | | | | | | | | | | | |
| Second | -75 | -68 | -61 | -54 | -47 | -40 | -33 | -26 | -19 | -12 | -5 | | | | | | | | | | | | |

## REFERENCES


[1] Robert M. Mason, "An Encoding Algorithm and Tables for the Digital Analysis of Harmony, *Journal of Research in Music Education,* Vol. XVIII, No. 3, (Fall 1969), pp. 286-300, (II) Vol. XVII, No. 4, (Winter 1969), pp. 369-387.

[2] A. W. Horton, Jr., "An Introduction to Computer Binary Arithmetic," *Bell Telephone System Monograph 3050* (1956).

[3] Joseph Shillinger, *Kaleidophone: New Resources of Melody & Harmony,* (Witmark, New York, 1940).

[4] John Riordan, *An Introduction to Combinatorial Analysis* (Princeton University Press, Princeton, NJ, 1980).

[5] *Grove's Dictionary,* Fifth Edition.

[6] Ferruccio Busoni, *Sketch of a New Esthetic of Music,* (1911).

[7] James Murray Barbour, "Synthetic Musical Scales," *The American Mathematical Monthly,* Vol. 36 (Mar. 1929) pp. 155-160.

[8] Robert M. Mason, "Enumeration of Synthetic Musical Scales by Matrix Algebra and a Catalogue of Busoni Scales," *Journal of Music Theory,* Vol. 14/1 (Yale University, Spring 1970) pp. 92-126.

[9] James Murray Barbour, "Musical Scales and their Classification," *The Journal of the Acoustical Society of America* Vol. 21, No. 6, (Nov. 1949) pp. 586-589.

[10] Nicolas Slonimsky, *Thesaurus of Scales and Melodic Patterns* (Coleman-Ross Co., Inc., New York, 1947) pp. 137-154.

[11] Thorvald Otterström, *A Theory of Modulation* (The University of Chicago Press, Chicago, Illinois, 1935) pp. 130-143.

[12] Howard Hanson, *Harmonic Materials of Modern Music* (Appleton-Century-Crofts, Inc., New York, 1960) p.2.

[13] Franklin W. Robinson, *Aural Harmony Revised* (Hill-Coleman, New York, 1936) p. 30.

[14] Robert M. Mason, "A Formula, Nomogram, and Tables for Determining Musical Interval Relationships," *Journal of Research in Music Education,* Vol. XV, No. 2 (Summer 1967) pp. 110-119.

*To regard the ART of composition in the light of a mere game of chance, puzzles thoughtful students as to where the ART comes in! The fact of the existence of a rule requiring a composition to end in the principal key in which it begins, certainly demands* **choice** *of intermediate keys, and judging by the works of the Great Masters, very much of* **their** *ART has consisted in a careful selection of related keys, and their many devices of approach and adieu to them.*

*ALFRED RHODES, Curiosities of the Key-Board and the Staff, 1896*

PART II

# Chapter 3

# Background

## INTRODUCTORY REMARKS

Functionally speaking, there are two types of musical structures, **horizontal** and **vertical**. These in turn lead to two areas of theoretical analysis referred to as **contrapuntal** and **harmonic**. The material encompassed by the phrase "computer-assisted music analysis" includes those parts of modern music theory that have their basis in the classical theory of music analysis, that is, in strict counterpoint and traditional harmony. As understood in this book, music analysis basically consists of studying the composer's tonal manipulations and the resultant musical motions. Every competent music analyst meticulously probes and reflects on each composition under study. This must be done in order to identify organizational components of a composition and establish the functional and supportive relations that exist among various musical constructs. These constructs are intervals, chords, scales, phrases, and so forth. The present subdivision (Part II) of this book contains a quantitative theory of tonality and modulation for the twelve-tone equitempered system, with special emphasis being placed on the development of the subject through geometrical arguments. This theory is a prerequisite for building a dynamic computer methodology.

For the construction of a comprehensive theory of music that can explicate mankind's ability to compose--to analyze, produce, develop, and understand musical thoughts as a source of human impressions and emotions--extensive knowledge in the area of tonality and modulation is needed to support and clarify the knowledge of the grammatical rules of harmony and counterpoint. Fortunately, a certain branch of mathematics known as **vector analysis** is particularly appropriate for expressing quantitatively the principles and relationships in this area. As vector analysis has become a basic tool in the study of motion, an essential characteristic of musical voices as well as of physical objects, its use in the study of music permits the theory for the first time to advance sufficiently so that practical machine calculations can be made. The resulting calculus upholds the known and accepted properties of polytonality and atonality in addition to tonality, while at the same time preserving many other classical considerations. Moreover, it leads to the presentation of formalized procedures for transcribing in detail the content, structure, and timing of music.

The principal end result is a computer methodology for analyzing musical compositions and determining tonalities, modulations, and keys in terms of vector force diagrams and complex numbers. Since with the exception of the Exercises little previous knowledge of mathematics is assumed on the part of the reader, the student should experience little or no difficulty in becoming adept at handling vector terminology as he or she progresses through the remainder of the book. Using this theory, fast, practical, note-by-note computer-assisted music analysis becomes attainable. The new computer methodology enables the development of digital computer programs for measuring important musical parameters and discriminating among keys or other tonal groupings. Visual displays are recommended to supplement the analytical investigations. The geometrical treatment in the closing sections of the book is oriented towards the automatic statistical analysis of music as a time series, with emphasis on delimiting the areas wherein useful applications can be found. From this computer analysis various statistics bearing upon composers' styles or signatures can be determined. Although this approach does not have quite the same potential as Fourier analysis does, it requires less mathematical apparatus, and since it is a step in the direction of Fourier methods, it seems to represent an attractive compromise between complexity and capability. The concluding section suggests several promising directions for further exploration.

## ESSENTIAL PARAMETERS

A fundamental problem of the computer-oriented musical theorist is that of reducing a musical composition to the simplest possible terms that still will represent reliably the essential features of the composition being studied. Clearly, the reason for abstracting is to eliminate unimportant factors sufficiently for a detailed analysis of the remaining simplified situation to become possible. Such an idealized simplified version of an originally complicated situation often is called a "mathematical model." If such a model is made accurate enough, the results of calculations based upon it will agree with observations.

It is generally accepted [1] that a tone can be completely specified by its frequency, intensity, growth, steady state, decay, portamento, timbre, vibrato, and deviation. Any ultimate conception of musical tonality also has to take into account the complexities of aural harmonics and other psychoacoustic phenomena. But there are so many fundamental parameters and subprocesses potentially involved in musical audition--few of them well described or as yet clearly understood--that a psychoacoustic theory of musical tonality is not now attainable. [2] Nevertheless, on a gross level, a good theory of music needs only to encompass those tonal phenomena that can be distinguished consistently by various musical listeners. In this way it is possible to identify the most important parameters that control the general audition process.

It is a fundamental postulate of this work that features of music other than pitch, duration, and simultaneity are not essential in the basic audition process and thus, as second-order effects, can be eliminated safely from immediate consideration. Such a postulate is in keeping with the notion of mathematical modeling. So, after the appropriate simplifying assumptions have been made, a mathematical basis for music analysis by computers should permit a straightforward treatment of the essential features of musical compositions while stripping away inconsequential details. It should, for example, identify three separate critical instants in the musical process: (a) initiation of voices, (b) changes in pitch, and (c) termination of voices. It should, on the other hand, regard as less significant such transitional interstices as **singing** to **humming**, **staccato** to **legato**, **acute** to **grave**, **fortissimo** to **pianissimo**, and **arco** to **pizzicato**. The model underlying the computer methodology must be in reasonable accord with the traditional "laws" of music. An acceptable basis for music analysis by computers might be expected in addition to answer such questions as where, when, how, and why. In this context, where implies a coordinate system, when is tied to the fact that music is a metric, rythmical, and periodic phenomenon, and how links cause with effect. But in the last analysis, although the role of mathematics in musical research is to help describe where, when, and how, it is not able to explain why a certain musical result occurs.

Basic requirements for the mathematical model include:

1. Tonality and modulation must be measurable in numerical quantities that can be determined unambiguously;

2. Relative orientations of the various key families must be precisely specified;

3. Key must be a slowly changing function as the key signature is modified discontinuously by the insertion, or by the deletion of individual sharps or flats; and

4. Schemes for constructing a basis for the computer methodology that would introduce new or obtuse notions should be rejected in favor of one that employs a continuation of familiar physical concepts such as, for example, **distance**, **velocity**, and **acceleration** as applied to motion.

Other important criteria for a solid mathematical basis for automated music analysis are:

5. The tonality of a given passage must not depend on previous passages, although the sense of key--the effect of key on the mind of the listener--may;

6. Simple logical tests should be available to distinguish among musical intervals, chords, harmonies, sonorities, chromaticity/diatonicity, tonalities, keys, and modulations;

7. Meaningful numerical designations should be used wherever required to facilitate arithmetic;

8. Tonal assemblages should have easily recognizable coding patterns to simplify categorization; and

9. The architecture of the evolving computer methodology should have maximum compatibility with the concepts, formalism, and superstructure of classical theory.

## EXERCISES

**3.1** Prepare a general computer program to calculate the vibration-numbers of tones dividing an octave into N equitempered scale degrees. Provide a basis for both international and philosophical pitch. (Hint. Raise

$$2^{\frac{1}{N}} = e^{\frac{1}{N}\ln 2}$$

to higher integer powers for each subsequent degree.)

**3.2** How are the terms **pitch**, **duration**, **loudness**, **timbre**, and **texture** defined? In what ways do these characteristics of sound influence musical forms.

**3.3** Convert the standard two-tone commercial telephone signals given in Fig. 3.1 to the nearest applicable letter names. What combination tones are associated with these touch-tone pairs?

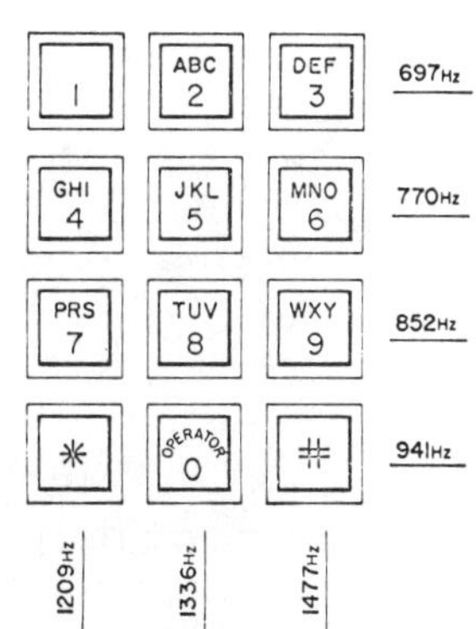


**Figure 3.1**

Matrix of telephone push buttons and associated frequencies.

## DECOMPOSITIONAL HYPOTHESIS

Musical tonality arose in the Renaissance and assumed a fixed and definite form during the lifetime of Rameau (1683-1764). Its effects have been known and studied for at least as long as the science of harmony. Moreover, historically the concept of tonality, as either a psychological or esthetic principle, has played a role in the literature almost as important as that of the concept of **triad.** The subject of tonality is concerned with all questions directly or indirectly bearing on key--the inner relationships that exist among chords within the key system and arise in part in the tonal interactions of the notes of the diatonic scales.

The term **tonality** is admittedly a vague one. In musical research the word has been used many times by many authors, starting with Fétis, but nearly always in a general sense without precise definition. Unfortunately, a nonquantitative assessment usually is not very meaningful. The use of quantitative methods, on the other hand, reduces bias, enhances consistency, and renders the analysis more explicit too. The term **tonality** to the author's knowledge has never been defined before with sufficient precision to allow for its direct measurement, although the study of tonality dates back more than a full century. This void perhaps is due to a lack of motivation as well as to a lack of a clear picture of what is meant by a "key." Although considerable evidence is presented in later chapters to indicate that a key is best thought of as an infinite sector of the complex plane and that a vectorial definition of tonality as a time derivative is justified, the meaning of the word tonality in this work may not at first seem to agree with the common notion nor to denote the thing that musicians are accustomed to recognize as tonality when confronted by a musical passage.

The word **tonality** can mean many things, of course. Both individual differences in musical perception and personal preferences or prejudices undoubtedly become important here. Tonality may mean at various levels a certain kind of key family, or the effect this family of sounds has on the human ear, or most important of all, the result of this effect in the mind of the listener. Yet, to those who read this book, tonality may come to mean a point in a space that localizes a latticework of harmonies,. embedded in an infinitely sheeted Riemann surface! Actually, this new viewpoint is for the most part consistent with the customary one, which regards tonality as the expression of the harmonic equivalence of all major scales, or of all minor scales, and regards major and minor keys as chord families based upon these scales--families whose members share a common relationship with a key center.

The fundamental hypothesis underlying this work is that the process by which a listener is able to interpret the tonality of each of the many musical phrases that he or she hears is a decompositional process. This means that the tonality of any syntactically compound constituent of a musical phrase is obtained as a function of the tonalities of the parts of that constituent, which is an application of the same principle of superposition that in another form applies to overlapping sound pressure waves or to the general linearity of solutions of the wave equation. Every piece of music is describable by a superposition of time-varying functions. In the present theory, it is postulated that a chord may be separated into individual tonalities that arise severally from its tonal constituents. In keeping with this hypothesis the tonality of chords, harmonies, or other constructs is taken to be a linear combination of their component subchords, subharmonies, or subconstructs. This hypothesis admittedly is probably too atomistic to be true in any large sense. Its attraction is that it defines tonality in a restricted, measurable way using lengths and angles and that the resulting theory is successful in describing and predicting certain musical phenomena.

## EXERCISES

**3.4** Write an expository essay on the topic **tonality.** Typed double space it should run from 5 to, at most, 10 pages.

**3.5** Use a compass to scribe a circle of convenient radius. Divide the circumference of this circle into twelve equal parts. Draw radii of the circle at these points. Use compass and straightedge only. Attach arrowheads at the outer ends of the twelve radii and label them with the designations $T_0$, $T_1$, ..., $T_{11}$ of the primitive tones. In how many ways can the labeling be done consistently?

## REFERENCES

[1] Harry F. Olson, "Electronic Music Synthesis for Recordings," *IEEE Spectrum* (Apr. 1971) pp. 18-30.

[2] Reinier Plomp, *Aspects of Tone Sensation: A Psychophysical Study,* (Academic Press, New York, 1976).

PART II

# Chapter 4

# Theory

*... traditional harmony systematizes only a very small proportion of all the possibilities of the twelve-tones and leaves all the rest in a state of chaos.*

*HOWARD HANSON, Harmonic Materials of Modern Music,* 1960

## VECTORS

**To serve** as a theoretical starting point, there is no reason why the twelve tones of the equitempered system should not be symmetrically placed about a center so that enharmonic equivalents coincide. This produces a well-known construction in one form called the "cycle of tempered fifths" (see Fig. 4.1a). Certainly it provides an obvious and necessary adjunct to the introduction of the familiar idea of key signatures, which in turn can be arranged in another circle, as shown in Fig. 4.1b, so that sound-alike keys, such as B♯ Major, C Major, and D♭♭ Major congregate. The advantage of this arrangement is that there arises an orderly succession of flat or sharp clusters in traversing the circle either clockwise or counterclockwise. Inspection of Fig. 4.1b suggests that in counterclockwise rotation, an additonal sharp appears for every thirty degrees of arc; in clockwise rotation an additional flat appears for every thirty degrees of arc. Thus, by unspoken convention, a sharp acts as a negative flat and a flat acts as a negative sharp.

In this book a related construction combines the advantages of both the principle of key signatures and the cycle of tempered fifths. First, a circle of unit radius is associated with the pitch wheel. Second, the idea that tones B and F, for example, are antipodal is brought to a sharper focus by representing them by arrows rather than by points. Thus, the center of the unit circle becomes a common point or "origin" from which the tone arrows are drawn. No two of the arrows shown in the resulting diagram (see Fig. 4.2) are equal. Granted that the length or "magnitude" of the arrows remains fixed, but the *direction* of the arrows changes with each successive fifth. It turns out that, because of this directivity, a general formulation of the principle of key signatures can be based upon the plane geometry of Fig. 4.2. This formulation leads naturally to a theory of the classical concept of tonality, and actually goes a considerable distance beyond.

**Figure 4.1a**

Cycle of tempered fifths or pitch wheel.

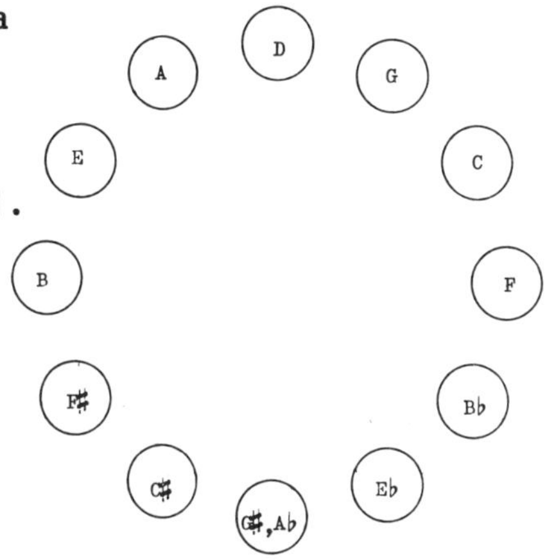

D
G
C
F
B♭
E♭
G♯,A♭
C♯
F♯
B
E
A

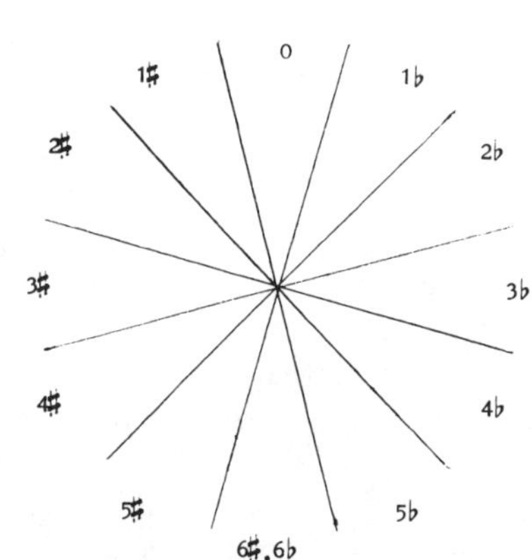


**Figure 4.1b**

Circular arrangement of key signatures.

**Figure 4.2**

Circularly disposed tone vectors based on the pitch wheel, inscribed in the unit circle of the x,y plane to form a "pitch compass."

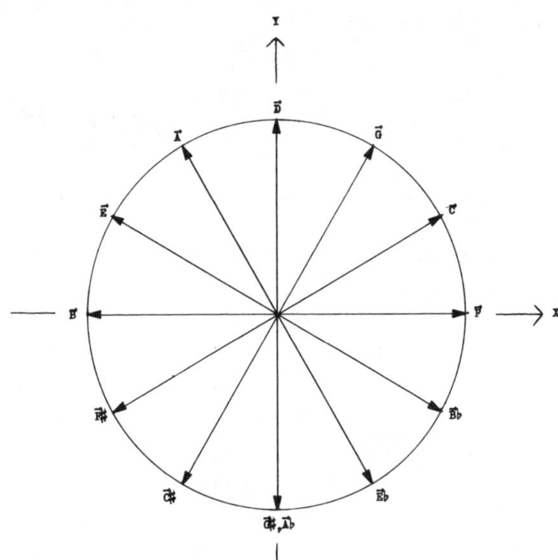


A mathematical name for directed line segments or arrows such as shown in these figures is "vector." The rules for handling vectors, such as:

TAIL HEAD

initial point terminal point

is the subject of a mathematical topic called "vector algebra." Before grappling with this topic, which treats quantities that have direction as well as magnitude, some introductory remarks and definitions are needed.

A "unit vector" in a particular direction is defined to be a vector of unit length, or of magnitude one, pointing in that direction. Usually the direction is calculated in degrees from a fixed reference direction along a line called the "polar axis." This axis corresponds to the horizontal line labeled "X" in Fig. 4.2. In this book the twelve primitive tones $T_0$, $T_1, \ldots, T_{11}$ are represented by unit vectors termed "tone vectors." In general, tone vectors are denoted by the corresponding literal printed either in boldface, such as **C**, **C♯**, **D♭**, **D**, ..., or (if handwritten) with a small arrow above it, such as $\vec{C}$, $\vec{C\sharp}$, $\vec{D\flat}$, $\vec{D}$, ..., with the understanding that each literal so designated represents both the magnitude and the direction of the musical quantity.

The diagram of Fig. 4.2 shows clearly that the direction of tone **B** is simply a reversal of the direction of tone **F**, something of the nature of a backfire. Also this diagram shows that the tone **D** can be considered to act directly upward, while **F♯** can be considered to act downward and to the left at an angle of thirty degrees (or 210 degrees) with the horizontal. The tone vectors **B** and **D** are of unit magnitude and are at right angles to each other. Under the assumption that oppositely directed tones balance each other and tend to produce a neutral condition that might be called "keylessness," it is easy to predict that such combinations as **B**, **D**, **F**, **G♯** will be keyless, since the tone vectors cancel in pairs.

The notion of a vector has been a valuable tool in understanding the physical relationships among forces, masses, and accelerations in the field of physics called classical mechanics. In fact, the subject of vector analysis greatly appeals to many professional engineers and students of the physical sciences because it provides a clearer mental conception of such quite fundamental ideas as motion, momentum, and velocity. In the remainder of the present section some of the more basic features of vector algebra, such as are immediately applicable to the present study, are illustrated. Examples throughout the rest of this book will apply these ideas in music theory. By placing reliance upon these examples, students who have some background in Harmony should be able to follow the theoretical discussions without any real difficulty. Perhaps the best place for those unfamiliar with vectors to begin their studies is with the little textbook **Understanding Vectors and Phase** by John F. Rider and Seymour D. Uslan.

The rules that apply to vectors are drawn from vector algebra:

I. Two vectors are said to be "equal" if and only if they have the same length and direction.

II. Two vectors may be added to produce a third vector called their "sum" or "resultant." The sum of vectors U and V is written U + V.

III. A vector may be multiplied by an ordinary number (called a "scalar") to form a longer or shorter vector with the same or opposite direction. Symbolically, the product of a scalar alpha $\alpha$ and a vector V is a vector $\alpha$V whose magnitude is $|\alpha|$, the "absolute value" of alpha, times as great as the magnitude of V and which is directed similarly or oppositely to V depending upon whether $\alpha$ is positive or negative.

IV. Any vector can be shifted to a new position without changing its length or direction.

These four rules, which also form the basis both for vector geometry and for the composition of physical forces, are clarified by drawing appropriate diagrams.

The sum S of two vectors U and V is defined according to the following scheme: Displace the vector V such that the tail of V is at the head of U, with the head of V pointing in the same direction as before. (The original V and the displaced V will be parallel to each other.) Then connect the tail of U to the head of the displaced vector V by an arrow. This new vector is the vector sum S = U + V. When a vector V is added to itself, a vector is obtained whose length or magnitude is twice as large and whose direction is unchanged. The difference U - V of two vectors is defined as the sum U + (-V) of the vector U and the "negative" -V of the vector V, which is a vector of equal magnitude and opposite direction to V. The "zero vector" is defined as a segment of zero length and indefinite direction. When a vector U is subtracted from itself, the zero vector is obtained and the resulting direction is an indeterminate quantity.

Two examples, shown in Fig. 4.3, display the mechanics of vector addition. The four-sided geometric figure appearing there whose opposite sides are equal and parallel gives its name to this kind of addition. Since the diagonal of the parallelogram represents either the sum U + V or the sum V + U, these vectors are the same. Consequently, the addition of vectors is a commutative operation (unchanged when the two summands are reversed) when performed according to the **parallelogram law**. Two or more vectors are added by the so-called "polygon method" shown in Fig. 4.3b. The Greek

**Figure 4.3** Vector addition.

(a) The parallelogram law.

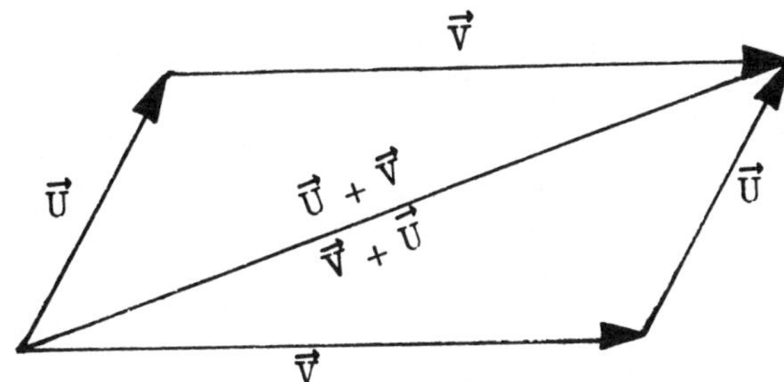


(b) The polygon method.

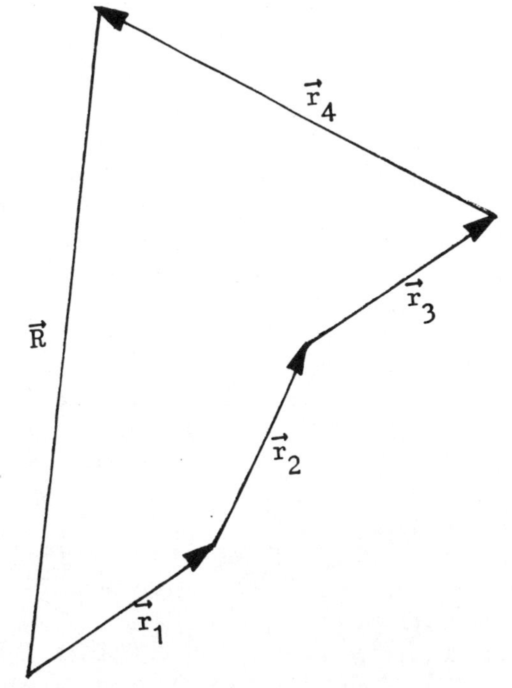

capital letter sigma is used to indicate such a sum; for example,

$$\sum_{k=1}^{n} r_k = r_1 + r_2 + \dots + r_n.$$

The sum $\mathbf{R} = \sum_{k=1}^{n} r_k$

of n separate vectors, taking account of their directions, is called the "resultant vector." The resultant joins the tail end of the first vector in the summation to the head end of the last vector in the summation. No matter what order is followed in lining up the arrows tail-to-head, the resultant will have the same magnitude and direction. This can be ascertained readily by experimentation. To solve a problem in vector addition graphically, it is necessary to draw the diagram carefully to scale using a ruler and protractor.

For clarity in dealing with musical vectors, however, it must be understood that the commutative law $\mathbf{U} + \mathbf{V} = \mathbf{V} + \mathbf{U}$ holds only if **U** and **V** are vertical structures that sound simultaneously. Otherwise, **U** + **V** will indicate that vertical structure **U** precedes vertical structure **V** in strict time sequence, and **V** + **U** will indicate that this happens the other way around. Of course, many of the quantities arising in music are not vectors, but rather are scalars. A scalar quantity is characterized by the fact that it has magnitude only. Scalar quantities, such as note durations or tone intensities, do not ordinarily have a direction. Consequently, scalars are added by the elementary rules of everyday arithmetic. For example, 2 beats + 5 beats = 7 beats. A vector quantity, on the other hand, is characterized by the fact that it has both magnitude and direction. A musical example is given by a quarter note D. The magnitude of this note is 1 beat. Moreover, since the scale of C major is laid out symmetrically in a half circle of the cycle of tempered fifths, as F,C,G,D,A,E,B, it is clear that the direction of the vector **D** that corresponds to the note D points precisely along the line of bisection of the key of C major. The central position of tone D in the key of C causes it to be the most deeply seated member of that key. Whereas the addition of only two sharps to the key signature is sufficient to alienate the tone C, the addition of four sharps, or four flats, is required in order to expel the tone D. More will be said about this subject later.

Given a plane, the "origin" is defined as an arbitrarily chosen point in that plane which is used as a fixed reference or benchmark. "Position vectors" are defined as vectors drawn from this origin point to various points (positions) in the plane. The "displacement," in distance and direction, of some point in the plane measured from the origin is a position vector that shall be denoted by the symbol **r**. When such a vector is shown graphically, it is represented by an arrow, whose initial point is at the origin and whose terminal point or tip is at the point in question. Graphical methods have many advantages: first, laborious calculations usually are not required, and second, those music analysts who are not very mathematically inclined often will find graphical methods easy to learn and intuitively appealing.

## EXERCISES

**4.1** The phase difference between any two individual tone vectors is the difference between their respective phase angles. Calculate the phase difference for successive degrees of the diatonic scales using Fig. 4.4 as a guide.

**4.2** Extend the pentatonic scale CDEFGA to form three different major scales. In what way do these extensions correspond to the sums 5 + 2, 1 + 5 + 1, and 2 + 5?

4.3 Determine the durations of the notes shown in Fig. 4.5 directly from the lengths of the vectors. What can be said for the duration of the segment labeled G + F?

4.4 Complete the following two diagrams.

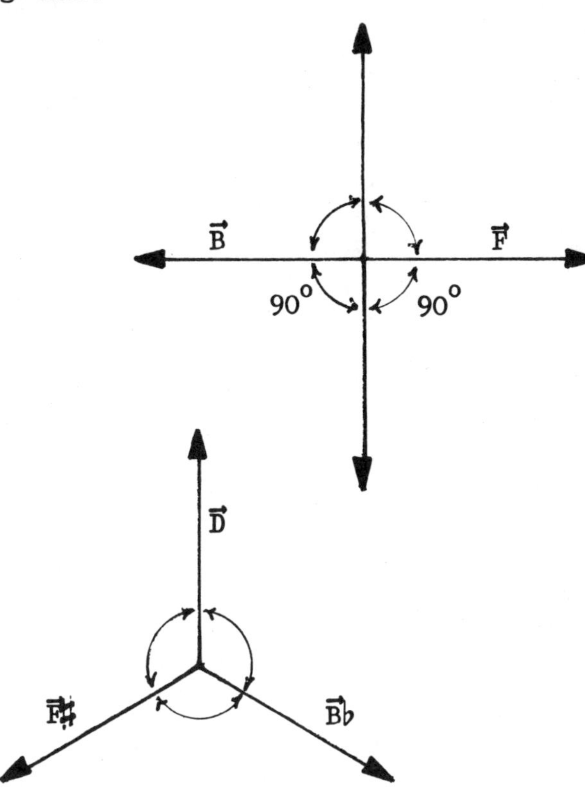


**Figure 4.4**

Relative phases of the twelve primitive tone vectors. Transposition thus amounts to a uniform phase shift.

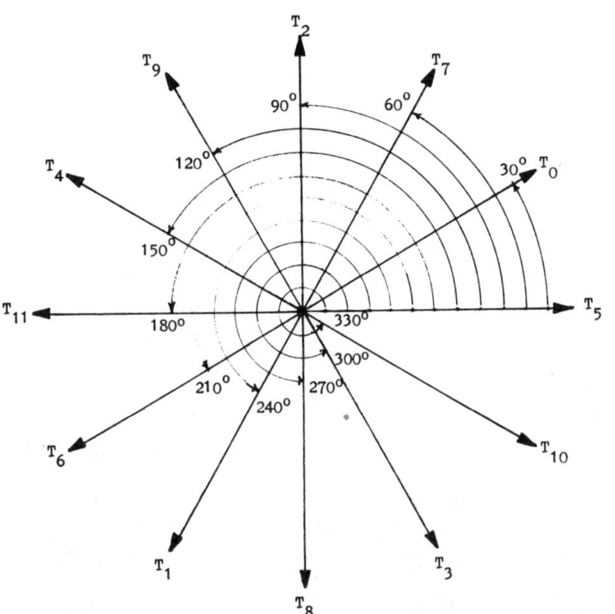


**Figure 4.5**

Typical tone vectors and magnitude (or duration) scale.

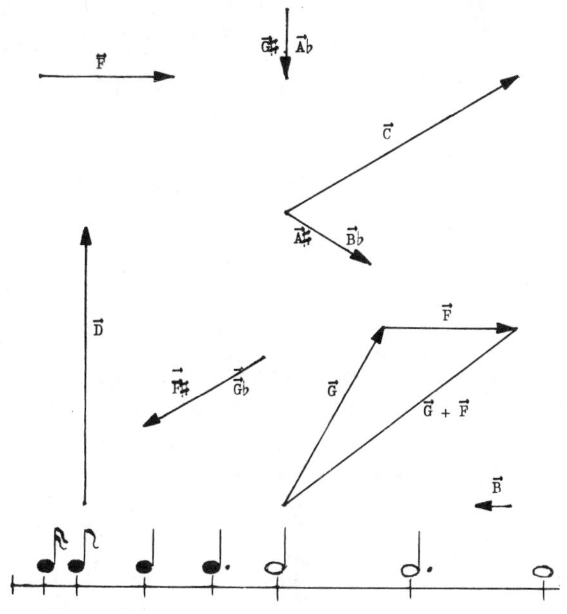


## BALANCE

In the previous section several tone arrows were added graphically in order to obtain their vector sum or "resultant." Using vector addition, the pitch compass can be applied to attach a value registering the condition of balance of any tone combination within the twelve-tone system. The term "balance" requires explicit definition. The balance referred to is a condition in which either all voices are silent, or the resultant of all voices is the zero vector. The value **zero** indicates perfect balance. Consider as an example the musical interval relationship known as the "tritone" or augmented fourth. If the tritone CF♯ is examined for balance, it will be discovered that the sum of its tone vectors C and F♯ is zero. The tone F♯ is represented by a vector whose direction is diametrically opposite to that of the vector representing the tone C. This may be expressed as F♯ = -C, where F♯ denotes the F♯ vector and C denotes the C vector. Hence, the tritone CF♯ is balanced. The tones C and F♯ neutralize each other, producing a listless, somewhat jarring, condition of keylessness. In like manner, the tones corresponding to <u>all</u> the tritones in the chromatic scale cancel in pairs. It may be concluded that the chromatic scale harmony is balanced.

As a third example, the major triad CEG will be examined for balance. The method is illustrated in Fig. 4.6. In the picture the three tone arrows C, E, and G shown at the left are added together in the vector diagram at the right. Clearly the major triad is not balanced. It is an example of an "unbalanced harmony." The diagrams of C maj 7, C min 7, and C7 shown in Fig. 4.7 are entirely typical of unbalanced systems. As a third example, consider the so-called Gypsy scale

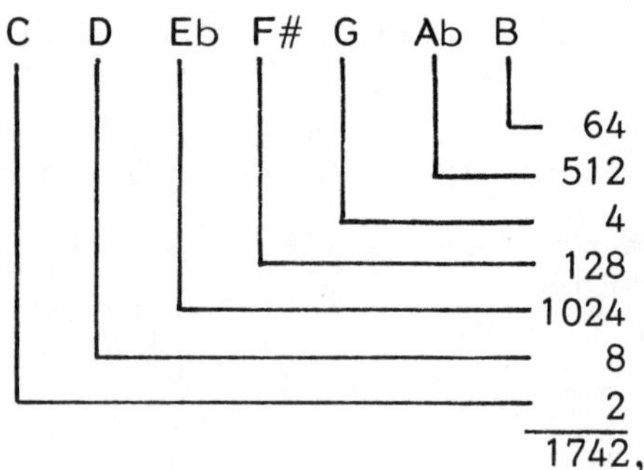


where the factored designation number 1742 = 871*2 shows characteristic 871 and level 2. This scale is a balanced harmony, since

$$C + D + E\flat + F\sharp + G + A\flat + B =$$

$$(C+F\sharp)+(D+A\flat)+(E\flat+G+B) = 0.$$

So, it has an indeterminate phase.

**Figure 4.6**

Testing a typical chord for tonal balance.

(a) The C major triad.

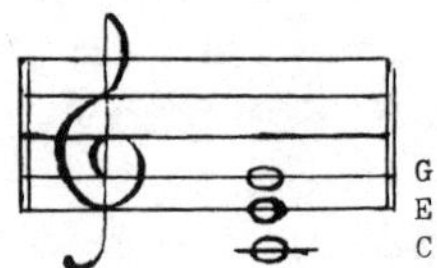


(b) The C major triad fan diagram.

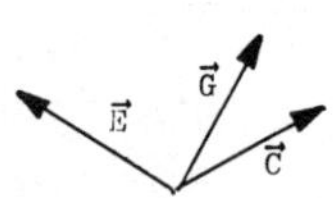


(c) The C major triad vector resultant.

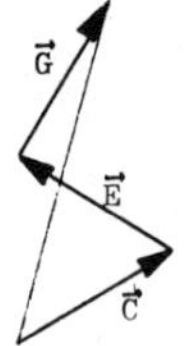


**Figure 4.7**

Unbalanced seventh chords in rectangular coordinates.

(a) C maj 7

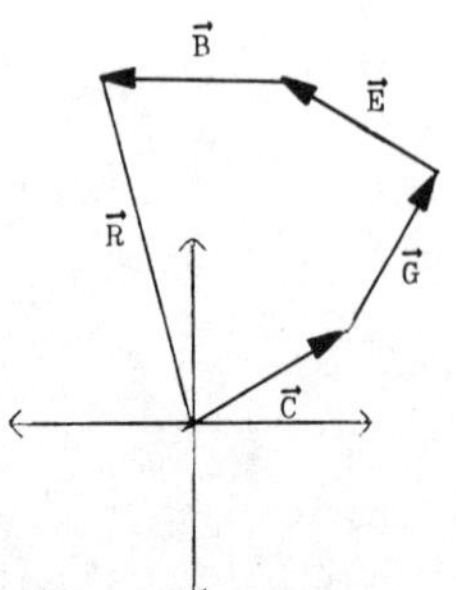


(b) C7

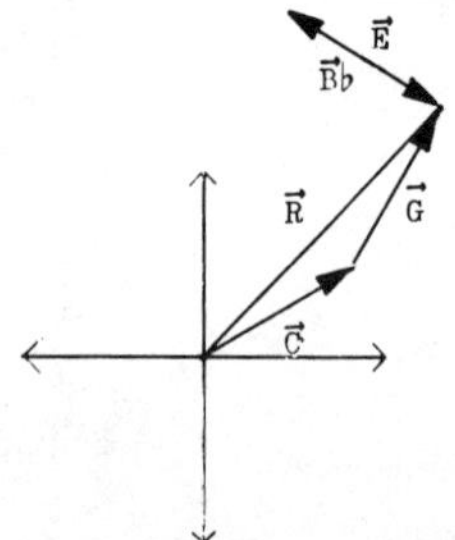


(c) C min 7

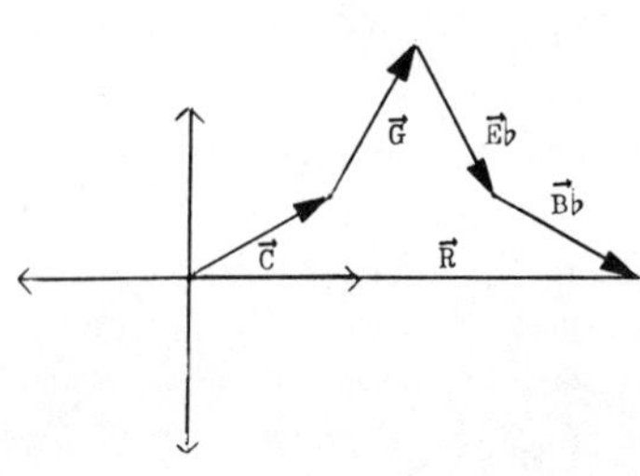

Figure 4.8

Fan diagrams of balanced sonorities.

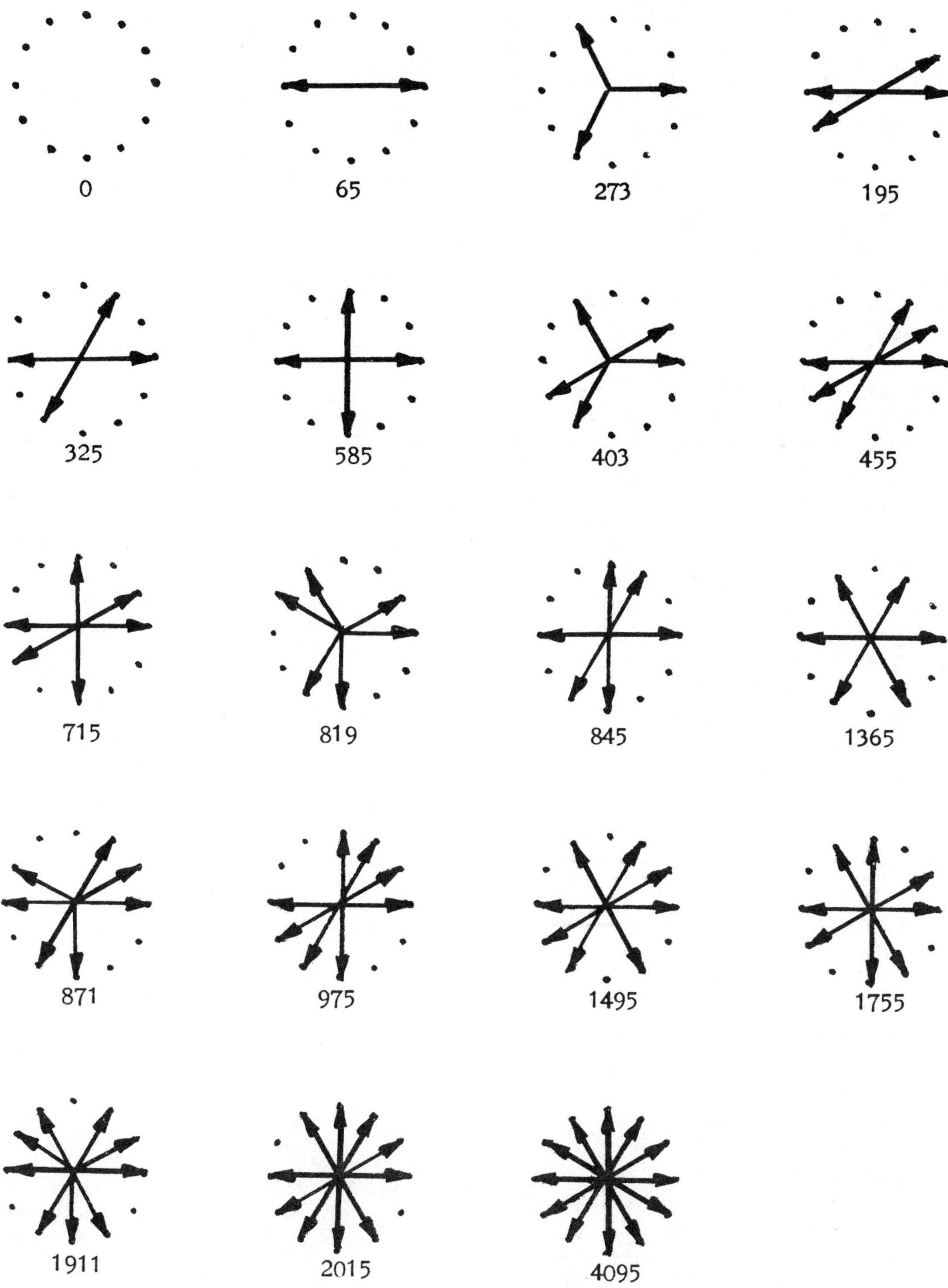

From the standpoint of tonal resultants, all tone combinations with the same total displacement have the same tonality (perhaps only in a certain context) and are synonymous with each other (perhaps only partly so). As a consequence, knowledge of the tonality does not uniquely characterize a chord or harmony. This fact is not unexpected. The reverse, however, is true. Knowledge of the chord does allow the tonality to be completely specified. It is easily verified that the components of the tritone dyad, the augmented triad, the diminished seventh tetrad, and so forth have a zero vector sum. Such zero-sum harmonies, and by extension, their sonorities, are said to be "balanced." Sonorities having perfect balance are listed in ascending order of characteristic number in Fig. 4.8. Clearly, any balanced subharmony may be discarded from a given harmony without affecting its tonal resultant. The balanced subharmony disappears from the vector sum. Thus, C + C♯ + F + A = C. Again, C+E+F♯+G♯+B = E+G♯+B = F♯+B. In a balanced harmony, all terms disappear from the vector sum leaving the zero vector, which corresponds to the null harmony.

The practical significance of the notion of balance is seen by considering a typical example. It is a matter of common musical experience that the diminished seventh harmony does not in isolation from context commit itself to a definite minor key. The ambivalent nature of this harmony has led to its employment in some extended operatic passages to heighten tension by dramatically suspending the listener, in mid-air, so to speak. A certain amount of context is revealed if the literal notation of the diminished seventh tetrad is specified. For example, given the harmony BDFG♯ and the harmony BDFA♭, it is rather easy to pick out which one is <u>not</u> in the key of A harmonic minor.

EXERCISES

4.5 Indicate by asterisks the subharmony that can be dropped from CD♯EF♯GA♯B according to the rule set forth above.

4.6 The regular polygon diagrams that follow confirm graphically the balance of the augmented triad and diminished-seventh sonorities, respectively. Using this same technique, verify that the remainder of the zero-sum sonorities listed are balanced.

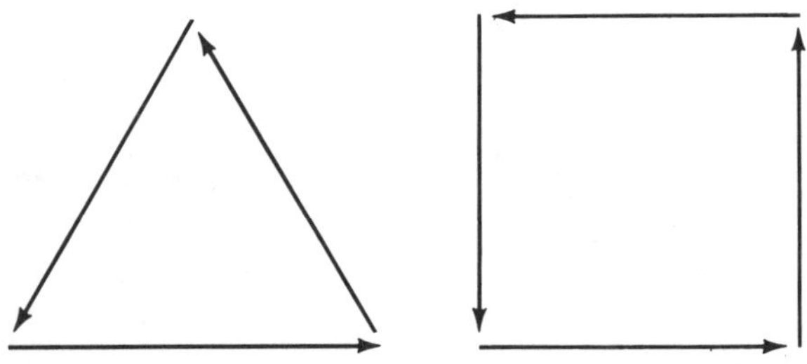

4.7 With the aid of balanced sonorities, it is possible to find all the harmonies whose total displacement coincides with that of a given harmony. Do so for the C major-seventh tetrad and for the D minor-seventh tetrad. What conclusions can be drawn from the results?

4.8 On the basis of the principle of tonal equilibrium, the two tones C and E at any instant are counterbalanced by the force of the tone G♯ or A♭. Use this fact to show algebraically that C + E = D.

4.9 (a) After being shifted to form the vector sum or resultant, the tone vectors pertaining to a given chord may be shifted back to their original position, so that their tails again are attached to the point of origin. When returned to this position, the vectors form a configuration resembling the ribs of a fan. Draw fan diagrams for a few familiar chords and show their resultants. (See Fig. 4.6) (b) Write a digital computer program to plot the fan diagrams and resultants of the 352 characteristic harmonies.

4.10 List all balanced subharmonies of the various heptadiatonic scale harmonies.

## NEGATION

The *Webster's Dictionary* defines the word "charm" as being an obsolete intransitive verb that once meant "to sound harmonically." This word seems well suited for revival as a noun for expressing concisely the idea of something falling conceptually between a chord and a harmony. Let T denote the set

$$\{T_0, T_1, \ldots, T_{11}\}$$

containing all of the twelve primitive tones $T_0, T_1, \ldots, T_{11}$.

Accordingly, a subset $H \subset T$ is called a "harmony"; an indexed subset $X \subset T \times J$, where $J = \{1,2,\ldots\}$, is called a "charm"; and a doubly indexed subset, $ç \subset T \times J \times J$, is a "chord." Hence, a charm is simply an expanded harmony in which some tones may be repeated; a chord is simply a charm in which an octave assignment is given to each element. Consequently, each harmony manifests itself in a multiplicity of charms, and each charm manifests itself in a multiplicity of chords.

Up to this point, voice doublings have been neglected completely since attention has centered upon harmonies and scales. To treat charms and chords, in which the same literal may appear more than once, tone arrows or vectors must be drawn for each replicate. This means that the doubling of tones is represented by two arrows of the same length drawn in the same direction. The tripling of tones is represented by three equal arrows, and so on. It follows that the resultant R of a charm X is a linear combination

$$R = a_0T_0 + a_1T_1 + \ldots + a_{11}T_{11}$$

of the twelve unit tone vectors $T_i$, where $i = 0,1,\ldots,11$. The coefficients $a_i$ appearing in the sum are always integers, usually positive or zero.

Recall that the tone vectors **C** and **F♯** are equal and opposite in sign. Each vector is the other's negative. As a result, the tritone charm X = CF♯, which is represented by the linear combination 1C + 1F♯, has the resultant

$$R_{CF\sharp} = 1C + 1F\sharp = 1C + 1(-C)$$
$$= 1C - 1C = (1 - 1)C = 0C = 0.$$

By definition, a charm that has a zero resultant is said to be "balanced." All tritones are balanced. A zero value arises also for other symmetrical charms such as the augmented triad (three-voiced) and the often used diminished-seventh tetrad (four-voiced). Here, as elsewhere, summation extends over all tones in the charm. So, if any tone were to be duplicated in these symmetrical charms, then the resulting charm would not be balanced. The tones of the wholetone scale, having the same magnitude and possessing six-fold rotational symmetry add to zero vectorially too. This process can be visualized as one in which the tritones cancel in pairs. (See Fig. 4.8, characteristic harmony 1365.)

Every vector has a negative. This means that for any tone arrow **T**, there is another tone arrow **X** such that **T + X = 0**, the zero vector. This magic arrow **X** is called the "negative" of **T** and is symbolized by the expression **-T**. As a consequence, there always must exist tones that can wipe out whatever effect on the tonality the tones of any charm might have when added vectorially to them. For example, consider the charm X with no replicated tones and therefore corresponding exactly to some harmony H. By combining with X the charm $\overline{X}$, corresponding to the complement harmony $\overline{H} = T - H$ whose designation is 4095 - H, the chromatic scale charm is obtained, which is balanced. Usually, however, there are other solutions. This is true because given a particular solution S, another solution can be obtained by adding a balanced structure to S. Therefore, the general solution can be written S + b, where b is a balanced set of tone vectors. Again take the charm X corresponding to the harmony H. By superimposing the charm $R^6(X)$ obtained by transposing H up an augmented fourth, another balanced charm is obtained.

EXAMPLE

Start with the C pentatonic scale harmony

$$H = (C, D, E, G, A).$$

First, form its complement

$$\overline{H} = (C\sharp, D\sharp, F, F\sharp, G\sharp, A\sharp, B).$$

Combine H and $\overline{H}$ to arrive at the chromatic scale harmony. Second, rotate H by $180^{o}$ to obtain

$$R^{6}(H) = (C\sharp, D\sharp, F\sharp, G\sharp, A\sharp).$$

Superimpose H and $R^{6}(H)$ to find the balanced charm

$$(C, C\sharp, D, D\sharp, E, F\sharp, G, G\sharp, A, A\sharp).$$

Finally, observe that $\overline{H}$ and $R^{6}(H)$ differ by a balanced tritone (F,B).

Remember that each harmony is represented by a nonnegative integer less than 4096 called its <u>designation</u>. Moreover, this number in turn is related to an equal or smaller nonnegative integer called the <u>characteristic</u>. These two quantities are connected by the formula:

DESIGNATION=CHARACTERISTIC*LEVEL

or $H = S * L$,

where the asterisk denotes multiplication modulo 4095. The value of the sonoral characteristic S is defined in terms of the designation number H as the minimum of the set of values H, 2H, 4H, 8H, 16H, 32H, 64H, 128H, 256H, 512H, 1024H, and 2048H when reduced with respect to the modulus 4095, which means that the quantity 4095 is subtracted from the indicated product as many times

Figure 4.9

Weighted keyboard chart.

(EXTENDED FORM)

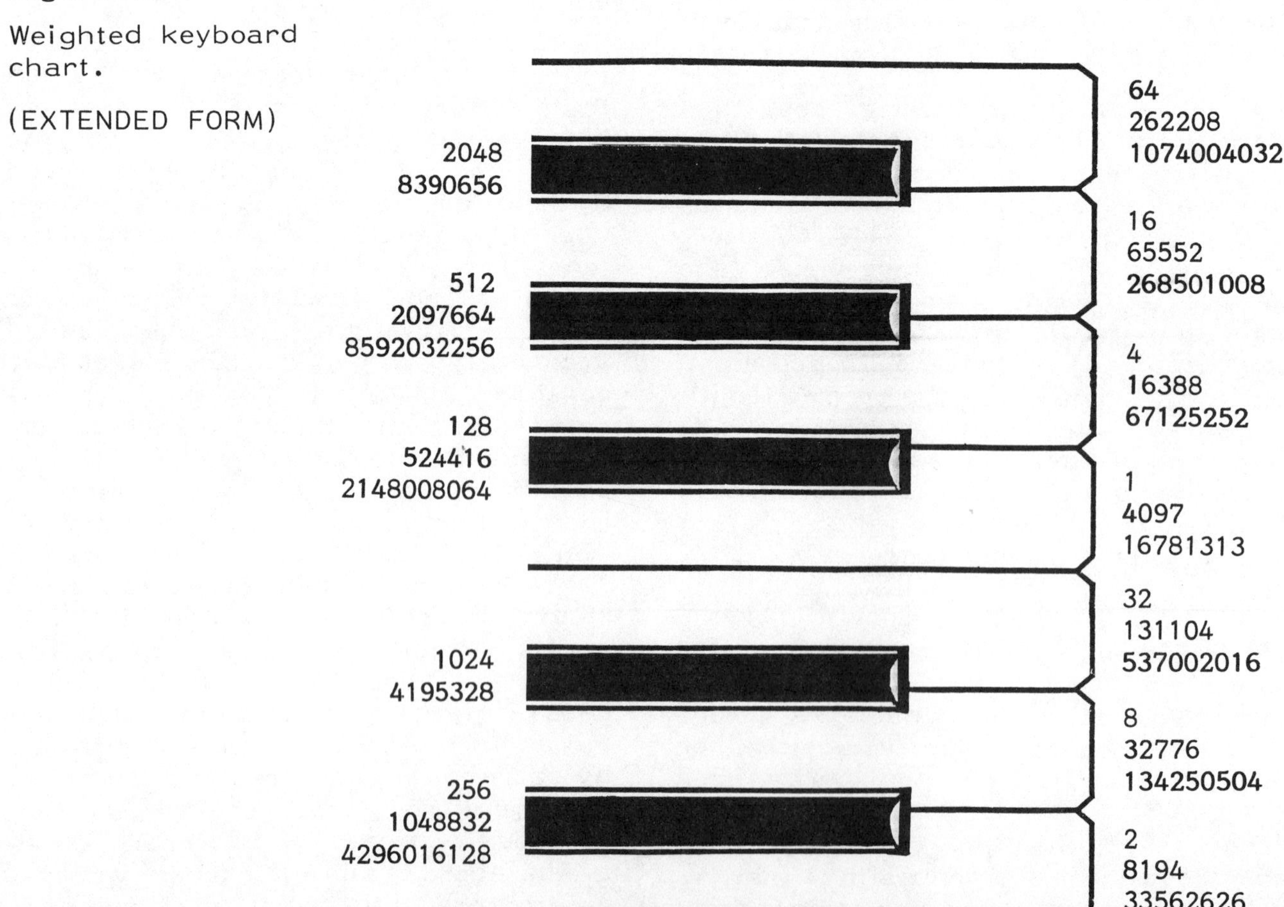

as possible without causing any change of sign and only the positive integer remainder is taken into further consideration. This numerical language makes it easier to talk about harmonies and sonorities with great precision.

Since the notion of a charm includes that of a harmony as a special case in which there is no replication of notes, it is worthwhile to try to extend the designative form of nomenclature, which thus far applies just to harmonies, to cover charms. This can be done in many ways. The way it is done in this book leads to each charm being represented by its own decimal integer, which will be called the "specification." Again this number is nonnegative, but this time there is no size limitation. Consider for example some chord CCEGCG, which is one embodiment of the charm EGGCCC. Here the note C appears three times, the note G twice, and the note E once. The specification is calculated by referring to Fig. 4.9. Simply take the third line adjacent to C, which contains the number 33562626, and add to it the number 16388 from the second line adjacent to G, and add to the result the number 32, which appears on the first line adjacent to E. The total, 33579046, is the specification of the charm EGGCCC. A useful feature of specific form is that if, and only if, the specification number N is less than or equal to 4095, then the charm is for practical purposes actually a harmony and the specification of the charm is identical to the harmonic designation.

Obviously, a certain amount of good information is lost in the process of going from chords to charms. For example, it is no longer possible to identify the inversions of chords or to distinguish between their open and closed positions when they are represented as charms. Still, charms have useful properties. They can provide enough significant detail about a piece of music to enable quite an extensive computer analysis of it, as will be demonstrated throughout this book. Such analysis covers much that is germain to the discovery of the tonal organization of the composition.

EXERCISES

**4.11** (a) Prove that every harmony having a short orbital period is balanced. (b) Is the converse true?

**4.12** (a) Find all balanced heptad harmonies. (b) List all balanced seven-note charms.

**4.13** Explain how numerical, literal, or other types of comparisons are to be carried out in each decision box of the following flow chart.

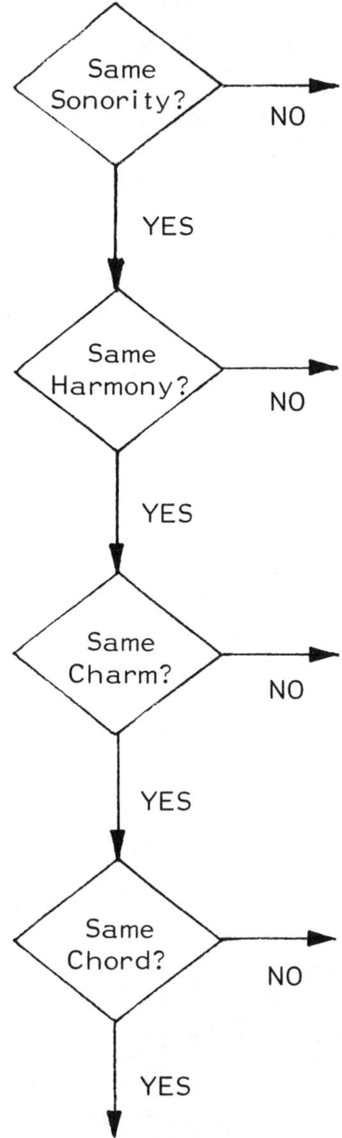

**4.14** (a) How can specification numbers be used to determine the repeat rate of identical chords within units of $\bar{m}$ chords? (b) How can designation numbers be used to establish the percentages of complete and incomplete triads within progressions of $\bar{m}$ harmonies. (c) How can weights and cardinalities be employed to identify different types of simultaneities?

**4.15** Design a program to provide chord lists in inflected alphabetic order defined by the collation sequences

A < B < C < D < E < F < G

and 𝄫 < ♭ < ♮ < ♯ < x,

with counts, and a cross index of temporal locations in the score.

## COORDINATE SYSTEMS

For a detailed analysis of displacement, tonality, and modulation, it is necessary to introduce a coordinate reference frame. The most commonly used system is a rectangular coordinate system as shown in Fig. 4.10. The point at which the x axis and the y axis cross is called the "origin of coordinates" or, simply, the "origin." As shown in Fig. 4.10a, the x,y plane is divided into four quadrants by the coordinate axes. Thus, the vector v pictured in Fig. 4.10b lies in the first quadrant, or quadrant I. As indicated, there is a unique decomposition of the vector v into its components x and y along the X and Y directions. The ratio y/v, where

$$v = |v| = \sqrt{x^2 + y^2}$$

is the length of the vector v, is called the "sine" of the angle θ, abbreviated sin θ; the ratio x/v, also important, is called the "cosine" of the angle θ, abbreviated cos θ (see Fig. 4.11a). For convenience, an abridged table of these two trigonmetric functions follows:

| angle θ | sin θ | cos θ |
|---|---|---|
| $0^\circ$ | 0.00000 | 1.00000 |
| $15^\circ$ | 0.25882 | 0.96593 |
| $30^\circ$ | 0.50000 | 0.86603 |
| $45^\circ$ | 0.70711 | 0.70711 |
| $60^\circ$ | 0.86603 | 0.50000 |
| $75^\circ$ | 0.96593 | 0.25882 |
| $90^\circ$ | 1.00000 | 0.00000 |
| $105^\circ$ | 0.96593 | -0.25882 |
| $120^\circ$ | 0.86603 | -0.50000 |
| $135^\circ$ | 0.70711 | -0.70711 |
| $150^\circ$ | 0.50000 | -0.86603 |
| $165^\circ$ | 0.25882 | -0.96593 |
| $180^\circ$ | 0.00000 | -1.00000 |
| $195^\circ$ | -0.25882 | -0.96593 |
| $210^\circ$ | -0.50000 | -0.86603 |
| $225^\circ$ | -0.70711 | -0.70711 |
| $240^\circ$ | -0.86603 | -0.50000 |
| $255^\circ$ | -0.96593 | -0.25882 |
| $270^\circ$ | -1.00000 | 0.00000 |
| $285^\circ$ | -0.96593 | 0.25882 |
| $300^\circ$ | -0.86603 | 0.50000 |
| $315^\circ$ | -0.70711 | 0.70711 |
| $330^\circ$ | -0.50000 | 0.86603 |
| $345^\circ$ | -0.25882 | 0.96593 |
| $360^\circ$ | 0.00000 | 1.00000 |

**Figure 4.10a**

Rectangular x,y coordinate system showing the four quadrants.

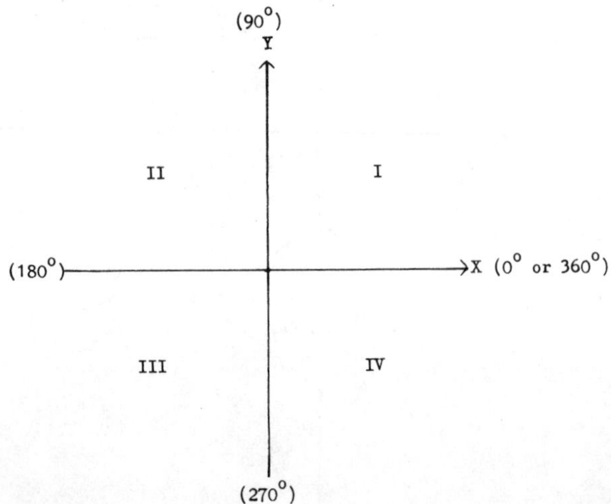


**Figure 4.10b**

Decomposition of a vector v.

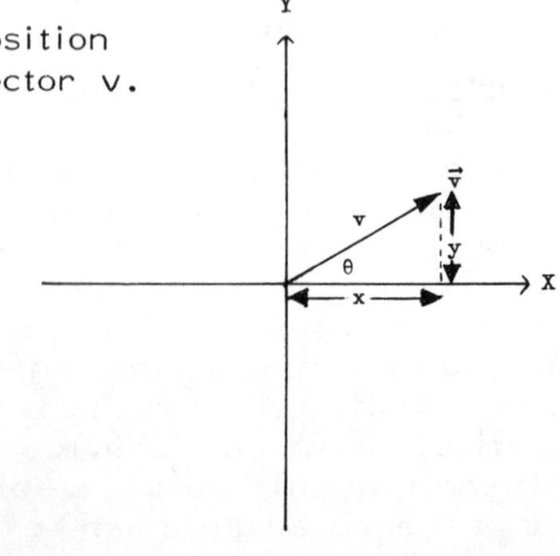

By methods taught in Analytic Geometry, the algebraic equation of the circle shown in Fig. 4.11b can be written as

$$x^2 + y^2 = r^2,$$

where r is the radius of the circle. If r = 1, then this circle is referred to as the **unit circle.** Concentric circles result when r is set equal to various real constants. (See Fig. 4.11c.)

When a point P in the plane is located by its distance r from an origin 0 and by the angle θ that the radius vector pointing from 0 to P makes with the horizontal axis, the system employed is called "polar coordinates." For music analysis--especially in problems involving questions of key center determination--polar coordinates usually are more convenient as a mathematical framework than are cartesian (rectangular) coordinates. The essential elements of the polar coordinate system are (a) the polar axis, and (b) the fixed point 0 on the polar axis that is used as a point of reference for angles. Conventionally the polar axis is drawn to the right. Because of the twelve-sided symmetry of the pitch wheel, the problem of tonal analysis is greatly simplified by introducing polar coordinates, with the origin placed at the center of symmetry. In order to conform with the standard stencil the coordinate system adopted in this book has its polar axis in the direction of the tone arrow F natural.

In the polar coordinate system, a point P is determined by the coordinate pair r, θ where the magnitude r can take any nonnegative value. As shown in Fig. 4.12, the angle θ is customarily considered to be positive when measured in the counterclockwise sense and negative, otherwise. An angle θ may have any numerical value. In the following chapters various data, including note names and duration values, will be read from musical scores and employed to reconstruct the tonal motion and to display the tonal organization of the music on a polar chart. Examples will show that it is both practical and informative to calculate literal notations and to determine keys in terms of polar coordinates. Polar coordinates are also very useful in describing the motion of the composition, but they are not always the most convenient coordinates in terms of which to find vector resultants.

**Figure 4.11a**

Trigonometric relationships.

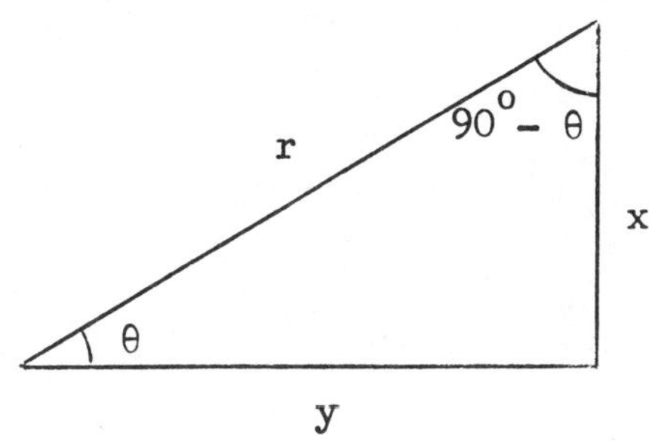


$\sin\theta = \text{sine}\ \theta = x/r,$

$\cos\theta = \text{cosine}\ \theta = y/r,$

$\tan\theta = \text{tangent}\ \theta = x/y.$

**Figure 4.11b**

Circle of radius r.

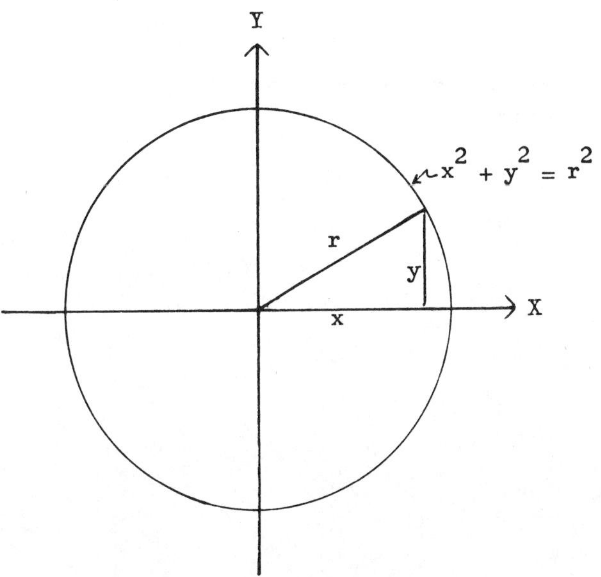

Figure 4.11c

Family of concentric circles.

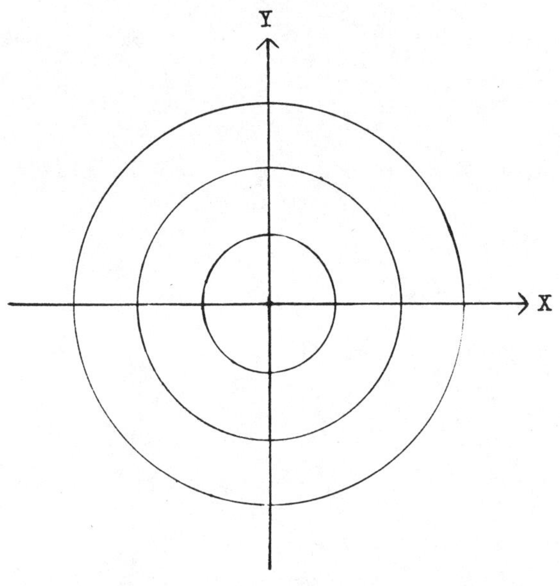


Figure 4.12

Angle convention in polar coordinate system.

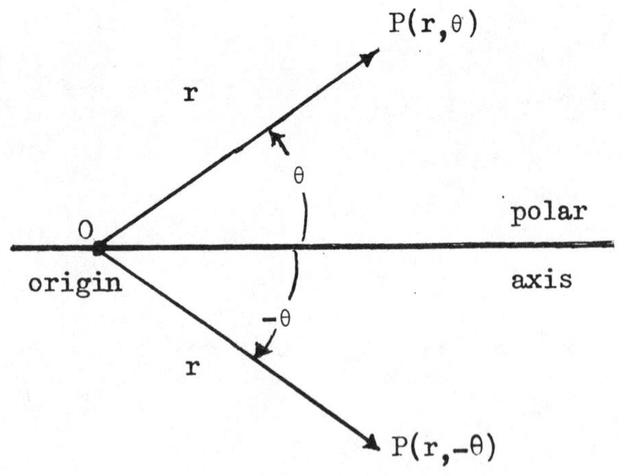


EXERCISES

**4.16** Prepare a table of values for the tangent function based upon the abridged table of values for the sine and cosine functions.

**4.17** For two vectors V and **W**, the squared magnitude of the vector sum **V** + **W** is

$$V^2 + W^2 + 2\ V\ W \cos\theta,$$

where $V = |\mathbf{V}|$ and $W = |\mathbf{W}|$ are the magnitudes of V and W, respectively, and θ is the included angle. Determine the resultants obtained by taking the primitive tones two at a time and check the answers graphically.

**4.18** Complete the table:

F = (0.00000, 1.00000),

C = (0.86603, 0.50000),

...

expressing the unit tone vectors in terms of their x and y components.

**4.19** Using the information obtained in the previous exercise, find the x, y components of harmony 102. Add the x components and y components separately to obtain the components of the resultant simple tonality. What is its amplitude? What is its phase angle?

**4.20** (a) What are the x, y coordinates of the dominant tetrad GBDF? (Hint: Locate G + B + D + F.) (b) What is its distance from the origin? (c) What are the polar coordinates of this point? (d) What are the sine and cosine of the angle between this vector and the polar axis?

**4.21** At time t = 1 sec, a point has r, θ coordinates of 3, 30°. At time 1.5 sec, its coordinates are 3, 90°. What is the change in position? Just what does this movement signify?

PART II

# Chapter 5

# Analysis

*'Tis not enough the voice be sound and clear, 'Tis modulation that must charm the ear.*

*LLOYD*

## TONAL DISPLACEMENT

It may be instructive at this juncture to describe briefly the geometric method by which it is possible to undertake the computer analysis of the motions of musical voices. The basic concept is to locate sequences of points that describe the composition at successive instants. First, it is necessary to introduce some new terminology.

In classical mechanics, a change in the position of a mass point, or of its associated position vector, is called a "displacement." Describing a displacement of a center of gravity, for example, is the customary initial step in describing a motion of a rigid body. To determine a displacement uniquely, simply ask both *how far* and in *what direction* is the point or vector in question displaced. Recall that such a displacement can be represented by a vector drawn along the direction of the motion, and the time extent of the motion can be represented by the length of this vector, measured from its initial point or "tail" to its terminal point or "head."

In the present theoretical development, displacement vectors are determined on the basis of tonality and duration. When they are summed vectorially they will form mathematical objects that will be termed "composition vectors." Composition vectors in music are exact analogues to what are named "composition vectors" in physics. Measurements of displacements of composition vectors in successive musical measures provide an excellent indication of tonal motion. The most important use of the displacement diagram is to exhibit the key relationship between successive notes or chords and to show the resultant amplitude and phase angle of various tonalities.

It will be most convenient to begin the study of musical motion by investigating the displacement of solo voices. The successive tones of even simple melodies are not usually spaced equally in time, but rather, progress rhythmically. In order to analyze a melody vectorially, it is useful and advantageous to consider the motion of a representative geometric point, called the "melody point," as it traces out or generates a melodic line. The first sound emitted by a solo voice displaces the melody point from its initial equilibrium position--the point of silence--which is taken as the origin. For example, the displacement of the melody point caused by sounding the initial tone C, for two successive beats, is considered as possessing direction as well as length. It is represented by a vector having two units of magnitude and forming an angle of $30^{\circ}$ with the polar axis. This vector is expressed **2C**, where the symbol **C** denotes the C vector, which is a primitive tone vector. The twelve tone vectors comprising the complete set to be used are the same radially outward directed straight line segments earlier referred to as the arrows of the pitch compass. A rest of any duration is represented by a displacement vector of zero length and an unspecified direction. This is called the "zero vector," denoted **0.** At each successive instant, the displacement of the melodic point from its central equilibrium position is the cumulative sum of the successive displacements it has undergone thus far; in other words, it is the current **melody vector.** The total displacement at time t, therefore, is found by vector addition.

## VOICE TRACKS

The melodic line generated by a solo voice is an example of a more general concept, namely, a **voice track.** In this work a voice is represented by a geometrical point (one having no dimension), while the voice track is a broken line (one having no thickness) or polygonal arc. The "voice track" is defined to be any path in the tonal displacement plane along which a voice point moves. Fig. 5.1 shows a convenient coordinate system for depicting voice tracks during computer analysis. The track shown in Fig. 5.2a is reminiscent of a Schillinger skyline graph; he represented tones by real numbers, however, and not by complex numbers or vectors. Due to this big limitation, Schillinger's graphical technique (see Fig. 5.2b) never progressed much beyond the pictorial stage, and for the most part its use has been abandoned. At any point in time an individual voice in a musical fabric is constrained either to be motionless (silent) or to move in one of the twelve directions specified by the radial tone vectors of Fig. 5.1. The total distance d traversed by an individual voice during a particular phrase is fixed only by its starting point and its ending point, and is independent of each of the intermediate steps. In other words, d is the length of the trend line.

Figure 5.1

A polar coordinate representation of the tonal displacement plane.

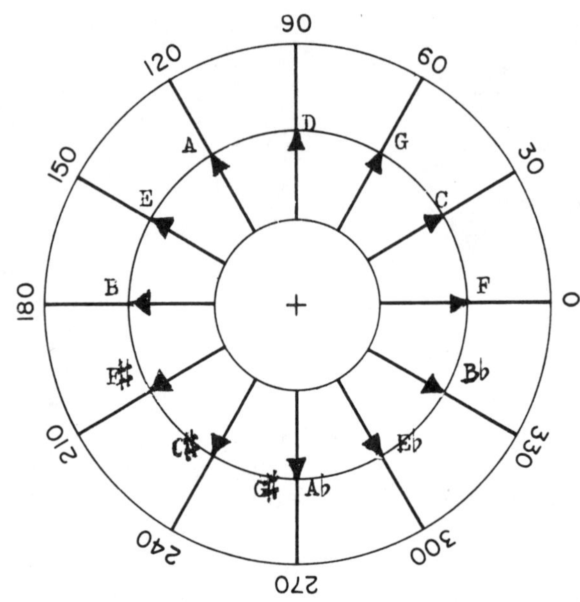


Figure 5.2a

An example of a voice track. The dashed line indicates the linear trend. Motion begins at the left. Consequently horizontal lines signify the note F and vertical lines signify the note D.

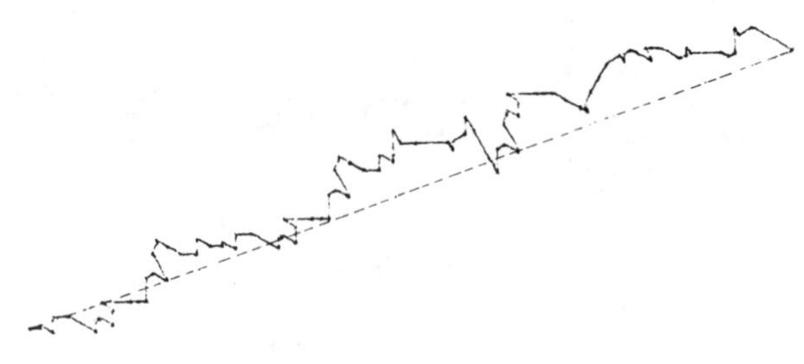

Figure 5.2b

A typical Cartesian plot of melody vs. time (after Shillinger). The skyline is formed by the "roofs" and sides of a collection of contiguous rectangles whose heights are proportional to the instantaneous value of the melody, which is a log-frequency or pitch varying musical sound, and where widths are proportional to the duration time of the corresponding notes [1]. Graphs of pitch against time now are used for preparing melodic lines for proof-listening.

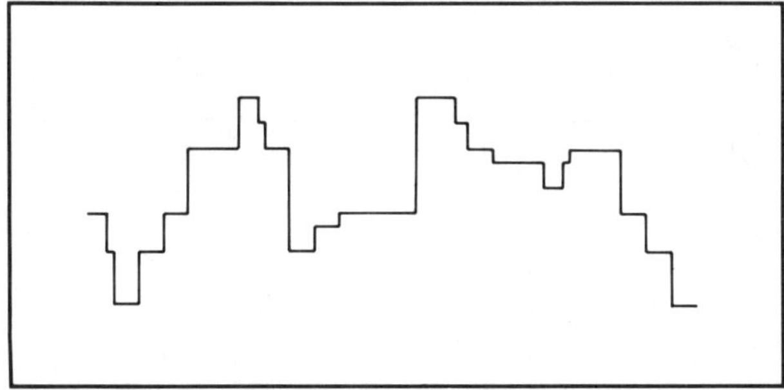

Therefore the successive displacement vectors entering into the voice track are not always along a radius from the origin. Every change of direction produces a point of deflection:

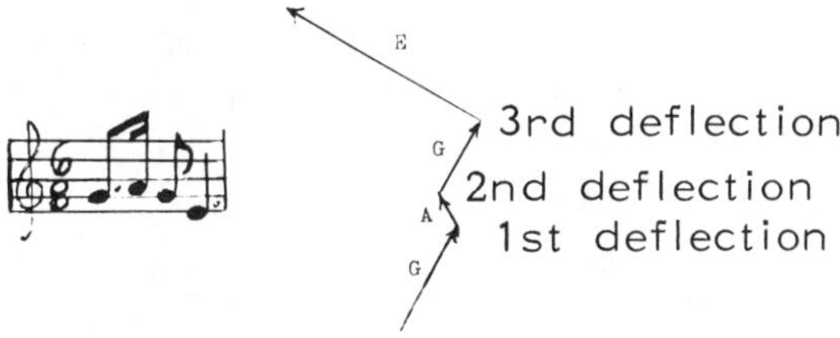


A typical melodic line is shown in Fig. 5.3. Many familiar melodies display such a striking directivity when plotted in two dimensions in accordance with the basic geometry of the displacement plane.

**Figure 5.3**

Silent Night.

Although the track exhibits some curvature, the trend line expresses the correct key (C major) with great precision.

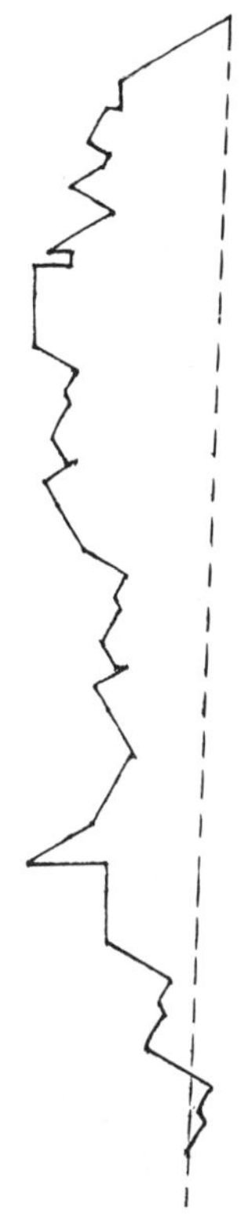

## EXERCISES

**5.1** (a) Show by a ruler and compass construction that the total displacement of the melody point brought about by playing the chromatic scale

C, C♯, D, D♯, E, F, F♯, G, G♯, A, A♯, B

(without closing on C) in sixteenth notes is the zero vector. (Hint: Let a sixteenth note value correspond to 1 inch.) (b) With a little practice, voice tracks can be plotted by hand rather quickly, on a chart or plain paper, using either a protractor or a simple chart tool called an aircraft navigation plotter. Repeat the construction of part (a) using one of these aids. (c) For what other musical scales or scale patterns will the same total displacement of zero be obtained?

**5.2** Indentify the melody graphed in Fig. 5.2.

## SIMPLE MELODIES

Associated with any note of a melody is exactly one of the unit tone vectors ..., B♭, F, C, G, D, A, E, B, F♯, ... each of which has a certain direction. So, it is clear that the direction of the arrow corresponding to the nth note in a melody does not always agree with that of the arrow corresponding to the n-1th note.

Thus far the motion of only solo or individual melodic voices has been described. In even a slightly more complicated situation, such as in a duet, voices will undergo other than parallel displacements. In order to construct a voice track type vector diagram for n-part harmony, the position of each voice is represented by a separate vector. The position of the first voice may be described with respect to the origin **0** by the position vector $r_1(t)$, where t denotes the time variable. Similarly, the position of the ith voice is given by the position vector $r_i(t)$. In drawing the vector diagram, the tones that are longer in duration again count more strongly; if one tone is sustained two beats to another's one, then its displacement vector will be twice as long. The process is continued in this fashion until all voice tracks have been drawn. The resultant for each voice will be equal to the sum of the displacement vectors describing the motion of that voice. This sum may be found by application of the **polygonal method.** The tail end of each displacement vector in turn is placed to the head end of its predecessor. The vector addition leading to the resultant is a kind of "eraser" that eliminates the previous record of the voice tracks. The transition to a multivoice array introduces no new difficulties, and to simplify the ensuing discussion the remainder of this book will be confined to the treatment of musical passages having only small numbers of voices. The resultant graphs are somewhat reminiscent of the charts showing the location, course, and velocity of ships in a convoy.

## EXERCISES

**5.3** Usually in a melody the end of any tone is also the beginning of the next one. Sometimes, however, a pause will occur between adjacent tones. This interruption to the flow of the melodic line is generally marked by a rest sign. The example given in Fig. 5.4 shows that some care must be taken, in the presence of melodic discontinuities, in order to label the time parameter correctly. Following the guidelines set by this example, index the voice track appearing in Fig. 5.3.

**5.4** It sometimes happens that the total displacement of the melody point for different melodies is identical. To illustrate, consider the following two melodic fragments:

Show that the trend lines for the first measure of each fragment coincide. This means that the total displacement due to a quarter note rest followed by a quarter note D equals the total displacement due to two successive displacements for C and E, each having a duration of one quarter note. Invent other examples of identical displacements.

### Figure 5.4

The effects of caesuras. At the four places marked by the numbers 1, 2, 3, and 4 the beats are the same.

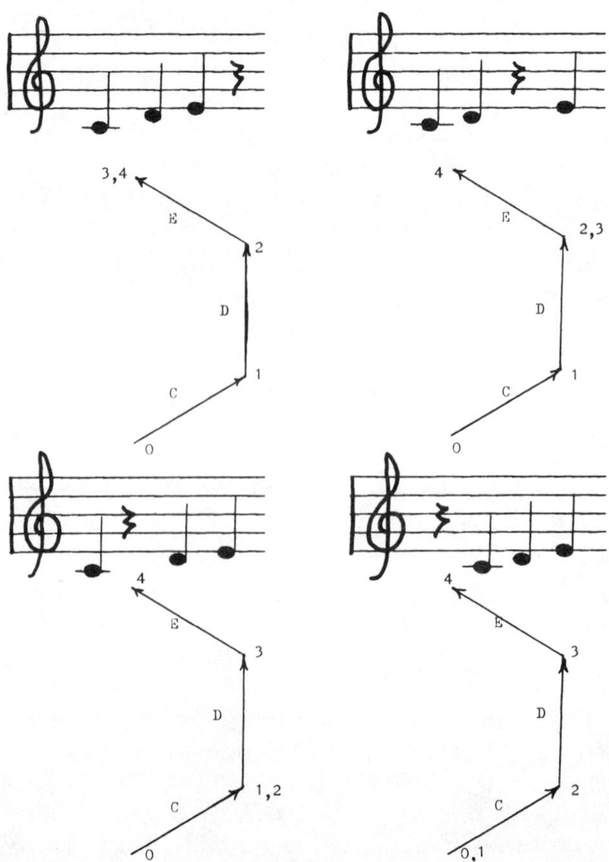

5.5 Artificial melodic attachments such as grace notes, mordants, and turns usually are thought to have only a transient effect, since they act over a short period. For this reason some music analysts like to pre-edit their input data before keying it in by stripping off such elements of ornamentation. Fig. 5.5 suggests a recommended alternative graphical solution to the question of how to handle such knick-knackery. Apply the suggestion to other cases.

Figure 5.5

Rather than to disregard a trill, accord its constituents equal duration values by averaging. The dashed arrow depicts the resultant.

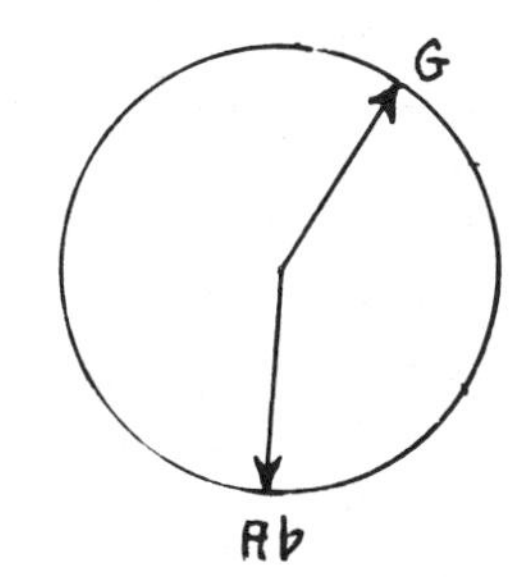


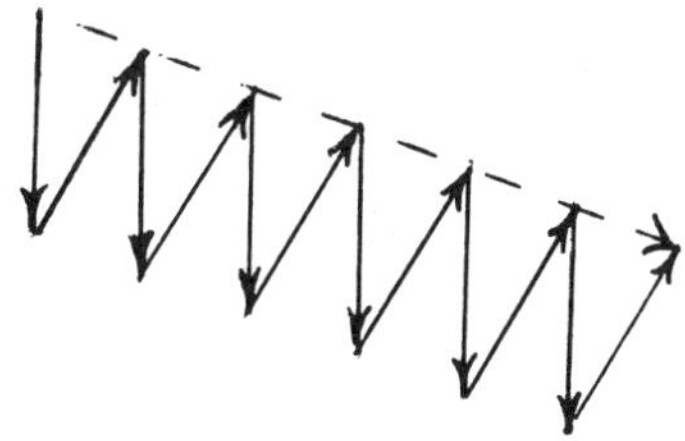

## COMPOSITION TRAJECTORIES

The theoretical basis for treating multivoice arrays was sketched in the preceding section. As explained there, the first step is to construct a displacement diagram for each vocal part separately, assuming that each voice is a vectorial quantity and that all voices may be combined, by using vector addition. Next, arrowheads may be labeled and tick marks or numbers placed on or alongside the shafts to indicate the time scale or clock synchronization. This procedure is valuable in studying counterpoint, especially, for in this application the music analyst wishes to follow the tracks of single voices or of a few related voices simultaneously. Now these individual voices may execute complicated gymnastics, even losing their identity. Or they may come and go while engaging in an "on-off" process. Sometimes it cannot be decided with surety at the outset just what tones are included in each part, that is, which notes are to be sung by the soprano, which notes are to be sung by the alto, and so on. Actually, for many pieces of music such a distinction has no meaning. Under these special circumstances another point, to be called the "composition point," carries the weight of the analysis, although it may be fruitful still to pursue vocal phrases or snatches of melody whose delineation then will be almost entirely subjective. A knowledge of the composition trajectory is usually helpful in obtaining a true description of the dynamic character of a musical work. This procedure is valuable also in studying harmony.

In considering the motion of complicated musical systems such as harmonic progressions, musicians traditionally have found it natural to distinguish one tone in each chord, for example the **root**, in order to characterize the motion of the composition as a whole. (Indeed, both Hindemith and Schillinger have introduced the luxury of allowing certain chords to have multiple roots.) The notion of tonal resultant retains the spirit of this accepted approach to analysis. The tonal resultant may be thought of as a fictitious tone, something like a root--a tone displaced to the position attained by the vector sum of the assemblage of tones in the chord or charm. The rule of vector addition can be applied to the case of many voices extending over time; the tones of the individual voices are combined from the beginning of the piece so as to yield their total cumulative displacement. This mathematical definition thus represents the composition vector at a particular moment as the sum of all of the tones that are being played or sung together at that time combined with the vector sum of all tones produced earlier. Each part is considered to be of equal importance in forming this sum. The "composition trajectory," which is the continuous path taken by the composition point as a function of the parameter **time**, assumes the place of one or more voice tracks, and when it is so substituted the tracks it replaces thenceforth can be disregarded. The composition point, being at each instant of time itself a vector resultant, sometimes can be located by elementary considerations of balance or symmetry. Because of the smoothing nature of its definition, the composition point often follows a less intricate path than do the individual parts.

The points P of the displacement plane are identified with the position vectors **R** measured from the fixed origin **0**. If the line segment drawn from the origin 0 to the point P is denoted by $\overline{0P}$, the corresponding position vector **R** is given by the **directed** line segment $\overline{0P}$. The composition point p is the terminus of a position vector r directed to the point (x,y) in the displacement plane. The length of this vector is given by

$$|r| = r = (x^2+y^2)^{\frac{1}{2}}.$$

The motion of the music is summed up in the location of the composition point at each instant, which is expressed in terms of its distance r from the fixed origin **0** and its angle θ with respect to the polar or x axis.

The composition point is free to move in a variety of ways, or it can remain stationary. It is natural to ask: When does the composition point move, and under what circumstances does it not move? From the time of initiation of a struck or sounding tone for the length of time the vibrations continue, the composition point moves in a straight line, assumedly under the action of some unknown force acting along the line of motion. A turning point of the path occurs at each appearance or disappearance of a tone from the audible signal. If a new tone is sounded, the composition as a whole is displaced from one position to another in the displacement plane. While no new tone appears or old tone disappears, the composition point, which is related to the center of gravity of the composition or "tonal center," is either at rest or in uniform motion. Speaking precisely, it will be at rest for balanced chords. So, from this standpoint, balanced structures contribute nothing to the movement.

When a musical composition is being performed, the composition point correspondingly undergoes a continual change of position relative to the origin of the displacement plane. The linear translatory motion of the composition point is set to be at a constant speed and constant heading for a specified time interval. At the end of this period a new speed and heading are obtained. In the solo case, the composition point will follow the motion of the melody point or voice track. For $\underline{n}$-voice harmony, the general motion of the composition point will be equivalent to the resultant motion of the $\underline{n}$ individual voice point motions. An alternate form of resultant for analyzing harmonic progressions is obtained if each of the vector sums is divided by the associated weight or cardinality so as to express all of them in equivalent numbers. This division produces a true center of gravity or "centroid." For the analysis of $\underline{n}$-part harmony, then, it is often realistic to consider only the problem of the motion of a single figmental tonal centroid.

The present approach to music analysis by computers regards a harmonic progression of length N as consisting of N + 2 components (the two new components being null harmonies placed at each end, the first at the beginning where time $t = t_0$ and the second at the end where time t = T). The theory entails partitioning the subject music passage from $t_0$, which corresponds to the origin of the polar plot, to T, which corresponds to the terminus of the plot, into a discrete sequence of message frames by means of a set of time points

$$t_0 = 0, t_1, \ldots, t_i, t_{i+1}, \ldots, t_N = T.$$

The "message frame" is defined as any interval of time over which the musical signal is constant. The length of these message frames expands and contracts as the music is played.

The partition in question is defined as that subdivision of time interval $[t_0, T]$ for which only steady-state sounds occur (that is, nothing new happens) on each open interval $(t_i, t_{i+1})$, with $i = 0, 1, \ldots, N-1$, and for which a musical change or discontinuity occurs at each precise moment $t_0, t_1, \ldots, t_N$. It follows that a musical composition is a **step function**, in musical component space. This function M has the form

$$M(t) = c_i, \quad t_i \leq t < t_{i+1}$$

for some subdivision of $[t_0, T]$ and some set of constant components $c_i$. These components are those constant sounding portions of a musical composition that are not contained in any larger constant sounding portion. Accordingly, a component usually differs from its immediate left and right neighbors. The computerized analysis of components is essentially sequential. As all music involves such components as elemental pieces, all music is amenable to computer analysis.

To help crystallize some of these new ideas, consider the musical example given in Fig. 5.6a,b. It is apparent that the voices all are moving in various directions. Although the four voice tracks depart from one another rather severely, the combined motion is more regulated, as shown by the path of the harmonic progression in Fig. 5.6c. This trajectory describes a path not unlike a cross *patée*. Notice that the symmetry is not to be registered with respect to the origin, but rather with respect to an offset point. On the outward half of the journey, from beats 1 through 6, the objective key is B minor. On the return trip, however, from beats 7 through 12, the ground just gained is relinquished because of an equal and opposite development in the direction of E# minor. A striking feature of this progression is that successive tonalities are about $90^\circ$ out of phase with (perpendicular to) their immediate predecessors.

In Fig. 5.6d the four separate voice tracks and the trajectory have been combined on a single graph, although again the voice tracks chart the course they would have had if each voice were sounding alone. During a single message frame the motion of the composition point is at a constant speed and heading for that time period which is specified by the duration of the component. At the end of this period a new speed and heading are specified by the next component. A complete cycle of the cross involves at most the territory of a halfplane, so that it is reasonable to regard it as lying in a single generalized key, namely, D major. In this simple example it is felt that some of the power and elegance of the vectorial method begins to become apparent.

**Figure 5.6a**

Enharmonic change is a semantic factor in this beautiful chord sequence.

PIANO TUNERS' PROGRESSION

Figure 5.6b

Voice tracks taken from x,y recorder plots. Each segment represents one quarter note time value. The straight line portions are associated with tones that repeat on successive beats. The original scale size for all voices was 5/3 beats per inch.

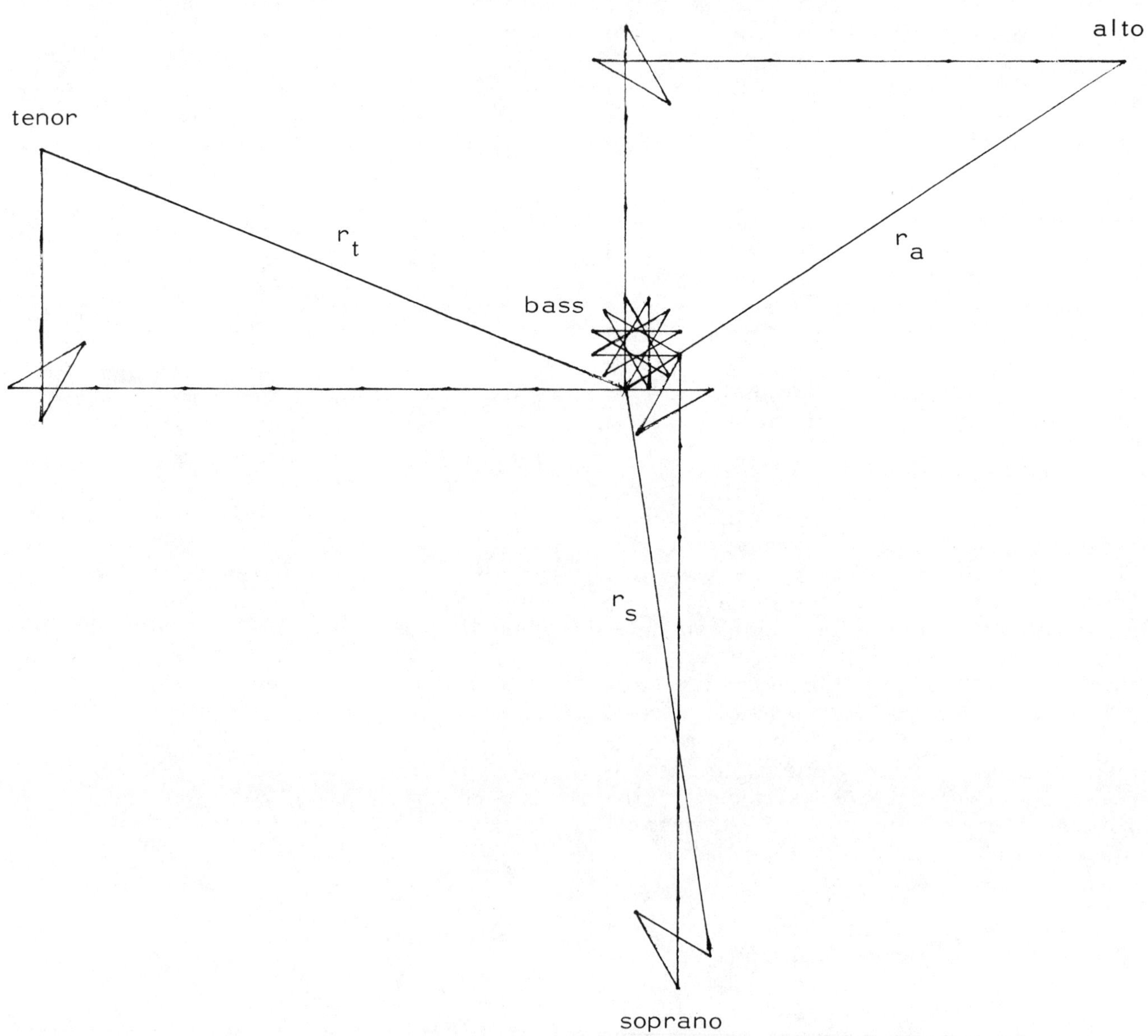

Figure 5.6c

Composition point trajectory for the Piano Tuners' Progression.

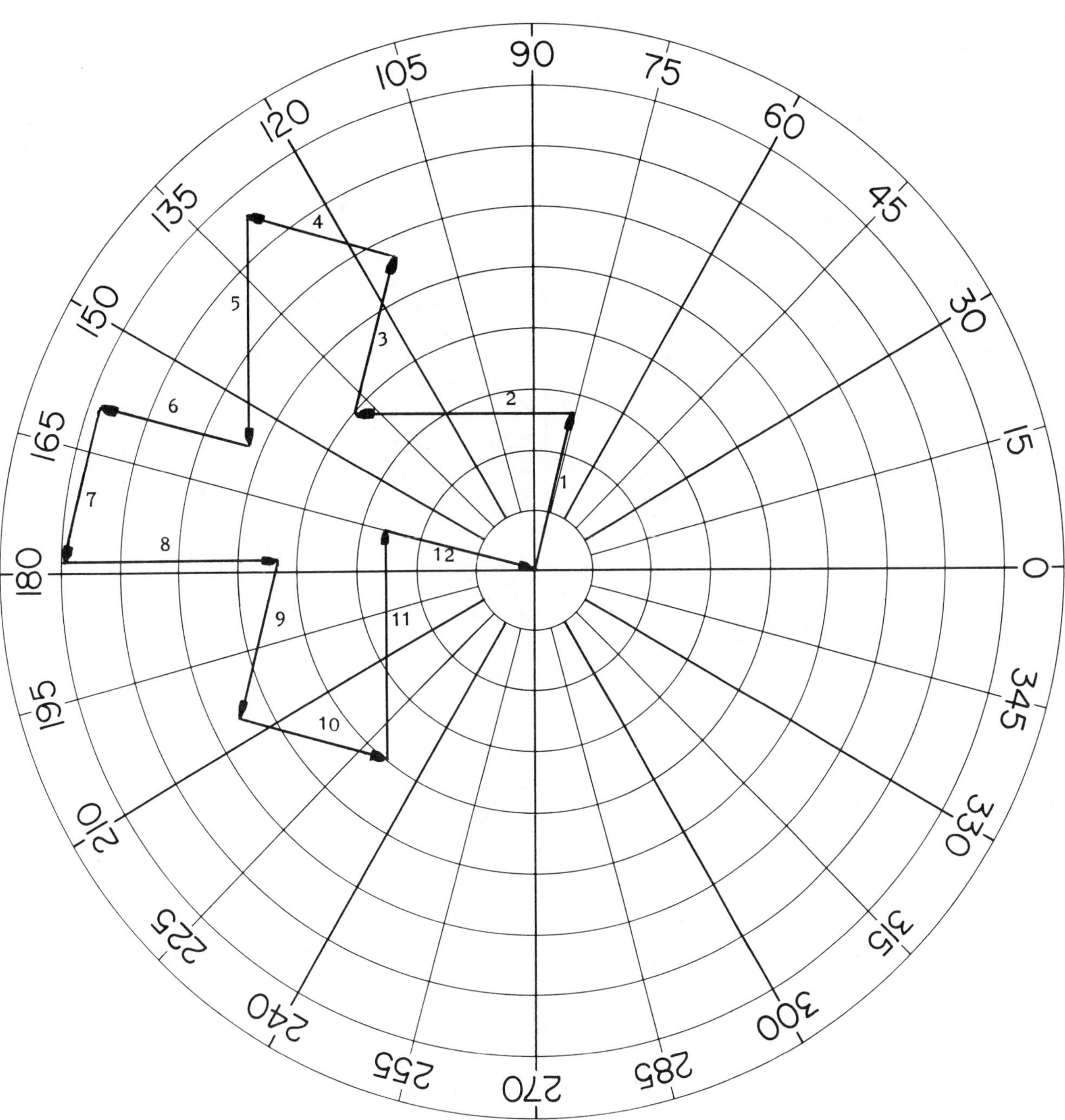

Figure 5.6d

Combination of composition trajectory and tracks made by the soprano, alto, tenor, and bass voices. The fundamental behaviour of the individual parts may be understood, crudely at least, from the standpoint of the amount of freedom of motion the four voices possess. Here the interactions of the separate parts are of no immediate importance since they all are cut from the same pattern. When interactions among voices become important, a more detailed discussion is required. In general, vocal parts may be considered singly or in aggregate or both.

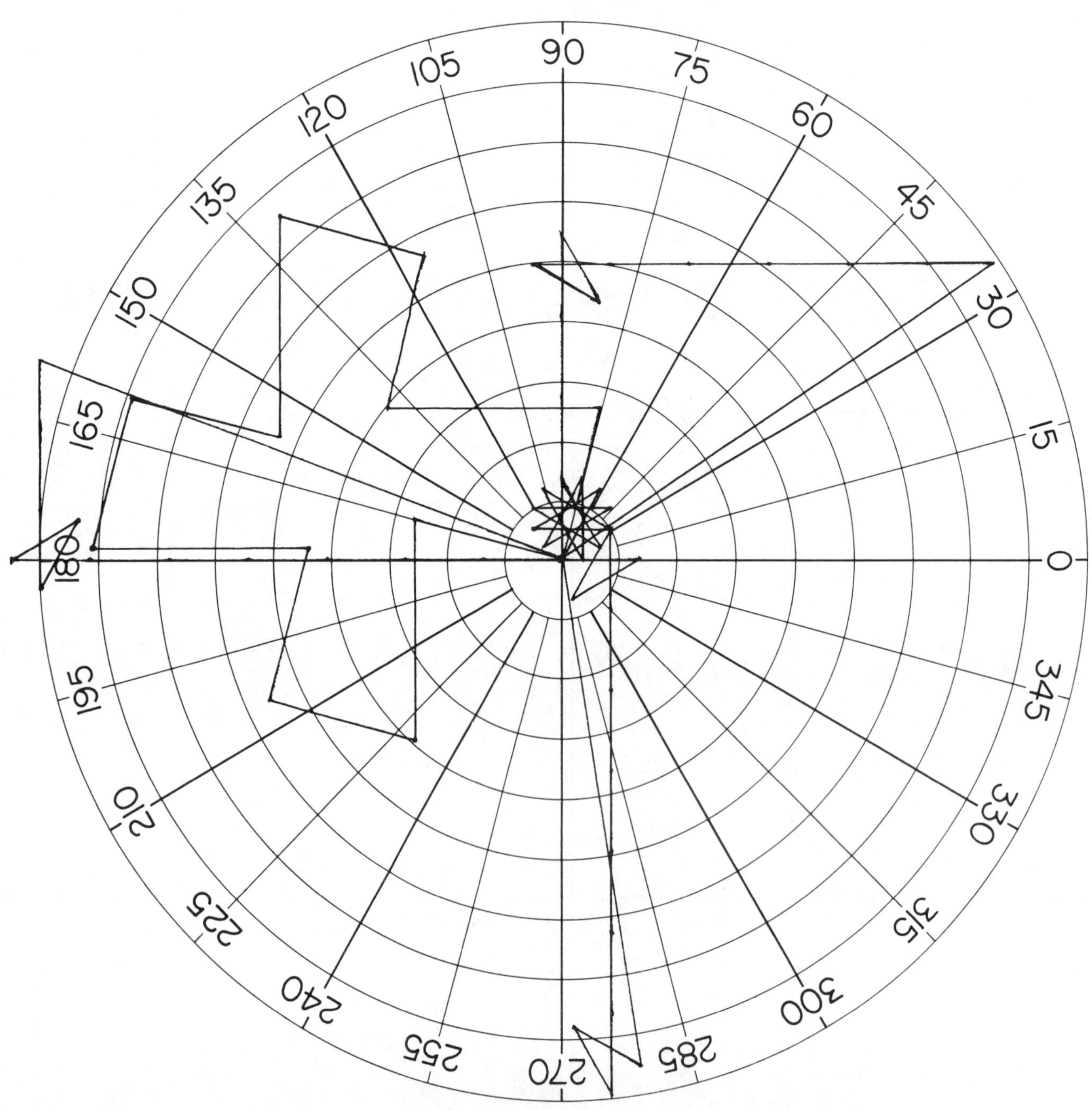

By the procedure just described, a picture or geometrical representation always can be associated with any piece of music. An entire composition can be mapped out painstakingly as a sequence of displacement vectors, one after another, each indicated by an arrow of the proper length and direction. The precise order in which these arrows are added is no longer immaterial. Moreover, there is apparently nothing to keep these composition trajectories from becoming quite elongated or even muddled. Innumerable trajectories would be required to graph all the existing musical literature. Such an enterprise would tax even the fastest computer and probably would contribute very little to the understanding of music. Nevertheless, when the procedure is applied to short passages using a small computer to share the burden, the results can be rather illuminating.

## EXERCISES

**5.6** (a) Prove that every musical composition has a unique decomposition into components. (b) Is the number of components in each such decomposition finite? (Hint. Consider both manuscript and performance analysis.)

**5.7** In what sense do voice tracks reveal the shallow structure and composition trajectories reveal the deep structure of a given musical passage?

**5.8** Show that the composition trajectories for FB → EC and FB → F♯A♯ are equal and opposite

**5.9** Prepare a polar chart showing the composition trajectory for Edward MacDowell's "To a Wild Rose," **Woodland Sketches**, Op. 51. Bear in mind that working by hand requires care in plotting for good results.

**5.10** Is it possible to determine voice tracks from charm sequence data?

## TIME PARAMETER

The discussion of the previous section provided a complete mathematical technique for describing the motions of composition points. There it was shown that, as time goes by, the composition point moves along a polygonal path in the tonal displacement plane, tracing out a trajectory that describes the changing state of the musical composition under scrutiny. Time formally becomes the natural parameter of the composition trajectory, rather than arc length; to each point on the polygonal curve there is associated at least one time value. For all times less than zero $(t < 0)$, silence reigns because the music is assumed to start at time zero. At time $t = 0$, the various instrumental voices, represented as a suitable number of time-dependent frequency-band-distributed tone sources, turn on.

Since the tonal motion imparted to the composition point by silence is most easily conceived to be one of absolute rest, the simplest motion of a melody, other than being quiescent, is to sustain a tone. This situation corresponds to one in which the melody point moves with a constant speed along a straight line segment of the voice track in the direction of some specific unit tone vector. A voice at rest is actually a trivial special case because, while mute, a voice "moves" at a constant **zero** speed in an **indeterminate** direction. But during the time interval that a voice is sustaining a definite fixed pitch, the situation is that of uniform rectilinear motion; the voice track is being generated at a constant speed and the direction of travel of the melody point is constant in time.

When every sounding voice is sustaining its assigned pitch, the composition point p will traverse a straight line portion of the composition trajectory in the direction of the resultant tonality. In general, the completed trajectory will be a broken line or polygon. The time parameter t advances in a natural order along the path, and each tonality vector is multiplied by a scalar time value proportional to the component duration.

Because elaborate electronic facilities, including equipment for making time measurements, probably will not be readily available to the music analyst, it is better at least for the student to begin analysis of music with the printed page, and perhaps later to shift to actual music, whether recorded or live. The procedure for the latter pursuit would be to sample the continuous signal at constant intervals of time $\Delta t$, taken sufficiently small to ensure a good approximation. During each sampling interval, the output would be held constant and equal to the exact value of the signal at the previous sampling instant. Despite the greater value of combined analog and digital processing of performed music for the accurate measurement of elementary acoustical parameters, a much simpler pedagogical course has been taken here since it would require extensive instrumentation to derive the necessary parameters from sound reproductions, or to collect good data at each time frame from live musical performances in a concert hall. Indeed, real-time analysis of performed music is limited to past samples only, since the future samples are not revealed in the present. On the other hand, the more leisurely analysis of music in manuscript form is unrestricted and a musical selection could just as well be studied backwards. or with time reversed, as forwards. When using only the score, however, it is not particularly difficult to separate a musical composition into discrete units although corresponding units in the sound pressure waveform are less readily identifiable.

In printed music or handwritten scores, units of time are defined by measures and their subdivisions. Consequently, for simplicity, tempo variations such as called for by **rubato** markings usually should be neglected in the first cut at music analysis by computers. For more precise investigations taking all these tempo variations into consideration, electronic clock pulses would be preferred. And the slowest pulse rate should be chosen for which sampling more frequently will not provide any significant additional information about the music. By sampling at constant intervals, status of the time slice is reassessed even if nothing has happened. Time units $\Delta t$, often denoted by T in books on sampled data systems [2],[3], are numbered in natural order and each tone is given the indices of the time units in which it occurs.

## EXERCISES

**5.11** The basic note lengths are indicated in Fig. 5.7 as rectangular pulses. Using graph paper, draw pulse diagrams for the following sums:

(a) 𝅗𝅥 + 3 𝅘𝅥 + 𝅝 =

(b) 𝅗𝅥. + 𝅘𝅥. + 8 𝅘𝅥𝅯 =

(c) 𝅝 + 3 𝅘𝅥 + 2 𝅗𝅥 =

(d) 3 𝅗𝅥 + 𝅝. + 4 𝅘𝅥 =

(e) 𝅘𝅥. + 6 𝅘𝅥 + 3 𝅗𝅥 =

(f) 2 𝅝 + 4 𝅘𝅥 + 12 𝅘𝅥𝅯 =

(g) 𝅘𝅥. + 8 𝅘𝅥𝅰 + 𝅗𝅥. =

(h) 𝅗𝅥 + 8 𝅘𝅥 + 16 𝅘𝅥𝅰 + 8 𝅘𝅥𝅱 =

(i) 8 𝅘𝅥𝅯 + 8 𝅘𝅥𝅰 + 16 𝅘𝅥𝅱 =

(j) 𝅗𝅥.. + 𝅘𝅥. + 4 𝅘𝅥𝅯 =

(k) 𝅝.. + 𝅘𝅥.. + 3 𝅘𝅥𝅯 =

**5.12** Determine the duration $\Delta t$ in milliseconds (one-thousandth seconds) of the following note values at a moderate tempo m.m. 𝅘𝅥 = 60 (sixty quarter notes per minute): (a) 32nd note, (b) 16th note, (c) 8th note, (d) quarter note, (e) half note, and (f) whole note.

Figure 5.7

Variable pulse lengths. A discontinuity in the signal occurs when the tone begins or ends, but not in between.

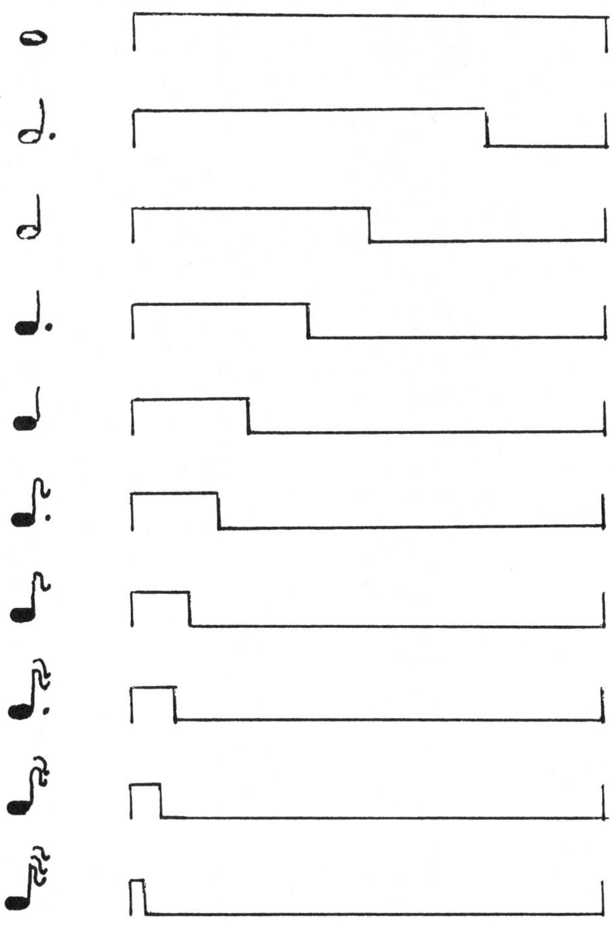

## AVERAGE TONALITY

From the standpoint of tonality, as opposed to that of key, the absolute position of the successive displacement vectors is not so important as their relative orientations. For this reason tonality is defined here as the rate at which displacement is changing. The tonality at any point of time tells where the composition is going and how fast it is getting there. The average tonality of a piece of music as a whole is determined solely by the total distance and direction traveled and the total time elapsed. Thus, the average tonality of the composition throughout is a time varying function expressing the rate of motion in displacement space of the point whose radius vector is the resultant $\mathbf{R} = \Sigma \mathbf{r}_k$. This point, called the "composition point" is located at the tip of the composition vector **R**. Consequently the variations of the position of a musical composition with time can be depicted graphically. It follows that tonality also can be represented by a vector diagram. The representation of tonality as a directed magnitude analogous to velocity is the true basis of the kinematic concept in musicology.

Tonality, being just a time rate of change, is comparable to a velocity in that it has direction and magnitude. At any instant the tonality can be represented by an arrow whose direction and length are continually altering. Notice that the tonality is constant except for instantaneous changes in direction that may be brought about by the appearance or the disappearance of tones.

If v is a given constant tonality vector and t is a positive length along the time axis, then vt is defined to be a displacement vector **r** in the same direction (and having the same sense) as v and of a length t times that of v. Analogously, in **mechanics**

$$\frac{\text{distance} = \text{rate} \times \text{time}}{r = v \times t}$$

and, in **music**

$$\frac{\text{displacement} = \text{tonality} \times \text{time}}{r = v \times t}$$

In the opposite derivation, the tonality is found by dividing the distance in the displacement plane between pairs of points on the composition trajectory by the time elapsed in going between these points. Hence, in the present theory, tonality and displacement are equally fundamental musical quantities.

In discussing problems of music analysis, it is sometimes of interest to follow the musical motion in **tonality space.** The "tonality plane" is defined as a two-dimensional Euclidean space of the same type as the tonal displacement plane, but having musical velocity coordinates instead of musical distance coordinates. The origin of the tonality plane corresponds to a composition point at rest in the displacement plane. The cartesian axes $v_x$ and $v_y$ of the tonality plane are assumed to be taken parallel to the x and y axes, respectively, of the displacement plane. As the composition point changes its motion along its trajectory in tonal displacement space, the musical velocity vector moves in tonality space.

The quantity $v_2 - v_1$, which is proportional to $m(v_2 - v_1)$, the **tonal impulse** (a term to be defined in Chapter 6), is a vector in the tonality plane. This vector joins the tips of vectors $v_1$ and $v_2$, and it is called the "relative tonality."

In many texts, the Greek capital letter **delta** ($\Delta$) is used to denote a "change in value" of a given parameter, or a "difference between" two measurements. Thus, "$\Delta t$," read delta t, means the **change in time.** In this book the letter v will be used to designate **tonality.** If the tonality of a musical passage at one time is represented by $v_0$ and at a later time by $v_1$, then the difference between these values, $v_1 - v_0$, represents the **change in tonality** that takes place. So, the expression "$\Delta v$" means the change in tonality. The delta symbol denotes a subtraction, namely, the difference between the final and initial values of some variable. The subscripted letter $t_0$, which is read t subzero, usually designates the initial instant or starting time, although this point of time may refer to any moment in the performance of a musical selection. Similarly, the letter $t_1$, or sometimes t without a subscript, designates the first instant, that is, any later point in time. By convention, $t_0 \leq t_1$.

To illustrate, if a performance of Tchaikovsky's "Romeo and Juliet" (**Fantasy-Overture**) starts at 8:30 p.m. and stops at 8:51 p.m., then the difference between these two times, that is, twenty-one minutes, represents the elapsed time, and it is denoted in conventional fashion by

$$t = t_1 - t_0 = 21 \text{ min.}$$

The same notation applies to vectors. For example, take the position vector $\mathbf{r} = (x, y)$. The change $\Delta \mathbf{r}$ in the value of $\mathbf{r}$ is given by

$$\Delta r = (\Delta x, \Delta y) = \mathbf{r}_1 - \mathbf{r}_0 = (x_1 - x_0, y_1 - y_0).$$

Here, $\Delta r$ is called a "displacement vector." The corresponding time interval $\Delta t$ during which this change in position or displacement took place is again given by $\Delta t = t_1 - t_0$. This period is called the "elapsed time." Now for obvious reasons, it makes sense to identify the displacement of the composition point during the time interval $\Delta t$ with the change in position $\Delta \mathbf{r}$ of the position vector $\mathbf{r}$. The rate of change is the amount a quantity varies per unit time. This leads to a very important definition. The time rate of change $\Delta \mathbf{r}/\Delta t$ of displacement $\Delta \mathbf{r}$ of the composition point p during the interval between $t_0$ and $t_1 = t_0 + \Delta t$, during which time its position changes from $\mathbf{r}_0$ to $\mathbf{r}_1 = \mathbf{r}_0 + \Delta \mathbf{r}$, is given by

$$\mathbf{v}_{av} = \frac{\Delta \mathbf{r}}{\Delta t} = \frac{\mathbf{r}_1 - \mathbf{r}_0}{t_1 - t_0} = \left( \frac{x_1 - x_0}{t_1 - t_0}, \frac{y_1 - y_0}{t_1 - t_0} \right).$$

This quotient is called the "average tonality during the time interval $\Delta t$." Because of its strategic role in the development of a computer methodology for music analysis, this quotient will sometimes be referred to by the additional names "musical motion vector" and "tonality vector."

When a body in motion traverses equal distances in equal units of time $\Delta t$, its motion is described as being "uniform." For uniform motion in a straight line, the distance traveled is proportional to time (see Fig. 5.8). The velocity at a point of deflection or path turning point is undefined. Similar statements are applicable to musical motions. In dealing with voice tracks and composition trajectories, it is necessary to work with vectors that are localized, that is, have a definite point of application. For example, tonality vectors are localized in the **tonality plane** by fixing their initial points to the center or origin of the coordinate system. Displacement vectors, on the other hand, are localized in the **displacement plane** by attaching ends to tips in strict order of their appearance. This construction forms the polygonal path herein called the composition trajectory (or the voice track). At each resultant point, or fix, of the composition vector, a relative preferred notation is implied.

**Figure 5.8**

Displacement due to constant tonality.

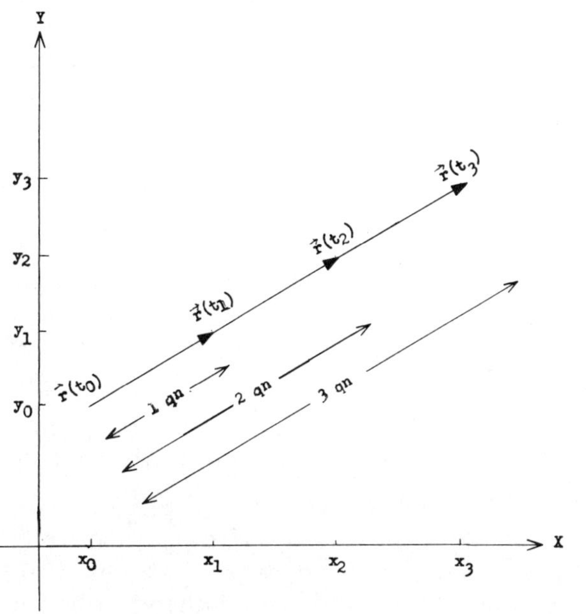


EXAMPLE

Consider the cadence DFGB → CEGC, where the dominant seventh chord is sustained for a quarter note and the tonic chord is sustained for a half note. The two tonalities are represented by the linear combinations

$$v_{V}7 = \ldots+1B+0E+0A+1D+1G+0C+1F+\ldots$$

$$= 1B+1D+1G+1F = B+D+G+F = D+G, \text{ and}$$

$$v_{I} = \ldots+0B+1E+0A+0D+1G+2C+0F+\ldots$$

$$= 1E+1G+2C = E+G+2C = D+G+C.$$

The two duration values are $\Delta t_{V}7=\frac{1}{4}$ and $\Delta t_{I}=\frac{1}{2}$. Consequently, the average tonality is given by

$$\frac{r_1 - r_0}{t_1 - t_0} = \frac{r_V 7 + r_I}{\Delta t_V 7 + \Delta t_I} =$$

$$\frac{v_V 7\ \Delta t_V 7 + v_I\ \Delta t_I}{\Delta t_V 7 + \Delta t_I} =$$

$$\frac{\frac{D+G}{4} + \frac{D+G+C}{2}}{\frac{3}{4}} =$$

$$\frac{D+G+2D+2G+2C}{3} =$$

$$D + G + \frac{2}{3}C$$

Now that the notion of average tonality has been introduced, it would be natural to ask whether it is possible to extend it to instantaneous values. The answer to this question is affirmative. To do so, however, requires a limiting process. Recall that the average tonality has been expressed as the difference between two composition vectors divided by the intervening time period. The "instantaneous tonality" v of point P at time t is defined as the limit of the average tonality as the increment of time approaches zero as a limit. In mathematical notation

$$v = \lim_{\Delta t \to 0} v_{av}\Big|_t = \lim_{\Delta t \to 0} \frac{\Delta r}{\Delta t}\Big|_t$$

$$= \lim_{\Delta t \to 0} \frac{r(t + \Delta t) - r(t)}{\Delta t} = \frac{dr}{dt}$$

where $|_t$ signifies that the limit is to be evaluated at that given point of time t at which the value of the instantaneous tonality is required, and $\frac{dr}{dt}$ is called a "time derivative." As the time interval $\Delta t$ decreases to zero, the tonality vector becomes tangent to the composition trajectory at t, so the instantaneous tonality is in the direction of the displacement. This means that, excluding points of deflection, the tonality is always tangent to the path of motion of the composition point. And although it paid to apply the limiting process once to see what would happen, there is no need as yet to work with the derivative since, aside from path turning points, the variables r and t are related linearly as $r = t\hat{r}$, where the caret ^ denotes a **unit** vector, namely, $\hat{r} = r/|r|$. In short, a nonzero vector is tangent to itself along its entire length.

The automotive age has accustomed everyone to the terms **velocity** and **acceleration.** Not everyone is aware, however, that these terms are defined as derivatives. Ordinary motions are often variable, for example, those of rockets. A curvilinear arc changes direction from point to point. So the situation for the automotive engineer or the rocket expert is often complicated. The good news is that the composition point progresses in uniform motion along each straight line segment or "leg" of its journey. A straight line segment has the same direction at all of its points (see Fig. 5.9). Consequently, the situation for the music analyst is considerably simpler, at least for the time being. All derivatives are the quotients of finite magnitudes rather than quotients of infinitesimals. It may be concluded that the tonality does not vary between arrowheads. This is obvious since nothing new happens inside a message frame. The same result holds for modulation, as explained in the next chapter. Things will become more complicated when realistic wave forms, transients, attack, and decay are no longer neglected.

Figure 5.9

Tangents to curvilinear arc.

Tangents to polygonal arc.

## EXERCISES

**5.13** Given the metronome setting **m.m.** ♩ = 120, which assigns to each quarter note a duration of one 1/120th of a minute, find the largest value of $\Delta t$ commensurate with the rhythmic subdivisions of Exercise 5.12, expressing the answer in milliseconds (msec.).

**5.14** (a) The time signature $\frac{3}{4}$ indicates that there are three quarter note beats per measure; a tempo marking of **m.m.** ♩ = 180 indicates three quarter notes per second, that is, 3 qn/sec. What is the corresponding speed in measures per second? (b) What is the length of a half note in $\frac{4}{4}$ time in units of beats? (c) What is the length of a dotted eight note in $\frac{3}{4}$ time at a metronome setting of **m.m.** ♩ = 100 in units of seconds?

**5.15** (a) When does music stand still? (b) When is musical motion uniform?

**5.16** A given high-fidelity phonograph turntable rotates at a uniform speed. Does the motion of the stylus or needle relative to the record grooves decrease or increase in its speed as the record plays? Why does this change have no effect on the musical tempo? What effect might it have on the fidelity?

**5.17** How should a digital computer be programmed to determine the proportion of notes and rests of a certain duration in a musical sample?

**5.16** Is the average tonality of a composition affected by a uniform change in tempo? Explain.

**5.17** List possible situations in which consideration of the average tonality for an entire passage or composition would be required.

**5.18** What questions might be answered better by reversing time and plotting a composition trajectory from a given point of time into the past?

## REFERENCES

[1] J. Schillinger, *The Schillinger System of Musical Composition,* Vol. 1 (Carl Fischer, Inc., New York, 1946) p. xix.

[2] Bernard Gold and Charles M. Rader, *Digital Processing of Signals* (McGraw-Hill Book Company, New York, 1969) p. 3.

[3] Harry S. Black, *Modulation Theory* (Van Nostrand Reinhold Company, New York, 1953) p. 38.

*Another chord that frequently appears with the tonic and dominant is the submediant, in a I-VI-V-I progression. Here, however, in contrast to the II, III, and IV of the three basic progressions [I-II-V-I, I-III-V-I, I-IV-V-I], the submediant has no harmonic asociation with either the tonic or dominant, and consequently imparts a weaker impulse to the progression*

*ADELE T. KATZ, Challenge to Musical Tradition, 1945*

PART II

# Chapter 6 Modulation

## KEY SIGNATURES, CLOSED HALFPLANES, AND SECTORS

The grouping of sharps or flats that usually appears immediately to the right of the clef sign is termed the "key signature." Naming a key signature is like specifying a trump suit in contract bridge. It effects a reordering of the hierarchy of values and a restructuring of what is meaningful. While it is in effect, such a signature determines the enharmonic value of certain notes, for example, a single sharp customarily indicates that until further notice every F that follows should be played as an F♯. Each such proviso may be cancelled temporarily by the appearance of a natural sign, or more permanently by the specification of a new key signature. Now that the idea of a displacement plane has been discussed, it will be fruitful to ask whether some region of relevance can be assigned to each key signature.

Unquestionably the reader is familiar with the circular arrangement of key signatures. From a glance at Fig 6.1 it is obvious that every sharp in a key signature stands for a counterclockwise rotation and every flat in the signature stands for a clockwise rotation. Looking at the matter another way, each 30$^{o}$ of mechanical rotation produces a corresponding change in the key signature of one inflection. This fact gives support to the intuitive feeling that neighboring keys somehow touch. After some thought it becomes clear that at every boundary between two adjacent major keys there must be a discontinuity in the key signature function. In other words, at the precise point of leaving one major key and entering its neighbor, the key signature function has to take an integer jump, which changes its total number of sharps or flats by plus or minus one.

**Figure 6.1.**

Circular chart of key signatures.

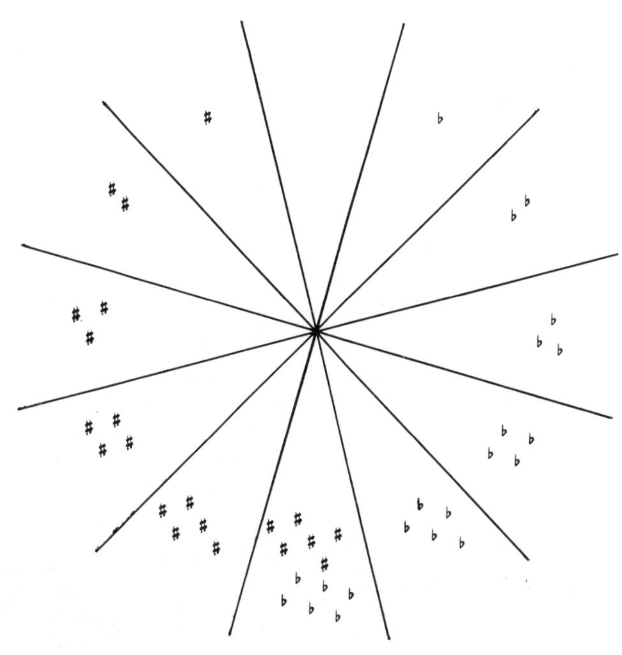

Collateral evidence supporting the conjecture that neighboring keys touch is gained from the construction shown in Fig. 6.2. Here the tones of the C major scale are seen to fall in what mathematicians call the "closed upper halfplane." The tones of the G major scale, on the other hand, lie in a halfplane that is offset from the horizontal by a $30^{\circ}$ angle, counterclockwise, whereas the tones of the F major scale lie in a different halfplane that is tilted $30^{\circ}$ clockwise. These halfplanes may be thought of as regions of influence of the various major keys. It soon becomes apparent that all of the major scales are likewise shifted symmetrically about a central reference point. Moreover, any particular point in the plane is held in condominium by several key halfplanes. This observation suggests that it might be possible to assign a subregion of higher relevance to each major key, such as depicted in Fig. 6.3.

Figure 6.2.

Key relevant regions of the displacement plane viewed as overlapping halfplanes.

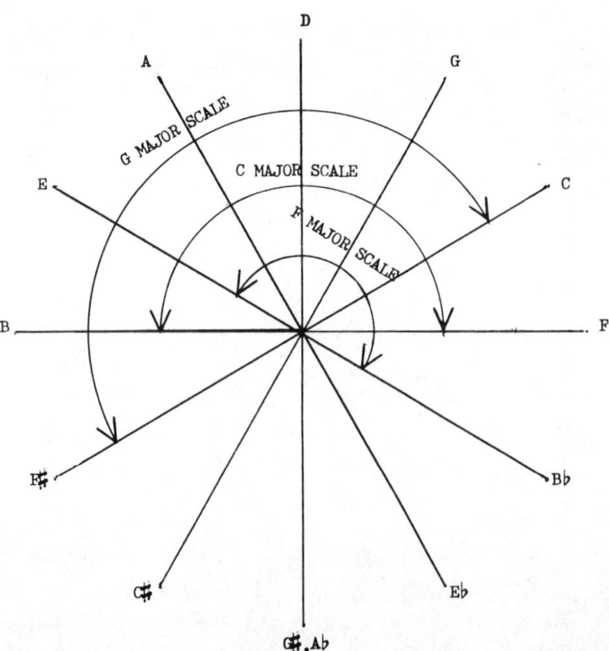


Figure 6.3.

Wedge shaped key sector forming the core of a major key region of influence.

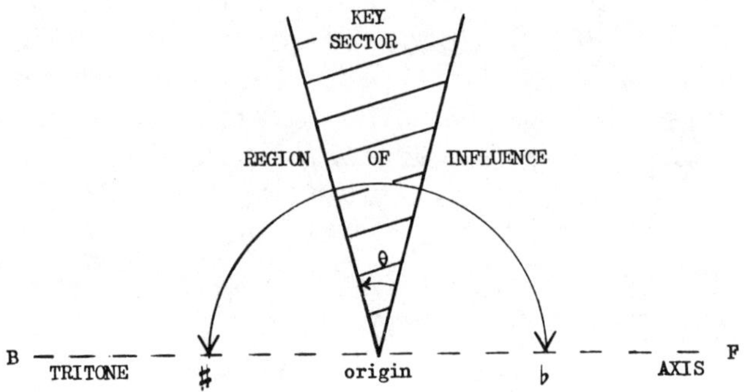


In this diagram the dashed line BF defines the upper halfplane. This line will be called the "tritone axis" of the key of C major. The curved arrow describes the region of influence of the key of C major. This region is shown to extend beyond a hypothetical sector of C major into the lands of sharps and flats. The Greek letter θ designates the unknown angular width of this sector. Luckily it is possible to solve for this quantity. To find the value of θ it is necessary to realize that C major is, after all, no more important than is any other key. Recall that transposition to a new key is equivalent to a planar rotation. Also recall that there are exactly twelve harmonically distinct major scales. Clearly the C major sector is bounded on each side by neighboring sectors belonging to G major and F major. So, the space alloted to C major's region of influence by the halfplane assigned to the C major scale must be reduced to allow room for twelve equal sectors. This condition results in a value for theta of $\theta = 360^{\circ}/12 = 30^{\circ}$. Moreover, it is reasonable to require that the contraction from a halfplane to a sector be performed symmetrically, because to do anything else would be difficult to justify theoretically. Accordingly, the C major sector is confined to the area that lies between the two halflines that emanate from the origin as rays situated at angles of $75^{\circ}$ and $105^{\circ}$ with the line BF, which coincides with the horizontal or polar axis. The azimuthal coverage of the key of C (refer to Fig. 6.4) is therefore from 75° to 105°.

Figure 6.4.

Range and azimuth coverage of each major key sector.

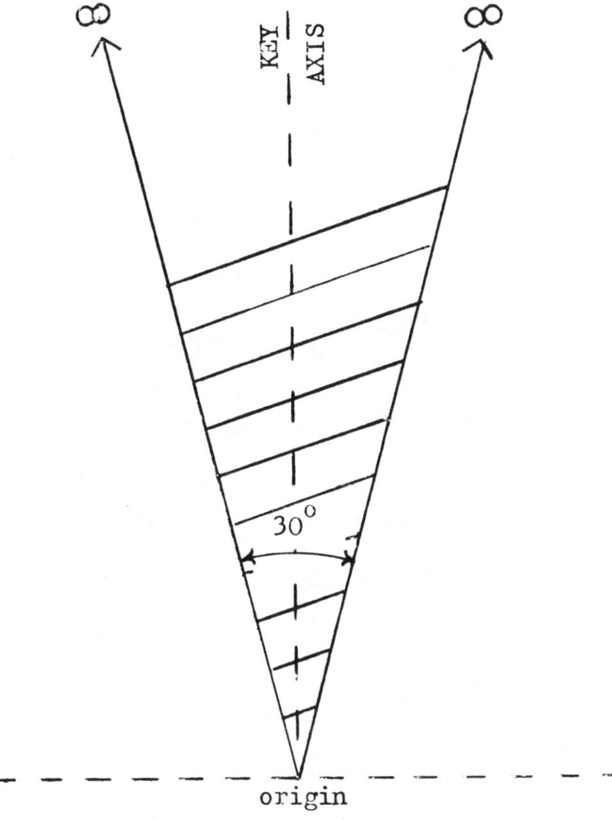


By a similar argument it can be shown that to each major key there corresponds a region of influence, or halfplane, lying to one side of the tritone axis of the key and constituting the **generalized key** domain. Moreover, centrally located within each such region there exists a subregion, or sector, relevant to the **enlarged key signature.** Thus, there are two fundamental regions in the displacement plane that pertain to each major key, the second and smaller one being included in the first.

Figure 6.5 contains a diagram that may help in visualizing the situation. Its examination reveals several pieces of information. The first

Figure 6.5

Pitch compass, key sectors, and key halfplanes. The sectors widen and the influence of neighboring sectors diminishes as the point of observation approaches infinity along any key axis.

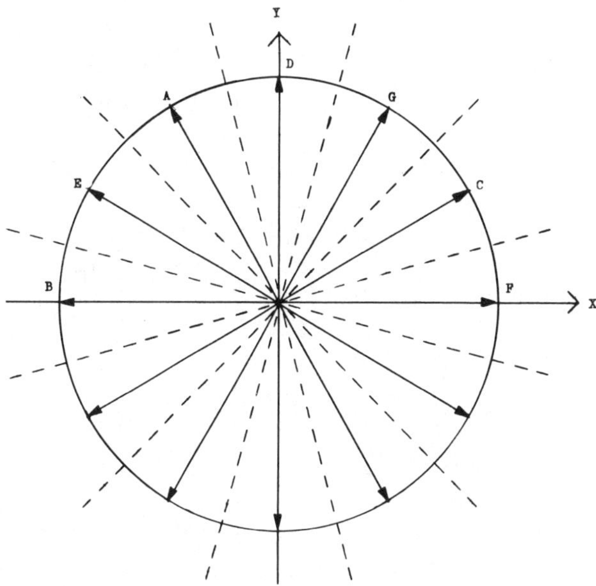


fact is that each key sector falls within the regions of influence of several other keys. For example, the C major sector is a satellite of the keys F, G, B♭, D, E♭, and A major, since it is situated within the halfplanes belonging to these keys. A startling fact also is evident from Fig. 6.5, namely, that the key of C has no definite outer boundary. Fig. 6.5 shows also that the circular 180° arc FCGDAEB is centered upon the tone D. This is another surprise. For it might be thought **à priori** that the bisector of the key of C should be either its tonic C or its dominant G. (Both of these tones, of course, are in the larger sector formed by the closed upper halfplane.) Because of its importance to the key of C major, which remains to be demonstrated, the tone vector D will come to have a familiar significance as an arrow pointing along the bisector or "key axis" of the key of C major. Oddly enough, by repeating the note D, the composer creates a tonal effect that pushes the listener in a definite direction--the key of C becomes more credible.

When two tones are sounded, whether simultaneously or successively, they will have their maximum effect on establishing the listener's sense of key when they are identical. In this case the two tones act in the same direction, and so the magnitude of their vector resultant will be proportional to the sum of their durations.

Note that at the origin there is a point of indecision or "dead" zone. It follows that the origin may be thought of as belonging to all key sectors. So the minimum effect will be produced when two tones are sounded six halfsteps apart. In this case the tones act in precisely opposite directions, and so the magnitude of their vector resultant will be proportional to the difference of their durations.

It is sometimes informative to trace the advance (or retreat) of a composition point along a sequence of straight line segments into the various major key sectors of the displacement plane. For example, Fig. 6.6a illustrates that the melody of "Yankee Doodle," although it pursues a broken line course, still maintains a pronounced single-mindedness of purpose as it passes along a fixed corridor on a heading about ten degrees off the key axis. When this familiar national air is played in C major, the melody point describes a radially outbound course from the origin toward a much deeper tonal commitment to the key of C. That a D-going course indeed characterizes the key of C is evidenced by the fact that two well-known harmonic progressions also depart from the origin (the seat of keylessness) in this same direction, which is orthogonal (at right angles) to the FB tritone axis, as shown in Fig. 6.6b,c. In both cases, the primary beam of displacements proceeds in the direction of the tone vector **D**. Thus, the key of C appears to be a stable objective with this vertical key axis. Such directivity, typical of tonal works, is readily evident also in Fig. 6.7, which shows the geometry of the computer-assisted analysis of a representative Bach chorale. Beginning at the origin, with antecedent silence, the displacement curve rises quite rapidly with the passage of time on an approximate 130° heading until some farthest point is reached at the conclusion of the composition, with consequent silence. There is again no deviation of purpose, because the trajectory does not fold back but, rather, maintains a constant angle relative to the polar coordinate system, although it clearly consists of what seems to be an irregular sequence of perturbations or jog-like advances along the trend line. Close

**Figure 6.6a.**

Yankee Doodle's "ride."

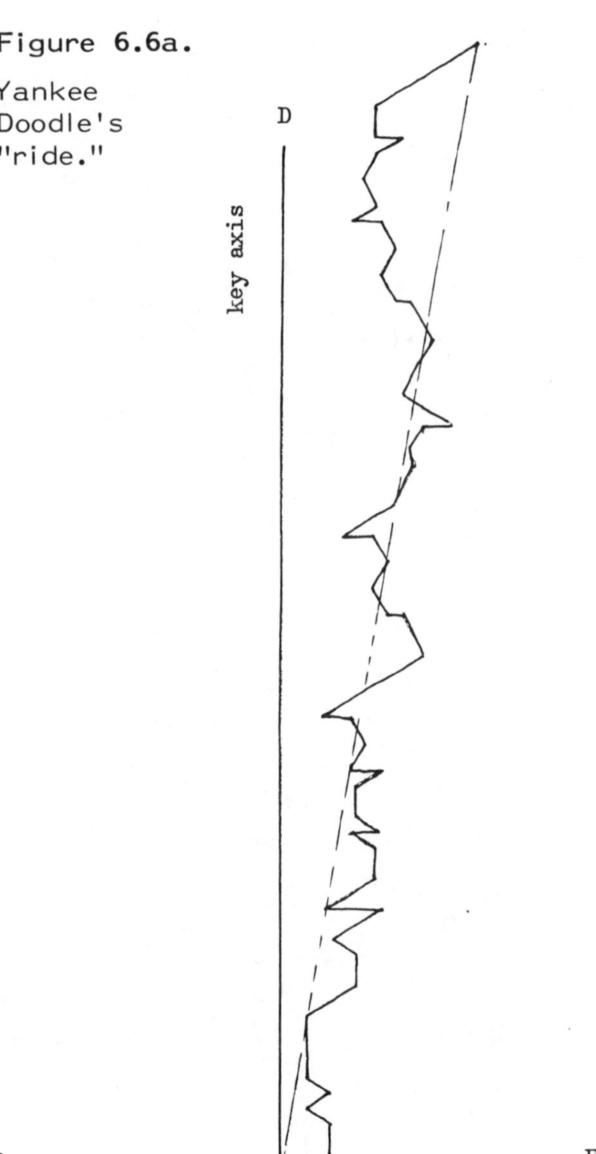

inspection reveals that although the preponderance of average tonalities may be in this same general direction, individual tonalities in quite different directions are to be observed. Therefore, such a graph when completed serves as a convenient "road map" or travel guide to the composition.

Position, direction, and distance are the basic elements of all navigation, land, air, sea, etc. Accordingly, the reader is cautioned that a possible source of confusion may arise from failure to distinguish between two equally important, but different, navigational functions: (a) the specification of compass directions along the path of the composition trajectory (these are tonality phases), and (b) the charting of geographical divisions of the displacement plane (these are keys). So it becomes necessary for the musical "skipper" as well as the ship captain to make use of such practical aids to navigation as those shown in Fig. 6.8.

**Figure 6.6b.**

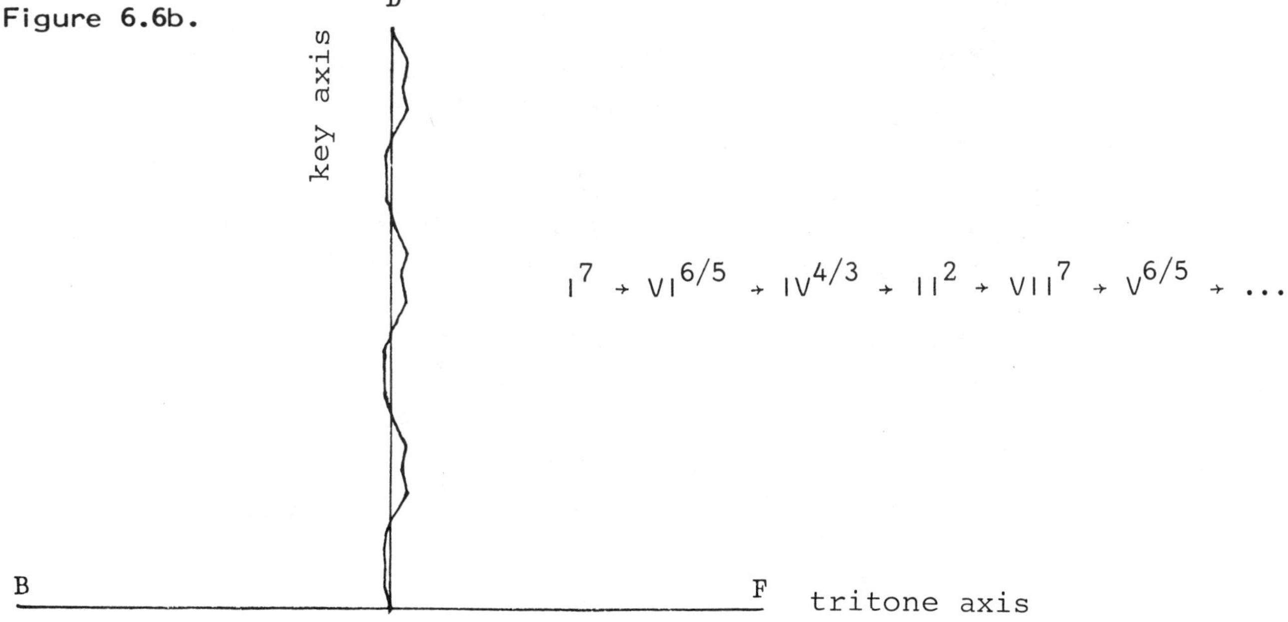


**Figure 6.6c.**

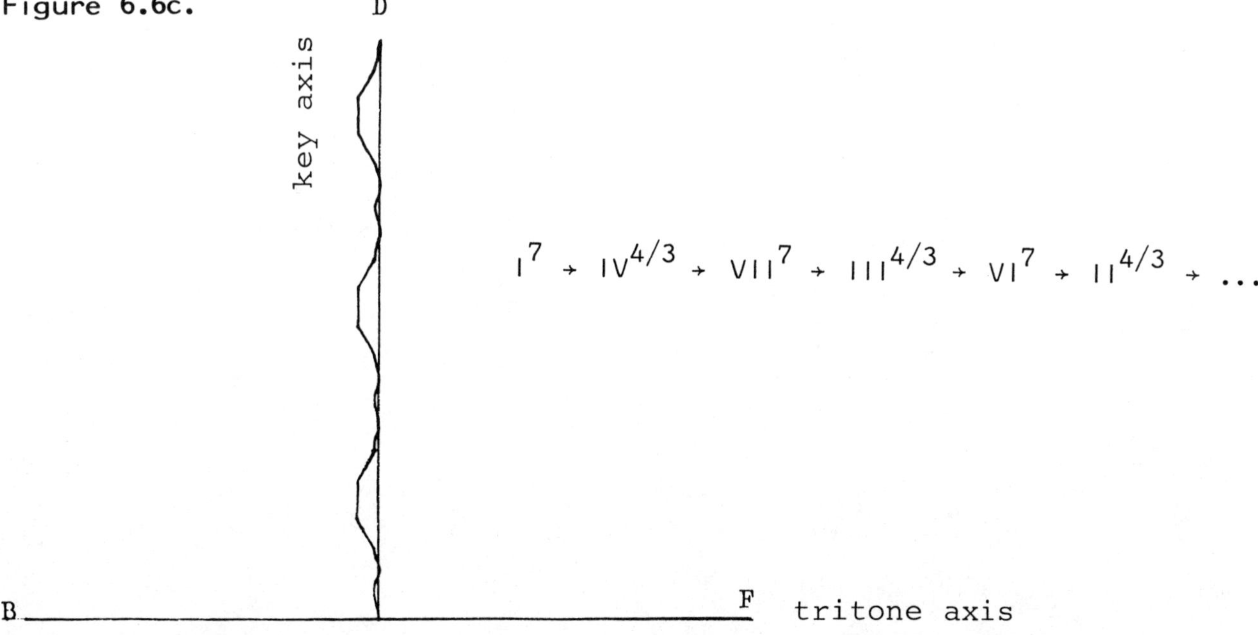

Figure 6.7.

**Bach Chorale No. 3:** *"Ach Gott, vom Himmel sieh' darein."* Direction is a good indicator of key.

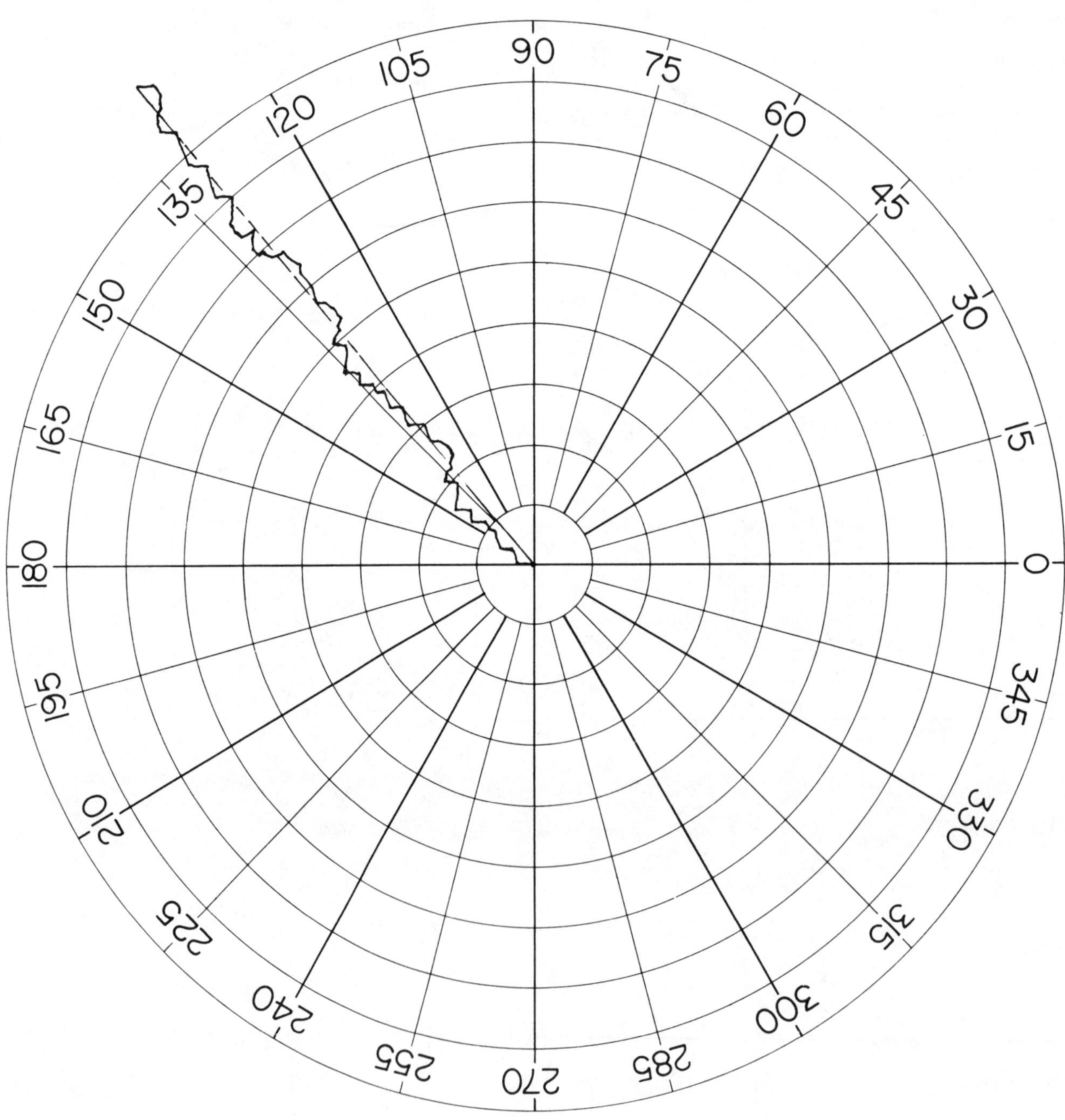

**Figure 6.8a.**

A mariner's compass card showing the 32 points of direction and the 360 degrees of the circle.

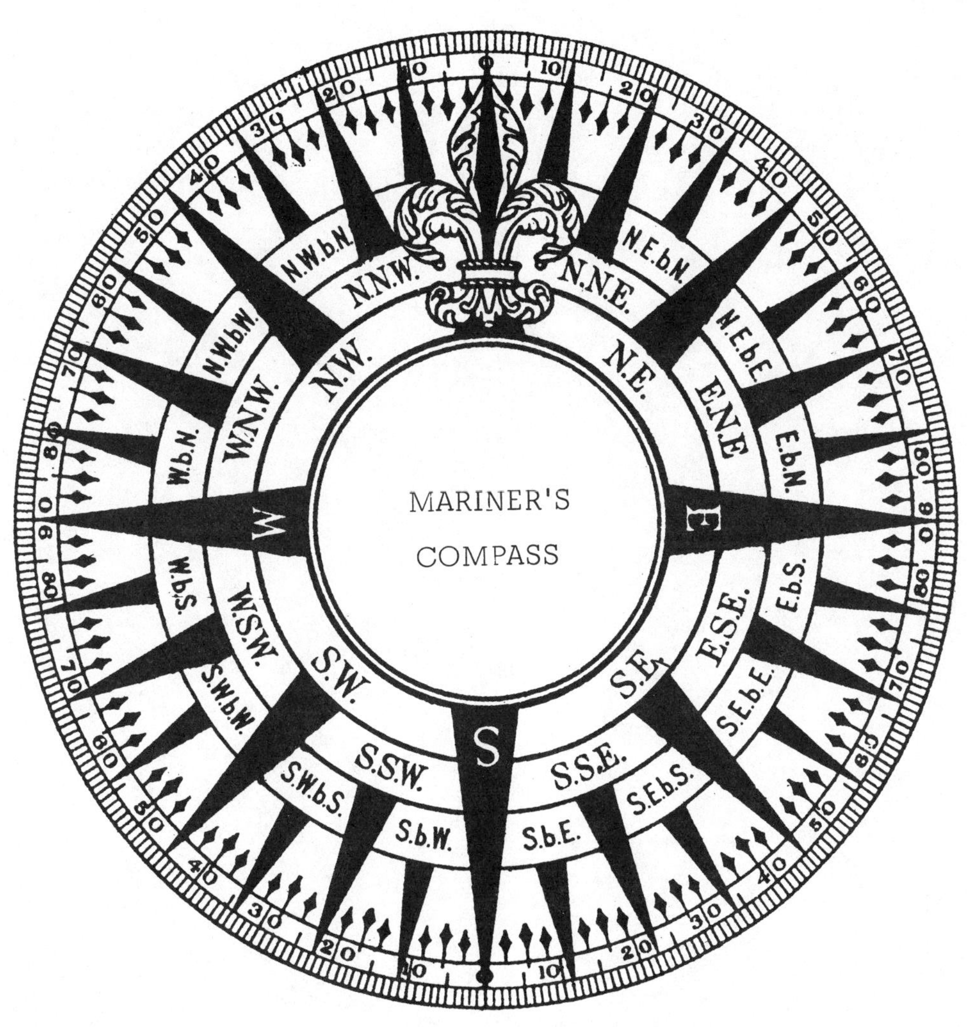

Figure 6.8b.

Navigation plot of an attempt to photograph a bottom mounted acoustic array.

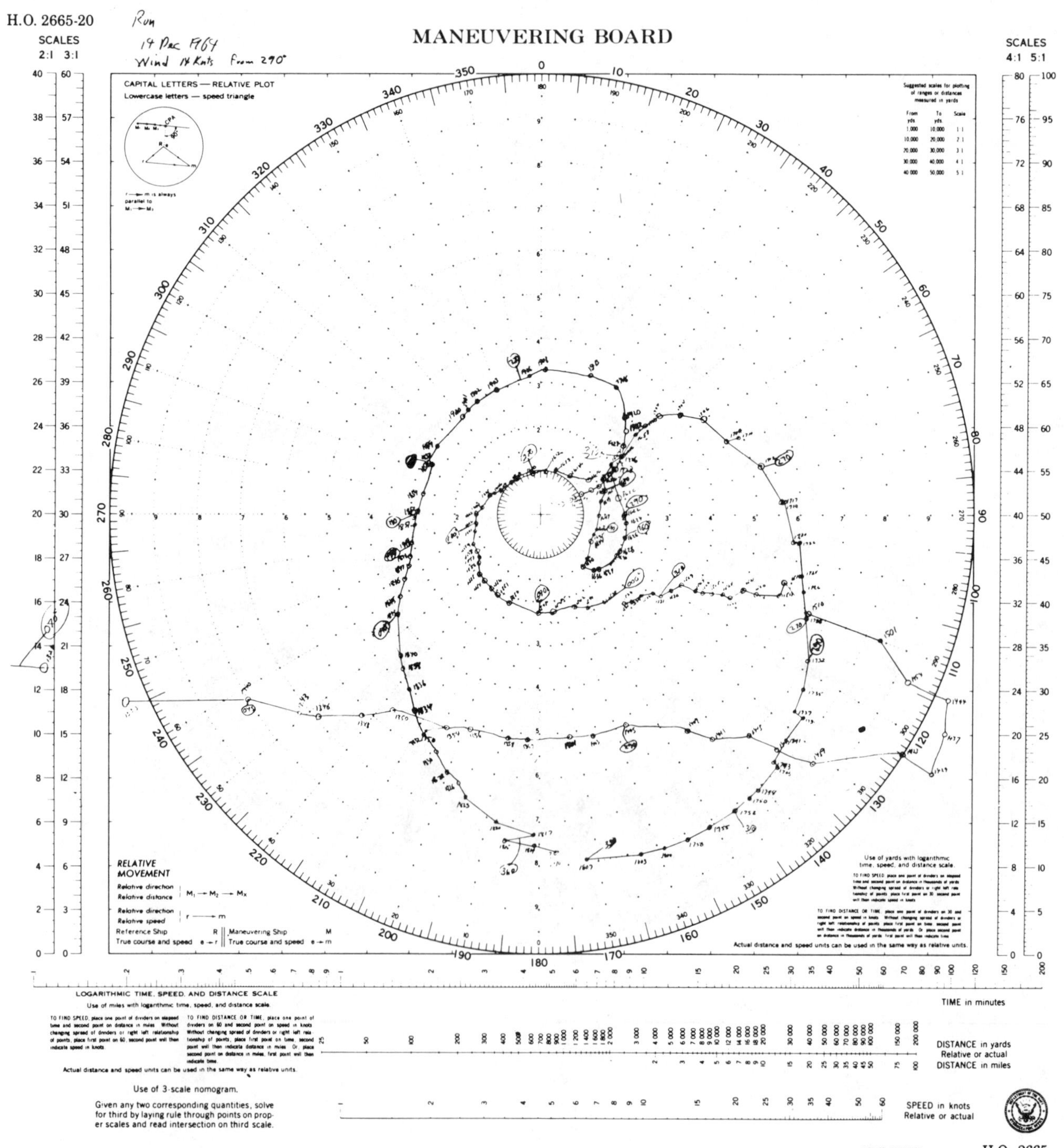

## EXERCISES

**6.1** What meanings have the following nautical terms: (1) constant helming, (2) leg, (3) zig, (4) bearing, (5) range, (6) azimuth, (7) traverse sailing, (8) line of position, (9) dead reckoning position, (10) tack, (11) fix, and (12) course line? Do they have musical analogues?

**6.2** Have all diatonic scales regions of influence?

**6.3** Calculate the azimuth angle coverage for each characteristic Busoni scale listed in Table III of Chapter 2.

**6.4** Musical structures whose resultant vectors coincide have the same amplitude and phase. They are said to be "in phase" and to be of the same "tonality." Those musical structures whose resultant vectors are symmetrically located with respect to the origin have the same amplitude and opposite phase. They are said to be "$180^{\circ}$ out of phase" and to be of the "opposite tonality." Prove the following: **(a)** A chord is of the same tonality as itself and any balanced chord combined. **(b)** A harmony and its complement are of opposite tonality. **(c)** A charm and its negative are of opposite tonality. **(d)** The negative of a complement harmony equals the complement of a negative harmony. **(e)** A harmony and its negative complement are of the same tonality.

**6.5** A pentatonic scale sector is symmetrically embedded in the C major halfplane. What is its azimuth coverage in degrees of arc? What is its key axis? Does it have a tritone axis? In what sense is it more restricted than its symmetric extension to a major key? Wherein lies its strength? (Hint: Apply statement (e) above; check with statement (b).)

**6.6** The possible reaches of a harmony

$$H = \{T_{j_1}, T_{j_2}, \ldots, T_{j_n}\}$$

under N-tuplings are given by the expression

$$R(H) = \{a_{j_1}T_{j_1} + a_{j_2}T_{j_2} + \ldots + a_{j_n}T_{j_n} :$$

$$a_{j_n} \text{ nonnegative integers } \leq N\}.$$

Graph this set, which is a convex cone, for H = {C,E,G} and N = 2, that is, permitting at most doublings. What is the azimuth coverage of R({C,E,G}) in degrees and in radians?

**6.7** Examine the variants of the well-known tune "Yankee Doodle" given in **Grove's Dictionary** [1] using vectors to determine the influence of small differences or melodic perturbations on track. Apply mathematical techniques to establish nearness or neighborliness of the variants.

## PROJECTION

At any particular moment in the performance of a musical composition the entire previous history of motion of the composition point has relevance for determining key relationships. Usually key sector penetration begins with the very first component and the sector selection is immediately reinforced by the next few components. Therefore, it would seem that the number of notes required to establish the key in such a case would be quite small. Nevertheless, to reach a clearcut decision regarding the key is a logical impossibility, despite the availability of perfect knowledge of the key sector, simply because the sectors are all shared by different major and minor keys. Because this fact has never been truly understood, there are many examples of academic debate concerning the probable intended key of a large assortment of particular musical passages.

It is possible to solve a related problem and to produce a key profile, with relatively few computer instructions, using a projection technique equivalent to forming an **in-**

ner product [2] of each ensuing composition vector with every possible major and/or minor key axis. (Minor key axes are derived in Chapter 7.) The resulting set of profiles tells at a glance the extent of key indebtedness at each stage of the composition. A large positive value somewhere along the profile indicates that the composition is more deeply committed to that key than does a small positive value. A zero value indicates key neutrality; a negative value, an antagonistic relationship. For clarity, however, negative values--which are redundant--will be suppressed.

The polar chart in Fig. 6.9b provides a quick look into the hidden key relationships of the opening measures of Beethoven's **First Symphony**.

The trajectory initally proceeds in the direction 37.369°; this heading is the phase of the first tonality, which is imparted by the tonal impulse 3C+G. (The formula for calculating the tonal impulse is derived in a later section.) Next the trajectory turns slightly to the right. This movement produces a new heading 17.374°, which corresponds to the phase of the second tonality, caused by the impulse 3F+2G♭. At this point an intermediate stage is reached in the progressive change of the tonal pattern. A shift in phase abruptly alters the course to the left and brings the composition point from the sector centered upon note C into the sector centered upon note G. In traversing this segment the composition point must cross the sector centered on the interval CG. Thus, in turn the composition point lies in the B♭ major, G minor, and F major key sectors. A different direction is taken during the message frame of each component as the trajectory slowly turns and proceeds outbound until the excerpt concludes with a little flurry of activity.

**Figure 6.9a.**

When extended to eight measures, the composition trajectory pictured in the next panel is seen to finish two cycles of a roughly sinusoidal oscillation about the trend line. Accordingly, it may be conjectured that in a given context a particular chord is a "rest" chord if it brings the composition back onto the established course.

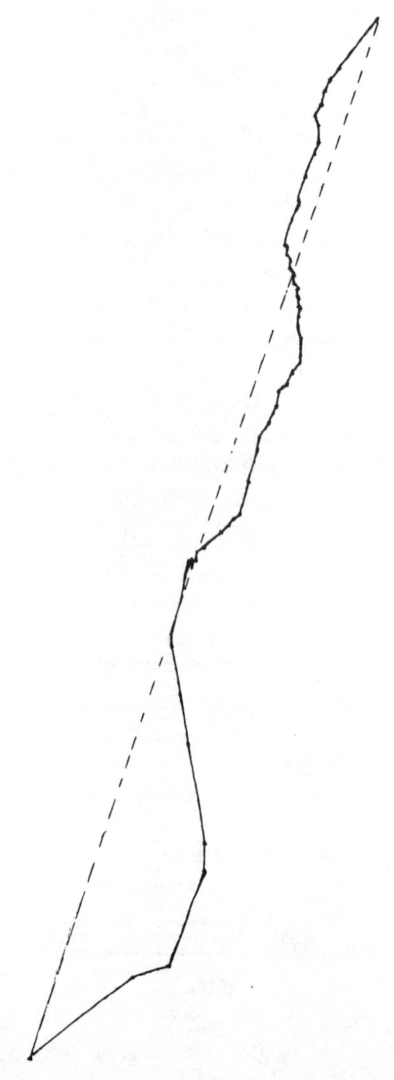

**Figure 6.9b.**
The composition trajectory for the first four measures of Beethoven's "First Symphony" (as transcribed for piano) graphed in polar coordinates.

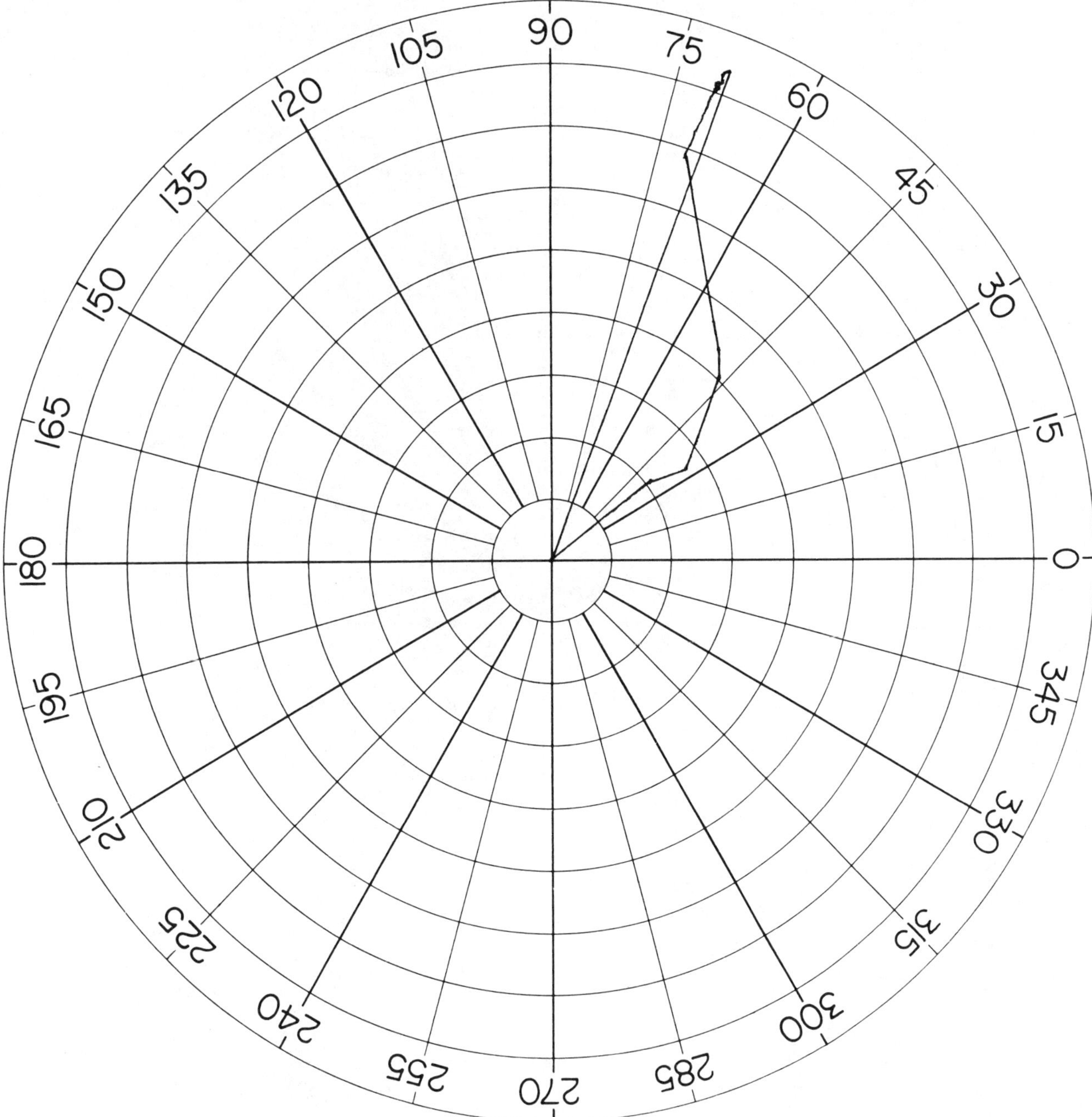


To construct a key profile, compute the projection of each successive composition vector **r** on various key axes. This can be done either by calculating inner products or graphically, as shown in Fig. 6.10, by dropping perpendiculars from the tip R of the composition vector to each key axis in turn to determine the component of **r** along this key axis. Because of the uniform spacing between pairs of adjacent key axes, the set of successive key profiles can be regarded as a family of sinusoidal functions. This representation is the subject of Fig. 6.11. By this means the interplay of competing key involvements is revealed. Certainly, construction of a set of key profiles results in a more dynamic conception of what is going on musically than does the wishful pursuit of such an impossible objective as trying to determine key uniquely.

Figure 6.10

The heavy line segments are the projections along the key axes of the composition vector at the end of the seventh nonsilent component. The outer endpoints of these segments all lie on a circle, called the "circle of projection."

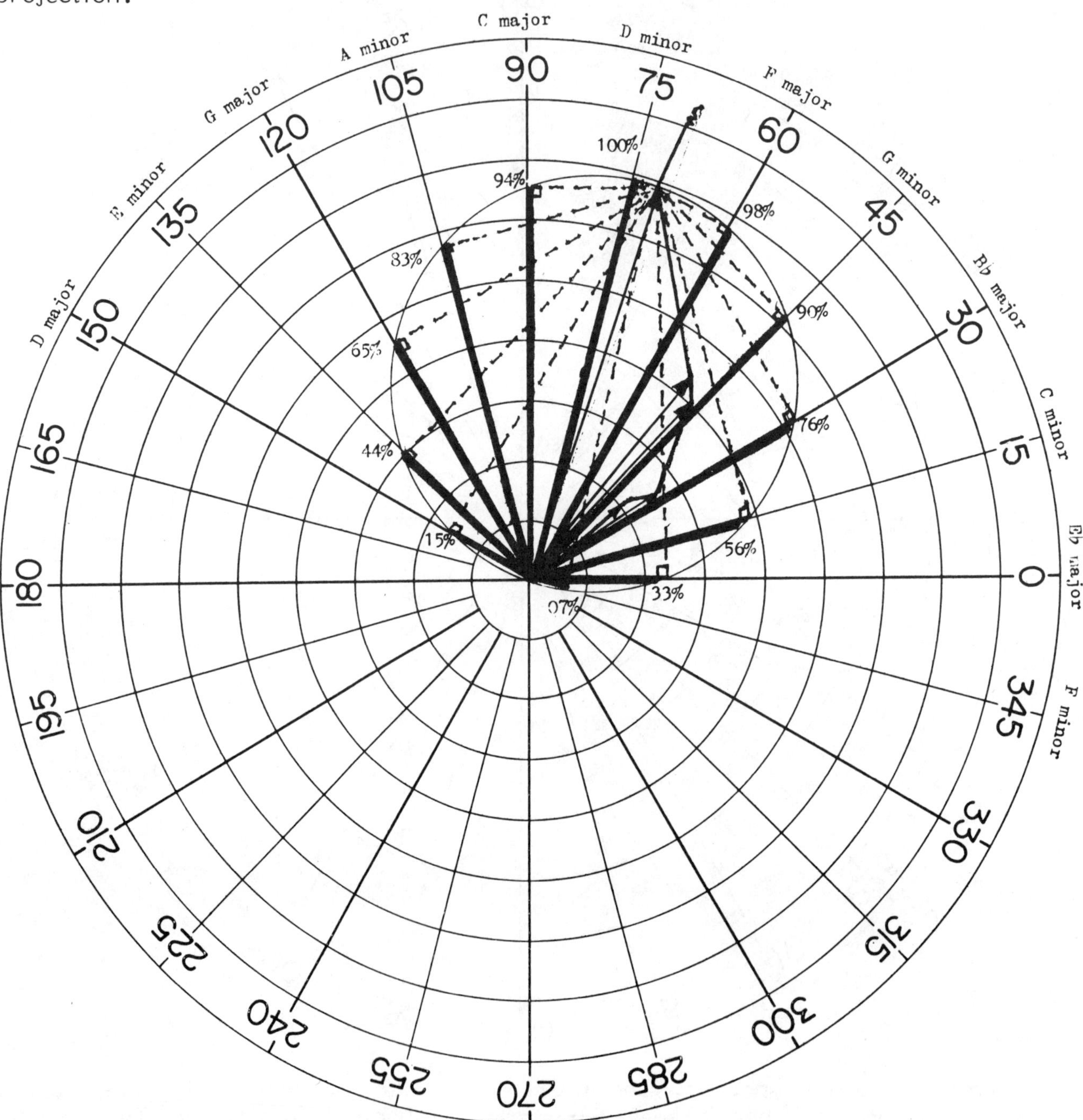


An interesting function called the "absolute penetration" $\alpha$ of the composition point p relative to the major and minor key axes

$$k_1, k_2, \ldots, k_{24}$$

is shown in Fig. 6.12. It is computed using the formula

$$\alpha = 10 \log_{10} r \cos(\theta - k),$$

where the quantity $r \cos(\theta - k)$ represents the projection of the composition vector r upon each of the unit vectors $\hat{k}_1, \hat{k}_2, \ldots, \hat{k}_{24}$ along the 24 key axes. Absolute penetration varies with the position of the composition vector at distinct points of the trajectory.

**Figure 6.11**

In the broadest of terms, it appears from these key profiles that measures one, two, and three are 54% to 94%, and measures four, five, six, seven, and eight are 93% to 96%, in the key of C major.

100% locus

| | Hb | Ab | f | Eb | c | Bb | g | F | d | C | a | G | e | D |
|---|---|---|---|---|---|---|---|---|---|---|---|---|---|---|
| 00 | 13 | 30 | 61 | 79 | 92 | 99 | 99 | 92 | 79 | 61 | 30 | 13 | | |
| 01 | 21 | 46 | 67 | 84 | 95 | 00 | 98 | 89 | 74 | 54 | 31 | 05 | | |
| 02 | | 24 | 48 | 69 | 85 | 96 | 00 | 97 | 88 | 72 | 52 | 28 | 02 | |
| 03 | | 17 | 42 | 64 | 81 | 94 | 00 | 99 | 91 | 77 | 53 | 35 | 10 | |
| 04 | | | 21 | 45 | 67 | 84 | 95 | 00 | 98 | 89 | 74 | 54 | 31 | 05 |
| 05 | | | 13 | 39 | 61 | 80 | 93 | 99 | 99 | 92 | 79 | 61 | 30 | 13 |
| 06 | | | 07 | 33 | 56 | 76 | 90 | 98 | 00 | 94 | 83 | 65 | 44 | 19 |
| 07 | | | 05 | 31 | 55 | 74 | 89 | 98 | 00 | 95 | 84 | 67 | 45 | 21 |
| 08 | | | 06 | 31 | 55 | 75 | 89 | 98 | 00 | 95 | 84 | 66 | 45 | 20 |
| 09 | | | 06 | 32 | 55 | 75 | 90 | 98 | 00 | 95 | 83 | 66 | 44 | 20 |
| 10 | | | 05 | 31 | 54 | 74 | 89 | 98 | 00 | 95 | 84 | 67 | 46 | 21 |
| 11 | | | 07 | 32 | 56 | 75 | 90 | 98 | 00 | 95 | 83 | 66 | 44 | 19 |
| 12 | | | 06 | 32 | 55 | 75 | 90 | 98 | 00 | 95 | 83 | 66 | 45 | 20 |
| 13 | | | 07 | 33 | 56 | 76 | 90 | 98 | 00 | 94 | 83 | 65 | 44 | 19 |
| 14 | | | 09 | 35 | 58 | 77 | 91 | 99 | 00 | 94 | 82 | 64 | 42 | 17 |
| 15 | | | 10 | 36 | 59 | 78 | 91 | 99 | 99 | 93 | 81 | 63 | 41 | 16 |
| 16 | | | 11 | 36 | 59 | 78 | 91 | 99 | 99 | 93 | 81 | 63 | 41 | 16 |
| 17 | | | 11 | 37 | 59 | 78 | 92 | 99 | 99 | 93 | 80 | 62 | 40 | 15 |
| 18 | | | 11 | 36 | 59 | 78 | 91 | 99 | 99 | 93 | 81 | 63 | 41 | 15 |
| 19 | | | 10 | 35 | 58 | 77 | 91 | 99 | 99 | 93 | 81 | 63 | 41 | 16 |
| 20 | | | 10 | 35 | 58 | 77 | 91 | 99 | 00 | 94 | 81 | 64 | 41 | 16 |
| 21 | | | 10 | 36 | 59 | 78 | 91 | 99 | 99 | 93 | 81 | 63 | 41 | 16 |
| 22 | | | 10 | 36 | 59 | 78 | 91 | 99 | 99 | 93 | 81 | 63 | 41 | 16 |
| 23 | | | 10 | 35 | 58 | 77 | 91 | 99 | 99 | 94 | 81 | 63 | 41 | 16 |
| 24 | | | 11 | 36 | 59 | 78 | 91 | 99 | 99 | 93 | 81 | 63 | 40 | 15 |
| 25 | | | 11 | 36 | 59 | 78 | 91 | 99 | 99 | 93 | 81 | 63 | 40 | 15 |
| 26 | | | 11 | 37 | 59 | 78 | 92 | 99 | 99 | 93 | 80 | 62 | 40 | 15 |
| 27 | | | 11 | 36 | 59 | 78 | 92 | 99 | 99 | 93 | 81 | 63 | 40 | 15 |
| 28 | | | 10 | 35 | 58 | 77 | 91 | 99 | 00 | 94 | 81 | 64 | 41 | 17 |
| 29 | | | 09 | 34 | 58 | 77 | 91 | 99 | 00 | 94 | 82 | 64 | 42 | 17 |
| 30 | | | 09 | 34 | 57 | 77 | 91 | 99 | 00 | 94 | 82 | 64 | 42 | 17 |
| 31 | | | 09 | 34 | 57 | 77 | 91 | 99 | 00 | 94 | 82 | 64 | 42 | 17 |
| 32 | | | 08 | 34 | 57 | 76 | 90 | 99 | 00 | 94 | 82 | 65 | 43 | 18 |
| 33 | | | 08 | 34 | 57 | 76 | 90 | 99 | 00 | 94 | 82 | 65 | 43 | 18 |
| 34 | | | 08 | 33 | 56 | 76 | 90 | 98 | 00 | 94 | 83 | 65 | 43 | 18 |
| 35 | | | 08 | 33 | 56 | 76 | 90 | 99 | 00 | 94 | 83 | 65 | 43 | 19 |
| 36 | | | 07 | 32 | 56 | 75 | 90 | 98 | 00 | 95 | 83 | 66 | 44 | 19 |
| 37 | | | 07 | 32 | 56 | 75 | 90 | 98 | 00 | 95 | 83 | 66 | 44 | 20 |
| 38 | | | 06 | 31 | 55 | 75 | 89 | 98 | 00 | 95 | 84 | 67 | 45 | 20 |
| 39 | | | 06 | 31 | 55 | 75 | 89 | 98 | 00 | 95 | 84 | 67 | 45 | 20 |
| 40 | | | 05 | 30 | 54 | 74 | 89 | 98 | 00 | 95 | 84 | 67 | 46 | 21 |
| 41 | | | 05 | 30 | 54 | 74 | 89 | 98 | 00 | 95 | 84 | 67 | 46 | 21 |
| 42 | | | 04 | 30 | 54 | 74 | 89 | 98 | 00 | 95 | 84 | 68 | 46 | 22 |
| 43 | | | 04 | 30 | 54 | 74 | 89 | 98 | 00 | 95 | 84 | 68 | 46 | 22 |
| 44 | | | 04 | 30 | 54 | 74 | 89 | 98 | 00 | 95 | 84 | 68 | 46 | 22 |
| 45 | | | 04 | 30 | 54 | 74 | 89 | 98 | 00 | 95 | 84 | 67 | 46 | 22 |
| 46 | | | 04 | 30 | 54 | 74 | 89 | 98 | 00 | 95 | 84 | 68 | 46 | 22 |
| 47 | | | 04 | 30 | 54 | 74 | 89 | 98 | 00 | 95 | 84 | 68 | 46 | 22 |
| 48 | | | 04 | 30 | 54 | 74 | 89 | 98 | 00 | 95 | 84 | 68 | 46 | 22 |
| 49 | | | 04 | 30 | 54 | 74 | 89 | 98 | 00 | 95 | 84 | 68 | 46 | 22 |
| 50 | | | 04 | 30 | 53 | 74 | 89 | 98 | 00 | 95 | 84 | 68 | 46 | 22 |
| 51 | | | 04 | 29 | 53 | 73 | 88 | 97 | 00 | 96 | 85 | 68 | 47 | 22 |
| 52 | | | 03 | 29 | 53 | 73 | 88 | 97 | 00 | 96 | 85 | 69 | 47 | 23 |
| 53 | | | 04 | 29 | 53 | 73 | 88 | 97 | 00 | 96 | 85 | 68 | 47 | 22 |
| 54 | | | 03 | 29 | 53 | 73 | 88 | 97 | 00 | 96 | 85 | 68 | 47 | 23 |
| 55 | | | 04 | 29 | 53 | 73 | 88 | 97 | 00 | 96 | 85 | 68 | 47 | 22 |
| 56 | | | 04 | 30 | 54 | 74 | 89 | 98 | 00 | 95 | 84 | 68 | 46 | 22 |
| 57 | | | 06 | 32 | 55 | 75 | 90 | 98 | 00 | 95 | 83 | 66 | 45 | 20 |

← 7th nonsilent component (row 06)

100% locus

| | Gb | Ab | f | Eb | a | Bb | g | F | d | C | a | G | e | D |
|---|---|---|---|---|---|---|---|---|---|---|---|---|---|---|
| 02 | 03 | 04 | 06 | 07 | 03 | 03 | 03 | 09 | 07 | 06 | 04 | 03 | | |
| 01 | 03 | 06 | 08 | 09 | 02 | 09 | 01 | 09 | 01 | 07 | 04 | ·03 | | |
| 02 | | 05 | 03 | 10 | 11 | 11 | 11 | 11 | 11 | 10 | 04 | 06 | ·04 | |
| 03 | | 04 | 03 | 10 | 11 | 11 | 12 | 12 | 11 | 10 | 09 | 07 | 01 | |
| 04 | | | 06 | 09 | 11 | 12 | 12 | 13 | 13 | 12 | 11 | 12 | 08 | 02 |
| 05 | | | 04 | 09 | 11 | 12 | 13 | 13 | 13 | 13 | 12 | 11 | 09 | 04 |
| 06 | | | 02 | 09 | 11 | 12 | 13 | 13 | 14 | 13 | 13 | 12 | 10 | 06 |
| 07 | | | 03 | 09 | 12 | 13 | 14 | 14 | 14 | 14 | 13 | 13 | 11 | 07 |
| 08 | | | 02 | 09 | 12 | 13 | 14 | 14 | 14 | 14 | 14 | 13 | 11 | 07 |
| 09 | | | 02 | 09 | 12 | 13 | 14 | 14 | 14 | 14 | 13 | 12 | 11 | 07 |
| 10 | | | 01 | 09 | 12 | 13 | 14 | 14 | 14 | 14 | 14 | 13 | 11 | 08 |
| 11 | | | 03 | 09 | 12 | 13 | 14 | 14 | 14 | 14 | 14 | 13 | 11 | 07 |
| 12 | | | 04 | 09 | 12 | 13 | 14 | 14 | 14 | 14 | 14 | 13 | 11 | 07 |
| 13 | | | 03 | 10 | 12 | 13 | 14 | 15 | 14 | 14 | 14 | 13 | 11 | 07 |
| 14 | | | 04 | 10 | 12 | 13 | 14 | 15 | 15 | 14 | 14 | 13 | 11 | 07 |
| 15 | | | 05 | 10 | 12 | 14 | 14 | 15 | 15 | 14 | 14 | 13 | 11 | 07 |
| 16 | | | 05 | 10 | 12 | 14 | 14 | 15 | 15 | 14 | 14 | 13 | 11 | 07 |
| 17 | | | 05 | 10 | 13 | 14 | 14 | 15 | 15 | 14 | 14 | 13 | 11 | 07 |
| 18 | | | 05 | 11 | 13 | 14 | 15 | 15 | 15 | 15 | 14 | 13 | 11 | 07 |
| 19 | | | 05 | 11 | 13 | 14 | 15 | 15 | 15 | 15 | 14 | 13 | 11 | 07 |
| 20 | | | 05 | 11 | 13 | 14 | 15 | 15 | 15 | 15 | 14 | 13 | 12 | 07 |
| 21 | | | 06 | 11 | 13 | 14 | 15 | 15 | 15 | 15 | 15 | 13 | 12 | 07 |
| 22 | | | 06 | 11 | 13 | 14 | 15 | 16 | 16 | 15 | 15 | 14 | 12 | 08 |
| 23 | | | 06 | 11 | 13 | 15 | 15 | 16 | 16 | 15 | 15 | 14 | 12 | 08 |
| 24 | | | 06 | 11 | 13 | 15 | 15 | 16 | 16 | 15 | 15 | 14 | 12 | 08 |
| 25 | | | 06 | 11 | 14 | 15 | 15 | 16 | 16 | 15 | 15 | 14 | 12 | 08 |
| 26 | | | 06 | 11 | 14 | 15 | 15 | 16 | 16 | 16 | 15 | 14 | 12 | 08 |
| 27 | | | 06 | 11 | 14 | 15 | 16 | 16 | 16 | 16 | 15 | 14 | 12 | 08 |
| 28 | | | 06 | 11 | 14 | 15 | 16 | 16 | 16 | 16 | 15 | 14 | 12 | 08 |
| 29 | | | 06 | 11 | 14 | 15 | 16 | 16 | 16 | 16 | 15 | 14 | 12 | 08 |
| 30 | | | 06 | 11 | 14 | 15 | 16 | 16 | 16 | 16 | 15 | 14 | 12 | 08 |
| 31 | | | 07 | 11 | 14 | 15 | 16 | 16 | 16 | 16 | 15 | 14 | 12 | 09 |
| 32 | | | 05 | 11 | 14 | 15 | 16 | 16 | 16 | 16 | 15 | 14 | 12 | 05 |
| 33 | | | 05 | 11 | 14 | 15 | 16 | 16 | 16 | 16 | 15 | 14 | 13 | 09 |
| 34 | | | 05 | 11 | 14 | 15 | 16 | 16 | 16 | 16 | 15 | 14 | 13 | 09 |
| 35 | | | 05 | 11 | 14 | 15 | 16 | 16 | 16 | 16 | 15 | 14 | 13 | 09 |
| 36 | | | 04 | 11 | 14 | 15 | 16 | 16 | 16 | 16 | 15 | 14 | 13 | 09 |
| 37 | | | 04 | 11 | 14 | 15 | 16 | 16 | 16 | 16 | 16 | 15 | 13 | 09· |
| 38 | | | 04 | 11 | 14 | 15 | 16 | 16 | 16 | 16 | 16 | 15 | 13 | 09 |
| 39 | | | 04 | 11 | 14 | 15 | 16 | 16 | 16 | 16 | 16 | 15 | 13 | 09 |
| 40 | | | 03 | 11 | 14 | 15 | 16 | 16 | 16 | 16 | 16 | 15 | 13 | 10 |
| 41 | | | 02 | 11 | 14 | 15 | 16 | 16 | 16 | 16 | 16 | 15 | 13 | 10 |
| 42 | | | 03 | 11 | 14 | 15 | 16 | 16 | 16 | 16 | 16 | 15 | 13 | 10 |
| 43 | | | 03 | 11 | 14 | 15 | 16 | 16 | 17 | 16 | 16 | 15 | 13 | 10 |
| 44 | | | 03 | 11 | 14 | 15 | 16 | 17 | 17 | 16 | 16 | 15 | 13 | 10 |
| 45 | | | 03 | 11 | 14 | 15 | 16 | 17 | 17 | 16 | 16 | 15 | 13 | 10 |
| 46 | | | 03 | 11 | 14 | 15 | 16 | 17 | 17 | 16 | 16 | 15 | 13 | 10 |
| 47 | | | 03 | 12 | 14 | 15 | 16 | 17 | 17 | 17 | 16 | 15 | 13 | 10 |
| 48 | | | 03 | 12 | 14 | 16 | 16 | 17 | 17 | 17 | 16 | 15 | 14 | 10 |
| 49 | | | 03 | 12 | 14 | 16 | 16 | 17 | 17 | 17 | 16 | 15 | 14 | 10 |
| 50 | | | 03 | 12 | 14 | 16 | 16 | 17 | 17 | 17 | 16 | 15 | 14 | 10 |
| 51 | | | 03 | 12 | 14 | 15 | 16 | 17 | 17 | 17 | 16 | 15 | 14 | 10 |
| 52 | | | 02 | 12 | 14 | 16 | 17 | 17 | 17 | 17 | 16 | 15 | 14 | 11 |
| 53 | | | 03 | 12 | 14 | 16 | 17 | 17 | 17 | 17 | 16 | 15 | 14 | 11 |
| 54 | | | 03 | 12 | 14 | 16 | 17 | 17 | 17 | 17 | 16 | 16 | 14 | 11 |
| 55 | | | 03 | 12 | 14 | 16 | 17 | 17 | 17 | 17 | 17 | 16 | 14 | 11 |
| 56 | | | 04 | 12 | 15 | 16 | 17 | 17 | 17 | 17 | 17 | 16 | 14 | 11 |
| 57 | | | 05 | 13 | 15 | 15 | 17 | 17 | 18 | 17 | 17 | 16 | 14 | 11 |

Figure 6.12a

The straight vertical sides of this topographic view, provided by a plotter printout of the absolute penetration function, support the conclusion that little or no modulation occurs after the opening two measures. It is evident from the values that the "highest ground" is attained in the key of D minor, with both F major and C major being strong contenders.

Figure 6.12b

Presented here are curves depicting the absolute penetration function, historically developed along the major key axes. The dots at the top mark the component interstices. The parallelism obtained for measures four through eight indicates the tonal nature of the work and consequently attests to the validity of the mathematical model.

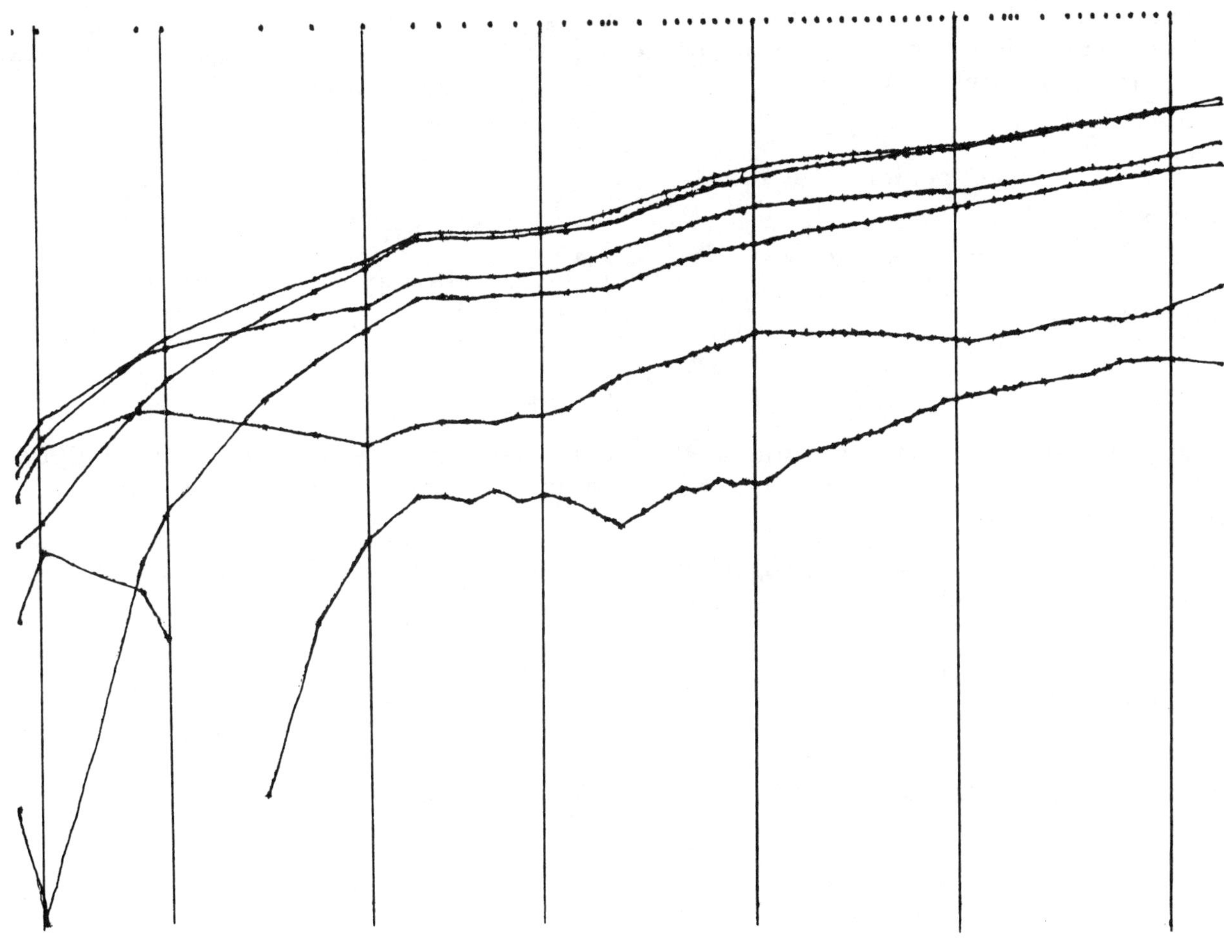

EXERCISES

6.8 A question that arises frequently in music analysis concerns the influence of chords or chord constituents upon the tonality and hence upon the key. Shirlaw [3] gives two examples of passages that are throughout in A minor despite the problematic appearance of G natural in one of them. Is he right in this determination? Return to this problem after reading Chapter 7.

MODULATION

There is some confusion and occasional disagreement among music educators and theorists concerning the meaning of modulation and associated concepts and terminology. The opposing views of Walter Piston [4] and Roger Sessions [5] on what constitutes a bona fide modulation are representative of two legitimate viewpoints. The discussion that follows may shed additional light on this old question, and the definition proposed for **average modulation** provides an interesting justification of the earlier meanings of the term modulation used by these two authors.

In the present book "modulation" is defined as the rate at which tonality changes, or as the change in tonality per unit time. Thus modulation also is a vector quantity. In exact analogy to the definition of average tonality given previously, the "average modulation" over any time interval $\Delta t$ equals the change of tonality during the interval divided by the length of that interval. The time rate of change of tonality of the composition point p during the time interval between

$$t_o \text{ and } t_1 = t_o + \Delta t,$$

during which time period its tonality changes from

$$v_o \text{ to } v_1 = v_o + \Delta v$$

is given by

$$\frac{\Delta v}{\Delta t} = \frac{v_1 - v_0}{t_1 - t_0}.$$

Here, $v_1$ is the tonality at the end of time interval $\Delta t$, and $v_0$ is the tonality at the beginning.

Therefore, the average modulation during the time interval $\Delta t$ is defined as

$$a_{av} = \frac{\Delta v}{\Delta t} = \frac{v_1 - v_0}{t_1 - t_0},$$

a vector whose direction is that of $\Delta v$ and whose magnitude is the magnitude of $\Delta v$ divided by $\Delta t$. In other words,

Average tonality EQUALS $\frac{\text{Distance traversed by the composition,}}{\text{Time elapsed}}$

and

Average modulation EQUALS $\frac{\text{Change in tonality}}{\text{Time elapsed}}$.

Derivatives other than the first are referred to as "higher derivatives" of a function. By elementary calculus the **instantaneous tonality** of the composition point has been defined as $v = \frac{dr}{dt}$, which is a first derivative. As modulation bears the same relation to tonality that tonality bears to displacement, the "instantaneous modulation" is defined as the limit of the average modulation as the time increment $\Delta t$ approaches zero.

$$\mathbf{a} = \lim_{\Delta t \to 0} a_{av} = \lim_{\Delta t \to 0} \frac{\Delta v}{\Delta t} = \frac{dv}{dt}.$$

As the time rate of change of tonality is modulation, the time rate of change of the time rate of change of displacement is again the modulation. In mathematical notation

$$\mathbf{a} = \frac{dv}{dt} = \frac{d^2r}{dt^2}.$$

Thus, modulation is the second derivative of the displacement with respect to time and the first derivative of the tonality with respect to time. That is, write

$$\dot{r} \text{ for } \frac{dr}{dt} \text{ and } \ddot{r} \text{ for } \frac{d^2r}{dt^2},$$

then modulation may be put concisely $\mathbf{a} = \dot{v} = \ddot{r}$.

EXAMPLE

Consider the resolution GBDF → CGCE in quarter notes. Schematically,

```
         → F →
gained { → D → }  lost
         → B →
         → G → G →
             → E →
    gained { → C → }  lost
             → C →
```

(See table on next page.)

The first tonality to be analyzed is G + B + D + F, which collapses to G + D. The next and last tonality is C + G + C + E, which becomes C + G + D. The instantaneous modulation evaluated precisely at time t = 0.250 is given by

$$\mathbf{a}(t) = \mathbf{a}(0.250)$$

$$= \lim_{\Delta t \to 0} \frac{v_2 - v_1}{\Delta t}$$

$$= \lim_{\Delta t \to 0} \frac{C+G+D-(G+D)}{\Delta t}$$

$$= \lim_{\Delta t \to 0} \frac{C}{\Delta t} = \infty .$$

Such infinite values of the instantaneous modulation always will arise at points of discontinuity of the tonality function. But this apparent flaw occurs naturally in manuscript analysis.

| TIME $t$ | DISPLACEMENT $r$ | AVERAGE TONALITY $\frac{r_i - r_{i-1}}{t}$ | AVERAGE MODULATION $\frac{v_i - v_{i-1}}{t}$ |
|---|---|---|---|
| 0.000 | $r_0 = 0$ | $v_0 = 0$ | $a_0 = 0$ |
| 0.250 | $r_1 = \frac{G+B+D+F}{4}$ | $v_1 = G+B+D+F$ | $a_1 = 4(G+D)$ |
| | $= \frac{G+D}{4}$ | $= G+D$ | |
| 0.500 | $r_2 = \frac{G+D}{4} + \frac{C+G+C+E}{4}$ | $v_2 = C+G+C+E$ | $a_2 = 4C$ |
| | $= \frac{C+2G+2D}{4}$ | $= C+G+D$ | |
| 0.750 | $r_3 = \frac{C+2G+2D}{4}$ | $v_3 = 0$ | $a_3 = -4(C+G+D)$ |

## EXERCISES

**6.9** The music of Johann Sebastian Bach exhibits an appreciable number of cadences. Gannett's useful book [6] gives operational data on this. Assuming that the tones obey the parallelogram law, calculate the displacement for selected examples as a function of time and plot it. From the shape of the curve, deduce values for the average tonality and average modulation.

**6.10** Explain how concepts of average modulation and instantaneous modulation strengthen and weld together the apparently conflicting points of view of Piston and Sessions regarding the nature of modulation.

**6.11** The broken chord C,E,G,C, G,E,C,C is played (up and down) in eighth notes. What is the instantaneous modulation approaching the end of the measure? What is the total modulation?

**6.12** The chromatic scale (ascending) is played from C to D♯ inclusive in 0.5 seconds. Find the average tonality. Find the average modulation.

## TONAL IMPULSE AND MUSICAL MOMENTUM

In many physical situations a very large force F may act on a single particle (for example, a golf ball) during a fairly brief, but nonzero, time interval $\Delta t$. This force may be negligible or zero at all other times, yet produce an observable change in motion at the instant of its application. The sudden blow, which causes the motion, is called an "impulsive force." The concept of an impulsive force is known to every physicist. The same underlying idea also probably is familiar to most musicians. A pianist knows from practical experience that when a key is struck the resulting collision between the felt hammer head and the wire string occurs during a very short time interval. Initially at rest, the string moves only a relatively small distance while the force is acting, but continues to vibrate after contact is broken, because of inertia, until a second damping force is applied. The same thing holds for other percussion instruments, such as the drum or xylophone; the time of impact is very short and the force has a high peak value. An even better example is provided by a switched tone [7], which rises instantly from zero to unit amplitude at the time the key is depressed and drops instantly back to zero when the key is released. The organ signal is approximately a rectangular pulse with instantaneous rise time. The discontinuities occurring at each end of the pulse can be viewed as the impulsive response of a zero-order hold, which can be decomposed into two tandem unit step functions as shown in Fig. 6.13.

Figure 6.13

At impact time an ideal organ tone has a discontinuous tonality. The impulse delivered to set the organ tone sounding can be cancelled only by application of an equal and opposite impulse. Similarly, for manuscript analysis, a musical tone is regarded as resulting from a quick blow of force

$$m\ v\ \delta(t),$$

where the force function $F = F(t)$ has the magnitude $F = |F| = \delta$ of the "Dirac delta function." This function is defined by taking the limit as $\varepsilon \to 0$ of

$$\delta_\varepsilon(t) = \begin{cases} 0, & t \leq t_1 \\ 1/\varepsilon, & t_1 < t < t_1 + \varepsilon \\ 0, & t_1 \leq t. \end{cases}$$

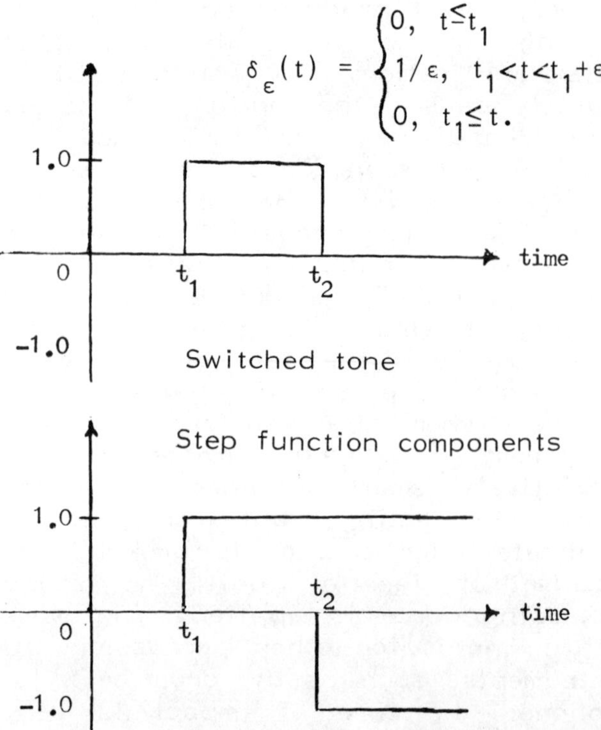


Implicit in the organization of symbols on a printed page of musical text is the assumption that music can be described to a sufficient degree of approximation by a sequence of overlapping rectangular pulse trains. That is, given a number of pulse generators of prescribed frequencies

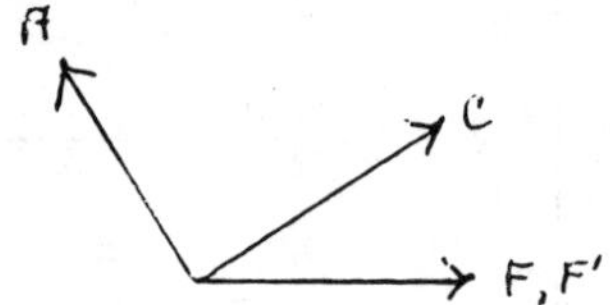


and a timing mechanism or diagram

for cueing organ tones, each level of which may be viewed as a train of box-car pulses

it becomes possible to synthesize music electronically. By attaching a characteristic decay curve to these pulse trains, it is possible to distort or filter the resulting signal in order to mimic the sound of other instruments, such as the piano

For discussions of music analysis based upon the assumption that the tone produced by each particular generator is a rectangular pulse, it is clear that tones do not vary with time. Such analysis is termed "manuscript analysis." In practice, however, the tones from any musical instrument are almost never constant in any parameter. Variations in loudness alone may be caused by room acoustic conditions, the resonance structure of the instrument, or sound equipment instabilities. But the chief source of fluctuation is that of transients due to scraping, plucking, hammering, or blowing. When these real effects are taken into consideration, even slightly, such analysis is termed "performance analysis."

The motion of a particle of mass m along a straight line in some plane under the action of a force **F** is given by the vector equation

$$F = \frac{d(mv)}{dt}.$$

The mechanical interpretation of this equation is that the time rate of change $\frac{d}{dt}$ of the momentum mv equals the unbalanced force **F**. This statement is known as **Newton's second law**. It would be natural to ask whether this equation can be used meaningfully in discussing musical, as well as mechanical problems. The evident success of this analogy rests upon the close identification of the notion of musical modulation with that of mechanical acceleration.

For any given motion of a musical composition, all musical variables (displacement, tonality, and modulation) so far associated with the composition point are functions of time. Although the displacement at a particular point of time has been found to depend on the entire previous history of the composition, the tonality depends on only the actual status of motion associated with the thrust of the music at each specific instant. In the preceding section, the instantaneous tonality (musical velocity) was defined as the quantity

$$v = \frac{dr}{dt}$$

and the instantaneous modulation (musical acceleration) as the quantity

$$a = \frac{dv}{dt} = \frac{d^2r}{dt^2}.$$

Now it will be useful to define two additional quantities, the <u>musical momentum</u> and the <u>tonal impulse</u>.

The "musical momentum" is defined as the quantity

$$p = mv = m\frac{dr}{dt},$$

which is the product of the mass m of the composition point, assumed to be constant, and the tonality. Beginning with the assumption that Newton's second law holds true for music, substitute **p** to obtain

$$F = \frac{dp}{dt} = \frac{d(mv)}{dt} = \frac{d}{dt}\left(m\frac{dr}{dt}\right).$$

Since the mass is assumed constant, it follows that **F** = m**a**. Consequently, the applied force is proportional to the musical modulation. Moreover, it follows that $F = m\frac{dv}{dt}$. This equation states that the applied force is proportional to the time rate of change of the musical tonality. Now, multiply both sides of

$$F = \frac{dp}{dt}$$

by dt, and integrate with respect to time t from $t_1$ to $t_2$ to obtain the resulting equation

$$\int_{t_1}^{t_2} F\,dt = p\Big|_{t_1}^{t_2} = mv\Big|_{t_1}^{t_2}.$$

For an impulsive force **F** this time integral is called the "impulse." Here the impulse lasts for the time interval $\Delta t = t_2 - t_1$. Evaluating the term appearing on the right-hand side of the impulse momentum equation yields

$$\int_{t_1}^{t_2} F dt = mv(t_2) - mv(t_1)$$
$$= mv_2 - mv_1,$$

so that the **mechanical impulse** is equal to the change in momentum between the times $t_1$ and $t_2$. By analogy, the "tonal impulse" is proportional to the change in tonality. Clearly, both the musical momentum **mv** and the tonal impulse $mv_2 - mv_1$ are vector quantities.

Admittedly it is a fiction to assign a mass m to the composition point, but it is a convenient fiction. No further harm is done by putting $m = 1$ as a simplification, even though after setting $mv = v$ musical momentum and tonality become indistinguishable. For the present it suffices to allow the musical momentum to have the same magnitude and direction as the tonality, and even to be expressed in the same physical units. Whenever it becomes necessary to separate the two quantities dimensionally, this can be done easily by attaching a physical unit to musical mass. The "musical speed" of the music is defined as the absolute value $|v| = v$ of the musical velocity, which may be identified also as the amplitude of the tonality.

For musical mass $m = 1$, the impulse momentum equation becomes

$$\int_{t_1}^{t_2} F dt = mv_2 - mv_1$$
$$= m(v_2 - v_1)$$
$$= 1(v_2 - v_1)$$
$$= v_2 - v_1,$$

where $v_2$ and $v_1$ are the tonalities at times $t_2$ and $t_1$, respectively. This equation states that the tonal impulse of a force F which acts during a vanishingly small time interval $\Delta t = t_2 - t_1$ is equal to the resulting change in tonality of the composition point on which the force acts. After experiencing such an impulsive force, the composition point coasts at constant musical velocity until the next path turning point, which comes at the instant the next tonal impulse or "kick" occurs. Generally speaking, the more notes appearing together, the more vigorous the musical motion will be. When the impulse acting on a composition point is zero, the music has a constant tonality. During such periods, the composition point undergoes rectilinear motion. At a turning point of the composition trajectory, the tonal impulse may be found by subtracting vectorially the initial momentum from the terminal momentum. Thus, the impulse can be represented graphically in a vector diagram as

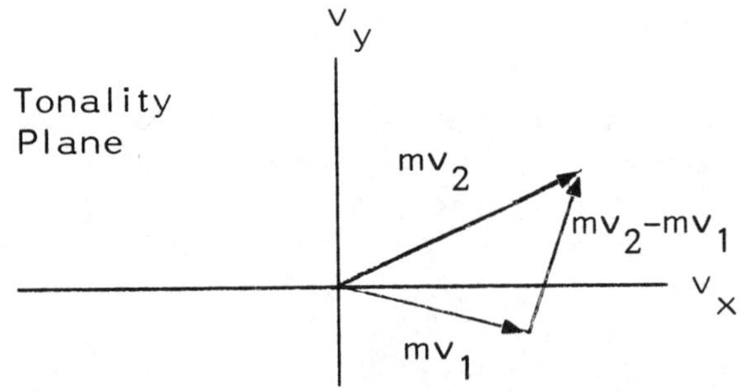


Taking advantage of tonal impulse as an parameter additional to modulation, tonality, and displacement makes it easier to study an individual composer's style as a function of composition trajectory. All four of these music variables--composition, tonality, modulation, and tonal impulse--can be thought of as being vectors hinged at some origin and fluctuating in direction.

## EXAMPLE

The composition trajectories for both "Yankee Doodle" and the Bach **chorale** have almost zero curvature, that is, they have an extremely large radius of curvature. This means that the average direction of impulse is roughly constant with respect to time. In the progression plotted in Fig. 6.14, which in part provides an expanded view of the first portion of Fig. 6.6b, a subtle change of tonal direction is brought about through a gradual shift of tonal impulse. This allows a possible continuation of the progression as either a tonal or a real sequence. In the former case, the key of C is maintained; otherwise, the key of B♭ is chosen as a replacement. As shown, an abrupt correction BDFA is required at the upper extremity to reassert the original key. Otherwise, the path of the trajectory maintains its near circularity. The following table illustrates the impulse calculation for this harmonic progression.

| DISPLACEMENT r | TONALITY v | TONAL IMPULSE Δv |
|---|---|---|
| 0 | | C+E+G+B = D+A |
| | C+E+G+B | |
| C+E+G+B = D+A | | A–B = A+F = G |
| | C+E+G+A | |
| 2D+2A+G | | F–G = F+D♭ = Eb |
| | C+E+F+A | |
| 3D+2A+2G | | D–E = D+B♭ = C |
| | C+D+F+A | |
| 4D+3G+2A+C | | B♭–C = B♭+G♭ = A♭ |
| | B♭+D+F+A | |
| 4D+4G+2A+2C | | –(B♭+D+F+A) = –(C+G) = G♭+D♭ |

In the general case this calculation becomes rather cumbersome without the aid of a digital computer.

Figure 6.14 Sequence showing nearly constant curvature of trajectory.

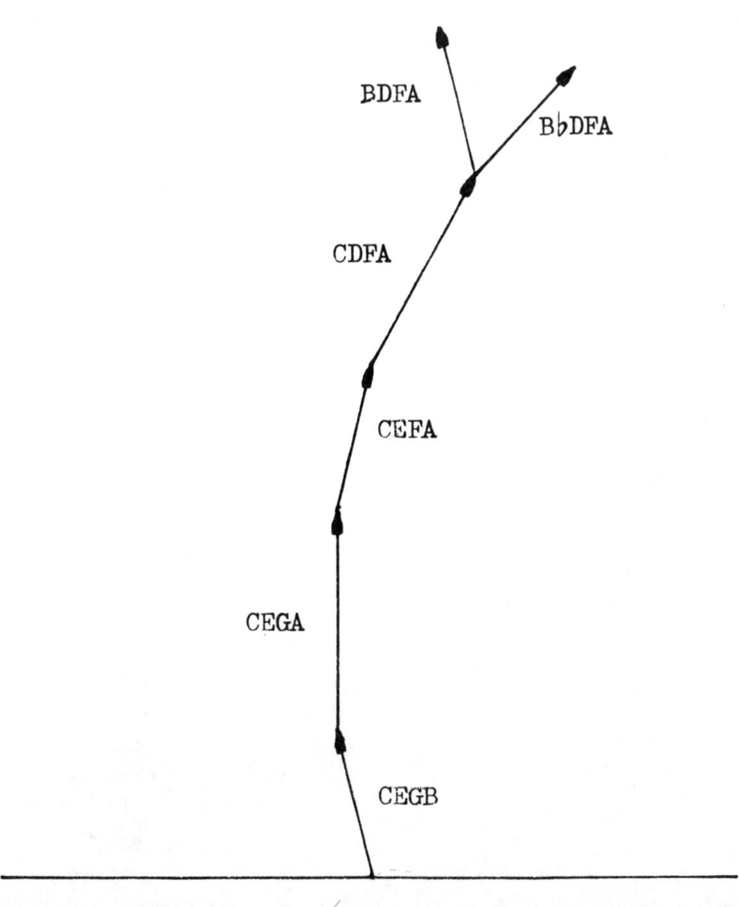

In manuscript analysis the composition point is imagined to engage in polygonal motion, as though the surface of the displacement plane were frictionless. The musical acceleration, or modulation, is zero for periods of uniform linear motion and becomes infinite at path turning points or corners. It becomes necessary to examine the tonal impulses, which cause such abrupt changes in movement. The ideal impulse produces an instantaneous change in both musical momentum and tonality, but no change in position or displacement. The impulse momentum equation is treated in the limit in which $\Delta t$ approaches zero, so that the displacement vector **r** is a constant during the impact. At the instant a force is applied, the momentum of the composition point changes discontinuously and work is done. In the limit, as the time interval $\Delta t$ approaches zero, the total impulse is delivered to the composition point at once. Thus the interval of integration $[t_1, t_2]$ becomes infinitesimally small, during which time the composition point is set into a new motion; the force **F** tends to infinity in such a way that the change in momentum remains finite. In performance analysis, on the other hand, the displacement plane can be treated as having a nonzero coefficient of friction. Also, variable forces are needed to model organic growth and decay realistically.

## EXERCISES

**6.13** The kinematics entailed in manuscript analysis reduces to a pure impulse problem involving only isolated instantaneous changes of tonality. The essential novelty of this idea lies in the suddenness of these changes. Considered either as a function of time or of trajectory length, tonality is discontinuous. Using the formulas

Tonality

$$v = ve^{i\phi}$$

Amplitude

$$v = |v| = \sqrt{v_x^2 + v_y^2}$$

Phase

$$\phi = \arg v = \arctan \frac{v_y}{v_x},$$

compute v, v, and $\phi$ for the triads I, II, III, IV, V, VI, VII in C major.

**6.14** Compute the impulse value of the cadence X → Y for each intersection of row X and column Y in the chart

| X \ Y | I | II | III | IV | V | VI | VII |
|---|---|---|---|---|---|---|---|
| I | | | | | | | |
| II | | | | | | | |
| III | | | | | | | |
| IV | | | | | | | |
| V | | | | | | | |
| VI | | | | | | | |
| VII | | | | | | | |

(Hint. First solve this problem for the case of three-part harmony. Then, expanding the table as necessary, redo the problem for four voices.)

**6.15** One of the advantages of this operational definition of tonal impulse is its apparent agreement with a qualitative statement by Katz [8]. Substantiate this assertion using data from the preceding exercise.

**6.16** Consequently it could be argued with some justification that the concept of tonal impulse has been foreshadowed in the musical literature, if it were not for the fact that in the work cited Katz speaks of many different kinds of impulse, such as **harmonic, melodic, rhythmic, contrapuntal, thematic, motivic, creative, fundamental, dynamic, dramatic, psychological, musical, romantic, chromatic,** and **emotional** without formally defining any of these terms. Supply these missing definitions.

**6.17** Analyze the following progressions with regard to tonal impulse:

(a) CGEB → CGEB♭ → CGE♭B♭ → CG♭E♭B♭ → BF♯D♯A♯ → BF♯D♯A → BF♯DA → ...

(b) CGEB → CGEA → CFEA → CFDA → BFDA → BFDG → BEDG → BECG → AECG → ...

(c) DF♯AC♯ → DF♯GB → C♯EGB → C♯EF♯A → BDF♯A → BDEG♯ → AC♯EA,

and

(d) EB♭DG → FACE → FBDG → GCE.

**6.18** Tonal impulses and musical momenta may be combined by vector addition or resolved into components by projection in the same manner as displacements or tonalities. Consider a solo voice, at rest at the initial instant, which is acted upon by a sequence of tonal impulses according to the following table

| t (sec) | 0 | 1 | 2 | 3 | 4 | 5 | 6 | 7 | 8 |
|---|---|---|---|---|---|---|---|---|---|
| Impulse | C | E | F♯ | B♭+F | A | B | C♯ | F+C | F♯ |

Draw the displacement trajectory. What is the melody?

**6.19** Illustrate the effect of four successive quarternotes, all having the same pitch, when played by an organist (1) staccato, (2) legato, (3) extreme legato, and (4) tied.

## SLIDING DISC ANALOGY

Friction occurs in many problems of mechanics. It is a resistive force that opposes motion. When a checker player advances his draughts they immediately come to rest because of friction. This force is just a simple push, such as would be exerted by an index finger. But a hockey puck will slide a considerable distance, because it is struck harder and the coefficient of friction for ice is smaller than that for a checker board. When a hockey puck traverses an icy surface it loses energy not only to the water crystals with which it comes in contact, but also to internal motion of its own molecules. These two examples illustrate a fundamental law of physics: Uniform motion in a straight line continues as long as the resultant of all the forces acting on a body is zero. If a force acts for a brief time only, it will cause a body to accelerate, and thus to acquire a certain final velocity. A hockey stick imparts such an impulsive force. Another impulsive force occurs when a tuning fork is struck and caused to vibrate in a repetitive manner. Because of internal friction the tone of the tuning fork is characterized by a decay curve. The magnitude of friction is given by empirical laws, and its direction is opposite to the change in position of the body. Around any closed path, friction opposes motion at every step, and thus a net amount of work is accomplished. The work done can be written in the form of an integral $\int \mathbf{F}.d\mathbf{r}$, where dr is the vector representing the displacement caused by the force **F**. This expression formulates the criterion commonly used for measuring work as the product of the frictional force **F** on the body and the corresponding horizontal displacement dr.

Even more important to the world than friction is **energy**, a vital unifying concept in modern physics. As is always the case in irreversible processes, energy is consumed by friction. Thus, energy cannot increase, but only decrease with time. This loss of usable energy is called the "dissipation of energy." When a sliding disc slows down, it loses **kinetic energy** (energy of motion), it does work against the force of friction. When water runs downhill it loses **potential energy** (energy of position or height). The energy as so defined possesses a minimum value for certain relative positions of the water. The simplest musical significance that can be attached to the energy of a composition is that it represents in some way the creative drive or vis viva of a musical "work." The postulation of the existence of a creative force may provide useful insight into the music of classical composers. According to Ernst Křenek [9], the melodies that make up the fabric of polyphony can be understood as "manifestations of a stream of energy the fluctuations of which are made perceptible in the tones through which the melodic lines proceed." By identifying upward motion with increase of energy and downward motion with the opposite, he is led to regard large melodic skips as sudden changes of energy and stepwise motions as gradual changes. With characteristic insight Křenek continues: "Since complete canceling out each other of energy created and expended is ideally seen as the net result of any musical process, a situation in which the energy level is zero must not be reached before the melody is meant to come to its end."

It is convenient to regard a musical composition as a disc moving on a smooth flat surface. This surface is afforded by the displacement plane. At first, this idea may seem somewhat artificial. It is certainly foreign to traditional harmony. In keeping with this sliding disc analogy, it is convenient to think of the composer as participating in a game against nature. Play begins with a small endowment of creative energy. This bankroll of energy can be used to obtain voice movements. By wise expenditures, the composer can optimize gains. Each musical composition will tend to its lowest energy level at its conclusion, where it indeed comes to rest just as its fuel supply is exhausted. The composition disc can be brought from one position to another in many ways; assuming that there is a frictional or dissipative force; the work done in this process depends not only on the initial and final states, but also on the path taken.

In the present theory, two kinds of music analysis have been distinguished: manuscript and performance analysis. For manuscript work, it will be assumed that (a) the displacement plane is a frictionless surface, and (b) the composition disc is subjected only to impulsive forces. It follows from these assumptions that the resulting musical motion is uniform and that the tonality takes on a sequence of constant values. For performance work, it will be assumed that (a) the displacement plane has a nonzero coefficient of friction, and (b) the composition disc is subjected to time varying forces. It follows from these assumptions that the resulting musical motion is nonuniform and that the tonality is a continually changing function of time.

The sliding disc analogy, which encompasses both kinds of music analysis, is based on a number of basic assumptions that now are listed.

<u>ASSUMPTION 1</u>: The composition disc is a point particle of mass m having no extension in space.

<u>ASSUMPTION 2</u>: The transfer of the composition disc may be accompanied by a frictional loss of energy.

<u>ASSUMPTION 3</u>: The work done by the force of creative energy may depend on the path taken.

<u>ASSUMPTION 4</u>: The frictional force exerted by the tonal displacement plane on the composition disc, if not negligible, may be variable in magnitude or depend on the tonality amplitude, and acts in a direction always opposing the motion.

<u>ASSUMPTION 5</u>: The energy required to move the composition disc need not be just the sum of the energies required to move the separate voice discs in the displacement plane, because when these energies are added up, part of the total could represent mutual interaction of the voices.

<u>ASSUMPTION 6</u>: The total energy expended during a transition of the composition disc is the sum of the kinetic energies of the entire ensem-

ble of voices, as if concentrated at the center of voices, plus the kinetic energy of motion about the center.

ASSUMPTION 7: Less energy is required if a simultaneous movement of two voice discs occurs such that the resultant motion of the composition disc is minimized.

ASSUMPTION 8: The total energy of any piece of music gradually decreases as it is performed and diminishing monotonically, eventually reaches zero (see Fig. 6.15).

Figure 6.15

Decrease with time of creative energy in the initial four measures of Beethoven's **First Symphony**, as transcribed for piano.

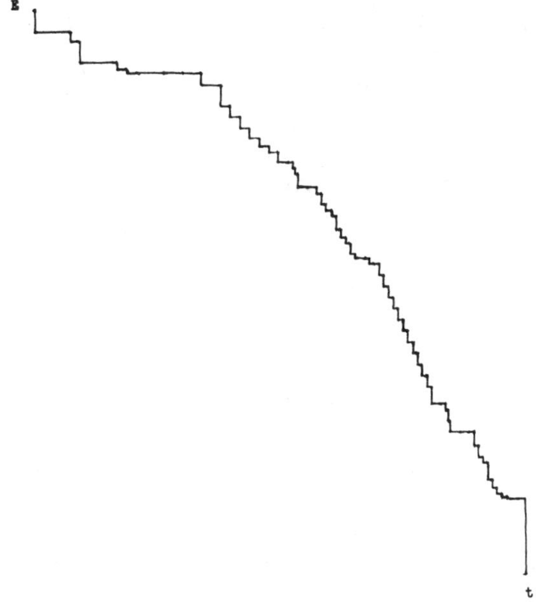


The resulting analogy provides an idealization of the approximate behavior of musical voices in keeping with the previously developed mathematical model. The composition disc is imagined to slide, or to be pushed about, on the upper surface of the displacement plane; its motion giving a clear picture of the musical movement. Such a disc can be transported from one position to another by a certain expenditure of creative energy. In manuscript analysis all fuel is consumed in short bursts to provide course corrections to the composition disc similar to those provided for space probes and satellites by rocket engines. In performance analysis the composition disc continually does work against the nonconservative (dissipative) force of friction. Either way, the composer must profitably use up the total quantity of creative energy available at the beginning of the piece. The composition point will continue to move at command until the conclusion of the musical composition, but leaving a continually dwindling stock of energy. It will become evident that the sliding disc analogy provides a stepping stone to a detailed analysis of the impetuous motion of musical voices.

## WORK AND ENERGY

In classical mechanics, "work" is defined by the formula

$$W = \int_{r_0}^{r_1} F.dr,$$

where $r_0$ is the position of the physical object being worked upon at the beginning of its motion, $r_1$ is the position of this object at the conclusion of its motion, and the dot "." signifies the inner product operation. Work is done only when the object is moved. Moreover, experimentation has demonstrated conclusively that no work is done during periods of constant (or zero) velocity, because during these periods there is no unbalanced force, so F is zero. In the preceding sections it is suggested that tonality is musical velocity. Additionally, it is postulated that modulation is musical acceleration. By Newton's second law, acceleration is proportional to the applied force. Consequently, if Newton's law applies, then work is done on the composition disc during modulation. In manuscript analysis, however, work is confined to that infinitesimal displacement dr of the tip of the composition vector r that arises when the impulsive force F, which acts for only an instant, has a nonzero value, for example, at path turning points.

Energy is the capacity to do work. Two kinds of energy are recognized in classical mechanics: **kinetic** (the energy of motion) and **potential** (the energy of position or distortion). The formula for kinetic energy T is

$$T = \tfrac{1}{2}mv^2,$$

where $v = |\mathbf{v}|$ is the amplitude of the velocity vector $\mathbf{v}$ of an object of mass m. Another name for v is "speed." Without going into the details, it is possible to express the work W done by the impulsive force F as the difference in kinetic energies. Thus

$$W = T_1 - T_0 = \tfrac{1}{2}mv_1^{\,2} - \tfrac{1}{2}mv_0^{\,2}$$

where the values $v_0^{\,2}$ and $v_1^{\,2}$ are the squares of the speeds at the start and end of the motion, respectively.

EXERCISES

**6.20** Calculate work done during the perfect cadence GBDF → CGCE. (Hint. Consider the lengths of the vectors in the following diagram.)

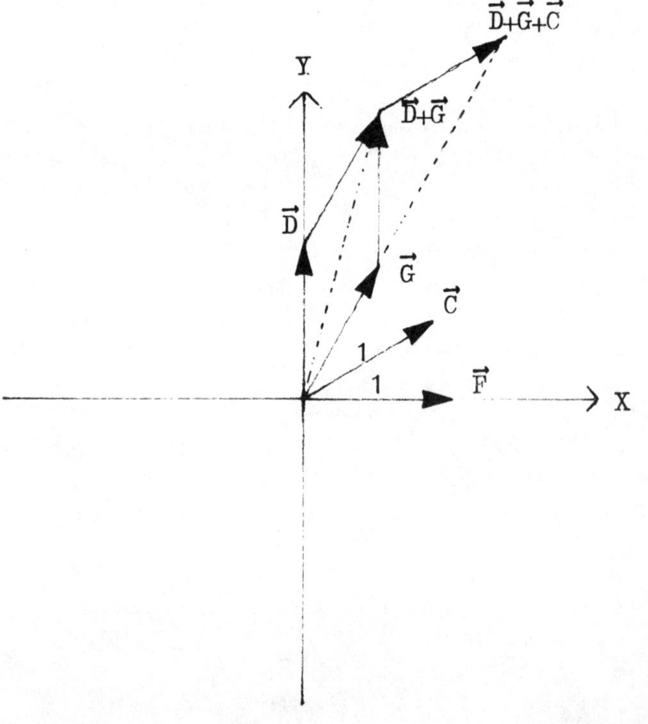


**6.21** The total work done while playing the ascending one octave C major scale is calculated as follows (m = 1):

$$W_{\}C} = \tfrac{1}{2}(1)1^2 - 0 = \tfrac{1}{2}$$

$$W_{CD} = W_{DE} = W_{EF} = \ldots = W_{BC} =$$

$$\tfrac{1}{2}(1)1^2 - \tfrac{1}{2}(1)1^2 = 0$$

$$W_{C\}} = 0 - \tfrac{1}{2}(1)1^2 = -\tfrac{1}{2}$$

which gives

$$W = W_{\}C} + W_{CD} + \ldots + W_{C\}} =$$

$$\tfrac{1}{2} + (-\tfrac{1}{2}) = 0.$$

What can be said about the total work done in performing any complete musical composition?

**6.22** (a) Should it be easier to follow silence by a chord of n tones or a chord of n+1 tones? (b) Will a chord having n tones persist as readily as one having n+1 tones? (c) Do all harmonies commute with silence?

**6.23** Which charm progression, GBD → GBE → GCE or GBD → GCE, requires more energy?

**6.24** Write an original piece of music illustrating the conversion of a given fixed amount of creative energy to directionally applied energy. Plan to modify the tonality of the moving composition disc to assure the arrival of the composition at a preselected point of the displacement plane.

## OFF-COURSE TENSION AND HARMONIC IMBALANCE

In exploring the many relationships that exist among chords and melodies, it long ago became apparent to people interested in music that certain classes of tones can be assigned the semantic features "active" (creating stress or demanding subsequent resolution through voice movement) or "passive" (providing some relief from prior tensions or removing barriers to other developments). Carolyn A. Alchin [10] has called the tendency of an active tone to resolve to a rest tone **tonal magnetism.** In modal analysis a change of polarity of select tones must be taken into account, as evidenced by the example shown in Fig. 6.16. In this illustration an interchange in roles of attraction and repulsion occurs between tones A and G. This switch demonstrates that if, indeed, there is a magnetic principle at work in music, then it must be supported by some kind of time-varying field. Further, if this field is attached to the tonality plane, then presumably it must be a central field. Someday experiments in auditory perception may reveal why it is natural for certain musical phrases to create a feeling of stability and well-being, and for others to generate a sense of instability and uneasiness.

Figure 6.16

Two possible types of active and passive roles. Note symmetry.

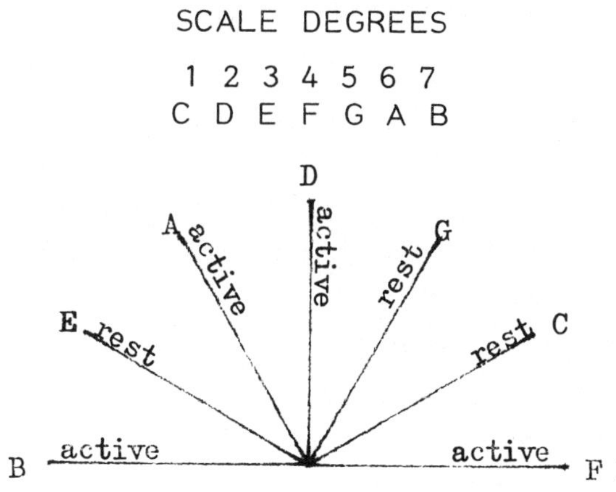

SCALE DEGREES

1 2 3 4 5 6 7
C D E F G A B

D: active; A: active; G: rest; E: rest; C: rest; B: active; F: active

C Major

SCALE DEGREES

1 2 3 4 5 6 7
A B C D E F G

D: active; A: rest; G: active; E: rest; C: rest; B: active; F: active

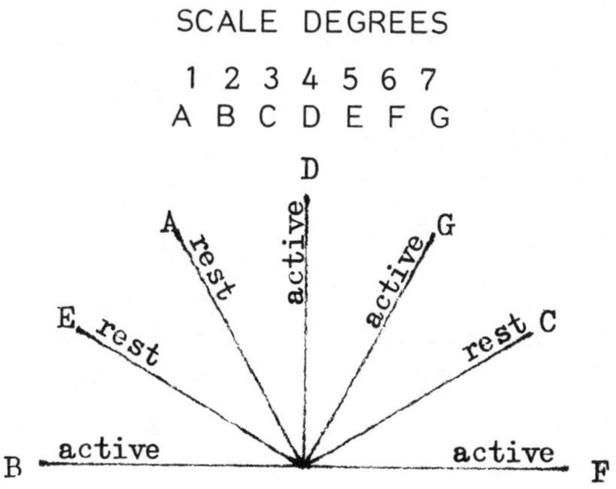

A Minor (natural form)

The manner in which tones (and chords) stray from the course established by their particular musical context can be understood from Fig. 6.17. Here an inspection of the trajectory formed by the notes of the C major scale, when played in their customary order, suggests that in tonal music another kind of tension might occur, one that would be positively correlated with distance of offset, when that distance is measured perpendicularly to the course line, MN. A "global course line" is defined by construction as being the linear extension of the shaft of the total resultant vector--that vector which stretches from the point of origin to the final destination point of the composition. Depending on the circumstances, "local course lines" could be drawn to include other straight line segments obtained by picking suitable pairs of turning points along the trajectory and joining the two elements of each pair by an arrow. This procedure might be useful in analyzing short sections of a long piece of music. Generally speaking, it is on the basis of changes in offset that a tone (or chord) is best described as "going on" or "off course." Notice that every course line happens to divide the displacement plane into two separate regions, a left-hand side tending towards sharps and a right-hand side tending towards flats. Tonalities that point to the right of the course line will be called **dextral**; those that point to the left, **sinistral**. Tonalities coincident with the course line itself or any tonality parallel thereto will be referred to as **"sagital."** Thus, in Fig. 6.17, reading from the bottom up, **C**, **F**, **G**, and **C** are dextral tonalities and **D**, **E**, **A**, and **B** are sinistral tonalities; no sagital tonalities are present.

At the endpoints of any trajectory the offset will be zero. At the start of the C major scale, whether ascending or descending, the composition disc experiences an impulsive force that thrusts it outwards; while at the other end of the scale, it experiences the reverse effect. Similar course deviations give rise to differences in offset all along the C major scale trajectory. Fig. 6.18 provides a significant clue to their interpretation. Taken together the two figures illustrate the main points involved in trajectory analysis; no modifications are necessary in order to fit the argument to multivoice arrays. Now inspection of Fig. 6.17 shows that from point 0 to point 1 the offset increases, calling for course corrections to be

**Figure 6.17**

Trajectory of the one-octave ascending C major scale. The course line, MN, coincides with the total resultant vector

$$R = C+D+E+F+G+A+B+C,$$

which in this case is the sum of eight primitive tone vectors.

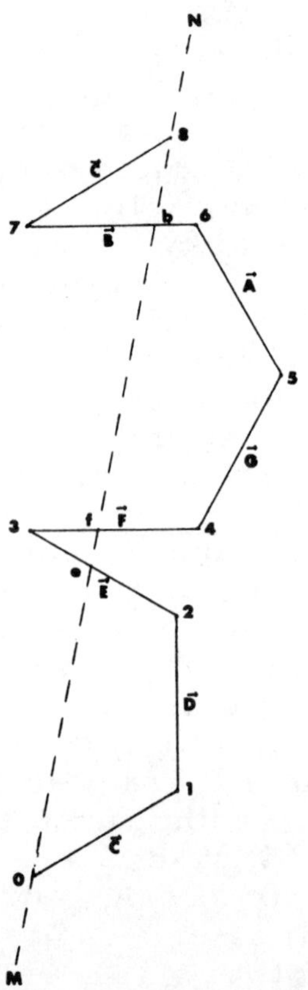


made both at point 1 and again at point 2 to reduce the perpendicular distance to the course line and allay any associated tension on the part of the listener. Theoretically, the movement of a composition disc after it has received an impulsive blow is controlled by its own mechanical inertia. Along segment E this inertia causes the composition disc to overshoot the mark at point e, thus putting the progression of major scale degrees off course again at point 3. Two more similar reversals in offset occur at points f and b, where the vectors F and B have zero crossings.

**Figure 6.18**

A simple way of interpreting the offset is to rotate the diagram until the course line coincides with the vertical axis.

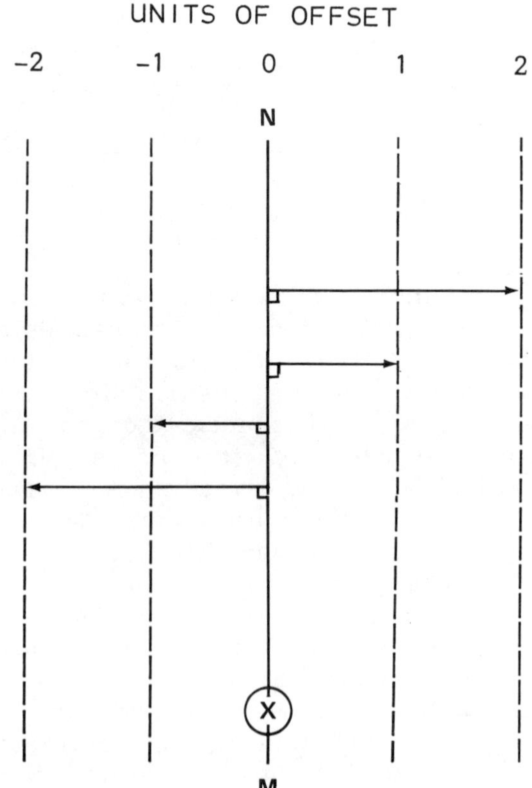


The phrase **off-course tension** might be a good name for the domain of various listener response states corresponding to the complete range of possible offset distances. Clearly, the off-course tension is a minimum on the course line, indeed it can reasonably be postulated as zero there, since silence, which usually is considered to be a condition of repose, occurs at the two endpoints where the offset is zero. Moreover, off-course tension should be a non-negative function, which at least near the trajectory increases monotonically with the distance of offset. This increase continues up to a certain point, if not indefinitely. The approximate nature of off-course tension functions for individual listeners can be determined, if at all, only through psychometric methods. Fig. 6.19 presents two possibilities.

The "absolute harmonic imbalance" can be defined as the difference between the sum of areas generated on the left and the sum of those generated on the right of the course line by the moving composition point as it traces relevant portions of the composition trajectory (the shaded areas of Fig. 6.20). The "coefficient of harmonic imbalance" is this same quantity divided by the total amount of area to be found on both sides of the course line. Multiplication by 100 converts the value of the coefficient to a "relative harmonic imbalance" expressed as a percentage.

The present treatment of the subject of off-course tension is mainly qualitative. This sketchy approach is justifiable for now because of the lack of sufficient psychoacoustic data. Nevertheless, by this time it should be becoming increasingly evident that a significant number of topics in elementary music theory can be illuminated by simple geometric considerations.

Figure 6.20

Harmonic imbalance in the one-octave ascending C major scale.

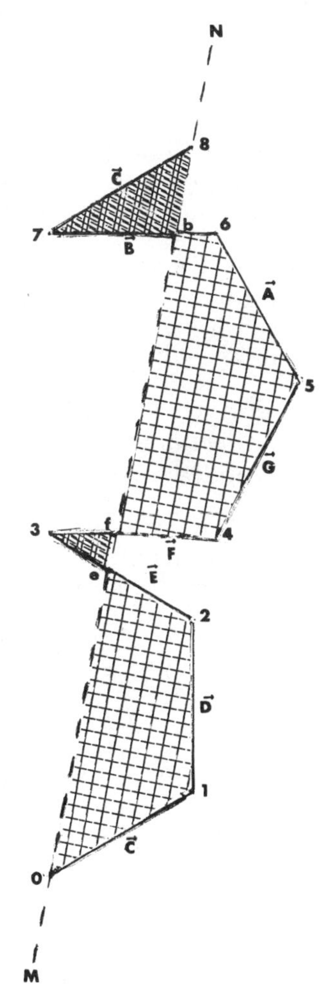


Figure 6.19

Plausible off-course tension function candidates.

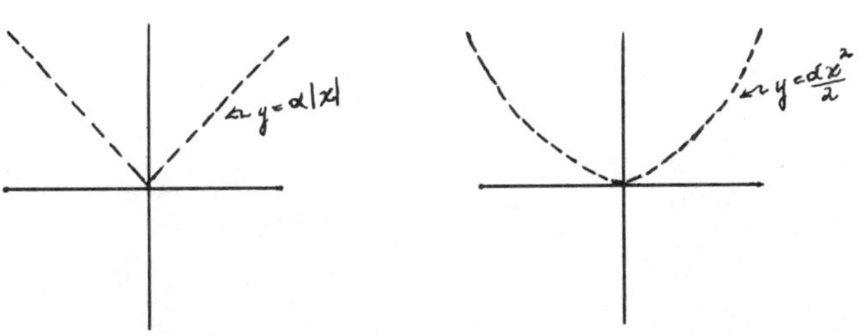


EXERCISES

6.25 (a) Draw the trajectory for the one-octave descending C major scale. (b) Construct a diagram showing the harmonic imbalance of this scale. (c) How does the result relate to that in Fig. 6.20?

6.26 What sort of general statements apply to the relationship of trajectories when a musical composition is reversed?

REFERENCES

[1] *Grove's Dictionary of Music and Musicians,* 5th Edition, Vol. IX.

[2] John A. Eisele and Robert M. Mason, *Applied Matrix and Tensor Analysis* (John Wiley & Sons, Inc., New York, 1970).

[3] Matthew Shirlaw, *The Theory of Harmony* (Novelle & Co., Ltd., London) p. 228.

[4] Walter Piston, *Harmony,* 3rd Ed. (W. W. Norton & Co., Inc., New York, 1969).

[5] Roger Sessions, *Harmonic Practice,* (Harcourt, Brace & World, Inc., New York, 1951)

[6] Kent Gannett, *Bach's Harmonic Progressions: Ten Thousand Examples* (Oliver Ditson Co., 1942) pp. 1-50.

[7] Richard H. Dorf, *Electronic Musical Instruments* (Radio Magazines, Inc., Mineola, New York, 1954)

[8] Adele T. Katz, *Challenge to Musical Tradition* (Putnam & Co., Ltd., London, 1947) p. 11.

[9] Ernst Křenek, *Tonal Counterpoint* (Boosey and Hawkes, Inc., 1958) pp. 6-7.

[10] Carolyn A. Alchin, *Applied Harmony,* Part I (L. R. Jones, Publisher, Los Angeles, California, 1935) p. 31.

*It should not be overlooked that harmonies with multiple meaning--the 'vagrants'--may occasionally proceed in conflict with the theory of root progressions. This is one of the short-comings of every theory--and this theory cannot claim to be an exception; no theory can exclude everything that is wrong, poor, or even detestable, or include everything that is right, good, or beautiful.*

*ARNOLD SCHOENBERG,* ***Structural Functions of Harmony,*** *Revised Edition, 1969*

PART II

# Chapter 7 Modeling

## IMAGINARY AND COMPLEX NUMBERS

The displacement plane can be regarded as a complex plane, as shown in Fig. 7.1. It is often convenient to think of a point in this plane, which is sometimes also called the Gaussian plane, or more briefly the z plane, not only as a composition vector, r, which extends from the origin to the composition point, but also as being represented by a complex number z. Thus, $z = a + bi$, where the presence of the imaginary unit $i = \sqrt{-1}$ distinguishes the complex quantity $a + bi$ from the corresponding real quantities a and b. Every displacement vector is attached to a point on the complex plane. As a result, every composition point corresponds to a complex number. Let $w = u + iv$ and $z = x + iy$. Accordingly, the equation $w = z$ implies two separate equalities, one stating that the real parts are equal ($u = x$) and the other that the imaginary parts are equal ($v = y$). Often the relationship between the two complex variables w and z is more complicated. For example, sometimes

$$w = z^n + a_1 z^{n-1} + \dots + a_{n-1} z + a_n,$$

which is a polynomial in z.

Of particular interest are the complex numbers that correspond to the twelve unit tone vectors. Geometrically, these arrows point to the vertices of a regular twelve-sided polygon, or **duodecagon,** which is inscribed in the unit circle centered at the origin of the complex plane. Each solution of the complex polynomial equation $z^{12} = 1$ provides the coordinates of such a vector. It follows from the Fundamental Theorem of Algebra that there are precisely twelve distinct solutions to this equation. These solutions, collectively called the twelve "twelfth roots of unity," are found simply by substituting the integers 0, 1, ..., 11 for k in the expression:

$$w_k = \cos \frac{k\pi}{6} + i \sin \frac{k\pi}{6}.$$

A harmony can be regarded as a plane figure, such as a fan diagram, by selecting a subset of the set of twelve twelfth roots of unity.

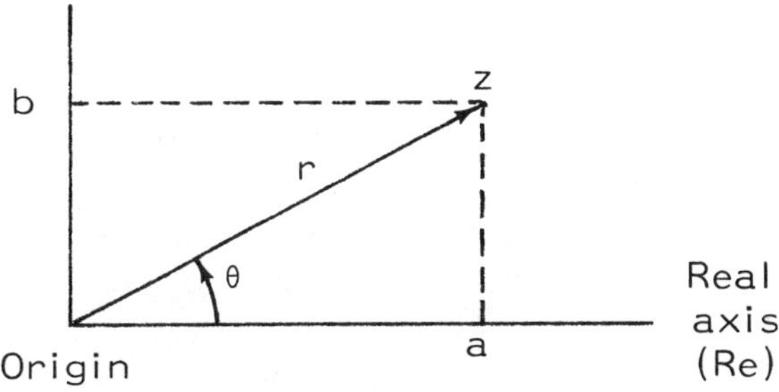


Figure 7.1

This is the **Argand diagram** of the displacement vector **r.** The angle $\theta = \arg z$ is called the "argument" of the complex number z. As indicated, this angle is measured from the real (or **polar**) axis. The vector **r** has length

$$r = |\mathbf{r}| = (a^2+b^2)^{\frac{1}{2}}.$$

A glance at Fig. 7.1 confirms that the composition point z can be located by its cartesian coordinates a and b and also by the length r and the angle θ that the vector **r** makes with the real axis. The Pythagorean theorem states that

$$r^2 = a^2 + b^2.$$

Moreover, $\tan\theta = b/a = \mathrm{Im}\, z/\mathrm{Re}\, z$, the ratio of the imaginary part to the real part of z. The quantities $r = |z|$ (the absolute value of the complex number z) and θ (the argument of the complex number z) have a close connection with the exponential function $e^z = \exp(z)$ for a complex variable z. To be exact, $z = a + bi = r \exp(i\theta)$. It is easier to add and subtract in the form $z = a + bi$ and to multiply and divide in the form $z = r \exp(i\theta)$. The scalar quantities r and θ appearing in $r \exp(i\theta)$ determine the distance and direction of the composition point as a function of time. The formulas $\exp(i\theta) = \cos\theta + i \sin\theta$ and $\exp(-i\theta) = \cos\theta - i\sin\theta$ due to Euler relate the exponential to the trigonometric functions.

Writing $z = a + bi$ and $w = c + di$, their sum becomes

$$z + w = (a + c) + (b + d)i.$$

Writing $z = r_1 \exp(i\theta_1)$ and $w = r_2 \exp(i\theta_2)$, their product becomes

$$zw = (a + bi)(c + di) =$$
$$(ac - bd) + (ad + bc)i =$$
$$(r_1 e^{i\theta_1})(r_2 e^{i\theta_2}) =$$
$$r_1 r_2 e^{i(\theta_1 + \theta_2)}.$$

That is, the magnitude of the product of two complex numbers is the product of their magnitudes; the argument of the product of two complex numbers is the sum of their arguments.

The complex number a + bi is closely related to its **complex conjugate,** a − bi. Graphically, the vector representing the complex conjugate $\bar{z}$ of a complex number z is the mirror image of the vector r representing the number itself, with reflection occurring through the x-axis, the axis of reals, or as it sometimes is called, the "polar axis." In general, the complex conjugate of a complex number is obtained by changing the algebraic sign of the imaginary unit i wherever it appears in the number. The sum of a complex number z and its conjugate $\bar{z}$ is real, because the imaginary parts cancel:

$$a + bi + a - bi =$$
$$a + a + bi - bi = 2a.$$

Similarly, the product $z\bar{z}$ is also real since

$$r \exp(i\theta)\, r \exp(-i\theta) =$$
$$r^2 \exp(i\theta) \exp(-i\theta) =$$
$$r^2 \exp(i\theta - i\theta) =$$
$$r^2 \exp(0) = r^2 \times 1 = r^2.$$

It follows that

$$\sqrt{z\bar{z}} = |z|,$$
$$(z + \bar{z})/2 = \mathrm{Re}\, z,$$
$$\text{and } (z - \bar{z})/2i = \mathrm{Im}\, z.$$

## RIEMANN SURFACES

In studying the musical notions of displacement, tonality, and modulation, profitable use can be made of

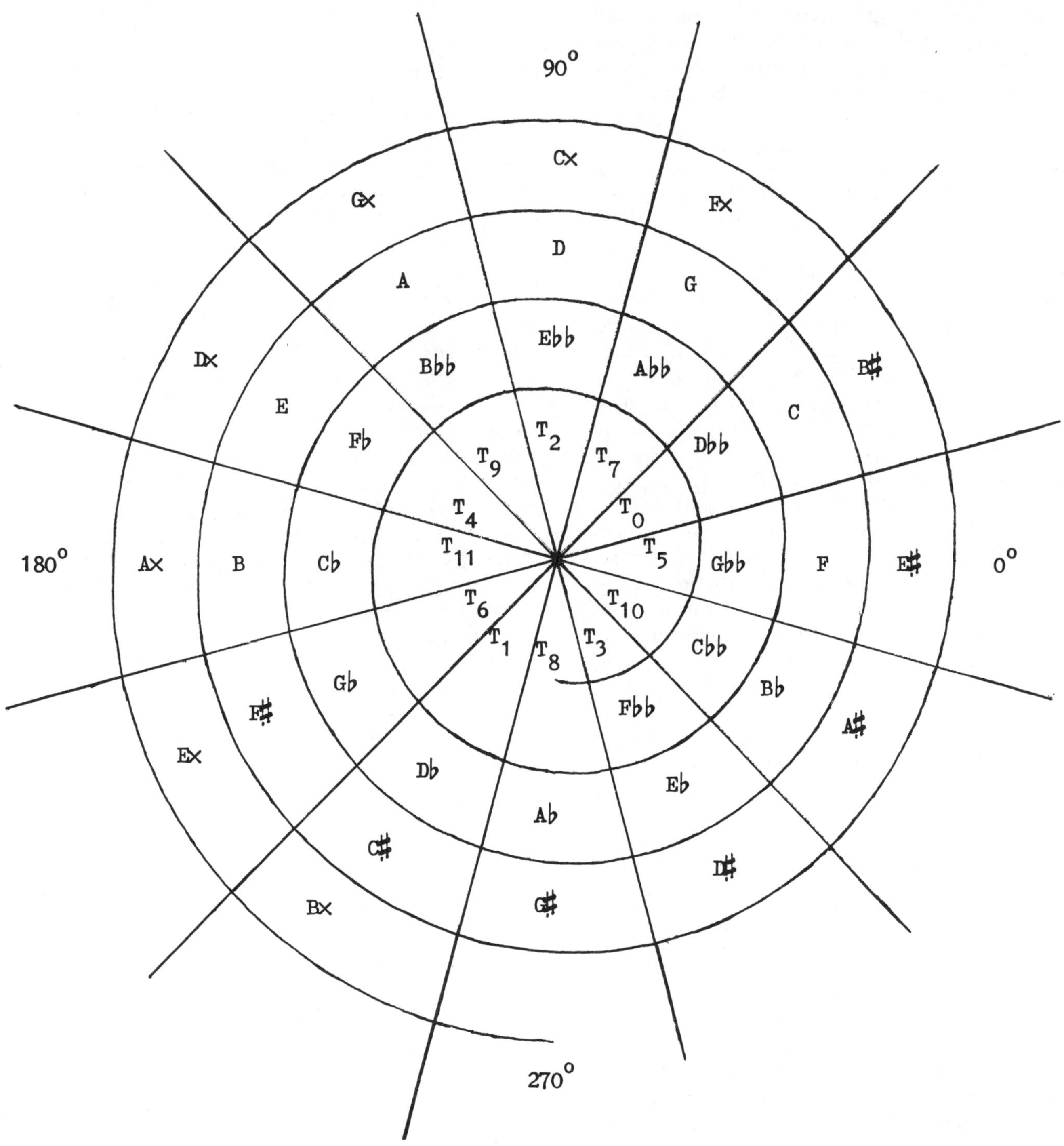


Figure 7.2

The spiral ramp. From F♭♭, innermost on the spiral, the enchained fifths follow in natural sequence to Bx. Literals appearing in the same radial sector are said to be "enharmonic equivalents," because they map onto the same primitive tone. With one exception, this enharmonic mapping associates exactly three literals with each tone. The sole exception is that only two literals, G♯ and A♭, map onto $T_8$.

the mathematical concept of the complex plane, although rigorous pursuit of this subject would involve developing or adapting a great deal of additional theoretical machinery. By reference to Fig. 7.2, the literals of the spiral ramp can be found to correspond to the twelve primitive tones. These tones have been assumed to lie on the unit circle at the vertices of an inscribed regular duodecagon; they correspond, as shown in Fig. 7.3, to the twelve twelfth roots of unity. Because the literal scale repeats the same tones enharmonically each time the ramp position advances $360^{\circ}$, musical notation, (and consequently) displacement, tonality, and modulation are multiple-valued functions of the corresponding angle. Fortunately, this type of situation long has been recognized in other fields, so that mathematical theory years ago evolved to the point where it often treats the complex plane as an infinite family of overlaid planes, or more formally, as the sheets of a **Riemann surface.** Consequently, the fact that the z plane reflects the periodicity of the literal scale makes it very useful in automated music analysis. As a rule, however, textbooks on complex analysis do not talk about the concept of a Riemann surface unless it is being applied to a certain type of function called an **analytic function.** The fact the the function w = arg z is not analytic should not bother the music student. After all, a person can find some comfort in the fact that it is harmonic!

The function w = arg z can be represented by a Riemann surface, but it turns out to be a somewhat unusual surface since w is real-valued. In mathematical terms, a "branch" or single-valued representation of a multiple-valued function having a branch point at z = 0 is obtained by cutting the complex plane along a straight line that connects the origin with the point at infinity. The line chosen to connect these two branch points is called a "branch line" or "cut" of the Riemann surface. Such a cut separates the Riemann surface into a number of sheets. Fig. 7.3c shows

**Figure 7.3a**

Diagrammatic representation of the mapping from the literal chain to the pitch wheel. Equal segments of the line are replotted as equal arcs of the circle. The underlying transformation corresponds to the composition $k = h \circ g \circ f \circ e$,

where the function $e: (L,\leq) \rightarrow P$ maps the literal chain of perfect fifths onto the Pythagorean system of natural fifths, the function $f: P \rightarrow Q$ retunes the natural fifths in equitempered intonation, the function $g: Q \rightarrow R$ transforms the equitempered fifths into residue classes with respect to octave congruence, and the function $h: R \rightarrow S$ places these classes in one-to-one correspondence with the spokes of the pitch wheel, which in turn can be identified with the radial sectors of the spiral ramp by the relation of enharmonic equivalence.

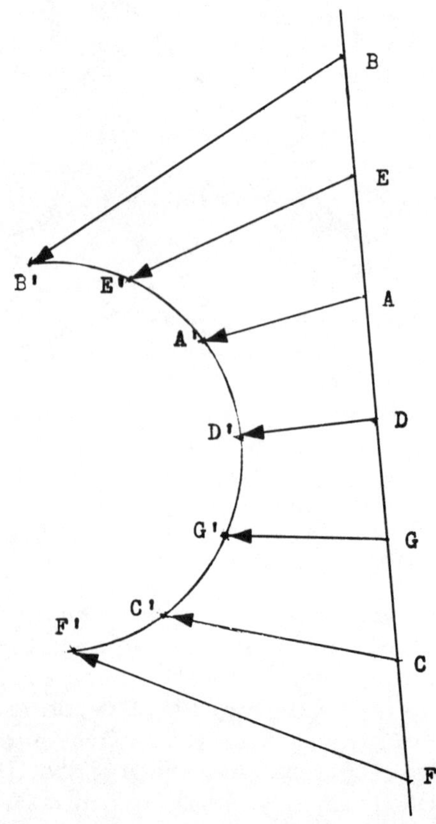

Figure 7.3b

Relationship between the w-plane and the z-plane when $z = e^{iw}$.

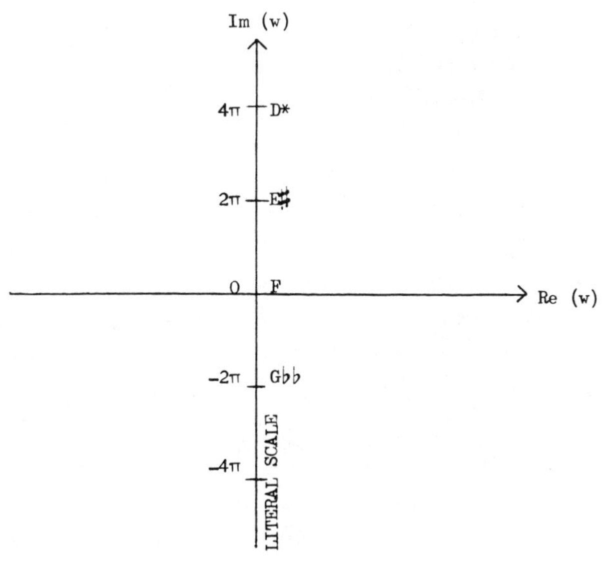


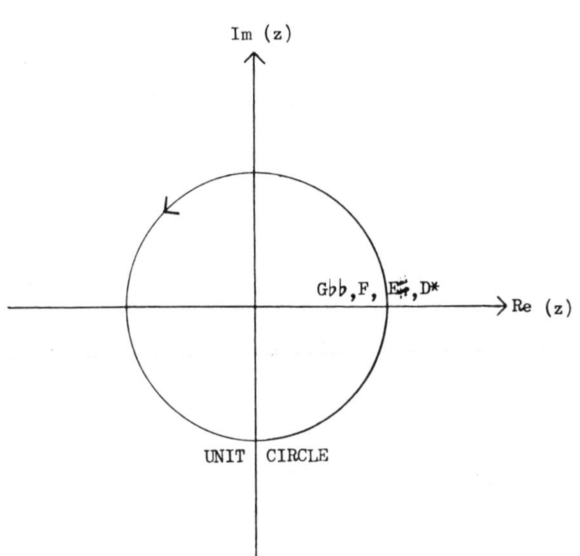


a branch cut in which the complex z plane is slit along the imaginary axis from 0 to $-\infty i$. This cut separates the Riemann surface for the function w = arg z into a number of sheets. As indicated in the figure, one of these sheets bears the literals of the stencil for the extended key of C major. For this branch of the argument function, it is true that

$$\arg 1 = 0, \ \arg i = \pi/2,$$
$$\text{and } \arg(-1) = \pi.$$

At the same time, by an assumption made earlier,

$$\mathbf{F} = \exp(0i), \ \mathbf{D} = \exp(\pi i/2),$$
$$\text{and } \mathbf{B} = \exp(\pi i).$$

It follows that

$$\mathbf{F} = \exp(i \arg 1), \ \mathbf{D} = \exp(i \arg i),$$
$$\text{and } \mathbf{B} = \exp[i \arg(-1)].$$

It also follows that

$$\mathbf{G}\flat\flat = e^{i(\arg 1 - 2\pi)},$$

$$\mathbf{E}\flat\flat = e^{i(\arg i - 2\pi)},$$

$$\text{and } \mathbf{C}\flat = e^{i[\arg(-1) - 2\pi]},$$

where the angles lie on the sheet below, and

$$\mathbf{E}\sharp = e^{i(\arg 1 + 2\pi)},$$

$$\mathbf{C}\times = e^{i(\arg i + 2\pi)},$$

$$\text{and } \mathbf{A}\times = e^{i[\arg(-1) + 2\pi]},$$

where the angles lie on the sheet above.

In this manner, the stencil

(G♯|A♭)C♯F♯BEADGCFB♭E♭

is related to a single portion of a Riemann surface of infinitely many sheets and having a branch point at z = 0. The adjacent sheets of this surface are attached to each other so that they form an endless spiral ramp (refer again to Fig. 7.2). The situation would resemble what one might see on a tour through the exhibit areas of the Guggenheim Museum in New York City, if, instead of pictures, the individual elements of the literal alphabet were to be on display. The origin itself is not a point of the Riemann surface for w = arg z, but rather, is centrally located somewhere in the rampwell.

Figure 7.3c

Branch cut for the sheet corresponding to the generalized key of C major and its stencil.

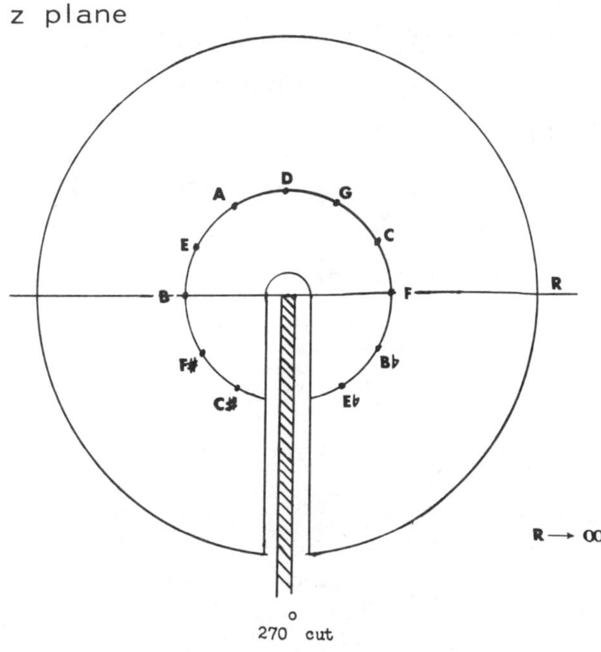


The various dials of Fig. 7.4 illustrate 24 different branch lines along which the complex displacement plane can be cut. Each branch cut supports several stencils. In the first case, the cut extends along the real axis from the point $-\infty$ to the point zero. Careful examination of the configurations of literals appearing in columns to the right of the dials reveals that for certain dials two enharmonically equivalent values appear on opposing sides of the branch cut. This same circumstance is implicit in Fig. 7.3c, where the complex plane was cut along the negative imaginary axis. If the sheet of the Riemann surface and the branch of w = arg z corresponding to the canonical stencil are chosen, then $T_8$ = A♭ on the right bank of the cut and $T_8$ = G♯ on the left bank in this picture. Consequently, as the second and successive even numbered dial rows reveal, any spelling ambiguity that may arise with respect to a few chords on key sector boundaries is ruled out completely on key sector interiors. For example, if arg z lies between $0^\circ$ and $30^\circ$, then each tonality belonging to this common region must have a unique spelling because reference is made to the same stencil. Moreover, the notational ambiguity, which arises only at sector boundaries, can be resolved in every case by postulating that both the left and right boundary literals are equally acceptable.

The extensive information of Fig. 7.4 has been condensed and summarized for clarity in Fig. 7.5a. The first sector of this superchart is formed by the set of all points z of the displacement plane such that $z \neq 0$ and one value of arg $z = \theta$ satisfies the inequality

$$0^\circ \leq \theta < 30^\circ.$$

Notice that the two stencils for this sector given in Fig. 7.4 have been reduced from the $360^\circ$ arc they occupy there, so as to fit entirely into the $30^\circ$ subtended arc of Fig. 7.5a. From this new vantage point, it is possible to determine every feasible notation quickly, by reading it off the stencil wheel. For example, consider the dominant seventh harmony (designation 77). This harmony is spelled in different ways depending upon the current value of $\theta$.

It should be emphasized that the more highly inflected spellings are not nonsense, but rather indicate that the composition point z, in its push to the borders of the key of C major, has trespassed even beyond them. This example shows that the constant orthographic representation or spelling of chords and harmonies called "true" notation has to be abandoned in favor of "relative" notations, in certain extreme cases where tonality becomes divorced from key.

Now an added dividend appears. Again referring to Fig. 7.5a, it is clear that the C harmonic minor scale can be spelled only in the first quadrant, that is, for arguments $\theta$ on the range $0^\circ$ through

Figure 7.4
Development of stencils by branch cuts in the complex displacement plane.

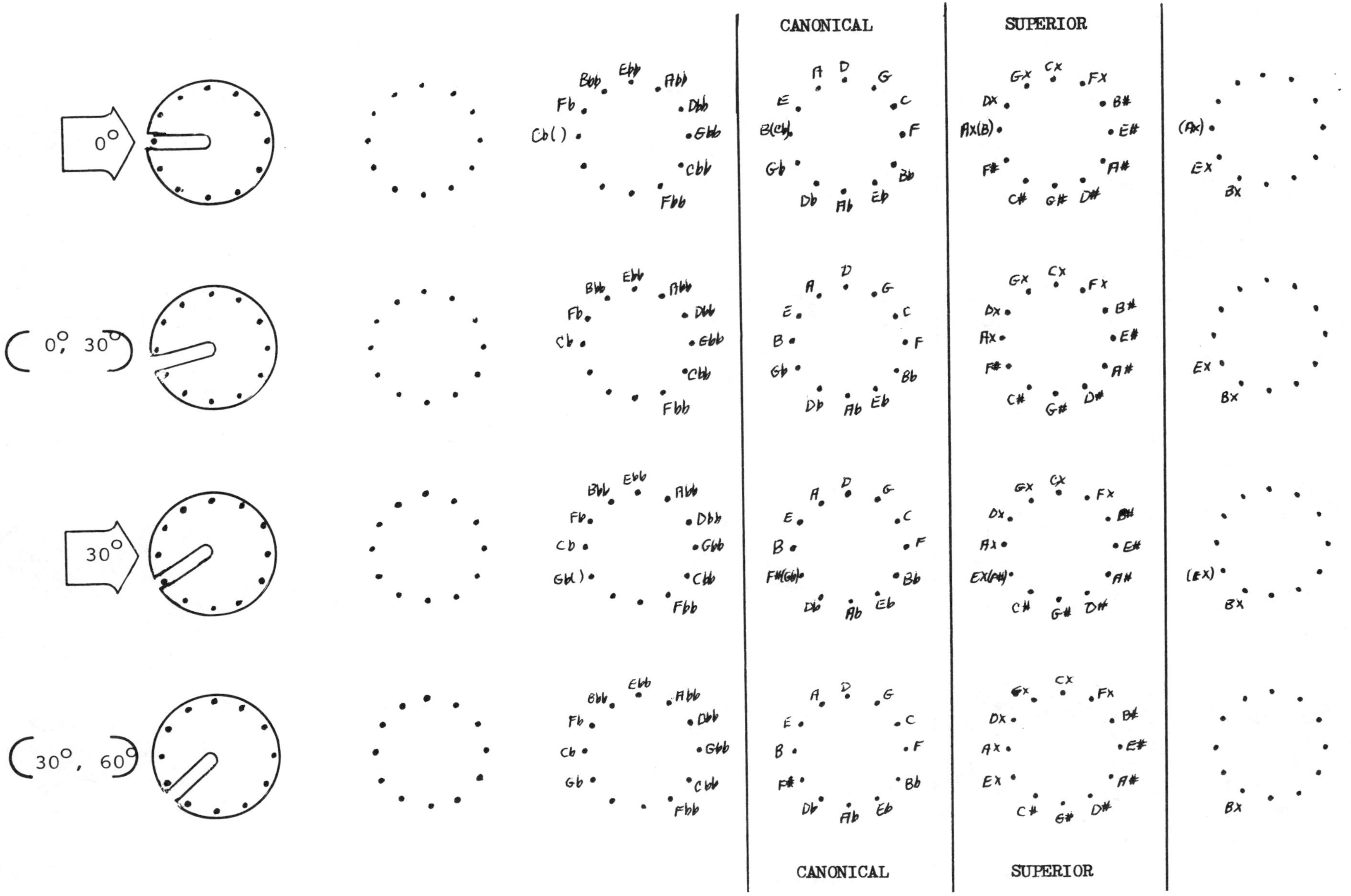

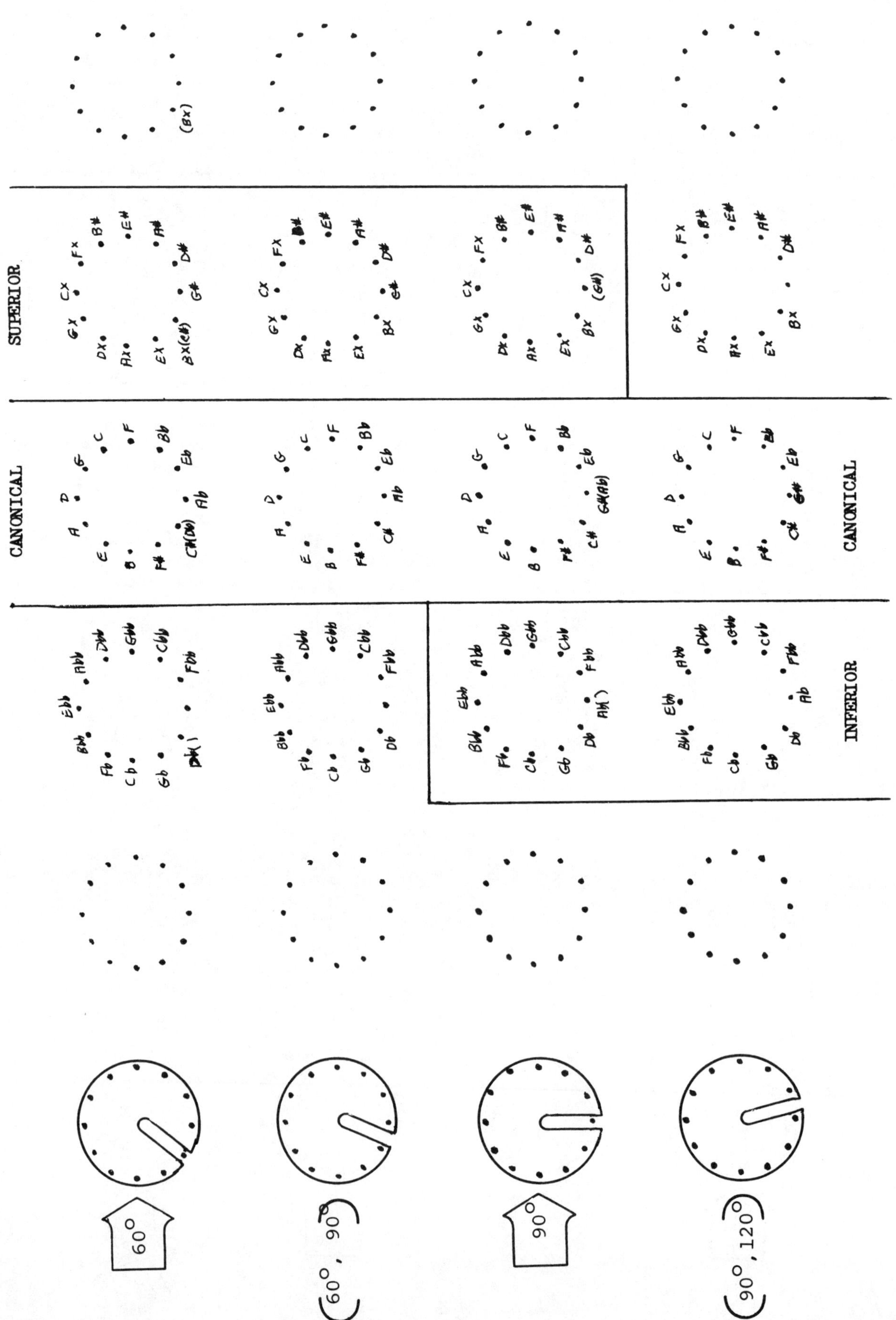
SUPERIOR
CANONICAL
INFERIOR
CANONICAL
60°
(60°, 90°)
90°
(90°, 120°)

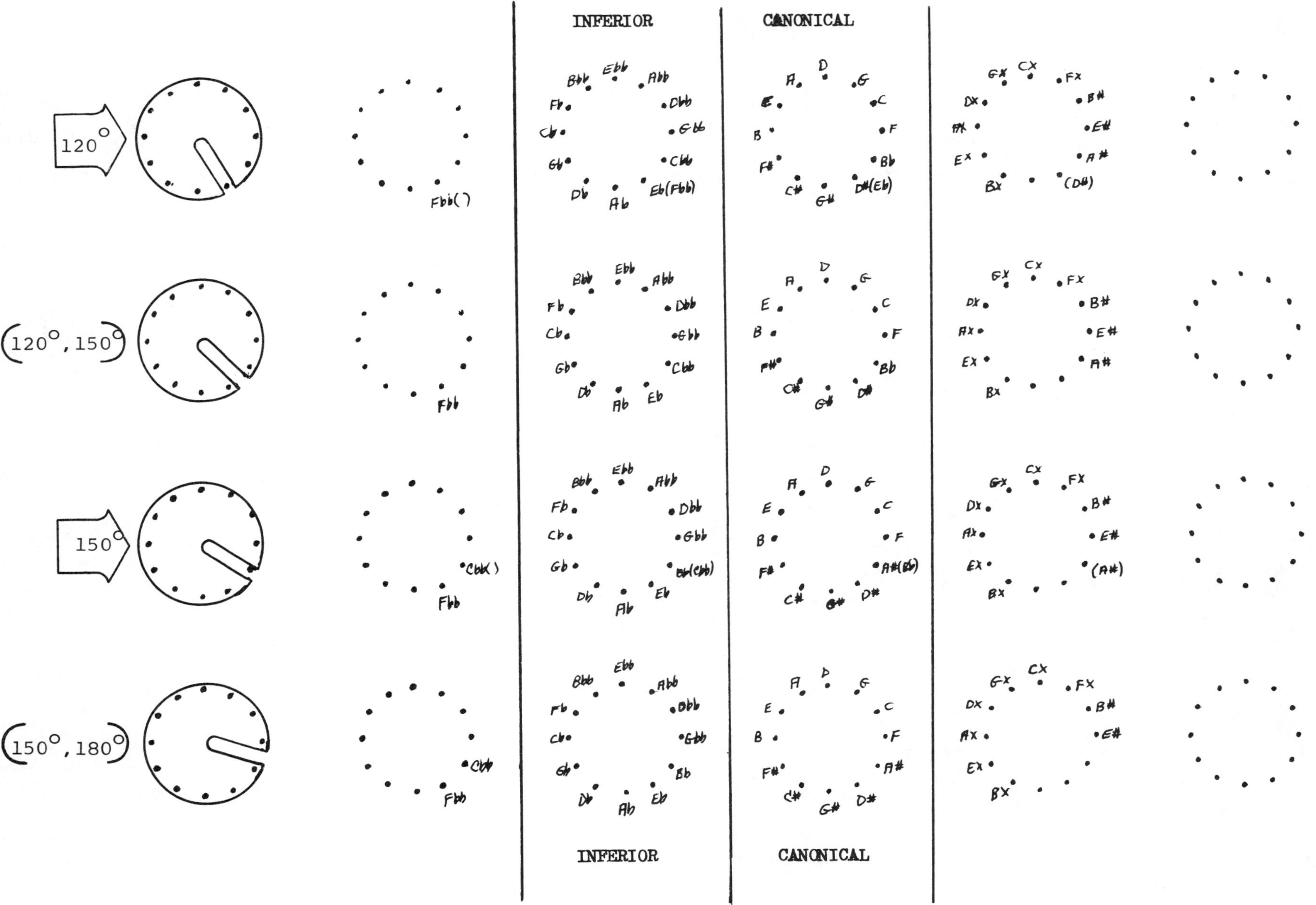
INFERIOR
CANONICAL
120°
(120°, 150°)
150°
(150°, 180°)
INFERIOR
CANONICAL

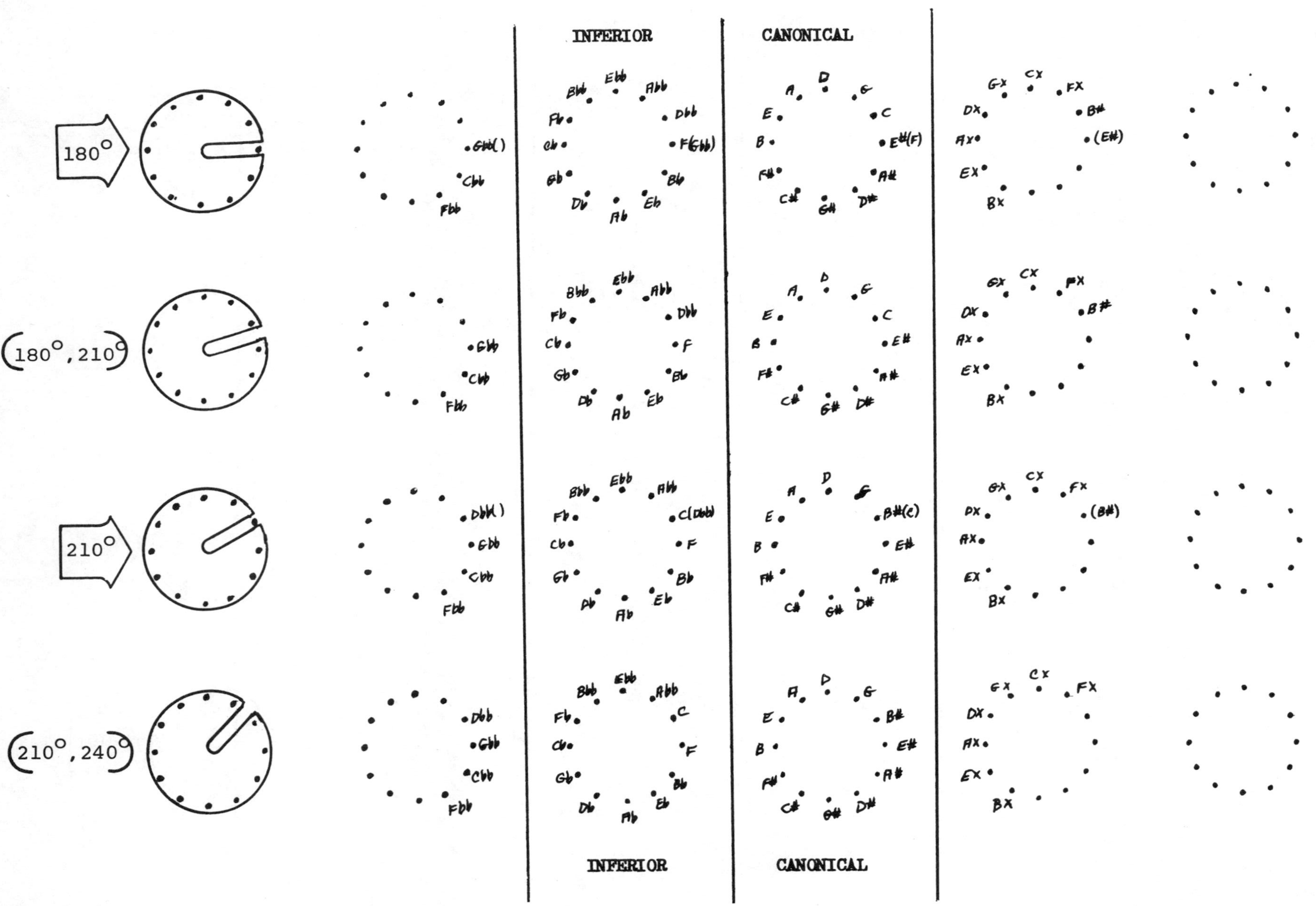
INFERIOR
CANONICAL
180°
(180°, 210°)
210°
(210°, 240°)
INFERIOR
CANONICAL

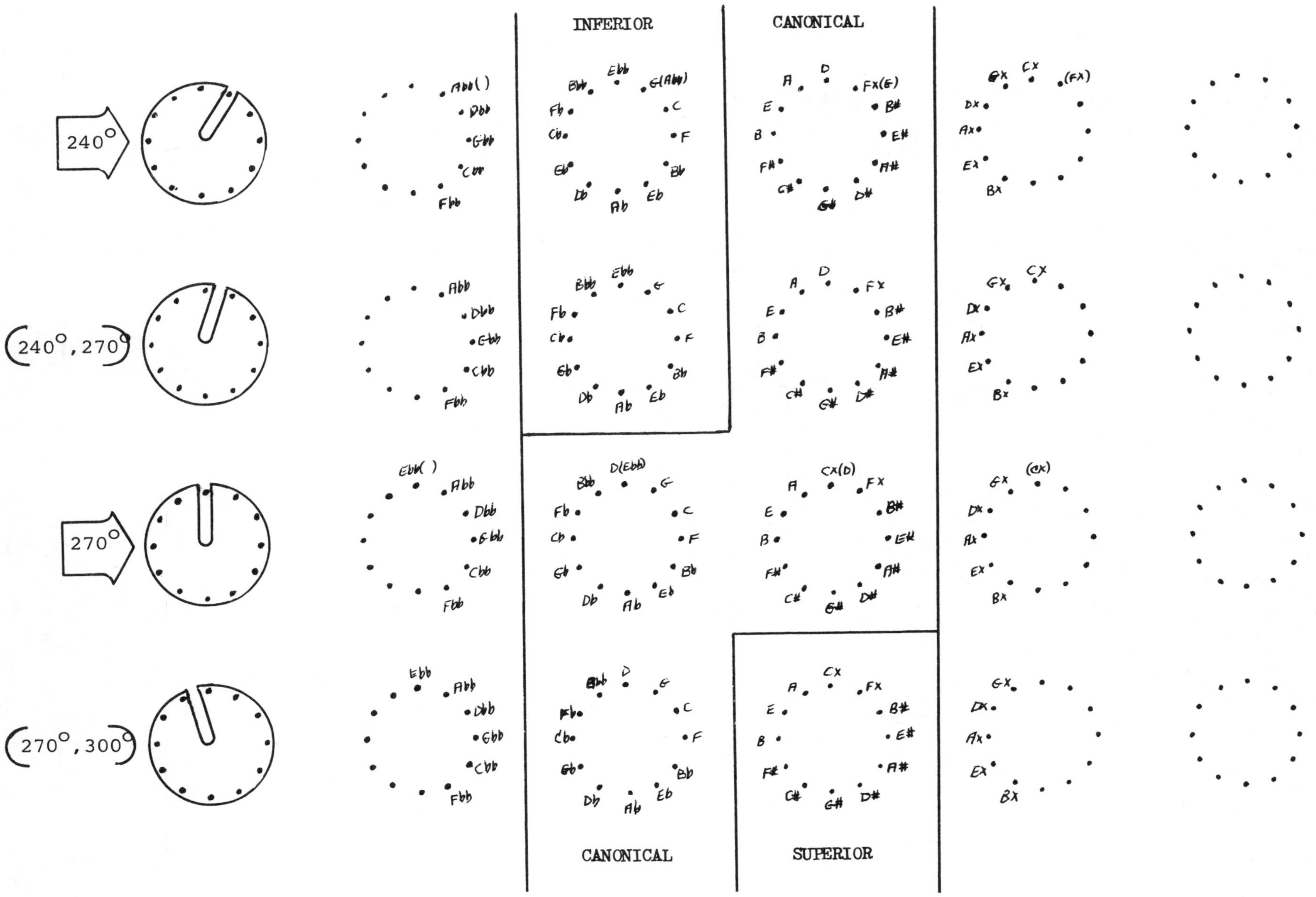
INFERIOR
CANONICAL
CANONICAL
SUPERIOR
240°
(240°, 270°)
270°
(270°, 300°)

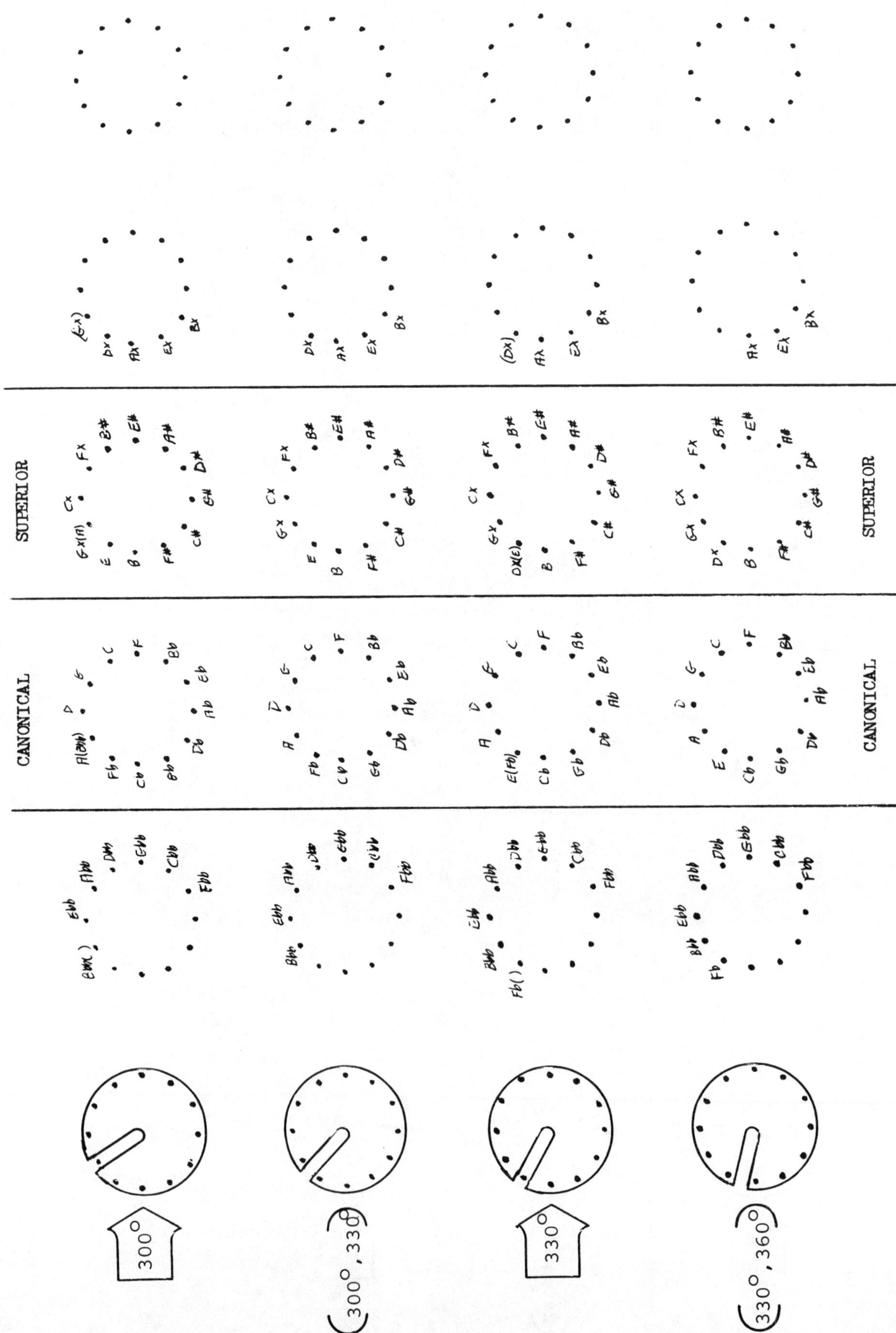
CANONICAL
SUPERIOR
CANONICAL
SUPERIOR
300°
(300°, 330°)
330°
(330°, 360°)

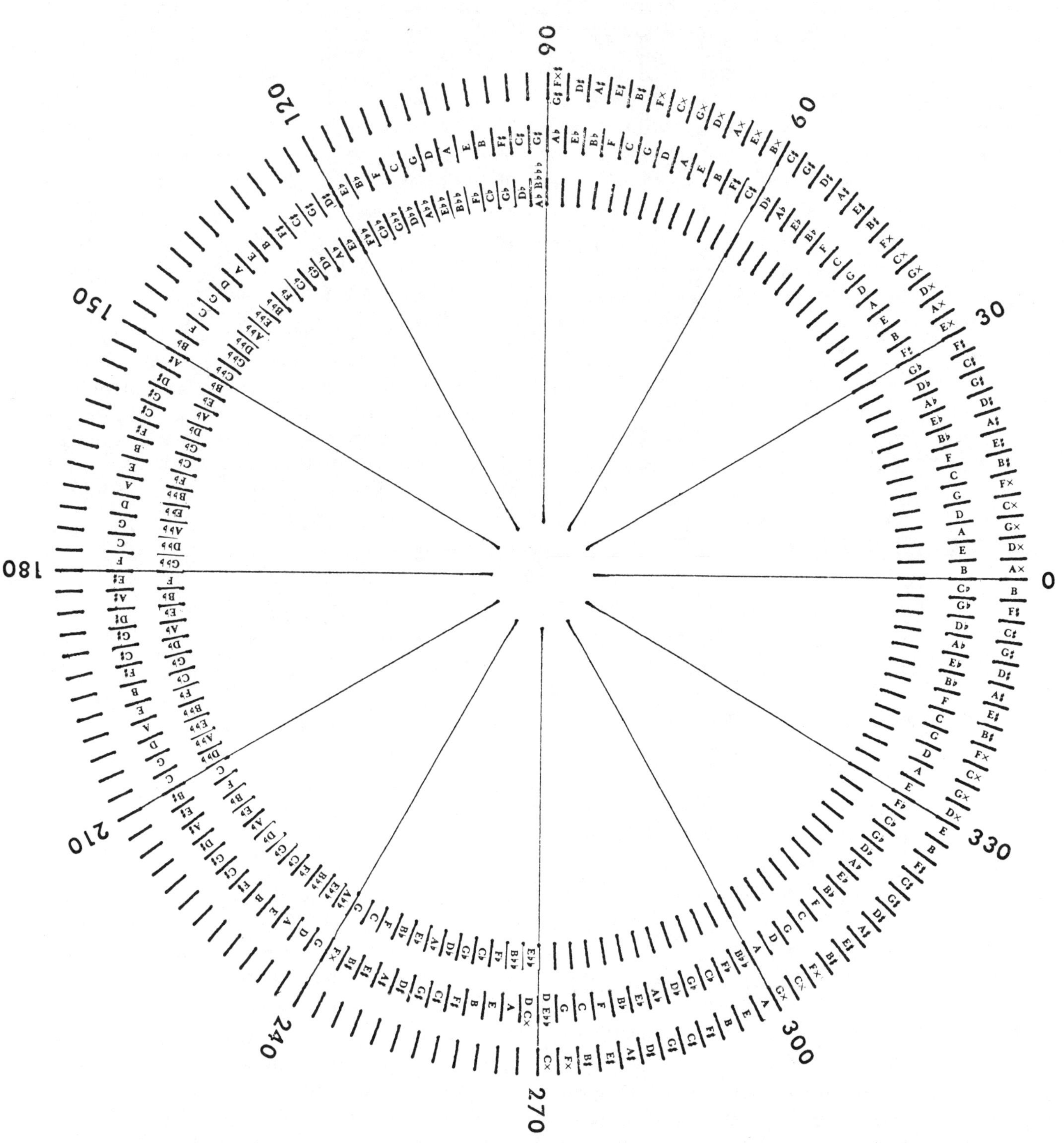


Figure 7.5a

Stencil wheel, showing arrangement of inferior, canonical, and superior literal sets on inner, middle, and outer rims, respectively.

$90^{\circ}$. The remaining harmonic minor scales behave the same way. Thus, there is a blending of the major and minor domains. In Fig. 7.5b the three cases--upper or **superior**, middle or **canonical**, and lower or **inferior**--are arranged separately in a way that may illuminate the orthographic synthesis routines given in a later chapter.

Figure 7.5b

Three possible levels of musical notation are illustrated by vertical passage down these three parallel Riemann sheets.

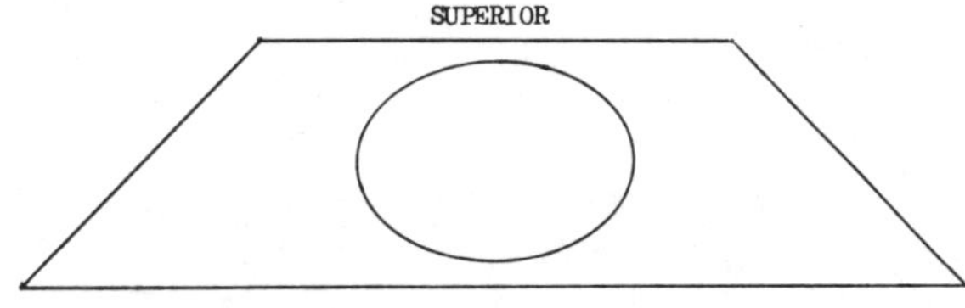


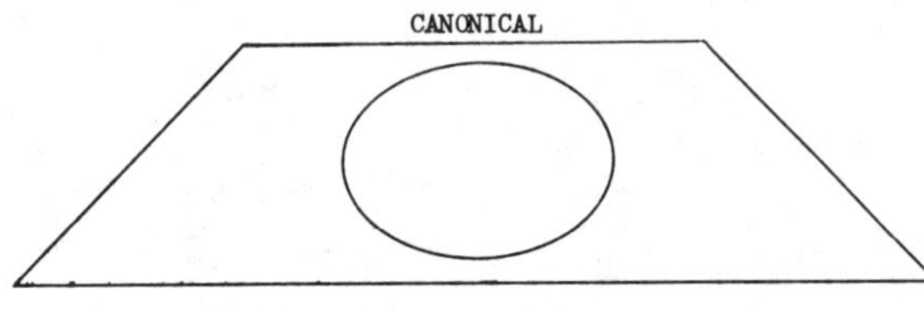


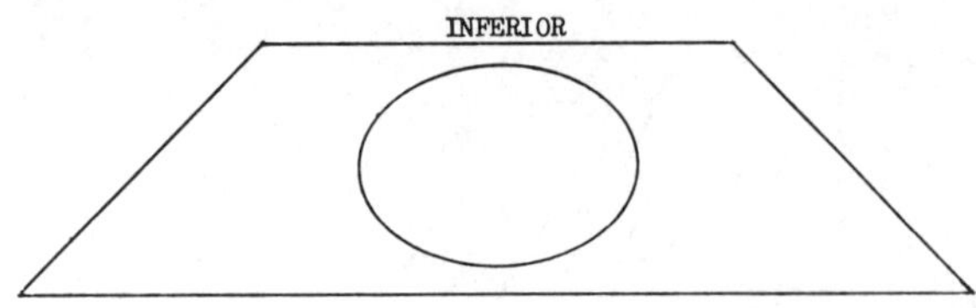


It is quite possible that many readers will not be content with just mathematical arguments and would prefer to see some tangible results before deciding to accept the complex conceptual framework that is presented here as a computer methodology for supporting music analysis. To meet this expected reaction, the next three sections will undertake a fairly lengthy demonstration of the application of the Riemann surface idea to various practical topics, such as the calculation of stencils, the construction of generalized keys, the creation of true and relative preferred notations, the determination of exact points of enharmonic change, the analysis of curvature of trajectories, and the assessment of some published examples of modulation.

The problem of the next section is to reduce the information contained in the stencil wheel (see Fig. 7.5a) to more manageable terms. The result is a simple tableau, which despite its simplicity is so amply endowed with notational richness that it sustains most of the following investigations into the basic aspects of music analysis. Of these aspects, the various roles of the dominant seventh harmony merit early special attention.

EXERCISES

**7.1** Derive the major and harmonic minor key axes.

**7.2** Why do major scales and their relative minor scales (harmonic form) have the same signature, but a different domain?

**7.3** Produce a formula for the domain of a charm in terms of its notational span.

**7.4** Apparent notational ambiguity arises (as expected) when the composition point passes through the origin or is situated on the boundary line between two sectors. Discuss this topic thoroughly bringing to bear all relevant theory.

**7.5** A function $w = w(z)$ of the complex variable $z = x + iy$ is said to be "analytic" at a point on the z plane if and only if the function and its first derivative are finite and single-valued there. If the derivative $f'(z)$ exists at every point z of a region R, then $f(z)$ is said to be "analytic in R." A necessary condition that

$$w = f(z) = u(x,y) + iv(x,y)$$

be analytic in a region R is that

u and v satisfy the Cauchy-Riemann equations

$$\frac{\partial u}{\partial x} = \frac{\partial v}{\partial y}, \quad \frac{\partial u}{\partial y} = \frac{-\partial v}{\partial x}$$

there. Show that w = arg z is not an analytic function.

**7.6** Functions, such as u(x,y) and v(x,y) in 7.5, that satisfy Laplace's equation

$$\frac{\partial^2 \psi}{\partial x^2} + \frac{\partial^2 \psi}{\partial y^2} = 0$$

in a region R are said to be "harmonic functions in R." Show that w = arg z is harmonic in the complex plane.

## GENERALIZED KEYS

Since a formal discussion of modulation requires a precise understanding of the meaning of several terms that until now could not be defined except in a vague way, these terms will be reviewed and made more precise. The first term to require tightening up is **stencil.** For the 35-literal alphabet, exactly 24 basic stencils are possible. These stencils are displayed in counterclockwise order in the "tableau" of Fig. 7.6, which aptly consolidates the information previously given in the wheel of Fig. 7.5a. The stencil tableau consists of a literal array whose spatial coverage ranges from -270 to 450 degrees. Notice that the inferior stencils are designated by letters a,b,c,d,e,f; the canonical stencils, by letters g,h,i,j,k,l,m,n,o,p,q,r; and the superior stencils, by letters s,t,u,v,w,x. The problem of assigning a stencil is solved in the following way.

Each given tonality--and consequently each harmony, charm, or chord--has a stencil. This stencil, which yields the true preferred notation, is identified by the phase of the respective tonality. The tonality of the C major scale harmony has a phase of 90°. It so happens that this value falls between rows l and m of the tableau. As a result, the C major scale stencil has thirteen literals

|B♭|E♭|A♭/G♯|C♯|F♯|B|E|A|D|G|C|F|.

On the other hand, the D harmonic minor scale tonality has phase 75°. The choice of stencil this time is clearcut; it is row l

|B♭|E♭|A♭|C♯|F♯|B|E|A|D|G|C|F|.

The C augmented triad tonality has indeterminate phase. Therefore, any stencil may be used for it. The same rule applies to any other balanced tonality. In general, the stencil associated with a given tonality is derived from that row or pair of adjacent rows of the stencil tableau that corresponds to the phase of the tonality.

Next consider the revised term **key.** By strict definition, a "key" is that region of the complex displacement plane prescribed by rows of the stencil tableau for which the spelling of a tonality does not deviate from the preferred spelling based on the associated stencil. For example, the C major scale stencil (a merger of rows l and m) requires the spelling CDEFGAB. This identical spelling is allowed only by rows j,k,l,m,n,o. So it follows that the region of the complex plane for which $\theta$ = arg z satisfies $0 \leq \theta \leq \pi$ (or, the closed upper half plane) corresponds to the key of C major. As a result, the C major key axis, which is determined by bisection, is the positive imaginary axis, that is, the vertical ray extending upward from the origin. As a second example, the A harmonic minor scale harmony ABCDEFG♯ has the phase $\theta$ = arg(**A+B+C+D+E+F+G♯**). After removing the balanced diminished seventh component **B + D + F + G♯** = 0 and substituting **C + E = D,** arg z becomes $\theta$ = arg(**A + D**) or $\theta = 105°$. Hence, the tonality of the A harmon-

## STENCIL TABLEAU

| Standard Stencil | A♯ | D♯ | G♯ | C♯ | F♯ | B | E | A | D | G | C | F |
|---|---|---|---|---|---|---|---|---|---|---|---|---|
| Binary Weights | 2048 | 1024 | 512 | 256 | 128 | 64 | 32 | 16 | 8 | 4 | 2 | 1 |
| Sector | | | | | | | | | | | | |
| I] a [-270,-240] | C♭♭ | F♭♭ | A♭ | D♭ | G♭ | C♭ | F♭ | B♭♭ | E♭♭ | A♭♭ | D♭♭ | G♭♭ |
| I] b [-240,-210] | C♭♭ | E♭ | A♭ | D♭ | G♭ | C♭ | F♭ | B♭♭ | E♭♭ | A♭♭ | D♭♭ | G♭♭ |
| I] c [-210,-180] | B♭ | E♭ | A♭ | D♭ | G♭ | C♭ | F♭ | B♭♭ | E♭♭ | A♭♭ | D♭♭ | G♭♭ |
| I] d [-180,-150] | B♭ | E♭ | A♭ | D♭ | G♭ | C♭ | F♭ | B♭♭ | E♭♭ | A♭♭ | D♭♭ | F |
| I] e [-150,-120] | B♭ | E♭ | A♭ | D♭ | G♭ | C♭ | F♭ | B♭♭ | E♭♭ | A♭♭ | C | F |
| I] f [-120,-90] | B♭ | E♭ | A♭ | D♭ | G♭ | C♭ | F♭ | B♭♭ | E♭♭ | G | C | F |
| C] g [-90,-60] | B♭ | E♭ | A♭ | D♭ | G♭ | C♭ | F♭ | B♭♭ | D | G | C | F |
| C] h [-60,-30] | B♭ | E♭ | A♭ | D♭ | G♭ | C♭ | F♭ | A | D | G | C | F |
| C] i [-30,0] | B♭ | E♭ | A♭ | D♭ | G♭ | C♭ | E | A | D | G | C | F |
| C] j [0,30] | B♭ | E♭ | A♭ | D♭ | G♭ | B | E | A | D | G | C | F |
| C] k [30,60] | B♭ | E♭ | A♭ | D♭ | F♯ | B | E | A | D | G | C | F |
| C] l [60,90] | B♭ | E♭ | A♭ | C♯ | F♯ | B | E | A | D | G | C | F |
| C] m [90,120] | B♭ | E♭ | G♯ | C♯ | F♯ | B | E | A | D | G | C | F |
| C] n [120,150] | B♭ | D♯ | G♯ | C♯ | F♯ | B | E | A | D | G | C | F |
| C] o [150,180] | A♯ | D♯ | G♯ | C♯ | F♯ | B | E | A | D | G | C | F |
| C] p [180,210] | A♯ | D♯ | G♯ | C♯ | F♯ | B | E | A | D | G | C | E♯ |
| C] q [210,240] | A♯ | D♯ | G♯ | C♯ | F♯ | B | E | A | D | G | B♯ | E♯ |
| C] r [240,270] | A♯ | D♯ | G♯ | C♯ | F♯ | B | E | A | D | Fx | B♯ | E♯ |
| S] s [270,300] | A♯ | D♯ | G♯ | C♯ | F♯ | B | E | A | Cx | Fx | B♯ | E♯ |
| S] t [300,330] | A♯ | D♯ | G♯ | C♯ | F♯ | B | E | Gx | Cx | Fx | B♯ | E♯ |
| S] u [330,360] | A♯ | D♯ | G♯ | C♯ | F♯ | B | Dx | Gx | Cx | Fx | B♯ | E♯ |
| S] v [360,390] | A♯ | D♯ | G♯ | C♯ | F♯ | Ax | Dx | Gx | Cx | Fx | B♯ | E♯ |
| S] w [390,420] | A♯ | D♯ | G♯ | C♯ | Ex | Ax | Dx | Gx | Cx | Fx | B♯ | E♯ |
| S] x [420,450] | A♯ | D♯ | G♯ | Bx | Ex | Ax | Dx | Gx | Cx | Fx | B♯ | E♯ |

I] Inferior  C] Canonical  S] Superior

Figure 7.6

Literal array containing generalized key regions and used for validating preferred notations in accordance with the perfect orthographic principle. The construction of every row of the tableau is based upon the choice of an appropriate sheet of the Riemann surface on which the function $w = \arg z$ is defined.

ic minor scale harmony has phase 105°. This value is the key axis and corresponds to row m of the stencil tableau. Accordingly, the A harmonic minor scale stencil is

|B♭|E♭|G♯|C♯|F♯|B|E|A|D|G|C|F|.

Again by definition, the key of A harmonic minor is that region of the complex displacement or z-plane which refers to those rows of the tableau that permit the same true preferred spelling as that called for by the associated stencil. Only rows m,n, and o permit this spelling. It is concluded that the region of the complex plane for which $\theta = \arg z$ satisfies the inequality $\pi/2 \leq \theta \leq \pi$ (or the closed second quadrant) corresponds to the key of A harmonic minor. The bisector of this region is the ray with slope minus one issuing from the origin, that is, the 135° line. Note that for the major scale harmony the **bisector** and **tonality phase angle** coincide. This result is not true for the harmonic minor scale harmony. (See Fig. 7.7.)

A final new definition is forthcoming based on the preceding ones and locking them into place. This is the fundamental concept of a generalized key. A "generalized key" is defined to be that region of the complex plane corresponding to a given key and including not only the literals of the preferred spelling of the underlying tonality, as prescribed by the associated stencil and naturally extended into adjacent rows of the stencil tableau, but also those literals, not required to spell the tonality, that appear in these rows. The members of this set form what might be called the "field of accidentals" of the generalized key. To illustrate, for the key of C major

| | | | | | | | | | | | | | |
|---|---|---|---|---|---|---|---|---|---|---|---|---|---|
| C] j | [0,30] | B♭ | E♭ | A♭ | D♭ | G♭ | B | E | A | D | G | C | F |
| C] k | [30,60] | B♭ | E♭ | A♭ | D♭ | F♯ | B | E | A | D | G | C | F |
| C] l | [60,90] | B♭ | E♭ | A♭ | C♯ | F♯ | B | E | A | D | G | C | F |
| C] m | [90,120] | B♭ | E♭ | G♯ | C♯ | F♯ | B | E | A | D | G | C | F |
| C] n | [120,150] | B♭ | D♯ | G♯ | C♯ | F♯ | B | E | A | D | G | C | F |
| C] o | [150,180] | A♯ | D♯ | G♯ | C♯ | F♯ | B | E | A | D | G | C | F |

and for the key of C harmonic minor

| | | | | | | | | | | | | | |
|---|---|---|---|---|---|---|---|---|---|---|---|---|---|
| C] j | [0,30] | B♭ | E♭ | A♭ | D♭ | G♭ | B | E | A | D | G | C | F |
| C] k | [30,60] | B♭ | E♭ | A♭ | D♭ | F♯ | B | E | A | D | G | C | F |
| C] l | [60,90] | B♭ | E♭ | A♭ | C♯ | F♯ | B | E | A | D | G | C | F |

KEY AXIS LOCATOR CHART

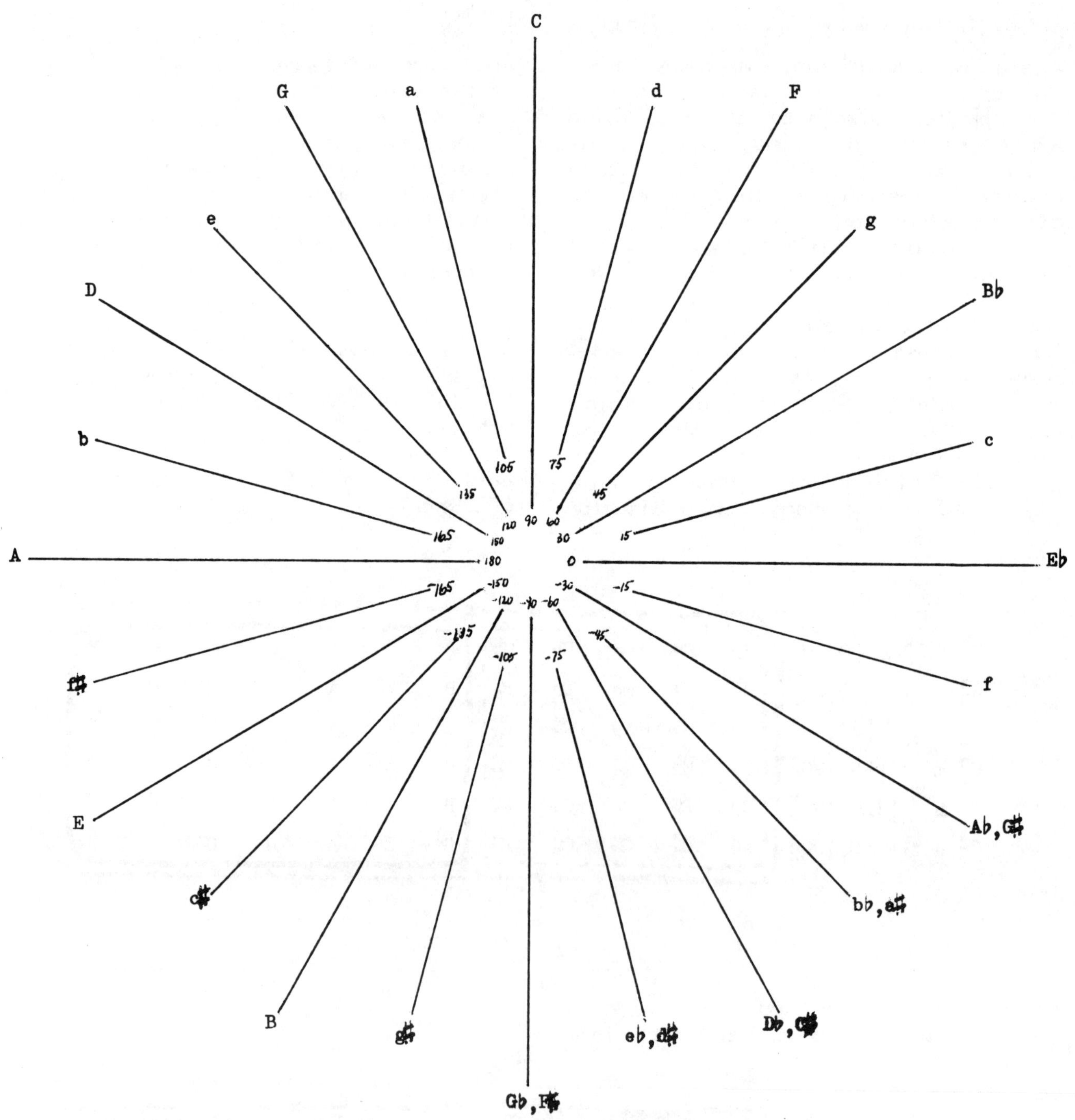


Figure 7.7

Directory of major and minor key axes in the complex displacement plane. Recall that by their construction the minor keys have a more limited angular coverage (only $90^{\circ}$) than do the major keys (a full $180^{\circ}$). Although the boundaries of keys can be found exactly, their interiors--the key regions--are ambiguous because of overlap.

| | A♯ | D♯ | G♯ | C♯ | F♯ | B | E | A | D | G | C | F |
|---|---|---|---|---|---|---|---|---|---|---|---|---|
| Standard Stencil | A♯ | D♯ | G♯ | C♯ | F♯ | B | E | A | D | G | C | F |
| Binary Weights | 2048 | 1024 | 512 | 256 | 128 | 64 | 32 | 16 | 8 | 4 | 2 | 1 |
| Sector | | | | | | | | | | | | |
| I] a [-270,-240] | C♭♭ | F♭♭ | A♭ | D♭ | G♭ | C♭ | F♭ | B♭♭ | E♭♭ | A♭♭ | D♭♭ | G♭♭ |
| I] b [-240,-210] | C♭♭ | E♭ | A♭ | D♭ | G♭ | C♭ | F♭ | B♭♭ | E♭♭ | A♭♭ | D♭♭ | G♭♭ |
| I] c [-210,-180] | B♭ | E♭ | A♭ | D♭ | G♭ | C♭ | F♭ | B♭♭ | E♭♭ | A♭♭ | D♭♭ | G♭♭ |
| I] d [-180,-150] | B♭ | E♭ | A♭ | D♭ | G♭ | C♭ | F♭ | B♭♭ | E♭♭ | A♭♭ | D♭♭ | F |
| I] e [-150,-120] | B♭ | E♭ | A♭ | D♭ | G♭ | C♭ | F♭ | B♭♭ | E♭♭ | A♭♭ | C | F |
| I] f [-150,-90] | B♭ | E♭ | A♭ | D♭ | G♭ | C♭ | F♭ | B♭♭ | E♭♭ | G | C | F |
| C] g [-90,-60] | B♭ | E♭ | A♭ | D♭ | G♭ | C♭ | F♭ | B♭♭ | D | G | C | F |
| C] h [-60,-30] | B♭ | E♭ | A♭ | D♭ | G♭ | C♭ | F♭ | A | D | G | C | F |
| C] i [-30,0] | B♭ | E♭ | A♭ | D♭ | G♭ | C♭ | E | A | D | G | C | F |
| C] j [0,30] | B♭ | E♭ | A♭ | D♭ | G♭ | B | E | A | D | G | C | F |
| C] k [30,60] | B♭ | E♭ | A♭ | D♭ | F♯ | B | E | A | D | G | C | F |
| C] l [60,90] | B♭ | E♭ | A♭ | C♯ | F♯ | B | E | A | D | G | C | F |
| C] m [90,120] | B♭ | E♭ | G♯ | C♯ | F♯ | B | E | A | D | G | C | F |
| C] n [120,150] | B♭ | D♯ | G♯ | C♯ | F♯ | B | E | A | D | G | C | F |
| C] o [150,180] | A♯ | D♯ | G♯ | C♯ | F♯ | B | E | A | D | G | C | F |
| C] p [180,210] | A♯ | D♯ | G♯ | C♯ | F♯ | B | E | A | D | G | C | E♯ |
| C] q [210,240] | A♯ | D♯ | G♯ | C♯ | F♯ | B | E | A | D | G | B♯ | E♯ |
| C] r [240,270] | A♯ | D♯ | G♯ | C♯ | F♯ | B | E | A | D | F× | B♯ | E♯ |
| S] s [270,300] | A♯ | D♯ | G♯ | C♯ | F♯ | B | E | A | C× | F× | B♯ | E♯ |
| S] t [300,330] | A♯ | D♯ | G♯ | C♯ | F♯ | B | E | G× | C× | F× | B♯ | E♯ |
| S] u [330,360] | A♯ | D♯ | G♯ | C♯ | F♯ | B | D× | G× | C× | F× | B♯ | E♯ |
| S] v [360,390] | A♯ | D♯ | G♯ | C♯ | F♯ | A× | D× | G× | C× | F× | B♯ | E♯ |
| S] w [390,420] | A♯ | D♯ | G♯ | C♯ | E× | A× | D× | G× | C× | F× | B♯ | E♯ |
| S] x [420,450] | A♯ | D♯ | G♯ | B× | E× | A× | D× | G× | C× | F× | B♯ | E♯ |

I] Inferior C] Canonical S] Superior

Figure 7.8

Stencil tableau showing the four different preferred spellings of harmony 77 in the generalized key of B major. Note that of these the one designated the German sixth chord (the augmented sixth built on the flat submediant) is the most probable.

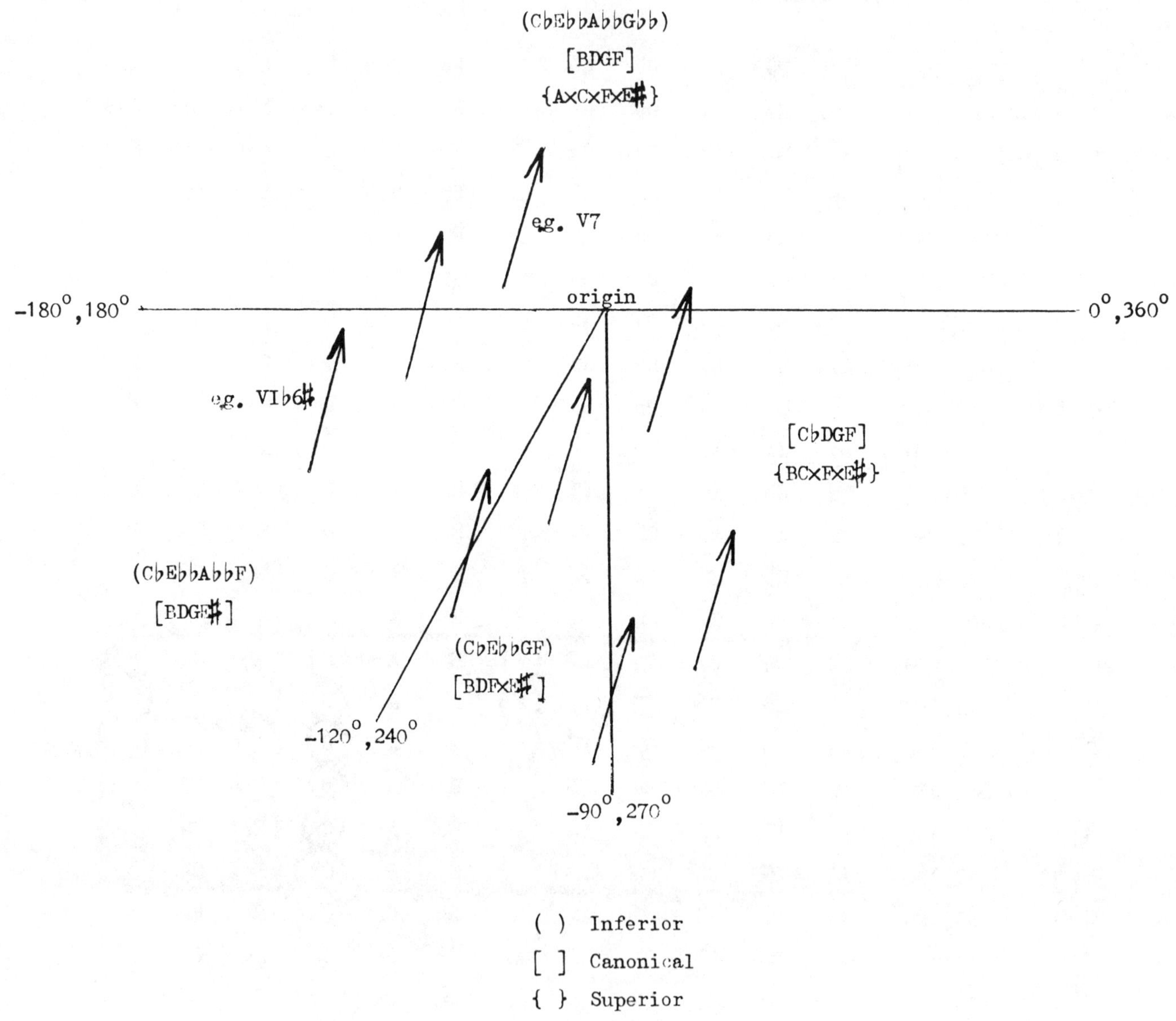


Figure 7.9

Regions of the tonal displacement plane having different preferred notations for harmony 77. Arrows of phase 75° show possible localizations of harmony 77 with respect to the center of the coordinate system. Points of enharmonic change are determined precisely by boundary crossings, but do not always accompany a key sector departure or entry.

where the **generalized key** is represented by the barbed enclosure, the **key** is designated by the solid enclosure, and the **field of accidentals** is indicated by the dashed enclosure.

The stencil tableau of Fig. 7.6 allows the deduction of much data of interest about key relationships. The boundary lines mark angles of $30^{o}k$, where the multiplier $k = 0, 1, 2, \ldots$, separating distinct regions of notational uniformity as well as delimiting generalized keys. It is useful to see which notations can be continued across these boundaries. The proper answer to this question is essential to a thorough understanding of the theory of enharmonic exchange because the spellings and therefore the roles of chords may change significantly as the variable composition point p moves in the z-plane from one region of notational uniformity into another.

Basic texts in traditional harmony almost always cover the matter of German augmented sixth chords. But, unfortunately, heretofore no precise estimates of their effects could be given. The fact that the spelling that leads to this interpretation of a chord arises naturally as a preferred notation reveals a great deal about the chord's auditory nature. For example, the two tonalities spelled GBDE♯ and GBDF are theoretically (in equitemperament), and indeed often practically, interchangeable. Nevertheless, if regarded as being preferred notations, these spellings instantly can provide a useful insight into key relationships that otherwise might remain hidden if the notes are interpreted along conventional harmonic lines. As shown in Fig. 7.8, there are two additional preferred spellings for harmony 77 that arise in the generalized key of B major. These are FxBDE♯ and FxBCxE♯. Notice that the spellings FxBDE♯ and GBDE♯ are confined to the B major region, whereas the spellings GBDF and FxBCxE♯ continue outside the region.

This occurrence of varied spellings leads to an apparent dilemma. From one point of view (all of C major), harmony 77 is written BDGF; from another point of view (part of B major), the same harmony 77 is written BDGE♯. But there is a way out of trouble. The exact spelling of a musical component in relative preferred notation depends completely on the particular points z of the path that are encountered by the variable composition point p, while the composition trajectory is being generated. This fact is illustrated by Fig. 7.9. If z is a point lying on the sector $0^{o} \leq \arg z \leq 180^{o}$, i.e., the upper half plane associated with the generalized key of C major, then the harmony is represented by the canonical notation BDGF. Otherwise, it has a different notation. As indicated, the effect of crossing any boundary is to relax one literal constraint and to tighten another. Similar boundaries can be found for any chord by referring to the thresholds of enharmonic exchange that are indicated by the dotted lines in Fig. 7.8.

The next few pages contain a short musical example. It is intended to illustrate and reinforce several important aspects of the new computer methodology so far revealed.

LITTLE PRELUDE

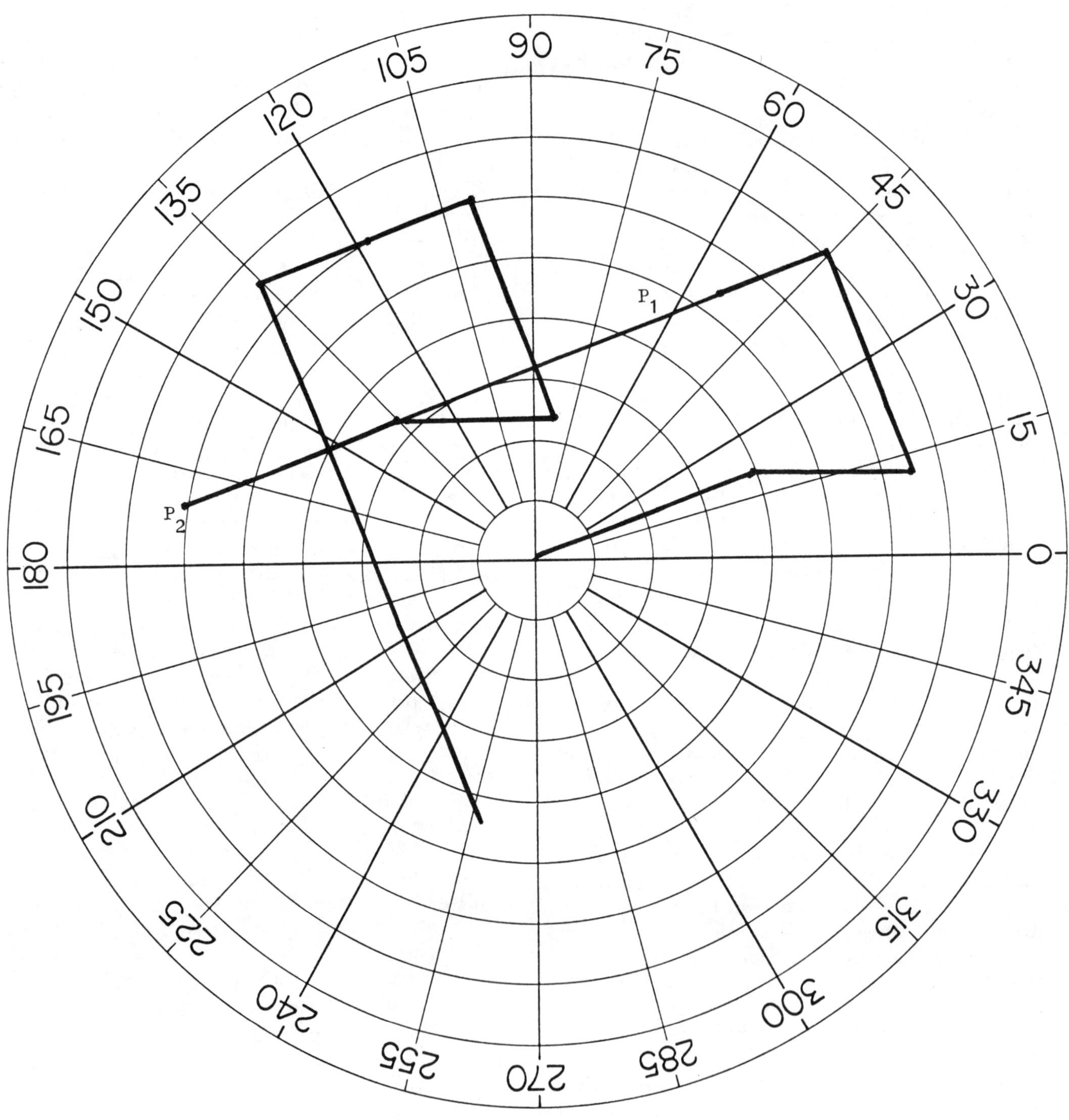


Figure 7.10

The trajectory for the **Little Prelude** travels a jagged course in getting from the key signature sector of three flats to the key signature sector of six sharps. At point $P_1$ the path crosses the D♭/C♯ enharmonic threshold; at point $P_2$ there is a phase reversal.

The complete data file can be read out for verification. This listing is the first segment of a component-by-component analysis of the "Little Prelude," produced by the programs for music analysis given in Chapter 9. These include

40 Phonetic Notation

41 Inferior True Notation

42 Canonical True Notation

43 Superior True Notation

44 Inferior Relative Notation

45 Canonical Relative Notation

46 Superior Relative Notation

Here the original music, expressed in phonetic notation, has been numerically coded to form the data file.

```
N              x        Δt
00 2 68 3 2 0 1.000
01 1 1 58 4 0 1.000
02 5 5 2 6 0 1.000
03 19 5 29 19 0 0.500
04 19 5 29 19 0 2.500
05 2 68 3 2 0 1.000
06 1 1 58 4 0 1.000
07 5 5 2 6 0 1.000
08 19 5 29 19 0 0.500
09 19 5 29 19 0 0.500
10 58 58 2 68 58 0 2.000
```

At any instant the harmonic designation H has 4096 possible values, the pitch level L has 12 possible values, the sonoral characteristic S has 352 possible values, and the charm specification Q has an unlimited number of possible values.

```
N        Q          S    L    H
00 00000000009222 0025X1024 1030
01 00000000004617 0073X0512 0521
02 00000000065586 0025X0002 0050
03 00000000524688 0025X0016 0400
04 00000000524688 0025X0016 0400
05 00000000009222 0025X1024 1030
06 00000000004617 0073X0512 0521
07 00000000065586 0025X0002 0050
08 00000000524688 0025X0016 0400
09 00000000524688 0025X0016 0400
10 00859203328 2 0019X0512 1538
```

The absolute key penetration function slants to the right, indicating a short-term shift in key signature.

| N | Gb | eb | Db | bb | Ab | f | Eb | c | Bb | g | F | d | C | a | G | e | D | b | A | f# | E | c# | B | g# | F# |
|---|---|---|---|---|---|---|---|---|---|---|---|---|---|---|---|---|---|---|---|---|---|---|---|---|---|
| 00 | | | -03 | 00 | 02 | 03 | 04 | 04 | 04 | 04 | 03 | 02 | 00 | -05 | | | | | | | | | | | |
| 01 | | -05 | 01 | 04 | 05 | 06 | 06 | 06 | 06 | 06 | 05 | 03 | 00 | | | | | | | | | | | | |
| 02 | | | | -99 | 01 | 04 | 05 | 06 | 07 | 07 | 07 | 06 | 05 | 04 | 01 | | | | | | | | | | |
| 03 | | | | | | -05 | 00 | 02 | 03 | 04 | 04 | 04 | 04 | 03 | 02 | 00 | -03 | | | | | | | | |
| 04 | 01 | | | | | | | | | | | | | 01 | 05 | 07 | 09 | 09 | 09 | 09 | 09 | 08 | 07 | 05 | 01 |
| 05 | -05 | | | | | | | | | | | | | 02 | 05 | 06 | 07 | 03 | 08 | 08 | 08 | 07 | 05 | 03 | -05 |
| 06 | -05 | | | | | | | | | | | | | 00 | 03 | 05 | 06 | 06 | 07 | 07 | 06 | 05 | 04 | 02 | -05 |
| 07 | | | | | | | | | | | | -01 | 03 | 06 | 07 | 07 | 08 | 08 | 07 | 07 | 06 | 04 | -00 | | |
| 08 | | | | | | | | | | | | | 01 | 05 | 07 | 08 | 09 | 09 | 09 | 09 | 08 | 07 | 05 | -00 | |
| 09 | 10 | 10 | 09 | 07 | 04 | | | | | | | | | | | | | -06 | 05 | 08 | 09 | 10 | 10 | 10 | 10 |
| 10 | 14 | 14 | 13 | 12 | 11 | 09 | 03 | | | | | | | | | | | | | 06 | 10 | 12 | 13 | 13 | 14 |

The boundary of the six-or-greater regions serves to pinpoint those keys that tend to stand out conspicuously above the others.

| N | Gb | eb | Db | bb | Ab | f | Eb | c | Bb | g | F | d | C | a | G | e | D | b | A | f# | E | c# | B | g# | F# |
|---|---|---|---|---|---|---|---|---|---|---|---|---|---|---|---|---|---|---|---|---|---|---|---|---|---|
| 00 | | | -03 | 00 | 02 | 03 | 04 | 04 | 04 | 04 | 03 | 02 | 00 | -05 | | | | | | | | | | | |
| 01 | | -05 | 01 | 04 | 05 | 06 | 06 | 06 | 06 | 06 | 05 | 03 | 00 | | | | | | | | | | | | |
| 02 | | | | -99 | 01 | 04 | 05 | 06 | 07 | 07 | 07 | 06 | 05 | 04 | 01 | | | | | | | | | | |
| 03 | | | | | | -05 | 00 | 02 | 03 | 04 | 04 | 04 | 04 | 03 | 02 | 00 | -03 | | | | | | | | |
| 04 | 01 | | | | | | | | | | | | | 01 | 05 | 07 | 09 | 09 | 09 | 09 | 09 | 08 | 07 | 05 | 01 |
| 05 | -09 | | | | | | | | | | | | | 02 | 05 | 06 | 07 | 08 | 00 | 08 | 08 | 07 | 05 | 03 | -05 |
| 06 | -05 | | | | | | | | | | | | | 00 | 03 | 05 | 06 | 06 | 07 | 07 | 06 | 05 | 04 | 02 | -05 |
| 07 | | | | | | | | | | | | -01 | 03 | 06 | 07 | 07 | 08 | 08 | 07 | 07 | 06 | 04 | -00 | | |
| 08 | | | | | | | | | | | | | 01 | 05 | 07 | 08 | 09 | 09 | 09 | 09 | 08 | 07 | 05 | -00 | |
| 09 | 10 | 10 | 09 | 07 | 04 | | | | | | | | | | | | | -06 | 05 | 08 | 09 | 10 | 10 | 10 | 10 |
| 10 | 14 | 14 | 13 | 12 | 11 | 09 | 03 | | | | | | | | | | | | | 06 | 10 | 12 | 13 | 13 | 14 |

| P | TI | TC | TS |
|---|---|---|---|
| C E♭ G C | C E♭ G C | C E♭ G C | B♯ D♯ Fx B♯ |
| F F A♭ D | F F A♭ D | F F A♭ D | E♯ E♯ G♯ Cx |
| A A C E | B♯ B♯ D♯ F♭ | A A C E | A A C E |
| F♯ A C♯ F♯ | G♭ B♯ D♭ G♭ | F♯ A C♯ F♯ | F♯ A C♯ F♯ |
| F♯ A C♯ F♯ | G♭ B♯ D♭ G♭ | F♯ A C♯ F♯ | F♯ A C♯ F♯ |
| C E♭ G C | C E♭ G C | C E♭ G C | B♯ D♯ Fx B♯ |
| F F A♭ D | F F A♭ D | F F A♭ D | E♯ E♯ G♯ Cx |
| A A C E | B♯ B♯ D♯ F♭ | A A C E | A A C E |
| F♯ A C♯ F♯ | G♭ B♯ D♭ G♭ | F♯ A C♯ F♯ | F♯ A C♯ F♯ |
| F♯ A C♯ F♯ | G♭ B♯ D♭ G♭ | F♯ A C♯ F♯ | F♯ A C♯ F♯ |
| A♭ A♭ C E♭ A♭ | A♭ A♭ C E♭ A♭ | A♭ A♭ C E♭ A♭ | G♯ G♯ B♯ D♯ G♯ |

| P | RI | RC | RS |
|---|---|---|---|
| C E♭ G C | C E♭ G C | C E♭ G C | B♯ D♯ Fx B♯ |
| F F A♭ D | F F A♭ D | F F A♭ D | E♯ E♯ G♯ Cx |
| A A C E | A A C E | A A C E | Gx Gx B♯ Dx |
| F♯ A C♯ F♯ | F♯ A D♭ F♯ | F♯ A D♭ F♯ | Ex Gx C♯ Ex |
| F♯ A C♯ F♯ | G♭ B♯ D♭ G♭ | F♯ A C♯ F♯ | F♯ A C♯ F♯ |
| C E♭ G C | D♯ E♭ A♯ D♯ | C D♯ G C | C D♯ G C |
| F F A♭ D | F F A♭ D | F F A♭ D | E♯ E♯ G♯ Cx |
| A A C E | B♯ B♯ D♯ F♭ | A A C E | A A C E |
| F♯ A C♯ F♯ | G♭ B♯ D♭ G♭ | F♯ A C♯ F♯ | F♯ A C♯ F♯ |
| F♯ A C♯ F♯ | G♭ B♯ D♭ G♭ | F♯ A C♯ F♯ | F♯ A C♯ F♯ |
| A♭ A♭ C E♭ A♭ | A♭ A♭ C E♭ A♭ | G♯ G♯ B♯ D♯ G♯ | G♯ G♯ B♯ D♯ G♯ |

P: phonetic I: inferior
T: true C: canonical
R: relative S: superior

## EXERCISES

**7.7** Explain how the stencil tableau of Fig. 7.6 is derived from the stencil wheel of Fig. 7.5a. What sector corresponds to the standard stencil?

**7.8** What accidentals are in the generalized keys of (a) F major and (b) C♯ harmonic minor?

**7.9** What generalized harmonic minor keys are included in the generalized key of A♭ major?

**7.10** In what way does the generalized key of C harmonic minor differ from the generalized key of C melodic minor?

**7.11** Debate the question: Should the harmonic scale be regarded as an independent diatonic scale, or rather as simply a variation of the conventional major scale?

**7.12** Using the stencil tableau, illustrate the notion of enharmonically equivalent keys.

**7.13** Find the field of accidentals for (a) the wholetone scale CDEF♯G♯A♯, (b) the wholetone scale FGABC♯D♯, and (c) the chromatic scale B♯C♯DD♯EE♯F♯GG♯AA♯B.

**7.14** Define the term "field of essentials" as relating to a generalized key. Is it larger or smaller than the associated field of accidentals? Using this concept, find and express a necessary and sufficient condition for a literal to belong to a given generalized key.

**7.15** For the 35-literal alphabet, the stencil tableau covers 720 degrees in azimuth. Extend the tableau as required for the 49-literal alphabet.

**7.16** In the C major sector, the enlarged key signature is found from the stencil tableau (rows l and m) to contain three sharps and three flats:

```
G♯  C♯  F♯  B   E   A   D   G   C   F   B♭  E♭  A♭ —chromatic
            |   |   |   |   |   |   |
            B   E   A   D   G   C   F —diatonic
                |   |   |   |   |
                E   A   D   G   C — pentatonic.
```

Identify the (a) seven regular degrees and (b) six auxiliary--not chromatic--degrees, two of which are enharmonically equivalent. Make the same identification for assorted diatonic scales.

**7.17** Find all preferred notations (inferior, canonical, and superior) for each of the following expressions:

(a) H = 1365,

(b) H = 127*128,

(c) Q = 10,666,

(d) $ii^7$ in G♯/A♭ minor,

(e) F×C♭DG♭♭,

(f) Scriabin's mystic chord, and

(g) $\{T_0, T_1, T_2\}$.

(<u>Hint</u>. First determine θ).

**7.18** The problem of musical notation, although often ignored, is not trivial. Upon it nevertheless hinges the basic question of practicality for a completely general computer methodology for music analysis. But once understood, the perfect orthographic principle is quite simple. Its method of application may be summarized as a list of topics:

Riemann surface
displacement plane
vector resultant
phase reversal
branch cut
Riemann sheet
applicable stencil
preferred notation
stencil tableau
generalized key
field of accidentals.

Trace through this list and expand each item into a short paragraph devoted to an explanation of the given topic.

**7.19** J.A. Hamilton [1] defined the word **equivocal** as a "term applied to such chords as, by a mere change in the notation, may belong to several keys." Refine this definition.

| Standard Stencil | A# | D# | G# | C# | F# | B | E | A | D | G | C | F |
|---|---|---|---|---|---|---|---|---|---|---|---|---|
| Binary Weights | 2048 | 1024 | 512 | 256 | 128 | 64 | 32 | 16 | 8 | 4 | 2 | 1 |
| Sector | | | | | | | | | | | | |
| I] a [-270,-240] | | | Ab | Db | | Cb | Fb | | | Abb | Dbb | Gbb |
| I] b [-240,-210] | | | Ab | Db | | Cb | Fb | | | Abb | Dbb | Gbb |
| I] c [-210,-180] | | | Ab | Db | | Cb | Fb | | | Abb | Dbb | Gbb |
| I] d [-180,-150] | | | Ab | Db | | Cb | Fb | | | Abb | Dbb | F |
| I] e [-150,-120] | | | Ab | Db | | Cb | Fb | | | Abb | C | F |
| I] f [-150,-90] | | | Ab | Db | | Cb | Fb | | | G | C | F |
| C] g [-90,-60] | | | Ab | Db | | Cb | Fb | | | G | C | F |
| C] h [-60,-30] | | | Ab | Db | | Cb | Fb | | | G | C | F |
| C] i [-30,0] | | | Ab | Db | | Cb | E | | | G | C | F |
| C] j [0,30] | | | Ab | Db | | B | E | | | G | C | F |
| C] k [30,60] | | | Ab | Db | | B | E | | | G | C | F |
| C] l [60,90] | | | Ab | C# | | B | E | | | G | C | F |
| C] m [90,120] | | | G# | C# | | B | E | | | G | C | F |
| C] n [120,150] | | | G# | C# | | B | E | | | G | C | F |
| C] o [150,180] | | | G# | C# | | B | E | | | G | C | F |
| C] p [180,210] | | | G# | C# | | B | E | | | G | C | E# |
| C] q [210,240] | | | G# | C# | | B | E | | | G | B# | E# |
| C] r [240,270] | | | G# | C# | | B | E | | | Fx | B# | E# |
| S] s [270,300] | | | G# | C# | | B | E | | | Fx | B# | E# |
| S] t [300,330] | | | G# | C# | | B | E | | | Fx | B# | E# |
| S] u [330,360] | | | G# | C# | | B | Dx | | | Fx | B# | E# |
| S] v [360,390] | | | G# | C# | | Ax | Dx | | | Fx | B# | E# |
| S] w [390,420] | | | G# | C# | | Ax | Dx | | | Fx | B# | E# |
| S] x [420,450] | | | G# | Bx | | Ax | Dx | | | Fx | B# | E# |

I] Inferior C] Canonical S] Superior

Figure 7.11

Stencil tableau restricted to the notes of the Gypsy scale (harmony 871). The spellings in rows j and k and their transposes in rows v and w account for this harmony's quasi-diatonicity.

**7.20** What accounts for changes in key? What accounts for changes in tonality?

**7.21** Is it possible to alter chords without causing changes in the trajectory? Give examples.

**7.22** (a) What different spellings for harmony 266 occur in the stencil tableau? (b) To which sectors do they apply? (c) Are they all proper? (d) Are they all feasible? (e) Are they all true? (f) If the answer to any of the last three questions is "yes," generalize; otherwise, list exceptions. (g) Where are the enharmonic thresholds located?

**7.23** By working along lines similar to those leading to Fig. 7.11, show that the balanced harmonies are about equally distributed among the classes diatonic, quasi-diatonic, and chromatic.

**7.24** Which of the following charm successions can be justified notationally? (a) GGDB♯ → CGCE, (b) GGBE♭ → CGCE, (c) FACD♯ → EGCE, (d) FACE♭ → EGCE? This exercise demonstrates the importance of finding out which notations are theoretically admissible within the context of the musical statement under analysis.

**7.25** Are the chord progressions CEG → CEG# → CEA and CEA → CEA♭ → CEG correctly notated? (Hint. If the algebraic sign of the time parameter t were to be reversed at the end, then the composition would retrace its path.)

**7.26** Write a program to calculate the proportion of accidentals in musical input text. To what types of theoretical questions is it applicable?

## CURVATURE OF TRAJECTORY

The first step of orthographic analysis is to read in the data assuming that the study material has been written phonetically, that is, without regard to the principles of preferred notation advocated in this text. The second step is to compute the trajectory, which has two primary uses: (a) to make the musical meaning of the composition clear, and (b) to show the underlying grammatical construction. The third step is to determine from the trajectory the value of two angles--the phase $\omega$ of the immediate tonality vector and the argument $\theta$ showing the direction of the composition vector--at points of the path corresponding to every completed message frame. The fourth step, which often will be the last step, is to apply the perfect orthographic principle to obtain the proper stencils with which to spell each chord in both true and relative preferred notation, using context where necessary to resolve questions of indeterminacy. Always bear in mind that the resultant spelling depends on the winding number of the path in order to establish which sheet of the Riemann surface the composition point is currently traversing. This is a basic theoretical requirement.

As a first example consider the harmonic progression

A♯EG♯C♯ → BEG♯ → G♯DF♯B → ADF♯ → F♯CEA → GCE → EB♭DG → FB♭D → ....

This progression forms a real sequence from which escape is quite difficult. When coded for computer input, the charm data has the appearance

```
59,6,39,29,0,1;
7,6,39,0,1;
39,4,19,7,0,1;
5,4,19,0,1;
19,2,6,5,0,1;
3,2,6,0,1;
59,4,3,8,0,1;
1,59,4,0,1;
```

when the passage is played in quarter notes. As this coding system is a straightforward numerical substitution, it is not deserving of further explanation in the present section. Next, consider the related progression

A♯EG♯C♯ → BEG♯ → G♯DF♯B → C♯F♯A♯ → F♯CEA → GCE → EB♭DG → ADF♯ →

..., which seems to offer greater hope of recovery. This sequence is coded

59,6,39,29,0,1;
7,6,39,0,1;
39,4,19,7,0,1;
29,19,59,0,1;
19,2,6,5,0,1;
3,2,6,0,1;
59,4,3,8,0,1;
5,4,19,0,1.

Input of these statements concludes the first step.

The result of the second step--to compute the trajectory--is shown in Fig. 7.12. From the diagrams it is clear that in both cases the composer has intended to take advantage of the angular variation of key and so to travel a symmetric path into a region of fewer sharps. In order to obtain an idea about the grammatical construction of the two passages, it is necessary to complete the third step by determining the value of the phases ω and arguments θ. These values are

| CASE 1 | | CASE 2 | |
|---|---|---|---|
| ω | θ | ω | θ |
| 255.0 | -105.0 | 255.0 | -105.0 |
| 195.0 | -135.0 | 195.0 | -135.0 |
| 195.0 | -145.9 | 195.0 | -145.9 |
| 135.0 | -165.0 | 255.0 | -135.0 |
| 135.0 | -178.9 | 135.0 | -151.1 |
| 75.0 | 165.0 | 75.0 | -165.0 |
| 75.0 | 148.9 | 75.0 | 175.9 |
| 15.0 | 135.0 | 135.0 | 165.0 |

Figure 7.12

Two real sequences exhibiting partially developed six- and three-fold symmetry.

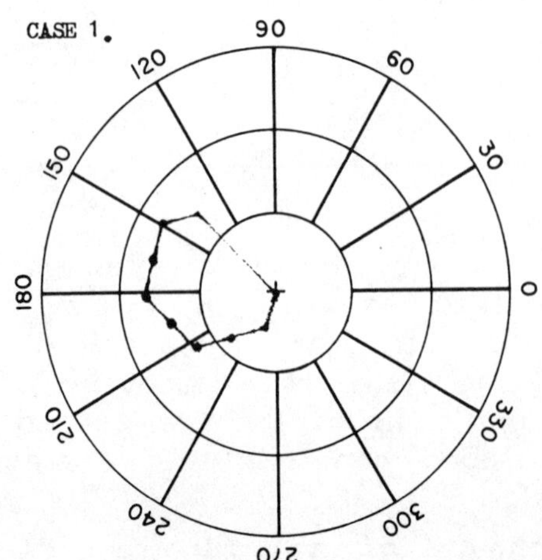


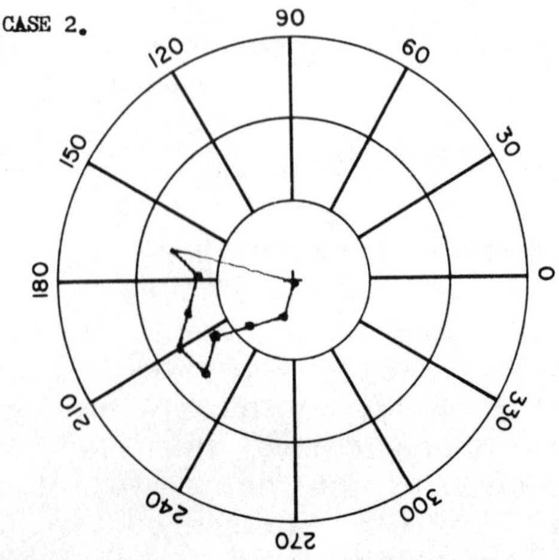

Remember that true preferred notation is a function of the local slope of the trajectory and that relative preferred notation is a function of the global position of the composition point in the displacement plane. Both kinds of notation depend upon a choice of sheet of the Riemann surface. Moreover, the exact amount of the shift in argument is dependent on the direction and magnitude of the motion, and therefore the consequent changes in key can be different for different tonalities. For this reason, it should be recognized that a composition requires integration time to build up a new sense of key, or for that matter, to tear down an old one. To conclude the analysis, a direct application of the stencil tableau shows that the true and relative notations are in complete agreement for Case 1. This parallelism shows that notational stresses have not yet had a sufficient time to accumulate. On the other hand, a discrepancy arises for Case 2 on the penultimate chord, which in relative terminology becomes EA#DG. This small deviation provides an escape route, and the second progression can be easily terminated as

A#EG#C# → BEG# → G#DF#B → C#F#A#
→ F#CEA → GCE → EA#DG → ABDF#
→ G#BDF → .....

It may be instructive to examine the changes in key that occur when a composition point describes various closed curves in the z-plane. And so, another example comparing two cases has been chosen to help clarify the discussion. The motion illustrated is approximately circular.

Case 1--Let z describe the closed curve shown in Fig. 7.13. After leaving the origin, the composition point moves out along the tone vector **D#**. Since z then passes around the origin once in the clockwise direction, it follows that the key signature function adds 12 flats. Had z passed around the origin once in a counterclockwise direction, then this function would have added 12 sharps.

Case 2--Let z describe the closed curve shown in Fig. 7.14. This time upon departing the origin, the composition point maintains a heading along the tone vector **A**. When it reaches the end of the first chord it again starts a slow $360^{o}$ turn. Since the origin is exterior to this closed curve, it turns out that the number of sharps decreases going from $\underline{\alpha}$ to $\underline{\beta}$ and increases going from $\underline{\beta}$ to $\underline{\alpha}$, so that the total effect on the key signature is zero!

| Path segment | Phase | |
|---|---|---|
| | Case 1 | Case 2 |
| 1 | 300 | 120 |
| 2 | (240,270) | 150 |
| 3 | (210,240) | (150,180) |
| 4 | (180,210) | 150 |
| 5 | (150,180) | (120,150) |
| 6 | (120,150) | (120,150) |
| 7 | 120 | 120 |
| 8 | (90,120) | (90,120) |
| 9 | (60,90) | (90,120) |
| 10 | (30,60) | (60,90) |
| 11 | (0,30) | (60,90) |
| 12 | (330,360) | 90 |
| 13 | 300 | 120 |
| 14 | (240,270) | 150 |

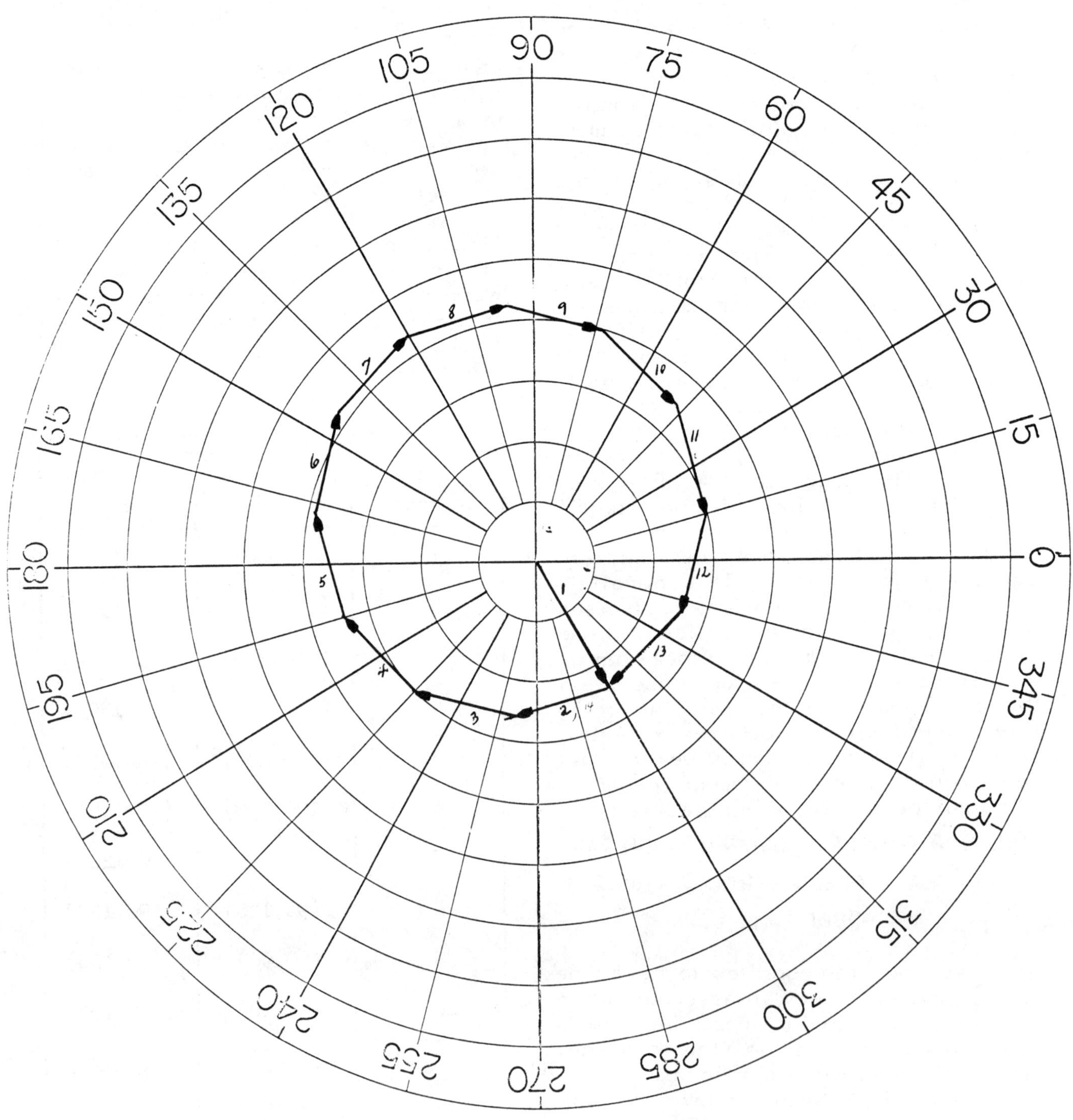


Figure 7.13
(Case 1) In this chord sequence,

$D\sharp m^{6/4} \rightarrow B^7 \rightarrow E^{4/3} \rightarrow A^7 \rightarrow D^{4/3} \rightarrow G^7 \rightarrow C^{4/3} \rightarrow F^7 \rightarrow \ldots,$

the composition trajectory is shifted so that its path encircles the origin. Since the center of the coordinate system is enclosed by the contour, the argument of the variable point z decreases by $2\pi$ as the composition point completes the circuit.

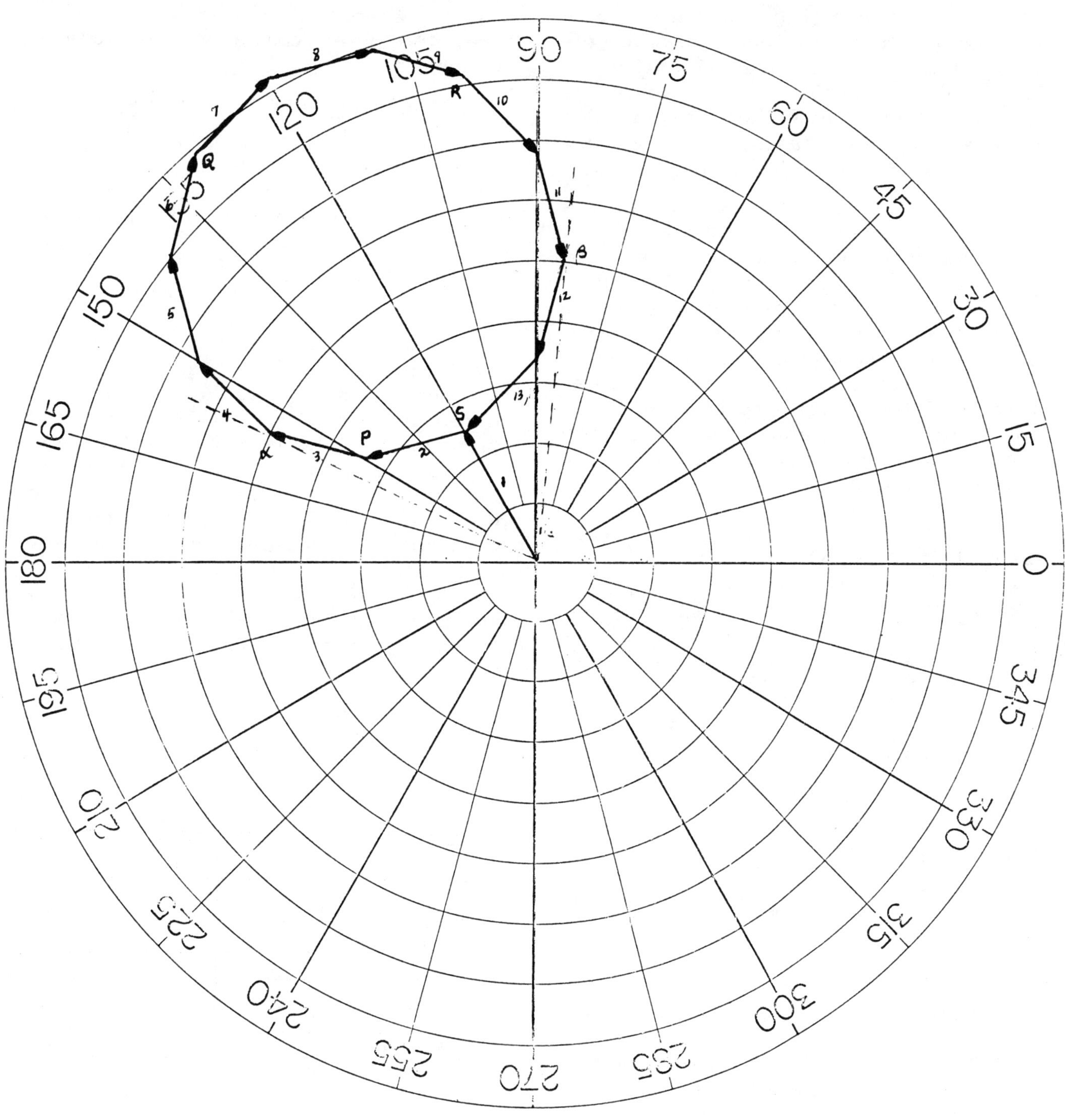


Figure 7.14

(Case 2) In this chord sequence,

$Am^{6/4} \rightarrow B^{4/3} \rightarrow E^{7} \rightarrow A^{4/3} \rightarrow$

$D^{7} \rightarrow G^{4/3} \rightarrow C^{7} \rightarrow F^{4/3} \rightarrow \ldots,$

the composition trajectory undergoes an initial offset before circling. As a result, the angle $\theta$ is restricted to the sector bounded by the rays through points $\alpha$ and $\beta$. Except for the first tonality (along arrow 1), which is of equal magnitude, but of opposite direction to that of Case 1, all corresponding tonalities are identical for the two cases.

It is not surprising that this relocalization has an orthographic effect. Despite the near identity of the two progressions, their spellings are not the same. The disagreement between the two cases is caused by the paths crossing different sectors.

This example is important for several reasons. First, it illustrates how the theory of complex variables can be applied in conjunction with other mathematical principles in order to strengthen yet simplify music analysis using computers. Second, it provides valuable insight into the nature of the tonal process, namely, the total key change over a closed loop trajectory not containing the origin is zero.

CASE 1 (Conclusion)

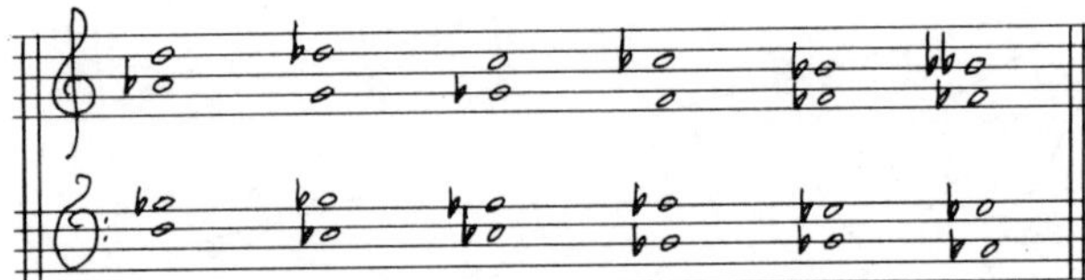

CASE 2 (Conclusion)

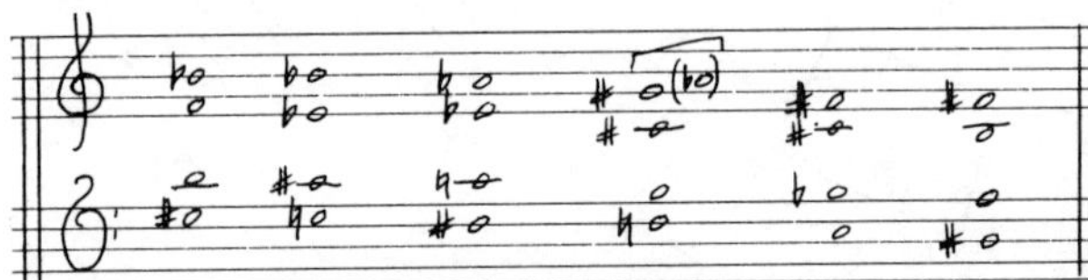

## EXERCISES

7.27 An implicit assumption underlies the first example of this section. What is it? Is it valid?

7.28 For the second example: (a) How many different stencils are required for Case 1? for Case 2? (b) What happens at points P, Q, R, and S in Fig. 7.14? (c) Explain how these two cases illustrate grammatical differences, inadequately identified in strictly phonetically spelled renditions. (d) When extended does either case return to a previously occupied notational state? (e) Draw and label each successive Case 1 and Case 2 composition vector.

7.29 When both r and θ vary with time, the polar components of tonality are

$$v_r = \frac{dr}{dt} \text{ and } v_\theta = r\,\frac{d\theta}{dt},$$

where $\frac{dr}{dt}$ denotes the time rate of change of the radial component r of z and $\frac{d\theta}{dt}$ is the limit of the ratio

$$w_{av} = \frac{\theta_2 - \theta_1}{t_2 - t_1} = \frac{\Delta\theta}{\Delta t}$$

as Δt approaches zero. In this expression it is assumed that θ changes from $\theta_1$ to $\theta_2$ as time t increases from $t_1$ to $t_2$ and the quantity $w_{av}$ is termed the "average angular tonality." Assume that all durations are quarter notes and plot the average angular tonality function, expressed in flats per beat, for the (dominant) seventh chords in the second example, taken consecutively two at a time. How do the graphs for Case 1 and Case 2 differ?

7.30 Complete the following table:

| $\vec{R}$ | $\vec{v}_i$ | $\vec{v}_{i+1} - \vec{v}_i$ |
|---|---|---|
| 0 | | |
| | $\vec{C} + \vec{E} + \vec{G} + \vec{Bb}$ | |
| $\vec{C} + \vec{E} + \vec{G} + \vec{Bb} = \vec{C} + \vec{G}$ | | $\vec{F} - \vec{G} = \vec{F} + \vec{Db} = \vec{Eb}$ |
| | $\vec{F} + \vec{A} + \vec{C} + \vec{Eb}$ | |
| $\vec{F} + 2\vec{C} + \vec{G}$ | | $\vec{Db} - \vec{C} = \vec{Gb} + \vec{Bb} = \vec{Ab}$ |
| | $\vec{Bb} + \vec{D} + \vec{F} + \vec{Ab}$ | |
| $\vec{Bb} + 2\vec{F} + 2\vec{C} + \vec{G}$ | | $\vec{Eb} - \vec{F} = \vec{Cb} + \vec{Eb} = \vec{Db}$ |
| | $\vec{Eb} + \vec{G} + \vec{Bb} + \vec{Db}$ | |

7.31 Outline a scientific approach to the study of various composers' spelling habits.

7.32 Write the chord sequence

$$T_0T_7T_{10}T_2,\ T_{11}T_6T_9T_1,$$
$$T_{10}T_5T_8T_0,\ \ldots$$

in (a) phonetic form, (b) true form, and (c) relative form. Terminate the sequence taking advantage of the build-up of notational stresses.

## EXAMPLES OF MODULATION

An effective way to learn about and to advance the art of modulation is to study the methods from the past. By analyzing carefully the examples of such theoreticians as Cornell, Foote, Otterström, and Reger, it is possible to extract many useful ideas and principles of successful modulation. One of the many points to be observed is the importance of the topological concept of winding number. It is clear that where a modulation must lead directly to a more distant key in the same number of measures, the curvature of the trajectory must be greater. Any change of key involving the addition of more than twelve sharps or twelve flats will require a fully circuitous course. The trajectory will wrap around the origin entirely thereby completing a $360^{\circ}$ sector. To such a curve--whether it be a circle or a spiral--is assigned a winding number of plus or minus unity.

It is interesting to apply this idea to the collection of one hundred examples of modulation given by Reger in [2]. In Fig. 7.15, all plots are drawn in polar coordinates, with time as the parameter of the polygonal arc. In each graph the data are normalized to a time zero, which corresponds to a new starting point for each musical example. To assume that the value of time is reset to zero is to assume a complete recalibration of the data that involves a shift of the origin. This shift corresponds to a reorientation of the mental set of the listener--something like that required of a jury when the judge orders it to ignore some inadmissible testimony of a witness. Figuratively speaking, this recalibration adjusts the listener's key pointer to the left-hand limit of his or her span of memory gate.

The trajectories of Fig. 7.15 clearly illustrate the importance of bending or curvature to modulation. Notice in particular the necessity of encircling the origin in a counterclockwise (clockwise) direction to the attainment of a new key with a greater number of sharps (flats) than that of the old key. In many of the examples this bending culminates in a striking parallelism of the last segment of path to some particular key axis, major or minor. This, however, is an expression of the ultimate tonality and does not illuminate the ultimate key. Some light on the final key reached is cast by the argument of the last resultant. That is to say, the determination of target key depends on several factors, one of which is the direction of the trajectory endpoint as seen from the origin.

Certain theoretical calculations were necessary to achieve the constructions shown in Fig. 7.15. In order to perform a partial check on their validity, it is advisable to find out what, if anything, can be learned about Reger's examples from inspection of the polar diagrams, before consulting the index to the examples that immediately follows the figure. First, it is evident that the trajectories shown in diagrams 1 through 12 chart the course of the composition point as it turns more and more to the left, in an obvious attempt to attain target keys having more and more sharps in their key signature. In each of these diagrams the essential features of Reger's musical rendition are portrayed, although the actual notes employed remain hidden from the eyes of the analyst. After all, the actual notes are readily available in the score and are not especially pertinent at this stage to a quest for greater understanding of the modulatory process. What is pertinent, it is claimed, is an anomaly that the careful reader may by this point already have noticed in Reger's examples 8 through 12, and elsewhere. In these curves, which still satisfactorily describe the motion of the composition point over time, the path curiously fails to circumnavigate the origin. This fact reveals that the winding number of the path is not monotonically increasing. Although Reger's examples 8 through 12 are substantially correct, their respective diagrams indicate that what is being done somehow falls short of his stated aims.

The first conclusion from this investigation, therefore, is that in these five cases, at least, Reger's modulations are going to miss the target sharp keys and land instead in enharmonically equivalent flat keys. Certainly this slip will create an unwanted twist in the notation. Only through explicit analysis based upon both computer calculations and music theoretical considerations can this conclusion be reached. In all such instances, luckily, the anomaly can be avoided by prolonging certain chords. This possibility indicates that target keys, and probably the listener's key sense as well, are strongly dependent upon the dwell time, which is not very startling. Such a course correction is illustrated by the dotted line in the diagram for example 10.

The remainder of Reger's 100 examples resemble his initial twelve, but they sometimes are modified by a bending toward the right, thereby increasing the number of flats, instead of bending to the left. Almost always the modulation is completed in no more than two measures. Because of this length restriction, gains in the turn rate and decreases in the turn radius occur with each deeper penetration of the positively or negatively inflected realms. Especially apparent from the "square corner turns" in the higher numbered examples is the intention by Reger to achieve maximum performance modulations. He has remarked in the preface to his book that "Of course, all the examples of modulation will allow of other solutions; but I doubt whether such other solutions will always be shorter--i.e. 'more to the point' and more logical than those given ...". Further examination shows that occasionally the examples deviate from the original flight path or quickly reverse turn at some point (see diagrams 28 and 30 in Fig. 7.15). Such occurrences might mark the appearance of special chords, for example, the **Neapolitan sixth**, and thus they may merit close scrutiny.

In actual music, as opposed to textbook examples, the basis for determining the key reached by modulation, while finite, will be very broad, even when it is reckoned only from the last explicitly stated key signature instead of going all the way back to the beginning of the piece. The exposed anomaly assumes that the first arrow always is fastened to the origin and that each arrow other than the first is linked to its immediate predecessor to form a chain of vectors. As a consequence, it makes a big difference whether or not a phrase as short as these examples by Reger occurs at the beginning of the composition, before the key sense is saturated by a repetition of similarly directed tonalities. For this reason it may be profitable to shift the origin from time to time as the analysis proceeds, perhaps at various rates to model different memory retention spans. If this were done, then the resultant displacement would no longer represent the complete cumulative development of the composition at any point of time, but rather, only the recent past. And the resulting segmented graph would reject the influence of the previous development in favor of recently established tonal lines. Although this question is not pertinent to the development of the present computer methodology, it would seem to be an appropriate area for exploration.

Figure 7.15.
Reger paths in the complex displacement plane.

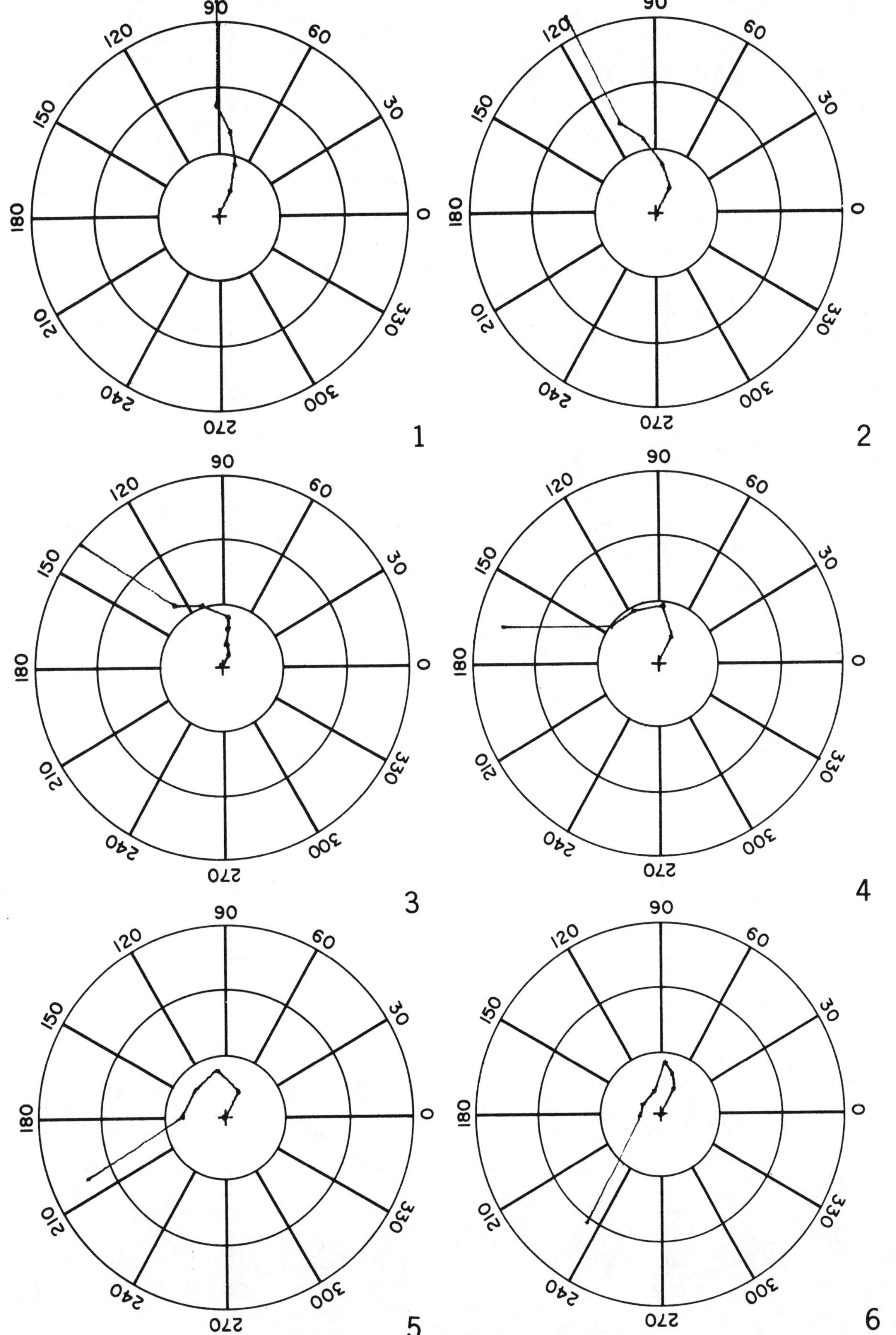

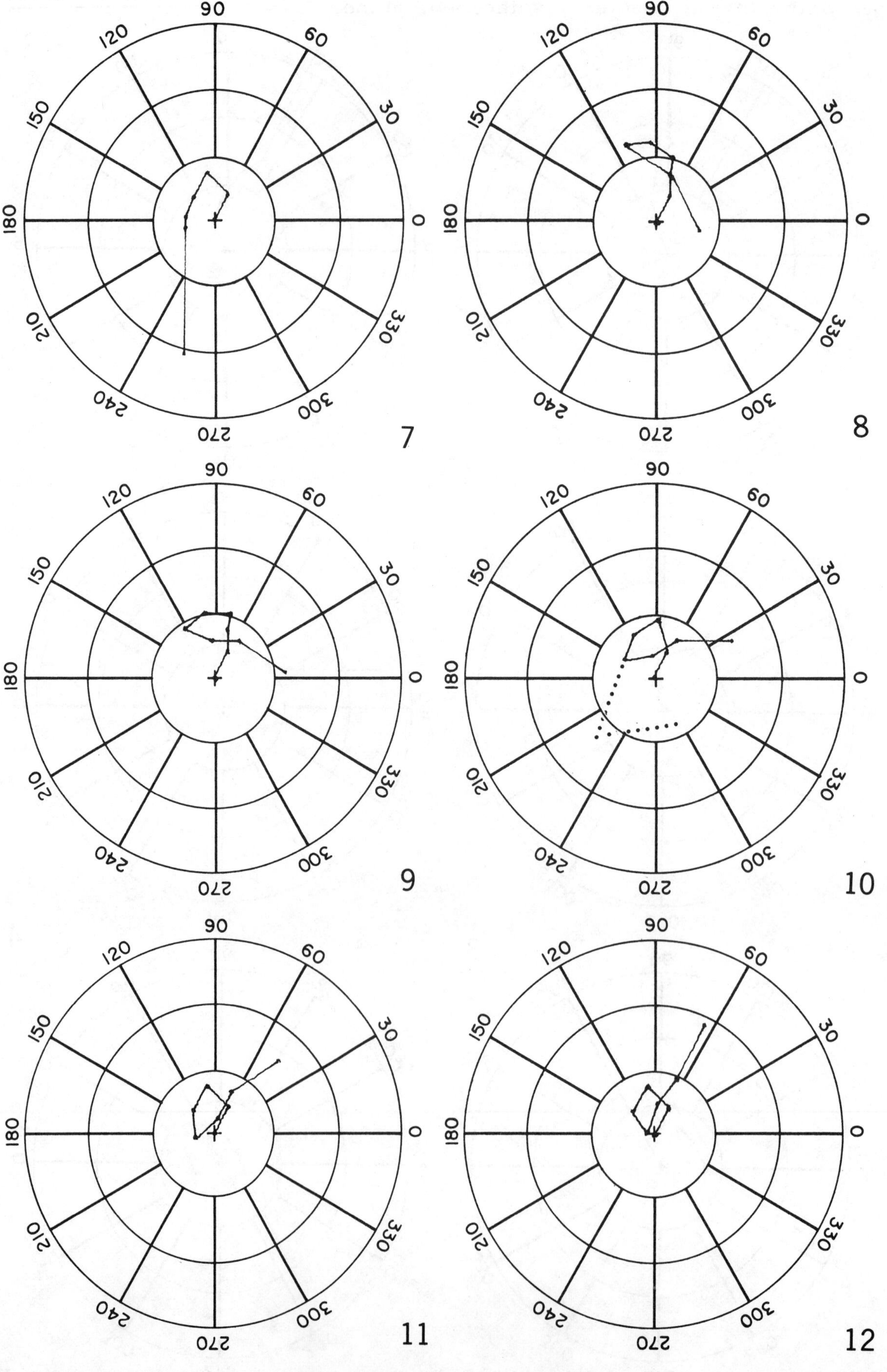
90
60
30
0
330
300
270
240
210
180
150
120
7
8
9
10
11
12

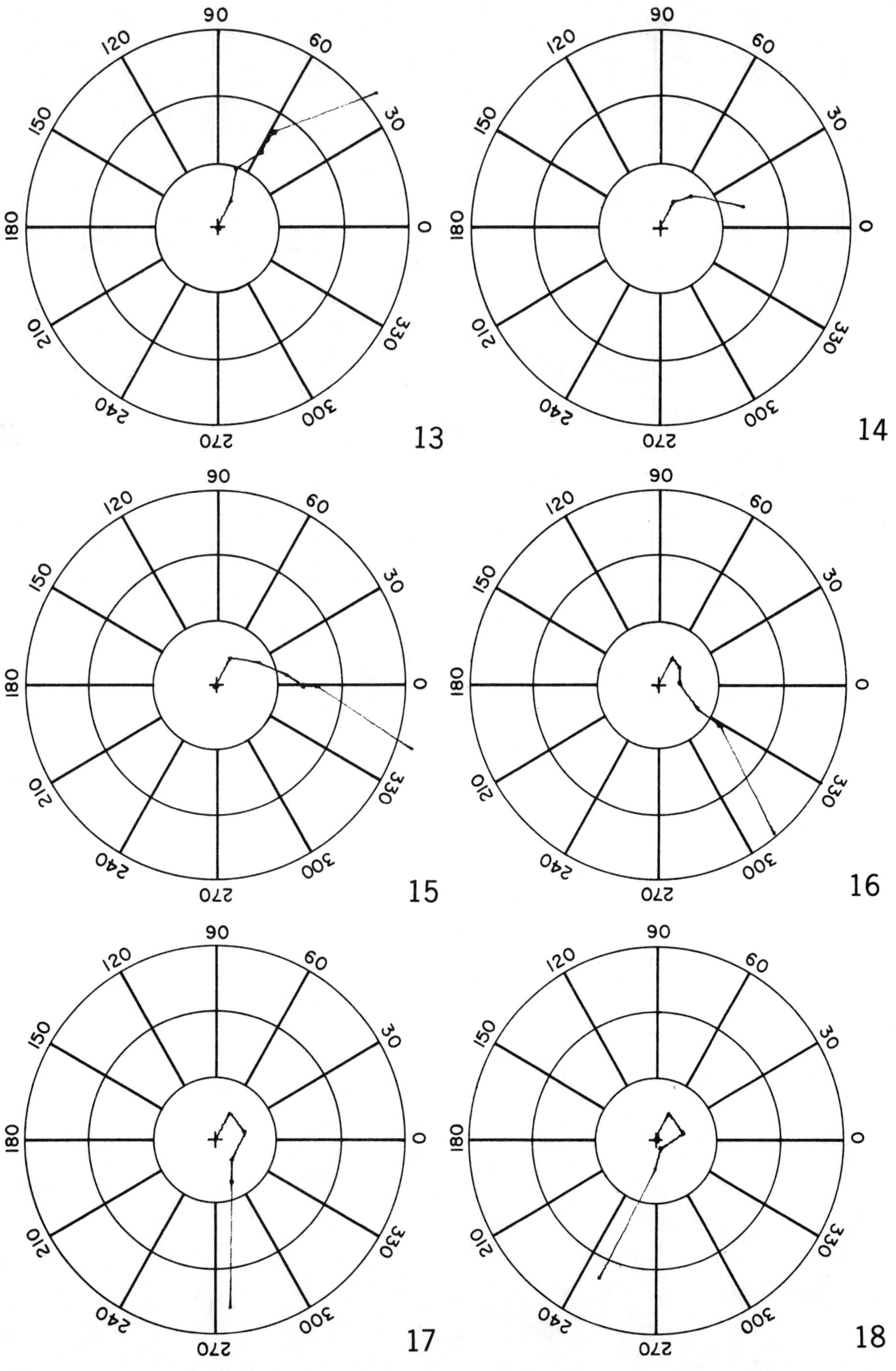
90
60
30
0
330
300
270
240
210
180
150
120
13
14
15
16
17
18

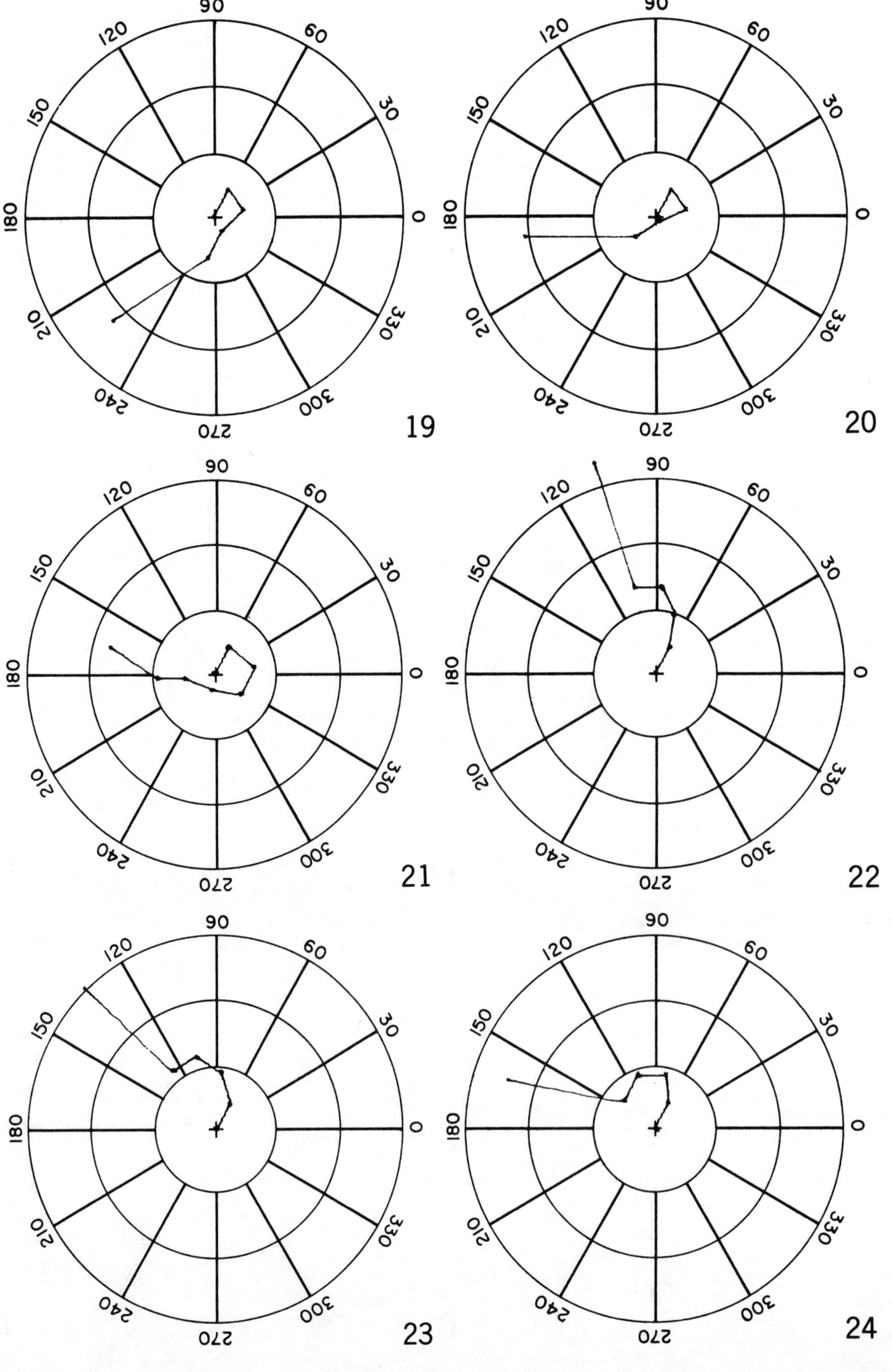
90
120
60
150
30
180
0
210
330
240
300
270
19
20
21
22
23
24

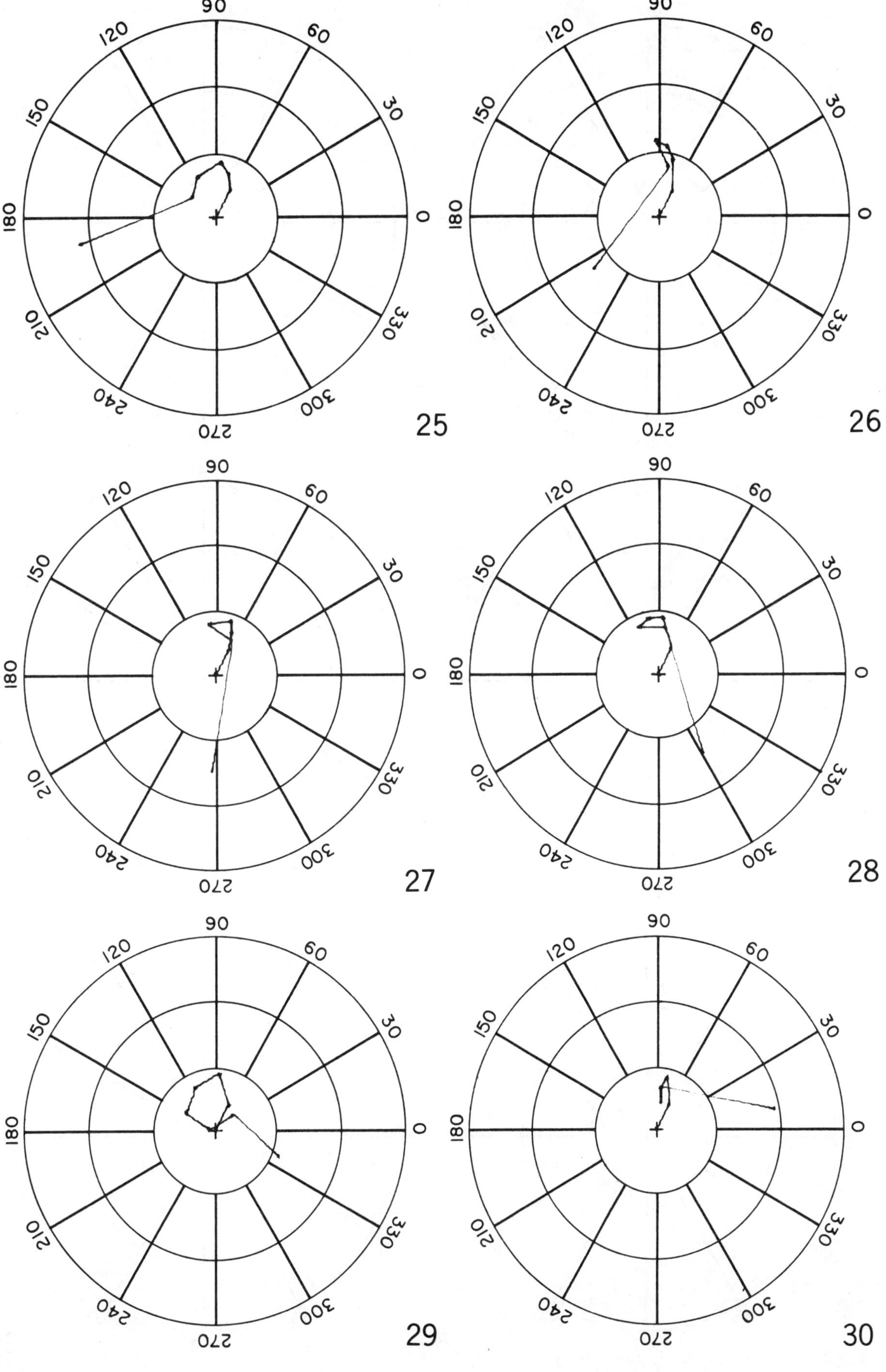
90
60
30
0
330
300
270
240
210
180
150
120
25
26
27
28
29
30

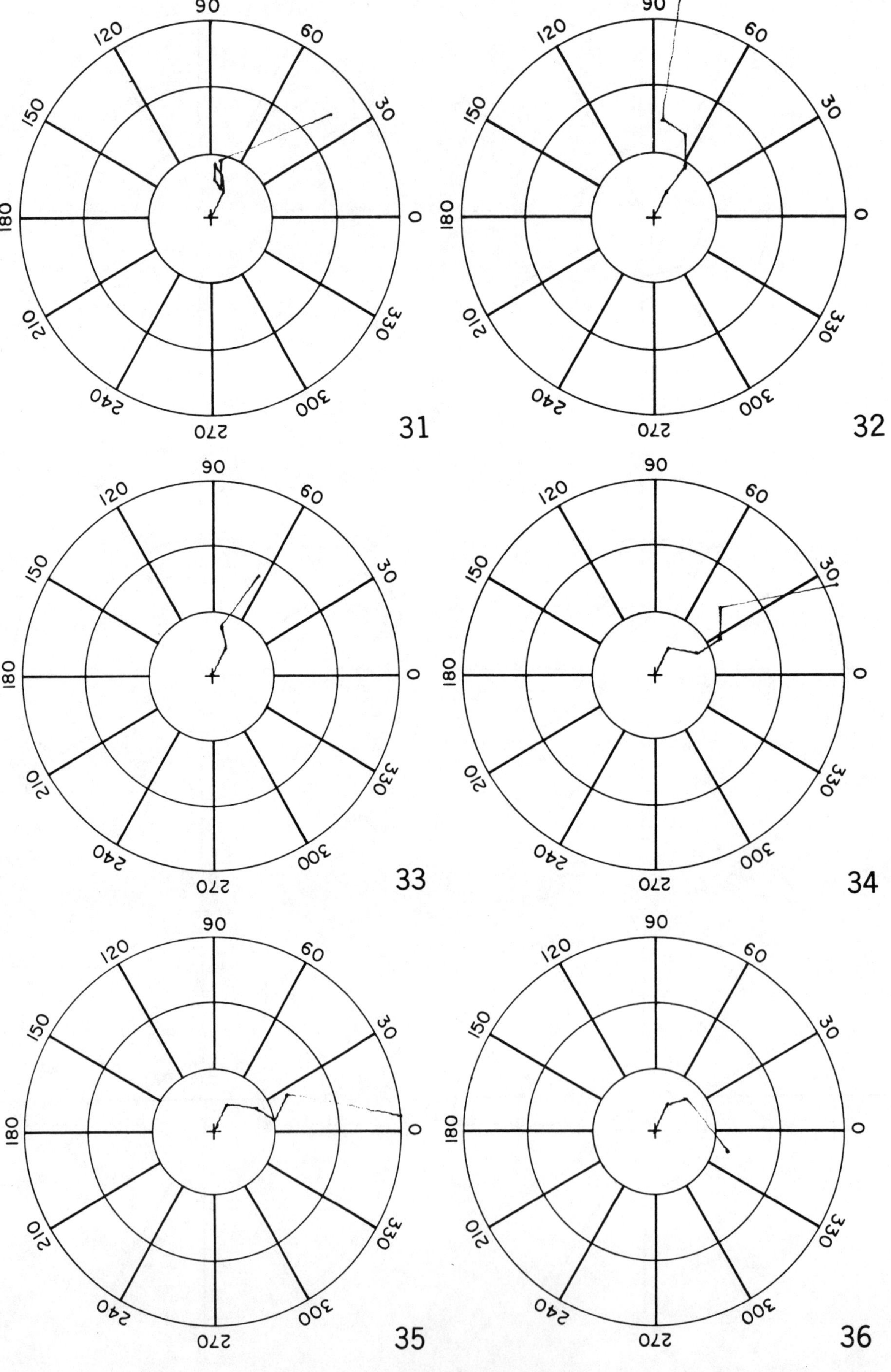
90
60
30
0
330
300
270
240
210
180
150
120
31
32
33
34
35
36

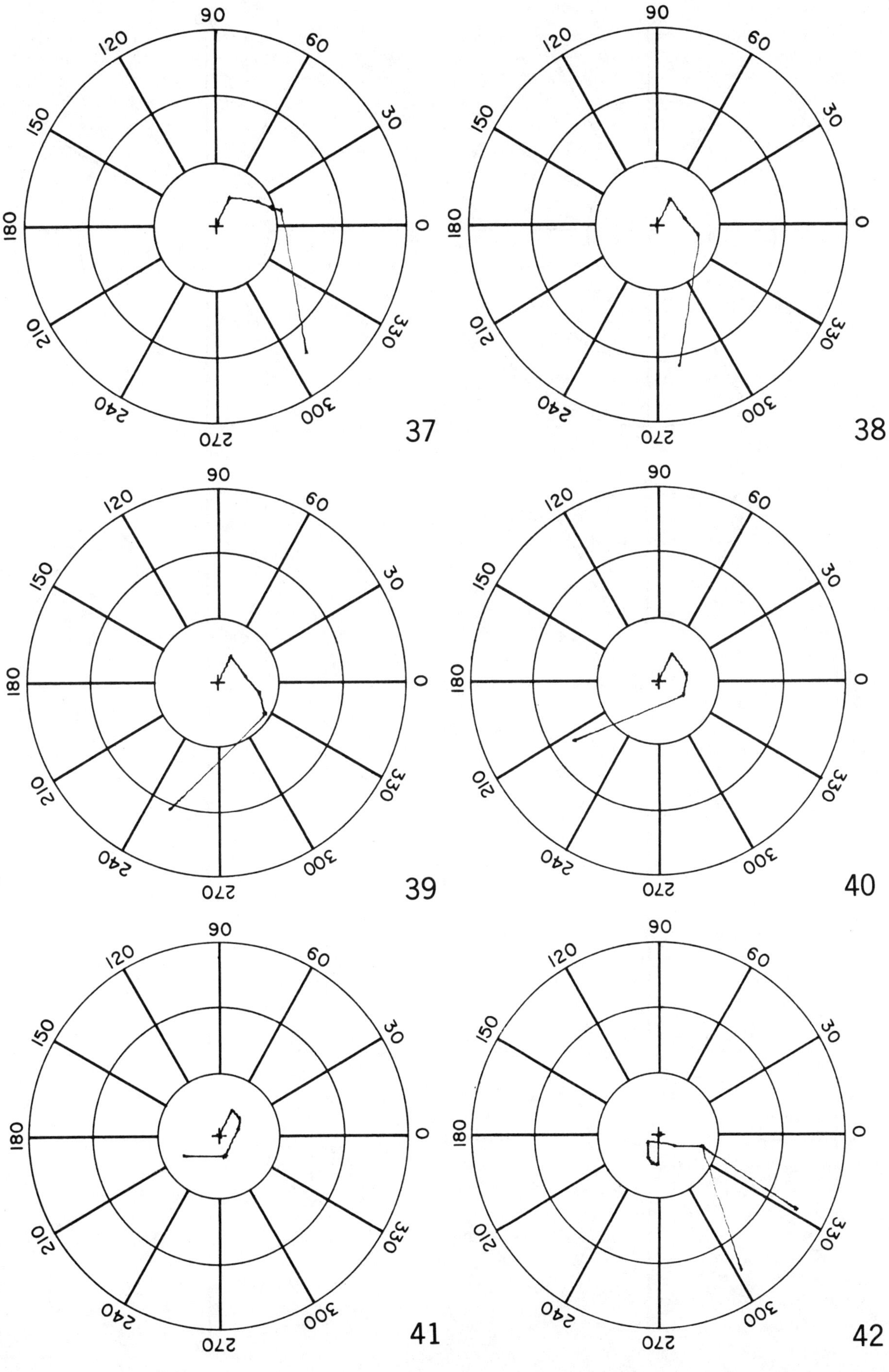
90
120
60
150
30
180
0
210
330
240
300
270
37
38
39
40
41
42

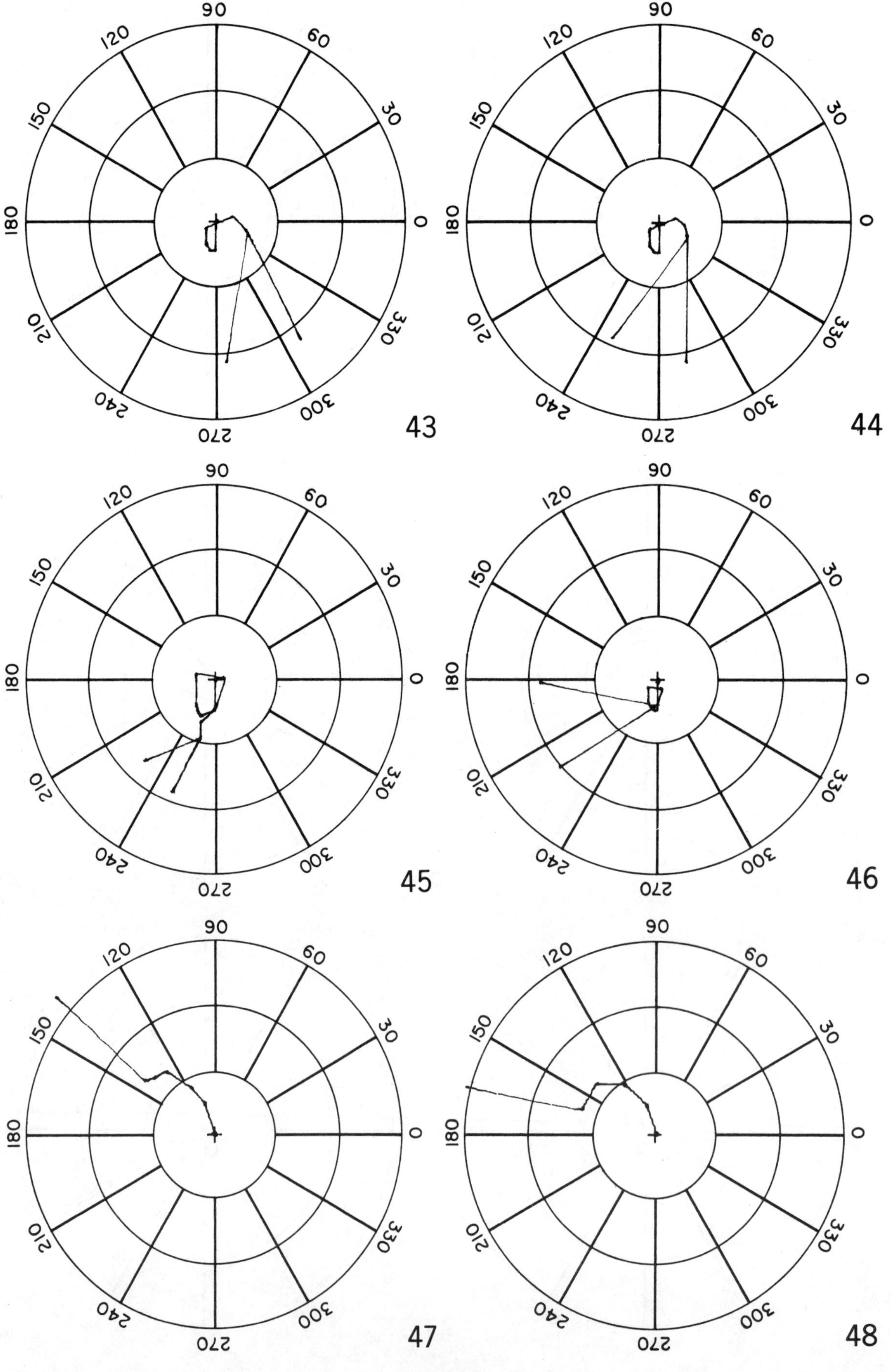
90
120
60
150
30
180
0
210
330
240
300
270
43
44
45
46
47
48

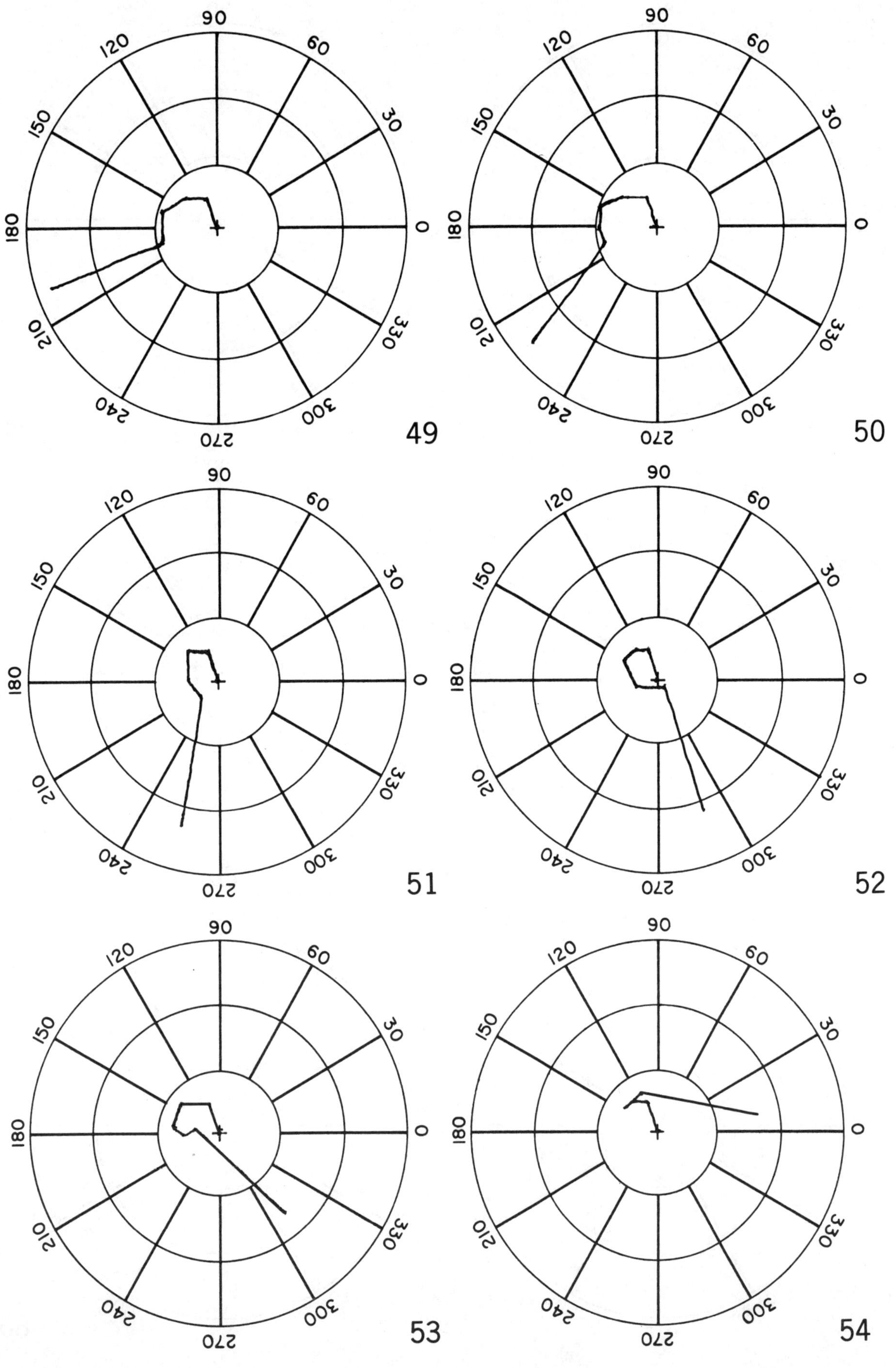
90
60
30
0
330
300
270
240
210
180
150
120
49
50
51
52
53
54

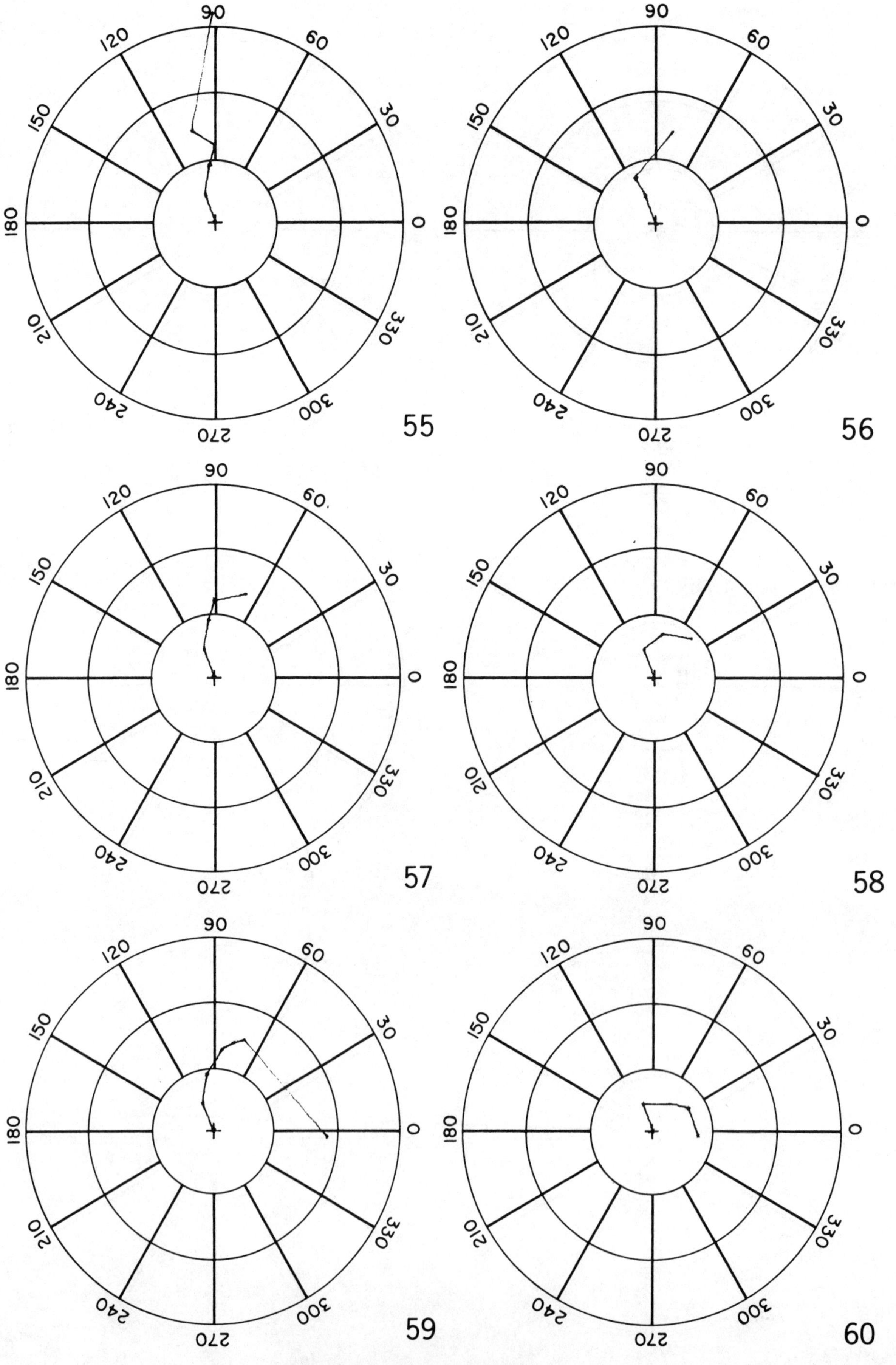
90
120
60
150
30
180
0
210
330
240
300
270
55
56
57
58
59
60

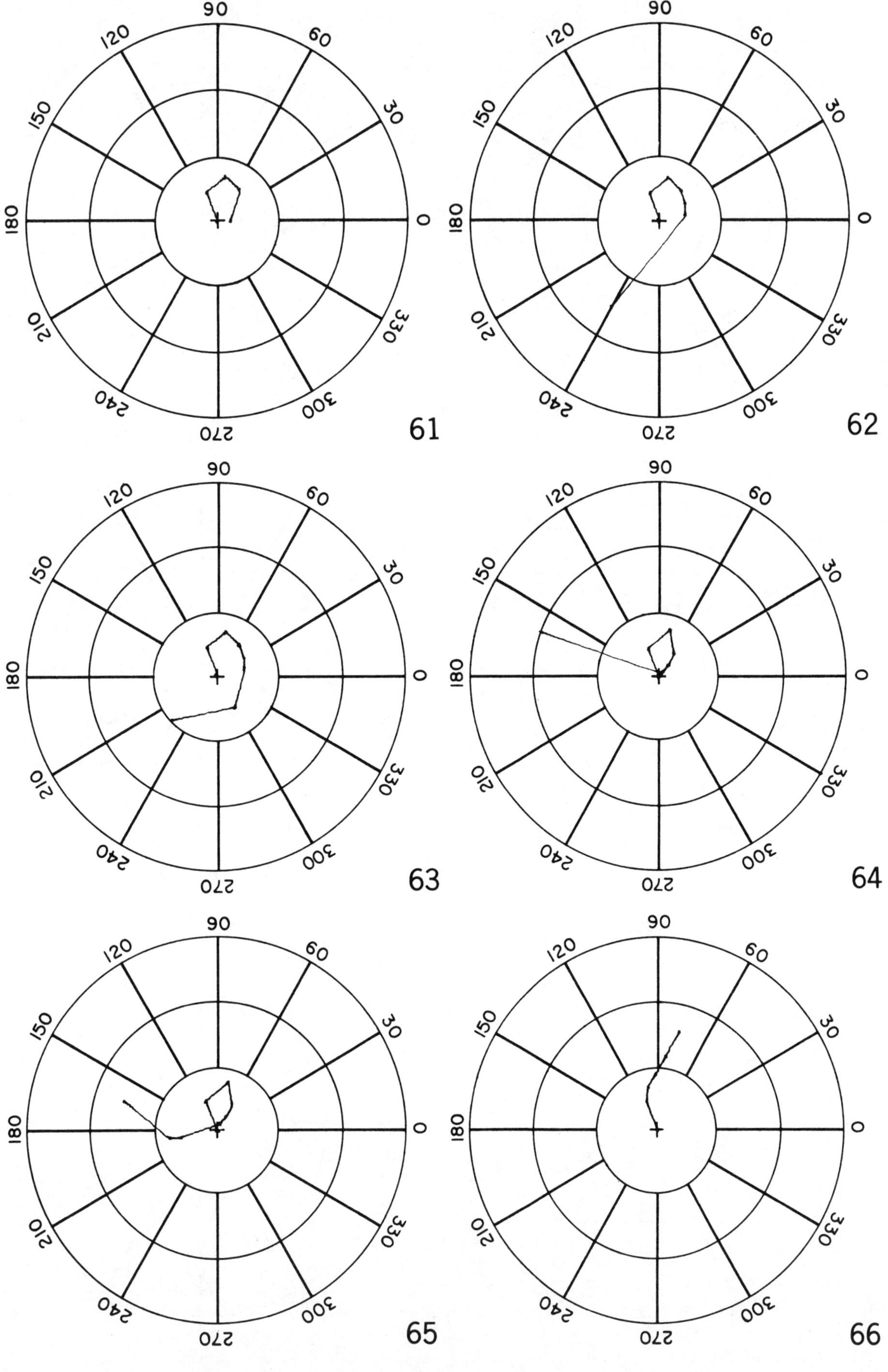
90
60
30
0
330
300
270
240
210
180
150
120
61
62
63
64
65
66

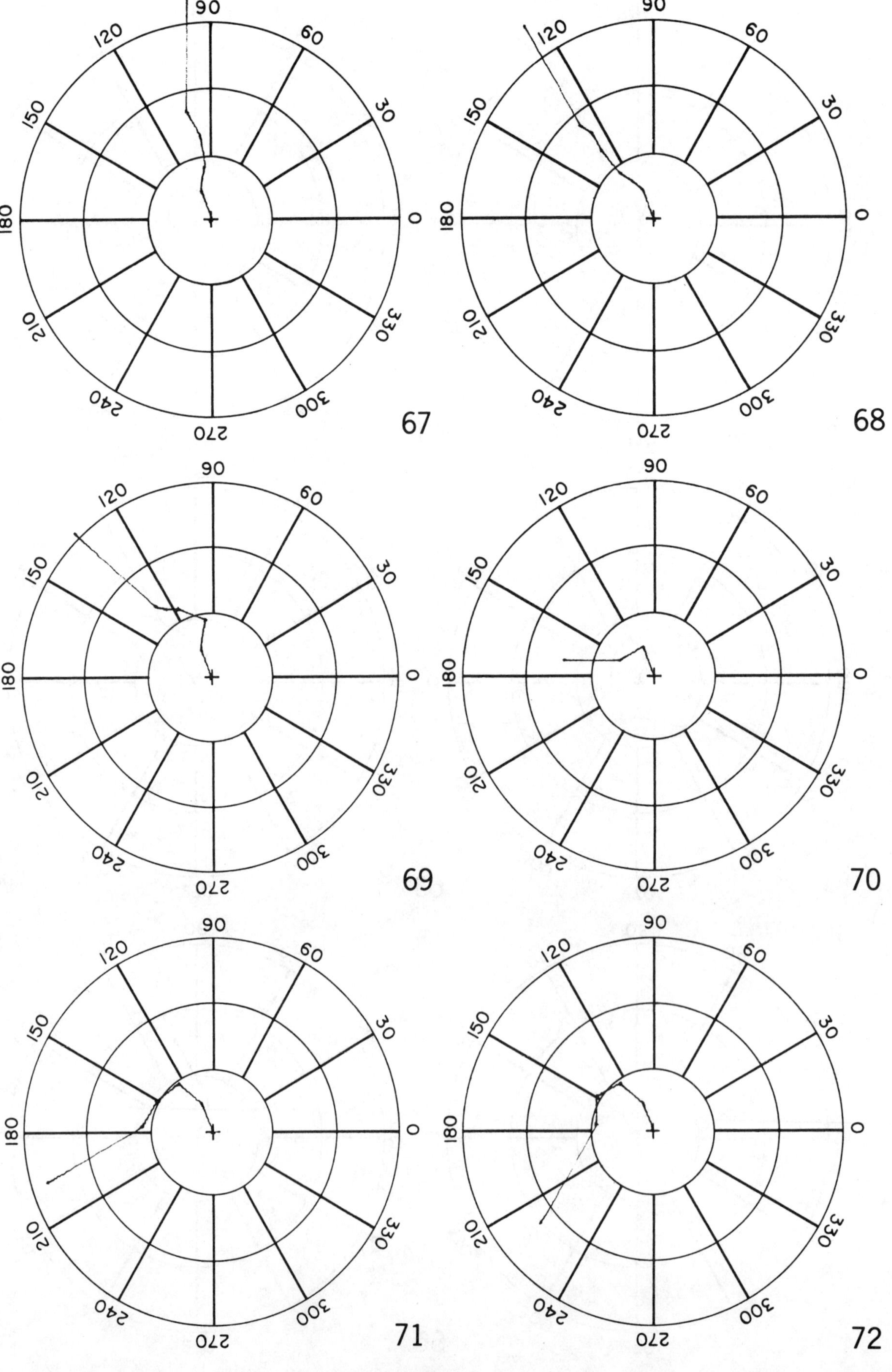

90
120
60
150
30
180
0
210
330
240
300
270
67
68
69
70
71
72

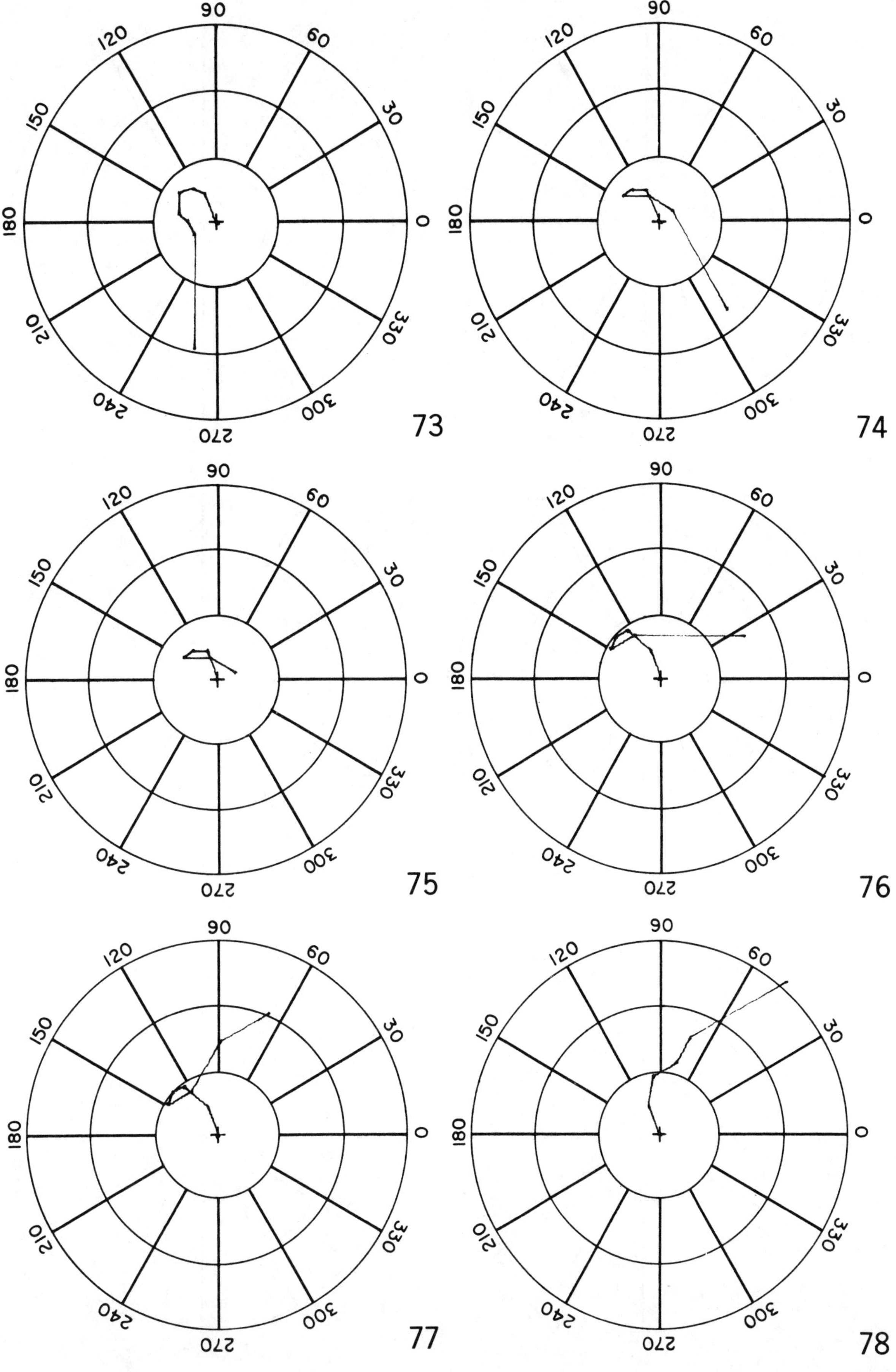
90
60
30
0
330
300
270
240
210
180
150
120
73
74
75
76
77
78

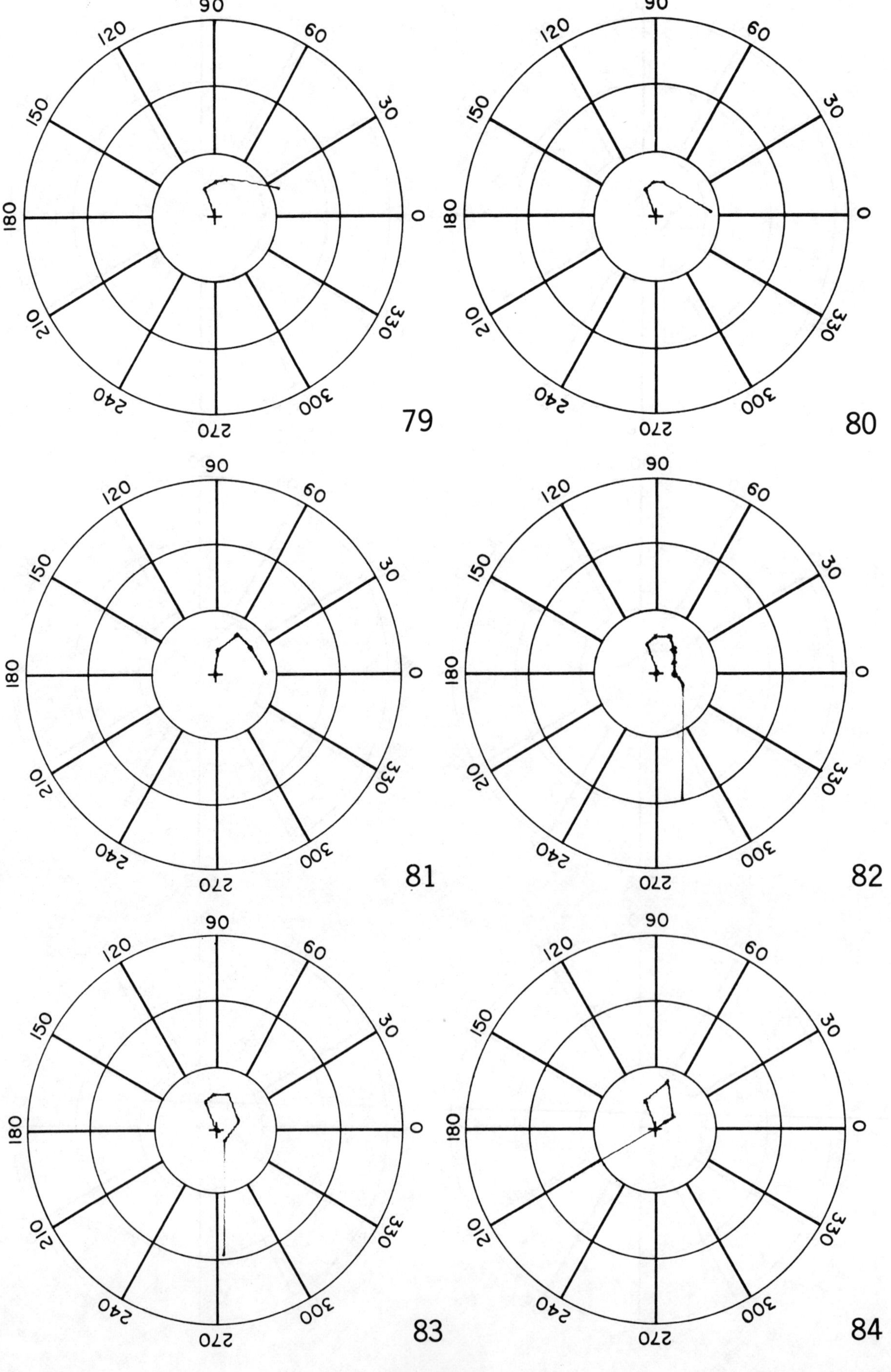
90
120
60
150
30
180
0
210
330
240
300
270
79
80
81
82
83
84

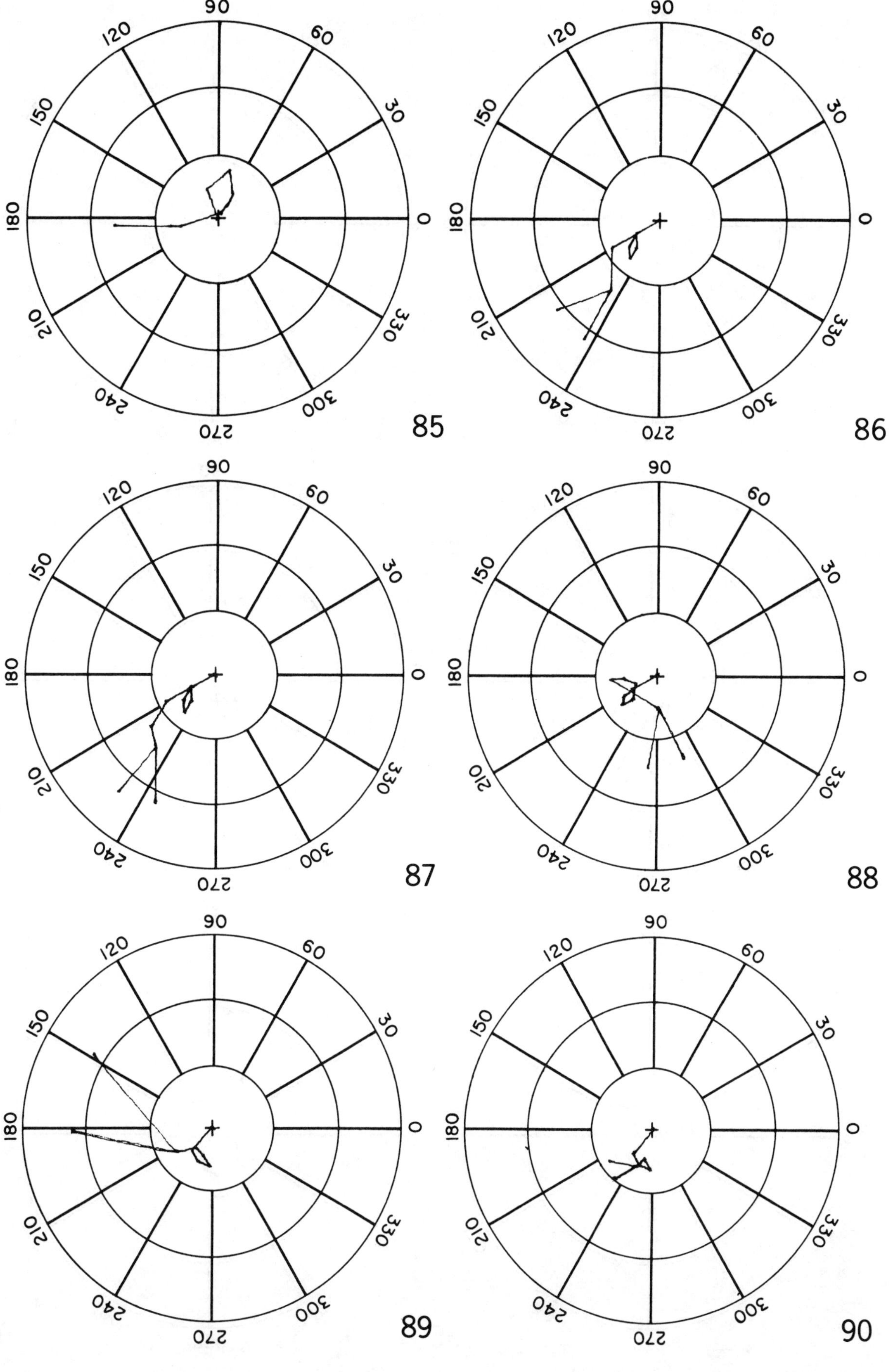

90
120
60
150
30
180
0
210
330
240
300
270
85
86
87
88
89
90

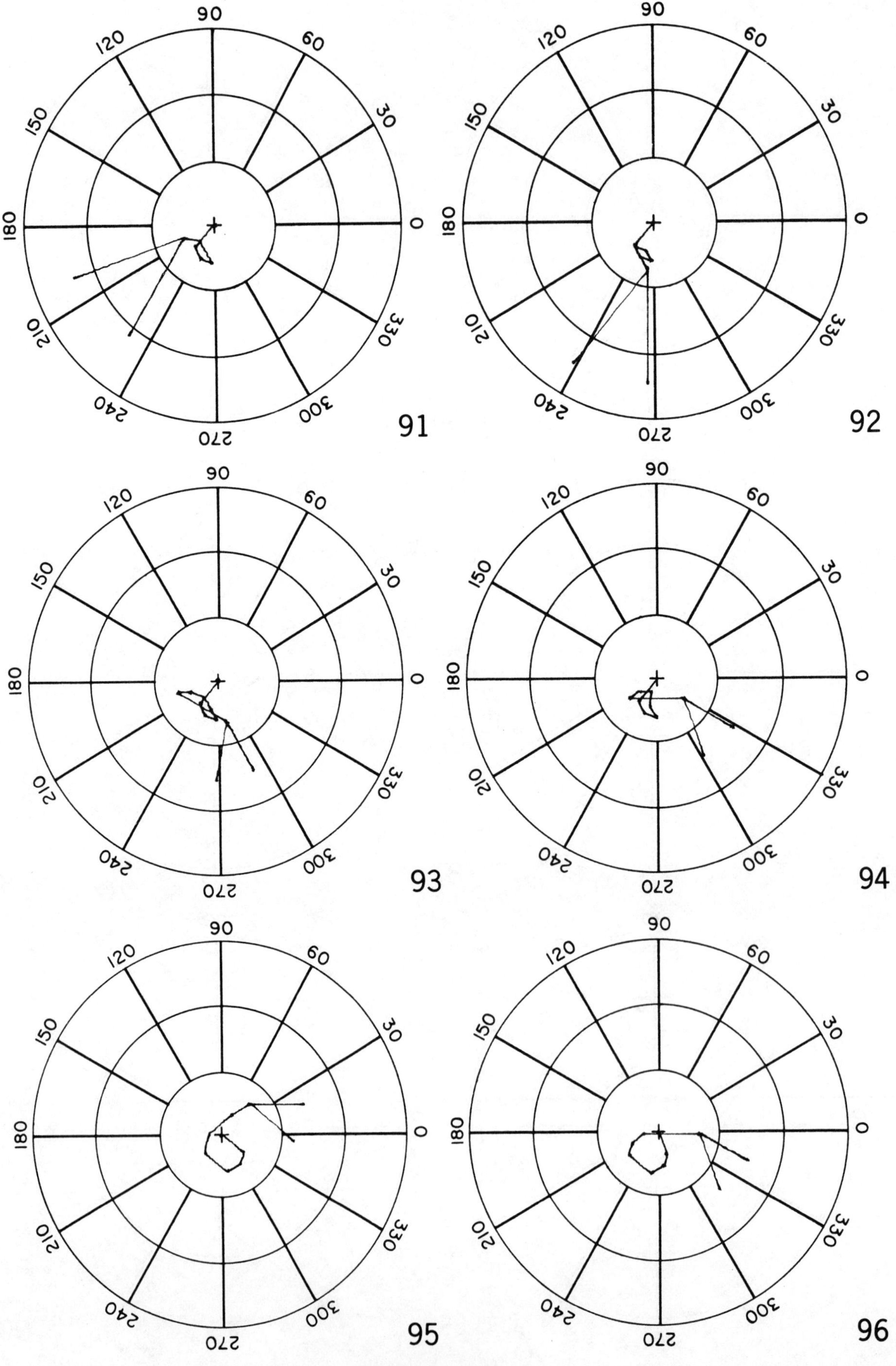
90
60
30
0
330
300
270
240
210
180
150
120
91
92
93
94
95
96

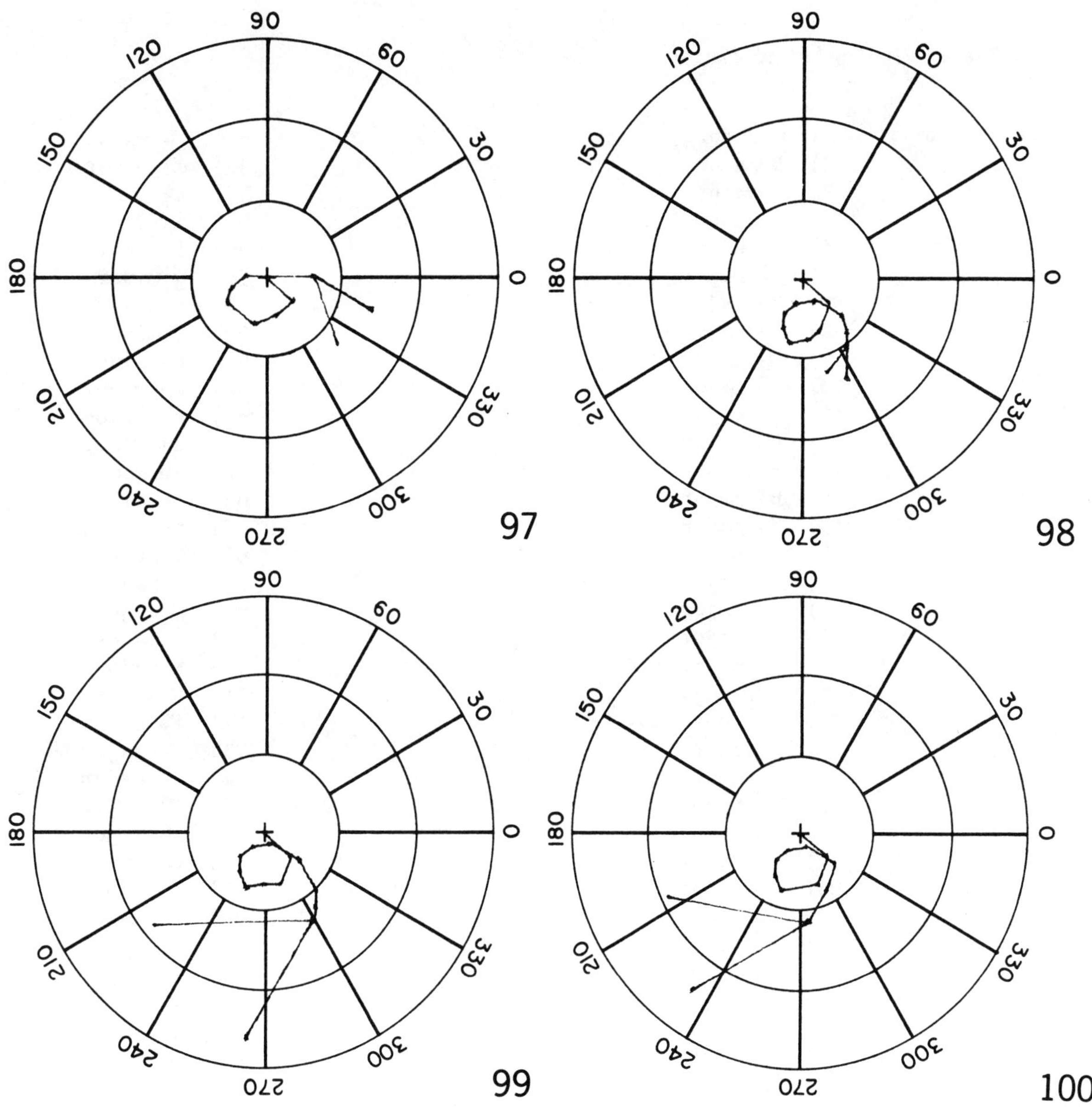
90
60
30
0
330
300
270
240
210
180
150
120
97
98
99
100

Index to Reger's Examples in Modulation

a) From C major to:
1) G major
2) D major
3) A major
4) E major
5) B major
6) F♯ major
7) C♯ major
8) G♯ major
9) D♯ major
10) A♯ major
11) E♯ major
12) B♯ major
13) F major
14) B♭ major
15) E♭ major
16) A♭ major
17) D♭ major
18) G♭ major
19) C♭ major
20) F♭ major
21) B♭♭ major
22) a minor
23) e minor
24) b minor
25) f♯ minor
26) c♯ minor
27) g♯ minor
28) d♯ minor
29) a♯ minor
30) e♯ minor
31) b♯ minor
32) d minor
33) g minor
34) c minor
35) f minor
36) b♭ minor
37) e♭ minor
38) a♭ minor
39) d♭ minor
40) g♭ minor
41) c♭ minor

b) From c♯ minor to:
42) E♭ major (e♭ minor)
43) A♭ major (a♭ minor)
44) D♭ major (d♭ minor)
45) G♭ major (g♭ minor)
46) C♭ major (c♭ minor)

c) From a minor to:
47) e minor
48) b minor
49) f♯ minor
50) c♯ minor
51) g♯ minor
52) d♯ minor
53) a♯ minor
54) e♯ minor
55) d minor
56) g minor
57) c minor
58) f minor
59) b♭ minor
60) e♭ minor
61) a♭ minor
62) d♭ minor
63) g♭ minor
64) c♭ minor
65) f♭ minor
66) C major
67) G major
68) D major
69) A major
70) E major
71) B major
72) F♯ major
73) C♯ major
74) G♯ major
75) D♯ major
76) A♯ major
77) E♯ major
78) F major
79) B♭ major
80) E♭ major
81) A♭ major
82) D♭ major
83) G♭ major
84) C♭ major
85) F♭ major

From C♭ major to:
86) F♯ major (f♯ minor)
87) C♯ major (c♯ minor)
88) G♯ major (g♯ minor)

From d♭ minor to:
89) E major (e minor)
90) B major (b minor)
91) F♯ major (f♯ minor)
92) C♯ major (c♯ minor)
93) G♯ major (g♯ minor)
94) D♯ major (d♯ minor)

From a♯ minor to:
95) B♭ major (b♭ minor)
96) E♭ major (e♭ minor)
97) A♭ major (a♭ minor)
98) D♭ major (d♭ minor)
99) G♭ major (g♭ minor)
100) C♭ major (c♭ minor)

## EXERCISES

**7.33** Based upon an examination of the relative turn capability of counterclockwise versus clockwise directions shown in these diagrams, does it appear that Reger was more at home when writing in the sharp keys or in the flat keys?

**7.34** In examples 42 through 46, and again in examples 86 through 100, the bifurcation of trajectory has resulted simply from the combination of two cases, and has no other special significance. Determine theoretically which fork of the trajectory, inside or outside, corresponds to the minor ending.

**7.35** Using insights provided by Fig. 7.15, continue to analyze the rest of Reger's 100 examples. Initiate changes to correct any observed deviation from his stated intentions. Suitably annotate each chart with arguments of z and preferred notations, especially identifying Neapolitan sixth chords and other harmonies causing abrupt changes of key.

**7.36** Under what circumstances can prolongation in time lead to an enharmonic modification? Cite cases discovered in the previous exercise and elsewhere. It would be natural to wonder to what extent the human ear can be trained to distinguish such nice shades of meaningful difference. The answer to this question is open for investigation by experimental psychologists.

**7.37** Some musicians think that chords A♭CE♭A♭ and G♯B♯D♯G♯ sound the same on the piano. Admittedly they do in isolation from context. Show how this thinking may have to be adjusted, given that the listener's frame of reference includes a perfect knowledge of the spelling of the preceding chord and a belief that the composer has not acted rashly.

**7.38** The preceding analysis of the modulation examples given by Reger indicates that his objectives are not always completely satisfied. Suggest ways in which a rationale encompassing additional musical parameters might explain away some of the apparent shortcomings.

## REFERENCES

[1] J. A. Hamilton, *Hamilton's Celebrated Dictionary* (S. T. Gordon, New York, 1866) p. 60.

[2] Max Reger, *On the Theory of Modulation*, (New York, 1948).

*We have, however, attempted to make our programs mirror the progressive character of musical comprehension--by which we mean that as a fugue subject proceeds the listener's ideas about its metre and key become more and more definite, and may indeed crystallize well before the end of a long subject.*

*H. C. Longuet-Higgens and M. J. Steedman, "On Interpreting Bach," in* ***Machine Intelligence*** *6, American Elsevier Publ. Co., New York, 1971, p. 223.*

PART II

# Chapter 8

# Methodology

## AMPLITUDES AND PHASE ANGLES

The foregoing sections have shown how to derive the resultant tonalities for various charms and harmonies, starting with the basic tone vectors and employing the concept of vector addition. It has been shown that most chords have definite phases, but for balanced chords, the phase angle is indeterminate. So far as the present investigation is concerned, the word **tonality** is used in three mutually consistent expressions: the tonality plane, the tonality phase, and the tonality amplitude.

The tonality plane is formed by taking rational combinations of the twelve unit tone vectors, which are identified with the twelfth roots of unity. These twelve vectors, however, are not linearly independent over the rational field, and consequently cannot be said to form a basis for the space. By the "amplitude" of a tonality is meant the length of its associated tonality vector. Tonalities are more or less intense according to their amplitudes. Thus, by dividing by the total time T the maximum range or distance D from the origin attained by the composition in its controlled meandering across the displacement plane, an estimate of the devotedness or dedication to a particular key is obtained, which tends to establish the degree of a composer's singleness of purpose. This estimate is sometimes the amplitude of the average tonality.

When successive chords have different tonalities, the result may be due to a change of amplitude, or phase, or both. The use of amplitude and phase information avoids making any particular hypotheses about the underlying key or changes from key to key--both of which concepts are almost meaningless for much modern music. Therefore, the central problem of tonal analysis is to find the amplitude v and phase $\phi$ of each resultant tonality. Once again consideration may be restricted to vectors in a fixed plane, so that each vector has only two components.

As described in Chapter 4, vector addition can be used to associate a vector, termed the **tonality vector**, with every one of the 4096 members of the harmonic tonality. The resulting tabulation serves as well for "simple chords," that is, those chords in which doubling does not occur. Each summation extends over all the tones of the harmony. Every vector sum calculated leads to an amplitude and a phase angle, which together define a position in the tonality plane, which can be plotted. The assembly of all such points is displayed in Fig. 8.1. A second display, in Fig. 8.2, reorients these tonality points with respect to an x,y coordinate system, and a third, in Fig. 8.3, places them in the polar coordinate system. From this representation it is comparatively easy to relate the points to the reference key-axis system and to identify those points corresponding to subharmonies of the key of C major. These points are extracted and labeled in Fig. 8.4. The four charts reduce the work entailed in determining the tonal impulse or in finding the true preferred notation for simple chords. Moreover, the pretty patterns produced by plotting the vector resultants of various sets of harmonies may suggest novel approaches to musical composition.

Figure 8.1

The distribution of simple tonalities in the tonality plane. Each point represents the tip of a vector emanating from the origin, which is located at the center of symmetry of the distribution.

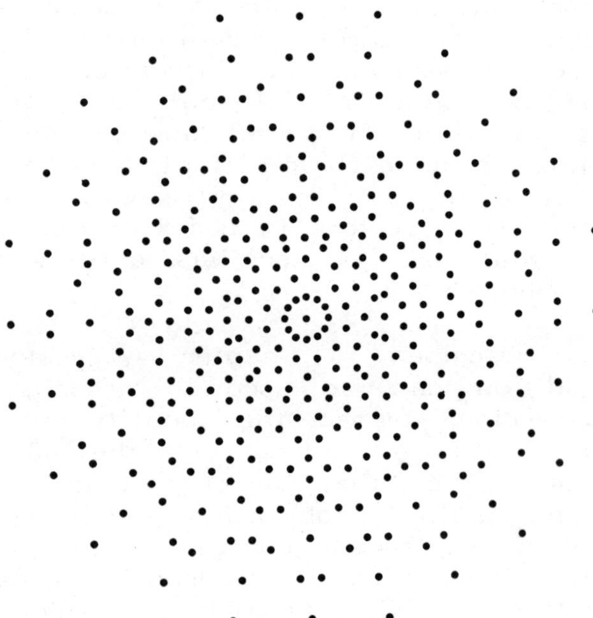

Figure 8.2

System of simple tonalities overlaid with unit-square grid.

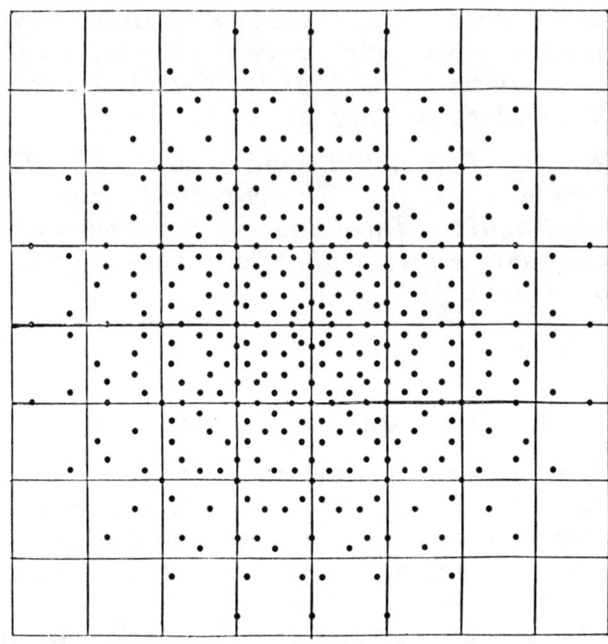

Figure 8.3

The simple chords corresponding to the subharmonies of the C major scale are emphasized against a background of smaller dots in this rendition using polar coordinates.

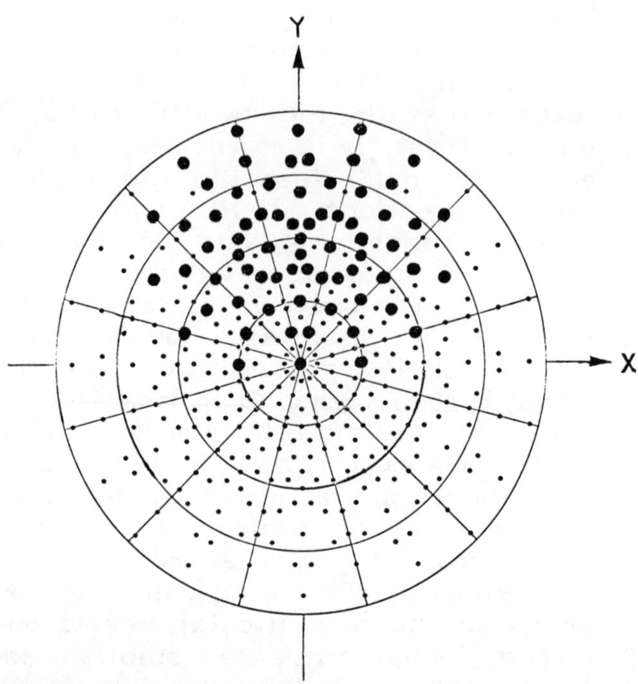

Figure 8.4

Ring array of left and right, inner and outer harmonies in the key of C major. The spatial relationship of simple tonalities in any major key, for that matter, are made up of two like families of concentric circles. Notice the straight lines too.

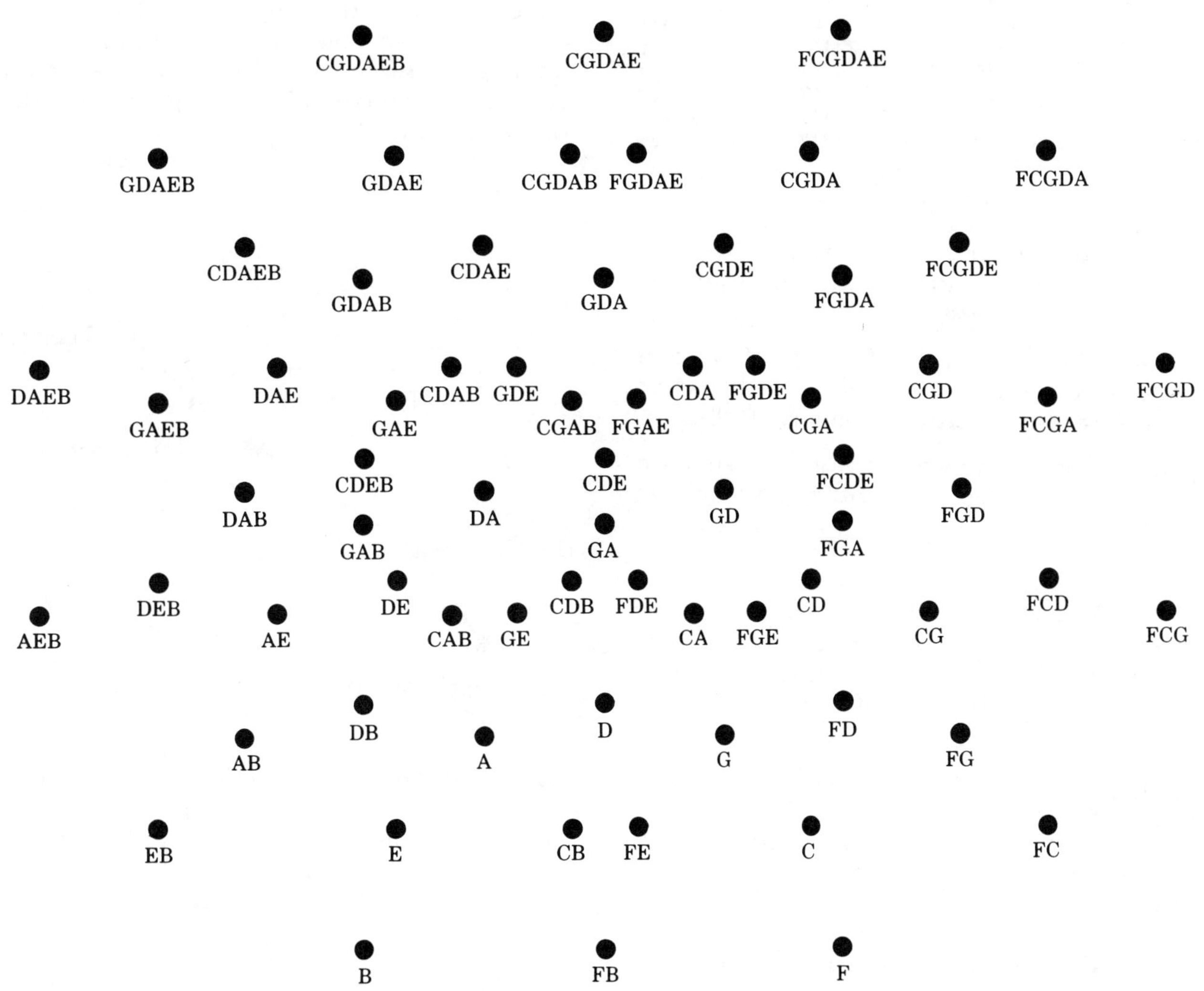


EXERCISES

**8.1** (a) Find one other harmony having the same tonality as C, E, DF, BD, DC, AG, ED, DGF, EDC, BAD, AGC, EAG, ADGF, BADG, ADGC, EADG, and EADGC. (b) Find two other harmonies having the same tonality as G, A, GC, AC, EG, EA, DGC, ADC, EDG, EAD, EDGC, and EADC. (c) Find three other harmonies having the same tonality as D, and ADG. (d) Find all other harmonies having the same tonality as AG, and AD. (Hint. All harmonies must be subharmonies of the C major scale harmony.)

**8.2** In Fig. 8.4 where are harmonies I, II, III, IV, V, VI, and VII located? Where are harmonies I-7, II-7, III-7, IV-7, V-7, VI-7, and VII-7 located?

**8.3** Show how the following substitution tables were obtained by invoking the symmetries of Fig. 8.4.

| INDENTICAL | HORIZONTAL | VERTICAL | CENTRAL |
|---|---|---|---|
| I | VI | I | VI |
| II | V | II | V |
| III | IV | III7 | II7 |
| IV | III | II7 | III7 |
| V | II | V | II |
| VI | I | VI | I |
| VII | VII | VI7 | VI7 |
| I7 | IV7 | I7 | IV7 |
| II7 | III7 | IV | III |
| III7 | II7 | III | IV |
| IV7 | I7 | IV7 | I7 |
| V7 | VII7 | V7 | VII7 |
| VI7 | VI7 | VII | VII |
| VII7 | V7 | VII7 | V7 |

Extend these transformations to include all C major scale subharmonies.

**8.4** What points of Fig. 8.4 are associated with the subharmonies of the pentatonic scale harmony CDEGA?

**8.5** Construct a diagram similar to Fig. 8.4 for the harmonic minor scale.

**8.6** Often the phase angle of a chord can be determined at least approximately without going through the complete details of the calculation for $\theta$.

Example. For the C major scale, determine the phases of triads I through VII and sevenths I-7 through VII-7. The solution is obtained by noting that the endnotes of major thirds coalesce and those of diminished fifths vanish. The results may be tabulated

RELATIVE POSITIONS OF COMMON C MAJOR SCALE SUBHARMONIES

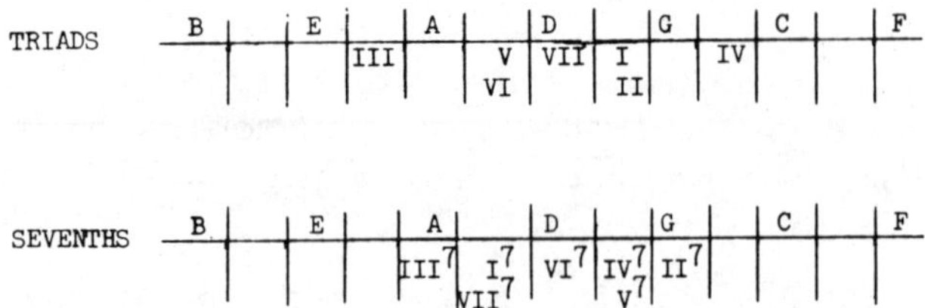


(a) Identify the mediant, dominant-submediant, tonic-supertonic, and subdominant portions of the C major halfplane. (b) For the G harmonic minor scale, determine the phases of triads i through vii and sevenths i-7 through vii-7. (c) Comment on the symmetry, or lack of it, in the two cases--major and minor.

**8.7** (a) An automobile, driven from Washington, D.C., to New York City, travels at a different constant speed between each of the major cities shown below. By choosing tonalities appropriately, plan a musical paraphrase of this journey. How does it sound?

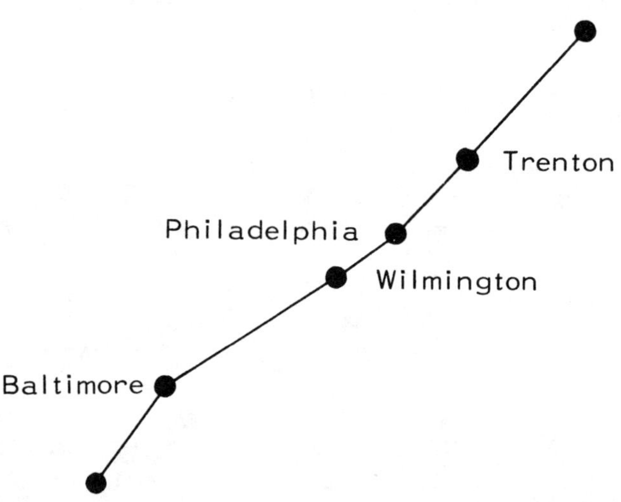


(b) Reduce the number of terms in the following vector sums to obtain simpler expressions:

(a) $\vec{G} + \vec{A\flat} + \vec{A} + \vec{B\flat} + \vec{D} + \vec{F} + \vec{F\sharp}$

(b) $\vec{A} + \vec{B} + \vec{C} + \vec{D} + \vec{E} + \vec{G} + \vec{G\sharp}$

(c) $\vec{A} + \vec{B} + \vec{C} + \vec{C\sharp} + \vec{D} + \vec{E} + \vec{F}$

(d) $\vec{A\flat} + \vec{B\flat\flat} + \vec{B\flat} + \vec{C\flat} + \vec{D\flat} + \vec{F} + \vec{G\flat}$

(e) $\vec{E} + \vec{F\sharp} + \vec{G} + \vec{A} + \vec{B\flat} + \vec{B} + \vec{D}$

(f) $\vec{D\sharp} + \vec{E} + \vec{E\sharp} + \vec{F\sharp} + \vec{G} + \vec{G\sharp} + \vec{B}$

(g) $\vec{D} + \vec{E} + \vec{F} + \vec{F\sharp} + \vec{G} + \vec{A\flat} + \vec{A} + \vec{B\flat} + \vec{C} + \vec{C\sharp}(\vec{D\flat})$

(h) $\vec{A\sharp} + \vec{D\sharp} + \vec{E} + \vec{E\sharp} + \vec{F\sharp} + \vec{F\times} + \vec{G\sharp}$

(i) $\vec{A} + \vec{B\flat} + \vec{B} + \vec{D} + \vec{E} + \vec{F} + \vec{F\sharp} + \vec{G}$

(j) $\vec{C} + \vec{D} + \vec{E\flat} + \vec{E} + \vec{F} + \vec{G} + \vec{B\flat}$

(k) $\vec{F} + \vec{G\flat} + \vec{G} + \vec{A\flat} + \vec{A} + \vec{B\flat} + \vec{C} + \vec{D\flat}$

(l) $\vec{D} + \vec{E} + \vec{F} + \vec{G} + \vec{A\flat} + \vec{A} + \vec{B\flat} + \vec{B} + \vec{C} + \vec{C\sharp}$

(m) $\vec{E} + \vec{F} + \vec{F\sharp} + \vec{G} + \vec{G\sharp} + \vec{A} + \vec{C\sharp} + \vec{D}$

(n) $\vec{A} + \vec{B\flat} + \vec{B} + \vec{C} + \vec{D} + \vec{E} + \vec{G}$

(o) $\vec{D} + \vec{F} + \vec{F\sharp} + \vec{G} + \vec{A} + \vec{B\flat} + \vec{B} + \vec{C}$

(p) $\vec{F\times} + \vec{B\sharp} + \vec{C\times} + \vec{D\sharp} + \vec{D\times} + \vec{E\sharp} + \vec{E\times}$

(q) $\vec{A} + \vec{B\flat} + \vec{B} + \vec{C} + \vec{D} + \vec{E\flat} + \vec{E} + \vec{F} + \vec{F\sharp} + \vec{G\sharp}(\vec{A\flat})$

## TONALITY DIAGRAMS

On the following pages appears a complete collection of tonality diagrams for harmonies situated in the first sector, $[0^o, 30^o)$, of the tonality plane. This range is bisected by the C minor key axis and covers parts of the B♭ major and E♭ major key sectors. Each diagram constitutes a hierarchal decomposition of the tonality indicated by the phase and amplitude heading given at the upper right of the diagram. Each diagram expresses the inclusion relationship holding among those simple chords, or harmonies, characterized by the property of being phase and amplitude matched. Accordingly, all the labeled vertices in a particular diagram correspond to a single value of v and of ϕ, and consequently correspond to a single point in the tonality plane. Similar tonality diagrams for other sectors have identical structures and can be found by rotational transposition of the labeling notations.

Keep in mind that some simple and compound chords can have the same tonality. For example, B♭ + 2E♭, which is compound, equals B♭ + E♭ + D♭ + F, which is simple. One more thing: Inspection of the diagram headed PHASE 15.00000°, AMPLITUDE 1.93185 reveals that the simple chords B♭DF, CE♭G, DFA♭C, E♭GB♭D, and FACE♭ have the same tonality! This fact is noteworthy. It means that the mathematical model upholds the well established traditional connections found among the tonic triad (I), the supertonic triad (II), the subdominant seventh (IV-7), and the dominant seventh (V-7) in major keys. Also, it upholds those connections linking the tonic triad (i) and the supertonic seventh (ii-7) in minor keys. It is reassuring that such evidence exists in support of the claim that the present theory of tonality is in good agreement with the classical view held by composers who adhered to the major and minor key principle.

INDEX TO THE TONALITY DIAGRAMS

| Phase | Amplitude | Number of Elements |
|---|---|---|
| 0.00000 | 0.26795 | 2 |
| | 0.73205 | 12 |
| | 1.00000 | 60 |
| | 1.73205 | 20 |
| | 2.00000 | 10 |
| | 2.73205 | 12 |
| | 3.73205 | 2 |
| 2.37366 | 3.23483 | 2 |
| 3.43495 | 2.23607 | 6 |
| 5.10391 | 1.50597 | 12 |
| 6.20602 | 1.23931 | 6 |
| 7.08866 | 1.88040 | 2 |
| 8.79398 | 2.39417 | 12 |
| 9.89609 | 2.90931 | 6 |
| 15.00000 | 0.51764 | 36 |
| | 0.89658 | 4 |
| | 1.03528 | 1 |
| | 1.41421 | 36 |
| | 1.93185 | 36 |
| | 2.44949 | 4 |
| | 2.82843 | 1 |
| | 3.34607 | 4 |
| | 3.86370 | 1 |
| 20.10391 | 2.90931 | 6 |
| 21.20602 | 2.39417 | 12 |
| 22.91134 | 1.88040 | 2 |
| 23.79398 | 1.23931 | 6 |
| 24.89609 | 1.50597 | 12 |
| 26.56505 | 2.23607 | 6 |
| 27.62634 | 3.23483 | 2 |

PHASE 0.00000

AMPLITUDE 0.26795

**Note.** All phase angles are given in degrees.

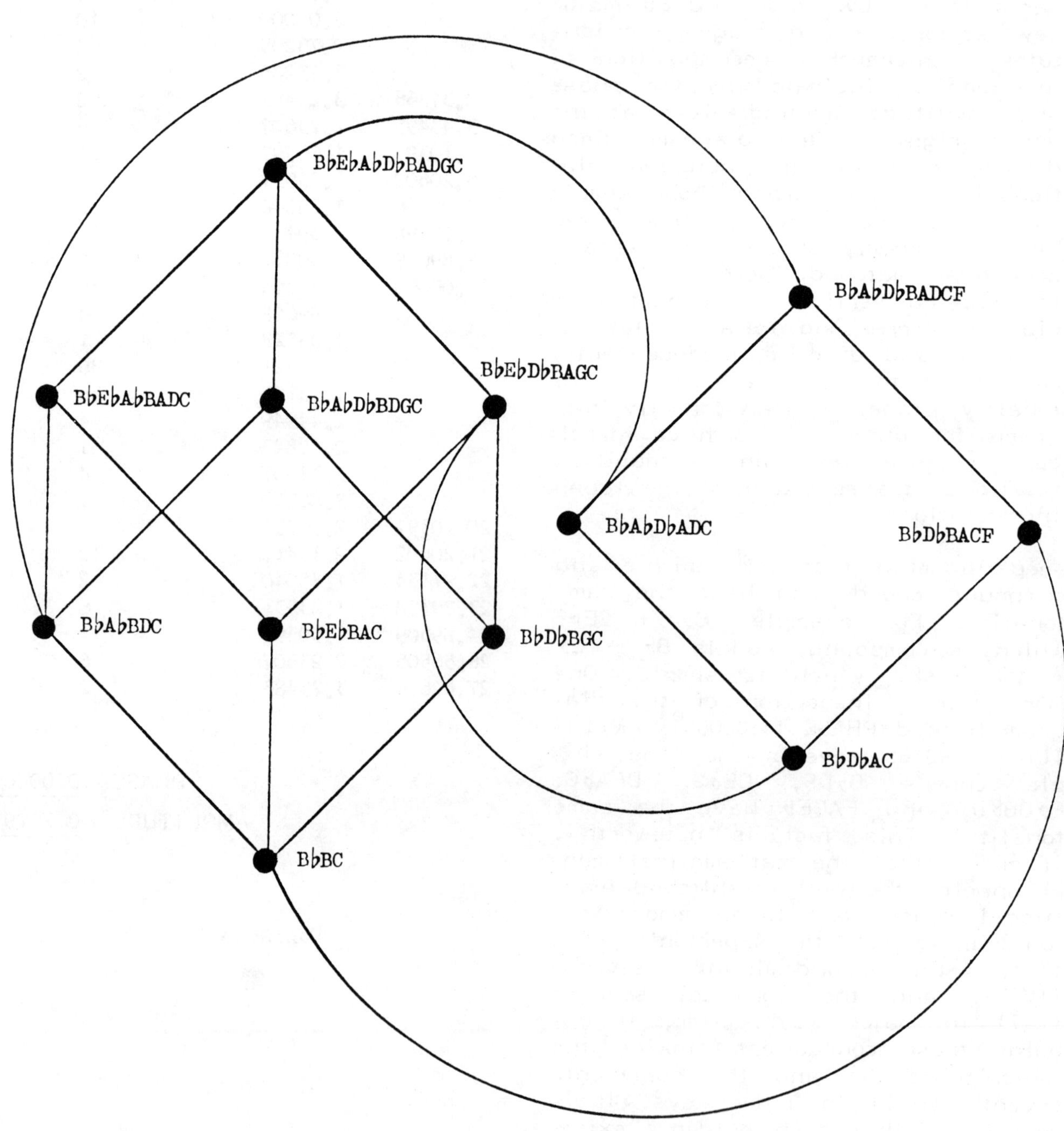
PHASE 0.00000
AMPLITUDE 0.73205
B♭E♭A♭D♭BADGC
B♭A♭D♭BADCF
B♭E♭A♭BADC
B♭A♭D♭BDGC
B♭E♭D♭BAGC
B♭A♭D♭ADC
B♭D♭BACF
B♭A♭BDC
B♭E♭BAC
B♭D♭BGC
B♭D♭AC
B♭BC

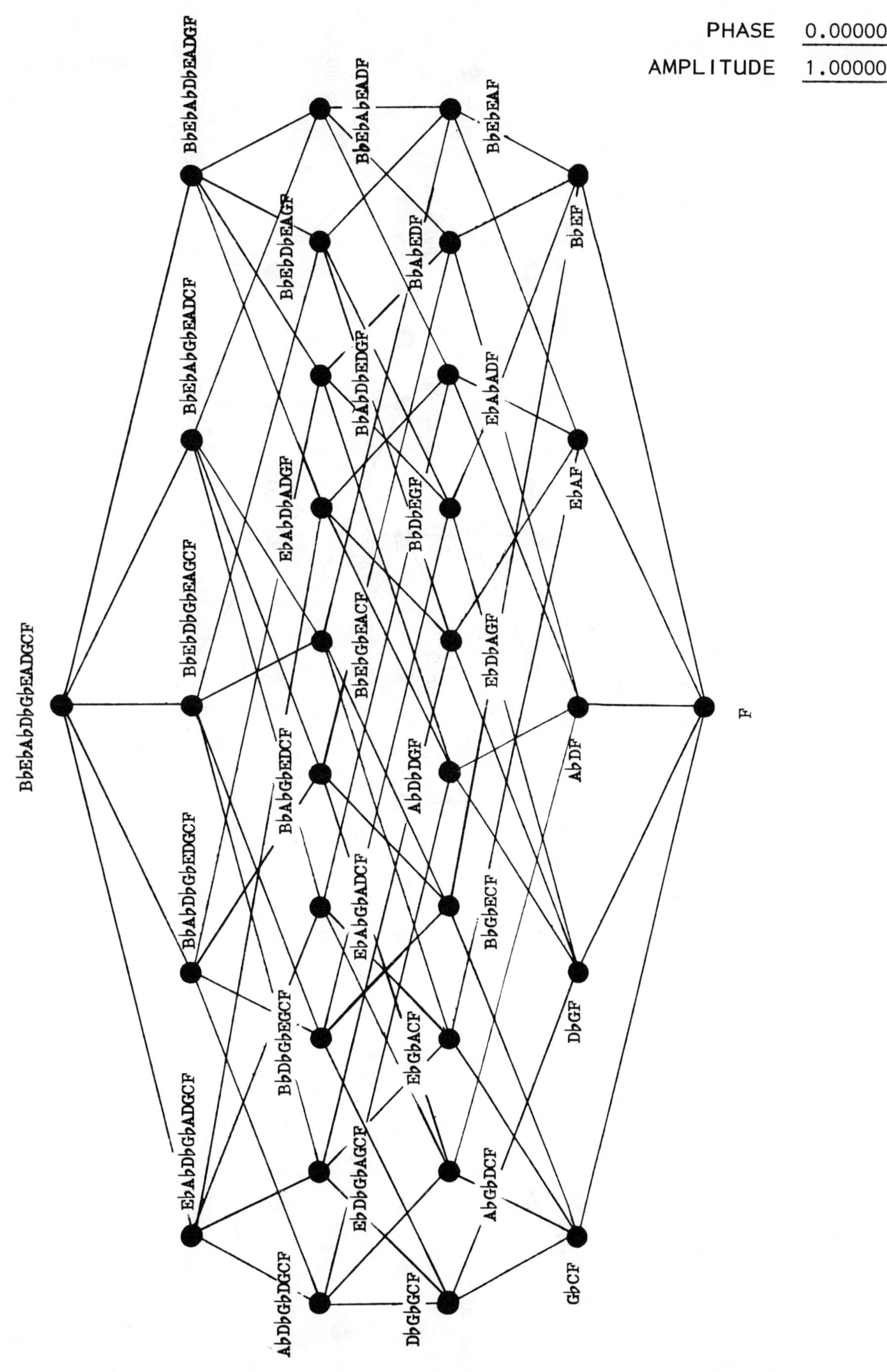
PHASE 0.00000
AMPLITUDE 1.00000
B♭E♭A♭D♭G♭EADGCF
B♭E♭A♭D♭EADGF
B♭E♭A♭G♭EADCF
B♭E♭D♭G♭EAGCF
B♭A♭D♭G♭EDGCF
E♭A♭D♭G♭ADGCF
B♭E♭D♭EAGF
E♭A♭D♭ADGF
B♭A♭G♭EDCF
B♭D♭G♭EGCF
A♭D♭G♭DGCF
B♭E♭A♭EADF
B♭A♭D♭EDGF
B♭E♭G♭EACF
E♭A♭G♭ADCF
E♭D♭G♭AGCF
B♭A♭EDF
B♭D♭EGF
A♭D♭DGF
E♭G♭ACF
D♭G♭GCF
B♭E♭EAF
E♭A♭ADF
E♭D♭AGF
B♭G♭ECF
A♭G♭DCF
B♭EF
E♭AF
A♭DF
D♭GF
G♭CF
F

PHASE 0.00000

AMPLITUDE 1.00000

(continued)

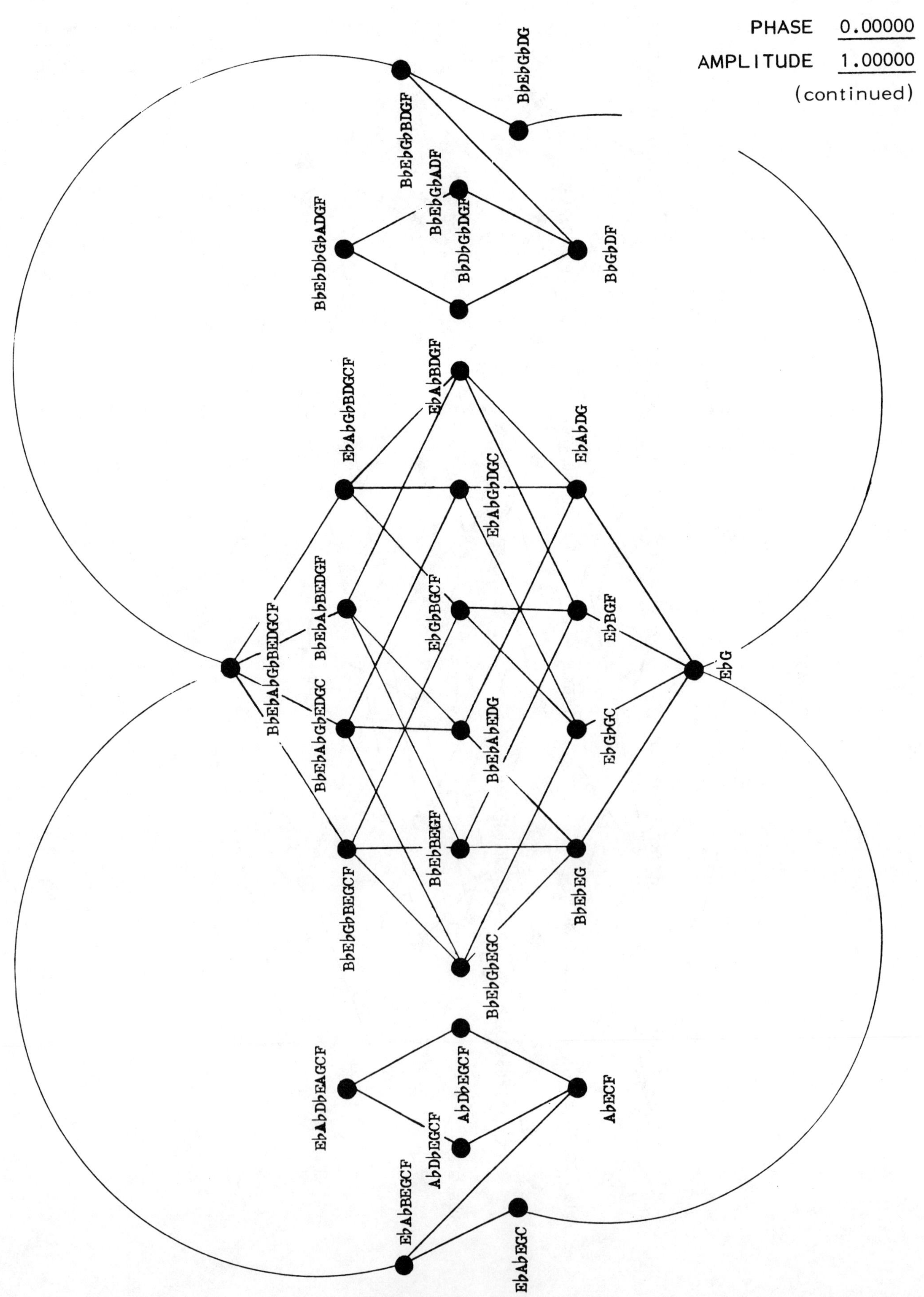

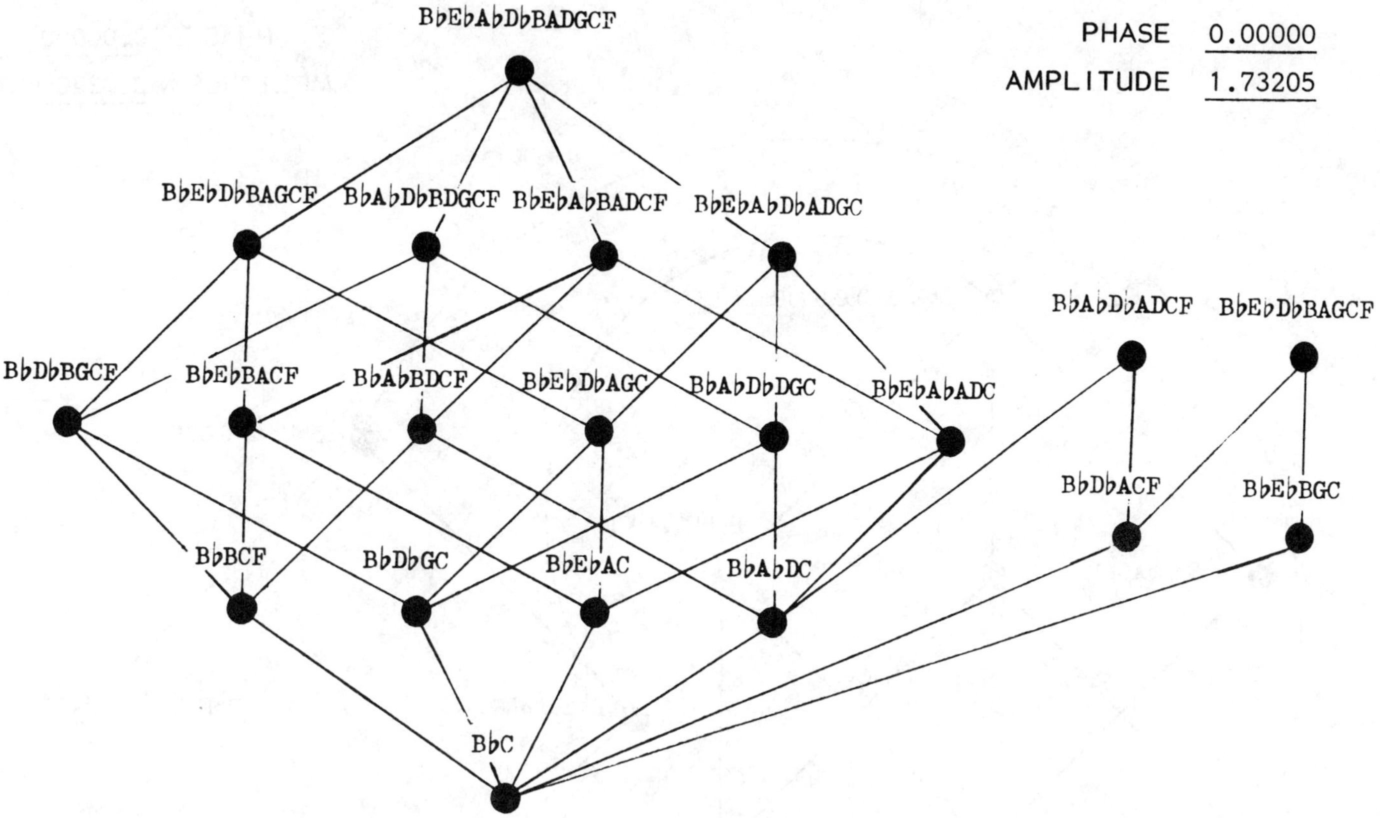
B♭E♭A♭D♭BADGCF
PHASE 0.00000
AMPLITUDE 1.73205
B♭E♭D♭BAGCF
B♭A♭D♭BDGCF
B♭E♭A♭BADCF
B♭E♭A♭D♭ADGC
B♭A♭D♭ADCF
B♭E♭D♭BAGCF
B♭D♭BGCF
B♭E♭BACF
B♭A♭BDCF
B♭E♭D♭AGC
B♭A♭D♭DGC
B♭E♭A♭ADC
B♭D♭ACF
B♭E♭BGC
B♭BCF
B♭D♭GC
B♭E♭AC
B♭A♭DC
B♭C

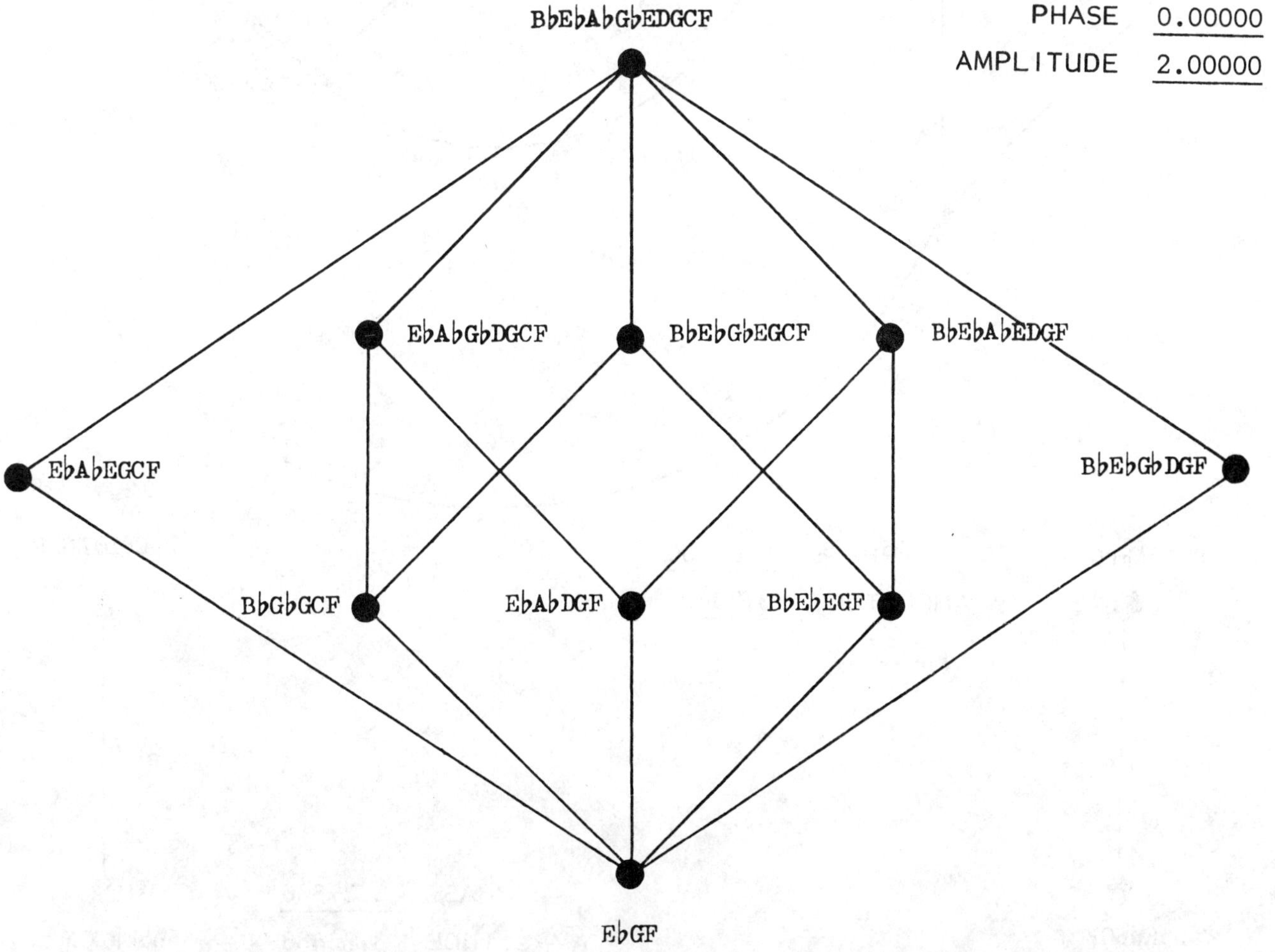
B♭E♭A♭G♭EDGCF
PHASE 0.00000
AMPLITUDE 2.00000
E♭A♭G♭DGCF
B♭E♭G♭EGCF
B♭E♭A♭EDGF
E♭A♭EGCF
B♭E♭G♭DGF
B♭G♭GCF
E♭A♭DGF
B♭E♭EGF
E♭GF

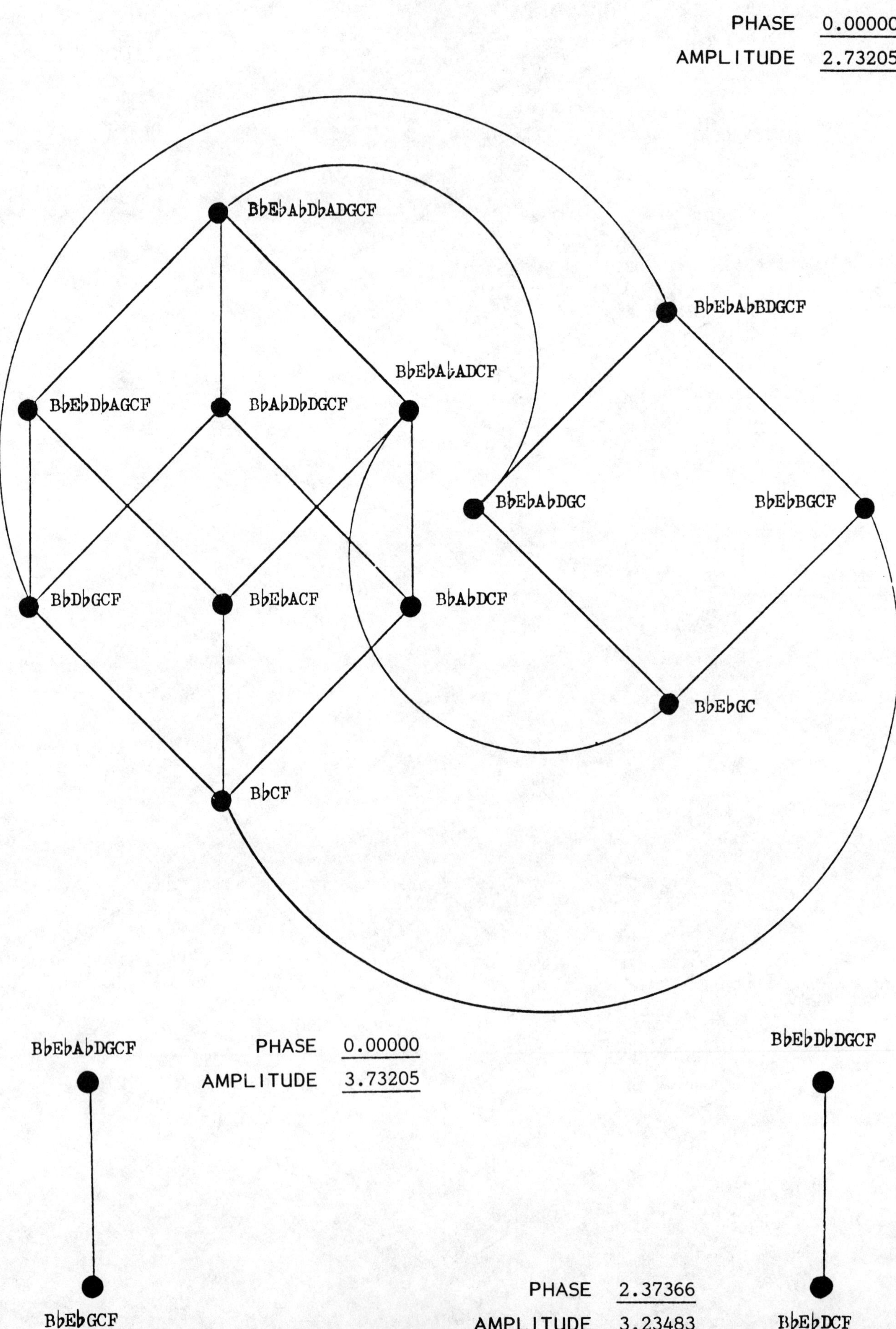
PHASE 0.00000
AMPLITUDE 2.73205
B♭E♭A♭D♭ADGCF
B♭E♭A♭BDGCF
B♭E♭A♭ADCF
B♭E♭D♭AGCF
B♭A♭D♭DGCF
B♭E♭A♭DGC
B♭E♭BGCF
B♭D♭GCF
B♭E♭ACF
B♭A♭DCF
B♭E♭GC
B♭CF
B♭E♭A♭DGCF
PHASE 0.00000
AMPLITUDE 3.73205
B♭E♭D♭DGCF
B♭E♭GCF
PHASE 2.37366
AMPLITUDE 3.23483
B♭E♭DCF

PHASE 3.43495

AMPLITUDE 2.23607

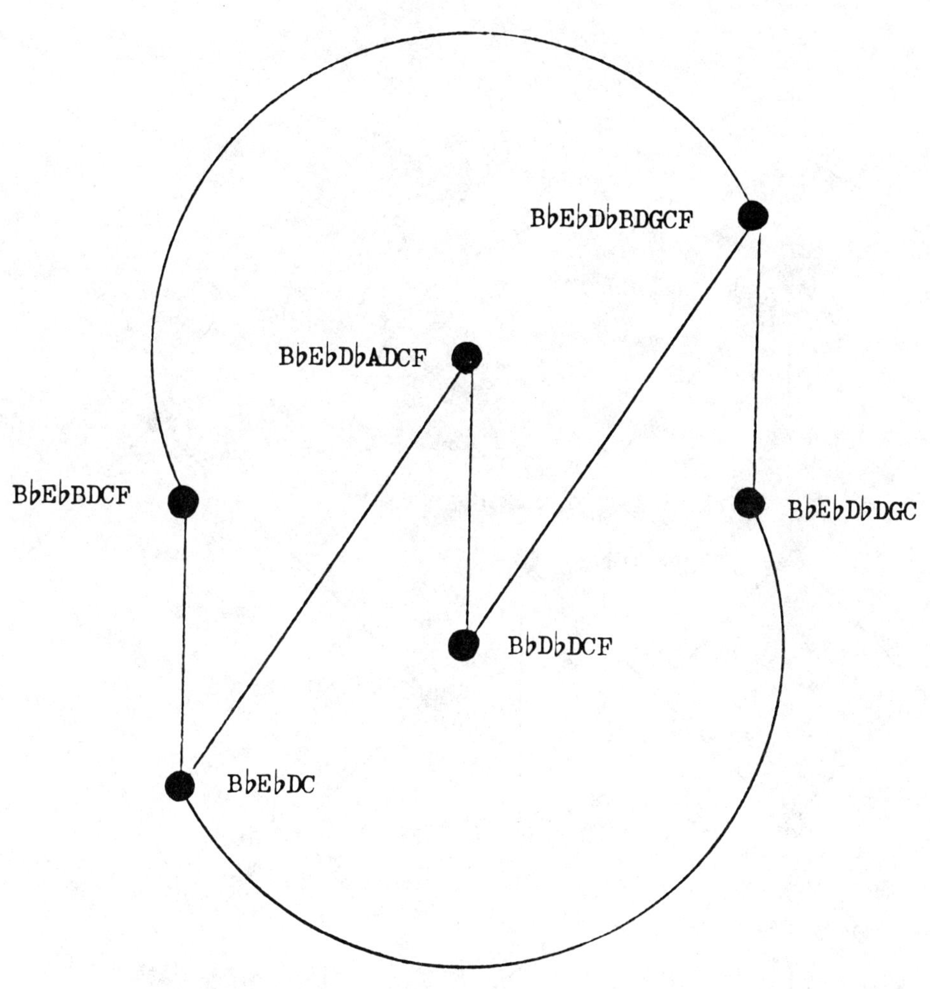

PHASE 5.10391

AMPLITUDE 1.50597

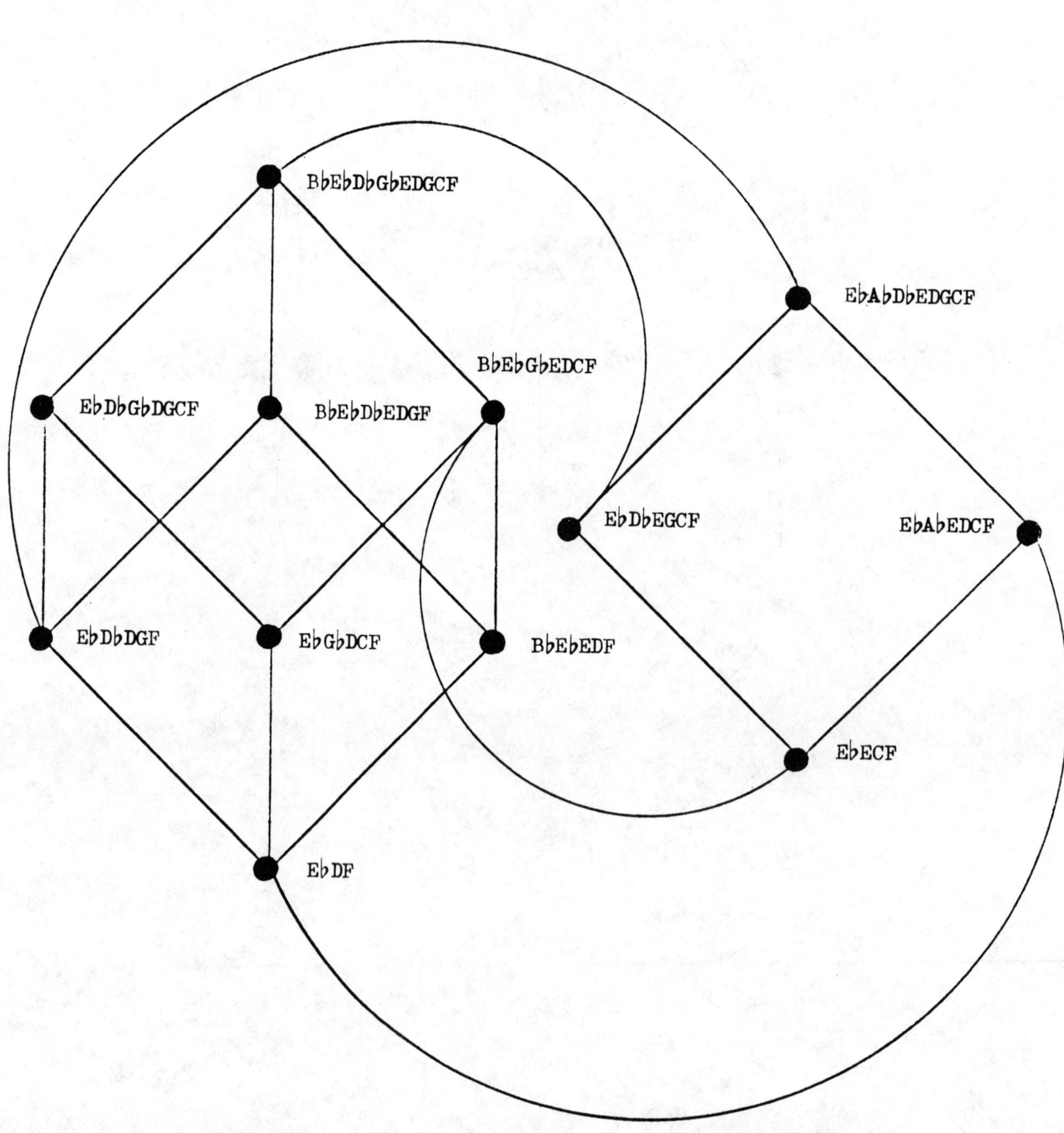

PHASE 6.20602

AMPLITUDE 1.23931

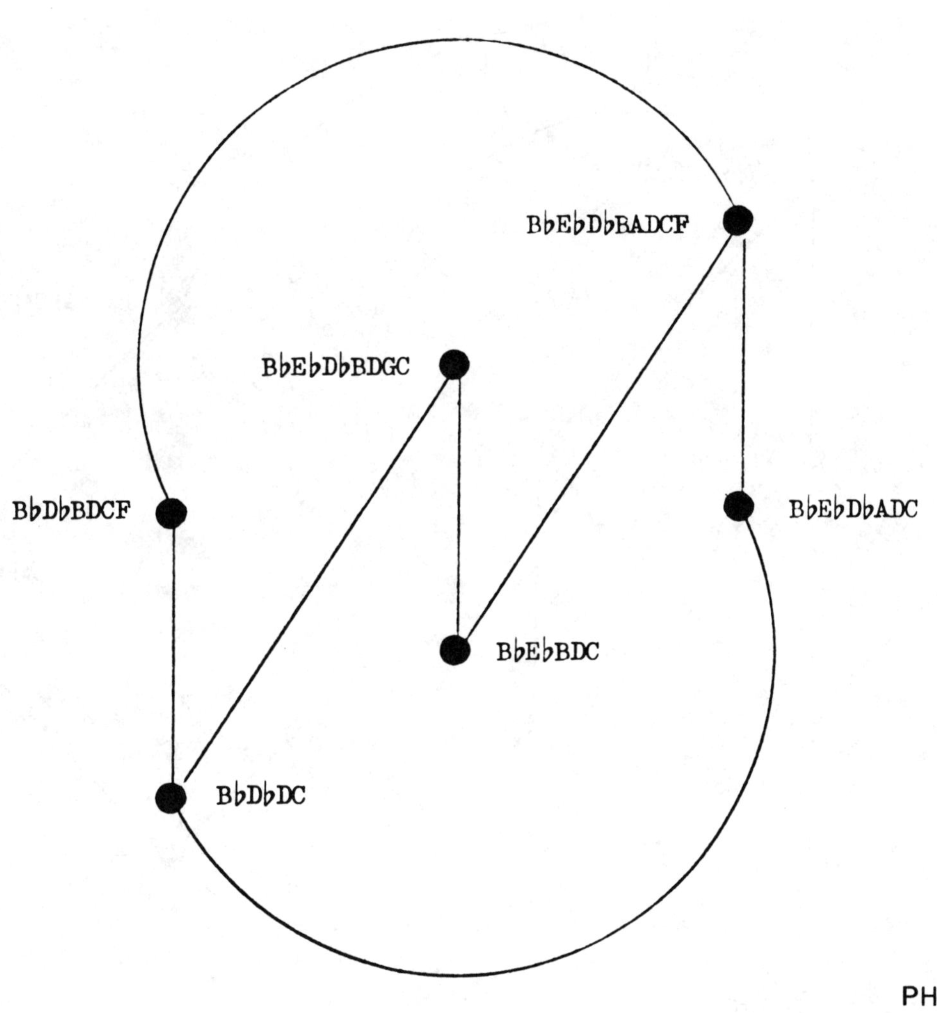


PHASE 7.08866

AMPLITUDE 1.88040

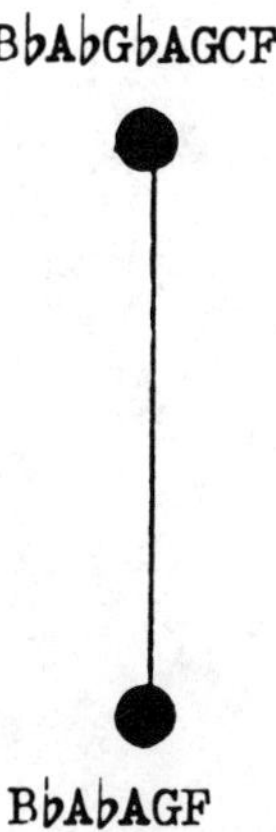

PHASE 8.79398

AMPLITUDE 2.39417

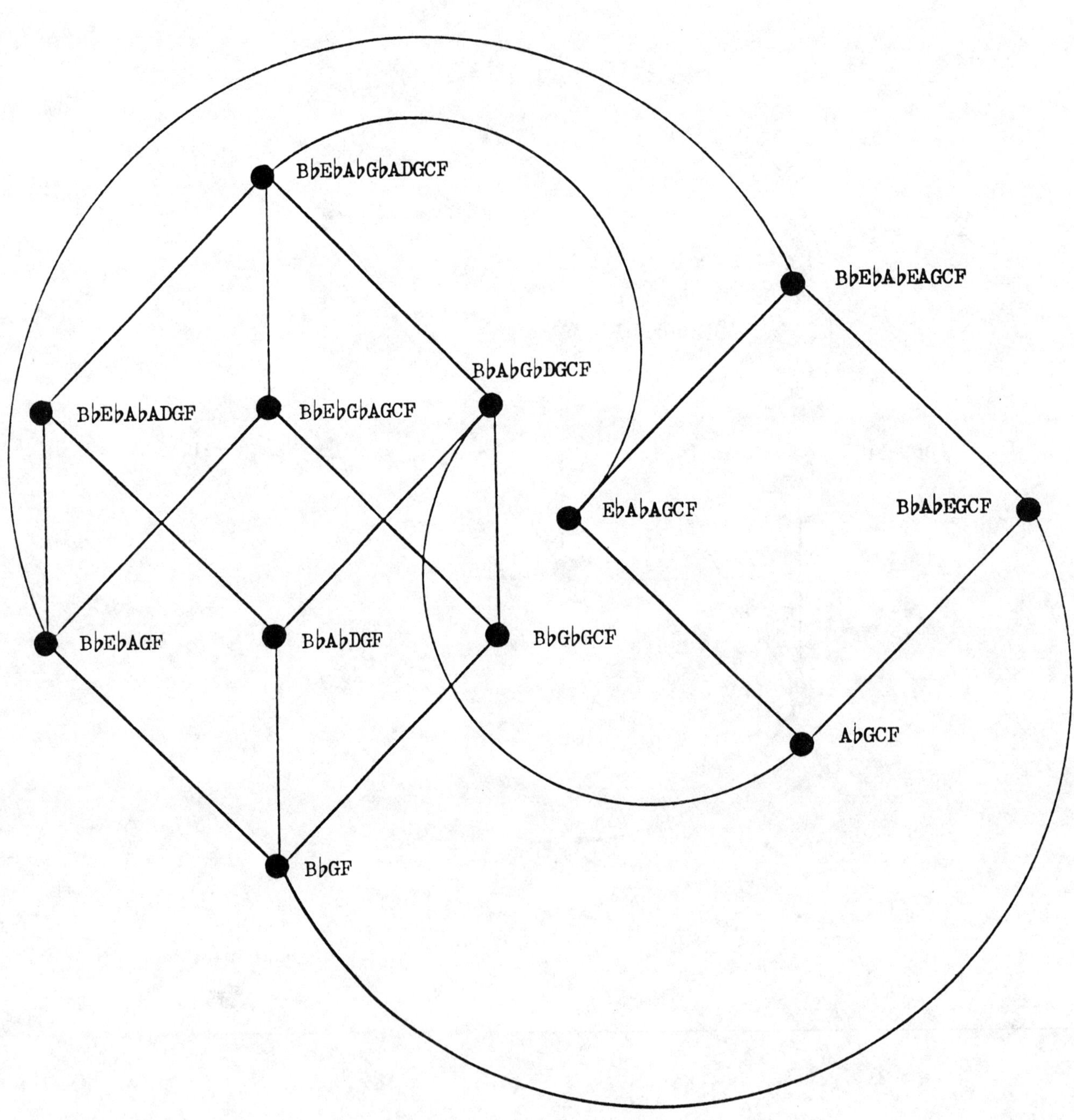

PHASE 9.89609

AMPLITUDE 2.90931

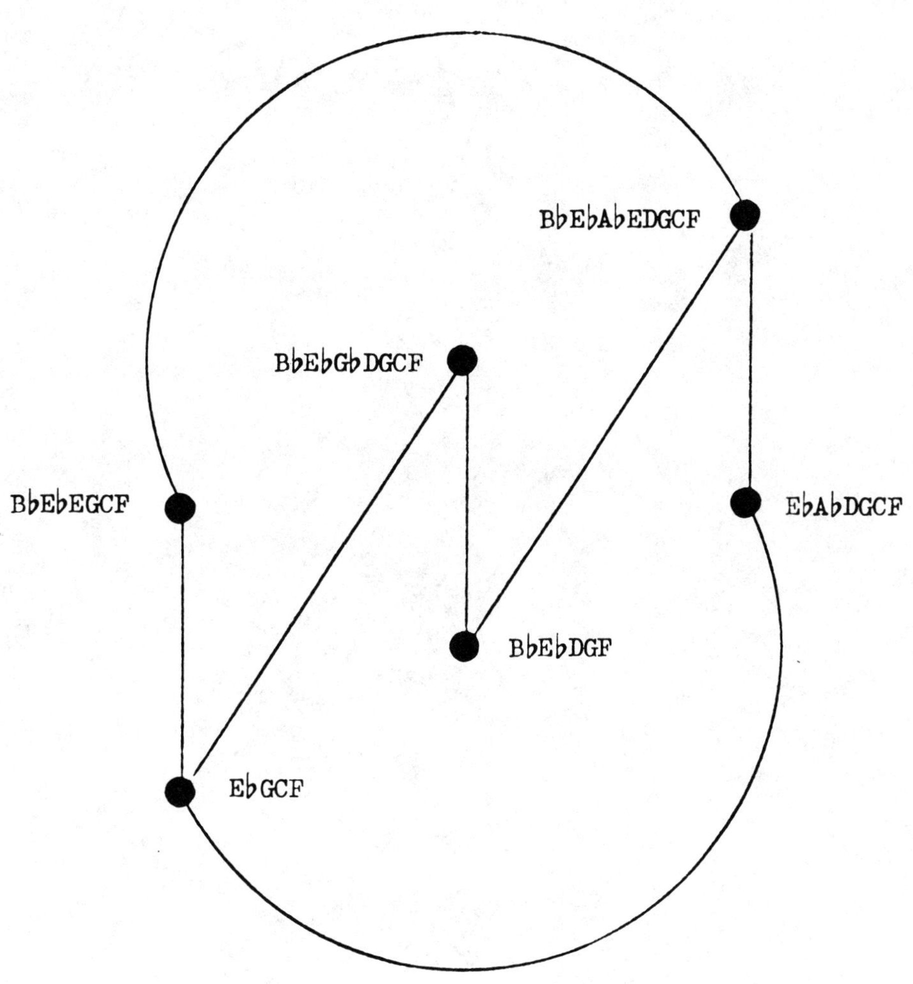

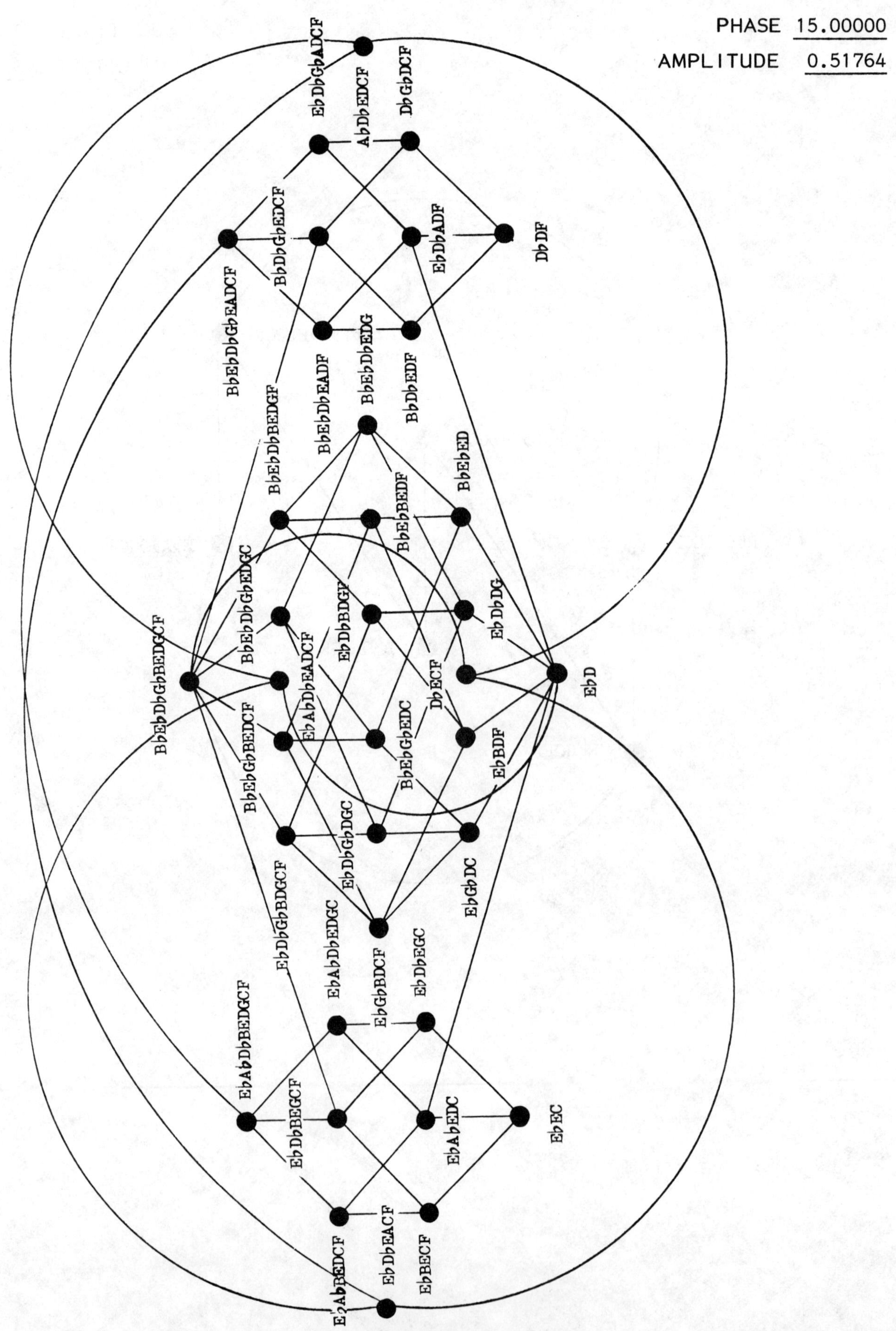
PHASE 15.00000
AMPLITUDE 0.51764
E♭D♭G♭ADCF
A♭D♭EDCF
D♭G♭DCF
B♭D♭G♭EDCF
E♭D♭ADF
D♭DF
B♭E♭D♭G♭EADCF
B♭E♭D♭EDG
B♭E♭D♭EADF
B♭D♭EDF
B♭E♭D♭BEDGF
B♭E♭ED
B♭E♭BEDF
B♭E♭D♭G♭EDGC
E♭D♭BDGF
E♭D♭DG
B♭E♭D♭G♭BEDGCF
E♭A♭D♭EADCF
D♭ECF
E♭D
B♭E♭G♭BEDCF
B♭E♭G♭EDC
E♭BDF
E♭D♭G♭DGC
E♭G♭DC
E♭D♭G♭BDGCF
E♭A♭D♭EDGC
E♭G♭BDCF
E♭D♭EGC
E♭A♭D♭BEDGCF
E♭D♭BEGCF
E♭A♭EDC
E♭EC
E♭D♭EACF
E♭A♭BEDCF
E♭BECF

PHASE 15.00000

AMPLITUDE 0.89658

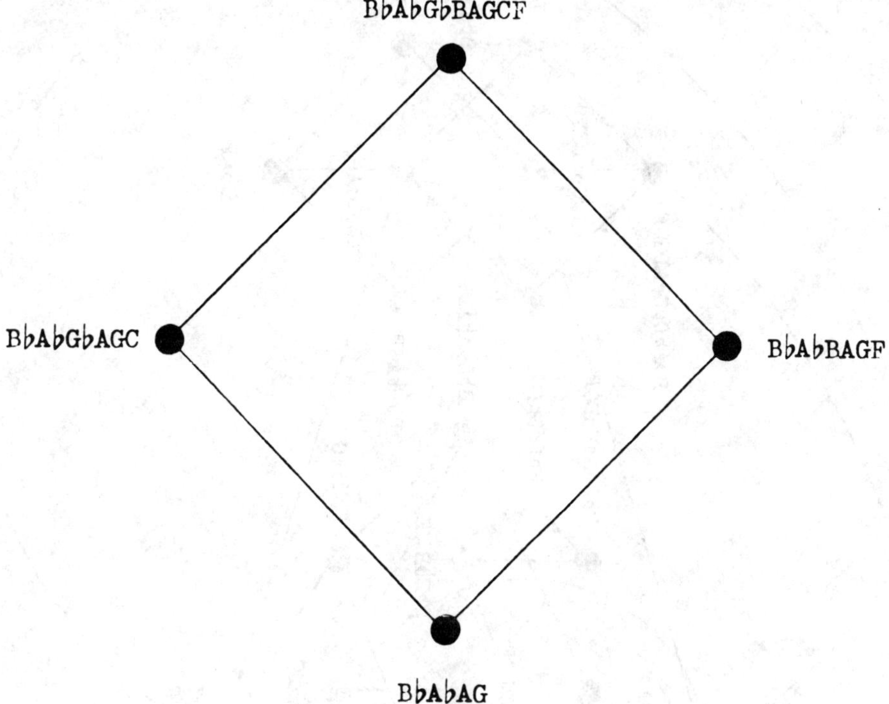


E♭D♭EDCF

PHASE 15.00000

AMPLITUDE 1.03528

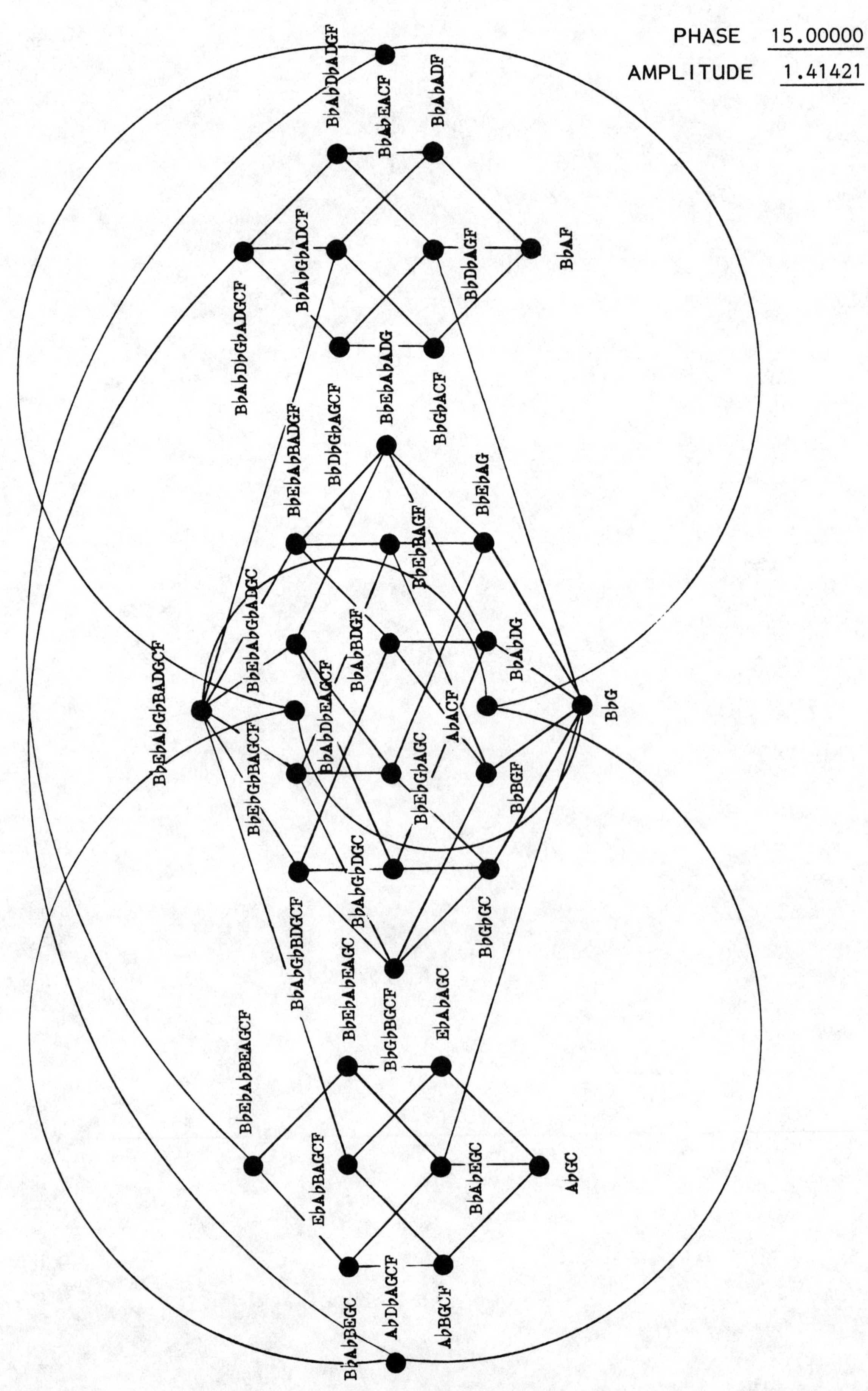
PHASE 15.00000
AMPLITUDE 1.41421
BbAbDbADGF
BbAbEACF
BbAbADF
BbAbGbADCF
BbDbAGF
BbAF
BbAbDbGbADGCF
BbEbAbADG
BbGbACF
BbEbAbBADGF
BbDbGbAGCF
BbEbAG
BbEbBAGF
BbEbAbGbADGC
BbAbBDGF
BbAbDG
BbEbAbGbBADGCF
BbEbAbGbADGC
BbAbDbEAGCF
AbACF
BbG
BbEbGbBAGCF
BbEbGbAGC
BbBGF
BbAbGbDGC
BbGbGC
BbAbGbBDGCF
BbEbAbEAGC
EbAbAGC
BbGbBGCF
BbEbAbBEAGCF
EbAbBAGCF
BbAbEGC
AbGC
BbAbBEGC
AbDbAGCF
AbBGCF

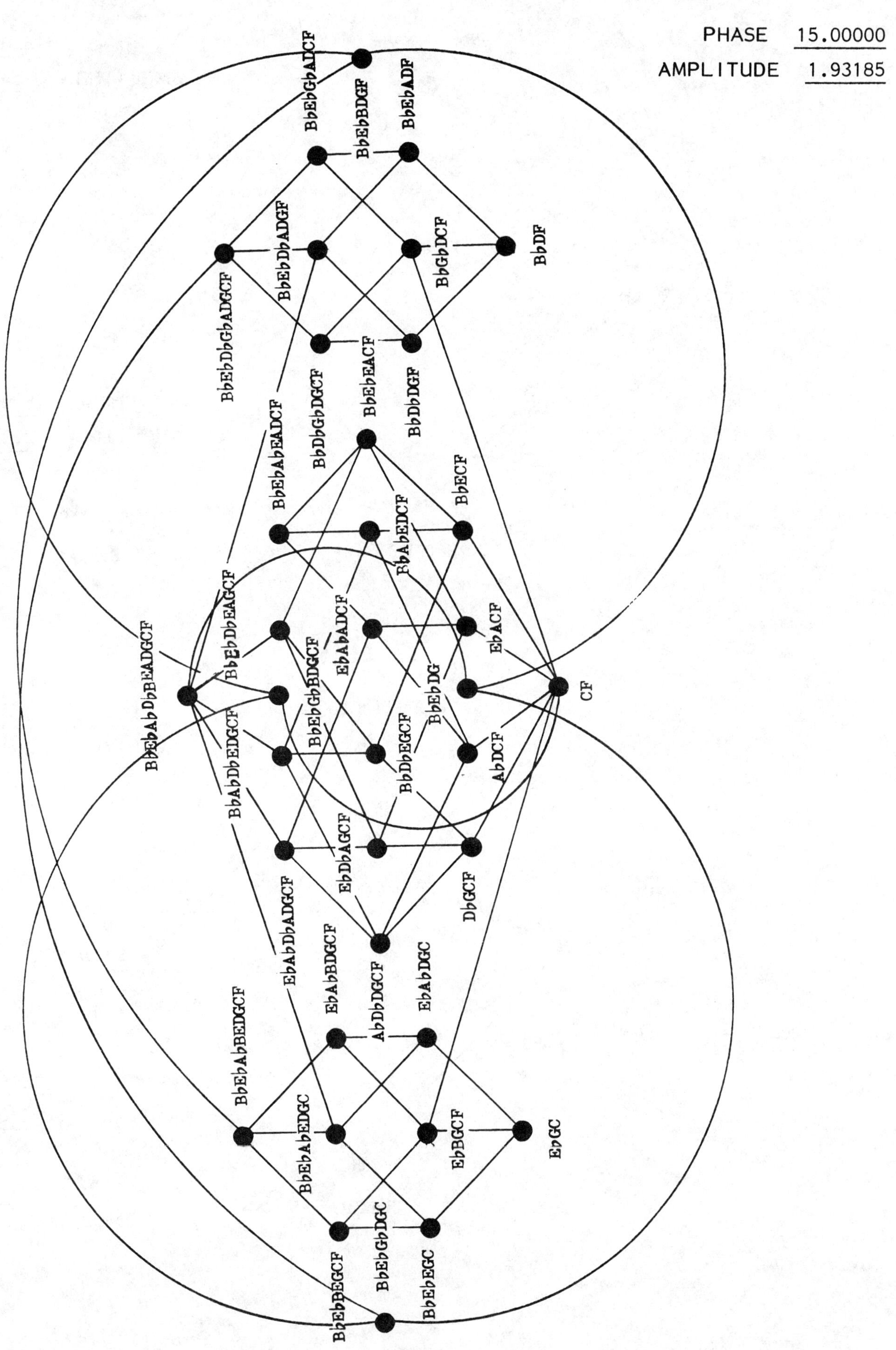
PHASE 15.00000
AMPLITUDE 1.93185
B♭E♭G♭ADCF
B♭E♭BDGF
B♭E♭ADF
B♭E♭D♭ADGF
B♭G♭DCF
B♭DF
B♭E♭D♭G♭ADGCF
B♭E♭EACF
B♭D♭G♭DGCF
B♭D♭DGF
B♭E♭A♭EADCF
B♭ECF
B♭A♭EDCF
B♭E♭D♭EAGCF
E♭A♭ADCF
E♭ACF
B♭E♭A♭D♭BEADGCF
B♭E♭G♭BDGCF
B♭E♭DG
CF
B♭A♭D♭EDGCF
B♭E♭G♭BDGCF
B♭D♭EGCF
A♭DCF
B♭A♭D♭
E♭D♭AGCF
D♭GCF
E♭A♭D♭ADGCF
E♭A♭BDGCF
A♭D♭DGCF
E♭A♭DGC
B♭E♭A♭BEDGCF
B♭E♭A♭EDGC
E♭BGCF
E♭GC
B♭E♭G♭DGC
B♭E♭BEGCF
B♭E♭EGC

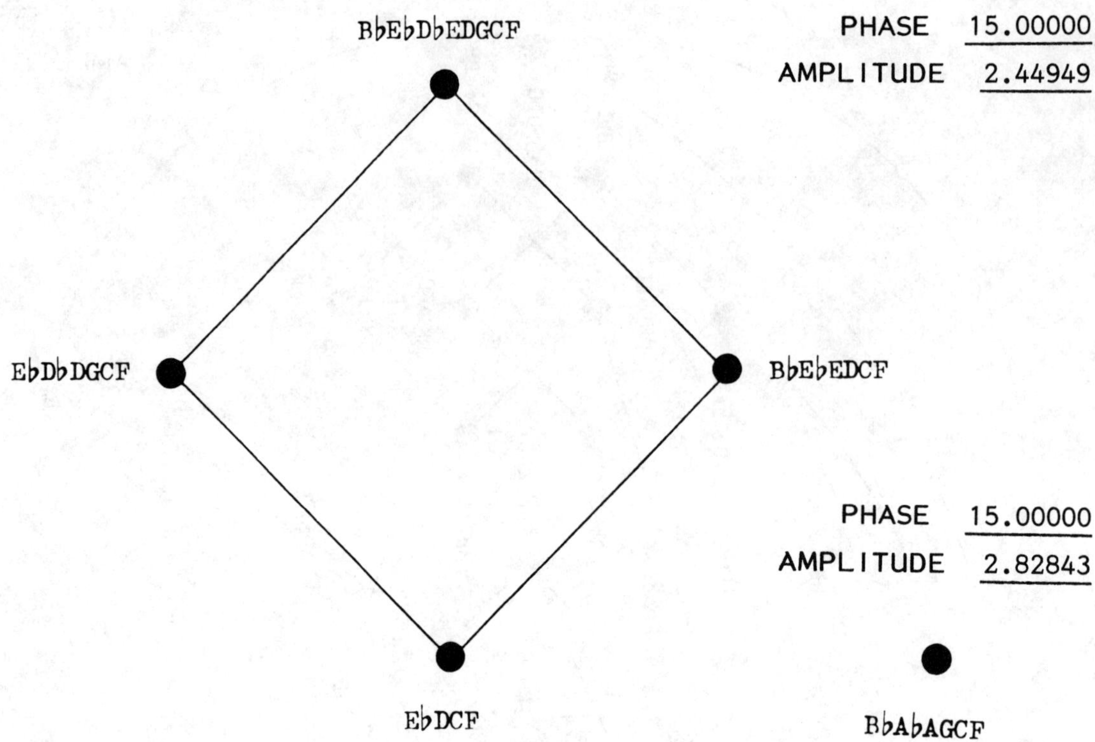
B♭E♭D♭EDGCF
PHASE 15.00000
AMPLITUDE 2.44949
E♭D♭DGCF
B♭E♭EDCF
PHASE 15.00000
AMPLITUDE 2.82843
E♭DCF
B♭A♭AGCF

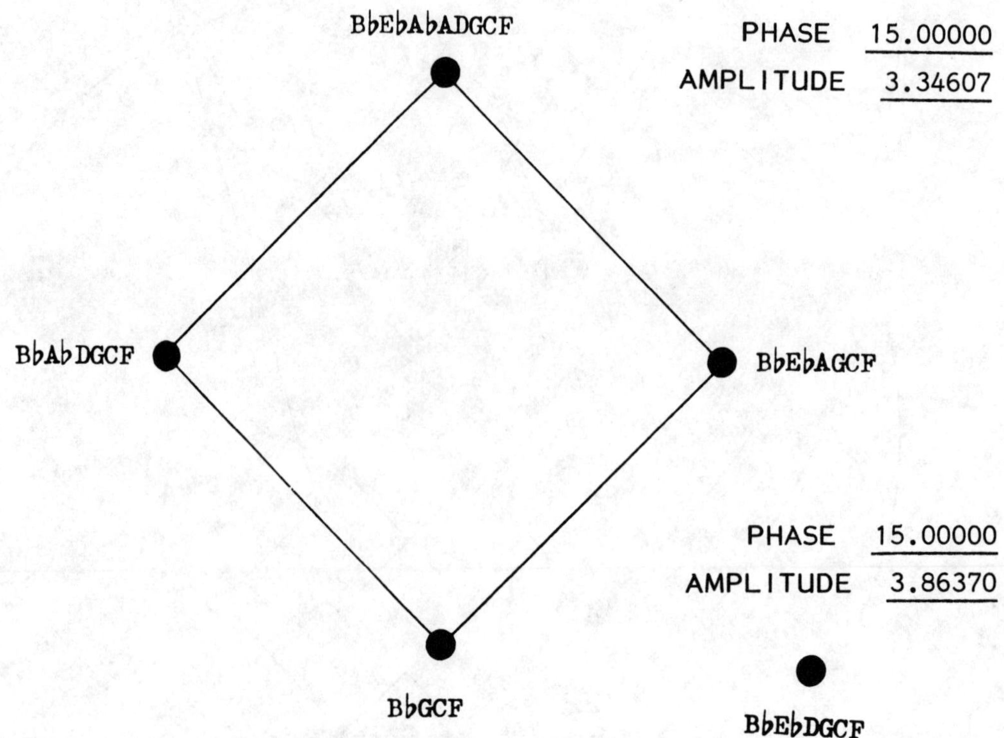
B♭E♭A♭ADGCF
PHASE 15.00000
AMPLITUDE 3.34607
B♭A♭DGCF
B♭E♭AGCF
PHASE 15.00000
AMPLITUDE 3.86370
B♭GCF
B♭E♭DGCF

PHASE 20.10391

AMPLITUDE 2.90931

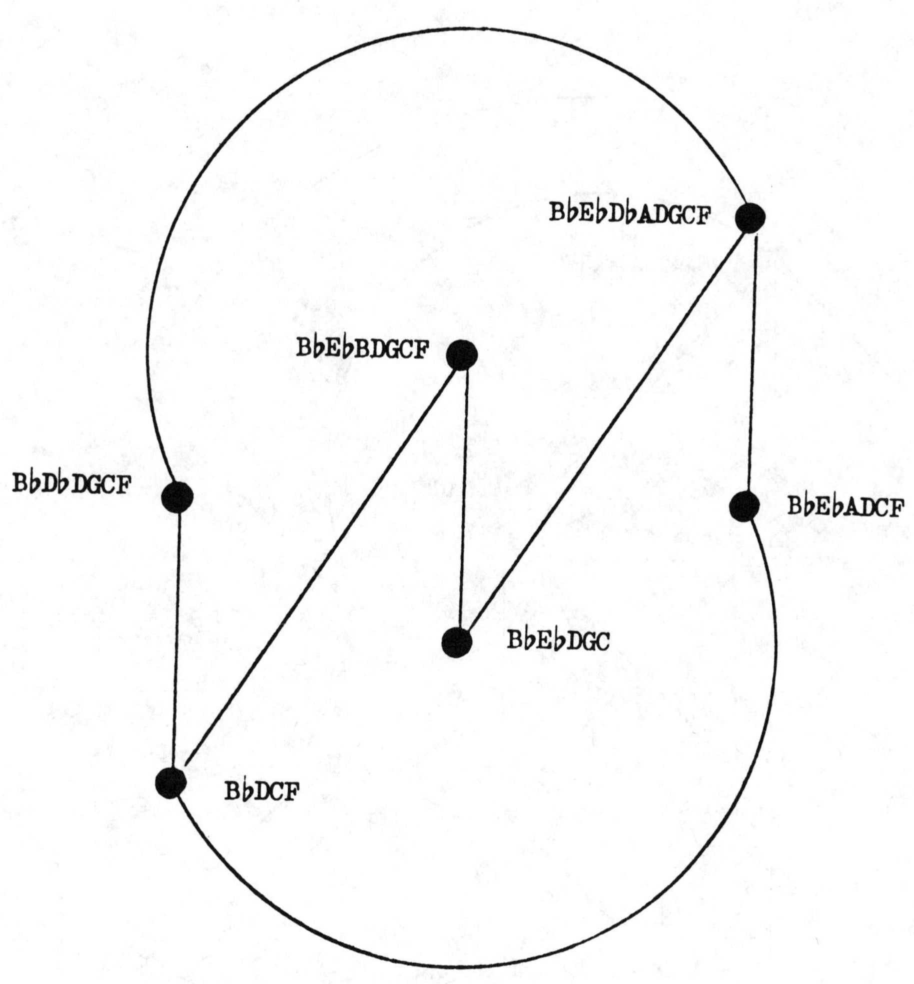

PHASE 21.20602

AMPLITUDE 2.39417

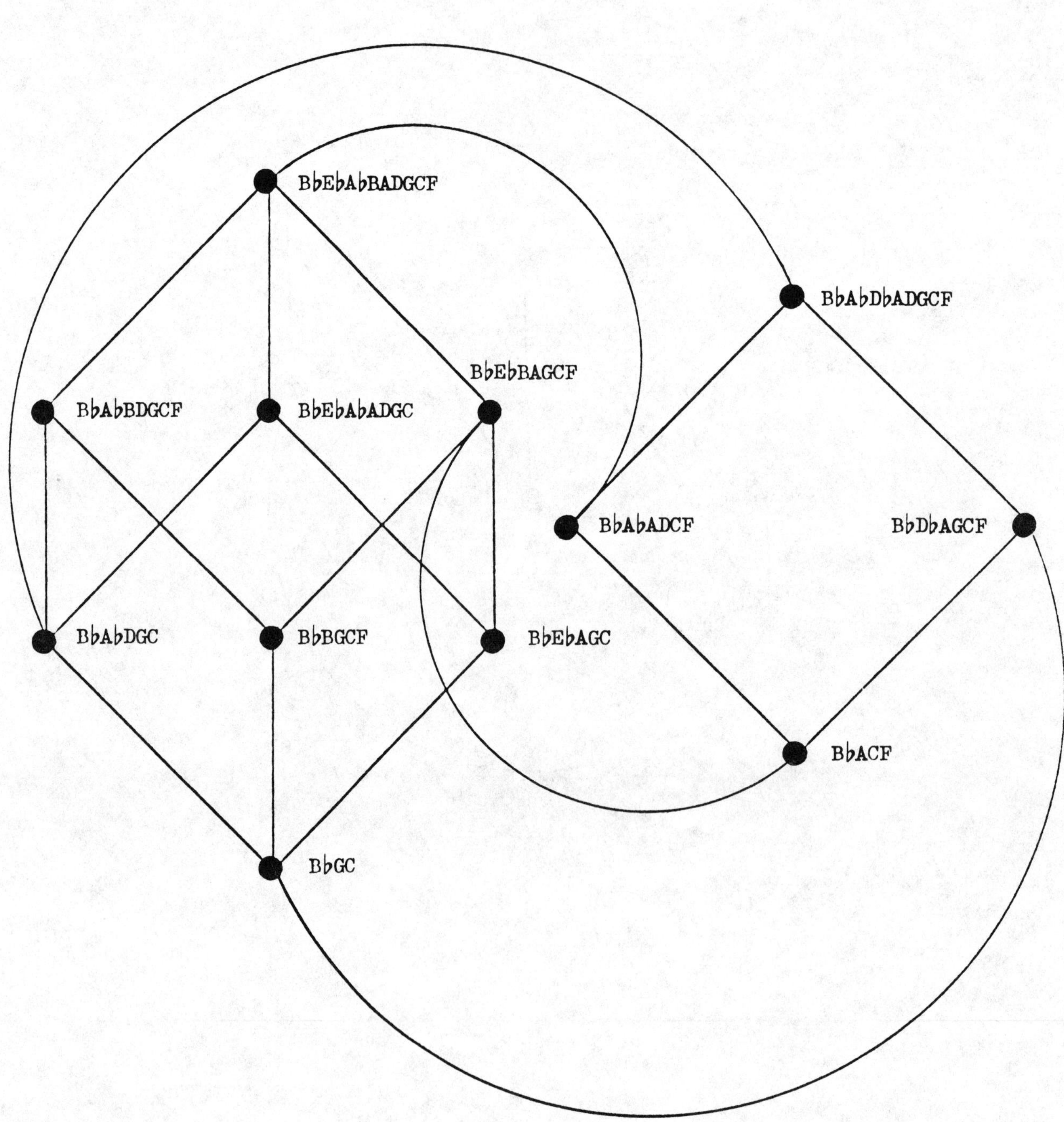

PHASE 22.91134
AMPLITUDE 1.88040

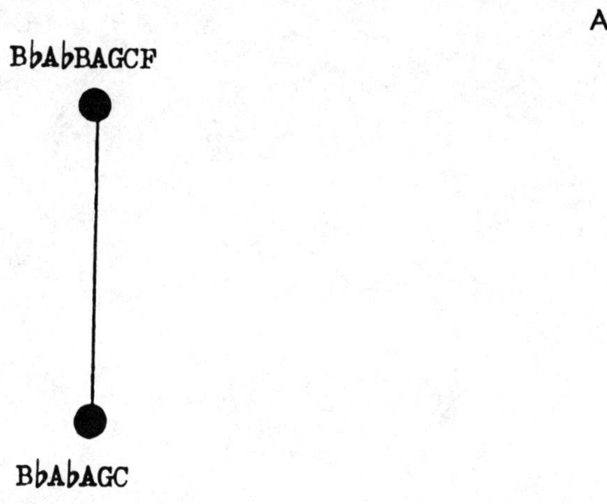


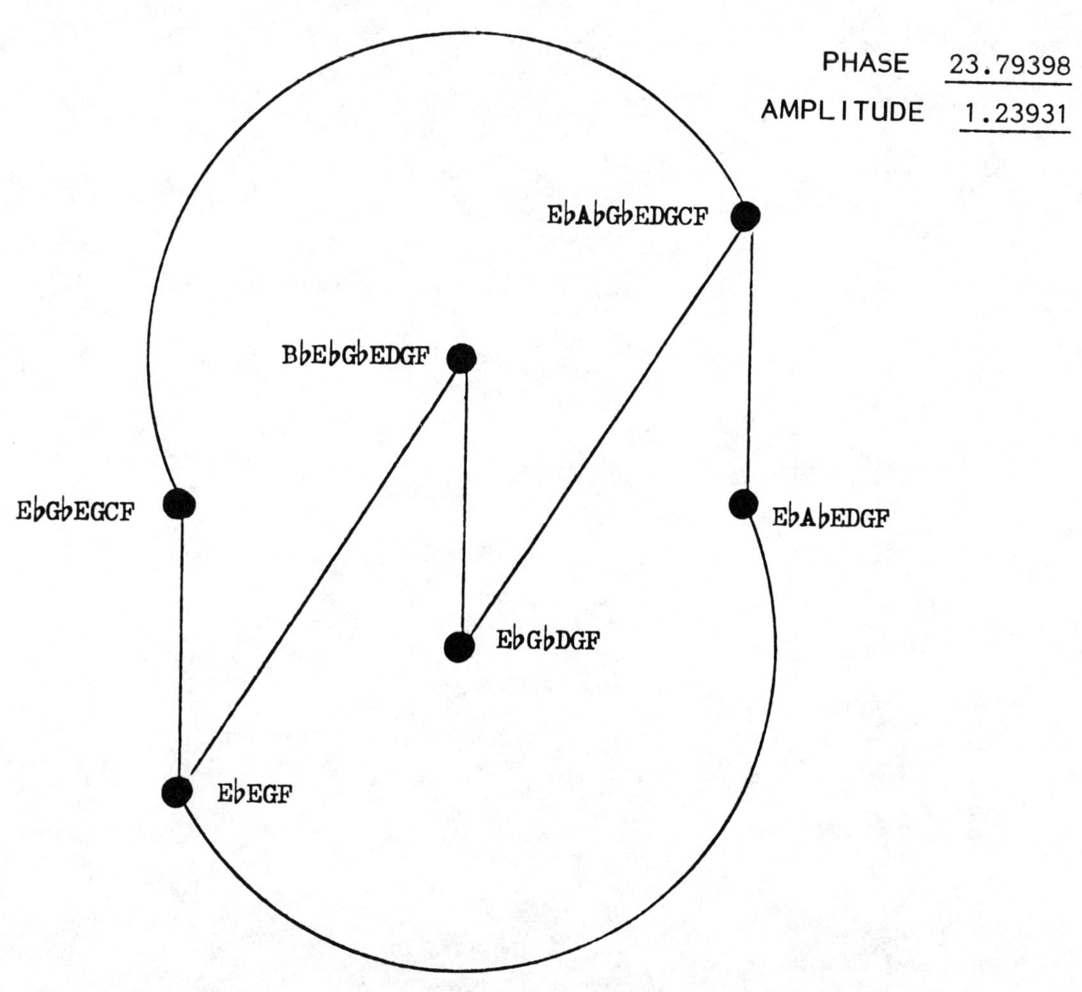

PHASE 24.89609

AMPLITUDE 1.50597

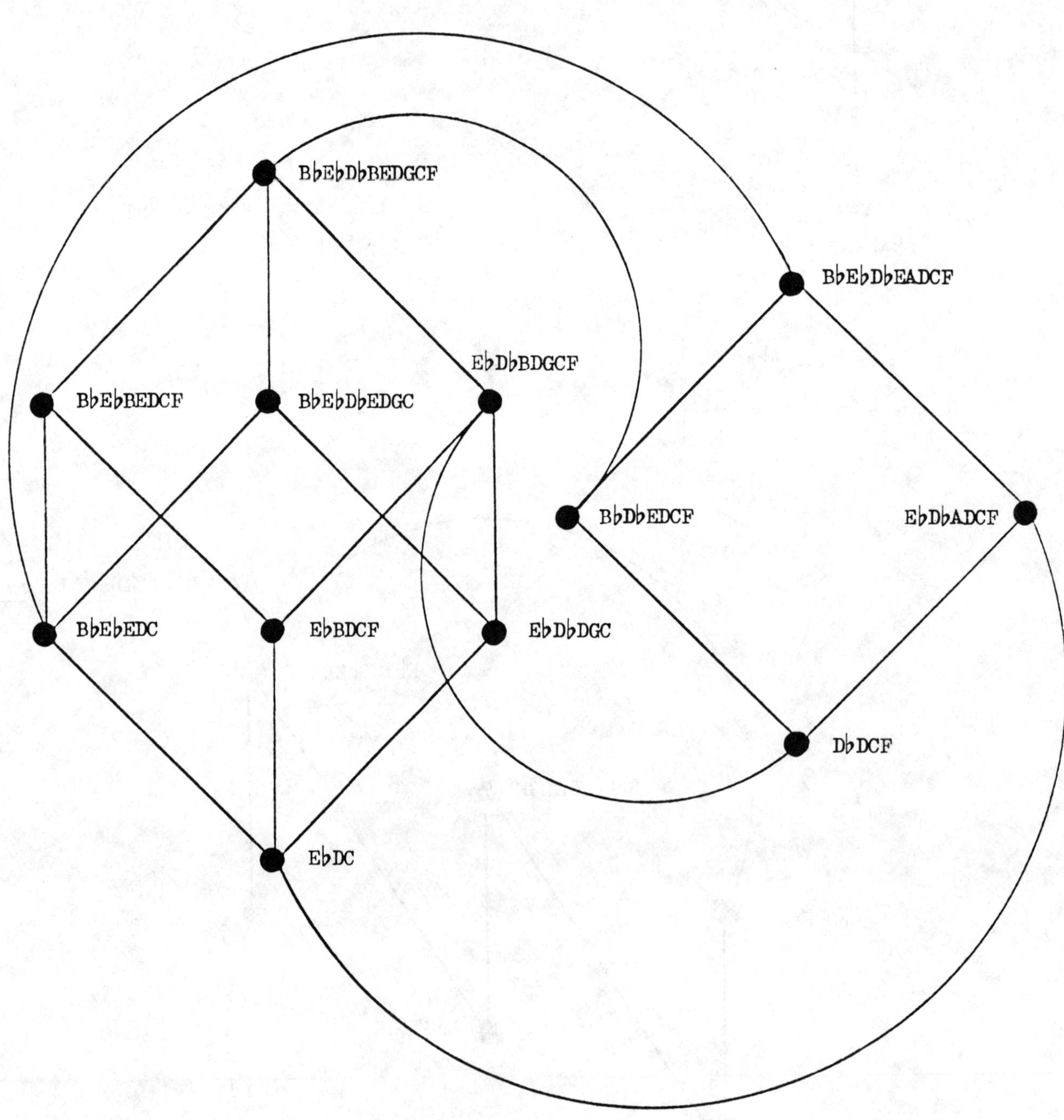

PHASE 26.56505
AMPLITUDE 2.23607

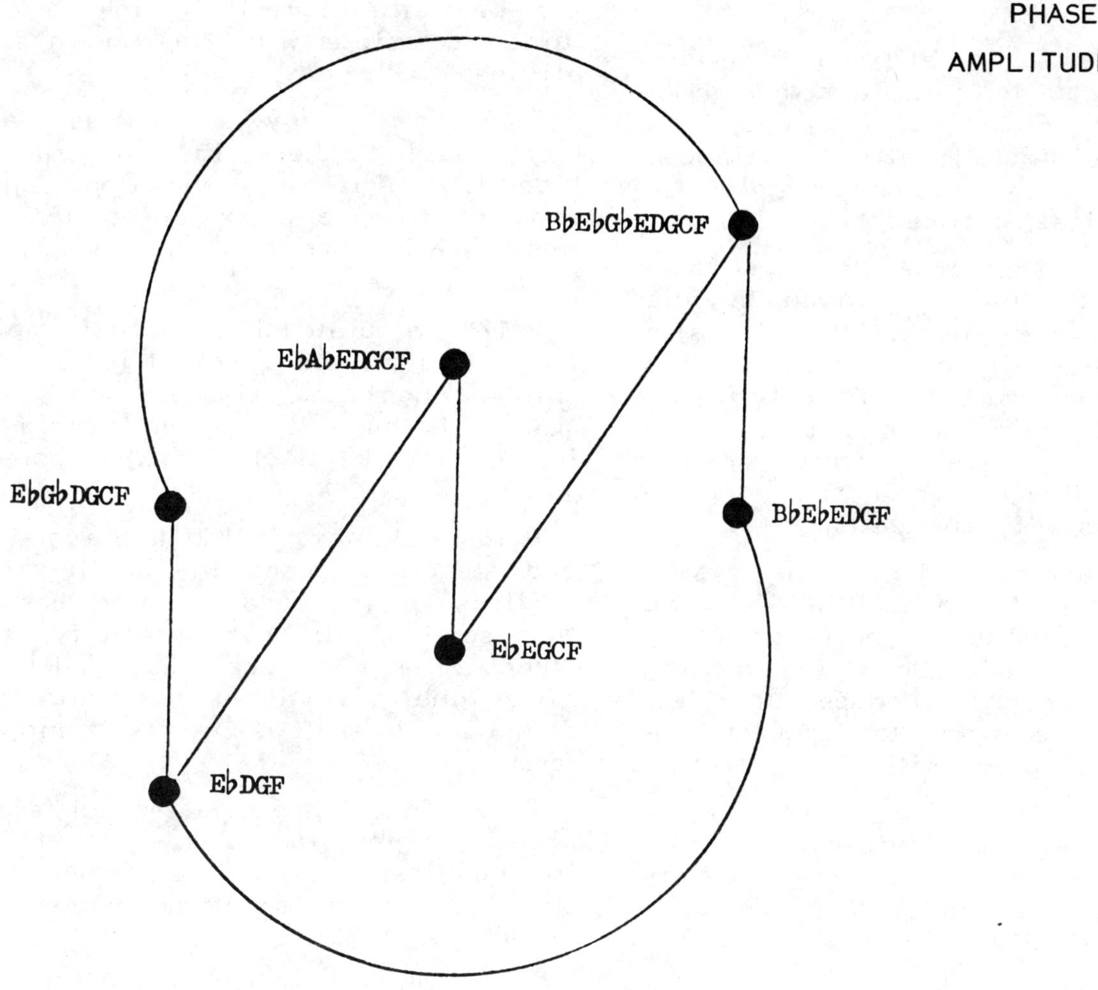


PHASE 27.62634
AMPLITUDE 3.23483

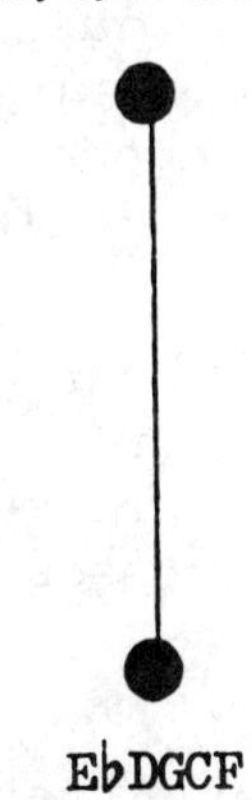

## EXERCISES

**8.8** Draw a tonality diagram for the characteristic balanced harmonies (see Fig. 4.8). Extend this drawing to include all the balanced harmonies. Is either diagram a (mathematical) lattice?

**8.9** (a) Transpose the first sector tonality diagrams given in this section to $[75^o, 105^o]$, the C major sector. Are all the common chords of C major represented? (b) Transpose the first sector tonality diagrams to the sector corresponding to the standard stencil and annotate the results with chromaticity indices.

**8.10** For convenience the system of tonalities for phase $0.00000^o$ and amplitude 1.00000 is represented by two subdiagrams. Draw the missing lines that can be deduced from the inclusion relation to connect the main subdiagram with its continuation.

**8.11** Where do good sounding harmonies congregate in the tonality diagrams? Why is this characteristic theoretically important?

**8.12** Write a musical composition whose trajectory starts at the origin and proceeds along a straight line to the displacement point $(12.0, 0^o)$.

**8.13** (a) Compose a harmonic progression that is confined to the first sector and has tonalities of successively decreasing amplitudes. (b) Construct a chord sequence that employs tonalities of successively increasing phases.

**8.14** Write a short passage whose trajectory begins at the origin and ends near the point $(8.0, 15^o)$ such that the path crosses the $15^o$ line at each step.

**8.15** (a) Do the tonalities of each diagram sound equally impressive? If so, rank the tonality diagrams using the scale:

| Bland | Piquant |
|---|---|
| 0.0 | 1.0 |

(b) Does the numerical ranking obtained correlate with the known amplitudes?

**8.16** How many tonalities are there having phase $15^o$ and amplitude 1.0? Write a composition using some of them and excluding tonalities of all other phases and amplitudes.

**8.17** Calculate the tonality amplitudes and phases of the triads, sevenths, augmented sixths, and augmented fifths, diatonic and chromatic, in the keys of C major and C minor.

**8.18** (a) Why couldn't the standard stencil be used in labeling the vertices of the tonality diagrams of this section? (b) For simplicity, the stencil that has been used will be given the promotional name "deluxe stencil." Present it in its standard form.

**8.19** There are sixteen different phase angles for simple tonalities in the first sector. How many additional angles arise if doublings are permitted?

**8.20** Which vertices of each tonality diagram have (a) diatonic (b) chromatic labels?

**8.21** Enumerate the simple tonalities forming distinct vertices in a major key. Do the same problem for a harmonic minor key.

**8.22** How many distinct simple tonalities are there in the (a) twelve-tone equitempered system and (b) nineteen-tone equitempered system.

**8.23** How many different harmonies are capable of neutralizing the vector C + E + G and thus correspond to simple tonalities of equal amplitude and opposite phase.

**8.24** A tonality is said to be "intricate" if and only it does not coincide with a simple tonality. Give examples of various intricate tonalities.

**8.25** When all tones sounding in a chord are sustained, the displacement vector can vary only in magnitude alone, with whatever direction it has remaining constant. Yet there are more interesting ways of holding a set course while maintaining a uniform speed. Recall that the tonality v expresses the rate at which the composition is changing its position in both magnitude and direction. Also, recall that by assumption the musical momentum mv changes only whenever the tonality changes, since the mass m has a constant value, unity. It is reasonably simple to restrict the tonal palette to eliminate unwanted modulations and by using just a few different tonalities to achieve an austere effect. In the example entitled **Brief Interlude**, only three impulses are applied to the coasting composition disc to start it in motion and to return it to its initial position at the origin. This low number is by no means a typical value for a musical composition to have. The result is that modulation is effected at only three places, which lie at the vertices of a triangle.

The tonalities in each phrase of **Brief Interlude** have been phase and amplitude matched intentionally to result in perfect tracking of two key axes. A plot of this composition is shown in Fig. 8.5. The resulting trajectory is perhaps too stable. Compose several variations on the basic pattern supplied by the composition **Brief Interlude** adding harmonic or contrapuntal frills gradually. Make the eight measure phrase more elaborate from one repetition to the next. Continue the process until both amplitudes and phases are changing from component to component. Show how the composition trajectory is changed by each subsequent refinement.

```
00 4 1 78 0-2.000
01 2 68 1 5 0-1.000
02 4 1 78 0-1.000
03 68 1 5 2 0 4.000
04 68 1 5 2 0-2.000
05 4 1 78 0-1.000
06 68 1 5 2 0-1.000
07 1 78 4 0 4.000
08 1 78 4 0-2.000
09 1 58 2 4 0-1.000
10 1 58 2 4 0-1.000
11 3 2 68 0-2.000
12 68 3 2 0-1.000
13 78 68 3 4 0-1.000
14 2 68 3 0-2.000
15 2 68 1 5 0-1.000
16 5 68 1 2 0-1.000
17 4 1 78 0 4.000
18 48 38 78 0-2.000
19 48 1 58 28 0-1.000
20 48 38 78 0-1.000
21 28 48 1 58 0 4.000
22 28 48 1 58 0-2.000
23 48 38 78 0-1.000
24 28 48 1 58 0-1.000
25 78 48 38 0 4.000
26 78 48 38 0-2.000
27 58 78 48 6 0-1.000
28 58 78 48 6 0-1.000
29 58 28 68 0-2.000
30 28 68 58 0-1.000
31 78 28 68 38 0-1.000
32 58 68 28 0-2.000
33 48 1 58 28 0-1.000
34 28 1 58 48 0-1.000
35 48 38 78 0 4.000
36 4 19 5 0-2.000
37 29 6 3 5 0-1.000
38 4 19 5 0-1.000
39 29 6 3 5 0 4.000
40 29 6 3 5 0-2.000
41 4 19 5 0-1.000
42 29 6 3 5 0-1.000
43 4 19 5 0 4.000
44 4 19 5 0-2.000
45 2 6 19 5 0-1.000
46 2 6 19 5 0-1.000
47 6 3 7 0-1.000
48 7 6 3 0-1.000
49 3 7 19 4 0-2.000
50 5 6 3 29 0-2.000
51 29 6 3 5 0-1.000
52 29 6 3 5 0-1.000
53 4 19 5 0 4.000
```

Figure 8.5

Once again the displacement vectors form the sides of a regular closed polygon--this time a triangle. Upon the upper side of the triangle, which is obviously equilateral, the composition point moves outward from the origin at an angle of exactly $15^{o}$ from the horizontal. This ray--the C minor key axis--forms the boundary line between the Bb and Eb major key sectors. So far **Brief Interlude** has had a constant tonality, but in practice a variety of tonalities (a broken line path) is more likely to be used. In nautical terminology, the ship has sailed a straight course without maneuvering.

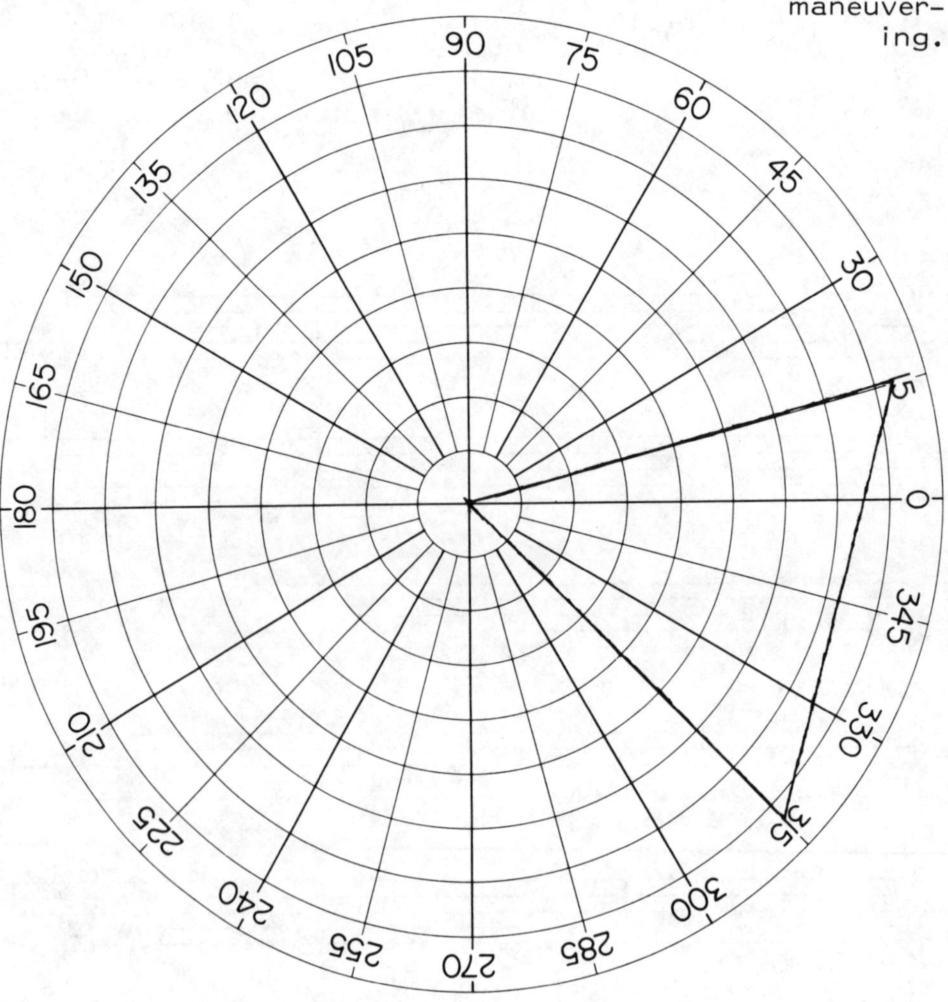

During the first phase the composition moves into the right halfplane at a constant angle of climb and a constant rate of musical speed, continuing its rightward movement further, until eventually after eight measures, it swings downward, making a hard right turn. At this point the second phase of the composition is initiated. After this maneuver, the prescribed heading of the composition is $-105^{o}$. The path angle is held to this value until the second and final turning point is reached. Along the second side of the triangle, the composition crosses a sector boundary. This crossover results in the key signature function experiencing a jump discontinuity. The magnitude of the jump is unity, that is, a flat is added to the signature. After traveling an equal distance, the composition swings back, making another hard right turn, and finally reaches the origin again. This last phase consists of a straight-in path until impact. At the point of origin the composition ends. Should the last side be extended, the key would change from positive (A♭|D♭ major) to negative (D|G major) and pass through zero in the process. Or, upon regaining the starting point, the composition could repeat its journey around the perimeter, thus providing an eternal character to the triangle.

The total duration of the composition **Brief Interlude** is 24 measures or 96 beats. The complete trajectory is based on a sequence of 54 components, numbered 00 through 53, generated by the application of just three separate impulses to the composition disc.

```
00 02.000 03 03
01 03.000 04 04
02 04.000 03 03
03 08.000 04 04
04 10.000 04 04
05 11.000 03 03
06 12.000 04 04
07 16.000 03 03
08 18.000 03 03
09 19.000 04 04
10 20.000 04 04
11 22.000 03 03
12 23.000 03 03
13 24.000 04 04
14 26.000 03 03
15 27.000 04 04
16 28.000 04 04
17 32.000 02 02
18 34.000 05 04
19 35.000 04 04
20 36.000 03 03
21 40.000 04 04
22 42.000 04 04
23 43.000 03 03
24 44.000 04 04
25 48.000 03 03
26 50.000 03 03
27 51.000 04 04
28 52.000 04 04
29 54.000 03 03
30 55.000 03 03
31 56.000 04 04
32 58.000 03 03
33 59.000 04 04
34 60.000 04 04
35 64.000 03 03
36 66.000 03 03
37 67.000 04 04
38 68.000 03 03
39 72.000 04 04
40 74.000 04 04
41 75.000 03 03
42 76.000 04 04
43 80.000 03 03
44 82.000 03 03
45 83.000 04 04
46 84.000 04 04
47 85.000 03 03
48 86.000 03 03
49 88.000 04 04
50 90.000 04 04
51 91.000 04 04
52 92.000 04 04
53 96.000 03 03
```

```
00 0000000002057 0019X2048 2057
01 0000000001043 0077X1024 1043
02 0000000002057 0019X2048 2057
03 0000000001043 0077X1024 1043
04 0000000001043 0077X1024 1043
05 0000000002057 0019X2048 2057
06 0000000001043 0077X1024 1043
07 0000000002057 0019X2048 2057
08 0000000002057 0019X2048 2057
09 0000000000523 0089X0512 0523
10 0000000000523 0089X0512 0523
11 0000000001030 0025X1024 1030
12 0000000001030 0025X1024 1030
13 0000000003084 0051X1024 3084
14 0000000001030 0025X1024 1030
15 0000000001043 0077X1024 1043
16 0000000001043 0077X1024 1043
17 0000000000065 0065X0001 0065
18 0000001051040 0077X0032 2464
19 0000000000833 0077X0064 0833
20 0000000002432 0019X0128 2432
21 0000000000833 0077X0064 0833
22 0000000000833 0077X0064 0833
23 0000000002432 0019X0128 2432
24 0000000000833 0077X0064 0833
25 0000000002432 0019X0128 2432
26 0000000002432 0019X0128 2432
27 0000000002848 0089X0032 2848
28 0000000002848 0089X0032 2848
29 0000000001600 0025X0064 1600
30 0000000001600 0025X0064 1600
31 0000000003264 0051X0064 3264
32 0000000001600 0025X0064 1600
33 0000000000833 0077X0064 0833
34 0000000000833 0077X0064 0833
35 0000000002432 0019X0128 2432
36 0000000000152 0019X0008 0152
37 0000000000308 0077X0004 0308
38 0000000000152 0019X0008 0152
39 0000000000308 0077X0004 0308
40 0000000000308 0077X0004 0308
41 0000000000152 0019X0008 0152
42 0000000000308 0077X0004 0308
43 0000000000152 0019X0008 0152
44 0000000000152 0019X0008 0152
45 0000000000178 0089X0002 0178
46 0000000000178 0089X0002 0178
47 0000000000100 0025X0004 0100
48 0000000000100 0025X0004 0100
49 0000000000204 0051X0004 0204
50 0000000000308 0077X0004 0308
51 0000000000308 0077X0004 0308
52 0000000000308 0077X0004 0308
53 0000000000152 0019X0008 0152
```

```
00 1.932 015.000 003.864 015.000
01 1.932 015.000 005.796 015.000
02 1.932 015.000 007.727 015.000
03 1.932 015.000 015.455 015.000
04 1.932 015.000 019.319 015.000
05 1.932 015.000 021.250 015.000
06 1.932 015.000 023.182 015.000
07 1.932 015.000 030.910 015.000
08 1.932 015.000 034.773 015.000
09 1.932 015.000 036.705 015.000
10 1.932 015.000 038.637 015.000
11 1.932 015.000 042.501 015.000
12 1.932 015.000 044.433 015.000
13 1.932 015.000 046.364 015.000
14 1.932 015.000 050.228 015.000
15 1.932 015.000 052.160 015.000
16 1.932 015.000 054.092 015.000
17 1.932 015.000 061.819 015.000
18 1.932-105.000 059.981 011.802
19 1.932-105.000 059.135 010.131
20 1.932-105.000 058.341 008.413
21 1.932-105.000 055.723 001.102
22 1.932-105.000 054.777-002.784
23 1.932-105.000 054.401-004.773
24 1.932-105.000 054.092-006.787
25 1.932-105.000 053.537-015.000
26 1.932-105.000 053.676-019.128
27 1.932-105.000 053.850-021.178
28 1.932-105.000 054.092-023.213
29 1.932-105.000 054.777-027.216
30 1.932-105.000 055.219-029.176
31 1.932-105.000 055.723-031.102
32 1.932-105.000 056.916-034.842
33 1.932-105.000 057.600-036.650
34 1.932-105.000 058.341-038.413
35 1.932-105.000 061.819-045.000
36 1.932 135.000 057.956-045.000
37 1.932 135.000 056.024-045.000
38 1.932 135.000 054.092-045.000
39 1.932 135.000 046.364-045.000
40 1.932 135.000 042.501-045.000
41 1.932 135.000 040.569-045.000
42 1.932 135.000 038.637-045.000
43 1.932 135.000 030.910-045.000
44 1.932 135.000 027.046-045.000
45 1.932 135.000 025.114-045.000
46 1.932 135.000 023.182-045.000
47 1.932 135.000 021.250-045.000
48 1.932 135.000 019.319-045.000
49 1.932 135.000 015.455-045.000
50 1.932 135.000 011.591-045.000
51 1.932 135.000 009.659-045.000
52 1.932 135.000 007.727-045.000
53 1.932 135.000 000.000-136.941
```

```
00 3.864 003.864
01 1.932 005.796
02 1.932 007.727
03 7.727 015.455
04 3.864 019.319
05 1.932 021.250
06 1.932 023.182
07 7.727 030.910
08 3.864 034.773
09 1.932 036.705
10 1.932 038.637
11 3.864 042.501
12 1.932 044.433
13 1.932 046.364
14 3.864 050.228
15 1.932 052.160
16 1.932 054.092
17 7.727 061.819
18 3.864 065.683
19 1.932 067.615
20 1.932 069.547
21 7.727 077.274
22 3.864 081.138
23 1.932 083.070
24 1.932 085.001
25 7.727 092.729
26 3.864 096.593
27 1.932 098.524
28 1.932 100.456
29 3.864 104.320
30 1.932 106.252
31 1.932 108.184
32 3.864 112.047
33 1.932 113.979
34 1.932 115.911
35 7.727 123.639
36 3.864 127.502
37 1.932 129.434
38 1.932 131.366
39 7.727 139.093
40 3.864 142.957
41 1.932 144.889
42 1.932 146.821
43 7.727 154.548
44 3.864 158.412
45 1.932 160.344
46 1.932 162.276
47 1.932 164.207
48 1.932 166.139
49 3.864 170.003
50 3.864 173.867
51 1.932 175.799
52 1.932 177.730
53 7.727 185.458
```

The column of characteristics reveals that the sonoral content of the piece **Brief Interlude** is rather limited.

A noticeable phase change occurs at every vertex of the triangle. That these three turning points are audibly detectable can be demonstrated by asking someone to listen for "corners" while the piece is played. Note that each heading change is equivalent to $-120^{o}$. No phase change is observed except at the vertices of the triangle.

```
00      00 26 50 71 87 97 00 97 87 71 50 26
01      00 26 50 71 87 97 00 97 87 71 50 26
02      00 26 50 71 87 97 00 97 87 71 50 26
03      00 26 50 71 87 97 00 97 87 71 50 26 00
04      00 26 50 71 87 97 00 97 87 71 50 26 00
05      00 26 50 71 87 97 00 97 87 71 50 26 00
06      00 26 50 71 87 97 00 97 87 71 50 26 00
07      00 26 50 71 87 97 00 97 87 71 50 26
08      00 26 50 71 87 97 00 97 87 71 50 26
09      00 26 50 71 87 97 00 97 87 71 50 26
10      00 26 50 71 87 97 00 97 87 71 50 26
11      00 26 50 71 87 97 00 97 87 71 50 26
12      00 26 50 71 87 97 00 97 87 71 50 26
13      00 26 50 71 87 97 00 97 87 71 50 26
14      00 26 50 71 87 97 00 97 87 71 50 26
15      00 26 50 71 87 97 00 97 87 71 50 26
16      00 26 50 71 87 97 00 97 87 71 50 26 00
17      00 26 50 71 87 97 00 97 87 71 50 26
18      06 31 55 75 89 98 00 95 84 67 45 20
19      08 34 57 76 91 98 00 94 82 64 42 18
20      11 37 60 78 92 99 99 93 80 62 40 15
21      24 48 69 86 96 00 97 88 72 52 28 02
22 05 31 54 74 89 98 00 95 84 67 46 21                                        05
23 08 34 57 76 90 98 00 94 82 65 43 18                                        08
24 12 37 60 79 92 99 99 93 80 62 39 14                                        12
25 26 50 71 87 97 00 97 87 71 50 26                                        00 26
26 33 56 76 90 98 00 94 83 65 44 19                                        07 33
27 36 59 78 91 99 99 93 81 63 40 15                                        11 36
28 39 62 80 93 99 99 92 79 60 37 12                                        14 39
29 46 67 84 95 00 98 89 74 54 31 05                                        21 46
30 49 70 86 96 00 97 87 72 51 27 01                                        24 49
31 52 72 88 97 00 96 86 69 48 24                                        02 28 52
32 57 76 91 98 00 94 82 64 43 18                                        08 34 57
33 60 78 92 99 99 93 80 62 40 15                                        12 37 60
34 62 80 93 99 99 92 78 60 37 11                                        15 40 62
35 71 87 97 00 97 87 71 50 26                                        00 26 50 71
36 71 87 97 00 97 87 71 50 26                                        00 26 50 71
37 71 87 97 00 97 87 71 50 26                                        00 26 50 71
38 71 87 97 00 97 87 71 50 26                                        00 26 50 71
39 71 87 97 00 97 87 71 50 26                                        00 26 50 71
40 71 87 97 00 97 87 71 50 26                                        00 26 50 71
41 71 87 97 00 97 87 71 50 26                                        00 26 50 71
42 71 87 97 00 97 87 71 50 26                                        00 26 50 71
43 71 87 97 00 97 87 71 50 26                                        00 26 50 71
44 71 87 97 00 97 87 71 50 26                                        00 26 50 71
45 71 87 97 00 97 87 71 50 26                                        00 26 50 71
46 71 87 97 00 97 87 71 50 26                                        00 26 50 71
47 71 87 97 00 97 87 71 50 26                                        00 26 50 71
48 71 87 97 00 97 87 71 50 26                                        00 26 50 71
49 71 87 97 00 97 87 71 50 26                                        00 26 50 71
50 71 87 97 00 97 87 71 50 26                                        00 26 50 71
51 71 87 97 00 97 87 71 50 26                                        00 26 50 71
52 71 87 97 00 97 87 71 50 26                                        00 26 50 71
53 68 47 23                                        03 29 53 73 88 97 00 96 85 68
```

In this printout the symbol 00 standing between two nonzero numbers represents 100%. By proceeding along the lines containing this value it can be seen that the entire composition is centered on the F minor (f) key axis and is symmetrically situated within the B♭ minor (b♭) quadrant. The numbers on the last line have no meaning, since the origin has indeterminate phase.

```
00    -96 00 02 04 05 05 05 05 05 04 02 00
01    -96 01 04 06 07 07 07 07 07 06 04 01
02    -95 03 05 07 08 08 08 08 08 07 05 03
03    -00 06 08 10 11 11 11 11 11 10 08 06-93
04    -00 06 09 11 12 12 12 12 12 11 09 06-92
05    -00 07 10 11 12 13 13 13 12 11 10 07-00
06    -00 07 10 12 13 13 13 13 13 12 10 07-91
07    -92 09 11 13 14 14 14 14 14 13 11 09
08    -91 09 12 13 14 15 15 15 14 13 12 09
09    -91 09 12 14 15 15 15 15 15 14 12 09
10    -89 10 12 14 15 15 15 15 15 14 12 10
11    -90 10 13 14 15 16 16 16 15 14 13 10
12    -90 10 13 14 15 16 16 16 15 14 13 10
13    -90 10 13 15 16 16 16 16 16 15 13 10
14    -89 11 14 15 16 16 17 16 16 15 14 11
15    -89 11 14 15 16 17 17 17 16 15 14 11
16    -89 11 14 15 16 17 17 17 16 15 14 11-00
17    -89 12 14 16 17 17 17 17 17 16 14 12
18     05 12 15 16 17 17 17 17 17 16 14 10
19     07 13 15 16 17 17 17 17 16 15 14 10
20     08 13 15 16 17 17 17 17 16 15 13 09
21     11 14 15 16 17 17 17 16 16 14 11 00
22 04 12 14 16 16 17 17 17 16 15 13 10                                    04
23 06 12 14 16 16 17 17 17 16 15 13 09                                    06
24 08 13 15 16 16 17 17 17 16 15 13 08                                    08
25 11 14 15 16 17 17 17 16 15 14 11                                   -87 11
26 12 14 16 16 17 17 17 16 15 13 10                                    05 12
27 12 15 16 16 17 17 17 16 15 13 09                                    07 12
28 13 15 16 17 17 17 16 16 15 13 08                                    08 13
29 13 15 16 17 17 17 16 16 14 12 04                                    10 13
30 14 15 16 17 17 17 16 15 14 11-01                                    11 14
31 14 16 16 17 17 17 16 15 14 11                                    00 11 14
32 15 16 17 17 17 17 16 15 13 10                                    06 12 15
33 15 16 17 17 17 17 16 15 13 09                                    08 13 15
34 15 16 17 17 17 17 16 15 13 08                                    09 13 15
35 16 17 17 17 17 17 16 14 12                                   -87 12 14 16
36 16 17 17 17 17 17 16 14 11                                   -87 11 14 16
37 15 16 17 17 17 16 15 14 11                                   -87 11 14 15
38 15 16 17 17 17 16 15 14 11                                   -87 11 14 15
39 15 16 16 16 16 16 15 13 10                                   -88 10 13 15
40 14 15 16 16 16 15 14 13 10                                   -85 10 13 14
41 14 15 15 16 15 15 14 13 10                                   -86 10 13 14
42 14 15 15 15 15 15 14 12 10                                   -86 10 12 14
43 13 14 14 14 14 14 13 11 09                                   -87 09 11 13
44 12 13 14 14 14 13 12 11 08                                   -86 08 11 12
45 12 13 13 14 13 13 12 10 08                                   -86 08 10 12
46 12 13 13 13 13 13 12 10 07                                   -86 07 10 12
47 11 12 13 13 13 12 11 10 07                                   -87 07 10 11
48 11 12 12 12 12 12 11 09 06                                   -86 06 09 11
49 10 11 11 11 11 11 10 08 06                                   -85 06 08 10
50 09 10 10 10 10 10 09 07 04                                   -85 04 07 09
51 08 09 09 09 09 09 08 06 03                                   -85 03 06 08
52 07 08 08 08 08 08 07 05 03                                   -85 03 05 07
53-86-88-91                                          -99-90-87-86-85-84-84-84-85-86
```

The absolute penetration function, tabulated here, is related to the previous printout by the formula given on p. 108.

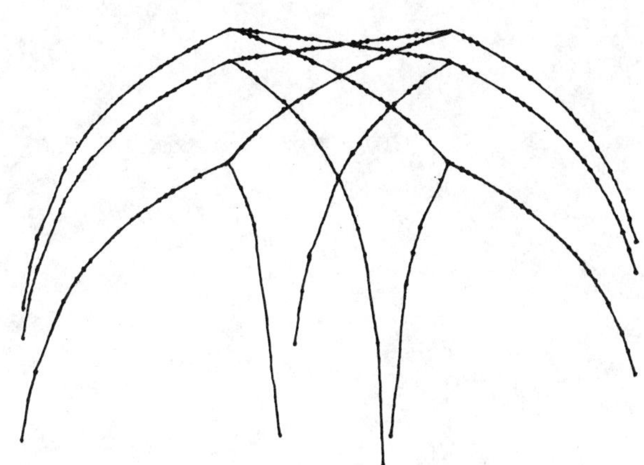

This absolute penetration function history looks like something on display in a haberdashery window.

Merely three tonality phases characterize the **Brief Interlude** trajectory. According to this printout, the initial phase has components

$$v_x = +001.866, \quad v_y = +000.500;$$

the middle phase,

$$v_x = -000.500, \quad v_y = -001.866;$$

and the terminal phase,

$$v_x = -001.366, \quad v_y = +001.366.$$

```
00 001.866 000.500 003.732 001.000
01 001.866 000.500 005.598 001.500
02 001.866 000.500 007.464 002.000
03 001.866 000.500 014.928 004.000
04 001.866 000.500 018.660 005.000
05 001.866 000.500 020.526 005.500
06 001.866 000.500 022.392 006.000
07 001.866 000.500 029.856 008.000
08 001.866 000.500 033.588 009.000
09 001.866 000.500 035.454 009.500
10 001.866 000.500 037.321 010.000
11 001.866 000.500 041.053 011.000
12 001.866 000.500 042.919 011.500
13 001.866 000.500 044.785 012.000
14 001.866 000.500 048.517 013.000
15 001.866 000.500 050.383 013.500
16 001.866 000.500 052.249 014.000
17 001.866 000.500 059.713 016.000
18-000.500-001.866 058.713 012.268
19-000.500-001.866 058.213 010.402
20-000.500-001.866 057.713 008.536
21-000.500-001.866 055.713 001.072
22-000.500-001.866 054.713-002.660
23-000.500-001.866 054.213-004.526
24-000.500-001.866 053.713-006.392
25-000.500-001.866 051.713-013.856
26-000.500-001.866 050.713-017.588
27-000.500-001.866 050.213-019.454
28-000.500-001.866 049.713-021.321
29-000.500-001.866 048.713-025.053
30-000.500-001.866 048.213-026.919
31-000.500-001.866 047.713-028.785
32-000.500-001.866 046.713-032.517
33-000.500-001.866 046.213-034.383
34-000.500-001.866 045.713-036.249
35-000.500-001.866 043.713-043.713
36-001.366 001.366 040.981-040.981
37-001.366 001.366 039.615-039.615
38-001.366 001.366 038.249-038.249
39-001.366 001.366 032.785-032.785
40-001.366 001.366 030.053-030.053
41-001.366 001.366 028.687-028.687
42-001.366 001.366 027.321-027.321
43-001.366 001.366 021.856-021.856
44-001.366 001.366 019.124-019.124
45-001.366 001.366 017.758-017.758
46-001.366 001.366 016.392-016.392
47-001.366 001.366 015.026-015.026
48-001.366 001.366 013.660-013.660
49-001.366 001.366 010.928-010.928
50-001.366 001.366 008.196-008.196
51-001.366 001.366 006.830-006.830
52-001.366 001.366 005.464-005.464
53-001.366 001.366 000.000 000.000
```

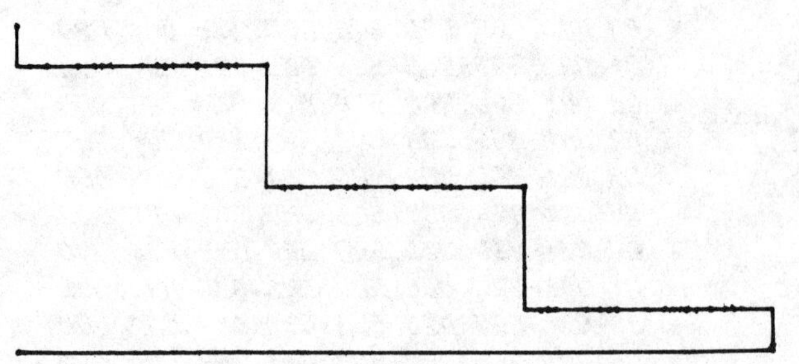

The inertia accompanying the rectilinear motion along the sides of the **Brief Interlude** triangle necessitates two energy expenditures to change the direction of that motion. These losses are in addition to the smaller amounts required for starting and stopping.

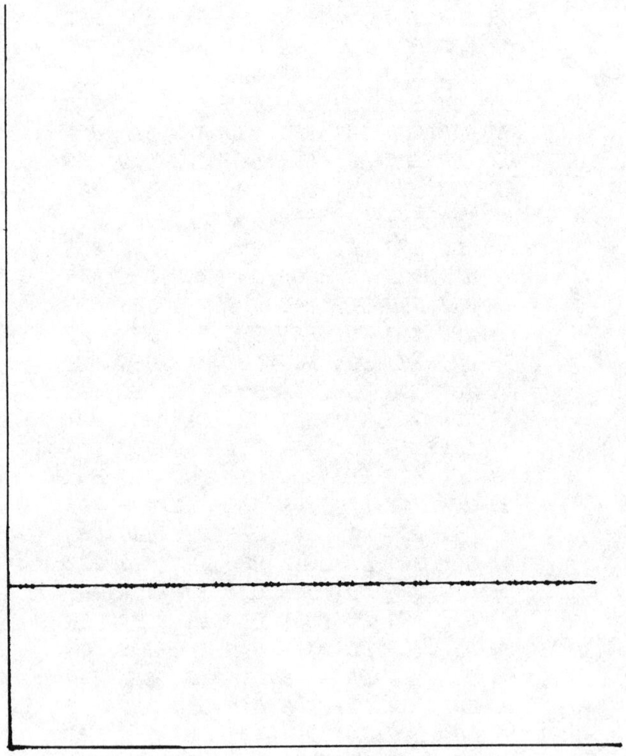

As predicted, the computer plot of the tonality amplitudes for **Brief Interlude** is a constant function. The dots mark the inception of components.

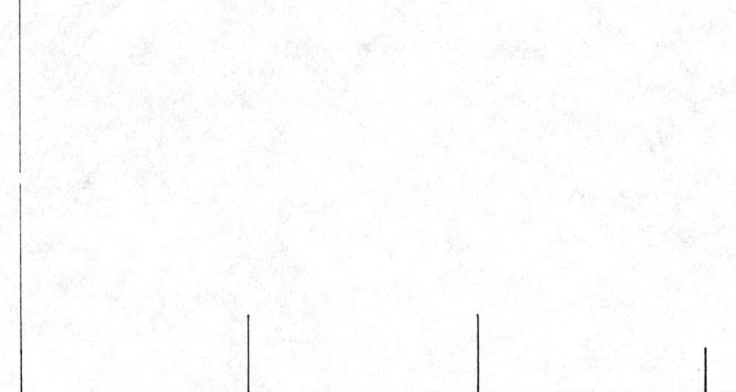

In addition to the three tonal impulses of nonzero magnitude described in the text, there is a fourth impulse necessary at the end to bring the composition point to a stop.

| | | |
|---|---|---|
| 00 | DFB♭ | DFB♭ |
| 01 | CE♭FA | CE♭FA |
| 02 | DFB♭ | DFB♭ |
| 03 | E♭FAC | E♭FAC |
| 04 | E♭FAC | E♭FAC |
| 05 | DFB♭ | DFB♭ |
| 06 | E♭FAC | E♭FAC |
| 07 | FB♭D | FB♭D |
| 08 | FB♭D | FB♭D |
| 09 | FA♭CD | FA♭CD |
| 10 | FA♭CD | FA♭CD |
| 11 | GCE♭ | GCE♭ |
| 12 | E♭GC | E♭GC |
| 13 | B♭E♭GD | B♭E♭GD |
| 14 | CE♭G | CE♭G |
| 15 | CE♭FA | CE♭FA |
| 16 | AE♭FC | AE♭FC |
| 17 | DFB♭ | DFB♭ |
| 18 | D♭G♭B♭ C♯F♯A♯ | D♭G♭B♭ |
| 19 | D♭FA♭C♭ C♯E♯G♯B | D♭FA♭B |
| 20 | D♭G♭B♭ C♯F♯A♯ | D♭G♭B♭ |
| 21 | C♭D♭FA♭ BC♯E♯G♯ | BD♭FA♭ |
| 22 | C♭D♭FA♭ BC♯E♯G♯ | C♭D♭FA♭ BC♯E♯G♯ |
| 23 | D♭G♭B♭ C♯F♯A♯ | D♭G♭B♭ C♯F♯A♯ |
| 24 | C♭D♭FA♭ BC♯E♯G♯ | C♭D♭FA♭ BC♯E♯G♯ |
| 25 | B♭D♭G♭ A♯C♯F♯ | B♭D♭G♭ A♯C♯F♯ |
| 26 | B♭D♭G♭ A♯C♯F♯ | B♭D♭G♭ A♯C♯F♯ |
| 27 | A♭B♭D♭F♭ G♯A♯C♯E | A♭B♭D♭E G♯A♯C♯Dx |
| 28 | A♭B♭D♭F♭ G♯A♯C♯E | A♭B♭D♭E G♯A♯C♯Dx |
| 29 | A♭C♭E♭ G♯BD♯ | A♭C♭E♭ G♯BD♯ |
| 30 | C♭E♭A♭ BD♯G♯ | C♭E♭A♭ BD♯G♯ |
| 31 | B♭C♭E♭G♭ A♯BD♯F♯ | B♭C♭E♭G♭ A♯BD♯F♯ |
| 32 | A♭E♭C♭ G♯D♯B | A♭E♭C♭ G♯D♯B |
| 33 | D♭FA♭C♭ C♯E♯G♯B | D♭FA♭C♭ C♯E♯G♯B |
| 34 | C♭FA♭D♭ BE♯G♯C♯ | C♭FA♭D♭ BE♯G♯C♯ |
| 35 | D♭G♭B♭ C♯F♯A♯ | D♭G♭B♭ C♯F♯A♯ |
| 36 | DF♯A | DG♭A CxF♯Gx |
| 37 | C♯EGA | D♭F♭GA C♯EFxGx |
| 38 | DF♯A | DG♭A CxF♯Gx |
| 39 | C♯EGA | D♭F♭GA C♯EFxGx |
| 40 | C♯EGA | D♭F♭GA C♯EFxGx |
| 41 | DF♯A | DG♭A CxF♯Gx |
| 42 | C♯EGA | D♭F♭GA C♯EFxGx |
| 43 | DF♯A | DG♭A CxF♯Gx |
| 44 | DF♯A | DG♭A CxF♯Gx |
| 45 | CEF♯A | CF♭G♭A B♯EF♯Gx |
| 46 | CEF♯A | CF♭G♭A B♯EF♯Gx |
| 47 | EGB | F♭GC♭ EFxB |
| 48 | BEG | C♭F♭G BEFx |
| 49 | GBF♯D | GC♭G♭D FxBF♯Cx |
| 50 | AEGC♯ | AF♭GD♭ GxEFxC♯ |
| 51 | C♯EGA | D♭F♭GA C♯EFxGx |
| 52 | C♯EGA | D♭F♭GA C♯EFxGx |
| 53 | DF♯A | E♯G♭B♯ DF♯A |

The key penetration depth achieved by **Brief Interlude** makes it difficult to alter the key even though a new line of chords expressed the desirability of such a change. This statement is clarified by a comparison of the relative preferred notations on the right with the true preferred notations on the left.

## TONALITY

In this section a brief introduction will be given to the characterization of tonal works preliminary to their analysis by computers. All such pieces show at least to some degree a structural analogy. One of the more important facts concerning such music is that over short periods of time it exhibits remarkable phase stability. That is, in most tonal works, the composition point, while making a succession of short tacks to starboard and port, steadily navigates a readily visible channel in the displacement plane. In the general case, the composition point will pursue a zigzag or undulatory course over a sequence of such channels and, over long periods of time, will cover a considerable distance before coming to a stop. The finished trajectory is made up of many relatively pedestrian advances, all of which are in the same general direction. This directness constitutes a characteristic feature of the older classical music displaying tonality, in contrast to the newer twelve-tone or serial music displaying atonality. The composition trajectories for many different works of the same type are not only similar in appearance, but sometimes can be brought almost into coincidence by a suitable change in scale factor. Trajectories of both sorts are rather simple in gross form.

Fig. 8.6 and 8.7 show, in polar coordinates, the tonal organization of two short compositions by Vincent Persichetti [1]. Notice the successive lines of development. Along these straight lines of displacement the listener supposedly may have time to recognize and adjust to the change of tonal direction. During these periods of path linearity and mental reorientation, the listener clearly is being conditioned to accept further tonal development in the same general direction. Yet this development does not always materialize. The paths suddenly turn, after reaching a stage that in the composer's opinion evidently assures fulfillment of one or more tonal objectives. Between turns the conditioning increases the listener's susceptibility to the next modulatory sensation and the aural impact is heightened by the alternate cessation and precipitation of centripetal forces. By using such graphic representations the music analyst can be especially watchful for the beginnings of modulatory activity.

Figure 8.6

Persichetti, "Our Father, whose creative will,..." **General Hymn No. 1**, Opus 68.

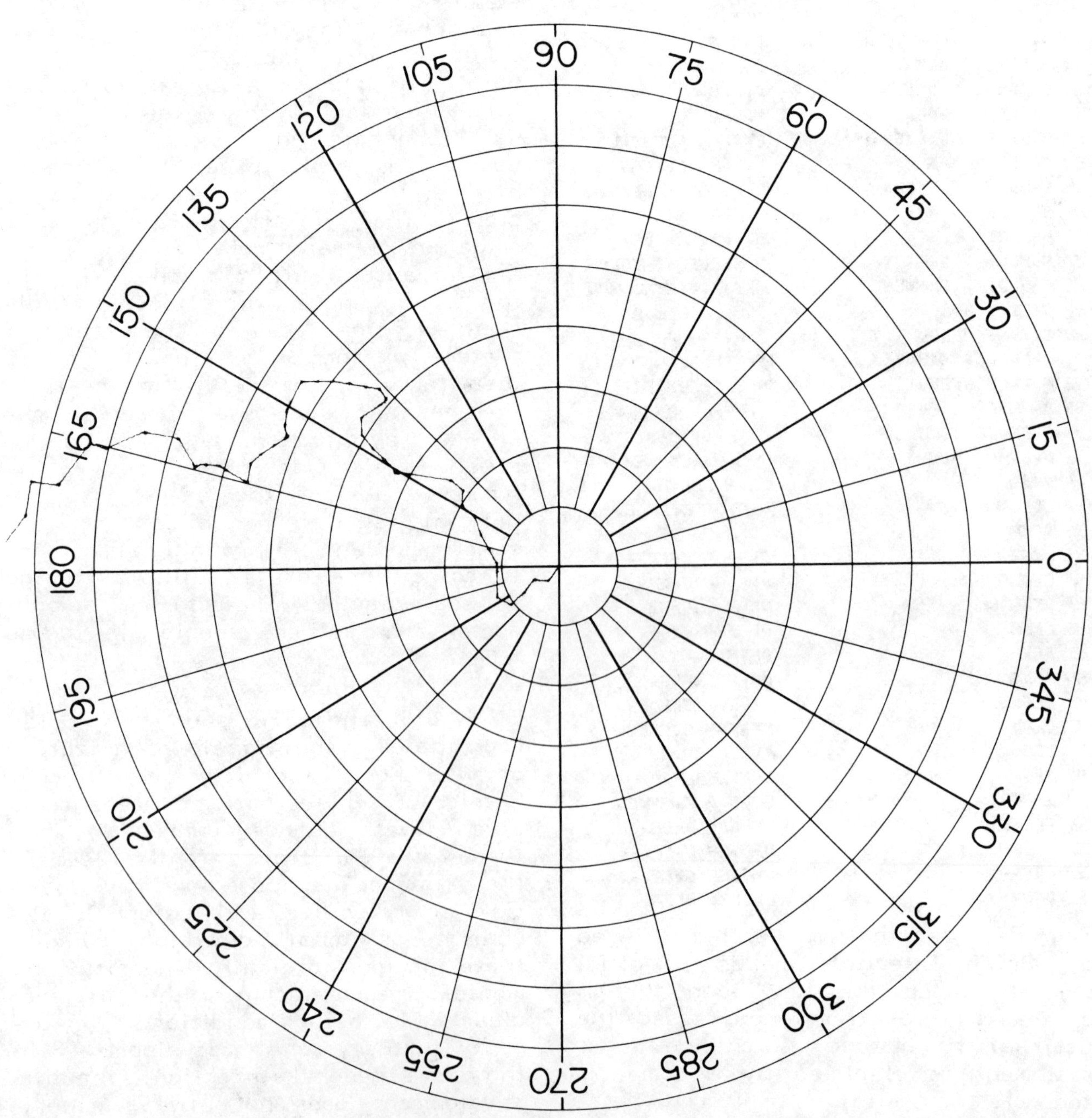

**Figure 8.7**

Persichetti, "Round me falls the night,..." General Hymn No. 2, Opus 68.

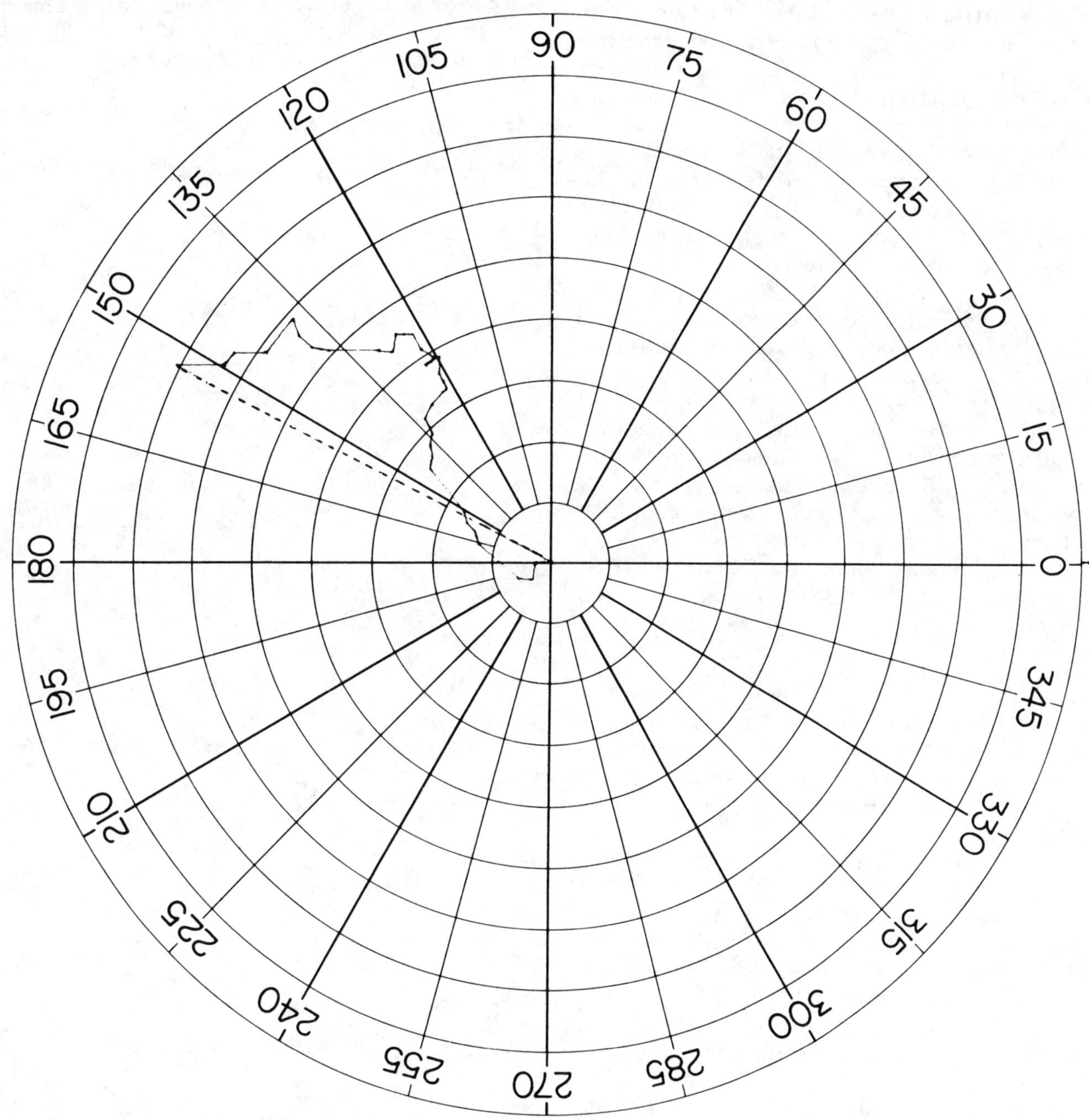


EXERCISES

**8.26** The curve in Fig. 8.7 exhibits three distinct phases. The first is a linear segment with angle 120°, the second is a linear segment with angle 90°, and the third is a linear segment with angle 180°. Trace the occurrence of these segments in the original composition, citing measure numbers. To what tonalities do they correspond? As indicated by the dashed line, the average displacement is at the angle 153°. With what key is this direction associated? What other conclusions can be reached?

## POLYTONALITY

Before proceeding to a discussion of the atonal regime, a short description will be interposed of the mathematical procedure that can be used in conjunction with decomposition along key axes to study polytonality. This will be done for the benefit of those who may wish to form some idea of this procedure, but without going into actual detailed examples. While polytonal works vary considerably, they can be described generally as being stratified into more than one key. The effect of the occurrence of such simultaneous key strata is that the primary aura of tonality should be weakened and the tonal amplitude reduced. By applying a procedure reminiscent of, but less frowned upon than an accountant keeping two separate sets of books, the composer attempts to satisfy the tonal requirements of each separate stratum independently and also tries to provide an intelligible work across the lines of stratification.

Consider the chord CEGB♭D♭G♭, which is spelled with respect to the E♭ major stencil and is simultaneously in the generalized keys of C major and G♭ major. It is composed of two nonoverlapping major triad subchords, CEG and B♭D♭G♭. The first subchord CEG represents a vector component C + E + G = D + G at a 75° angle; the second subchord B♭D♭G♭ represents another vector component B♭ + D♭ + G♭ = A♭ + D♭ at an angle of 255° (or -105°). The directions of the two subchords, which can be regarded as being along the Dm and A♭m key axes respectively, therefore are opposite, and since the magnitudes of the two subchords are the same, because they are both major triads, the total tonal effect is indeterminate, that is,

C + E + G + B♭ + D♭ + G♭ =

(C + G♭) + (E + B♭) + (G + D♭) = 0.

It is not difficult to check this vector addition. In Fig. 8.8 the two subchords CEG and B♭D♭G♭ are laid off graphically to scale in the proper directions from a common starting point. The sum of the two resultants is obviously zero.

**Figure 8.8**

Virtual pair production.

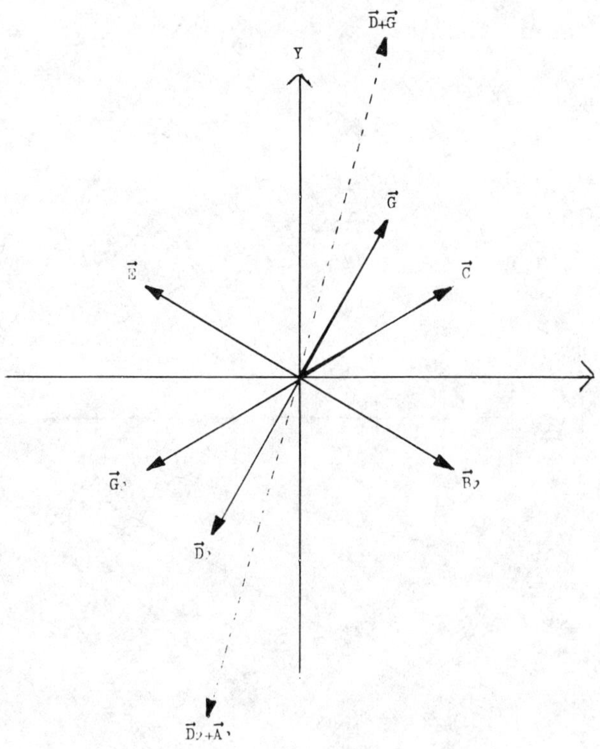

TERSE LAMENT

Figure 8.9

The path of the composition trajectory has several marked turning points. To achieve tonal unity the composition point strives to re-establish the inital course line at the end, but misses, presumably by a "cat's eyebrow."

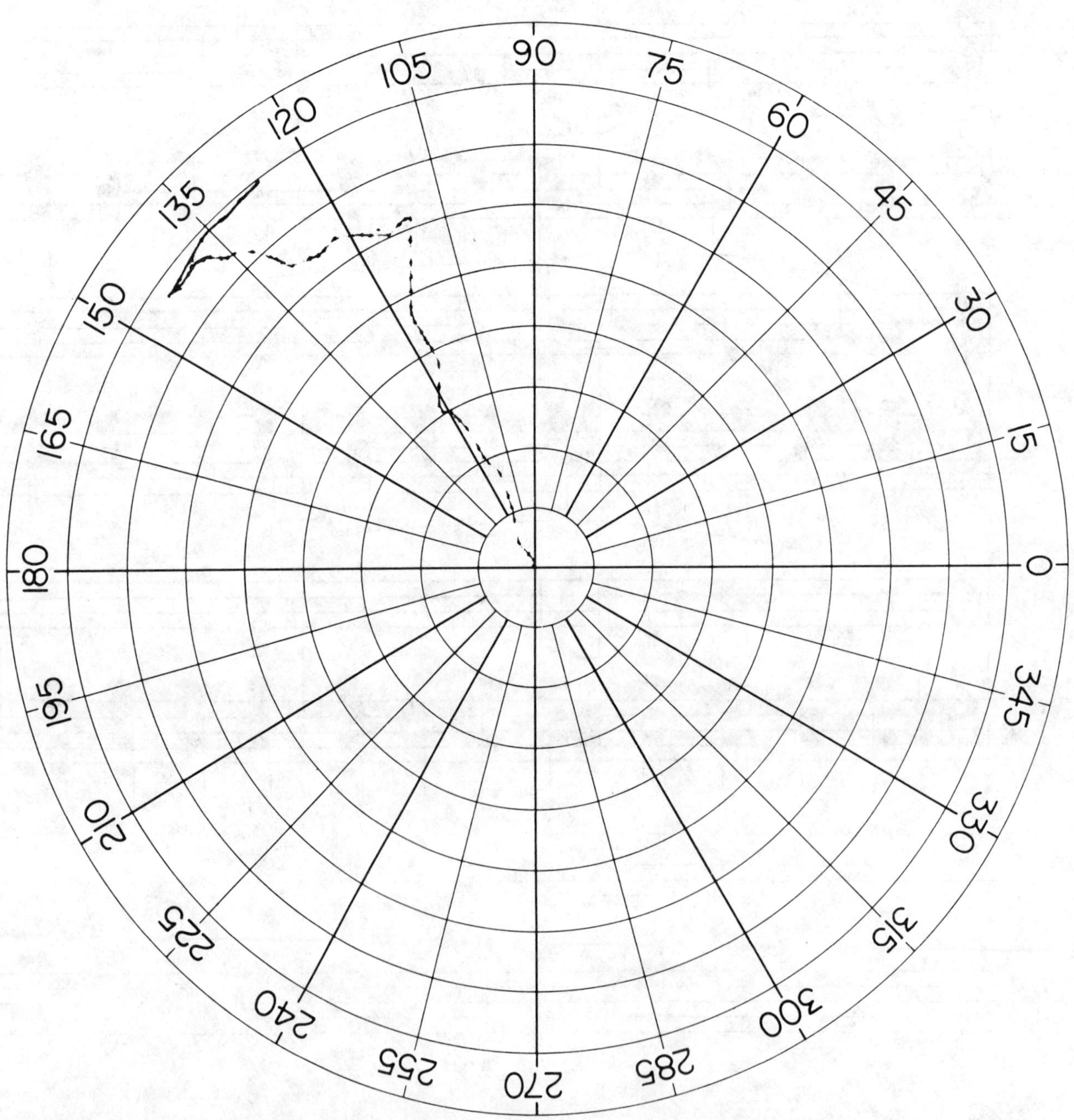

Figure 8.10

The uneven brickwork in the walls of this relative penetration function printout shows perturbing forces at work trying to weaken the supporting tonal structure.

```
00    00 26 50 71 87 97 00 97 87 71 50 26
01       00 26 50 71 87 97 00 97 87 71 50 26
02          13 38 61 79 92 99 99 92 79 61 38 13
03       08 33 57 76 90 98 00 94 82 65 43 18
04       13 38 61 79 92 99 99 93 80 61 39 13
05       13 39 61 80 93 99 99 92 79 61 38 13
06       14 39 62 80 93 99 99 92 79 60 37 12
07       09 34 58 77 91 99 00 94 82 64 42 17
08       07 32 56 75 90 98 00 95 83 66 44 19
09       06 32 55 75 90 98 00 95 83 66 45 20
10       05 31 54 74 89 98 00 95 84 67 45 21
11       03 29 53 73 88 97 00 96 85 68 47 23
12       02 28 52 72 88 97 00 96 86 69 48 24
13       01 27 51 72 87 97 00 96 86 70 49 25
14          23 48 69 85 96 00 97 88 73 52 28 03
15          23 48 69 85 96 00 97 88 73 52 29 03
16          25 49 70 86 96 00 97 87 71 51 27 01
17       02 28 52 72 88 97 00 96 86 69 48 24
18       07 32 56 75 90 98 00 95 83 66 44 19
19       06 32 55 75 90 98 00 95 83 66 44 20
20       06 32 55 75 90 98 00 95 83 66 45 20
21       06 32 55 75 89 98 00 95 83 66 45 20
22       06 32 55 75 89 98 00 95 84 66 45 20
23       05 31 54 74 89 98 00 95 84 67 45 21
24       06 31 55 75 89 98 00 95 84 67 45 20
25       07 32 56 75 90 98 00 95 83 66 44 19
26       09 34 57 77 91 98 00 94 82 64 42 17
27       11 36 59 78 91 99 99 93 81 63 41 16
28       12 38 60 79 92 99 99 93 80 61 39 14
29       15 40 62 80 93 99 99 92 78 59 37 11
30       17 42 64 82 94 00 99 91 77 58 35 09
31       15 40 63 81 93 99 99 91 78 59 36 11
32       13 39 61 80 93 99 99 92 79 61 38 13
33       10 35 58 77 91 99 00 94 81 64 42 17
34       05 31 54 74 89 98 00 95 84 67 45 21
35       03 29 53 73 88 97 00 96 85 69 47 23
36       01 27 51 71 87 97 00 96 86 70 49 25
37          22 46 68 84 95 00 98 89 74 53 30 04
38          18 43 65 82 94 00 98 90 76 57 34 08
39          16 41 63 81 93 99 99 91 77 59 36 10
40          14 39 61 80 93 99 99 92 79 60 38 13
41          09 34 57 77 91 98 00 94 82 64 42 17
42          07 33 56 76 90 98 00 94 83 65 43 19
43          07 32 56 75 90 98 00 95 83 66 44 19
44          06 32 55 75 90 98 00 95 83 66 44 20
45          04 29 53 73 88 97 00 96 85 68 47 22
46          00 26 50 71 87 97 00 97 87 71 50 26
47             24 49 70 86 96 00 97 87 72 51 27 02
48             24 48 69 85 96 00 97 88 72 52 28 02
49             22 46 68 84 95 00 98 89 74 53 30 04
50             20 45 67 84 95 00 98 89 75 55 31 06
51             18 43 64 82 94 00 98 91 76 57 34 08
52             16 41 63 81 93 99 99 91 78 59 36 10
53             12 38 60 79 92 99 99 93 80 61 39 14
54             10 35 58 77 91 99 00 94 81 64 41 16
55             12 37 60 79 92 99 99 93 80 62 39 14
56             15 40 62 80 93 99 99 92 78 60 37 12
67             19 44 66 83 95 00 98 90 75 56 32 07
58             24 48 69 85 96 00 97 88 72 52 28 02
59          03 29 53 73 88 97 00 96 85 68 47 22
60          09 35 58 77 91 99 00 94 82 64 42 17
61          15 40 62 80 93 99 99 92 78 59 37 11
```

Figure 8.11

The array for the absolute penetration function conforms in outline to that of the relative penetration function.

```
00  -05 -06 -03 -01 -00 -00 -00 -00 -00 -01 -03 -06
01      -01 -03 -00 01  02  02  02  02  02  01  -00 -03
02          -03 01  03  04  05  05  05  05  04  03  01  -03
03      -03 03  05  06  07  08  08  07  07  06  04  00
04      00  04  06  07  08  08  08  08  07  06  04  00
05      00  05  07  08  09  09  09  09  08  07  05  00
06      02  06  08  09  10  10  10  10  09  08  06  01
07      00  06  09  10  11  11  11  11  10  09  07  03
08      00  06  09  10  11  11  11  11  10  09  08  04
09      00  07  09  10  11  12  12  11  11  10  08  05
10      00  07  10  11  12  12  12  12  12  11  09  05
11      -01 07  10  11  12  12  13  12  12  11  09  06
12      -03 07  10  11  12  13  13  13  12  11  10  07
13      -05 07  10  11  12  13  13  13  12  11  10  07
14          07  10  11  12  13  13  13  12  12  10  08  -02
15          07  10  12  12  13  13  13  13  12  10  08  -02
16          07  10  12  13  13  13  13  13  12  10  08  -07
17      -02 08  11  12  13  13  14  13  13  12  10  07
18      02  09  11  13  13  14  14  14  13  12  10  07
19      02  09  12  13  14  14  14  14  13  12  11  07
20      02  09  12  13  14  14  14  14  14  13  11  07
21      02  09  12  13  14  14  14  14  14  13  11  07
22      02  10  12  13  14  14  15  14  14  13  11  08
23      02  10  12  13  14  15  15  15  14  13  11  08
24      02  10  12  14  14  15  15  15  14  13  11  08
25      03  10  12  14  15  15  15  15  14  13  11  08
26      05  11  13  14  15  15  15  15  14  13  11  08
27      06  11  13  14  15  15  15  15  14  13  11  07
28      06  11  13  15  15  16  16  15  15  13  11  07
29      08  12  14  15  16  16  16  15  15  14  11  06
30      08  12  14  15  16  16  16  16  15  14  11  06
31      08  12  14  15  16  16  16  16  15  14  12  06
32      07  12  14  15  16  16  16  16  15  14  12  07
33      06  11  14  15  16  15  16  16  15  14  12  08
34      03  11  13  15  16  16  16  16  15  14  13  09
35      01  11  13  15  16  16  16  16  15  14  13  10
36      -05 10  13  15  16  16  16  16  16  15  13  10
37          10  13  15  16  16  16  16  16  15  14  11  02
38          09  13  14  15  16  16  16  16  15  14  11  05
39          08  12  14  15  16  16  16  16  15  14  12  06
40          08  12  14  15  16  16  16  16  15  14  12  07
41          06  12  14  15  16  16  16  16  15  14  13  09
42          05  12  14  15  16  16  16  16  16  15  13  09
43          05  12  14  15  16  16  16  16  16  15  13  09
44          04  12  14  15  16  16  17  16  16  15  13  10
45          02  11  14  15  16  17  17  17  16  15  13  10
46          -07 11  14  15  16  17  17  17  16  15  14  11
47              11  14  15  16  17  17  17  16  15  14  11  -00
48              11  14  15  16  17  17  17  16  15  14  11  01
49              10  14  15  16  17  17  17  16  16  14  12  03
50              10  14  15  16  17  17  17  17  16  14  12  04
51              10  13  15  16  17  17  17  17  16  15  12  06
52              09  13  15  16  17  17  17  17  16  15  13  07
53              08  13  15  16  17  17  17  17  16  15  13  08
54              07  13  15  16  17  17  17  17  16  15  13  09
55              08  13  15  16  17  17  17  17  16  15  13  08
56              09  13  15  16  17  17  17  17  16  15  13  08
57              10  14  15  16  17  17  17  17  16  15  12  05
58              11  14  16  16  17  17  17  17  16  14  12  01
59          03  12  14  16  17  17  17  17  16  15  14  11
60          07  13  15  16  17  17  17  17  16  15  13  09
61          09  13  15  16  17  17  17  17  16  15  13  08
```

Figure 8.12

The absolute penetration history for **Terse Lament** shows three major keys vying for ascendancy. Fragments of curves at the bottom suggest hidden tonal nuances.

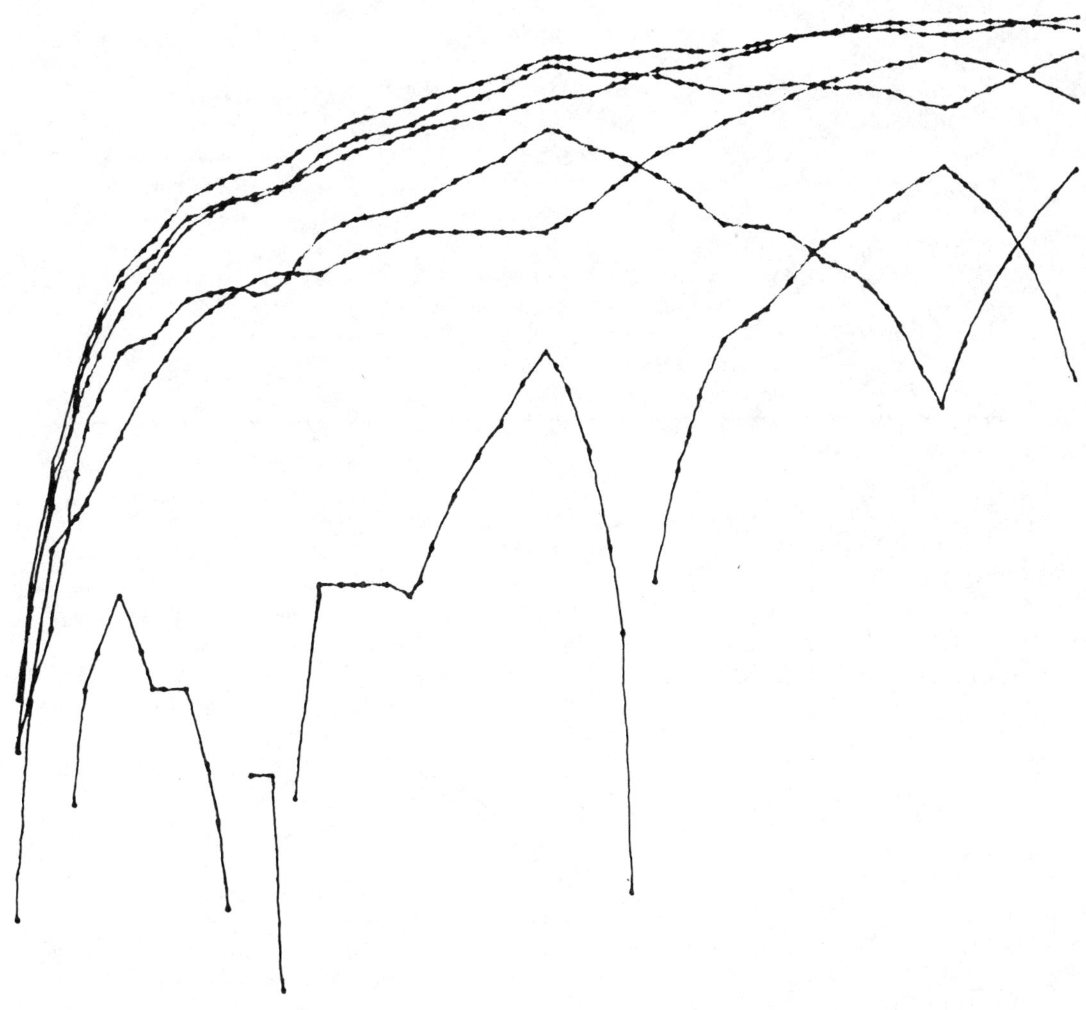

Figure 8.13

A decrease in energy occurs at every point of applied tonal impulse.

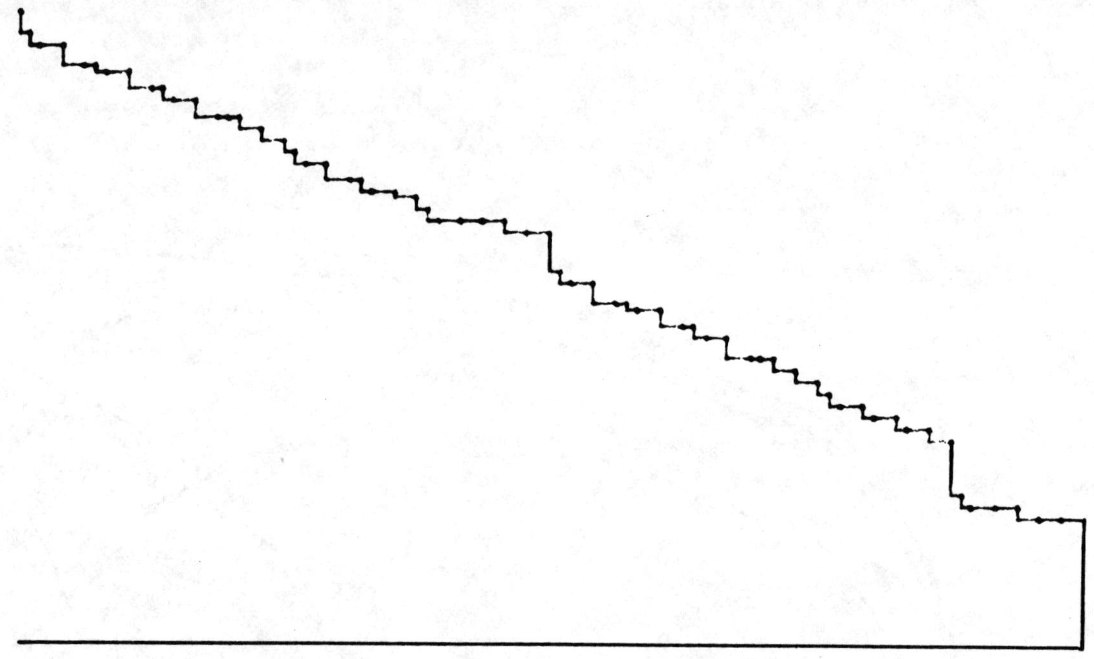

Figure 8.14

A balanced variety of tonal amplitudes appears in the composition.

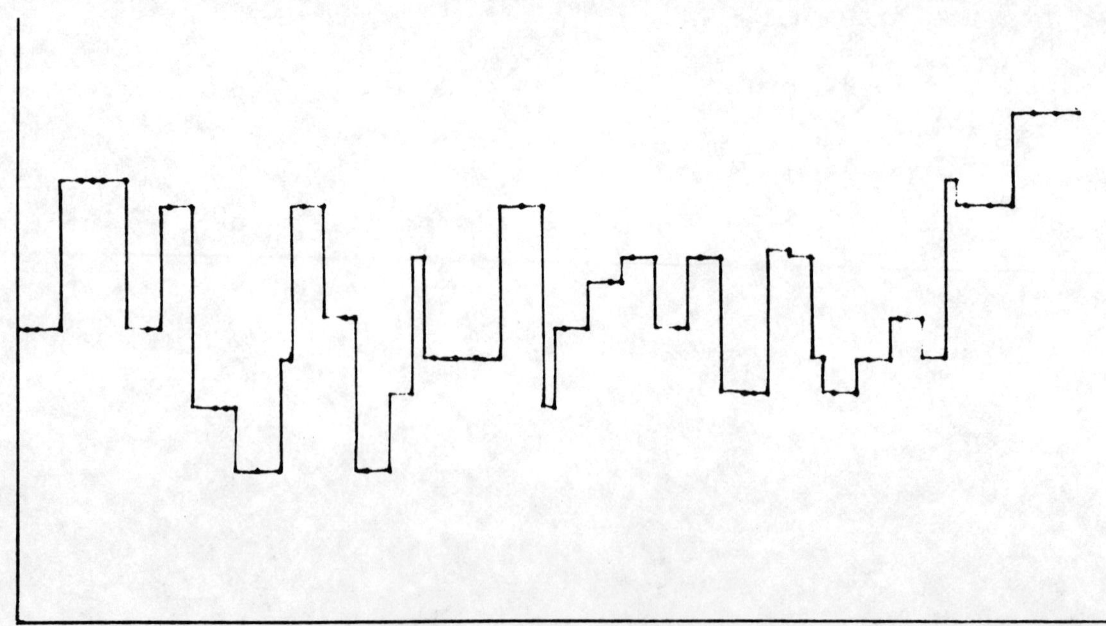

Figure 8.15

This is an impulse magnitude graph for the composition **Terse Lament.** One unusual feature is the abnormally high count of zero impulse points, which appear uniformly along the horizontal time axis. These can be attributed to the rhythmic repetition of chords in the accompaniment. Notice that three extreme impulses are about equally spaced and build up linearly to a climax near the conclusion of the piece.

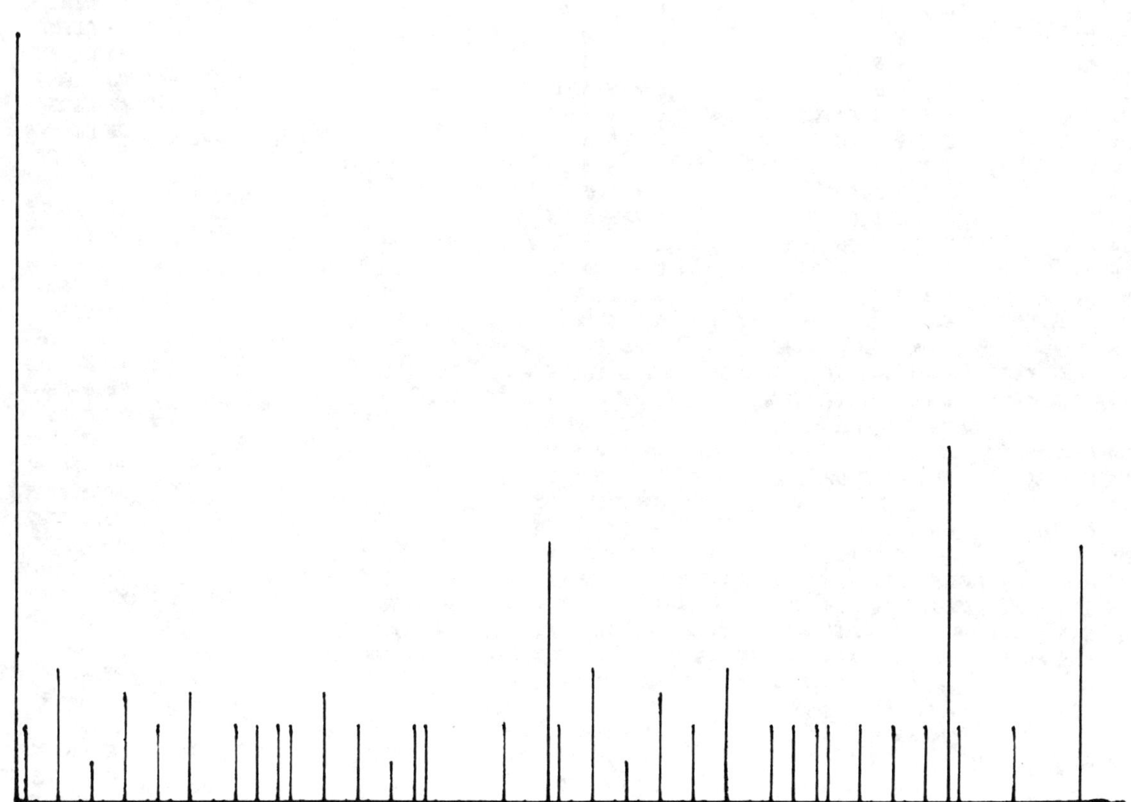

Figure 8.16

This output of inferior, canonical, and superior true notations (in left-to-right order of columns) illustrates what can happen with an improper tab setting. Its correction is left as an exercise.

```
00 Dbb Fb Abb Cb              C E G B            C E G B
01 Dbb Fb Abb Cb Gb           C E G B F#         C E G B F#
02 Dbb Fb Abb Cb Gb           C E G B F#         C E G B F#
03 Dbb Fb Abb Cb Ebb          C E G B D          C E G B D
04 Dbb Fb Abb Cb Ebb          C E G B D          C E G B D
05 Dbb Fb Abb Cb Bbb          C E G B A          C E G B A
06 Dbb Fb Abb Cb Bbb          C E G B A          C E G B A
07 Dbb Fb Abb Cb Gb           C E G B F#         C E G B F#
08 Dbb Fb Abb Cb Gb           C E G B F#         C E G B F#
09 Dbb Fb Abb Cb Fb           C E G B E          C E G B E
10 Dbb Fb Abb Cb Fb           C E G B E          C E G B E
11 Dbb Fb Abb Cb Db           C E G B C#         C E G B C#
12 Dbb Fb Abb Cb Db           C E G B C#         C E G B C#
13 Dbb Fb Abb Cb Db           C E G B C#         C E G B C#
14 Cb Fb Abb Bb Db            B E G A# C#        B E G A# C#
15 Cb Fb Abb Cbb              B E G Bb           B E G Bb
16 CbbBb FbE AbbG BbbA        BbA# EDx GFx AGx       BbA# EDx GFx AGx
17 CbbBb FbE AbbG BbbA EbbD   BbA# EDx GFx AGx DCx   BbA# EDx GFx AGx DCx
18 CbbBb FbE AbbG BbbA EbbD   BbA# EDx GFx AGx DCx   BbA# EDx GFx AGx DCx
19 Cbb Fb Abb Bbb Cb          Bb E G A B         Bb E G A B
20 Cbb Fb Abb Bbb Cb          Bb E G A B         Bb E G A B
21 Cbb Fb Abb Bbb Db          Bb E G A C#        Bb E G A C#
22 Cbb Fb Abb Bbb Db          Bb E G A C#        Bb E G A C#
23 Cbb Fb Abb Bbb Gb          Bb E G A F#        Bb E G A F#
24 Bbb Ebb Gbb Bbb Gb         A D F A F#         A D F A F#
25 BbbA EbbD GbbF BbbA AbB#bG#AAGx DCx FE# AGx G#AbFx#GAGx DCx FE# AGx G#AbFx#G#
26 BbbA EbbD GbbF BbbA AbB#bG#AAGx DCx FE# AGx G#AbFx#GAGx DCx FE# AGx G#AbFx#G#
27 BbbA EbbD GbbF BbbA AbB#bG#AAGx DCx FE# AGx G#AbFx#GAGx DCx FE# AGx G#AbFx#G#
28 BbbA EbbD GbbF BbbA AbB#bG#AAGx DCx FE# AGx G#AbFx#GAGx DCx FE# AGx G#AbFx#G#
29 BbbA EbbD GbbF BbbA        AGx DCx FE# AGx    AGx DCx FE# AGx
30 BbbA EbbD GbbF BbbA        AGx DCx FE# AGx    AGx DCx FE# AGx
31 Eb Gb Cb Ebb               D# F# B D          D# F# B D
32 Eb Gb Cb Ebb Ab            D# F# B D G#       D# F# B D G#
33 Eb Gb Cb Ebb Ab            D# F# B D G#       D# F# B D G#
34 Eb Gb Cb Ebb Fb            D# F# B D E        D# F# B D E
35 Eb Gb Cb Ebb Fb            D# F# B D E        D# F# B D E
36 Eb Gb Cb Ebb Cb            D# F# B D B        D# F# B D B
37 Eb Gb Cb Ebb Cb            D# F# B D B        D# F# B D B
38 Eb Gb Cb Ebb Ab            D# F# B D G#       D# F# B D G#
39 Eb Gb Cb Ebb Ab            D# F# B D G#       D# F# B D G#
40 Eb Gb Cb Ebb Gb            D# F# B D F#       D# F# B D F#
41 Eb Gb Cb Ebb Gb            D# F# B D F#       D# F# B D F#
42 Eb Gb Cb Ebb Ebb           D# F# B D D        D# F# B D D
43 Eb Gb Cb Ebb Ebb           D# F# B D D        D# F# B D D
44 Eb Gb Cb Ebb Ebb           D# F# B D D        D# F# B D D
45 Ebb Gb Cb Db Ebb           D F# B C# D        D F# B C# D
46 Ebb Gb Cb Db               D F# B C#          D F# B C#
47 Db Gb Cb CDbb              C# F# B B#C        C# F# B B#C
48 Db Gb Cb Dbb Ebb           C# F# B C D        C# F# B C D
49 Db Gb Cb Dbb Ebb           C# F# B C D        C# F# B C D
50 Db Gb Cb CDbb              C# F# B B#C        C# F# B B#C
51 Db Gb Cb CDbb              C# F# B B#C        C# F# B B#C
52 Db Gb Cb C Eb              C# F# B B# D#      C# F# B B# D#
53 Db Gb Cb C Eb              C# F# B B# D#      C# F# B B# D#
54 Db Gb Cb CDbb              C# F# B B#C        C# F# B B#C
55 C F A C                    B# E# Gx B#        B# E# Gx B#
56 C F A C E                  B# E# Gx B# Dx     B# E# Gx B# Dx
57 C F A C E                  B# E# Gx B# Dx     B# E# Gx B# Dx
58 C F A C E                  B# E# Gx B# Dx     B# E# Gx B# Dx
59 F C F A C E                E# B# E# Gx B# Dx  E# B# E# Gx B# Dx
60 F C F A C E                E# B# E# Gx B# Dx  E# B# E# Gx B# Dx
61 F C F A C E                E# B# E# Gx B# Dx  E# B# E# Gx B# Dx
```

Figure 8.17

It is debatable whether the computer performs its task of devising and printing preferred notations through application of artificial intelligence.

```
00 CEGB
01 CEGBF#
02 CEGBF#
03 CEGBD
04 CEGBD
05 CEGBA
06 CEGBA
07 CEGBF#
08 CEGBF#
09 CEGBE
10 CEGBE
11 CEGBC#
12 CEGBC#
13 CEGBC#
14 BEGA#C#
15 BEGBb
16 BbEGA
17 BbEGAD
18 BbEGAD
19 BbEGAB
20 BbEGAB
21 BbEGAC#
22 BbEGAC#
23 BbEGAF#
24 ADFAF#
25 ADFAG#
26 ADFAG#
27 ADFAG#
28 ADFAG#
29 ADFA
30 ADFA
31 EbF#BD
32 EbF#BDG#
33 EbF#BDG#
34 EbF#BDE
35 EbF#BDE
36 EbF#BDB
37 D#F#BDB
38 D#F#BDG#
39 D#F#BDG#
40 D#F#BDF#
41 D#F#BDF#
42 D#F#BDD
43 D#F#BDD
44 D#F#BDD
45 DF#BC#D
46 DF#BC#
47 C#F#BC
48 C#F#BCD
49 C#F#BCD
50 C#F#BC
51 C#F#BC
52 C#F#BCD#
53 C#F#BCD#
54 C#F#BC
55 CFAC
56 CFACE
57 CFACE
58 CFACE
59 FCFACE
60 FCFACE
61 FCFACE
```

## EXERCISES

**8.27** (a) Draw the 100% locus in Fig. 8.10. (b) Comment on the significance, if any, of its irregularity.

**8.28** (a) Draw several contour level lines in Fig. 8.11. (b) What is suggested by their appearance?

**8.29** Is **Terse Lament** a polytonal work? (Hint. Considered separately, the melody might call for a signature of three sharps; the accompaniment, for a signature of one flat. Pursue this concept of stratification further, by graphing the tracks of melody and accompaniment independently. Also, investigate the possibilities of decomposition along various pairs of major and minor key axes.)

**8.30** Frequently it is convenient to write a chord using sharps instead of flats, or vice versa. To illustrate, the chord CEGB♭D♭G♭ may be written as CEGA♯C♯F♯, which is the **Petrushka chord.** (a) What are the implications of this enharmonic change? (Hint. Consider geometry, the stencil, generalized keys, and key axes.) (b) Cite further cases of the tritone relation in bitonal works.

## ATONALITY

In previous sections it was illustrated that musical compositions which are classified as tonal works (having a key center) tend to concentrate on tonalities having the same general phase. Usually, in fact, they are constructed to advance the composition point through one or more relatively narrow corridors. The essential difference between tonal and atonal (having no key center) compositions is that in the former the composition point is biased and so traverses large distances, whereas in the latter the composition point is fair and hugs the equilibrium polar region. Many atonal works contain basic recurrent patterns called "tone rows," which are obtained by permuting the elements of the chromatic scale to form a series of twelve literals. These literals are then applied at various pitch levels, high and low, in accordance with predetermined transformations of the basic tone row. Often these transformations are mathematical **group** operations [2]. The basic tenet of the atonal doctrine is that there is to be no preferred tone. In terms of the present exposition, all directions in the displacement plane are to be of equal importance. Nevertheless, it is obvious that, depending upon the dwell times of various tones as determined from their durations, a twelve-tone row can be biased to any key. For example, if the basic tone row is simply the one-octave ascending chromatic scale starting on C, then it can be warped into the key of C major merely by playing each black key as though it were a grace note.

One authority, Kassler [3], has applied the theory of mathematical linguistics to the strict analysis of serial music. By using Iverson notation--a symbolic formalism that now has blossomed into a widely known and highly regarded programming language named APL (A Programming Language)--Kassler has been able to untangle highly coordinated serial compositions and, through careful examination, reveal a good deal of variability. In so doing he has contributed much to an understanding of the way in which works of great musical value and significance are put together using the four basic forms of an atonal tone row: original, inverted, retrograde, and inverted retrograde. Much of this work bearing on how tone rows are structured and combined is relevant to algorithms for computer-assisted music analysis [4]. More recently Kassler has been concerned with an explication of tonality in Shenkerian analysis.

Another eminent musicologist, Forte, has investigated the structure of the music of Anton Webern. In dealing with the atonal works of various composers, Forte's approach has relied extensively on SNOBOL [5], a string-manipulation language developed at Bell Telephone Laboratories, which is ideally suited to the performance of certain research functions in the humanities involving character sequences or strings. The first stage of Forte's research entails encoding the complete score in Bauer-Mengelberg notation--the so-called **Ford-Columbia** representation. During the second stage the encoded information is preprocessed by an analytic reading program for atonal music.

As shown in Fig. 8.18 and 8.19, the path of a typical atonal composition trajectory bears a striking similarity to that of a particle of dust suspended in mid-air, which experiences violent impulses due to the thermal agitation of the surrounding gas molecules. The particle of dust is said to undergo **Brownian motion** [6]. Since the composition point is propagated in the displacement plane in an apparently random manner for many atonal works, atonality may be regarded as the most efficient way of encoding musical meaning according to principles of information theory.

The continuous broken line in Fig. 8.20 represents a portion of the Křenek path plotted in Fig. 8.18. As with all atonal music, this trajectory fragment portrays an extremely complicated musical motion. Nevertheless, it is not impossible to analyze this complicated motion in detail. Gross inspection of the polar plot in Fig. 8.20 reveals that this work may be atonal only in the sense that the absolute penetration function is not allowed to grow without limit. Signs are quite visible under somewhat closer scrutiny that the musical signal, by means of the sequential pattern of components chosen, tends alternately to reinforce one particular phase of tonality and then its opposite.

In the very beginning there is an immediate although tentative thrust in the northeastern direction. Right away the composition point reverses its direction of travel. As though satisfied with the success of its test thrust, the composition point next makes a much bolder intrusion to the vicinity of the objective attained earlier only to fall back almost to a halfway position. A similar behavior can be seen again as the composition point strikes out into the first quadrant and retreats back into the fourth quadrant a third time. In the returning section of each complete transit, the sense of key that has been effectively built up in the patient listener's mind is efficiently and quickly dismantled.

Figure 8.18

Trajectory for the first fifteen measures of Křenek's atonal piece, **Dancing Toys.** Much crisscrossing produces a weakness of key. Notice the apparently random phase shifts.

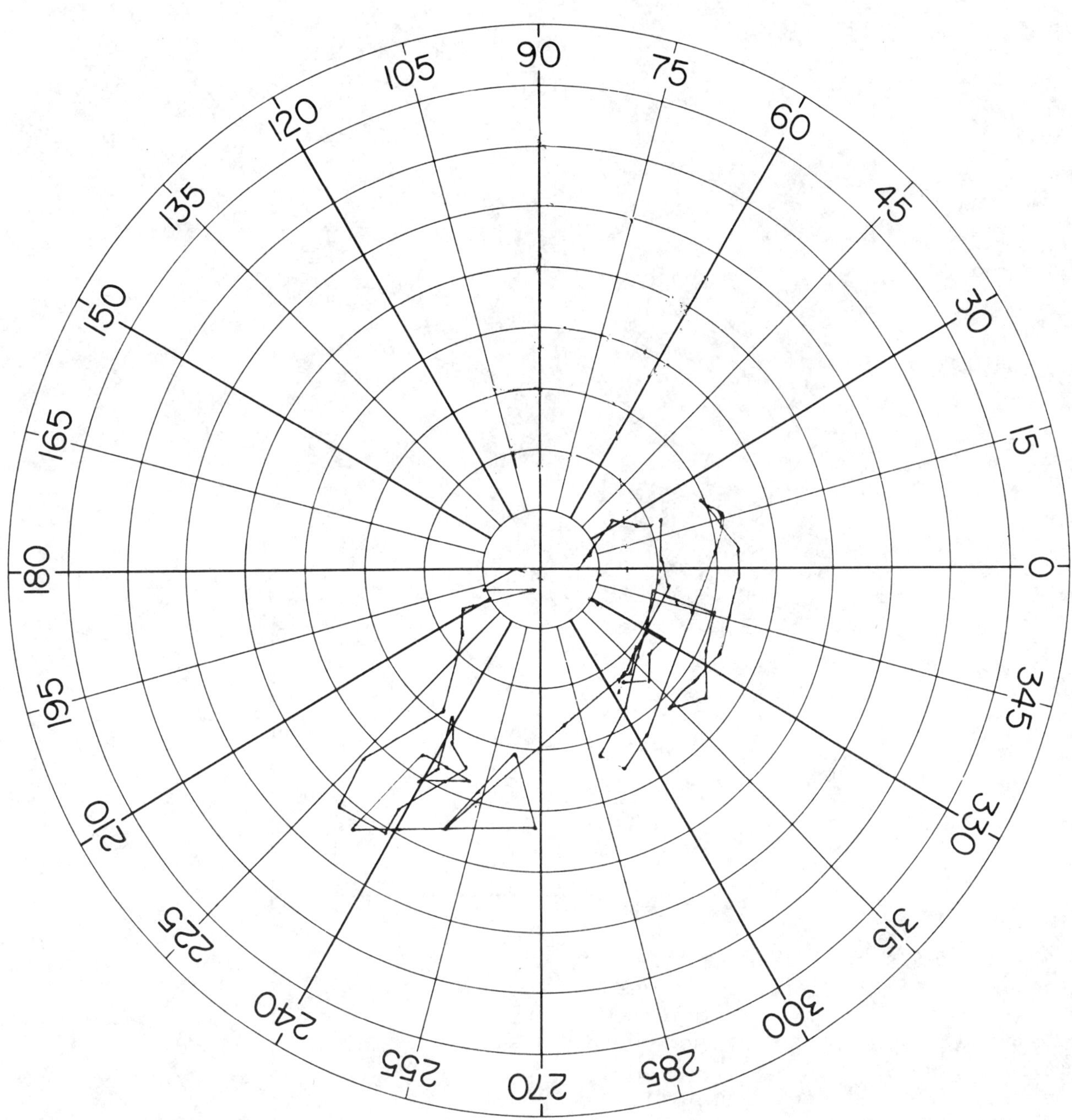

Figure 8.19

Trajectory of a single particle in Brownian motion. Each line segment joining two dots represents the displacement of the particle in a uniform time interval. (See, for example, [7].)

Figure 8.20

Biased random motion in Křenek displacements. The arrows represent the favored directions of translation of the composition disc. Such deliberate bipolar phasing of tonalities enables the listener's appetite for sweets to be partially appeased.

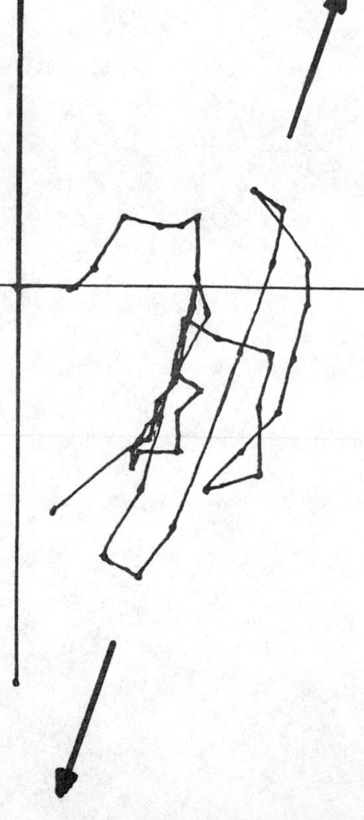

The arrows added to the chart in Fig. 8.20 summarize the overall tendency. The fact that certain trajectory segments project differently on two orthogonal axes proves that the displacements do have a preferred direction in spite of their apparent irregularity. Owing to the abrupt changes of direction of the trajectory, which are brought about by phase reversals, the average tonality achieved in the Southwestern part can be regarded as having a negative value, as it is about $180^{\circ}$ out of phase with the Northeastern part.

It is clear that an atonal composition should always be as prone to move in one direction as another. Even for pieces written in the tonal regime a glance at the charted movement often reveals that the composition trajectory continually undergoes both small and large deflections from its set course. As a first approximation, therefore, the motion of the tonal composition point may be considered to be the vector sum of a Brownian motion and a uniform motion of drift at a constant translational rate equal to the average tonality. These two quantities combine vectorially to give a total displacement that is partly stochastic and partly deterministic. For example, in Fig. 8.21, the tonalities chosen are not completely random; instead there is a preponderance of tonality components toward the upper right caused by unbalanced tonal impulses drawn from the first quadrant only. So, the trajectory remains fairly linear. Despite this apparent randomness, close scrutiny of representative musical excerpts written in either genre will show that musical motion, although sometimes irregular, is not at all haphazard, unless the composer is actually erratic. At this juncture the advantages of using a vectorial principle for organizing keys and structuring tonalities should be evident.

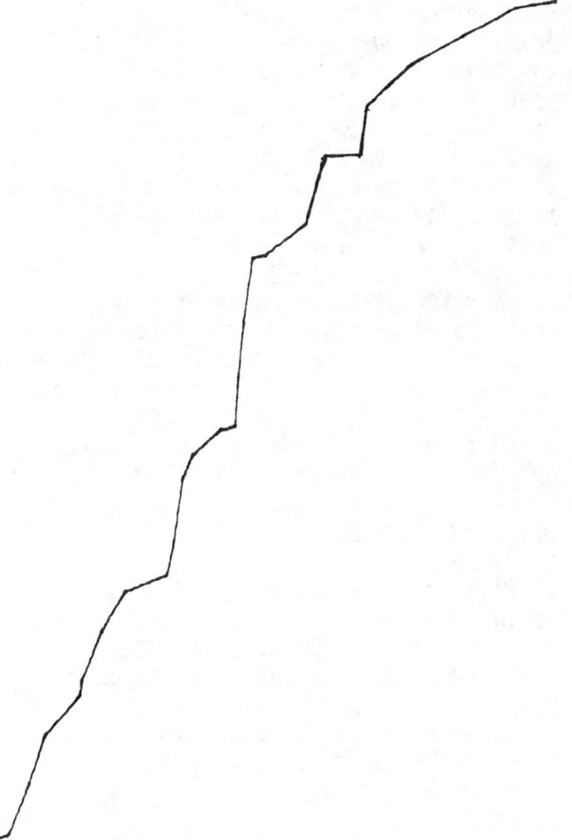

Figure 8.21

Trajectory of a single particle in combined Brownian motion and translation. Notice that the path seems to display a slight curvature, although the heading of $45^{\circ}$ is relatively stable. (Compare Fig. 6.9a.)

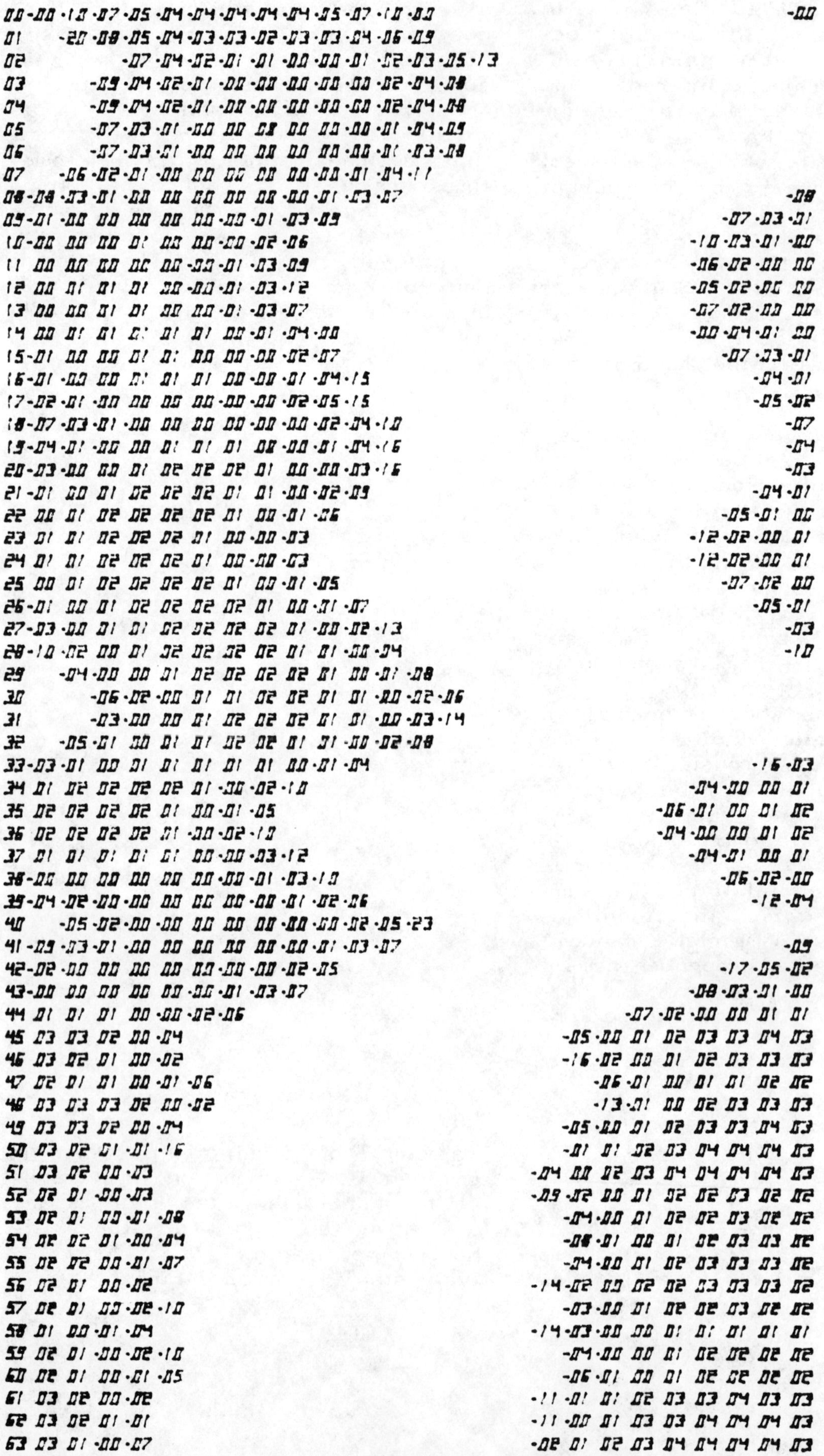

```
00-00 -10 -07 -05 -04 -04 -04 -04 -04 -05 -07 -10 -00                                 -00
01    -20 -08 -05 -04 -03 -03 -02 -03 -03 -04 -06 -09
02            -07 -04 -02 -01 -01 -00 -00 -01 -02 -03 -05 -13
03        -09 -04 -02 -01 -00 -00 -00 -00 -00 -02 -04 -08
04        -09 -04 -02 -01 -00 -00 -00 -00 -00 -02 -04 -08
05        -07 -03 -01 -00  00  00  00  00 -00 -01 -04 -09
06        -07 -03 -01 -00  00  00  00  00 -00 -01 -03 -08
07    -06 -02 -01 -00  00  00  00  00 -00 -01 -04 -11
08-08 -03 -01 -00  00  00  00  00 -00 -01 -03 -07                                      -08
09-01 -00  00  00  00  00 -00 -01 -03 -09                                      -07 -03 -01
10-00  00  00  01  00  00 -00 -02 -06                                      -10 -03 -01 -00
11 00  00  00  00  00 -00 -01 -03 -09                                      -06 -02 -00  00
12 00  01  01  01  00 -00 -01 -03 -12                                      -05 -02 -00  00
13 00  00  01  01  00  00 -01 -03 -07                                      -07 -02 -00  00
14 00  01  01  01  01  01  00 -01 -04 -00                                  -00 -04 -01  00
15-01  00  00  01  01  00  00 -00 -02 -07                                      -07 -03 -01
16-01 -00  00  01  01  01  00 -00 -01 -04 -15                                      -04 -01
17-02 -01 -00  00  00  00 -00 -00 -02 -05 -15                                      -05 -02
18-07 -03 -01 -00  00  00  00 -00 -00 -02 -04 -10                                      -07
19-04 -01 -00  00  01  01  01  00 -00 -01 -04 -16                                      -04
20-03 -00  00  01  02  02  02  01  00 -00 -03 -16                                      -03
21-01  00  01  02  02  02  01  01 -00 -02 -09                                      -04 -01
22 00  01  02  02  02  02  01  00 -01 -06                                      -05 -01  00
23 01  01  02  02  02  01  00 -00 -03                                      -12 -02 -00  01
24 01  01  02  02  02  01  00 -00 -03                                      -12 -02 -00  01
25 00  01  02  02  02  02  01  00 -01 -05                                      -07 -02  00
26-01  00  01  02  02  02  02  01  00 -01 -07                                      -05 -01
27-03 -00  01  01  02  02  02  02  01 -00 -02 -13                                      -03
28-10 -02  00  01  02  02  02  02  01  01 -00 -04                                      -10
29    -04 -00  00  01  02  02  02  02  01  00 -01 -08
30            -06 -02 -00  01  01  02  02  01  01 -00 -02 -06
31            -03 -00  00  01  02  02  02  01  01 -00 -03 -14
32    -05 -01  00  01  01  02  02  01  01 -00 -02 -08
33-03 -01  00  01  01  01  01  01  00 -01 -04                                      -16 -03
34 01  02  02  02  02  01 -00 -02 -10                                  -04 -00  00  01
35 02  02  02  02  01  00 -01 -05                                  -06 -01  00  01  02
36 02  02  02  02  01 -00 -02 -10                                  -04 -00  00  01  02
37 01  01  01  01  01  00 -00 -03 -12                                  -04 -01  00  01
38-00  00  00  00  00  00 -00 -01 -03 -10                                  -06 -02 -00
39-04 -02 -00 -00  00  00  00 -00 -01 -02 -06                                  -12 -04
40    -05 -02 -00 -00  00  00  00 -00 -00 -02 -05 -23
41-09 -03 -01 -00  00  00  00  00 -00 -01 -03 -07                                      -09
42-02 -00  00  00  00  00 -00 -00 -02 -05                                  -17 -05 -02
43-00  00  00  00  00 -00 -01 -03 -07                              -08 -03 -01 -00
44 01  01  01  00 -00 -02 -06                          -07 -02 -00  00  01  01
45 03  03  02  00 -04                      -05 -00  01  02  03  03  04  03
46 03  02  01  00 -02                      -16 -02  00  01  02  03  03  03
47 02  01  01  00 -01 -06                      -06 -01  00  01  01  02  02
48 03  03  03  02  00 -02                      -13 -01  00  02  03  03  03
49 03  03  02  00 -04                      -05 -00  01  02  03  03  04  03
50 03  02  01 -01 -16                      -01  01  02  03  04  04  04  03
51 03  02  00 -03                      -04  00  02  03  04  04  04  04  03
52 02  01 -00 -03                      -09 -02  00  01  02  02  03  02  02
53 02  01  00 -01 -08                      -04 -00  01  02  02  03  02  02
54 02  02  01 -00 -04                      -08 -01  00  01  02  03  03  02
55 02  02  00 -01 -07                      -04 -00  01  02  03  03  03  02
56 02  01  00 -02                      -14 -02  00  02  02  03  03  03  02
57 02  01  00 -02 -10                      -03 -00  01  02  02  03  02  02
58 01  00 -01 -04                      -14 -03 -00  00  01  01  01  01  01
59 02  01 -00 -02 -10                      -04 -00  00  01  02  02  02  02
60 02  01  00 -01 -05                      -06 -01  00  01  02  02  02  02
61 03  02  00 -02                      -11 -01  01  02  03  03  04  03  03
62 03  02  01 -01                      -11 -00  01  03  03  04  04  04  03
63 03  01 -00 -07                      -02  01  02  03  04  04  04  04  03
```

Figure 8.22

Irregularity of the 100% locus is indicative of the degree of keylessness associated with atonal music. Notice that an abrupt change in structure occurs in measure eight where serrated edges give way to slightly uneven edges. Usually the absolute penetration plateaus that are formed by atonal compositions can be distinguished by their having low altitudes such as these.

Figure 8.23

Rapid fluctuations and relatively little overall height are two characteristics of the absolute penetration history of atonal works.

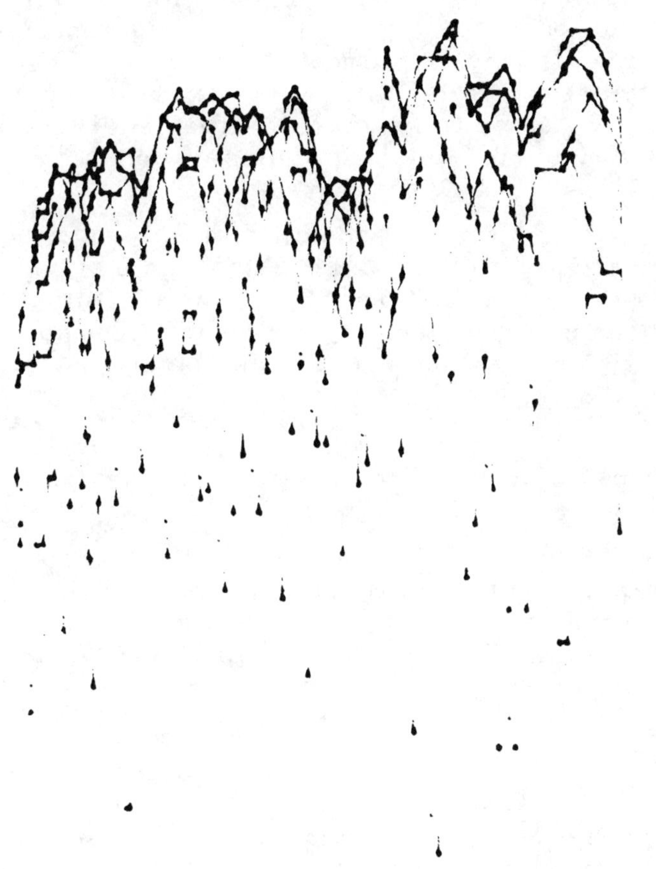

Figure 8.24

There is a fairly steady decrease in available energy.

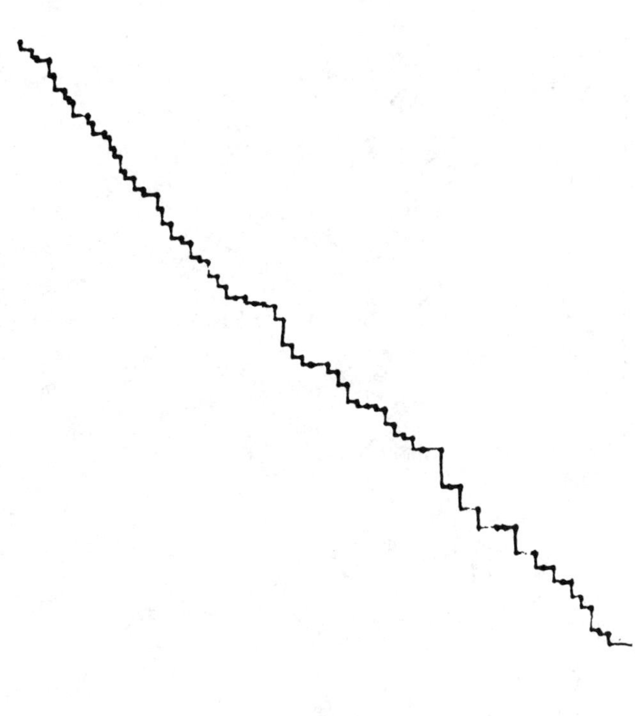

Figure 8.25

The tonality amplitudes for **Dancing Toys** present a pleasing visual pattern.

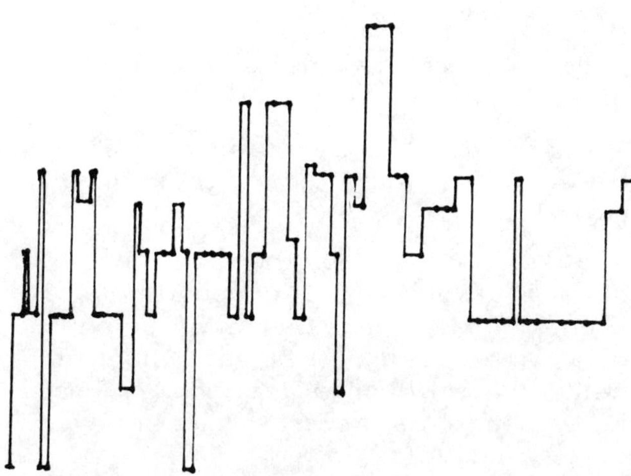

Figure 8.26

This graph illustrates the magnitude of the tonal impulse that is to be found at the start of each nonsilent component.

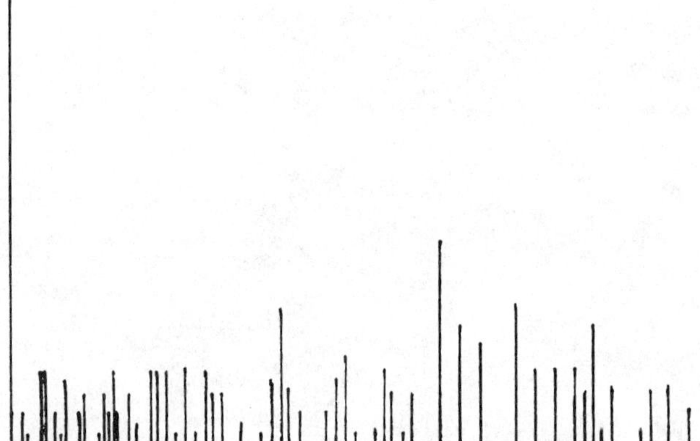

## EXERCISES

**8.31** New entrances of the basic tone row must be carefully phased into an atonal composition's overall serial organization in order to ensure that a minimum tonal amplitude is maintained during each measure. Using information theoretic terms, explain how atonal music makes the most economical use of a communication channel.

**8.32** Complete the above analysis of Křenek's **Dancing Toys.**

**8.33** Why are balanced chords the only vertical structures properly called atonal?

**8.34** Analyze another one or two of the twelve-tone compositions by Křenek [8]. Does the analysis support the claim that atonal music has no tonal organization, or does it appear that such music is very tightly organized?

**8.35** A useful estimate of the degree of tonal bias to be found in a given composition can be obtained by drawing a fan diagram of the entire composition, or of a sufficiently large random sample of it. The total lengths of the twelve arrows, drawn from their common origin, indicate the relative importance of each of the twelve tones in the composition. A **roundness chart** can be obtained from the fan diagram by fitting a smooth curve to the extremities of the twelve arrows. Apply this technique to the analysis of various tonal and atonal works.

**8.36** What mechanism is largely responsible for the atonality of a serial work. That is, what thing tends to restore a twelve-tone composition point to tonal equilibrium?

**8.37** Is the following selection a tonal work? (Hint. Calculate the trajectory of **Short Theme.**)

**8.38** In referring to the inadequacy of notation for the writing of music without keys, Krenek [9] states: "If we write the following phrase

EX. 8

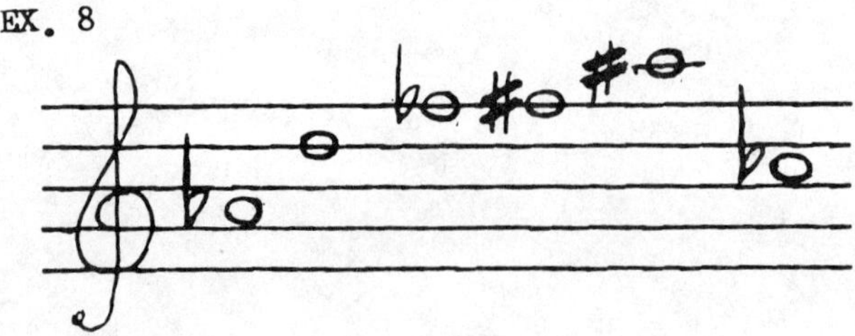

rather in the form:

EX. 9

we do so only from a desire for higher graphic clarity, not from considerations of tonal coordination." Criticize this remark, assuming that it is not cast in the editorial plural.

ANDANTE (con Ped.)
SHORT THEME
pp

**8.39** Draw the graph of a theoretical Brownian trajectory by this method: First, prepare a sequence of 600 random digits by copying numbers from a book--a telephone directory will serve the purpose if a table of random numbers is not handy. Then divide these digits into groupings of three. Next, affix algebraic signs to these groupings by flipping a fair coin (heads, +; tails, -). Finally take successive pairs of these triples to represent the x and y components of the successive displacements of the particle. Use the resulting chart as the basis for creating a brief musical work.

**8.40** (a) A drum majorette, in order to catch her twirling baton every time, must take steps of equal length randomly forward or backward. Where will she probably be standing after taking three steps? After four steps? (b) Show that the probability of her arriving just k steps away from her starting point on the <u>n</u>th step is given by the formula:

$$P_k = \frac{n!}{(\frac{n}{2} + \frac{k}{2})!(\frac{n}{2} - \frac{k}{2})!}(\frac{1}{2})^n$$

**8.41** As a first approximation, atonal music can be analyzed as a simple dispersion problem, either by considering a large number of composition points moving simultaneously or many successive displacements of a single composition point. Derive a random-walk formula for the displacement of an atonal composition point assuming that steps of each size are sufficiently numerous to be amenable to statistical treatment and may be taken in random directions in two dimensions. Use this formula to show that the root-mean-square displacement or standard deviation increases as $\sqrt{n}$, the square root of the number of components. (<u>Hint</u>. First observe that the displacements in any two directions perpendicular to each other are statistically independent. Next show that the probable position of an atonal composition point after the lapse of a given time interval is a function quite similar to a Gaussian error curve.)

**8.42** Which will tend more to express a definite key, a long or a short atonal work?

## REFERENCES

[1] V. Persichetti, *Hymns and Responses for the Church Year* (Elkan-Vogel Co., Inc., Philadelphia, Pennsylvania, 1956)

[2] E. J. Budden, *The Fascination of Groups* (The University Press, Cambridge, 1972)

[3] Michael Kassler, *The Decision of Arnold Schoenberg's Twelve-Note-Class System and Related Systems* (Princeton University, Princeton, New Jersey, 1961)

[4] Michael Kassler, "Decision of a Musical System" *Communications of the Association for Computing Machinery* <u>5</u>, 4 (1962)

[5] Allen Forte, *SNOBOL 3 Primer: An Introduction to the Computer Programminig Language* (MIT Press, Cambridge, Massachusetts, 1967)

[6] Robert M. Besançon, Ed., *The Encyclopedia of Physics*, Third Edition (Van Nostrand, Reinhold Co., New York, 1985) p. 154.

[7] Henry Semat, *Introduction to Atomic and Nuclear Physics* (Holt, Rinehart, and Winston, New York, 1966) pp. 56-61.

[8] Ernst Křenek, *12 Short Piano Pieces Written in the Twelve-Tone Technique*, Op. 83 (G. Schirmer, Inc., New York, 1939)

[9] Ernst Křenek, *Studies in Counterpoint* (G. Schirmer, Inc., New York, 1940) p. 2.

PART II

# Chapter 9

# Mechanization

*Fifty million answers can't be wrong.*
*J. P. M.*

## AUTOMATED MUSIC ANALYSIS

The rudimentary problems of music analysis typically are concerned with harmony, counterpoint, and form, with the movement of melodic lines, and under some conditions, with background accompaniment. The essential task of elementary music analysis is to obtain principles relating the motion of the musical composition under scrutiny to the ultimate causes of this motion. The analyst always would like to be able to achieve an understanding of the separate mechanisms and special influences that must have been responsible for creating a given effect or impression. To try to do so, some guiding principles must be discovered that will enable the analyst to relate the composition at one point of time with itself at a later point of time, regardless of the many details of what happens in between. In some cases it still may not be entirely clear how a foregoing development is related to the denouement of a later passage.

Ideally, the musical score supplies all of the information that will be needed for computing the motion of the composition point, that is, for finding the resultant vector R as a function of time $\underline{t}$, which is the first step in the present system of computer-assisted tonal analysis. Bear in mind, however, that tonality is only one of several factors contributing to the esthetic perceptibility of a musical selection. Ultimately it is necessary to introduce corrections to the analysis to take into proper account the finer details. The exact nature of these corrections will be the responsibility of the analyst.

As explained earlier, the second step in the proposed scheme for computer analysis of music is to construct a displacement diagram or **trajectory**, making use of voice tracks where meaningful. Eventually, when the analysis of the musical selection has been completed and graphical outputs obtained for inspection, the tonalities employed by the composer may be observed to group themselves more or less closely into extended linear patterns. This tendency becomes readily visible if histograms are prepared. For successful music analysis by computers, the amount of information coming out of such displays must be sufficient for intelligent thinking or decision making, and readily accessible to the user through uncomplicated interfacing, yet filtered enough so that the user readily can grasp its musical significance.

These three requirements are reminiscent of what happens in the concert hall during a recital. No performer ever knows exactly what goes on in the listener's mind. Nor does a composer ever know precisely what an interpreting artist thinks. Perhaps learning theory may provide a reasonable conceptual framework for studying the triadic, aural, composer-performer-listener relationship. As suggested by Fig. 9.1, music appreciation is a subjective act that depends on many factors--the musical signal, the sender, the receiver, noise, the type of feedback scheme, and the nature and the amount of à priori information known to the participants. Composing, performing, listening, even analyzing, are intellectual pursuits for some people and educational pastimes for others. Each person in the loop is engaged in an iterative, self-organizing, data analysis procedure (see Fig. 9.2). The ear, acting as a data-gathering element or **transducer**, translates musical utterances, which occur externally, into a form meaningful to the auditory cortex. With some practice and ear-training the listener improves at sorting incoming sound into meaningful chunks, to the point that he or she can process mentally (in real time) and simplify musical data, carefully structured by the composer (off-line) and precisely delineated in a data-reconstruction process by the performer (at the console), with a minimal loss of information.

Figure 9.1

The listener viewed as a learning machine. In utilizing context, human perception depends upon past experience as well as collaterally channeled information.

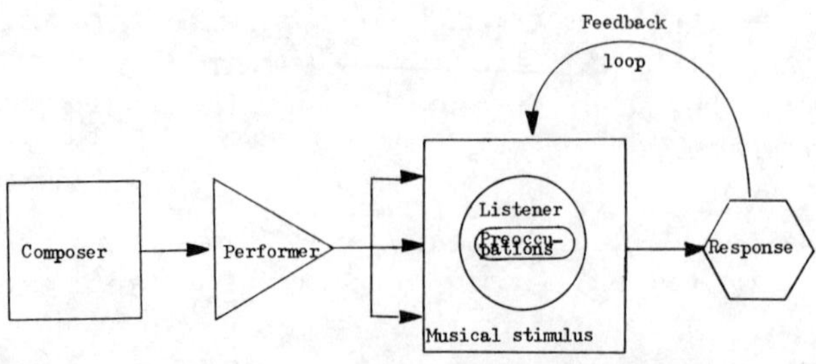


Unfortunately for the symphonic composer, there is no completely reliable method presently available by which to inform the members of the orchestra of how a new composition is to be rendered. If there were, there might be less need for studying music analysis and theory. Sometimes, however, an interpreter (for example, a conductor) actually can improve the composer's original concept of how the music should be performed. As indicated diagrammatically in Fig. 9.2, good analysis supports good performance; good performance improves audience understanding.

Figure 9.2

A schematic of the enlarged music analysis system.

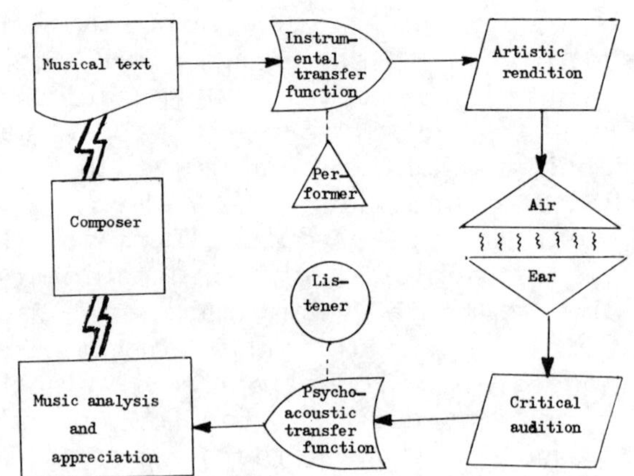


## LIFE HISTORIES

The graphical outputs that are produced by the methodology described in this book are intended to form the basis for further analysis. After the curves are plotted, many standard techniques may be applied. The graphs will help the musician to perceive the movement under study as a related whole and to organize the analytical approach to fit the situation. Characteristics of the composition trajectory can be studied statistically by treating the successive increments of the curve as a time series and applying Fourier methods to obtain time-averaged power spectra. As evidenced by the behavior of the composition point, a given piece of music may exhibit growth, development, evolution, progress, and most of all, a sense of direction. A piece of music is a tiny replica of a portion of the passing scenes and events of music history; indeed it is a time capsule capturing but a fleeting moment.

This computerized music analysis is based upon a blow-by-blow description, much like the oral commentary accompanying a slow motion, instant replay of a televised sports event. In a real sense, looking at one vertical component of a composition at a time is like viewing one frame of a motion picture film at a time. In effect, this means interrupting the performance, and taking a careful look at everthing at each time slice, before piecing all the segments back together. The life history of some compositions, viewed in slow motion, may mimic biological growth patterns. Initially the composition point experiences a period of deliberate motion, receives a certain impetus, then undergoes acceleration, and eventually slows down due to limiting factors affecting the growth rate. Finally, the musical phenomenon draws to a close as the composition trajectory asymptotically approaches some concluding direction.

The many computer printouts given in Fig. 9.3 and 9.4 are intended to provide a partial visualization of the total analytic potential of the computer methodology for music study presented here. The musical examples are taken from a book by Otterström [1].

The component listing provides a read-in check.

```
.00 68 3 78 68 0 1.000
01 4 3 78 68 0 1.000
02 2 19 5 49 0 1.000
03 7 3 7 6 0 1.000
04 78 3 2 6 0 1.000
05 78 3 48 1 0 1.000
06 58 58 48 1 0 1.000
07 5 3 2 68 0 1.000
08 78 38 2 68 0 1.000
09 78 1 78 48 0 1.000
10 39 6 7 29 0 1.000
11 3 69 7 299 0 1.000
12 19 19 7 49 0 1.000
13 199 6 59 29 0 1.000
14 39 49 39 7 0 1.000
15 19 49 39 7 0 1.000
16 1 68 58 2 0 1.000
17 38 48 38 78 0 1.000
18 48 48 1 58 0 1.000
19 68 78 68 38 0 1.000
20 48 78 68 38 0 1.000
21 28 58 48 1 0 1.000
22 78 78 48 38 0 1.000
23 58 28 1 58 0 1.000
24 38 48 38 78 0 1.000
25 1 68 58 2 0 1.000
26 3 68 58 2 0 1.000
27 3 4 3 7 0 1.000
28 2 68 3 2 0 1.000
29 2 1 7 4 0 1.000
30 2 3 2 68 0 1.000
31 2 19 5 4 0 1.000
32 7 3 7 4 0 1.000
33 78 19 2 6 0 1.000
34 5 1 2 6 0 1.000
35 78 1 78 4 0 1.000
36 1 1 5 2 0 1.000
37 6 5 2 1 0 1.000
38 4 5 4 1 0 1.000
39 4 5 2 1 0 1.000
40 4 3 7 19 0 1.000
41 4 3 7 3 0 1.000
42 29 3 5 19 0 1.000
43 29 3 5 6 0 1.000
44 4 19 5 29 0 1.000
45 19 19 5 4 0 1.000
46 6 19 5 6 0 1.000
47 4 19 5 19 0 1.000
48 48 38 78 1 0 1.000
49 48 38 78 6 0 1.000
50 2 1 5 1 0 1.000
51 2 1 5 68 0 1.000
52 78 1 78 2 0 1.000
53 78 1 78 48 0 1.000
54 5 48 1 2 0 1.000
55 5 48 1 78 0 1.000
56 39 2 6 7 0 1.000
57 39 2 6 2 0 1.000
58 5 2 1 4 0 1.000
59 5 2 1 2 0 1.000
60 4 4 1 78 0 1.000
61 4 68 38 78 0 1.000
62 2 68 1 78 0 1.000
63 78 4 1 78 0 1.000
64 68 68 3 78 0 4.000
```

OTTERSTROM ILLUSTRATION A

A

The devious path of the Illustration A trajectory suggests a connection with both the tonal and atonal regimes.

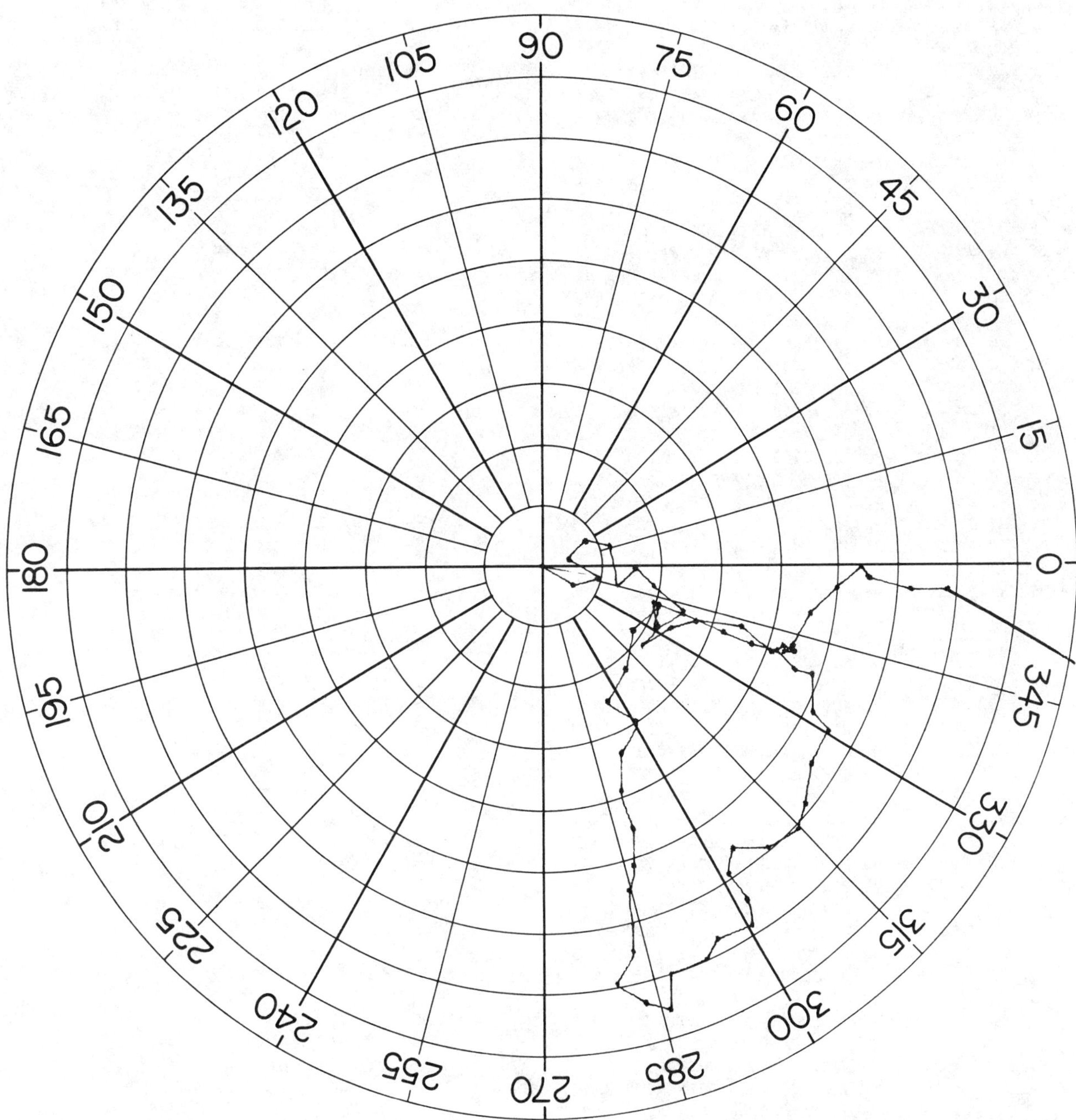

| | | | |
|---|---|---|---|
| 00 | 01.000 | 04 | 03 |
| 01 | 02.000 | 04 | 04 |
| 02 | 03.000 | 04 | 04 |
| 03 | 04.000 | 04 | 03 |
| 04 | 05.000 | 04 | 04 |
| 05 | 06.000 | 04 | 04 |
| 06 | 07.000 | 04 | 03 |
| 07 | 08.000 | 04 | 04 |
| 08 | 09.000 | 04 | 04 |
| 09 | 10.000 | 04 | 03 |
| 10 | 11.000 | 04 | 04 |
| 11 | 12.000 | 04 | 04 |
| 12 | 13.000 | 04 | 03 |
| 13 | 14.000 | 04 | 04 |
| 14 | 15.000 | 04 | 03 |
| 15 | 16.000 | 04 | 04 |
| 16 | 17.000 | 04 | 04 |
| 17 | 18.000 | 04 | 03 |
| 18 | 19.000 | 04 | 03 |
| 19 | 20.000 | 04 | 03 |
| 20 | 21.000 | 04 | 04 |
| 21 | 22.000 | 04 | 04 |
| 22 | 23.000 | 04 | 03 |
| 23 | 24.000 | 04 | 03 |
| 24 | 25.000 | 04 | 03 |
| 25 | 26.000 | 04 | 04 |
| 26 | 27.000 | 04 | 04 |
| 27 | 28.000 | 04 | 03 |
| 28 | 29.000 | 04 | 03 |
| 29 | 30.000 | 04 | 04 |
| 30 | 31.000 | 04 | 03 |
| 31 | 32.000 | 04 | 04 |
| 32 | 33.000 | 04 | 03 |
| 33 | 34.000 | 04 | 04 |
| 34 | 35.000 | 04 | 04 |
| 35 | 36.000 | 04 | 03 |
| 36 | 37.000 | 04 | 03 |
| 37 | 38.000 | 04 | 04 |
| 38 | 39.000 | 04 | 03 |
| 39 | 40.000 | 04 | 04 |
| 40 | 41.000 | 04 | 04 |
| 41 | 42.000 | 04 | 03 |
| 42 | 43.000 | 04 | 04 |
| 43 | 44.000 | 04 | 04 |
| 44 | 45.000 | 04 | 04 |
| 45 | 46.000 | 04 | 03 |
| 46 | 47.000 | 04 | 03 |
| 47 | 48.000 | 04 | 03 |
| 48 | 49.000 | 04 | 04 |
| 49 | 50.000 | 04 | 04 |
| 50 | 51.000 | 04 | 03 |
| 51 | 52.000 | 04 | 04 |
| 52 | 53.000 | 04 | 03 |
| 53 | 54.000 | 04 | 03 |
| 54 | 55.000 | 04 | 04 |
| 55 | 56.000 | 04 | 04 |
| 56 | 57.000 | 04 | 04 |
| 57 | 58.000 | 04 | 03 |
| 58 | 59.000 | 04 | 04 |
| 59 | 60.000 | 04 | 03 |
| 60 | 61.000 | 04 | 03 |
| 61 | 62.000 | 04 | 04 |
| 62 | 63.000 | 04 | 04 |
| 63 | 64.000 | 04 | 03 |
| 64 | 68.000 | 04 | 03 |

| | | | |
|---|---|---|---|
| 00 | 000004197380 | 0019X1024 | 3076 |
| 01 | 000000003004 | 0051X1024 | 3004 |
| 02 | 000000001170 | 0505X1024 | 1170 |
| 03 | 000000262244 | 0025X0004 | 0100 |
| 04 | 000000002086 | 0077X2048 | 2086 |
| 05 | 000000002309 | 0089X0256 | 2309 |
| 06 | 000002097921 | 0019X0256 | 0769 |
| 07 | 000000001046 | 0089X1024 | 1046 |
| 08 | 000000003202 | 0089X0128 | 3202 |
| 09 | 000008390913 | 0025X0256 | 2305 |
| 10 | 000000000864 | 0027X0032 | 0864 |
| 11 | 000000000077 | 0077X0001 | 0077 |
| 12 | 000000525504 | 0019X0064 | 1216 |
| 13 | 000000002340 | 0585X2048 | 2340 |
| 14 | 000002098752 | 0025X0064 | 1600 |
| 15 | 000000001728 | 0027X0064 | 1728 |
| 16 | 000000001539 | 0027X0512 | 1539 |
| 17 | 000000526720 | 0019X0128 | 2432 |
| 18 | 000001049345 | 0019X0256 | 0769 |
| 19 | 000004197504 | 0025X0128 | 3200 |
| 20 | 000000003456 | 0027X0128 | 3456 |
| 21 | 000000000833 | 0077X0064 | 0833 |
| 22 | 000008391040 | 0019X0128 | 2432 |
| 23 | 000002097729 | 0073X0064 | 0577 |
| 24 | 000000526720 | 0019X0128 | 2432 |
| 25 | 000000001539 | 0027X0512 | 1539 |
| 26 | 000000001542 | 0051X0512 | 1542 |
| 27 | 000000016460 | 0019X0004 | 0076 |
| 28 | 000000009222 | 0025X1024 | 1030 |
| 29 | 000000000075 | 0075X0001 | 0075 |
| 30 | 000000009222 | 0025X1024 | 1030 |
| 31 | 000000000154 | 0077X0002 | 0154 |
| 32 | 000000262220 | 0019X0004 | 0076 |
| 33 | 000000002210 | 0325X2048 | 2210 |
| 34 | 000000000051 | 0051X0001 | 0051 |
| 35 | 000008390665 | 0019X2048 | 2057 |
| 36 | 000000004115 | 0019X0001 | 0019 |
| 37 | 000000000051 | 0051X0001 | 0051 |
| 38 | 000000032793 | 0025X0001 | 0025 |
| 39 | 000000000027 | 0027X0001 | 0027 |
| 40 | 000000000204 | 0051X0004 | 0204 |
| 41 | 000000016460 | 0019X0004 | 0076 |
| 42 | 000000000404 | 0101X0004 | 0404 |
| 43 | 000000000308 | 0077X0004 | 0308 |
| 44 | 000000000408 | 0051X0008 | 0408 |
| 45 | 000000524440 | 0019X0008 | 0152 |
| 46 | 000000131248 | 0011X0016 | 0176 |
| 47 | 000000524440 | 0019X0008 | 0152 |
| 48 | 000000002433 | 0051X0128 | 2433 |
| 49 | 000000002464 | 0077X0032 | 2464 |
| 50 | 000000004115 | 0019X0001 | 0019 |
| 51 | 000000001043 | 0077X1024 | 1043 |
| 52 | 000008390659 | 0007X2048 | 2051 |
| 53 | 000008390913 | 0025X0256 | 2305 |
| 54 | 000000000275 | 0275X0001 | 0275 |
| 55 | 000000002321 | 0281X0256 | 2321 |
| 56 | 000000000610 | 0275X0032 | 0610 |
| 57 | 000000008738 | 0273X0512 | 0545 |
| 58 | 000000000027 | 0027X0001 | 0027 |
| 59 | 000000000211 | 0019X0001 | 0019 |
| 60 | 000000034825 | 0019X2048 | 2057 |
| 61 | 000000003208 | 0281X0128 | 3208 |
| 62 | 000000003075 | 0015X1024 | 3075 |
| 63 | 000008390665 | 0019X2048 | 2057 |
| 64 | 000004197380 | 0019X1024 | 3076 |

A table combining amplitude and phase angle with distance and direction gives immediate knowledge of tonality and key.

| | | | | |
|---|---|---|---|---|
| 00 | 2.732 | -030.000 | 002.732 | -031.000 |
| 01 | 1.932 | 015.000 | 004.320 | -011.565 |
| 02 | 0.000 | -012.043 | 004.320 | -011.565 |
| 03 | 2.732 | 150.000 | 001.932 | 015.000 |
| 04 | 1.932 | 045.000 | 003.732 | 030.000 |
| 05 | 1.932 | -015.000 | 005.279 | 015.000 |
| 06 | 2.909 | -040.104 | 005.796 | -015.000 |
| 07 | 1.932 | 045.000 | 006.965 | -001.102 |
| 08 | 1.932 | -045.000 | 008.464 | -010.200 |
| 09 | 2.909 | -039.896 | 011.086 | -017.676 |
| 10 | 2.732 | -150.000 | 005.464 | -030.000 |
| 11 | 1.932 | 075.000 | 005.156 | -010.241 |
| 12 | 2.909 | -140.104 | 000.011 | -035.206 |
| 13 | 0.000 | -162.645 | 000.011 | -036.206 |
| 14 | 2.909 | -039.056 | 005.659 | -051.870 |
| 15 | 2.732 | -120.000 | 010.574 | -055.220 |
| 16 | 2.732 | -030.000 | 013.299 | -058.423 |
| 17 | 2.732 | -120.000 | 014.795 | -057.769 |
| 18 | 2.732 | -090.000 | 017.356 | -071.193 |
| 19 | 2.909 | -050.096 | 020.264 | -070.059 |
| 20 | 2.732 | -090.000 | 022.865 | -073.229 |
| 21 | 1.932 | -105.000 | 024.529 | -075.605 |
| 22 | 2.394 | -081.206 | 025.912 | -076.102 |
| 23 | 2.000 | -090.000 | 026.859 | -077.056 |
| 24 | 2.732 | -120.000 | 030.914 | -080.509 |
| 25 | 2.732 | -030.000 | 032.715 | -076.613 |
| 26 | 1.932 | -015.000 | 033.575 | -073.915 |
| 27 | 2.732 | 050.000 | 031.059 | -072.518 |
| 28 | 2.909 | 020.104 | 031.862 | -067.152 |
| 29 | 1.732 | 060.000 | 030.040 | -064.516 |
| 30 | 2.909 | 020.104 | 030.459 | -059.059 |
| 31 | 1.932 | 105.000 | 029.556 | -057.997 |
| 32 | 2.394 | 120.794 | 026.230 | -050.515 |
| 33 | 0.000 | -051.710 | 026.230 | -050.615 |
| 34 | 1.932 | 075.000 | 024.537 | -055.400 |
| 35 | 2.732 | 000.000 | 025.563 | -050.547 |
| 36 | 2.732 | 030.000 | 027.166 | -044.854 |
| 37 | 1.932 | 075.000 | 026.250 | -041.195 |
| 38 | 2.909 | 060.104 | 024.071 | -035.459 |
| 39 | 2.732 | 060.000 | 024.761 | -025.153 |
| 40 | 1.932 | 135.000 | 022.509 | -027.834 |
| 41 | 2.732 | 050.000 | 021.758 | -021.461 |
| 42 | 1.414 | 165.000 | 020.353 | -021.909 |
| 43 | 1.932 | 135.000 | 018.601 | -019.575 |
| 44 | 1.932 | 165.000 | 016.575 | -020.104 |
| 45 | 2.394 | 150.794 | 014.233 | -015.919 |
| 46 | 3.356 | 156.206 | 010.507 | -010.717 |
| 47 | 2.394 | 150.794 | 008.515 | -010.018 |
| 48 | 1.932 | -075.000 | 005.704 | -007.526 |
| 49 | 1.932 | -135.000 | 009.312 | -019.045 |
| 50 | 2.732 | 030.000 | 010.601 | -025.115 |
| 51 | 1.932 | 015.000 | 012.142 | -017.235 |
| 52 | 3.633 | -007.911 | 015.720 | -016.634 |
| 53 | 2.909 | -019.096 | 018.429 | -020.209 |
| 54 | 1.000 | 030.000 | 015.004 | -017.901 |
| 55 | 1.000 | -030.000 | 020.063 | -018.500 |
| 56 | 1.000 | 150.000 | 019.117 | -019.451 |
| 57 | 1.000 | 030.000 | 019.782 | -017.249 |
| 58 | 2.732 | 060.000 | 020.556 | -009.802 |
| 59 | 2.909 | 030.896 | 022.550 | -004.155 |
| 60 | 2.394 | 030.794 | 024.357 | -000.315 |
| 61 | 1.000 | -060.000 | 024.077 | -002.304 |
| 62 | 3.346 | -015.000 | 026.150 | -003.801 |
| 63 | 2.732 | 000.000 | 030.377 | -003.465 |
| 64 | 2.732 | -030.000 | 040.945 | -010.313 |

The absolute key penetration function has undulating edges.

| N | Gb | eb | Db | Bb | Ab | f | Eb | c | Bb | g | F | d | C | a | f# | E | c# | B | g# | F# |
|---|---|---|---|---|---|---|---|---|---|---|---|---|---|---|---|---|---|---|---|---|
| 00 | 01 | 02 | 03 | 04 | 04 | 04 | 03 | 02 | 01 | -01 | -99 | | | | | | | | -01 | 01 |
| 01 | -00 | 02 | 04 | 05 | 06 | 06 | 06 | 05 | 05 | 03 | 01 | -05 | | | | | | | | -00 |
| 02 | -00 | 02 | 04 | 05 | 06 | 06 | 06 | 05 | 05 | 03 | 01 | -05 | | | | | | | | -00 |
| 03 | | -97 | -03 | -00 | 01 | 02 | 02 | 02 | 02 | 02 | 01 | -00 | -03 | | | | | | | |
| 04 | | | -94 | -00 | 02 | 04 | 05 | 05 | 05 | 05 | 05 | 04 | 02 | -00 | | | | | | |
| 05 | | -94 | 01 | 04 | 05 | 06 | 07 | 07 | 07 | 06 | 05 | 04 | 01 | | | | | | | |
| 06 | 01 | 04 | 06 | 07 | 07 | 07 | 07 | 07 | 06 | 04 | 01 | | | | | | | | -97 | 01 |
| 07 | -08 | 02 | 05 | 07 | 07 | 08 | 08 | 08 | 07 | 06 | 05 | 02 | | | | | | | | -08 |
| 08 | 01 | 05 | 07 | 08 | 09 | 09 | 09 | 08 | 08 | 06 | 04 | -01 | | | | | | | | 01 |
| 09 | 05 | 07 | 09 | 09 | 10 | 10 | 10 | 09 | 08 | 07 | 03 | | | | | | | | -02 | 05 |
| 10 | 06 | 08 | 09 | 09 | 09 | 09 | 09 | 08 | 06 | 03 | | | | | | | | -95 | 03 | 06 |
| 11 | 04 | 07 | 08 | 09 | 09 | 09 | 09 | 08 | 07 | 06 | 02 | | | | | | | | -02 | 04 |
| 12 | 06 | 07 | 08 | 08 | 09 | 08 | 08 | 07 | 05 | 00 | | | | | | | | -00 | 04 | 06 |
| 13 | 06 | 07 | 08 | 08 | 09 | 08 | 08 | 07 | 05 | 00 | | | | | | | | -00 | 04 | 06 |
| 14 | 08 | 09 | 09 | 09 | 09 | 08 | 07 | 05 | 01 | | | | | | | | 00 | 05 | 07 | 08 |
| 15 | 09 | 10 | 10 | 10 | 09 | 08 | 06 | 02 | | | | | | | | 00 | 05 | 08 | 09 | 09 |
| 16 | 10 | 11 | 11 | 11 | 10 | 09 | 08 | 05 | -04 | | | | | | | | 04 | 08 | 09 | 10 |
| 17 | 11 | 11 | 11 | 11 | 10 | 09 | 07 | 02 | | | | | | | | 03 | 07 | 09 | 10 | 11 |
| 18 | 12 | 12 | 12 | 11 | 11 | 09 | 07 | 00 | | | | | | | | 05 | 08 | 10 | 11 | 12 |
| 19 | 12 | 13 | 12 | 12 | 11 | 10 | 08 | 01 | | | | | | | | 05 | 09 | 11 | 12 | 12 |
| 20 | 13 | 13 | 13 | 13 | 12 | 10 | 08 | -01 | | | | | | | | 07 | 10 | 11 | 12 | 13 |
| 21 | 13 | 13 | 13 | 13 | 12 | 10 | 07 | | | | | | | | -05 | 08 | 10 | 12 | 13 | 13 |
| 22 | 14 | 14 | 14 | 13 | 12 | 11 | 08 | | | | | | | | -02 | 08 | 11 | 12 | 13 | 14 |
| 23 | 14 | 14 | 14 | 13 | 12 | 11 | 08 | | | | | | | | 00 | 09 | 11 | 13 | 14 | 14 |
| 24 | 14 | 14 | 14 | 14 | 12 | 11 | 07 | | | | | | | | 04 | 10 | 12 | 13 | 14 | 14 |
| 25 | 15 | 15 | 14 | 14 | 13 | 11 | 08 | | | | | | | | 00 | 09 | 12 | 13 | 14 | 15 |
| 26 | 15 | 15 | 15 | 14 | 13 | 12 | 09 | -01 | | | | | | | | 09 | 12 | 13 | 14 | 15 |
| 27 | 14 | 14 | 14 | 14 | 13 | 12 | 09 | 01 | | | | | | | | 08 | 11 | 13 | 14 | 14 |
| 28 | 14 | 14 | 14 | 14 | 13 | 12 | 10 | 06 | | | | | | | | 05 | 10 | 12 | 13 | 14 |
| 29 | 14 | 14 | 14 | 14 | 13 | 12 | 11 | 07 | | | | | | | | 03 | 10 | 12 | 13 | 14 |
| 30 | 14 | 14 | 14 | 14 | 14 | 13 | 11 | 09 | -03 | | | | | | | | 08 | 11 | 13 | 14 |
| 31 | 13 | 14 | 14 | 14 | 14 | 13 | 11 | 09 | 00 | | | | | | | | 08 | 11 | 12 | 13 |
| 32 | 13 | 14 | 14 | 14 | 13 | 12 | 11 | 08 | -01 | | | | | | | | 07 | 10 | 12 | 13 |
| 33 | 13 | 14 | 14 | 14 | 13 | 12 | 11 | 08 | -01 | | | | | | | | 07 | 10 | 12 | 13 |
| 34 | 13 | 13 | 13 | 13 | 13 | 12 | 11 | 09 | 03 | | | | | | | | 06 | 10 | 12 | 13 |
| 35 | 13 | 13 | 14 | 14 | 13 | 13 | 12 | 10 | 06 | | | | | | | | 04 | 09 | 11 | 13 |
| 36 | 12 | 13 | 14 | 14 | 14 | 13 | 12 | 11 | 08 | -11 | | | | | | | | 08 | 11 | 12 |
| 37 | 12 | 13 | 13 | 14 | 14 | 13 | 12 | 11 | 09 | 02 | | | | | | | | 07 | 10 | 12 |
| 38 | 11 | 12 | 13 | 13 | 13 | 13 | 13 | 12 | 10 | 06 | | | | | | | | 03 | 09 | 11 |
| 39 | 10 | 12 | 13 | 13 | 13 | 13 | 13 | 12 | 11 | 08 | -04 | | | | | | | | 07 | 10 |
| 40 | 10 | 11 | 12 | 13 | 13 | 13 | 13 | 12 | 10 | 08 | -00 | | | | | | | | 07 | 10 |
| 41 | 09 | 11 | 12 | 13 | 13 | 13 | 13 | 12 | 11 | 09 | 05 | | | | | | | | 03 | 09 |
| 42 | 08 | 10 | 12 | 12 | 13 | 13 | 12 | 12 | 10 | 09 | 04 | | | | | | | | 03 | 08 |
| 43 | 07 | 10 | 11 | 12 | 12 | 12 | 12 | 11 | 10 | 09 | 05 | | | | | | | | 01 | 07 |
| 44 | 07 | 09 | 11 | 11 | 12 | 12 | 11 | 11 | 10 | 08 | 04 | | | | | | | | 01 | 07 |
| 45 | 06 | 09 | 10 | 11 | 11 | 11 | 11 | 10 | 09 | 07 | 03 | | | | | | | | 00 | 06 |
| 46 | 05 | 07 | 09 | 09 | 10 | 10 | 10 | 09 | 08 | 06 | 03 | | | | | | | | -01 | 05 |
| 47 | 04 | 06 | 08 | 08 | 09 | 09 | 09 | 08 | 07 | 05 | 02 | | | | | | | | -03 | 04 |
| 48 | 06 | 08 | 09 | 09 | 09 | 09 | 09 | 08 | 07 | 04 | -03 | | | | | | | | 03 | 06 |
| 49 | 07 | 08 | 09 | 09 | 09 | 09 | 08 | 07 | 05 | -00 | | | | | | | | 01 | 05 | 07 |
| 50 | 06 | 08 | 09 | 09 | 10 | 10 | 09 | 09 | 07 | 05 | -00 | | | | | | | | 02 | 06 |
| 51 | 06 | 08 | 09 | 10 | 10 | 10 | 10 | 10 | 08 | 07 | 03 | | | | | | | | -00 | 06 |
| 52 | 06 | 09 | 10 | 11 | 11 | 11 | 11 | 11 | 10 | 08 | 05 | | | | | | | | -03 | 06 |
| 53 | 08 | 10 | 11 | 12 | 12 | 12 | 12 | 11 | 10 | 08 | 04 | | | | | | | | 02 | 08 |
| 54 | 07 | 10 | 11 | 12 | 12 | 12 | 12 | 12 | 11 | 09 | 06 | | | | | | | | -00 | 07 |
| 55 | 08 | 10 | 11 | 12 | 12 | 13 | 12 | 12 | 11 | 09 | 06 | | | | | | | | 00 | 08 |
| 56 | 08 | 10 | 11 | 12 | 12 | 12 | 12 | 11 | 10 | 09 | 05 | | | | | | | | 01 | 08 |
| 57 | 07 | 10 | 11 | 12 | 12 | 12 | 12 | 12 | 11 | 09 | 06 | | | | | | | | -01 | 07 |
| 58 | 05 | 09 | 11 | 12 | 12 | 13 | 13 | 12 | 11 | 10 | 08 | 02 | | | | | | | | 05 |
| 59 | 02 | 08 | 11 | 12 | 13 | 13 | 13 | 13 | 12 | 11 | 09 | 06 | | | | | | | | 02 |
| 60 | -08 | 08 | 10 | 12 | 13 | 13 | 13 | 13 | 13 | 12 | 10 | 07 | | | | | | | | -08 |
| 61 | 00 | 08 | 11 | 12 | 13 | 13 | 13 | 13 | 13 | 12 | 10 | 07 | | | | | | | | 00 |
| 62 | 02 | 09 | 11 | 13 | 14 | 14 | 14 | 14 | 13 | 12 | 10 | 07 | | | | | | | | 02 |
| 63 | 02 | 09 | 12 | 13 | 14 | 14 | 14 | 14 | 14 | 13 | 11 | 07 | | | | | | | | 02 |
| 64 | 08 | 12 | 14 | 15 | 15 | 16 | 16 | 15 | 14 | 13 | 11 | 05 | | | | | | | | 08 |

Hand-drawn contours of constant α bring prominence to the relief.

| N | Gb | eb | Db | bb | Ab | f | Eb | c | Bb | g | F | d | C | a | f# | E | c# | B | g# | F# |
|---|---|---|---|---|---|---|---|---|---|---|---|---|---|---|---|---|---|---|---|---|
| 00 | 01 | 02 | 03 | 04 | 04 | 04 | 03 | 02 | 01 | -01 | -99 | | | | | | | | -01 | 01 |
| 01 | -00 | 02 | 04 | 05 | 06 | 06 | 06 | 05 | 05 | 03 | 01 | -05 | | | | | | | | -00 |
| 02 | -00 | 02 | 04 | 05 | 06 | 06 | 06 | 05 | 05 | 03 | 01 | -05 | | | | | | | | -00 |
| 03 | | -97 | -03 | -00 | 01 | 02 | 02 | 02 | 02 | 02 | 01 | -00 | -03 | | | | | | | |
| 04 | | | -94 | -00 | 02 | 04 | 05 | 05 | 05 | 05 | 05 | 04 | 02 | -00 | | | | | | |
| 05 | | -94 | 01 | 04 | 05 | 06 | 07 | 07 | 07 | 06 | 05 | 04 | 01 | | | | | | | |
| 06 | 01 | 04 | 06 | 07 | 07 | 07 | 07 | 07 | 06 | 04 | 01 | | | | | | | | -97 | 01 |
| 07 | -08 | 02 | 05 | 07 | 07 | 07 | 08 | 08 | 07 | 06 | 05 | 02 | | | | | | | | -08 |
| 08 | 01 | 05 | 07 | 08 | 09 | 09 | 09 | 08 | 08 | 06 | 04 | -01 | | | | | | | | 01 |
| 09 | 05 | 07 | 09 | 09 | 10 | 10 | 10 | 09 | 08 | 07 | 03 | | | | | | | | -02 | 05 |
| 10 | 06 | 08 | 09 | 09 | 09 | 09 | 09 | 08 | 06 | 03 | | | | | | | | -95 | 03 | 06 |
| 11 | 04 | 07 | 08 | 09 | 09 | 09 | 09 | 08 | 07 | 06 | 02 | | | | | | | | -02 | 04 |
| 12 | 06 | 07 | 08 | 08 | 09 | 08 | 08 | 07 | 05 | 00 | | | | | | | | -00 | 04 | 06 |
| 13 | 06 | 07 | 08 | 08 | 09 | 08 | 08 | 07 | 05 | 00 | | | | | | | | -00 | 04 | 06 |
| 14 | 08 | 09 | 09 | 09 | 09 | 08 | 07 | 05 | 01 | | | | | | | | 00 | 05 | 07 | 08 |
| 15 | 09 | 10 | 10 | 10 | 09 | 08 | 06 | 02 | | | | | | | | 00 | 05 | 08 | 09 | 09 |
| 16 | 10 | 11 | 11 | 11 | 10 | 09 | 08 | 05 | -04 | | | | | | | | 04 | 08 | 09 | 10 |
| 17 | 11 | 11 | 11 | 11 | 10 | 09 | 07 | 02 | | | | | | | | 03 | 07 | 09 | 10 | 11 |
| 18 | 12 | 12 | 12 | 11 | 11 | 09 | 07 | 00 | | | | | | | | 05 | 08 | 10 | 11 | 12 |
| 19 | 12 | 13 | 12 | 12 | 11 | 10 | 08 | 01 | | | | | | | | 05 | 09 | 11 | 12 | 12 |
| 20 | 13 | 13 | 13 | 13 | 12 | 10 | 08 | -01 | | | | | | | | 07 | 10 | 11 | 12 | 13 |
| 21 | 13 | 13 | 13 | 13 | 12 | 10 | 07 | | | | | | | | -05 | 08 | 10 | 12 | 13 | 13 |
| 22 | 14 | 14 | 14 | 13 | 12 | 11 | 08 | | | | | | | | -02 | 08 | 11 | 12 | 13 | 14 |
| 23 | 14 | 14 | 14 | 13 | 12 | 11 | 08 | | | | | | | | 00 | 09 | 11 | 13 | 14 | 14 |
| 24 | 14 | 14 | 14 | 14 | 12 | 11 | 07 | | | | | | | | 04 | 10 | 12 | 13 | 14 | 14 |
| 25 | 15 | 15 | 14 | 14 | 13 | 11 | 08 | | | | | | | | 00 | 09 | 12 | 13 | 14 | 15 |
| 26 | 15 | 15 | 15 | 14 | 13 | 12 | 09 | -01 | | | | | | | | 09 | 12 | 13 | 14 | 15 |
| 27 | 14 | 14 | 14 | 14 | 13 | 12 | 09 | 01 | | | | | | | | 08 | 11 | 13 | 14 | 14 |
| 28 | 14 | 14 | 14 | 14 | 13 | 12 | 10 | 06 | | | | | | | | 05 | 10 | 12 | 13 | 14 |
| 29 | 14 | 14 | 14 | 14 | 13 | 12 | 11 | 07 | | | | | | | | 03 | 10 | 12 | 13 | 14 |
| 30 | 14 | 14 | 14 | 14 | 14 | 13 | 11 | 09 | -03 | | | | | | | | 08 | 11 | 13 | 14 |
| 31 | 13 | 14 | 14 | 14 | 14 | 13 | 11 | 09 | 00 | | | | | | | | 08 | 11 | 12 | 13 |
| 32 | 13 | 14 | 14 | 14 | 13 | 12 | 11 | 08 | -01 | | | | | | | | 07 | 10 | 12 | 13 |
| 33 | 13 | 14 | 14 | 14 | 13 | 12 | 11 | 08 | -01 | | | | | | | | 07 | 10 | 12 | 13 |
| 34 | 13 | 13 | 13 | 13 | 13 | 12 | 11 | 09 | 03 | | | | | | | | 06 | 10 | 12 | 13 |
| 35 | 13 | 13 | 14 | 14 | 13 | 13 | 12 | 10 | 06 | | | | | | | | 04 | 09 | 11 | 13 |
| 36 | 12 | 13 | 14 | 14 | 14 | 13 | 12 | 11 | 08 | -11 | | | | | | | | 08 | 11 | 12 |
| 37 | 12 | 13 | 13 | 14 | 14 | 13 | 12 | 11 | 09 | 02 | | | | | | | | 07 | 10 | 12 |
| 38 | 11 | 12 | 13 | 13 | 13 | 13 | 13 | 12 | 10 | 06 | | | | | | | | 03 | 09 | 11 |
| 39 | 10 | 12 | 13 | 13 | 13 | 13 | 13 | 12 | 11 | 08 | -04 | | | | | | | | 07 | 10 |
| 40 | 10 | 11 | 12 | 13 | 13 | 13 | 13 | 12 | 10 | 08 | -00 | | | | | | | | 07 | 10 |
| 41 | 09 | 11 | 12 | 13 | 13 | 13 | 13 | 12 | 11 | 09 | 05 | | | | | | | | 03 | 09 |
| 42 | 08 | 10 | 12 | 12 | 13 | 13 | 12 | 12 | 10 | 09 | 04 | | | | | | | | 03 | 08 |
| 43 | 07 | 10 | 11 | 12 | 12 | 12 | 12 | 11 | 10 | 09 | 05 | | | | | | | | 01 | 07 |
| 44 | 07 | 09 | 11 | 11 | 12 | 12 | 11 | 11 | 10 | 08 | 04 | | | | | | | | 01 | 07 |
| 45 | 06 | 09 | 10 | 11 | 11 | 11 | 11 | 10 | 09 | 07 | 03 | | | | | | | | 00 | 06 |
| 46 | 05 | 07 | 09 | 09 | 10 | 10 | 10 | 09 | 08 | 06 | 03 | | | | | | | | -01 | 05 |
| 47 | 04 | 06 | 08 | 08 | 09 | 09 | 09 | 08 | 07 | 05 | 02 | | | | | | | | -03 | 04 |
| 48 | 06 | 08 | 09 | 09 | 09 | 09 | 09 | 08 | 07 | 04 | -03 | | | | | | | | 03 | 06 |
| 49 | 07 | 08 | 09 | 09 | 09 | 09 | 08 | 07 | 05 | -00 | | | | | | | | 01 | 05 | 07 |
| 50 | 06 | 08 | 09 | 09 | 10 | 10 | 09 | 09 | 07 | 05 | -00 | | | | | | | | 02 | 06 |
| 51 | 06 | 08 | 09 | 10 | 10 | 10 | 10 | 10 | 08 | 07 | 03 | | | | | | | | -00 | 06 |
| 52 | 06 | 09 | 10 | 11 | 11 | 11 | 11 | 11 | 10 | 08 | 05 | | | | | | | | -03 | 06 |
| 53 | 08 | 10 | 11 | 12 | 12 | 12 | 12 | 11 | 10 | 08 | 04 | | | | | | | | 02 | 08 |
| 54 | 07 | 10 | 11 | 12 | 12 | 12 | 12 | 12 | 11 | 09 | 06 | | | | | | | | -00 | 07 |
| 55 | 08 | 10 | 11 | 12 | 12 | 13 | 12 | 12 | 11 | 09 | 06 | | | | | | | | 00 | 08 |
| 56 | 08 | 10 | 11 | 12 | 12 | 12 | 12 | 11 | 10 | 09 | 05 | | | | | | | | 01 | 08 |
| 57 | 07 | 10 | 11 | 12 | 12 | 12 | 12 | 12 | 11 | 09 | 06 | | | | | | | | -01 | 07 |
| 58 | 05 | 09 | 11 | 12 | 12 | 13 | 13 | 12 | 11 | 10 | 08 | 02 | | | | | | | | 05 |
| 59 | 02 | 08 | 11 | 12 | 13 | 13 | 13 | 13 | 12 | 11 | 09 | 06 | | | | | | | | 02 |
| 60 | -08 | 08 | 10 | 12 | 13 | 13 | 13 | 13 | 13 | 12 | 10 | 07 | | | | | | | | -08 |
| 61 | 00 | 08 | 11 | 12 | 13 | 13 | 13 | 13 | 13 | 12 | 10 | 07 | | | | | | | | 00 |
| 62 | 02 | 09 | 11 | 13 | 14 | 14 | 14 | 14 | 13 | 12 | 10 | 07 | | | | | | | | 02 |
| 63 | 02 | 09 | 12 | 13 | 14 | 14 | 14 | 14 | 14 | 13 | 11 | 07 | | | | | | | | 02 |
| 64 | 08 | 12 | 14 | 15 | 15 | 16 | 16 | 15 | 14 | 13 | 11 | 05 | | | | | | | | 08 |

There is an infeasible notation in the phonetic listing.

```
N
00 E♭ G B♭ E♭        05
01 D G B♭ E♭         06
02 C F♯ A D♯         10
03 B G B E           05
04 B♭ G C E          07
05 B♭ G D♭ F         07
06 A♭ A♭ D♭ F        05
07 A G C E♭          07
08 B♭ G♭ C E♭        07
09 B♭ F B♭ D♭        05
10 G♯ E B C♯         05
11 G E♯ B Cx         14
12 F♯ F♯ B D♯        05
13 Fx E A♯ C♯        10
14 G♯ D♯ G♯ B        05
15 F♯ D♯ G♯ B        05
16 F E♭ A♭ C         05
17 G♭ D♭ G♭ B♭       05
18 D♭ D♭ F A♭        05
19 E♭ B♭ E♭ G        05
20 D♭ B♭ E♭ G♭       05
21 C♭ A♭ D♭ F        07
22 B♭ B♭ D G         05
23 A♭ C♭ F A♭        07
24 G♭ D♭ G♭ B♭       05
25 F E♭ A♭ C         05
26 G E♭ A♭ C         06
27 G D G B           05
28 C E♭ G C          05
29 C F B D           07
30 C G C E♭          05
31 C F♯ A D          07
32 B G B D           05
33 B♭ F♯ C E         09
34 A F C E           06
35 B♭ F B♭ D         05
36 F F A C           05
37 E A C F           06
38 D A D F           05
39 D A C F           05
40 D G B F♯          06
41 D G B G           05
42 C♯ G A F♯         07
43 C♯ G A E          07
44 D F♯ A C♯         06
45 F♯ F♯ A D         05
46 E F♯ A E          04
47 D F♯ A F♯         05
48 D♭ G♭ B♭ F        06
49 D♭ G♭ B♭ E        11
50 C F A F           05
51 C F A E♭          07
52 B♭ F B♭ C         03
53 B♭ F B♭ D♭        05
54 A D♭ F C          09
55 A D♭ F B♭         09
56 G♯ C E B          09
57 G♯ C E C          09
58 A C F D           05
59 A C F C           05
60 D D F B♭          05
61 D E♭ G♭ B♭        09
62 C E♭ F B♭         04
63 B♭ D F B♭         05
64 D♭ D♭ F B♭        05
```

A historical development of the absolute penetration function along major key axis projections. To interpret these curves, it is necessary to relate them one by one to the columns corresponding to major keys in the printout on the previous page.

..............................................................................

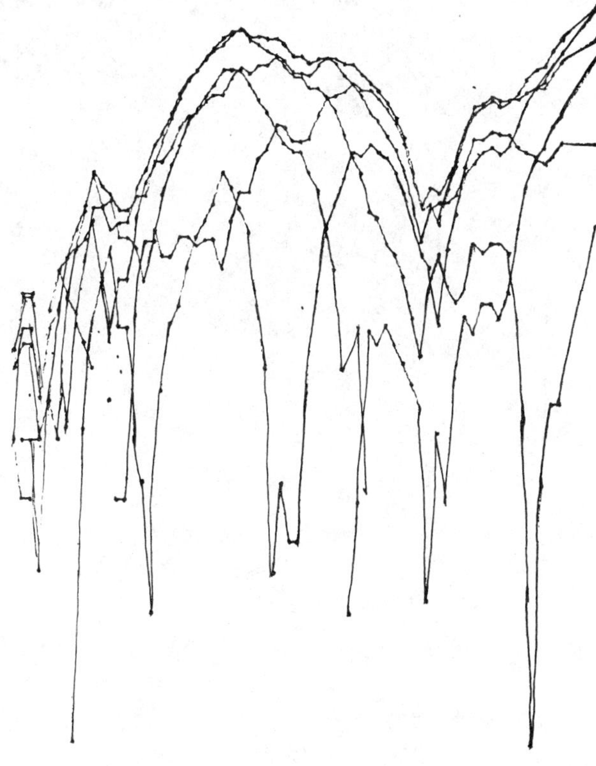

| | | | | | |
|---|---|---|---|---|---|
| 00 | 03.732 | 22 | 02.866 | 44 | 01.866 |
| 01 | 01.866 | 23 | 02.000 | 45 | 02.866 |
| 02 | 00.000 | 24 | 03.732 | 46 | 05.732 |
| 03 | 03.732 | 25 | 03.732 | 47 | 02.866 |
| 04 | 01.866 | 26 | 01.866 | 48 | 01.866 |
| 05 | 01.866 | 27 | 03.732 | 49 | 01.866 |
| 06 | 04.232 | 28 | 04.232 | 50 | 03.732 |
| 07 | 01.866 | 29 | 01.500 | 51 | 01.866 |
| 08 | 01.866 | 30 | 04.232 | 52 | 06.598 |
| 09 | 04.232 | 31 | 01.866 | 53 | 04.232 |
| 10 | 03.732 | 32 | 02.866 | 54 | 00.500 |
| 11 | 01.866 | 33 | 00.000 | 55 | 00.500 |
| 12 | 04.232 | 34 | 01.866 | 56 | 00.500 |
| 13 | 00.000 | 35 | 03.732 | 57 | 00.500 |
| 14 | 04.232 | 36 | 03.732 | 58 | 03.732 |
| 15 | 03.732 | 37 | 01.866 | 59 | 04.232 |
| 16 | 03.732 | 38 | 04.232 | 60 | 02.866 |
| 17 | 03.732 | 39 | 03.732 | 61 | 00.500 |
| 18 | 03.732 | 40 | 01.866 | 62 | 05.598 |
| 19 | 04.232 | 41 | 03.732 | 63 | 03.732 |
| 20 | 03.732 | 42 | 01.000 | 64 | 03.732 |
| 21 | 01.866 | 43 | 01.866 | | |

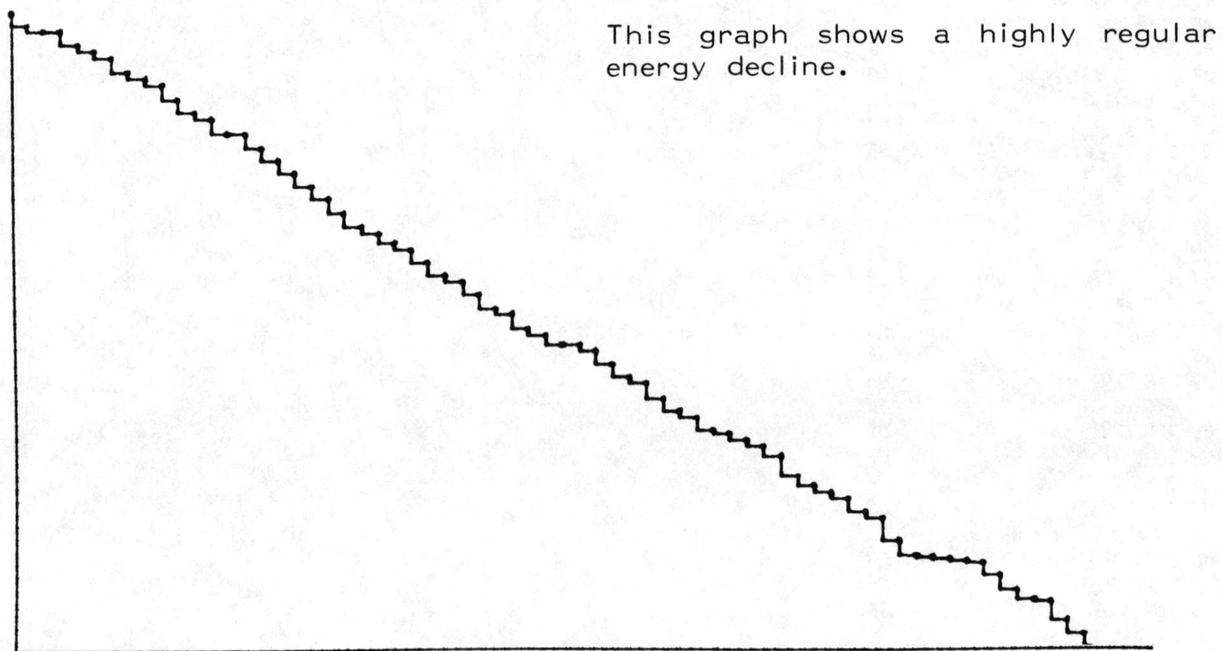

This graph shows a highly regular energy decline.

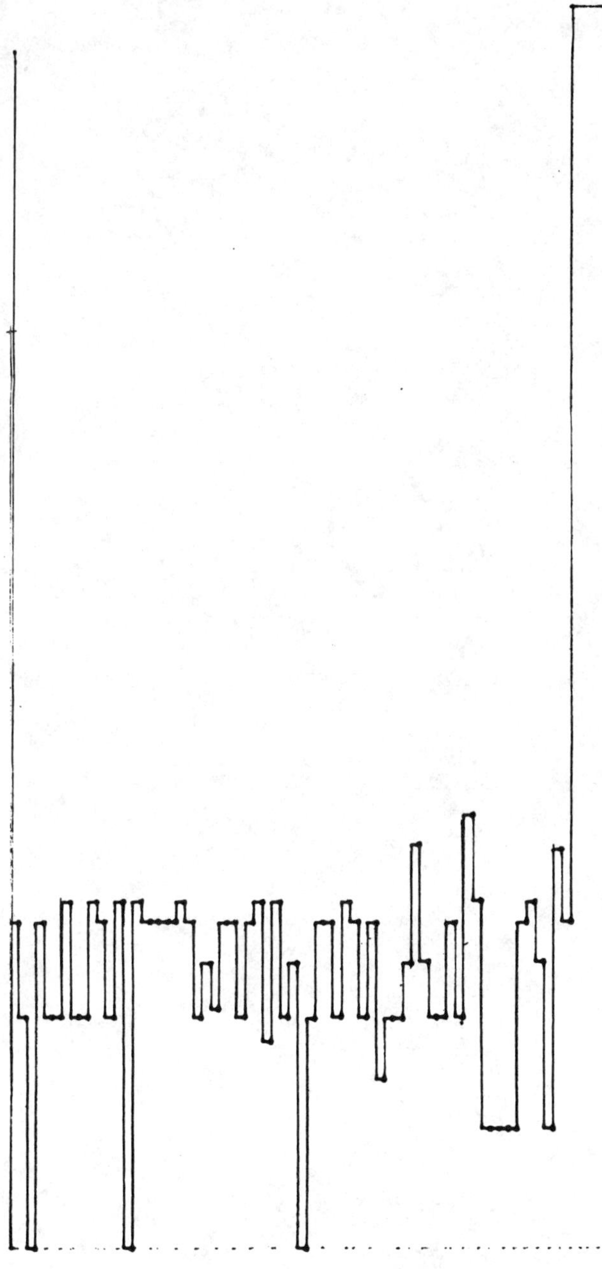

A history shows the fluctuations that occur in tonality amplitude.

This plot is a time sequence of tonal impulse amplitudes.

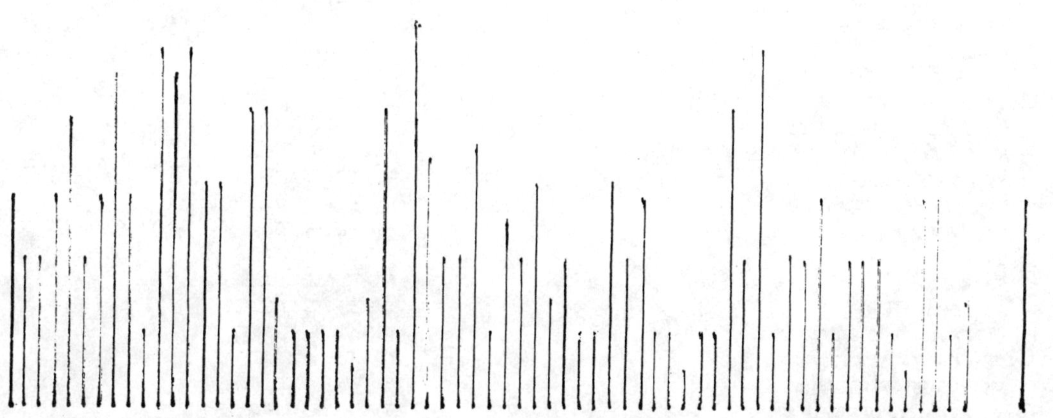

These true and relative preferred notations should be compared with the original phonetic spellings.

| | | |
|---|---|---|
| 00 | EbGBbEb D#FxA#D# | EbGBbEb D#FxA#D# |
| 01 | DEBbEb | DGBbEb CxFxA#D# |
| 02 | CGbAEb B#F#GxD# | CEbAEb B#F#GxD# |
| 03 | BGBE | BGBE |
| 04 | BbGCE | BbGCE |
| 05 | BbGDbF A#FxC#E# | BbGDbF |
| 06 | AbFbDbF G#G#C#E# | AbFbDbF G#G#C#E# |
| 07 | AGCEb | AGCEb GxFx[illegible] |
| 08 | BbGbCEb A#F#B#D# | BbGbCEb A#F#[illegible] |
| 09 | BbFBbDb A#E#A#C# | BbFBbDb A#E#A#C# |
| 10 | AbFbCbDb G#EBC# | AbEFbCbDb G#DxEBC# |
| 11 | GFBD | GFCbD FxE#BCx |
| 12 | GbGbCbEb F#F#BD# | GbGbCbEb F#F#BD# |
| 13 | A#FbBbDb G#EA#C# | GFbBbDb FxEA#C# |
| 14 | AbEbAbCb G#D#G#B | AbEbAbCb G#D#G#B |
| 15 | GbEbAbCb F#D#G#B | GbEbAbCb F#D#G#B |
| 16 | FEbAbC E#D#G#B# | FEbAbC E#D#G#B# |
| 17 | GbDbGbBb F#C#F#A# | GbDbGbBb F#C#F#A# |
| 18 | DbDbFAb C#C#E#G# | DbDbFAb C#C#E#G# |
| 19 | EbBbEbGb D#A#D#F# | EbBbEbGb D#A#D#F# |
| 20 | DbBbEbGb C#A#D#F# | DbBbEbGb C#A#D#F# |
| 21 | CbAbDbF BG#C#E# | CbAbDbF BG#C#E# |
| 22 | BbBbDbGb A#A#C#F# | BbBbDbGb A#A#C#F# |
| 23 | AbCbFAb G#BE#G# | AbCbFAb G#BE#G# |
| 24 | GbDbGbBb F#C#F#A# | GbDbGbBb F#C#F#A# |
| 25 | FEbAbC E#D#G#B# | FEbAbC E#D#G#B# |
| 26 | GEbAbC FxD#G#B# | GEbAbC FxD#G#B# |
| 27 | GDGB | GDGCb FxCxFxB |
| 28 | CEbGC | CEbGC B#D#FxB# |
| 29 | CFBD | CFCbD B#E#BCx |
| 30 | CGCEb | CGCEb B#FxB#D# |
| 31 | CF#AD | CGbAD B#F#GxCx |
| 32 | BGBD | CbECbD BFxBCx |
| 33 | BbGbCFb A#F#B#E | BbGbCFb A#F#B#E |
| 34 | AFCE | AFCFb GxE#B#E |
| 35 | BbFBbD A#E#A#Cx | BbFBbD A#E#A#Cx |
| 36 | FFAC | FFAC E#E#GxB# |
| 37 | EACF | FbACF EGxB#E# |
| 38 | DADF | DADF CxGxCxE# |
| 39 | DACF | DACF CxGxB#E# |
| 40 | DGBF# | DGCbGb CxFxBF# |
| 41 | DGBG | DGCbG CxFxBFx |
| 42 | C#GAF# | DbGAGb C#FxGxF# |
| 43 | C#GAE | DbGAE C#FxGxDx |
| 44 | DF#AC# | DGbADb CxF#GxC# |
| 45 | F#F#AD | GbGbAD F#F#GxCx |
| 46 | EF#AE | EGbAE DxF#GxDx |
| 47 | DF#AF# | DGbAGb CxF#GxF# |
| 48 | DbGbBbF C#F#A#E# | DbGbBbF C#F#A#E# |
| 49 | DbGbBbFb C#F#A#E | DbGbBbFb C#F#A#E |
| 50 | CFAF | CFAF B#E#GxE# |
| 51 | CFAEb | CFAEb B#E#GxD# |
| 52 | BbFBbC A#E#A#B# | BbFBbC A#E#A#B# |
| 53 | BbFBbDb A#E#A#C# | BbFBbDb A#E#A#C# |
| 54 | ADbFC | ADbFC GxC#E#B# |
| 55 | ADbFBb GxC#E#A# | ADbFBb GxC#E#A# |
| 56 | G#CEB | AbCECb G#B#DxB |
| 57 | AbCEC | AbCEC G#B#DxB# |
| 58 | ACFD | ACFD GxB#E#Cx |
| 59 | ACFC | ACFC GxB#E#B# |
| 60 | DDFBb | DDFBb CxCxE#A# |
| 61 | DEbGbBb CxD#F#A# | DEbGbBb CxD#F#A# |
| 62 | CEbFBb B#D#E#A# | CEbFBb B#D#E#A# |
| 63 | BbDFBb A#CxE#A# | BbDFBb A#CxE#A# |
| 64 | EbEbGBb D#D#FxA# | EbEbGBb D#D#FxA# |

OTTERSTROM ILLUSTRATION B

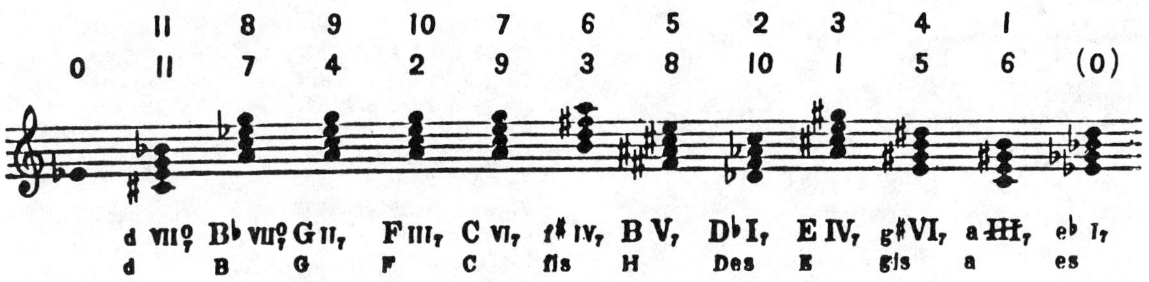

B

Printer output obtained as a byproduct of the input operation.

```
6.837868024  11
7.868024293  11
6.024415402  11
3.268024781  11
4.024681529  11
4.417840246  11
5.202468237  11
2.462350244  11
9.502432195  11
2.437370247  11
4.024473702  11
9.235024623  11
2.412150244  11
7.802426320  11
7.863402456  11
2.474370244  10
3.590244813  11
2.426340246  11
2.024419570  11
4.193979024  11
6.939290245  11
1.929024749  11
7.024629392  11
2.414858202  11
8.483878024  11
4.815802448  11
4.810243858  11
7.802415848  11
2.465293902  10
6.529502449  11
3.902449571  11
2.463974902  11
3.976024496  11
7.024296392  11
2.476394902  11
6.392990245  11
9.199490245  11
9.199290243  11
9.395902439  11
3.970245296  11
2.452965024  10
9.267024392  11
2.452140245  10
1.202444178  11
4.468387802  11
6.817802478  11
7.802468683  11
9.60         10
```

The data file.

```
00 68 3 78 68 0 1.000
01 4 3 78 68 0 1.000
02 29 3 78 6 0 1.000
03 4 1 5 1 0 1.000
04 5 3 2 68 0 1.000
05 78 1 78 4 0 1.000
06 68 1 5 29 0 1.000
07 4 1 78 4 0 1.000
08 68 2 5 2 0 1.000
09 68 2 3 78 0 1.000
10 6 2 3 5 0 1.000
11 4 2 19 5 0 1.000
12 3 2 19 59 0 1.000
13 3 7 3 7 0 1.000
14 7 7 3 4 0 1.000
15 4 7 3 7 0 1.000
16 49 2 3 5 0 1.000
17 6 2 3 5 0 1.000
18 1 2 1 5 0 1.000
19 4 4 1 78 0 1.000
20 2 6 3 2 0 1.000
21 78 6 3 4 0 1.000
22 5 6 3 2 0 1.000
23 7 4 3 7 0 1.000
24 4 1 3 59 0 1.000
25 48 1 3 7 0 1.000
26 2 6 3 4 0 1.000
27 6 6 3 2 0 1.000
28 4 19 5 7 0 1.000
29 4 19 39 79 0 1.000
30 29 69 39 29 0 1.000
31 59 6 19 29 0 1.000
32 7 49 19 7 0 1.000
33 6 29 39 29 0 1.000
34 1 48 58 2 0 1.000
35 38 48 38 78 0 1.000
36 48 48 1 58 0 1.000
37 48 58 48 1 0 1.000
38 38 58 48 78 0 1.000
39 1 58 48 58 0 1.000
40 6 5 29 39 0 1.000
41 6 5 29 5 0 1.000
42 49 5 7 39 0 1.000
43 49 5 7 19 0 1.000
44 6 39 7 49 0 1.000
45 6 39 7 6 0 1.000
46 49 6 39 7 0 1.000
47 29 6 39 29 0 1.000
48 7 6 39 49 0 1.000
49 7 6 39 299 0 1.000
50 59 49 199 49 0 1.000
51 59 49 199 29 0 1.000
52 39 49 39 59 0 1.000
53 39 49 39 7 0 1.000
54 5 29 6 29 0 1.000
55 5 29 6 5 0 1.000
56 39 2 6 7 0 1.000
57 39 2 6 2 0 1.000
58 5 2 1 4 0 1.000
59 5 2 1 2 0 1.000
60 4 4 1 78 0 1.000
61 4 68 38 78 0 1.000
62 2 68 1 78 0 1.000
63 78 4 1 78 0 1.000
64 68 68 3 78 0 4.000
```

The trajectory for **Illustration** B follows a meandering path also, reminiscent of the maneuvering board diagram shown in Fig. 6.8b.

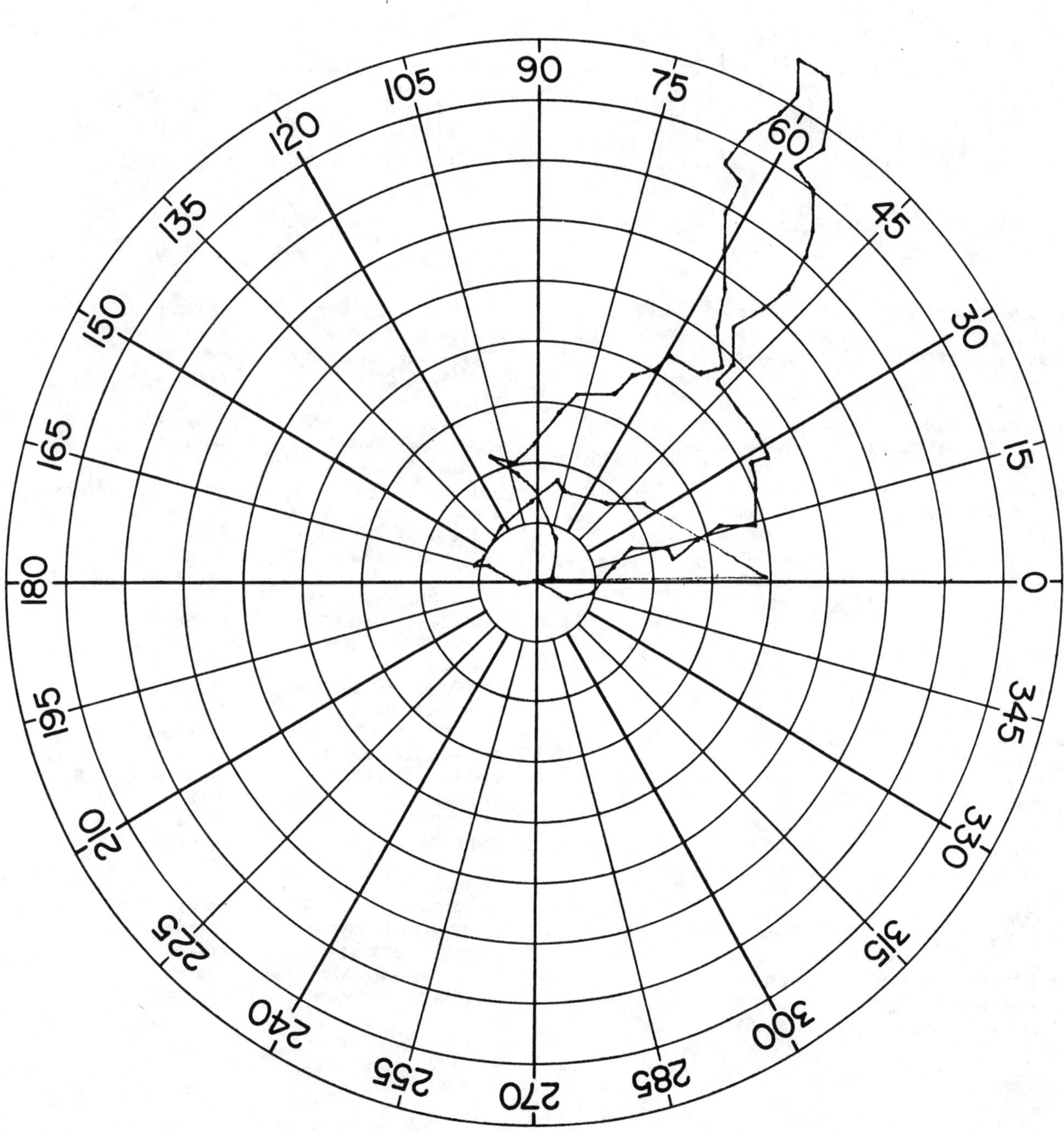

This impulse magnitude graph for Illustration B bears a close resemblance to that obtained for Illustration A.

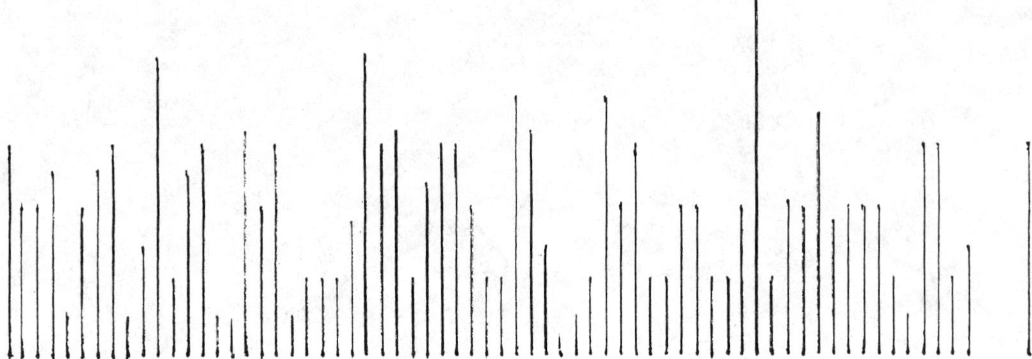

| | | | | | |
|---|---|---|---|---|---|
| 00 | EbGBbEb D#FxA#D# | EbGBbEb D#FxA#D# | 33 | FbDbAbDb EC#G#C# | EC#AbC# |
| 01 | DGBbEb | DGBbEb CxFxA#D# | 34 | FDbAbC E#C#G#B# | FC#AbC |
| 02 | DbAbbBbFb C#GA#E | DbGBbE C#FxA#Dx | 35 | GbDbGbBb F#C#F#A# | F#C#F#Bb |
| 03 | DFAF | DFAF | 36 | DbDbFAb C#C#E#G# | DbDbFAb |
| 04 | AGCEb | AGCEb | 37 | DbAbDbF C#G#C#E# | DbAbDbF |
| 05 | BbFBbD A#E#A#Cx | BbFBbD | 38 | GbAbDbBb F#G#C#A# | F#AbDbBb |
| 06 | EbFABbDb D#E#GxA#C# | EbFADb | 39 | FAbDbAb E#G#C#G# | FAbDbAb |
| 07 | DFBbD | DFBbD | 40 | FbBbbDbAb EAC#G# | EADbAb |
| 08 | EbGAC | EbCAC | 41 | EAC#A | EADbA |
| 09 | EbCGBb D#B#FxA# | EbCGBb | 42 | EbBbbCbAb D#ABG# | EbABAb |
| 10 | ECGA | ECGA | 43 | EbBbbCbGb D#ABF# | EbABF# |
| 11 | DCF#A | DCGbA | 44 | FbAbCbEb EG#BD# | EAbBEb |
| 12 | GCGbBb | GCGbBb | 45 | EG#BE | EAbBE |
| 13 | GBGB | GBGB | 46 | EbFbAbCb D#EG#B | EbEAbB |
| 14 | BBGD | BBGD | 47 | DbFbAbDb C#EG#C# | C#EG#C# |
| 15 | DBGB | DBGB | 48 | CbFbAbEb BEG#D# | BEG#Eb |
| 16 | EbCGA | EbCGA | 49 | BEG#D | BEG#D |
| 17 | ECGA | ECGA | 50 | BbEbGEb A#D#FxD# | BbEbGEb |
| 18 | FCFA | FCFA | 51 | BbEbGDb A#D#FxC# | BbEbGC# |
| 19 | DDFBb | DDFBb | 52 | AbEbAbBb G#D#G#A# | AbEbAbBb |
| 20 | CEGC | CEGC | 53 | AbEbAbCb G#D#G#B | AbEbAbB |
| 21 | BbEGD | BbEGD | 54 | BbDbFbDb A#C#EC# | BbDbFbDb A#C#EC# |
| 22 | AEGC | AEGC | 55 | AC#EA | AC#EA |
| 23 | BDGB | BDGB | 56 | G#CEB | G#CEB |
| 24 | DFGBb | DFGBb | 57 | AbCEC | G#CEC |
| 25 | C#FGB | DbFGB | 58 | ACFD | ACFD |
| 26 | CEGD | CEGD | 59 | ACFC | ACFC |
| 27 | EEGC | EEGC | 60 | DDFBb | DDFBb |
| 28 | DF#AB | DF#AB | 61 | DEbGbBb CxD#F#A# | DEbF#Bb |
| 29 | DGbAbC CxF#G#B# | DF#AbC | 62 | CEbFBb B#D#E#A# | CEbFBb |
| 30 | DbFAbDb C#E#G#C# | C#FAbC# | 63 | BbDbFBb A#C#E#A# | BbDbFBb |
| 31 | BbFbGbDb A#EF#C# | BbEF#C# | 64 | EbEbGBb D#D#FxA# | EbEbGBb |
| 32 | CbEbGbCb BD#F#B | BEbF#B | | | |

## EXERCISES

**9.1** Restate the components of Illustration A in phonetic notation.

**9.2** Exactly how many different charms, harmonies, and sonorities does Otterström employ in this example?

**9.3** Are there flaws in the following argument?

As everyone knows, when a musical performance is repeated, even under almost identical conditions, the second rendition is slightly different from the first. It is fortunate, therefore, that a delay in time makes very little difference in the esthetic value of a musical composition. If Beethoven's **Fifth Symphony** were to be started over again two hours later, or even two years later, by the same orchestra under the same conductor, then it would sound almost exactly the same way, subject to a slight variation in artistic performance and perhaps in audience sophistication. For this reason, a musical composition can be assumed to be reasonably invariant with respect to the passage of time. Thus, music qualifies, as much as any other signal, as a stationary process. Consequently, the theory of stochastic processes provides a mathematical basis for an analytic approach to determining the underlying regularities or laws of music by regarding music as a time series.

## MACHINE CALCULATION

Computers do not have to be large or expensive or nearby. The computer that is best suited to a given problem depends upon the circumstances under which the music analyst is working, the purpose, the needs of the study, and the size of the data base. The small computer system appears to be naturally suited to the needs of low-budget music departments. Since the low costs and ready availability of such machines are great advantages, they may open up a new frontier in musicology and music education. Considerable research time is saved by not having to wait one's turn for a big computer, and the cost of computer time on a big machine, especially when using a time-shared terminal, far exceeds that for a small machine.

Programmable calculators, or desktop computers, also appear to be well suited to classroom use for demonstrating and assisting elementary music analysis. Easy to use and completely self-contained, they form an ideal middle ground between a big system and a slide rule or pocket calculator. In the past few years a remarkable change has been taking place in their design and performance. These computers now can handle programs containing many thousands of instructions. The programs making up a library of certified music analysis functions can be stored easily on small magnetic cards, magnetic tape cassettes, or diskettes, depending upon the system, for later insertion into the computer memory. An X-Y plotter, controlled by and used in conjunction with the desk computer, can provide an excellent study tool for the music analyst. Using the combination, which incidentally can produce linear, log-log, and semilog plots, he or she is able to trace patterns of tonality and modulation without necessarily even hearing the composition.

Admittedly, factors such as the storage capacity or the computation speed and data read-out rate limit the amount of work that can be accomplished with these devices. Still, coupled with powerful visual aids, they allow the user to adjust his or her thinking immediately to account for any observed unusual features. When automatic plotting is coupled to computer assistance in routine music analysis procedures, the user has more time to be creative. Also, the advantage of being able to perform many logical and statistical operations required in the synthesis and analysis of music is offered. In the light of general musical application requirements, the small computer can effect a cost savings that could alter the whole economic picture for a small music conservatory or for an individual researcher.

Shown in Fig. 9.5 is perhaps the smallest useful music computation facility. On the left is the programmable calculator; on the right, the X-Y plotter. The block diagram of Fig. 9.6 shows the principal elements used to perform music analysis on the early version of a popular system. A modern programmable calculator or desk-top computer for individual use, has a powerful, although limited, internal memory and full programming capabilities; yet it requires little special training and few programming skills to operate. Although not applicable to a large data base, such a machine can be used to analyze music sequentially, using components. To demonstrate and emphasize the fact that even a programmable desk calculator or microcomputer can be a valuable study tool for the dynamic analysis of musical creations, every program presented in this book has been written for such a minimal system. No claim is made, however, that the programs have been coded optimally. Here and there in the collection to follow a program is prefaced by a general discussion of the function it is meant to perform. These brief reports may include program specifications or data formats, as well as certain other remarks necessary to explain the mechanics of individual programs.

A programmable calculator, like any other computer, large or small, requires a complete list of explicit instructions for each task. The conversion tables given in Fig. 9.7 concern the postulated logical/arithmetic order repertoire and relate the machine codes with their standard mnemonics. The meaning of each instruction is supplied in the following text.

Figure 9.5

A typical programmable calculator system with X-Y plotter.

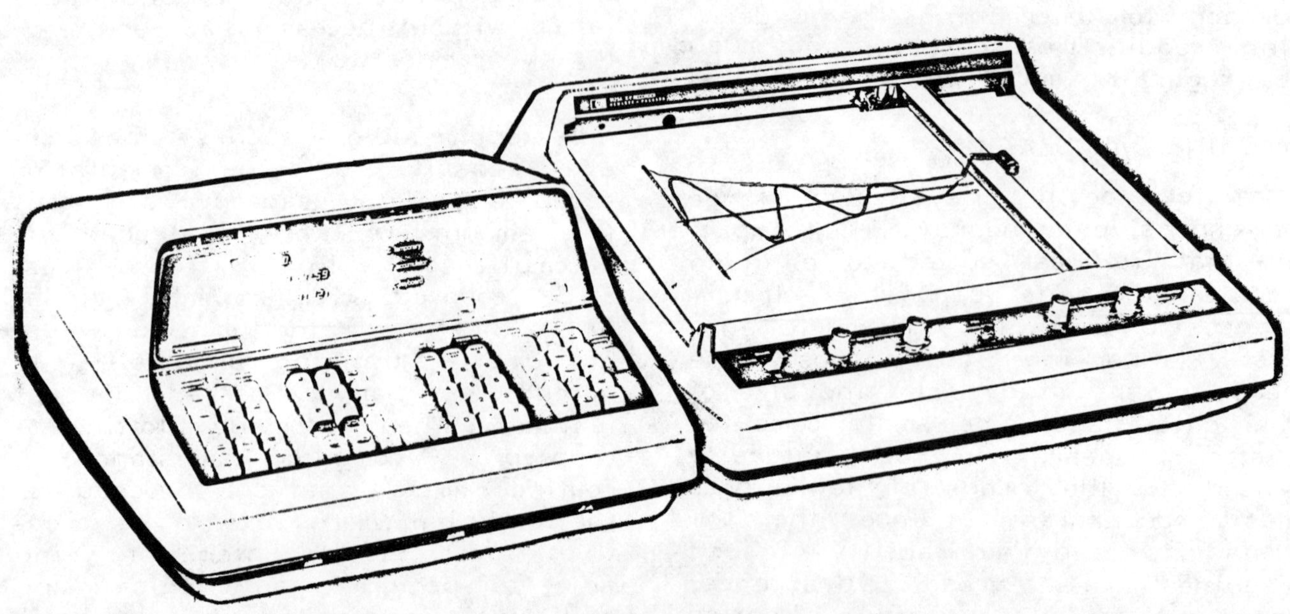

**Figure 9.6**

General layout of a modern computer-based, music-data-analysis facility. Checkmarks indicate which components were required in the preparation of this book.

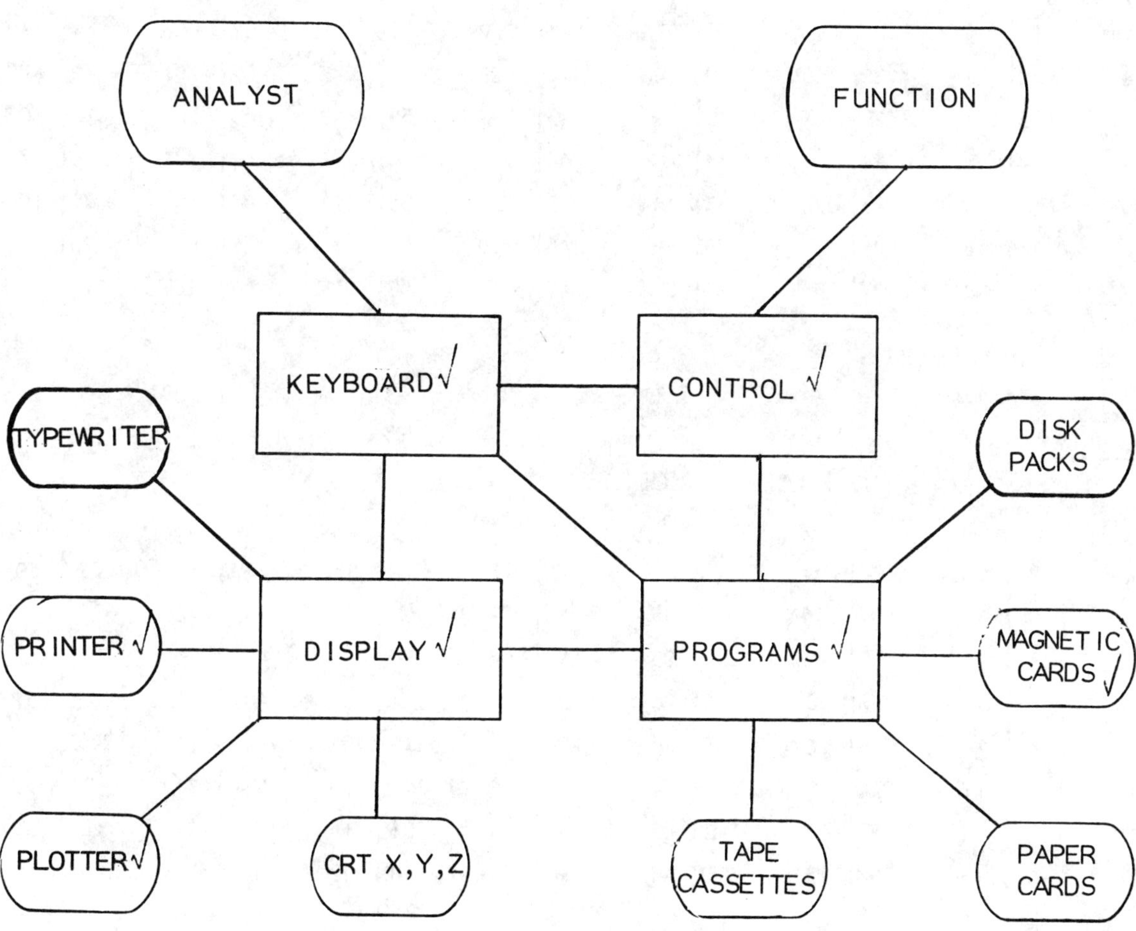

**Figure 9.7**

Tables for converting mnemonic symbols to machine codes, and vice versa. For present purposes, codes 51 and 77 are not assigned.

Table I

MACHINE CODES TO MNEMONIC SYMBOLS

| Code | Symbol | Code | Symbol | Code | Symbol | Code | Symbol | Code | Symbol | Code | Symbol | Code | Symbol | Code | Symbol |
|---|---|---|---|---|---|---|---|---|---|---|---|---|---|---|---|
| 00 | 0 | 10 | 8 | 20 | CLR | 30 | XEY | 40 | YTO | 50 | X=Y | 60 | AC+ | 70 | SIN |
| 01 | 1 | 11 | 9 | 21 | . | 31 | RDN | 41 | STP | 51 | | 61 | RCL | 71 | TAN |
| 02 | 2 | 12 | e | 22 | RUP | 32 | CHS | 42 | FMT | 52 | X<Y | 62 | POL | 72 | ARC |
| 03 | 3 | 13 | a | 23 | XTO | 33 | + | 43 | IFG | 53 | X>Y | 63 | AC– | 73 | COS |
| 04 | 4 | 14 | b | 24 | YE | 34 | – | 44 | GTO | 54 | SFL | 64 | INT | 74 | EXP |
| 05 | 5 | 15 | f | 25 | DN | 35 | DIV | 45 | PNT | 55 | \|Y\| | 65 | LN | 75 | LOG |
| 06 | 6 | 16 | c | 26 | EEX | 36 | × | 46 | END | 56 | π | 66 | RCT | 76 | √ |
| 07 | 7 | 17 | d | 27 | UP | 37 | CLX | 47 | CNT | 57 | PSE | 67 | HYP | 77 | |

Table II

MNEMONIC SYMBOLS TO MACHINE CODES

| Symbol | Code | Symbol | Code | Symbol | Code | Symbol | Code | Symbol | Code | Symbol | Code | Symbol | Code | Symbol | Code |
|---|---|---|---|---|---|---|---|---|---|---|---|---|---|---|---|
| 0 | 00 | 8 | 10 | AC– | 63 | . | 21 | HYP | 67 | + | 33 | SFL | 54 | X=Y | 50 |
| 1 | 01 | 9 | 11 | AC+ | 60 | DIV | 35 | IFG | 43 | PNT | 45 | SIN | 70 | | |
| 2 | 02 | a | 13 | ARC | 72 | DN | 25 | INT | 64 | POL | 62 | √ | 76 | X>Y | 53 |
| 3 | 03 | b | 14 | CHS | 32 | EEX | 26 | LN | 65 | PSE | 57 | STP | 41 | X<Y | 52 |
| 4 | 04 | c | 16 | CLR | 20 | END | 46 | LOG | 75 | RCL | 61 | | 77 | XTO | 23 |
| 5 | 05 | d | 17 | CLX | 37 | EXP | 74 | – | 34 | RCT | 66 | TAN | 71 | \|Y\| | 55 |
| 6 | 06 | e | 12 | CNT | 47 | FMT | 42 | × | 36 | RDN | 31 | UP | 27 | YE | 24 |
| 7 | 07 | f | 15 | COS | 73 | GTO | 44 | π | 56 | RUP | 22 | XEY | 30 | YTO | 40 |

## EXERCISES

**9.4** Standard input/output and mass storage devices include teletypes, paper-tape equipment, card-readers, magnetic tape units, disk packs, printers, controllers, front ends, displays, plotters, drums, and special interfaces. Describe some of these devices.

**9.5** What constraints on development programs and research goals in computer music presently are imposed by available resources and the technological state-of-the-art?

## IMPLEMENTATION

Although previously published studies afford little or no data for statistical analysis, computers are beginning to attract the attention of a growing number of musicologists for lengthy numerical calculations leading to semiquantitative discussion. Computers even make it possible for in depth analysis of several musical compositions simultaneously. Based upon today's rapidly emerging signal processing technology, computer programs and hybrid equipment can be set up to explore in a systematic fashion the interplay among numerous variables, including duration, pitch, attack, decay, tone quality, and loudness. The data processing requirements may be divided into four parts: (a) editing and reduction of musical data to machinable form, (b) information retrieval, (c) nonnumerical, numerical, and statistical calculations, and (d) graphic, tabular, and audio presentation of the results. As the number of completed analyses grows, libraries of musical texts ready for immediate input are being established at various research centers.

In developing those principles on which automated music analysis can be based, it is essential to have efficient methods for quantitatively describing displacement, tonality, and modulation. As graphical presentations usually are preferred to tables of numbers, the techniques of music analysis outlined in previous chapters of this book, which are not overly practical as a method for hand-calculation, would be programmed for machine calculation. Since these techniques are stated precisely, the methodology is amenable to easy mechanization. Sample programs have been devised and are presented in the following sections.

The motion of the composition point along its trajectory is hard to visualize without making use of some kind of apparatus to display its behavior in time by means of a moving diagram. In order to "see" the motion of the composition point, it is possible either to print out the decimal values or to plot them as points and lines, preferably on a cathode-ray tube (CRT) display. This type of on-line, video display terminal (VDT) output would be particularly convenient as an aid to teaching. The x,y coordinates of the composition point trajectory can be printed out or recorded on magnetic media for re-use in later steps of the processing. Modern techniques permit the central processor to control the plotting process automatically and to display all the resulting graphic material directly on a high resolution display screen from which it can be photographed or reduced to hard copy selectively. In such a display, designs might be evolved to show points, straight line segments, or arcs. The use of color is also a viable option.

A uniform procedure for formatting and inputting musical data is recommended. In this book the favored rule is that of bottom-up, left-right parsing. Think of a vertical cursor sliding from left to right along the pages of manuscript like a measure line or bar that has been detached and is free to float sideways on the musical staff. Next imagine a small dot, akin to the bouncing ball in audience sing-along projections, that is free to glide vertically along the cursor strip. The combined motion is shown in Fig. 9.8.

The musical data to be processed by the computer routines in this book are entered through the calculator keyboard sequentially in units called "messages" (see Fig. 9.9). A message transmission consists of an ordered sequence of key depressions arranged in accordance with the scheme for numerically coding the literal alphabet. The basis for this scheme is provided in Fig. 9.10. Several messages sometimes are combined to form a compound message. Messages provide useful data about musical sentences. Since each musical sentence may be interpreted in many ways, it follows that different kinds of messages may be needed in order to perform different kinds of analysis.

Figure 9.8

In parallel/serial forward scanning, tones sounding in parallel (chords) are entered in a sequence (from low to high pitch).

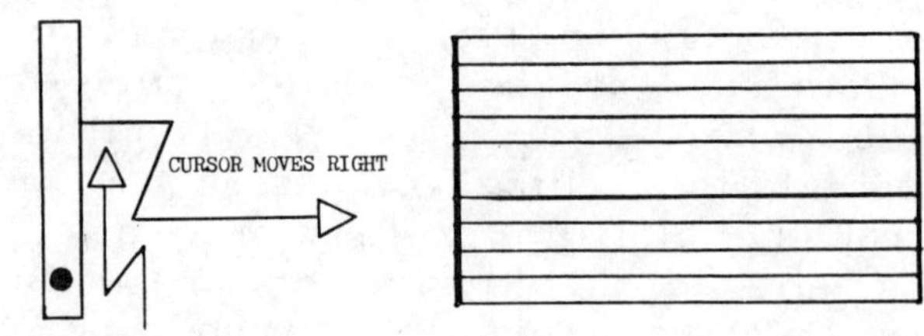


Figure 9.9

A numeric pad. During data read-in it is, of course, simple to cover the keytops with labels bearing the required letters and inflections.

Figure 9.10

The input sequencing procedure for a programmable calculator. Initially input of each measure of the musical text could require several minutes for completion. Experience may shorten this time considerably.

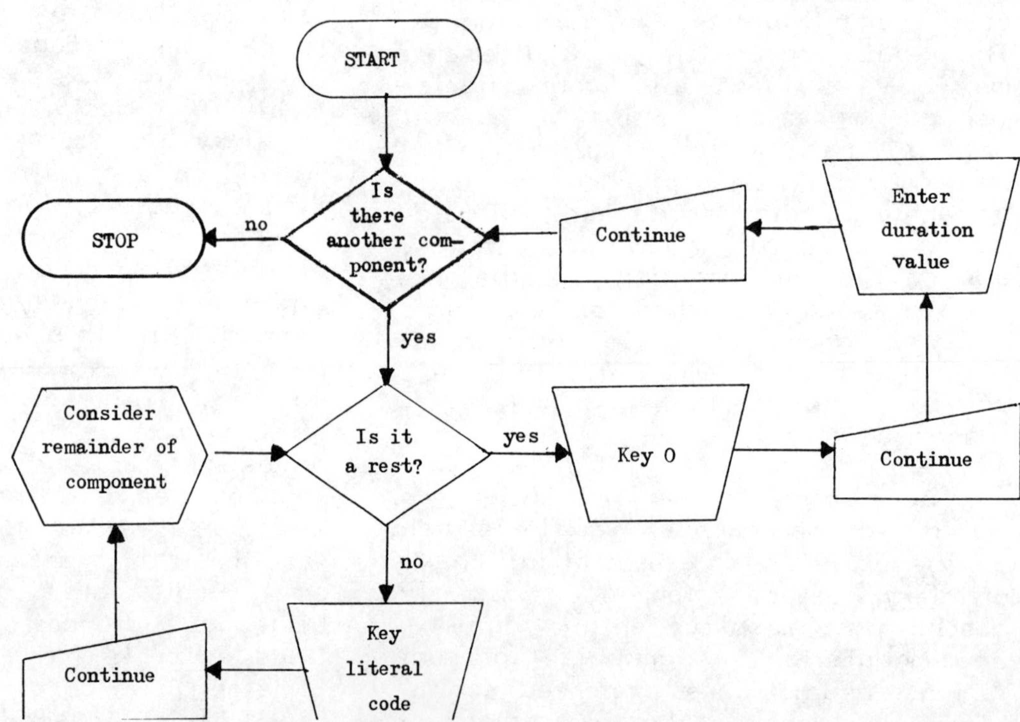

As shown in Fig. 9.11, each component is treated as a separate entity and gives rise to a short string of symbols, called a "data frame." The breakdown of a data frame is shown in Fig. 9.12. Here, the zero entry corresponds to a punctuation mark, which separates the sequence of literals making up the charm from the numerical value of the duration. Legal entries for the duration include:

| input | note |
|---|---|
| .25 | sixteenth |
| .33333 | triplet eighth |
| .5 | eighth |
| 1 | quarter |
| 2 | half |
| 4 | whole |
| 6 | dotted whole. |

As before, each character A, B, C, D, E, F, G, ♭, ♯ is assigned a one-decimal-digit code by which it must be referenced during computer processing. No literal code should be entered for rests. If the component contains either a ♭ or ♯ for any literal, then the keyboard entry of an "8" or a "9" as a part of that literal code will indicate the addition of a correction factor within the program. Moreover, if the literal field contains either a ♭♭ or a ♯♯, which stands for a double sharp (x), then the appropriate additional amount will be contributed to the value being accumulated. Striking the CLEAR X key will erase a particular entry after it is in the X register, and if this is done before pushing the CONTINUE key, a mistake can be deleted. After pushing the CONTINUE key, however, it will be too late for such a correction to be possible.

Following each zero marker, the user specifies the amount of time the composition spends on that component. The corresponding scaling factor inside the program is under user control and may be changed easily to enlarge or contract the size of the plotter output. Repeat chords may be re-entered, although it is not necessary to do so. Instead, consecutive duplicate entries may be abbreviated by combining them and summing their durations. For example,

2,6,3,2,0,1
⟩ 2,6,3,2,0,2.
2,2,3,6,0,1

As this example shows, abbreviation is permitted in coding components as long as charm meaning is not changed and enharmonic thresholds are not crossed during the message frame. Taking this short cut is usually not recommended, however.

Figure 9.11

Input for **Yankee Doodle** (see Fig. 6.6). The indicated keying sequence is 2, CONTINUE, 0, CONTINUE, 4, CONTINUE, 4, CONTINUE, 0, CONTINUE, and so on. Each individual zero key depression signifies that the next number entered will be a scalar multiplier proportional to the duration of that component.

| | |
|---|---|
| C: 2 0 4 | A: 5 0 2 |
| D: 4 0 2 | B: 7 0 2 |
| E: 6 0 2 | C: 2 0 4 |
| C: 2 0 2 | G: 3 0 3 |
| E: 6 0 2 | A: 5 0 1 |
| D: 4 0 4 | G: 3 0 2 |
| C: 2 0 4 | F: 1 0 2 |
| D: 4 0 2 | E: 6 0 4 |
| E: 6 0 2 | G: 3 0 4 |
| C: 2 0 4 | A: 5 0 3 |
| B: 7 0 4 | B: 7 0 1 |
| C: 2 0 4 | A: 5 0 2 |
| D: 4 0 2 | G: 3 0 2 |
| E: 6 0 2 | A: 5 0 2 |
| F: 1 0 2 | B: 7 0 2 |
| E: 6 0 2 | C: 2 0 2 |
| D: 4 0 2 | A: 5 0 2 |
| C: 2 0 2 | G: 3 0 2 |
| B: 7 0 2 | C: 2 0 2 |
| G: 3 0 2 | B: 7 0 2 |
| A: 5 0 2 | D: 4 0 2 |
| B: 7 0 2 | C: 2 0 8 |
| C: 2 0 8 | |
| A: 5 0 3 | |
| B: 7 0 1 | |
| A: 5 0 2 | |
| G: 3 0 2 | |

Figure 9.12

The essentials of the process for representing literals by numbers.

(a)

Input code structure.

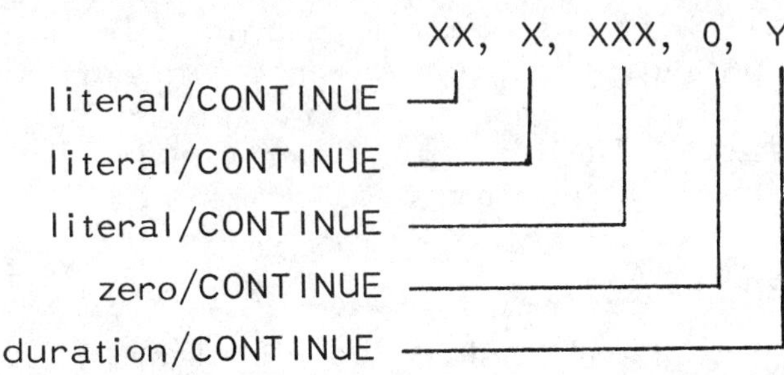


(b)

Examples of decimal-coded literals.

F = 1

C♯ = 29

G♭ = 38

D𝄪 = 499

A♭♭ = 588

E* = 6999

B♭♭♭ = 7888

(c)

Coding scheme for piano keyboard.

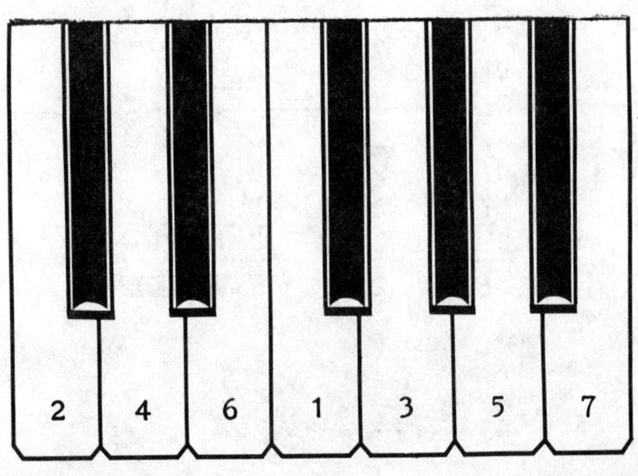


## EXERCISES

**9.6** No language should exist as an end unto itself. Prepare a report contrasting various current music input languages and illustrating their methods of achieving machine processable format.

**9.7** (a) Select a musical composition for study. (b) Dissect the composition into components to assure thorough analysis. (c) Examine each component for novelty and for significance to the musical passage. (d) Trace the evolution of each novel or significant feature.

**9.8** Sketch how to write an original program to provide a total view of a musical composition. Include its melodic functioning, harmonic complexity, organizational dispersion, timing, and intervallic relationships.

## INSTRUCTION REPERTOIRE

The following descriptions include all changes in the contents of the X, Y, and Z registers and all storage locations. It should be noted specifically that copying a quantity leaves the original unchanged. Unless otherwise stated, the letters x, y, and z denote the initial contents of X, Y, and Z. Storage registers are given the addresses 0, 1, ..., 9, a, ... f. All references to calculator keys should be visually reinforced by inspection of Fig. 9.12.

### Entry Keys

CL (CLEAR X)

Reset the X register to zero; remove ARC and HYPER conditions (unnecessary for a new entry).

CLR (CLEAR)

Reset the X, Y, Z, e and f registers to zero; remove ARC and HYPER conditions and clear the flag.

. (DECIMAL POINT)

Enter decimal point in X register (unnecessary for entry of integers).

Figure 9.12

Layout of a representative calculator keyboard. The keys of such a machine are clearly labeled; they are to be pushed individually.

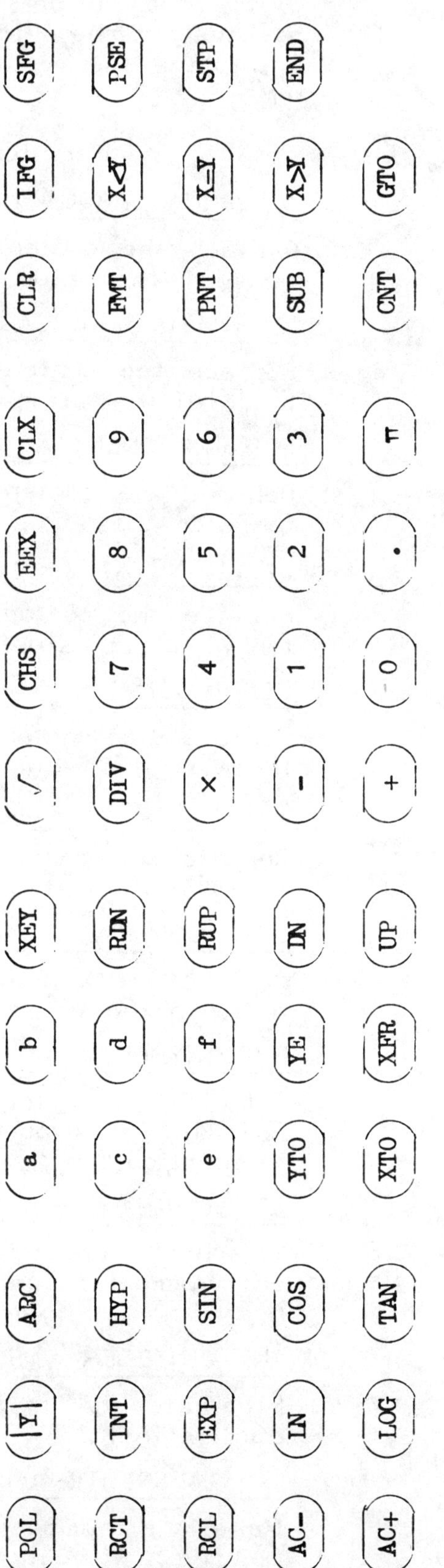

EEX (ENTER EXPONENT)

Cause the subsequent digits and change-sign entries to affect the exponent of the number contained in the X register. This operation overrides an existing decimal point.

CHS (CHANGE SIGN)

If ENTER EXP was pressed, change the sign of the exponent. Otherwise, change the sign of the number in X.

### Control Keys

RDN (ROLL DOWN)

Permute the contents of the X, Y, and Z registers, placing z in Y, y in X, and x in Z.

RUP (ROLL UP)

Permute the contents of the X, Y, and Z registers, placing x in Y, y in Z, and z in X.

DN (DOWN)

Place the contents of the Y register in the X register; then copy the contents of the Z register in the Y register.

UP (UP)

Place the contents of the Y register in the Z register; then copy the contents of the X register in the Y register.

XEY (X EXCHANGE Y)

Exchange the contents of the X register with those of the Y register.

### Arithmetic Keys

\+ (PLUS)

Add the number in the X register to the number in the Y register and place the result in the Y register.

\- (MINUS)

Subtract the number in the X register from the number in the Y register and place the result in the Y register.

X (TIMES)

Multiply the number in the Y register by the number in the X register and place the result in the Y register.

DIV (BY)

Divide the number in the Y register by the number in the X register and place the result in the Y register.

### Function Keys

√ (SQUARE ROOT X)

Replace the contents of the X register with the value $x^{\frac{1}{2}}$.

LN (NATURAL LOGARITHM X)

Replace the contents of the X register with the value $\ln x = \log_e x$.

EXP (EXPONENTIAL X)

Replace the contents of the X register with the value $e^x$

SIN (SINE X)

Replace the contents of the X register with the value sin x.

COS (COSINE X)

Replace the contents of the X register with the value cos x.

TAN (TANGENT X)

Replace the contents of the X register with the value tan x.

LOG (COMMON LOGARITHM X)

Replace the contents of the X register with the value $\log x = \log_{10} x$.

HYP (HYPER)

Interpret the trigonometric function following this prefix as a hyperbolic function.

ARC (ARC)

Interpret the trigonometric function or hyperbolic function following this prefix as an inverse function.

INT (INTEGER X)

Eliminate the fractional part of the number in X.

|Y| (ABSOLUTE VALUE Y)

Make the number in the Y register positive, without changing its magnitude.

### Coordinate Coversion Keys

POL (TO POLAR)

Replace the contents of the X register with the quantity:

$$r = \sqrt{x^2 + y^2};$$

replace the contents of the Y register with the quantity

$$\theta = \tan^{-1}(y/x).$$

RCT (TO RECTANGULAR)

Given r in X and θ in Y, replace the contents of the X register with the quantity $x = r \cos \theta$; replace the contents of the Y register with the quantity $y = r \sin \theta$.

### Vector Keys

AC+ (ACCUMULATE PLUS)

Add the number in the Y register to the number in the e register and place the result in the e register; add the number in the X register to the number in the f register and place the result in the f register.

AC- (ACCUMULATE MINUS)

Subtract the number in the Y register from the number in the e register and place the result in the e register; subtract the number in the X register from the number in the f register and place the result in the f register.

RCL (RECALL)

Copy the contents of the e register in the Y register and the contents of the f register in the X register.

### Store Keys

XTO (X TO)

Copy the contents of the X register in the storage location specified by the next keystroke.

YTO (Y TO)

Copy the contents of the Y register in the storage location specified by the next keystroke.

### Recall Keys

a,b,c,d,e,f

Copy the contents of the indicated alphabetically referenced registers in the X register.

YEX (Y EXCHANGE)

Exchange the contents of the Y register with the storage register 0, 1, ..., 9, a, ..., f indicated by the next keystroke.

### Program Control Keys

GTO (GO TO)

Transfer control to the program step addressed by the next two keystrokes.

X<Y (IF X < Y)

If $x < y$, transfer control to the program step addressed by the next two keystrokes provided that they specify an address or execute them if they are instructions; if $x \geq y$, skip the next two program steps.

X=Y (IF X = Y)

If $x = y$, transfer control to the program step addressed by the next two keystrokes provided that they specify an address or execute them if they are instructions; if $x \neq y$, skip the next two program steps.

X>Y (IF X > Y)

If $x > y$, transfer control to the program step addressed by the next two keystrokes provided that they specify an address or execute them if they are instructions; if $x \leq y$; skip the next two program steps.

SFL (SET FLAG)

Set a condition to be tested by the next IF FLAG.

IFG (IF FLAG)

If the flag condition has been set, clear it and transfer control to the program step addressed by the next two keystrokes provided that they specify an address or execute them if they are instructions. Otherwise, skip the next two program steps.

PSE (PAUSE)

Briefly display the X, Y, and Z registers during program execution. When depressed, cause STOP at next programmed PAUSE.

STP (STOP)

Interrupt program execution when used manually or as a program step.

END (END)

End record on magnetic card. Provide STOP and automatic GO TO (0)(0). This instruction is an obligatory last program step.

CNT (CONT)

Initiate program execution with the current address or serve as a space filler.

### Plotter and Printer Control Keys

FMT DN (FORMAT DOWN)

Without lifting the pen proceed in a straight line to the point specified by the numbers in the X and Y registers and plot that point.

FMT UP (FORMAT UP)

Without lowering the pen proceed in a straight line to the point specified by the numbers in the X and Y registers.

PNT (PRINT)

Record on electrosensitive paper that combination of numbers contained in the subset of the X, Y, and Z registers designated by buttons on the printer.

## EXTENDED MEMORY OPERATIONS

The Extended Memory Unit has 248 additional registers, numbered 0 to 247 inclusive, that can hold up to 3,472 program steps. Further, it provides both an indirect arithmetic and a subroutine capability. Subroutines can call other subroutines. This process is called "nesting." Subroutines can be nested 14 deep.

### Data Transfer Keys

FMT YTO (FORMAT Y TO)

Copy the contents of the Y register in the unprotected extended memory register specified by x.

FMT π (FORMAT PI)

Copy the contents of the extended memory register specified by x into the X register.

### Indirect Arithmetic Keys

FMT + (FORMAT PLUS)

Add the number in the Y register to the number in the unprotected extended memory register specified by x.

FMT - (FORMAT MINUS)

Subtract the number in the Y register from the number in the unprotected extended memory register specified by x.

FMT X (FORMAT TIMES)

Multiply the number in the unprotected extended memory register, specified by x, by the number in the Y register.

FMT DIV (FORMAT BY)

Divide the number in the unprotected extended memory register, specified by x, by the number in the Y register.

### Program Transfer Keys

FMT SFG (FORMAT SET FLAG)

Move the program protect line up next to the extended memory register specified by x.

FMT FMT (FORMAT FORMAT)

Transfer a program or subroutine from the calculator memory to the extended memory beginning with the first unprotected register assigning it the label x (two digit maximum). When the transfer is completed, the contents of the X register will be the address of the last protected extended memory register. The transferred routine must conclude with an END statement.

FMT GTO (FORMAT GO TO)

Recall to the calculator memory the protected program or subroutine identified by x. At the conclusion of this operation the X register will contain the address of the last extended memory register recalled.

### Subprogram Keys

FMT END (FORMAT END)

Terminate subroutine execution and return control to the calling routine at the step immediately after the FMT GTO that called the subroutine. At the conclusion of this operation the X register contains the address of the last extended memory register occupied by the calling program and the Y and Z registers are unchanged.

The instructions +, -, X, and DIV represent ordinary arithmetic operations. The first one, for example, causes the contents of the bottom two arithmetic registers, X and Y, to be added together and the resulting sum to be placed in the middle, or Y, register, which acts as the principal accumulator, containing the results of most arithmetic operations, thereby replacing the original summand. This operation does not disturb the prior contents of the top register, which is labeled Z. Similar meanings are attached to the remaining three arithmetic instructions. In addition to holding the addend, subtrahend, multiplier, or divisor in ordinary arithmetic operations, the X register serves as a buffer between the keyboard unit and the internal calculator memory.

The program control is advanced by one program step each time an instruction is selected. This consecutive sequencing can be altered in two ways--unconditionally, by a jump: GTO __, or by a subroutine entry: __FMT GTO, and conditionally by a comparison: X = Y, X < Y, or X > Y, or by a test: IFG. These conditionals enable the calculator to make logical decisions based on intermediate results. Using them, for example, the control can be caused to skip over certain instructions. Program steps normally are stored in registers 0 through 9 of the machine; those in the extra storage registers of the calculator, which are designated by the letters a, b, c, d, e, and f also can be reached by control sequence.

Each extended memory location is identified by an individual three-decimal-digit address by means of which data and instructions can be located as needed during a calculation. There are three visible arithmetic registers: X, Y, and Z. The X or "keyboard" register is used for adding, subtracting, multiplying, and dividing; the Z or "temporary" register is used for holding parameters (answers) during subroutine entries (returns). Special instructions are available for exponentiating, extracting square roots, taking logarithms or antilogarithms, and evaluating trigonmetric and hyperbolic functions. And the decimal point key and the pi key allow known amounts to be entered just as they would be written (see Fig. 9.13). The instructions AC+ and AC- tell the calculator to add or subtract the pair of numbers in the X and Y registers, which may be vector components, to or from the pair of numbers stored in the e and f registers. The instructions RCT and POL provide for transforming to rectangular coordinates from polar coordinates and vice versa.

Figure 9.13

The calculator's decimal point key allows amounts to be entered just as they would be written.

EXAMPLE 1

| Key | X |
|---|---|
| 1 | 1. |
| . | 1. |
| 5 | 1.5 |
| 3 | 1.53 |
| INT | 1. |

EXAMPLE 2

| Key | X |
|---|---|
| 0 | 0. |
| . | 0. |
| 7 | .7 |
| 2 | .72 |
| INT | 0. |

(a) The instruction INT forms the integer part of the number in the X register.

(b) In register display all numbers are alined automatically around a specified decimal point.

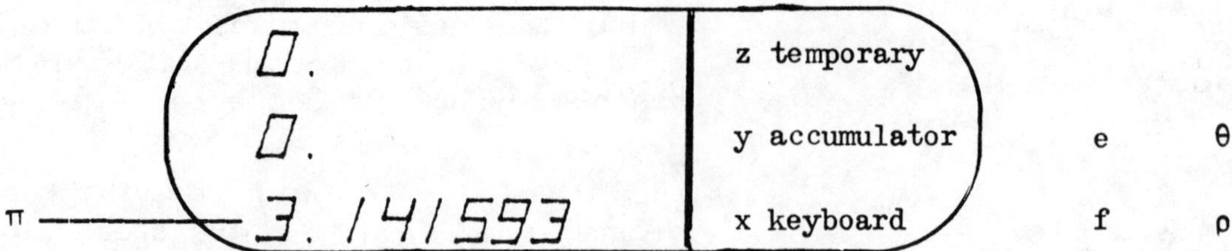


Plotting is achieved by using two basic operations, namely, FMT UP (pen up) and FMT DN (pen down). Here the FORMAT instruction causes the following UP or DOWN order to be interpreted as a plotter command. The pen may be raised or lowered under programmed control to mark any point on the plotter paper. The coordinates of the point to be plotted are specified by the contents of the X and Y registers. By combining these operations with others, the plotter can be utilized to generate reproducible graphics, charts, and line drawings annotated with optional alphanumeric symbols.

EXERCISES

**9.9** Program the following magnitude tests. Assume that p is a number in extended memory location 230 and that q is a number in calculator register f. As a further complication, assume that r is a number in calculator register 8.

(a)

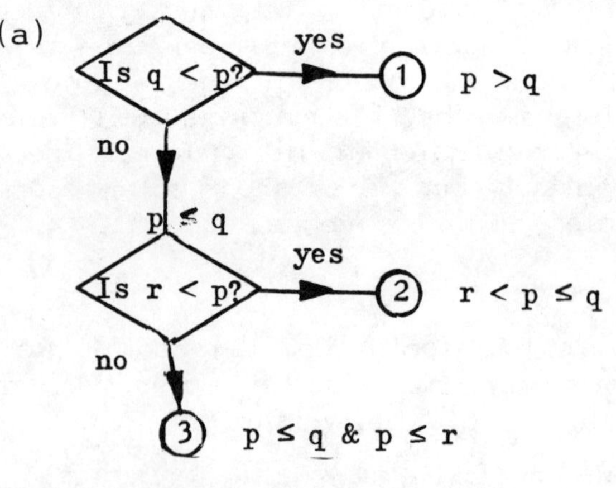


(b)

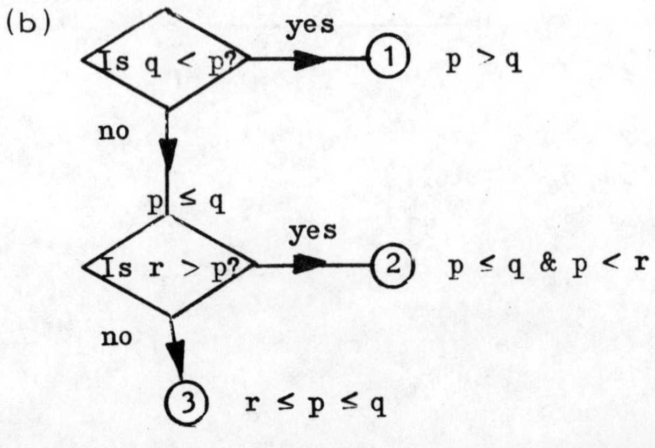


(c)

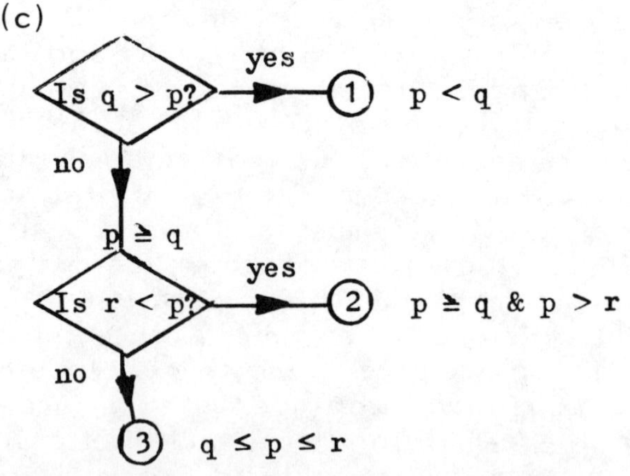


(d)

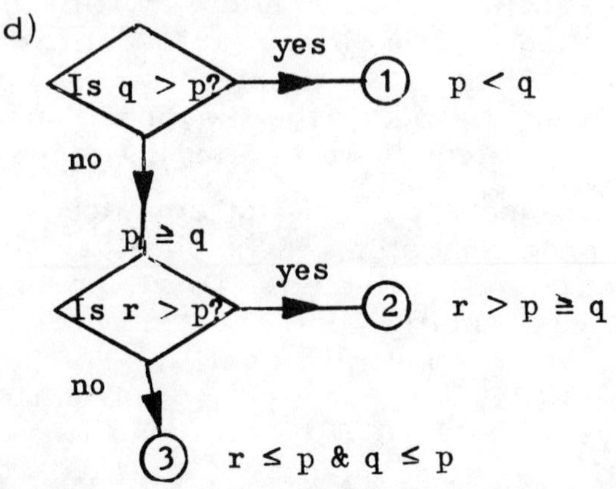

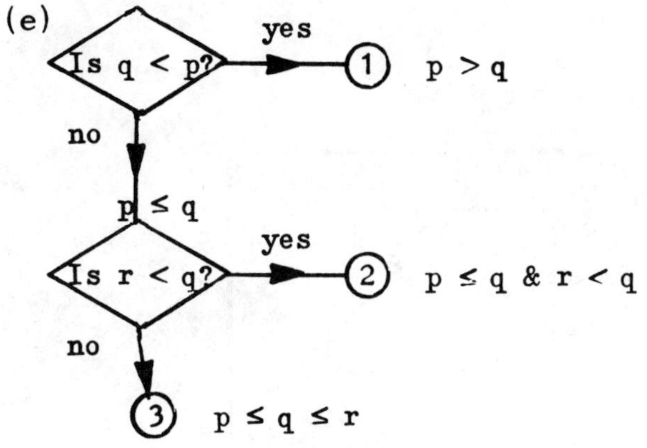


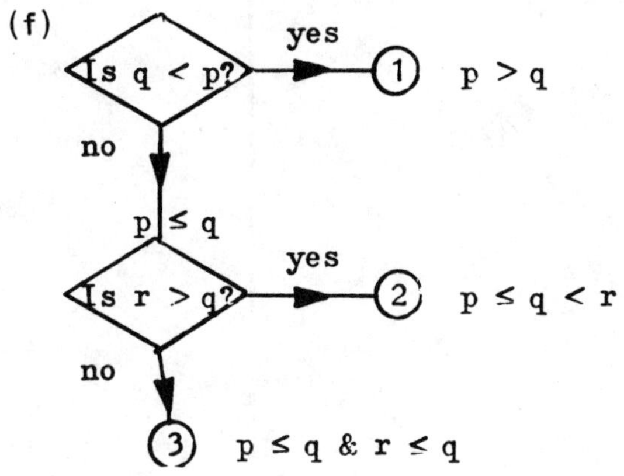


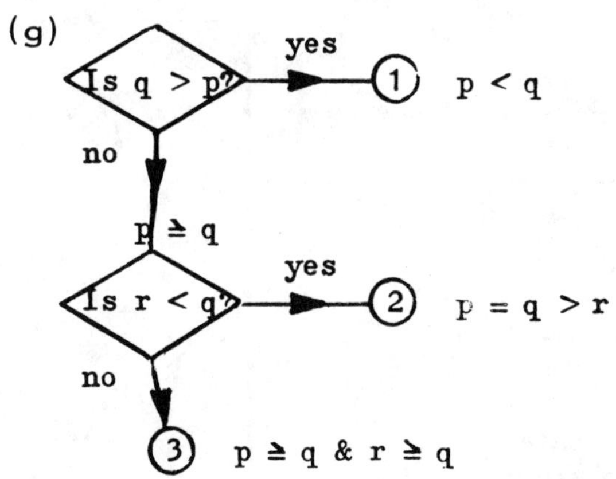


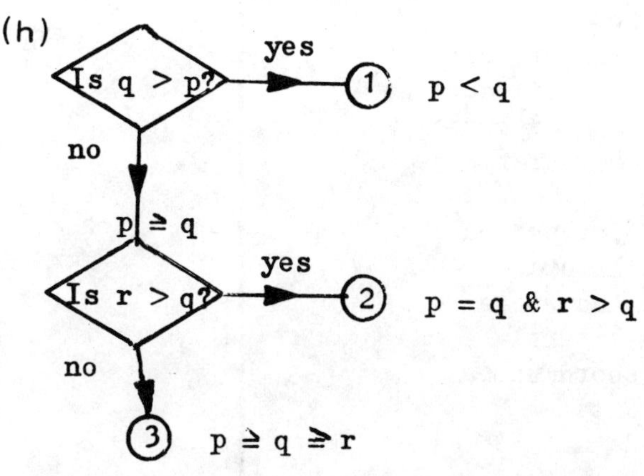


## SUBROUTINE DESCRIPTIONS

The basic requirement of music analysis is not a specific program that will be run only once; but rather, a general program that can be run over and over again. Such a program may consist of a collection or library of functional blocks, called "subroutines," each one of which carries out a particular function. A number of these subroutines can be stored simultaneously in the calculator memory and combinations of them can be related and tied together by one or more main programs to build up the analysis sequence as required.

The main programs and subroutines given in this section are intended to provide direct support for the accomplishment of the basic tasks of elementary music analysis as formulated in earlier parts of this book. Each subroutine treats a different problem or phase of a problem. Although essentially straightforward, they involve occasional tricks, which when well understood should stimulate the reader to think about efficient ways to increase the capability of the system or its descendents. Most of the instructions called for in these programs are self-explanatory. Some of them are clearly housekeeping instructions. In the program listings, the number to the left of each instruction is its memory address; the number to the right, its individual machine code in octal.

These simple tools will permit the music analyst to study many related facets of a musical composition in search for enlightenment. The subroutines are intended to operate together as a composite program. In their present modular form they can provide a valid point of departure for further theoretical development of the computer methodology by the reader. [The publisher encourages comments or recommendations that would increase its usefulness or extend its range of application.]

Figure 9.13

Functional elements of the computer methodology.

MAIN PROGRAMS

| | |
|---|---|
| 0 | Delineation |
| 1 | Component listing |
| 2 | Trajectory |
| 3 | Duration |
| 4 | Weight and cardinality |
| 5 | Specification |
| 6 | Characterization |
| 7 | Designation |
| 8 | Amplitude and phase |
| 9 | Distance and argument |
| 10 | Segment and path length |
| 11 | Relative penetration |
| 12 | Absolute penetration |
| 13 | Absolute penetration history |
| 14 | |
| 15 | |
| 16 | |
| 17 | |
| 18 | Tonality coordinates |
| 19 | Composition coordinates |
| 20 | Coded phonetic notation |
| 21 | Coded inferior true notation |
| 22 | Coded canonical true notation |
| 23 | Coded superior true notation |
| 24 | Coded inferior relative notation |
| 25 | Coded canonical relative notation |
| 26 | Coded superior relative notation |
| 27 | |
| 28 | |
| 29 | |
| 30 | Energy |
| 31 | Energy decline |
| 32 | Tonality amplitude |
| 33 | Impulse magnitude |
| 34 | |
| 35 | |
| 36 | |
| 37 | Span |
| 38 | |
| 39 | |
| 40 | Phonetic notation |
| 41 | Inferior true notation |
| 42 | Canonical true notation |
| 43 | Superior true notation |
| 44 | Inferior relative notation |
| 45 | Canonical relative notation |
| 46 | Superior relative notation |
| 47 | True preferred notation |
| 48 | Relative preferred notation |
| 49 | Data record |
| 50 | |
| 51 | |
| 52 | |
| 53 | |
| 54 | |
| 55 | |
| 56 | |
| 57 | |
| 58 | |
| 59 | |
| 60 | |
| 61 | |
| 62 | |
| 63 | |

DATA

64 - 69

SUBROUTINES

| | |
|---|---|
| 70 | Conclude |
| 71 | Reset |
| 72 | Tab |
| 73 | Weigh |
| 74 | Compute literal |
| 75 | Assemble literal |
| 76 | Switch |
| 77 | Encode literal |
| 78 | Resurrect coordinates |
| 79 | Save coordinates |
| 80 | Write number |
| 81 | Compute history |
| 82 | Displace |
| 83 | Evaluate |
| 84 | Get coordinates |
| 85 | Calculate span |
| 86 | Characterize |
| 87 | Specify |
| 88 | Round and truncate |
| 89 | Write numeral not one |
| 90 | Write signed number |
| 91 | Draw character |
| 92 | Write |
| 93 | Write inflection |
| 94 | Write literal |
| 95 | Clear and store |
| 96 | Fetch literal |
| 97 | Step coordinates |
| 98 | Pack data |
| 99 | Pack data |

Figure 9.14

Memory allocation chart.

| PROGRAM OR SUBROUTINE | EXTENDED MEMORY REGISTERS | DATA | EXTENDED MEMORY REGISTERS |
|---|---|---|---|
| 99 | [ 0, 7] | 69 | [170,179] |
| 98 | [ 8, 12] | 68 | [180,189] |
| 97 | [ 13, 18] | 67 | [190,199] |
| 96 | [ 19, 25] | 66 | [200,209] |
| 95 | [ 26, 27] | 65 | [210,219] |
| 94 | [ 28, 37] | 64 | [220,227] |
| 93 | [ 38, 43] | | |
| 92 | [ 44, 49] | | |
| 91 | [ 50, 58] | | |
| 90 | [ 59, 66] | | |
| 89 | [ 67, 74] | | |
| 88 | [ 75, 78] | | |
| 87 | [ 79, 88] | | |
| 86 | [ 89, 95] | | |
| 85 | [ 96,103] | | |
| 84 | [104,106] | | |
| 83 | [107,111] | | |
| 82 | [112,116] | | |
| 81 | [117,123] | | |
| 80 | [124,124] | | |
| 79 | [125,126] | | |
| 78 | [127,128] | | |
| 77 | [129,134] | | |
| 76 | [135,141] | | |
| 75 | [142,143] | | |
| 74 | [144,148] | | |
| 73 | [149,150] | | |
| 72 | [151,152] | | |
| 71 | [153,157] | | |
| 70 | [158,159] | | |
| 0,1, ... ,63 | [160,169] | | |

Figure 9.15

Interrelationship of subroutines.

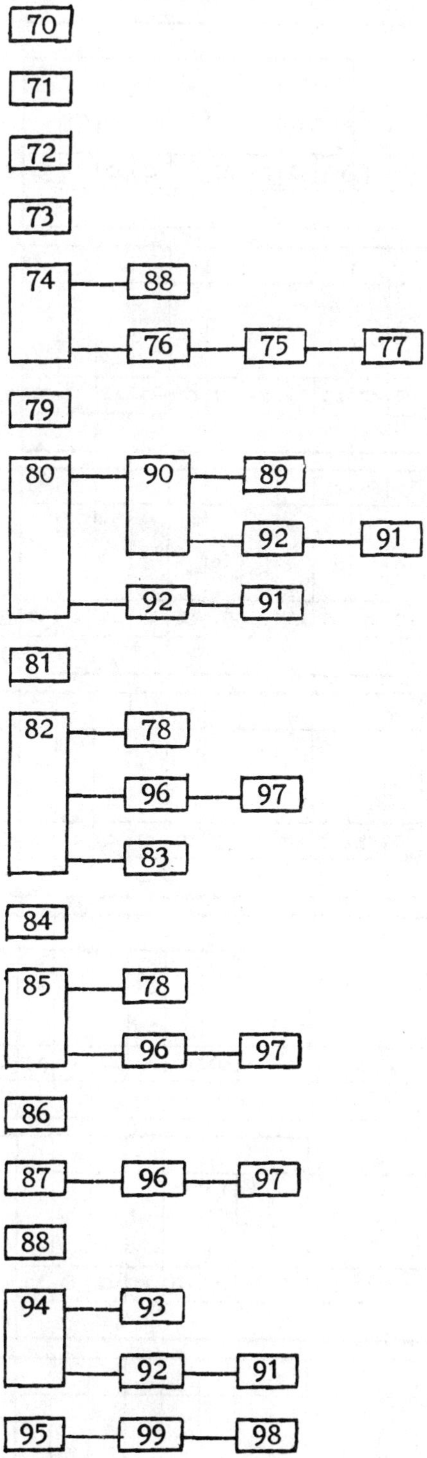

70
71
72
73
74 — 88
74 — 76 — 75 — 77
79
80 — 90 — 89
80 — 90 — 92 — 91
80 — 92 — 91
81
82 — 78
82 — 96 — 97
82 — 83
84
85 — 78
85 — 96 — 97
86
87 — 96 — 97
88
94 — 93
94 — 92 — 91
95 — 99 — 98

Figure 9.16

Sample programming sheet containing a layout of the directly programmable portion of the internal calculator memory.

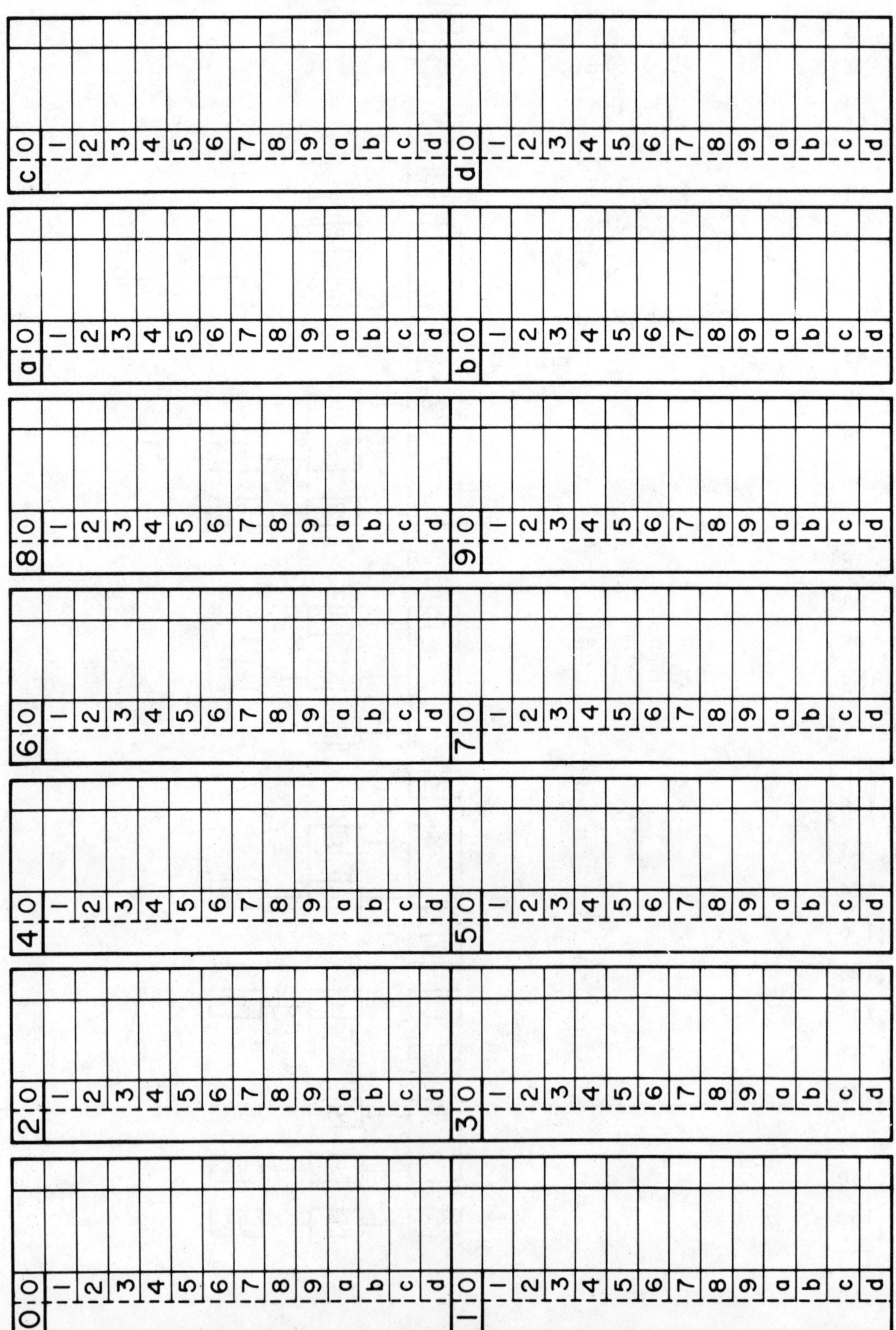

Decimal numbering ranging from 0 to 99 inclusive identifies the routines of this book. The music analysis system that follows utilizes both subroutines and main programs. Of these, a few are employed for orthographic synthesis, which is perhaps the most interesting part theoretically. The long table in Fig. 9.13 suggests the variety of other music analysis functions that is available in this book. Since the basic principles of the computer methodology, especially those of music orthography, have been discussed thoroughly in earlier chapters, it will not be necessary to reiterate them here. Before treating any of these routines in detail, it will be instructive to describe how they fit together. The allocation of storage registers in the extended memory to main programs, subroutines, data, and working locations is shown in the memory map of Fig. 9.14. In individual applications of this automated system for musical investigation, a few of these subroutines may be omitted, but in constructing a complete analysis they all must be entered in order not to ignore any element of importance. A flowchart, given in Fig. 9.15, shows how these subroutines are interrelated and summarizes the sequencing of the subroutine functions. Their application is consecutive in the order that the boxes are connected.

The present discussion of the music analysis routine collection is restricted to listings and capsule descriptions, with a few more words devoted to the more mathematical subroutines, if they are considered to be fundamental to the analytic process. In perusing these routines, remember that the numbers 0, 1, ..., 9; a, b, ..., f are the hexadecimal addresses of storage locations or registers internal to the programmable calculator. These registers are further compartmentalized into fourteen cells, all individually addressed as shown in Fig. 9.16, which are used for specifying program steps--either numerical digits or components of instructions.

To use the music analysis system, part of which can be kept in the extended memory unit indefinitely with the power disconnected, the operator first sets the programmable calculator and extended memory switches to the positions: DEGREES, FIXED POINT, POWER ON, RUN, FILE PROTECT OFF, DECIMAL WHEEL SETTING 6; the printer switches to the positions: ON, X; and the plotter switch to the position: ON. Next, he or she mounts a sheet of either plain white paper or coordinate paper on the surface of the plotting board, using as large a sheet as can be accommodated, and presses the CHART HOLD button to activate the electrostatic holddown of the paper. Then, he or she reads in the subroutines one at a time from magnetic cards or the keyboard into the calculator and transfers them into the extended memory. Finally, the user enters the notes of the musical passage under investigation literal-by-literal, using the numerical keyboard and pressing the CONTINUE button, which causes the appearance of a dot audibly signaling that the machine is ready for the next component to be entered.

All this information is transferred instantly to the waiting calculator, where it is stored in the extended memory. As often as a register is filled with packed data, its contents are printed. At the end, the operator concludes by filling the remainder of the last register used, or the entire next register, with zeros. A sample of the printout produced during the input of **Yankee Doodle** (see Fig. 9.11) is shown in Fig. 9.17. All subsequent outputs are based upon this one data file. Should more storage registers be required to accommodate the musical components for the given subject, the data file can be extended by segmentation and overlays during the computation.

The form of the following collection of music analysis routines, reflecting their various purposes in the computer methodology, is essentially

Figure 9.17

A numerical byproduct is written out during the data readin process, which can be used to check subsequent readins of the same text. Unfortunately, it is coded in a format that is difficult to decypher.

```
2.096404860   11
2.048604840   11
2.096404860   11
2.096709620   11
4.048604810   11
6.048404820   11
7.048304850   11
7.048219250   11
7.024504830   11
5.048704820   11
3.072502430   11
1.048609630   11
5.072702450   11
3.048504870   11
2.048504830   11
2.048704840   11
2.1920        11
          0.
```

a sequential arrangement of annotated listings, specifying the appropriate subroutine arguments and procedures. The main programs, data, subroutines, and initial data input package are placed in separate groupings. According to this plan, the total arrangement of functional elements is such as to permit the inclusion of indefinitely many additional main programs as they are acquired. A few more subroutines, if needed by the user, can be inserted after the initial data input phase is finished, by overlaying routines 95, 98, and 99.

## EXERCISES

**9.10** Write whatever subroutines are necessary to extend the present output character set to include the full upper case English alphabet.

**9.11** Another machine method for music spelling was invented by Longuet-Higgins and Steedman [2], which in its present form applies only to solo parts. (a) Program this method. (b) Extend the method to cover chords of varying durations.

**9.12** In block diagramming, rectangles indicate processing, oblique parallelograms indicate clerical operation, lozenges or diamonds indicate decision, and circles commonly are used to show connections between distant blocks. Following this convention, diagram the subroutines and main programs given in this section.

**9.13** To gain experience and to acquire a good working knowledge concerning the application of the main programs and the subroutines presented, which can be used both singly and in various combinations, develop appropriate test procedures to verify the correctness of each through codechecking.

**9.14** Check some favorite composer's spelling ability, comparing literal notations as they occur on the printed score with the corresponding preferred notations determined in accordance with the perfect orthographic principle.

**9.15** (a) Prepare a program to print out the tempo mark from a stored table based on the correspondence between M.M. and the tempo mark. (b) Why is this program of questionable validity?

**9.16** Work through various programs and subroutines in this section, listing the contents of the X, Y, and Z and other pertinent registers after each instruction.

**9.17** The programming skills to be acquired by working through the programs in this book will be immediately transferable to larger machines since the only differences are in computer languages, not in programming logic. Convert the software in this chapter to Basic, or some other available language, assuming that the data is available on floppy disks or other acceptable input medium.

## |0| DELINEATION

Program 0, which assigns a consecutive two-digit integer starting with 00 to each component of the prestored musical data, is the first main program. It usually is not begun until the subroutines are all stored in the extended memory and the data file has been loaded using Program 95. The instruction sequence consisting of step 19 through step 52 is a loop. So, the same process is reiterated for each component in the sample. This cyclic behavior is common to most of the main programs.

```
0:0: CLX 37    2:0:  6  06    4:0:  1  01
 :1: XTO 23     :1: FMT 42     :1:  +  33
 :2:  a  13     :2: GTO 44     :2: YTO 40
 :3: UP  27     :3:  3  03     :3:  a  13
 :4:  2  02     :4: RDN 31     :4:  9  11
 :5:  2  02     :5:  7  07     :5:  6  06
 :6:  8  10     :6:  0  00     :6: FMT 42
 :7: FMT 42     :7: FMT 42     :7: GTO 44
 :8: YTO 40     :8: GTO 44     :8:  f  15
 :9:  2  02     :9:  7  07     :9: UP  27
 :a:  4  04     :a:  2  02     :a: CLX 37
 :b:  4  04     :b: FMT 42     :b: X=Y 50
 :c: FMT 42     :c: GTO 44     :c:  1  01
 :d: YTO 40     :d:  a  13     :d:  9  11
1:0:  2  02    3:0: UP  27    5:0: GTO 44
 :1:  4  04     :1:  2  02     :1:  4  04
 :2:  5  05     :2: UP  27     :2:  4  04
 :3: FMT 42     :3:  9  11     :3: END 46
 :4: YTO 40     :4:  0  00
 :5:  7  07     :5: FMT 42
 :6:  1  01     :6: GTO 44
 :7: FMT 42     :7: SFL 54
 :8: GTO 44     :8:  9  11
 :9:  7  07     :9:  2  02
 :a:  9  11     :a: FMT 42
 :b: FMT 42     :b: GTO 44
 :c: GTO 44     :c:  a  13
 :d:  9  11     :d: UP  27
```

The output from this line numbering program invariably will be placed in the first column position on the plotter paper. The contents of the remaining columns may be selected or permuted at the convenience of the operator. The remaining column-printing programs are used singly or in combination and provide for their own indentation automatically.

To have the line number start at some other two-digit integer value MN, key in the sequence:

M<br>N<br>XTO<br>a<br>CLX<br>GTO<br>3<br>CNT

## |1| COMPONENT LISTING

Program 1, which records the input data in a free field format, can be extremely useful for checking the accuracy of the readin operation.

```
0:0:  7  07    2:0:  6  06    4:0:  4  04    6:0:  a  13    8:0:  2  02
 :1:  1  01     :1: FMT 42     :1:  6  06     :1: CLX 37     :1: FMT 42
 :2: FMT 42     :2: GTO 44     :2:  4  04     :2: UP  27     :2: GTO 44
 :3: GTO 44     :3:  f  15     :3: GTO 44     :3:  1  01     :3: GTO 44
 :4:  7  07     :4: UP  27     :4:  5  05     :4: UP  27     :4:  0  00
 :5: .2  02     :5: CLX 37     :5:  1  01     :5:  8  10     :5:  4  04
 :6: FMT 42     :6: X=Y 50     :6:  3  03     :6:  0  00     :6: END 46
 :7: GTO 44     :7:  5  05     :7: GTO 44     :7: FMT 42
 :8:  7  07     :8:  c  16     :8:  5  05     :8: GTO 44
 :9:  9  11     :9:  8  10     :9:  1  01     :9:  a  13
 :a: FMT 42     :a:  -  34     :a:  2  02     :a: UP  27
 :b: GTO 44     :b: CLX 37     :b: GTO 44     :b:  3  03
 :c:  9  11     :c: X>Y 53     :c:  5  05     :c: UP  27
 :d:  6  06     :d:  5  05     :d:  1  01     :d:  8  10
1:0: FMT 42    3:0:  0  00    5:0:  1  01    7:0:  8  10
 :1: GTO 44     :1:  7  07     :1: UP  27     :1: FMT 42
 :2:  3  03     :2:  2  02     :2:  f  15     :2: GTO 44
 :3:  2  02     :3:  -  34     :3: XEY 30     :3: IN  25
 :4: RDN 31     :4: CLX 37     :4: UP  27     :4:  1  01
 :5:  7  07     :5: X>Y 53     :5:  8  10     :5:  .  21
 :6:  0  00     :6:  4  04     :6:  0  00     :6:  3  03
 :7: FMT 42     :7:  a  13     :7: FMT 42     :7: UP  27
 :8: GTO 44     :8:  7  07     :8: GTO 44     :8:  9  11
 :9:  7  07     :9:  2  02     :9: GTO 44     :9:  0  00
 :a:  8  10     :a:  0  00     :a:  1  01     :a: FMT 42
 :b: FMT 42     :b:  -  34     :b:  d  17     :b: GTO 44
 :c: GTO 44     :c: CLX 37     :c:  e  12     :c: SFL 54
 :d:  9  11     :d: X>Y 53     :d: XTO 23     :d:  9  11
```

## |2| TRAJECTORY

Program 2 is used to plot all composition trajectories, so it does not print in column format. For each successive charm, the displacement is calculated and added to the previous resultant. The sum is a vector quantity that indicates the current position of the composition point. The new resultant is used to determine the x,y coordinates of the terminus of the next segment of the trajectory to be plotted. The corresponding line is drawn on the graph for the particular composition under investigation. After each displacement vector is plotted, the program control returns to step 0a and calls for the next piece of data.

Note that as the music analyst already has entered the data for each successive chord, there will be an opportunity to inspect the chart as it is being constructed and to identify each as-yet-unexplained occurrence. Needless to say, much charting can be done using manual procedures alone, but not very efficiently.

The polar diagrams distributed throughout this book amply demonstrate the salient capabilities of this valuable little computer program. An internal scale factor (incorporated in steps 04 through 08) may be adjusted as necessary to produce an acceptable size of plot. Specifically, its setting was 0050 for the Otterström illustration, 0060 for miscellaneous work, and 0080 for the Reger examples.

```
0:0: 7   07    2:0: 2   02    4:0: FMT 42    6:0: DN  25
  1: 1   01      1: 3   03      1: GTO 44      1: FMT 42
  2: FMT 42      2: 5   05      2: GTO 44      2: UP  27
  3: GTO 44      3: FMT 42      3: 0   00      3: STP 41
  4: 0   00      4: π   56      4: a   13      4: FMT 42
  5: 1   01      5: UP  27      5: 1   01      5: LN  25
  6: 5   05      6: a   13      6: 6   06      6: CLX 37
  7: 0   00      7: X   36      7: 0   00      7: UP  27
  8: XTO 23      8: 2   02      8: FMT 42      8: FMT 42
  9: a   13      9: 3   03      9: SFL 54      9: LN  25
  a: 7   07      a: 4   04      a: 2   02      a: FMT 42
  b: 9   11      b: FMT 42      b: 3   03      b: UP  27
  c: FMT 42      c: π   56      c: 5   05      c: STP 41
  d: GTO 44      d: UP  27      d: FMT 42      d: END 46
1:0: 9   11    3:0: a   13    5:0: π   56
  1: 6   06      1: X   36      1: UP  27
  2: FMT 42      2: DN  25      2: a   13
  3: GTO 44      3: FMT 42      3: X   36
  4: f   15      4: DN  25      4: 2   02
  5: UP  27      5: 1   01      5: 3   03
  6: CLX 37      6: XTO 23      6: 4   04
  7: X=Y 50      7: b   14      7: FMT 42
  8: 4   04      8: 8   10      8: π   56
  9: 5   05      9: 2   02      9: UP  27
  a: 7   07      a: FMT 42      a: a   13
  b: 8   10      b: GTO 44      b: X   36
  c: FMT 42      c: 8   10      c: DN  25
  d: GTO 44      d: 1   01      d: FMT 42
```

## |3| DURATION

Program 3 determines the total time elapsed by determining the amount of time accorded to each component and summing. The number of decimal places in the answers appearing to the left of the decimal point is 2; the number, to the right of the decimal point is 3. This arrangement is specified by the contents of program steps 30, 31, and 32.

```
0:0: 7   07    2:0: 2   02    4:0: 0   00
  1: 1   01      1: 9   11      1: 4   04
  2: FMT 42      2: FMT 42      2: CLX 37
  3: GTO 44      3: +   33      3: UP  27
  4: 7   07      4: FMT 42      4: 2   02
  5: 2   02      5: π   56      5: 4   04
  6: FMT 42      6: UP  27      6: 4   04
  7: GTO 44      7: 3   03      7: FMT 42
  8: 9   11      8: UP  27      8: YTO 40
  9: 6   06      9: [illegible] 9: 7   07
  a: FMT 42      a: 8   10      a: UP  27
  b: GTO 44      b: FMT 42      b: [illegible] 02
  c: f   15      c: GTO 44      c: [illegible] 02
  d: UP  27      d: DN  25      d: [illegible]
1:0: CLX 37    3:0: 2   02    5:0: FMT 42
  1: X=Y 50      1: .   21      1: +   33
  2: 1   01      2: 3   03      2: [illegible] 01
  3: 7   07      3: UP  27      3: [illegible] 06
  4: GTO 44      4: 9   11      4: [illegible] 00
  5: 0   00      5: 0   00      5: FMT 42
  6: 8   10      6: FMT 42      6: SFL 54
  7: e   12      7: GTO 44      7: STP 41
  8: UP  27      8: SFL 54      8: END 46
  9: CLX 37      9: 9   11
  a: X=Y 50      a: 2   02
  b: 4   04      b: FMT 42
  c: 2   02      c: GTO 44
  d: 2   02      d: GTO 44
```

The duration value for input components is limited to any fraction of the form n/12, with n going from 1 to 96. Generally, the basic equivalence is that one quarter note duration value equals 12/12 or unity.

## |4| WEIGHT AND CARDINALITY

Program 4 obtains and prints in parallel columns the integers corresponding to the chord weight, or number of tones in each component, and the harmonic cardinality, or number of distinct tones in each component.

```
0:0: 7   07    2:0: FMT 42    4:0: X>Y 53
  1: 1   01      1: GTO 44      1: 4   04
  2: FMT 42      2: 7   07      2: 7   07
  3: GTO 44      3: 3   03      3: -   34
  4: 7   07      4: FMT 42      4: GTO 44
  5: 9   11      5: GTO 44      5: 4   04
  6: FMT 42      6: 8   10      6: 0   00
  7: GTO 44      7: 0   00      7: YTO 40
  8: 9   11      8: FMT 42      8: f   15
  9: 6   06      9: GTO 44      9: 7   07
  a: FMT 42      a: 7   07      a: 3   03
  b: GTO 44      b: 8   10      b: FMT 42
  c: 6   06      c: FMT 42      c: GTO 44
  d: RDN 31      d: GTO 44      d: 9   11
1:0: 7   07    3:0: 8   10    5:0: 0   00
  1: 0   00      1: 7   07      1: FMT 42
  2: FMT 42      2: FMT 42      2: GTO 44
  3: GTO 44      3: GTO 44      3: SFL 54
  4: 7   07      4: 8   10      4: 9   11
  5: 2   02      5: 6   06      5: 2   02
  6: FMT 42      6: FMT 42      6: FMT 42
  7: GTO 44      7: GTO 44      7: GTO 44
  8: 7   07      8: DN  25      8: GTO 44
  9: 8   10      9: X   36      9: 0   00
  a: FMT 42      a: 4   04      a: 4   04
  b: GTO 44      b: 0   00      b: END 46
  c: 8   10      c: 9   11
  d: 7   07      d: 5   05
```

## |5| SPECIFICATION

Program 5, which computes and records the charm specification for each component, owes its apparent brevity to the fact that it makes direct call upon nine subroutines.

```
0:0: 7   07    2:0: 7   07
  1: 1   01      1: FMT 42
  2: FMT 42      2: GTO 44
  3: GTO 44      3: 9   11
  4: 7   07      4: 0   00
  5: 9   11      5: FMT 42
  6: FMT 42      6: GTO 44
  7: GTO 44      7: SFL 54
  8: 9   11      8: 9   11
  9: 6   06      9: 2   02
  a: FMT 42      a: FMT 42
  b: GTO 44      b: GTO 44
  c: 1   01      c: GTO 44
  d: 3   03      d: 0   00
1:0: RDN 31    3:0: 4   04
  1: 7   07      1: END 46
  2: 0   00
  3: FMT 42
  4: GTO 44
  5: 7   07
  6: 2   02
  7: FMT 42
  8: GTO 44
  9: 7   07
  a: 8   10
  b: FMT 42
  c: GTO 44
  d: 8   10
```

## |6| CHARACTERIZATION

Program 6 is probably the most important member of the battery of programs devoted to elementary harmonic principles. It provides a factorization of the harmonic designation for each component into its associated characteristic and level.

```
0¦0¦  7  07   2¦0¦  7  07   4¦0¦ GTO 44
 ¦1¦  1  01    ¦1¦ FMT 42    ¦1¦  a  13
 ¦2¦ FMT 42    ¦2¦ GTO 44    ¦2¦ UP  27
 ¦3¦ GTO 44    ¦3¦  8  10    ¦3¦  4  04
 ¦4¦  7  07    ¦4¦  6  06    ¦4¦ UP  27
 ¦5¦  9  11    ¦5¦ FMT 42    ¦5¦  9  11
 ¦6¦ FMT 42    ¦6¦ GTO 44    ¦6¦  0  00
 ¦7¦ GTO 44    ¦7¦  4  04    ¦7¦ FMT 42
 ¦8¦  9  11    ¦8¦ XTO 23    ¦8¦ GTO 44
 ¦9¦  6  06    ¦9¦  a  13    ¦9¦ SFL 54
 ¦a¦ FMT 42    ¦a¦ YE  24    ¦a¦  9  11
 ¦b¦ GTO 44    ¦b¦  a  13    ¦b¦  2  02
 ¦c¦  1  01    ¦c¦  9  11    ¦c¦ FMT 42
 ¦d¦  0  00    ¦d¦  0  00    ¦d¦ GTO 44
1¦0¦ RDN 31   3¦0¦ FMT 42   5¦0¦ GTO 44
 ¦1¦  7  07    ¦1¦ GTO 44    ¦1¦  0  00
 ¦2¦  0  00    ¦2¦  1  01    ¦2¦  4  04
 ¦3¦ FMT 42    ¦3¦  9  11    ¦3¦ END 46
 ¦4¦ GTO 44    ¦4¦  9  11
 ¦5¦  7  07    ¦5¦  3  03
 ¦6¦  2  02    ¦6¦  7  07
 ¦7¦ FMT 42    ¦7¦  7  07
 ¦8¦ GTO 44    ¦8¦  6  06
 ¦9¦  7  07    ¦9¦  4  04
 ¦a¦  8  10    ¦a¦ UP  27
 ¦b¦ FMT 42    ¦b¦  9  11
 ¦c¦ GTO 44    ¦c¦  2  02
 ¦d¦  8  10    ¦d¦ FMT 42
```

## |7| DESIGNATION

Program 7 can be used either independently or in conjunction with programs 0, 5, and 6. It produces and prints in a column the value of the harmonic designation corresponding to each component previously introduced as part of the input data.

```
0¦0¦  7  07   2¦0¦ FMT 42   4¦0¦ FMT 42
 ¦1¦  1  01    ¦1¦ GTO 44    ¦1¦ GTO 44
 ¦2¦ FMT 42    ¦2¦  8  10    ¦2¦ GTO 44
 ¦3¦ GTO 44    ¦3¦  6  06    ¦3¦  0  00
 ¦4¦  7  07    ¦4¦ FMT 42    ¦4¦  4  04
 ¦5¦  9  11    ¦5¦ GTO 44    ¦5¦ END 46
 ¦6¦ FMT 42    ¦6¦ DN  25
 ¦7¦ GTO 44    ¦7¦  X  36
 ¦8¦  9  11    ¦8¦  4  04
 ¦9¦  6  06    ¦9¦  0  00
 ¦a¦ FMT 42    ¦a¦  9  11
 ¦b¦ GTO 44    ¦b¦  5  05
 ¦c¦  5  05    ¦c¦ X>Y 53
 ¦d¦ RDN 31    ¦d¦  3  03
1¦0¦  7  07   3¦0¦  5  05
 ¦1¦  0  00    ¦1¦  -  34
 ¦2¦ FMT 42    ¦2¦ GTO 44
 ¦3¦ GTO 44    ¦3¦  2  02
 ¦4¦  7  07    ¦4¦  c  16
 ¦5¦  2  02    ¦5¦  4  04
 ¦6¦ FMT 42    ¦6¦ UP  27
 ¦7¦ GTO 44    ¦7¦  9  11
 ¦8¦  7  07    ¦8¦  0  00
 ¦9¦  8  10    ¦9¦ FMT 42
 ¦a¦ FMT 42    ¦a¦ GTO 44
 ¦b¦ GTO 44    ¦b¦ SFL 54
 ¦c¦  8  10    ¦c¦  9  11
 ¦d¦  7  07    ¦d¦  2  02
```

## |8| AMPLITUDE AND PHASE

Without question, program 8 can play a critical role in quantitative tonal analysis. The reason for this is simple. A knowledge of both the amplitude and the phase angle is necessary in order to specify the instantaneous tonality vector completely. The values obtained and printed by this program are correct to three decimal places.

```
0¦0¦  7  07   2¦0¦ FMT 42   4¦0¦ GTO 44   6¦0¦  9  11
 ¦1¦  1  01    ¦1¦ GTO 44    ¦1¦ DN  25    ¦1¦  2  02
 ¦2¦ FMT 42    ¦2¦  2  02    ¦2¦  1  01    ¦2¦ FMT 42
 ¦3¦ GTO 44    ¦3¦  3  03    ¦3¦  .  21    ¦3¦ GTO 44
 ¦4¦  7  07    ¦4¦  9  11    ¦4¦  3  03    ¦4¦ GTO 44
 ¦5¦  2  02    ¦5¦ FMT 42    ¦5¦ UP  27    ¦5¦  0  00
 ¦6¦ FMT 42    ¦6¦  π  56    ¦6¦  8  10    ¦6¦  4  04
 ¦7¦ GTO 44    ¦7¦ UP  27    ¦7¦  0  00    ¦7¦ END 46
 ¦8¦  7  07    ¦8¦  e  12    ¦8¦ FMT 42
 ¦9¦  9  11    ¦9¦ DIV 35    ¦9¦ GTO 44
 ¦a¦ FMT 42    ¦a¦  2  02    ¦a¦  a  13
 ¦b¦ GTO 44    ¦b¦  3  03    ¦b¦ UP  27
 ¦c¦  9  11    ¦c¦  8  10    ¦c¦  3  03
 ¦d¦  6  06    ¦d¦ FMT 42    ¦d¦ UP  27
1¦0¦ FMT 42   3¦0¦  π  56   5¦0¦  8  10
 ¦1¦ GTO 44    ¦1¦ UP  27    ¦1¦  8  10
 ¦2¦  1  01    ¦2¦  e  12    ¦2¦ FMT 42
 ¦3¦  4  04    ¦3¦ DIV 35    ¦3¦ GTO 44
 ¦4¦ RDN 31    ¦4¦ DN  25    ¦4¦ DN  25
 ¦5¦  7  07    ¦5¦ POL 62    ¦5¦  3  03
 ¦6¦  0  00    ¦6¦ YTO 40    ¦6¦  .  21
 ¦7¦ FMT 42    ¦7¦  a  13    ¦7¦  3  03
 ¦8¦ GTO 44    ¦8¦ UP  27    ¦8¦ UP  27
 ¦9¦  1  01    ¦9¦  3  03    ¦9¦  9  11
 ¦a¦ XTO 23    ¦a¦ UP  27    ¦a¦  0  00
 ¦b¦  b  14    ¦b¦  8  10    ¦b¦ FMT 42
 ¦c¦  8  10    ¦c¦  8  10    ¦c¦ GTO 44
 ¦d¦  2  02    ¦d¦ FMT 42    ¦d¦ SFL 54
```

## |9| DISTANCE AND ARGUMENT

Like program 8, program 9 is fundamental to quantitative tonal analysis. It is fundamental because the location of the composition point tells so much about the instantaneous key center. To know this location requires two facts--the distance of the composition point from the origin and the argument or angle of the composition vector with the polar axis. Of course, it should be recognized that the key is never uniquely determined. Every piece of music can be represented by a composition point or vector, the location of which varies with time. This vector at each instant projects into a dozen keys at once, being projected on each key axis to a varying degree.

```
0¦0¦  7  07   2¦0¦ FMT 42   4¦0¦  3  03   6¦0¦ FMT 42
 ¦1¦  1  01    ¦1¦ GTO 44    ¦1¦  .  21    ¦1¦ GTO 44
 ¦2¦ FMT 42    ¦2¦  8  10    ¦2¦  3  03    ¦2¦ GTO 44
 ¦3¦ GTO 44    ¦3¦  1  01    ¦3¦ UP  27    ¦3¦  0  00
 ¦4¦  7  07    ¦4¦ FMT 42    ¦4¦  8  10    ¦4¦  4  04
 ¦5¦  2  02    ¦5¦ GTO 44    ¦5¦  0  00    ¦5¦ END 46
 ¦6¦ FMT 42    ¦6¦ YTO 40    ¦6¦ FMT 42
 ¦7¦ GTO 44    ¦7¦  a  13    ¦7¦ GTO 44
 ¦8¦  7  07    ¦8¦  2  02    ¦8¦  a  13
 ¦9¦  9  11    ¦9¦  3  03    ¦9¦ UP  27
 ¦a¦ FMT 42    ¦a¦  5  05    ¦a¦  3  03
 ¦b¦ GTO 44    ¦b¦ FMT 42    ¦b¦ UP  27
 ¦c¦  9  11    ¦c¦  π  56    ¦c¦  8  10
 ¦d¦  6  06    ¦d¦ UP  27    ¦d¦  8  10
1¦0¦ FMT 42   3¦0¦  2  02   5¦0¦ FMT 42
 ¦1¦ GTO 44    ¦1¦  3  03    ¦1¦ GTO 44
 ¦2¦  1  01    ¦2¦  4  04    ¦2¦ DN  25
 ¦3¦  6  06    ¦3¦ FMT 42    ¦3¦  3  03
 ¦4¦ RDN 31    ¦4¦  π  56    ¦4¦  .  21
 ¦5¦  7  07    ¦5¦ POL 62    ¦5¦  3  03
 ¦6¦  0  00    ¦6¦ UP  27    ¦6¦ UP  27
 ¦7¦ FMT 42    ¦7¦  3  03    ¦7¦  9  11
 ¦8¦ GTO 44    ¦8¦ UP  27    ¦8¦  0  00
 ¦9¦  1  01    ¦9¦  8  10    ¦9¦ FMT 42
 ¦a¦ XTO 23    ¦a¦  8  10    ¦a¦ GTO 44
 ¦b¦  b  14    ¦b¦ FMT 42    ¦b¦ SFL 54
 ¦c¦  8  10    ¦c¦ GTO 44    ¦c¦  9  11
 ¦d¦  2  02    ¦d¦ DN  25    ¦d¦  2  02
```

Program 9 writes two fields of numbers. The first field contains the distance

$$R = |\sum r_i|,$$

where

$$r_i = v_i \Delta t_i = \sqrt{x_i^2 + y_i^2},$$

and the second, the argument $\theta = \arg z$, where

$$\theta = \arctan y/x \text{ and } z = x + iy.$$

## |10| SEGMENT AND PATH LENGTH

```
0:0:  7  07   2:0: FMT 42   4:0:  8  10   6:0:  3  03
 :1:  1  01    :1: GTO 44    :1:  8  10    :1: UP  27
 :2: FMT 42    :2:  2  02    :2: FMT 42    :2:  9  11
 :3: GTO 44    :3:  3  03    :3: GTO 44    :3:  0  00
 :4:  7  07    :4:  9  11    :4: DN  25    :4: FMT 42
 :5:  2  02    :5: FMT 42    :5:  1  01    :5: GTO 44
 :6: FMT 42    :6:  π  56    :6:  .  21    :6: SFL 54
 :7: GTO 44    :7: UP  27    :7:  3  03    :7:  9  11
 :8:  7  07    :8:  ×  36    :8: UP  27    :8:  2  02
 :9:  9  11    :9:  2  02    :9:  8  10    :9: FMT 42
 :a: FMT 42    :a:  3  03    :a:  0  00    :a: GTO 44
 :b: GTO 44    :b:  8  10    :b: FMT 42    :b: GTO 44
 :c:  9  11    :c: FMT 42    :c: GTO 44    :c:  0  00
 :d:  6  06    :d:  π  56    :d:  2  02    :d:  4  04
1:0: FMT 42   3:0: UP  27   5:0:  2  02   7:0: END 46
 :1: GTO 44    :1:  ×  36    :1:  9  11
 :2:  1  01    :2: DN  25    :2: FMT 42
 :3:  4  04    :3:  +  33    :3:  π  56
 :4: RDN 31    :4: DN  25    :4: UP  27
 :5:  7  07    :5:  √  76    :5:  3  03
 :6:  0  00    :6: UP  27    :6: UP  27
 :7: FMT 42    :7:  2  02    :7:  8  10
 :8: GTO 44    :8:  2  02    :8:  8  10
 :9:  1  01    :9:  9  11    :9: FMT 42
 :a: XTO 23    :a: FMT 42    :a: GTO 44
 :b:  b  14    :b:  +  33    :b: DN  25
 :c:  8  10    :c:  3  03    :c:  3  03
 :d:  2  02    :d: UP  27    :d:  .  21
```

## |11| RELATIVE PENETRATION

Program 11 produces an array of numbers. The layout of these numbers affords a bird's-eye view of the extent to which the composition vector is committed to various keys, as a function of component number. If a line, called the "100% locus," is drawn to connect those 00 values marking the maxima, then it is possible to visualize the relationship between the tonality and the musical structure of the composition readily in terms of key shifts.

```
0:0:  7  07   2:0: FMT 42   4:0: CLX 37   6:0:  2  02   8:0: END 46
 :1:  1  01    :1: GTO 44    :1: X>Y 53    :1:  7  07
 :2: FMT 42    :2:  8  10    :2:  7  07    :2:  5  05
 :3: GTO 44    :3:  1  01    :3:  2  02    :3: X>Y 53
 :4:  7  07    :4: FMT 42    :4:  2  02    :4:  2  02
 :5:  2  02    :5: GTO 44    :5: UP  27    :5:  b  14
 :6: FMT 42    :6:  9  11    :6:  8  10    :6: CLX 37
 :7: GTO 44    :7:  0  00    :7:  8  10    :7: XEY 30
 :8:  7  07    :8: CHS 32    :8: FMT 42    :8: SFL 54
 :9:  9  11    :9: XTO 23    :9: GTO 44    :9:  9  11
 :a: FMT 42    :a:  a  13    :a: DN  25    :a:  2  02
 :b: GTO 44    :b:  2  02    :b:  1  01    :b: FMT 42
 :c:  9  11    :c:  3  03    :c:  0  00    :c: GTO 44
 :d:  6  06    :d:  5  05    :d:  0  00    :d: GTO 44
1:0: FMT 42   3:0: FMT 42   5:0:  X  36   7:0:  0  00
 :1: GTO 44    :1:  π  56    :1:  2  02    :1:  4  04
 :2:  7  07    :2: UP  27    :2: UP  27    :2:  1  01
 :3:  5  05    :3:  2  02    :3:  8  10    :3:  0  00
 :4: RDN 31    :4:  3  03    :4:  0  00    :4:  8  10
 :5:  7  07    :5:  4  04    :5: FMT 42    :5: UP  27
 :6:  0  00    :6: FMT 42    :6: GTO 44    :6:  2  02
 :7: FMT 42    :7:  π  56    :7:  a  13    :7:  4  04
 :8: GTO 44    :8: POL 62    :8: UP  27    :8:  5  05
 :9:  1  01    :9:  a  13    :9:  1  01    :9: FMT 42
 :a: XTO 23    :a:  -  34    :a:  5  05    :a:  +  33
 :b:  b  14    :b: DN  25    :b:  +  33    :b: GTO 44
 :c:  8  10    :c: COS 73    :c: YTO 40    :c:  5  05
 :d:  2  02    :d: UP  27    :d:  a  13    :d:  7  07
```

## |12| ABSOLUTE PENETRATION

Program 12 prints out another array of numbers, closely related to the output from program 11. The numbers correspond to the function

$$\alpha = \log_{10} r \cos(\theta - k).$$

```
0:0:  7  07   2:0: FMT 42   4:0: COS 73   6:0: UP  27   8:0:  5  05
 :1:  1  01    :1: GTO 44    :1: UP  27    :1:  1  01    :1: FMT 42
 :2: FMT 42    :2:  8  10    :2: CLX 37    :2:  5  05    :2:  +  33
 :3: GTO 44    :3:  1  01    :3: X>Y 53    :3:  +  33    :3: GTO 44
 :4:  7  07    :4: FMT 42    :4:  7  07    :4: YTO 40    :4:  5  05
 :5:  2  02    :5: GTO 44    :5:  8  10    :5:  a  13    :5:  d  17
 :6: FMT 42    :6:  9  11    :6:  b  14    :6:  2  02    :6: END 46
 :7: GTO 44    :7:  0  00    :7:  X  36    :7:  7  07
 :8:  7  07    :8: CHS 32    :8: DN  25    :8:  5  05
 :9:  9  11    :9: XTO 23    :9: LOG 75    :9: X>Y 53
 :a: FMT 42    :a:  a  13    :a: UP  27    :a:  2  02
 :b: GTO 44    :b:  2  02    :b:  1  01    :b:  b  14
 :c:  9  11    :c:  3  03    :c:  0  00    :c: CLX 37
 :d:  6  06    :d:  5  05    :d:  X  36    :d: XEY 30
1:0: FMT 42   3:0: FMT 42   5:0:  2  02   7:0: SFL 54
 :1: GTO 44    :1:  π  56    :1: UP  27    :1:  9  11
 :2:  7  07    :2: UP  27    :2:  8  10    :2:  2  02
 :3:  5  05    :3:  2  02    :3:  8  10    :3: FMT 42
 :4: RDN 31    :4:  3  03    :4: FMT 42    :4: GTO 44
 :5:  7  07    :5:  4  04    :5: GTO 44    :5: GTO 44
 :6:  0  00    :6: FMT 42    :6: DN  25    :6:  0  00
 :7: FMT 42    :7:  π  56    :7:  2  02    :7:  4  04
 :8: GTO 44    :8: POL 62    :8: UP  27    :8:  1  01
 :9:  1  01    :9: XTO 23    :9:  8  10    :9:  0  00
 :a: XTO 23    :a:  b  14    :a:  0  00    :a:  8  10
 :b:  b  14    :b:  a  13    :b: FMT 42    :b: UP  27
 :c:  8  10    :c:  -  34    :c: GTO 44    :c:  2  02
 :d:  2  02    :d: DN  25    :d:  a  13    :d:  4  04
```

As evidenced more by examples than by substantiating theory, the resulting map--especially when highlighted by some hand-drawn contour lines--provides a prominent aerial view of the progress of the musical composition through time and how it casts its moving shadow on the surrounding terrain.

## |13| ABSOLUTE PENETRATION HISTORY

Program 13, which calls upon subroutines 71, 79, 96, 82, 81, and

```
0:0: CLX 37   2:0:  8  10   4:0:  X  36   6:0: FMT 42   8:0:  a  13
 :1: XTO 23    :1:  1  01    :1: DN  25    :1:  π  56    :1:  3  03
 :2:  a  13    :2: FMT 42    :2: LOG 75    :2: YE  24    :2:  5  05
 :3:  7  07    :3: GTO 44    :3: UP  27    :3:  b  14    :3:  5  05
 :4:  1  01    :4:  2  02    :4:  1  01    :4: FMT 42    :4: X>Y 53
 :5: FMT 42    :5:  3  03    :5:  0  00    :5: DN  25    :5:  0  00
 :6: GTO 44    :6:  5  05    :6:  0  00    :6: CLX 37    :6:  3  03
 :7:  7  07    :7: FMT 42    :7:  0  00    :7: X=Y 50    :7: CLX 37
 :8:  9  11    :8:  π  56    :8:  X  36    :8: FMT 42    :8: RDN 31
 :9: FMT 42    :9: UP  27    :9:  2  02    :9: UP  27    :9:  7  07
 :a: GTO 44    :a:  2  02    :a:  0  00    :a: GTO 44    :a:  0  00
 :b:  9  11    :b:  3  03    :b:  0  00    :b:  0  00    :b: FMT 42
 :c:  6  06    :c:  4  04    :c:  0  00    :c:  7  07    :c: GTO 44
 :d: FMT 42    :d: FMT 42    :d:  -  34    :d: FMT 42    :d: STP 41
1:0: GTO 44   3:0:  π  56   5:0: YTO 40   7:0: UP  27   9:0:  1  01
 :1:  f  15    :1: POL 62    :1:  b  14    :1: CLX 37    :1:  5  05
 :2: UP  27    :2: XTO 23    :2:  e  12    :2: UP  27    :2: GTO 44
 :3: CLX 37    :3:  b  14    :3: UP  27    :3: GTO 44    :3:  0  00
 :4: X=Y 50    :4:  a  13    :4:  0  00    :4:  5  05    :4:  1  01
 :5:  7  07    :5:  -  34    :5:  0  00    :5:  0  00    :5: END 46
 :6:  6  06    :6: DN  25    :6:  3  03    :6: FMT 42
 :7:  1  01    :7: COS 73    :7:  0  00    :7: UP  27
 :8: XTO 23    :8: UP  27    :8:  X  36    :8:  a  13
 :9:  b  14    :9: CLX 37    :9:  2  02    :9: UP  27
 :a:  8  10    :a: X>Y 53    :a:  2  02    :a:  3  03
 :b:  2  02    :b:  6  06    :b:  9  11    :b:  0  00
 :c: FMT 42    :c:  d  17    :c: FMT 42    :c:  +  33
 :d: GTO 44    :d:  b  14    :d:  +  33    :d: YTO 40
```

70, yields a multiple curve graph of the absolute penetration function along the major or minor key axes. The choice of major key axes is made by starting at step 00; the choice of minor key axes, by starting at step 90. The resulting semi-logarithmic plot can be stretched sideways be enlarging the automatic scale factor contained in steps 54 through 57 inclusive. The individual curves can be labeled by hand as the work progresses. Otherwise they are not very meaningful, although the overall shape of the ensemble tells much about the tonal regime by its general appearance.

## |18| TONALITY COORDINATES

This program calculates the components

$$v_x = \mathrm{Re}(v) \text{ and } v_y = \mathrm{Im}(v)$$

of the tonality vector $v = v_x + iv_y$.

To do so it calls upon ten different subroutines.

```
0:0:    7 07    2:0:  FMT 42    4:0:  GTO 44    6:0:    9 11
 :1:    1 01     :1:  GTO 44     :1:   DN 25     :1:    2 02
 :2:  FMT 42     :2:    2 02     :2:    3 03     :2:  FMT 42
 :3:  GTO 44     :3:    3 03     :3:    . 21     :3:  GTO 44
 :4:    7 07     :4:    9 11     :4:    3 03     :4:  GTO 44
 :5:    2 02     :5:  FMT 42     :5:   UP 27     :5:    0 00
 :6:  FMT 42     :6:    π 56     :6:    8 10     :6:    4 04
 :7:  GTO 44     :7:   UP 27     :7:    0 00     :7:  END 46
 :8:    7 07     :8:    e 12     :8:  FMT 42
 :9:    9 11     :9:  DIV 35     :9:  GTO 44
 :a:  FMT 42     :a:    2 02     :a:    a 13
 :b:  GTO 44     :b:    3 03     :b:   UP 27
 :c:    9 11     :c:    8 10     :c:    3 03
 :d:    6 06     :d:  FMT 42     :d:   UP 27
1:0:  FMT 42    3:0:    π 56    5:0:    8 10
 :1:  GTO 44     :1:   UP 27     :1:    8 10
 :2:    1 01     :2:    e 12     :2:  FMT 42
 :3:    6 06     :3:  DIV 35     :3:  GTO 44
 :4:  RDN 31     :4:   DN 25     :4:   DN 25
 :5:    7 07     :5:  CNT 47     :5:    3 03
 :6:    0 00     :6:  YTO 40     :6:    . 21
 :7:  FMT 42     :7:    a 13     :7:    3 03
 :8:  GTO 44     :8:   UP 27     :8:   UP 27
 :9:    1 01     :9:    3 03     :9:    9 11
 :a:  XTO 23     :a:   UP 27     :a:    0 00
 :b:    b 14     :b:    8 10     :b:  FMT 42
 :c:    8 10     :c:    8 10     :c:  GTO 44
 :d:    2 02     :d:  FMT 42     :d:  SFL 54
```

## |19| COMPOSITION COORDINATES

```
0:0:    7 07    2:0:  FMT 42    4:0:    3 03    6:0:  FMT 42
 :1:    1 01     :1:  GTO 44     :1:    . 21     :1:  GTO 44
 :2:  FMT 42     :2:    8 10     :2:    3 03     :2:  GTO 44
 :3:  GTO 44     :3:    1 01     :3:   UP 27     :3:    0 00
 :4:    7 07     :4:  FMT 42     :4:    8 10     :4:    4 04
 :5:    2 02     :5:  GTO 44     :5:    0 00     :5:  END 46
 :6:  FMT 42     :6:    2 02     :6:  FMT 42
 :7:  GTO 44     :7:    3 03     :7:  GTO 44
 :8:    7 07     :8:    5 05     :8:    a 13
 :9:    9 11     :9:  FMT 42     :9:   UP 27
 :a:  FMT 42     :a:    π 56     :a:    3 03
 :b:  GTO 44     :b:   UP 27     :b:   UP 27
 :c:    9 11     :c:    2 02     :c:    8 10
 :d:    6 06     :d:    3 03     :d:    8 10
1:0:  FMT 42    3:0:    9 09    5:0:  FMT 42
 :1:  GTO 44     :1:  FMT 42     :1:  GTO 44
 :2:    1 01     :2:    π 56     :2:   DN 25
 :3:    6 06     :3:  CNT 47     :3:    3 03
 :4:  RDN 31     :4:  YTO 40     :4:    . 21
 :5:    7 07     :5:    a 13     :5:    3 03
 :6:    0 00     :6:   UP 27     :6:   UP 27
 :7:  FMT 42     :7:    3 03     :7:    9 11
 :8:  GTO 44     :8:   UP 27     :8:    0 00
 :9:    1 01     :9:    8 10     :9:  FMT 42
 :a:  XTO 23     :a:    8 10     :a:  GTO 44
 :b:    b 14     :b:  FMT 42     :b:  SFL 54
 :c:    8 10     :c:  GTO 44     :c:    9 11
 :d:    2 02     :d:   DN 25     :d:    2 02
```

## |20| CODED PHONETIC NOTATION

```
0:0:    7 07    2:0:    6 06    4:0:    4 04    6:0:    2 02
 :1:    1 01     :1:  FMT 42     :1:    6 06     :1:  FMT 42
 :2:  FMT 42     :2:  GTO 44     :2:    4 04     :2:  GTO 44
 :3:  GTO 44     :3:    f 15     :3:  GTO 44     :3:  GTO 44
 :4:    7 07     :4:   UP 27     :4:    5 05     :4:    0 00
 :5:    2 02     :5:  CLX 37     :5:    1 01     :5:    4 04
 :6:  FMT 42     :6:  X=Y 50     :6:    3 03     :6:  END 46
 :7:  GTO 44     :7:    5 05     :7:  GTO 44
 :8:    7 07     :8:    c 16     :8:    5 05
 :9:    9 11     :9:    8 10     :9:    1 01
 :a:  FMT 42     :a:    - 34     :a:    2 02
 :b:  GTO 44     :b:  CLX 37     :b:  GTO 44
 :c:    9 11     :c:  X>Y 53     :c:    5 05
 :d:    6 06     :d:    5 05     :d:    1 01
1:0:  FMT 42    3:0:    0 00    5:0:    1 01
 :1:  GTO 44     :1:    7 07     :1:   UP 27
 :2:    2 02     :2:    2 02     :2:    f 15
 :3:    4 04     :3:    - 34     :3:  XEY 30
 :4:  RDN 31     :4:  CLX 37     :4:   UP 27
 :5:    7 07     :5:  X>Y 53     :5:    8 10
 :6:    0 00     :6:    4 04     :6:    0 00
 :7:  FMT 42     :7:    a 13     :7:  FMT 42
 :8:  GTO 44     :8:    7 07     :8:  GTO 44
 :9:    7 07     :9:    2 02     :9:  GTO 44
 :a:    8 10     :a:    0 00     :a:    1 01
 :b:  FMT 42     :b:    - 34     :b:    d 17
 :c:  GTO 44     :c:  CLX 37     :c:  SFL 54
 :d:    9 11     :d:  X>Y 53     :d:    9 11
```

## |21| CODED INFERIOR TRUE NOTATION

```
0:0:    7 07    2:0:  FMT 42    4:0:    8 10    6:0:  INT 64    8:0:  GTO 44
 :1:    1 01     :1:  GTO 44     :1:    4 04     :1:    - 34     :1:  GTO 44
 :2:  FMT 42     :2:    2 02     :2:    a 13     :2:  RDN 31     :2:    3 03
 :3:  GTO 44     :3:    3 03     :3:  XTO 23     :3:  XEY 30     :3:    6 06
 :4:    7 07     :4:    9 11     :4:    e 12     :4:    2 02     :4:  SFL 54
 :5:    2 02     :5:  FMT 42     :5:    8 10     :5:    2 02     :5:   9. 11
 :6:  FMT 42     :6:    π 56     :6:    3 03     :6:    9 11     :6:    2 02
 :7:  GTO 44     :7:   UP 27     :7:  FMT 42     :7:  FMT 42     :7:  FMT 42
 :8:    7 07     :8:    2 02     :8:  GTO 44     :8:  YTO 40     :8:  GTO 44
 :9:    9 11     :9:    3 03     :9:    6 06     :9:    1 01     :9:  GTO 44
 :a:  FMT 42     :a:    8 10     :a:  CHS 32     :a:  XEY 30     :a:    0 00
 :b:  GTO 44     :b:  FMT 42     :b:  XTO 23     :b:    9 11     :b:    4 04
 :c:    9 11     :c:    π 56     :c:    b 14     :c:    0 00     :c:  END 46
 :d:    6 06     :d:  POL 62     :d:    7 07     :d:  FMT 42
1:0:  FMT 42    3:0:  YTO 40    5:0:    4 04    7:0:  GTO 44
 :1:  GTO 44     :1:    a 13     :1:  FMT 42     :1:    2 02
 :2:    2 02     :2:    7 07     :2:  GTO 44     :2:    2 02
 :3:    4 04     :3:    8 10     :3:    f 15     :3:    9 11
 :4:  RDN 31     :4:  FMT 42     :4:   UP 27     :4:  FMT 42
 :5:    7 07     :5:  GTO 44     :5:  CLX 37     :5:    π 56
 :6:    0 00     :6:    9 11     :6:  X=Y 50     :6:  GTO 44
 :7:  FMT 42     :7:    6 06     :7:    7 07     :7:    5 05
 :8:  GTO 44     :8:  FMT 42     :8:    9 11     :8:    4 04
 :9:    1 01     :9:  GTO 44     :9:    1 01     :9:  CLX 37
 :a:  XTO 23     :a:    f 15     :a:    0 00     :a:   UP 27
 :b:    b 14     :b:  XEY 30     :b:    X 36     :b:    9 11
 :c:    8 10     :c:  CLX 37     :c:   DN 25     :c:    2 02
 :d:    2 02     :d:  X=Y 50     :d:   UP 27     :d:  FMT 42
```

## |22| CODED CANONICAL TRUE NOTATION

```
0:0:    7 07    2:0:  FMT 42    4:0:    8 10    6:0:  INT 64    8:0:  GTO 44
 :1:    1 01     :1:  GTO 44     :1:    4 04     :1:    - 34     :1:  GTO 44
 :2:  FMT 42     :2:    2 02     :2:    a 13     :2:  RDN 31     :2:    3 03
 :3:  GTO 44     :3:    3 03     :3:  XTO 23     :3:  XEY 30     :3:    6 06
 :4:    7 07     :4:    9 11     :4:    e 12     :4:    2 02     :4:  SFL 54
 :5:    2 02     :5:  FMT 42     :5:    8 10     :5:    2 02     :5:    9 11
 :6:  FMT 42     :6:    π 56     :6:    3 03     :6:    9 11     :6:    2 02
 :7:  GTO 44     :7:   UP 27     :7:  FMT 42     :7:  FMT 42     :7:  FMT 42
 :8:    7 07     :8:    2 02     :8:  GTO 44     :8:  YTO 40     :8:  GTO 44
 :9:    9 11     :9:    3 03     :9:  CLX 37     :9:    1 01     :9:  GTO 44
 :a:  FMT 42     :a:    8 10     :a:  CLX 37     :a:  XEY 30     :a:    0 00
 :b:  GTO 44     :b:  FMT 42     :b:  XTO 23     :b:    9 11     :b:    4 04
 :c:    9 11     :c:    π 56     :c:    b 14     :c:    0 00     :c:  END 46
 :d:    6 06     :d:  POL 62     :d:    7 07     :d:  FMT 42
1:0:  FMT 42    3:0:  YTO 40    5:0:    4 04    7:0:  GTO 44
 :1:  GTO 44     :1:    a 13     :1:  FMT 42     :1:    2 02
 :2:    2 02     :2:    7 07     :2:  GTO 44     :2:    2 02
 :3:    4 04     :3:    8 10     :3:    f 15     :3:    9 11
 :4:  RDN 31     :4:  FMT 42     :4:   UP 27     :4:  FMT 42
 :5:    7 07     :5:  GTO 44     :5:  CLX 37     :5:    π 56
 :6:    0 00     :6:    9 11     :6:  X=Y 50     :6:  GTO 44
 :7:  FMT 42     :7:    6 06     :7:    7 07     :7:    5 05
 :8:  GTO 44     :8:  FMT 42     :8:    9 11     :8:    4 04
 :9:    1 01     :9:  GTO 44     :9:    1 01     :9:  CLX 37
 :a:  XTO 23     :a:    f 15     :a:    0 00     :a:   UP 27
 :b:    b 14     :b:  XEY 30     :b:    X 36     :b:    9 11
 :c:    8 10     :c:  CLX 37     :c:   DN 25     :c:    2 02
 :d:    2 02     :d:  X=Y 50     :d:   UP 27     :d:  FMT 42
```

## |23| CODED SUPERIOR TRUE NOTATION

```
0:0:  7  07   2:0: FMT 42   4:0:  8  10   6:0: INT 64   8:0: GTO 44
 :1:  1  01    :1: GTO 44    :1:  4  04    :1:  -  34    :1: GTO 44
 :2: FMT 42    :2:  2  02    :2:  a  13    :2: RDN 31    :2:  3  03
 :3: GTO 44    :3:  3  03    :3: XTO 23    :3: XEY 30    :3:  6  06
 :4:  7  07    :4:  9  11    :4:  e  12    :4:  2  02    :4: SFL 54
 :5:  2  02    :5: FMT 42    :5:  8  10    :5:  2  02    :5:  9  11
 :6: FMT 42    :6:  π  56    :6:  3  03    :6:  9  11    :6:  2  02
 :7: GTO 44    :7: UP  27    :7: FMT 42    :7: FMT 42    :7: FMT 42
 :8:  7  07    :8:  2  02    :8: GTO 44    :8: YTO 40    :8: GTO 44
 :9:  9  11    :9:  3  03    :9: CLX 37    :9:  1  01    :9: GTO 44
 :a: FMT 42    :a:  8  10    :a:  6  06    :a: XEY 30    :a:  0  00
 :b: GTO 44    :b: FMT 42    :b: XTO 23    :b:  9  11    :b:  4  04
 :c:  9  11    :c:  π  56    :c:  b  14    :c:  0  00    :c: END 46
 :d:  6  06    :d: POL 62    :d:  7  07    :d: FMT 42
1:0: FMT 42   3:0: YTO 40   5:0:  4  04   7:0: GTO 44
 :1: GTO 44    :1:  a  13    :1: FMT 42    :1:  2  02
 :2:  2  02    :2:  7  07    :2: GTO 44    :2:  2  02
 :3:  4  04    :3:  8  10    :3:  f  15    :3:  9  11
 :4: RDN 31    :4: FMT 42    :4: UP  27    :4: FMT 42
 :5:  7  07    :5: GTO 44    :5: CLX 37    :5:  π  56
 :6:  0  00    :6:  9  11    :6: X=Y 50    :6: GTO 44
 :7: FMT 42    :7:  6  06    :7:  7  07    :7:  5  05
 :8: GTO 44    :8: FMT 42    :8:  9  11    :8:  4  04
 :9:  1  01    :9: GTO 44    :9:  1  01    :9: CLX 37
 :a: XTO 23    :a:  f  15    :a:  0  00    :a: UP  27
 :b:  b  14    :b: XEY 30    :b:  X  36    :b:  9  11
 :c:  8  10    :c: CLX 37    :c: DN  25    :c:  2  02
 :d:  2  02    :d: X=Y 50    :d: UP  27    :d: FMT 42
```

## |24| CODED INFERIOR RELATIVE NOTATION

```
0:0:  7  07   2:0: FMT 42   4:0:  f  15   6:0:  0  00   8:0: UP  27
 :1:  1  01    :1: GTO 44    :1: XEY 30    :1:  X  36    :1:  9  11
 :2: FMT 42    :2:  8  10    :2: CLX 37    :2: DN  25    :2:  2  02
 :3: GTO 44    :3:  1  01    :3: X=Y 50    :3: UP  27    :3: FMT 42
 :4:  7  07    :4: FMT 42    :4:  8  10    :4: INT 64    :4: GTO 44
 :5:  2  02    :5: GTO 44    :5:  8  10    :5:  -  34    :5: GTO 44
 :6: FMT 42    :6:  2  02    :6:  a  13    :6: RDN 31    :6:  3  03
 :7: GTO 44    :7:  3  03    :7: XTO 23    :7: XEY 30    :7:  a  13
 :8:  7  07    :8:  5  05    :8:  e  12    :8:  2  02    :8: SFL 54
 :9:  9  11    :9: FMT 42    :9:  8  10    :9:  2  02    :9:  9  11
 :a: FMT 42    :a:  π  56    :a:  3  03    :a:  9  11    :a:  2  02
 :b: GTO 44    :b: UP  27    :b: FMT 42    :b: FMT 42    :b: FMT 42
 :c:  9  11    :c:  2  02    :c: GTO 44    :c: YTO 40    :c: GTO 44
 :d:  6  06    :d:  3  03    :d:  6  06    :d:  1  01    :d: GTO 44
1:0: FMT 42   3:0:  4  04   5:0: CHS 32   7:0: XEY 30   9:0:  0  00
 :1: GTO 44    :1: FMT 42    :1: XTO 23    :1:  9  11    :1:  4  04
 :2:  2  02    :2:  π  56    :2:  b  14    :2:  0  00    :2: END 46
 :3:  4  04    :3: POL 62    :3:  7  07    :3: FMT 42
 :4: RDN 31    :4: YTO 40    :4:  4  04    :4: GTO 44
 :5:  7  07    :5:  a  13    :5: FMT 42    :5:  2  02
 :6:  0  00    :6:  7  07    :6: GTO 44    :6:  2  02
 :7: FMT 42    :7:  8  10    :7:  f  15    :7:  9  11
 :8: GTO 44    :8: FMT 42    :8: UP  27    :8: FMT 42
 :9:  1  01    :9: GTO 44    :9: CLX 37    :9:  π  56
 :a: XTO 23    :a:  9  11    :a: X=Y 50    :a: GTO 44
 :b:  b  14    :b:  6  06    :b:  7  07    :b:  5  05
 :c:  8  10    :c: FMT 42    :c:  d  17    :c:  8  10
 :d:  2  02    :d: GTO 44    :d:  1  01    :d: CLX 37
```

## |25| CODED CANONICAL RELATIVE NOTATION

```
0:0:  7  07   2:0: FMT 42   4:0:  f  15   6:0:  0  00   8:0: UP  27
 :1:  1  01    :1: GTO 44    :1: XEY 30    :1:  X  36    :1:  9  11
 :2: FMT 42    :2:  8  10    :2: CLX 37    :2: DN  25    :2:  2  02
 :3: GTO 44    :3:  1  01    :3: X=Y 50    :3: UP  27    :3: FMT 42
 :4:  7  07    :4: FMT 42    :4:  8  10    :4: INT 64    :4: GTO 44
 :5:  2  02    :5: GTO 44    :5:  8  10    :5:  -  34    :5: GTO 44
 :6: FMT 42    :6:  2  02    :6:  a  13    :6: RDN 31    :6:  3  03
 :7: GTO 44    :7:  3  03    :7: XTO 23    :7: XEY 30    :7:  a  13
 :8:  7  07    :8:  5  05    :8:  e  12    :8:  2  02    :8: SFL 54
 :9:  9  11    :9: FMT 42    :9:  8  10    :9:  2  02    :9:  9  11
 :a: FMT 42    :a:  π  56    :a:  3  03    :a:  9  11    :a:  2  02
 :b: GTO 44    :b: UP  27    :b: FMT 42    :b: FMT 42    :b: FMT 42
 :c:  9  11    :c:  2  02    :c: GTO 44    :c: YTO 40    :c: GTO 44
 :d:  6  06    :d:  3  03    :d: CLX 37    :d:  1  01    :d: GTO 44
1:0: FMT 42   3:0:  4  04   5:0: CLX 37   7:0: XEY 30   9:0:  0  00
 :1: GTO 44    :1: FMT 42    :1: XTO 23    :1:  9  11    :1:  4  04
 :2:  2  02    :2:  π  56    :2:  b  14    :2:  0  00    :2: END 46
 :3:  4  04    :3: POL 62    :3:  7  07    :3: FMT 42
 :4: RDN 31    :4: YTO 40    :4:  4  04    :4: GTO 44
 :5:  7  07    :5:  a  13    :5: FMT 42    :5:  2  02
 :6:  0  00    :6:  7  07    :6: GTO 44    :6:  2  02
 :7: FMT 42    :7:  8  10    :7:  f  15    :7:  9  11
 :8: GTO 44    :8: FMT 42    :8: UP  27    :8: FMT 42
 :9:  1  01    :9: GTO 44    :9: CLX 37    :9:  π  56
 :a: XTO 23    :a:  9  11    :a: X=Y 50    :a: GTO 44
 :b:  b  14    :b:  6  06    :b:  7  07    :b:  5  05
 :c:  8  10    :c: FMT 42    :c:  d  17    :c:  8  10
 :d:  2  02    :d: GTO 44    :d:  1  01    :d: CLX 37
```

## |26| CODED SUPERIOR RELATIVE NOTATION

```
0:0:  7  07   2:0: FMT 42   4:0:  f  15   6:0:  0  00   8:0: UP  27
 :1:  1  01    :1: GTO 44    :1: XEY 30    :1:  X  36    :1:  9  11
 :2: FMT 42    :2:  8  10    :2: CLX 37    :2: DN  25    :2:  2  02
 :3: GTO 44    :3:  1  01    :3: X=Y 50    :3: UP  27    :3: FMT 42
 :4:  7  07    :4: FMT 42    :4:  8  10    :4: INT 64    :4: GTO 44
 :5:  2  02    :5: GTO 44    :5:  8  10    :5:  -  34    :5: GTO 44
 :6: FMT 42    :6:  2  02    :6:  a  13    :6: RDN 31    :6:  3  03
 :7: GTO 44    :7:  3  03    :7: XTO 23    :7: XEY 30    :7:  a  13
 :8:  7  07    :8:  5  05    :8:  e  12    :8:  2  02    :8: SFL 54
 :9:  9  11    :9: FMT 42    :9:  8  10    :9:  2  02    :9:  9  11
 :a: FMT 42    :a:  π  56    :a:  3  03    :a:  9  11    :a:  2  02
 :b: GTO 44    :b: UP  27    :b: FMT 42    :b: FMT 42    :b: FMT 42
 :c:  9  11    :c:  2  02    :c: GTO 44    :c: YTO 40    :c: GTO 44
 :d:  6  06    :d:  3  03    :d: CLX 37    :d:  1  01    :d: GTO 44
1:0: FMT 42   3:0:  4  04   5:0:  6  06   7:0: XEY 30   9:0:  0  00
 :1: GTO 44    :1: FMT 42    :1: XTO 23    :1:  9  11    :1:  4  04
 :2:  2  02    :2:  π  56    :2:  b  14    :2:  0  00    :2: END 46
 :3:  4  04    :3: POL 62    :3:  7  07    :3: FMT 42
 :4: RDN 31    :4: YTO 40    :4:  4  04    :4: GTO 44
 :5:  7  07    :5:  a  13    :5: FMT 42    :5:  2  02
 :6:  0  00    :6:  7  07    :6: GTO 44    :6:  2  02
 :7: FMT 42    :7:  8  10    :7:  f  15    :7:  9  11
 :8: GTO 44    :8: FMT 42    :8: UP  27    :8: FMT 42
 :9:  1  01    :9: GTO 44    :9: CLX 37    :9:  π  56
 :a: XTO 23    :a:  9  11    :a: X=Y 50    :a: GTO 44
 :b:  b  14    :b:  6  06    :b:  7  07    :b:  5  05
 :c:  8  10    :c: FMT 42    :c:  d  17    :c:  8  10
 :d:  2  02    :d: GTO 44    :d:  1  01    :d: CLX 37
```

## |30| ENERGY

Program 30, which calls ten subroutines, is used to calculate the energy

$$E = \frac{mv^2}{2}$$

of each successive tonal impulse, under the assumption that the compositional mass is unity.

```
0:0:  7  07   2:0: GTO 44   4:0:  ×  36
 :1:  1  01    :1:  2  02    :1:  2  02
 :2: FMT 42    :2:  3  03    :2: DIV 35
 :3: GTO 44    :3:  9  11    :3:  3  03
 :4:  7  07    :4: FMT 42    :4: UP  27
 :5:  2  02    :5: DIV 35    :5:  8  10
 :6: FMT 42    :6:  2  02    :6:  8  10
 :7: GTO 44    :7:  3  03    :7: FMT 42
 :8:  7  07    :8:  8  10    :8: GTO 44
 :9:  9  11    :9: FMT 42    :9: DN  25
 :a: FMT 42    :a: DIV 35    :a:  2  02
 :b: GTO 44    :b:  8  10    :b:  .  21
 :c:  9  11    :c:  1  01    :c:  3  03
 :d:  6  06    :d: FMT 42    :d: UP  27
1:0: FMT 42   3:0: GTO 44   5:0:  9  11
 :1: GTO 44    :1:  2  02    :1:  0  00
 :2:  7  07    :2:  3  03    :2: FMT 42
 :3: RDN 31    :3:  1  01    :3: GTO 44
 :4:  7  07    :4: FMT 42    :4: SFL 54
 :5:  0  00    :5:  π  56    :5:  9  11
 :6: FMT 42    :6: UP  27    :6:  2  02
 :7: GTO 44    :7:  2  02    :7: FMT 42
 :8:  1  01    :8:  3  03    :8: GTO 44
 :9: XTO 23    :9:  0  00    :9: GTO 44
 :a:  b  14    :a: FMT 42    :a:  0  00
 :b:  8  10    :b:  π  56    :b:  4  04
 :c:  2  02    :c: POL 62    :c: END 46
 :d: FMT 42    :d: UP  27
```

## |31| ENERGY DECLINE

Program 31 provides a pictorial representation of the decline of creative energy with time, as it is expended to produce the required tonal impulses. The horizontal and vertical scale factors in program steps 57, 58, 59, 60, and 42, 43,

44, 45 respectively can be changed to reduce or to enlarge the plot. At the conclusion of the run, key in FMT UP.

```
0:0:  7  07   2:0:  2  02   4:0: POL 62   6:0:  9  11   8:0:  0  00
 :1:  1  01    :1: FMT 42    :1: UP  27    :1: FMT 42    :1:  3  03
 :2: FMT 42    :2: GTO 44    :2:  0  00    :2:  +  33    :2:  0  00
 :3: GTO 44    :3:  2  02    :3:  0  00    :3: FMT 42    :3:  ×  36
 :4: CLX 37    :4:  3  03    :4:  3  03    :4:  π  56    :4:  a  13
 :5: UP  27    :5:  9  11    :5:  0  00    :5: RDN 31    :5: XEY 30
 :6: FMT 42    :6: FMT 42    :6:  ×  36    :6:  a  13    :6:  -  34
 :7: DN  25    :7: DIV 35    :7:  a  13    :7: RUP 22    :7:  2  02
 :8: XTO 23    :8:  2  02    :8: XEY 30    :8: FMT 42    :8:  2  02
 :9:  a  13    :9:  3  03    :9:  -  34    :9: DN  25    :9:  9  11
 :a:  7  07    :a:  8  10    :a: YTO 40    :a: GTO 44    :a: FMT 42
 :b:  9  11    :b: FMT 42    :b:  a  13    :b:  0  00    :b:  π  56
 :c: FMT 42    :c: DIV 35    :c:  2  02    :c:  a  13    :c: FMT 42
 :d: GTO 44    :d:  8  10    :d:  2  02    :d:  2  02    :d: DN  25
1:0:  9  11   3:0:  1  01   5:0:  9  11   7:0:  3  03   9:0: CLX 47
 :1:  6  06    :1: FMT 42    :1: FMT 42    :1:  9  11    :1: FMT 42
 :2: FMT 42    :2: GTO 44    :2:  π  56    :2: FMT 42    :2: DN  25
 :3: GTO 44    :3:  2  02    :3: FMT 42    :3:  π  56    :3: FMT 42
 :4:  f  15    :4:  3  03    :4: DN  25    :4: UP  27    :4: UP  27
 :5: UP  27    :5:  1  01    :5:  •  12    :5:  2  02    :5: RDN 31
 :6: CLX 37    :6: FMT 42    :6: UP  27    :6:  3  03    :6:  7  07
 :7: X=Y 50    :7:  π  56    :7:  0  00    :7:  8  10    :7:  0  00
 :8:  6  06    :8: UP  27    :8:  0  00    :8: FMT 42    :8: FMT 42
 :9:  d  17    :9:  2  02    :9:  3  03    :9:  π  56    :9: GTO 44
 :a:  1  01    :a:  3  03    :a:  0  00    :a: POL 62    :a: END 46
 :b: XTO 23    :b:  0  00    :b:  ×  36    :b: UP  27
 :c:  b  14    :c: FMT 42    :c:  2  02    :c:  ×  36
 :d:  8  10    :d:  π  56    :d:  2  02    :d:  0  00
```

## |32| TONALITY AMPLITUDE

When using this program it may be necessary to restart the plot with a reduced horizontal scale in order to prevent running off the sheet of plotting paper. The scale factor is contained in program steps 64 through 67. The coordinate axes can be made into heavier lines by interrupting and restarting the program several times before the actual calculation has had time to begin.

```
0:0: CLX 37   2:0:  9  11   4:0:  2  02   6:0: FMT 42   8:0:  7  07
 :1: UP  27    :1: FMT 42    :1:  3  03    :1: DN  25    :1:  0  00
 :2: FMT 42    :2: GTO 44    :2:  8  10    :2:  •  12    :2: FMT 42
 :3: DN  25    :3:  9  11    :3: FMT 42    :3: UP  27    :3: GTO 44
 :4:  4  04    :4:  6  06    :4:  π  56    :4:  0  00    :4: END 46
 :5:  0  00    :5: FMT 42    :5: UP  27    :5:  0  00
 :6:  0  00    :6: GTO 44    :6:  •  12    :6:  3  03
 :7:  0  00    :7:  f  15    :7: DIV 35    :7:  0  00
 :8:  -  34    :8: UP  27    :8: DN  25    :8:  ×  36
 :9: CLX 37    :9: CLX 37    :9: POL 62    :9:  2  02
 :a: FMT 42    :a: X=Y 50    :a: UP  27    :a:  2  02
 :b: DN  25    :b:  7  07    :b:  0  00    :b:  9  11
 :c:  3  03    :c:  a  13    :c:  4  04    :c: FMT 42
 :d:  0  00    :d:  1  01    :d:  0  00    :d:  +  33
1:0:  0  00   3:0: XTO 23   5:0:  0  00   7:0: FMT 42
 :1:  0  00    :1:  b  14    :1:  ×  36    :1:  π  56
 :2: FMT 42    :2:  8  10    :2:  4  04    :2: RDN 31
 :3: DN  25    :3:  2  02    :3:  0  00    :3:  b  14
 :4: FMT 42    :4: FMT 42    :4:  0  00    :4: RUP 22
 :5: UP  27    :5: GTO 44    :5:  0  00    :5: FMT 42
 :6:  7  07    :6:  2  02    :6:  -  34    :6: DN  25
 :7:  1  01    :7:  3  03    :7: YTO 40    :7: GTO 44
 :8: FMT 42    :8:  9  11    :8:  b  14    :8:  1  01
 :9: GTO 44    :9: FMT 42    :9:  2  02    :9:  d  17
 :a: CLX 37    :a:  π  56    :a:  2  02    :a: FMT 42
 :b: XTO 23    :b: UP  27    :b:  9  11    :b: UP  27
 :c:  a  13    :c:  •  12    :c: FMT 42    :c: CLX 37
 :d:  7  07    :d: DIV 35    :d:  π  56    :d: RDN 31
```

## |33| IMPULSE MAGNITUDE

```
0:0: CLR 20   2:0:  9  11   4:0:  1  01   6:0: FMT 42   8:0:  +  33
 :1: FMT 42    :1:  6  06    :1: FMT 42    :1:  π  56    :1: GTO 44
 :2: DN  25    :2: FMT 42    :2: GTO 44    :2: FMT 42    :2:  1  01
 :3:  2  02    :3: GTO 44    :3:  2  02    :3: DN  25    :3:  a  13
 :4: EEX 26    :4:  f  15    :4:  3  03    :4: XEY 30    :4: SFG 54
 :5:  3  03    :5: UP  27    :5:  1  01    :5:  2  02    :5:  2  02
 :6:  -  34    :6: CLX 37    :6: FMT 42    :6: CHS 32    :6:  3  03
 :7: CLX 37    :7: X=Y 50    :7:  π  56    :7: EEX 26    :7:  9  11
 :8: FMT 42    :8:  8  10    :8: UP  27    :8:  3  03    :8: FMT 42
 :9: DN  25    :9:  4  04    :9:  2  02    :9: XEY 30    :9:  π  56
 :a:  3  03    :a:  1  01    :a:  3  03    :a: FMT 42    :a: UP  27
 :b: EEX 26    :b: XTO 23    :b:  0  00    :b: DN  25    :b:  2  02
 :c:  3  03    :c:  b  14    :c: FMT 42    :c: FMT 42    :c:  3  03
 :d: FMT 42    :d:  8  10    :d:  π  56    :d: UP  27    :d:  8  10
1:0: DN  25   3:0:  2  02   5:0: POL 62   7:0: IFG 43   9:0: GTO 44
 :1: FMT 42    :1: FMT 42    :1: UP  27    :1:  9  11    :1:  4  04
 :2: UP  27    :2: GTO 44    :2:  0  00    :2:  3  03    :2:  c  16
 :3:  7  07    :3:  2  02    :3:  1  01    :3:  •  12    :3: CLX 37
 :4:  1  01    :4:  3  03    :4:  0  00    :4: UP  27    :4: RDN 31
 :5: FMT 42    :5:  9  11    :5:  0  00    :5:  0  00    :5:  7  07
 :6: GTO 44    :6: FMT 42    :6:  ×  36    :6:  0  00    :6:  0  00
 :7: CLX 37    :7: DIV 35    :7:  2  02    :7:  3  03    :7: FMT 42
 :8: XTO 23    :8:  2  02    :8: EEX 26    :8:  0  00    :8: GTO 44
 :9:  a  13    :9:  3  03    :9:  3  03    :9:  ×  36    :9: END 46
 :a:  7  07    :a:  8  10    :a:  -  34    :a:  2  02
 :b:  9  11    :b: FMT 42    :b:  2  02    :b:  2  02
 :c: FMT 42    :c: DIV 35    :c:  2  02    :c:  9  11
 :d: GTO 44    :d:  8  10    :d:  9  11    :d: FMT 42
```

## |37| SPAN

```
0:0:  7  07   2:0: FMT 42
 :1:  1  01    :1: GTO 44
 :2: FMT 42    :2:  9  11
 :3: GTO 44    :3:  0  00
 :4:  7  07    :4: FMT 42
 :5:  9  11    :5: GTO 44
 :6: FMT 42    :6: SFL 54
 :7: GTO 44    :7:  9  11
 :8:  9  11    :8:  2  02
 :9:  6  06    :9: FMT 42
 :a: FMT 42    :a: GTO 44
 :b: GTO 44    :b: GTO 44
 :c:  3  03    :c:  0  00
 :d: RDN 31    :d:  4  04
1:0:  7  07   3:0: END 46
 :1:  0  00
 :2: FMT 42
 :3: GTO 44
 :4:  7  07
 :5:  2  02
 :6: FMT 42
 :7: GTO 44
 :8:  7  07
 :9:  8  10
 :a: FMT 42
 :b: GTO 44
 :c:  8  10
 :d:  5  05
```

## |40| PHONETIC NOTATION

```
0:0:  7  07   2:0:  6  06   4:0:  0  00
 :1:  1  01    :1: FMT 42    :1:  4  04
 :2: FMT 42    :2: GTO 44    :2: END 46
 :3: GTO 44    :3:  f  15
 :4:  7  07    :4: UP  27
 :5:  2  02    :5: CLX 37
 :6: FMT 42    :6: X=Y 50
 :7: GTO 44    :7:  3  03
 :8:  7  07    :8:  8  10
 :9:  9  11    :9:  9  11
 :a: FMT 42    :a:  4  04
 :b: GTO 44    :b: FMT 42
 :c:  9  11    :c: GTO 44
 :d:  6  06    :d: CLX 37
1:0: FMT 42   3:0: UP  27
 :1: GTO 44    :1:  9  11
 :2:  2  02    :2:  2  02
 :3:  4  04    :3: FMT 42
 :4: RDN 31    :4: GTO 44
 :5:  7  07    :5: GTO 44
 :6:  0  00    :6:  1  01
 :7: FMT 42    :7:  d  17
 :8: GTO 44    :8: SFL 54
 :9:  7  07    :9:  9  11
 :a:  8  10    :a:  2  02
 :b: FMT 42    :b: FMT 42
 :c: GTO 44    :c: GTO 44
 :d:  9  11    :d: GTO 44
```

## |41| INFERIOR TRUE NOTATION

Significant features of this program are retained in programs 42 and 43.

```
0:0: 7    07    2:0: FMT  42    4:0: 6    06    6:0: 3    03
 :1: 1    01     :1: GTO  44     :1: 2    02     :1: 6    06
 :2: FMT  42     :2: 2    02     :2: a    13     :2: SFL  54
 :3: GTO  44     :3: 3    03     :3: XTO  23     :3: 9    11
 :4: 7    07     :4: 9    11     :4: e    12     :4: 2    02
 :5: 2    02     :5: FMT  42     :5: 8    10     :5: FMT  42
 :6: FMT  42     :6: π    56     :6: 3    03     :6: GTO  44
 :7: GTO  44     :7: UP   27     :7: FMT  42     :7: GTO  44
 :8: 7    07     :8: 2    02     :8: GTO  44     :8: 0    00
 :9: 9    11     :9: 3    03     :9: 6    06     :9: 4    04
 :a: FMT  42     :a: 8    10     :a: CHS  32     :a: END  46
 :b: GTO  44     :b: FMT  42     :b: XTO  23
 :c: 9    11     :c: π    56     :c: b    14
 :d: 6    06     :d: POL  62     :d: 7    07
1:0: FMT  42    3:0: YTO  40    5:0: 4    04
 :1: GTO  44     :1: a    13     :1: FMT  42
 :2: 2    02     :2: 7    07     :2: GTO  44
 :3: 4    04     :3: 8    10     :3: 9    11
 :4: RDN  31     :4: FMT  42     :4: 4    04
 :5: 7    07     :5: GTO  44     :5: FMT  42
 :6: 0    00     :6: 9    11     :6: GTO  44
 :7: FMT  42     :7: 6    06     :7: CLX  37
 :8: GTO  44     :8: FMT  42     :8: UP   27
 :9: 1    01     :9: GTO  44     :9: 9    11
 :a: XTO  23     :a: f    15     :a: 2    02
 :b: b    14     :b: XEY  30     :b: FMT  42
 :c: 8    10     :c: CLX  37     :c: GTO  44
 :d: 2    02     :d: X=Y  50     :d: GTO  44
```

## |42| CANONICAL TRUE NOTATION

```
0:0: 7    07    2:0: FMT  42    4:0: 6    06    6:0: 3    03
 :1: 1    01     :1: GTO  44     :1: 2    02     :1: 6    06
 :2: FMT  42     :2: 2    02     :2: a    13     :2: SFL  54
 :3: GTO  44     :3: 3    03     :3: XTO  23     :3: 9    11
 :4: 7    07     :4: 9    11     :4: e    12     :4: 2    02
 :5: 2    02     :5: FMT  42     :5: 8    10     :5: FMT  42
 :6: FMT  42     :6: π    56     :6: 3    03     :6: GTO  44
 :7: GTO  44     :7: UP   27     :7: FMT  42     :7: GTO  44
 :8: 7    07     :8: 2    02     :8: GTO  44     :8: 0    00
 :9: 9    11     :9: 3    03     :9: CLX  37     :9: 4    04
 :a: FMT  42     :a: 8    10     :a: CLX  37     :a: END  46
 :b: GTO  44     :b: FMT  42     :b: XTO  23
 :c: 9    11     :c: π    56     :c: b    14
 :d: 6    06     :d: POL  62     :d: 7    07
1:0: FMT  42    3:0: YTO  40    5:0: 4    04
 :1: GTO  44     :1: a    13     :1: FMT  42
 :2: 2    02     :2: 7    07     :2: GTO  44
 :3: 4    04     :3: 8    10     :3: 9    11
 :4: RDN  31     :4: FMT  42     :4: 4    04
 :5: 7    07     :5: GTO  44     :5: FMT  42
 :6: 0    00     :6: 9    11     :6: GTO  44
 :7: FMT  42     :7: 6    06     :7: CLX  37
 :8: GTO  44     :8: FMT  42     :8: UP   27
 :9: 1    01     :9: GTO  44     :9: 9    11
 :a: XTO  23     :a: f    15     :a: 2    02
 :b: b    14     :b: XEY  30     :b: FMT  42
 :c: 8    10     :c: CLX  37     :c: GTO  44
 :d: 2    02     :d: X=Y  50     :d: GTO  44
```

## |43| SUPERIOR TRUE NOTATION

```
0:0: 7    07    2:0: FMT  42    4:0: 6    06    6:0: 3    03
 :1: 1    01     :1: GTO  44     :1: 2    02     :1: 6    06
 :2: FMT  42     :2: 2    02     :2: a    13     :2: SFL  54
 :3: GTO  44     :3: 3    03     :3: XTO  23     :3: 9    11
 :4: 7    07     :4: 9    11     :4: e    12     :4: 2    02
 :5: 2    02     :5: FMT  42     :5: 8    10     :5: FMT  42
 :6: FMT  42     :6: π    56     :6: 3    03     :6: GTO  44
 :7: GTO  44     :7: UP   27     :7: FMT  42     :7: GTO  44
 :8: 7    07     :8: 2    02     :8: GTO  44     :8: 0    00
 :9: 9    11     :9: 3    03     :9: CLX  37     :9: 4    04
 :a: FMT  42     :a: 8    10     :a: 6    06     :a: END  46
 :b: GTO  44     :b: FMT  42     :b: XTO  23
 :c: 9    11     :c: π    56     :c: b    14
 :d: 6    06     :d: POL  62     :d: 7    07
1:0: FMT  42    3:0: YTO  40    5:0: 4    04
 :1: GTO  44     :1: a    13     :1: FMT  42
 :2: 2    02     :2: 7    07     :2: GTO  44
 :3: 4    04     :3: 8    10     :3: 9    11
 :4: RDN  31     :4: FMT  42     :4: 4    04
 :5: 7    07     :5: GTO  44     :5: FMT  42
 :6: 0    00     :6: 9    11     :6: GTO  44
 :7: FMT  42     :7: 6    06     :7: CLX  37
 :8: GTO  44     :8: FMT  42     :8: UP   27
 :9: 1    01     :9: GTO  44     :9: 9    11
 :a: XTO  23     :a: f    15     :a: 2    02
 :b: b    14     :b: XEY  30     :b: FMT  42
 :c: 8    10     :c: CLX  37     :c: GTO  44
 :d: 2    02     :d: X=Y  50     :d: GTO  44
```

## |44| INFERIOR RELATIVE NOTATION

```
0:0: 7    07    2:0: FMT  42    4:0: f    15    6:0: 2    02
 :1: 1    01     :1: GTO  44     :1: XEY  30     :1: FMT  42
 :2: FMT  42     :2: 8    10     :2: CLX  37     :2: GTO  44
 :3: GTO  44     :3: 1    01     :3: X=Y  50     :3: GTO  44
 :4: 7    07     :4: FMT  42     :4: 6    06     :4: 3    03
 :5: 2    02     :5: GTO  44     :5: 6    06     :5: a    13
 :6: FMT  42     :6: 2    02     :6: a    13     :6: SFL  54
 :7: GTO  44     :7: 3    03     :7: XTO  23     :7: 9    11
 :8: 7    07     :8: 5    05     :8: e    12     :8: 2    02
 :9: 9    11     :9: FMT  42     :9: 8    10     :9: FMT  42
 :a: FMT  42     :a: π    56     :a: 3    03     :a: GTO  44
 :b: GTO  44     :b: UP   27     :b: FMT  42     :b: GTO  44
 :c: 9    11     :c: 2    02     :c: GTO  44     :c: 0    00
 :d: 6    06     :d: 3    03     :d: 6    06     :d: 4    04
1:0: FMT  42    3:0: 4    04    5:0: CHS  32    7:0: END  46
 :1: GTO  44     :1: FMT  42     :1: XTO  23
 :2: 2    02     :2: π    56     :2: b    14
 :3: 4    04     :3: POL  62     :3: 7    07
 :4: RDN  31     :4: YTO  40     :4: 4    04
 :5: 7    07     :5: a    13     :5: FMT  42
 :6: 0    00     :6: 7    07     :6: GTO  44
 :7: FMT  42     :7: 8    10     :7: 9    11
 :8: GTO  44     :8: FMT  42     :8: 4    04
 :9: 1    01     :9: GTO  44     :9: FMT  42
 :a: XTO  23     :a: 9    11     :a: GTO  44
 :b: b    14     :b: 6    06     :b: CLX  37
 :c: 8    10     :c: FMT  42     :c: UP   27
 :d: 2    02     :d: GTO  44     :d: 9    11
```

## |45| CANONICAL RELATIVE NOTATION

```
0:0: 7    07    2:0: FMT  42    4:0: f    15    6:0: 2    02
 :1: 1    01     :1: GTO  44     :1: XEY  30     :1: FMT  42
 :2: FMT  42     :2: 8    10     :2: CLX  37     :2: GTO  44
 :3: GTO  44     :3: 1    01     :3: X=Y  50     :3: GTO  44
 :4: 7    07     :4: FMT  42     :4: 6    06     :4: 3    03
 :5: 2    02     :5: GTO  44     :5: 6    06     :5: a    13
 :6: FMT  42     :6: 2    02     :6: a    13     :6: SFL  54
 :7: GTO  44     :7: 3    03     :7: XTO  23     :7: 9    11
 :8: 7    07     :8: 5    05     :8: e    12     :8: 2    02
 :9: 9    11     :9: FMT  42     :9: 8    10     :9: FMT  42
 :a: FMT  42     :a: π    56     :a: 3    03     :a: GTO  44
 :b: GTO  44     :b: UP   27     :b: FMT  42     :b: GTO  44
 :c: 9    11     :c: 2    02     :c: GTO  44     :c: 0    00
 :d: 6    06     :d: 3    03     :d: CLX  37     :d: 4    04
1:0: FMT  42    3:0: 4    04    5:0: CLX  37    7:0: END  46
 :1: GTO  44     :1: FMT  42     :1: XTO  23
 :2: 2    02     :2: π    56     :2: b    14
 :3: 4    04     :3: POL  62     :3: 7    07
 :4: RDN  31     :4: YTO  40     :4: 4    04
 :5: 7    07     :5: a    13     :5: FMT  42
 :6: 0    00     :6: 7    07     :6: GTO  44
 :7: FMT  42     :7: 8    10     :7: 9    11
 :8: GTO  44     :8: FMT  42     :8: 4    04
 :9: 1    01     :9: GTO  44     :9: FMT  42
 :a: XTO  23     :a: 9    11     :a: GTO  44
 :b: b    14     :b: 6    06     :b: CLX  37
 :c: 8    10     :c: FMT  42     :c: UP   27
 :d: 2    02     :d: GTO  44     :d: 9    11
```

## |46| SUPERIOR RELATIVE NOTATION

```
0:0: 7    07    2:0: FMT  42    4:0: f    15    6:0: 2    02
 :1: 1    01     :1: GTO  44     :1: XEY  30     :1: FMT  42
 :2: FMT  42     :2: 8    10     :2: CLX  37     :2: GTO  44
 :3: GTO  44     :3: 1    01     :3: X=Y  50     :3: GTO  44
 :4: 7    07     :4: FMT  42     :4: 6    06     :4: 3    03
 :5: 2    02     :5: GTO  44     :5: 6    06     :5: a    13
 :6: FMT  42     :6: 2    02     :6: a    13     :6: SFL  54
 :7: GTO  44     :7: 3    03     :7: XTO  23     :7: 9    11
 :8: 7    07     :8: 5    05     :8: e    12     :8: 2    02
 :9: 9    11     :9: FMT  42     :9: 8    10     :9: FMT  42
 :a: FMT  42     :a: π    56     :a: 3    03     :a: GTO  44
 :b: GTO  44     :b: UP   27     :b: FMT  42     :b: GTO  44
 :c: 9    11     :c: 2    02     :c: GTO  44     :c: 0    00
 :d: 6    06     :d: 3    03     :d: CLX  37     :d: 4    04
1:0: FMT  42    3:0: 4    04    5:0: 6    06    7:0: END  46
 :1: GTO  44     :1: FMT  42     :1: XTO  23
 :2: 2    02     :2: π    56     :2: b    14
 :3: 4    04     :3: POL  62     :3: 7    07
 :4: RDN  31     :4: YTO  40     :4: 4    04
 :5: 7    07     :5: a    13     :5: FMT  42
 :6: 0    00     :6: 7    07     :6: GTO  44
 :7: FMT  42     :7: 8    10     :7: 9    11
 :8: GTO  44     :8: FMT  42     :8: 4    04
 :9: 1    01     :9: GTO  44     :9: FMT  42
 :a: XTO  23     :a: 9    11     :a: GTO  44
 :b: b    14     :b: 6    06     :b: CLX  37
 :c: 8    10     :c: FMT  42     :c: UP   27
 :d: 2    02     :d: GTO  44     :d: 9    11
```

## |47| TRUE PREFERRED NOTATION

Manually key in

7
1
FMT
GTO
GTO
0
0
CNT

before starting this computation.

| Addr | Key | Code | Addr | Key | Code | Addr | Key | Code | Addr | Key | Code | Addr | Key | Code |
|---|---|---|---|---|---|---|---|---|---|---|---|---|---|---|
| 0:0 | 7 | 07 | 2:0 | 9 | 11 | 4:0 | XTO | 23 | 6:0 | FMT | 42 | 8:0 | 4 | 04 |
| :1 | 2 | 02 | :1 | FMT | 42 | :1 | b | 14 | :1 | GTO | 44 | :1 | 6 | 06 |
| :2 | FMT | 42 | :2 | π | 56 | :2 | a | 13 | :2 | 7 | 07 | :2 | XTO | 23 |
| :3 | GTO | 44 | :3 | UP | 27 | :3 | XTO | 23 | :3 | 8 | 10 | :3 | b | 14 |
| :4 | 7 | 07 | :4 | 2 | 02 | :4 | e | 12 | :4 | FMT | 42 | :4 | 8 | 10 |
| :5 | 9 | 11 | :5 | 3 | 03 | :5 | UP | 27 | :5 | GTO | 44 | :5 | 3 | 03 |
| :6 | FMT | 42 | :6 | 8 | 10 | :6 | CLX | 37 | :6 | 9 | 11 | :6 | FMT | 42 |
| :7 | GTO | 44 | :7 | FMT | 42 | :7 | X<Y | 52 | :7 | 6 | 06 | :7 | GTO | 44 |
| :8 | 9 | 11 | :8 | π | 56 | :8 | 7 | 07 | :8 | FMT | 42 | :8 | 7 | 07 |
| :9 | 6 | 06 | :9 | POL | 62 | :9 | a | 13 | :9 | GTO | 44 | :9 | 4 | 04 |
| :a | FMT | 42 | :a | YTO | 40 | :a | 8 | 10 | :a | f | 15 | :a | FMT | 42 |
| :b | GTO | 44 | :b | a | 13 | :b | 3 | 03 | :b | XEY | 30 | :b | GTO | 44 |
| :c | 4 | 04 | :c | 7 | 07 | :c | FMT | 42 | :c | CLX | 37 | :c | 9 | 11 |
| :d | 8 | 10 | :d | 8 | 10 | :d | GTO | 44 | :d | X=Y | 50 | :d | 4 | 04 |
| 1:0 | RDN | 31 | 3:0 | FMT | 42 | 5:0 | 7 | 07 | 7:0 | 9 | 11 | 9:0 | FMT | 42 |
| :1 | 7 | 07 | :1 | GTO | 44 | :1 | 4 | 04 | :1 | 5 | 05 | :1 | GTO | 44 |
| :2 | 0 | 00 | :2 | 9 | 11 | :2 | FMT | 42 | :2 | a | 13 | :2 | GTO | 44 |
| :3 | FMT | 42 | :3 | 6 | 06 | :3 | GTO | 44 | :3 | XTO | 23 | :3 | 6 | 06 |
| :4 | GTO | 44 | :4 | FMT | 42 | :4 | 9 | 11 | :4 | e | 12 | :4 | 6 | 06 |
| :5 | 1 | 01 | :5 | GTO | 44 | :5 | 4 | 04 | :5 | UP | 27 | :5 | SFL | 54 |
| :6 | XTO | 23 | :6 | f | 15 | :6 | FMT | 42 | :6 | CLX | 37 | :6 | 9 | 11 |
| :7 | b | 14 | :7 | XEY | 30 | :7 | GTO | 44 | :7 | X>Y | 53 | :7 | 2 | 02 |
| :8 | 8 | 10 | :8 | CLX | 37 | :8 | GTO | 44 | :8 | 8 | 10 | :8 | FMT | 42 |
| :9 | 2 | 02 | :9 | X=Y | 50 | :9 | 3 | 03 | :9 | 1 | 01 | :9 | GTO | 44 |
| :a | FMT | 42 | :a | 5 | 05 | :a | 2 | 02 | :a | XTO | 23 | :a | GTO | 44 |
| :b | GTO | 44 | :b | b | 14 | :b | UP | 27 | :b | b | 14 | :b | 0 | 00 |
| :c | 2 | 02 | :c | 6 | 06 | :c | 9 | 11 | :c | GTO | 44 | :c | 0 | 00 |
| :d | 3 | 03 | :d | CHS | 32 | :d | 2 | 02 | :d | 8 | 10 | :d | END | 46 |

| Addr | Key | Code | Addr | Key | Code | Addr | Key | Code | Addr | Key | Code | Addr | Key | Code |
|---|---|---|---|---|---|---|---|---|---|---|---|---|---|---|
| 0:0 | 7 | 07 | 2:0 | 5 | 05 | 4:0 | XTO | 23 | 6:0 | FMT | 42 | 8:0 | 4 | 04 |
| :1 | 2 | 02 | :1 | FMT | 42 | :1 | b | 14 | :1 | GTO | 44 | :1 | [illegible] | [illegible] |
| :2 | FMT | 42 | :2 | π | 56 | :2 | a | 13 | :2 | 7 | 07 | :2 | XTO | [illegible] |
| :3 | GTO | 44 | :3 | UP | 27 | :3 | XTO | 23 | :3 | 8 | 10 | :3 | [illegible] | [illegible] |
| :4 | 7 | 07 | :4 | 2 | 02 | :4 | e | 12 | :4 | FMT | 42 | :4 | [illegible] | [illegible] |
| :5 | 9 | 11 | :5 | 3 | 03 | :5 | UP | 27 | :5 | GTO | 44 | :5 | 3 | [illegible] |
| :6 | FMT | 42 | :6 | 4 | 04 | :6 | CLX | 37 | :6 | 9 | 11 | :6 | FMT | [illegible] |
| :7 | GTO | 44 | :7 | FMT | 42 | :7 | X<Y | 52 | :7 | 4 | 04 | :7 | GTO | [illegible] |
| :8 | 1 | 01 | :8 | π | 56 | :8 | 7 | 07 | :8 | FMT | 42 | :8 | [illegible] | [illegible] |
| :9 | XTO | 23 | :9 | POL | 62 | :9 | a | 13 | :9 | GTO | 44 | :9 | [illegible] | [illegible] |
| :a | b | 14 | :a | YTO | 40 | :a | 8 | 10 | :a | f | 15 | :a | [illegible] | [illegible] |
| :b | 8 | 10 | :b | a | 13 | :b | 3 | 03 | :b | XEY | 30 | :b | [illegible] | [illegible] |
| :c | 2 | 02 | :c | 7 | 07 | :c | FMT | 42 | :c | CLX | 37 | :c | [illegible] | [illegible] |
| :d | FMT | 42 | :d | 8 | 10 | :d | GTO | 44 | :d | X=Y | 50 | :d | [illegible] | [illegible] |
| 1:0 | GTO | 44 | 3:0 | FMT | 42 | 5:0 | 7 | 07 | 7:0 | 9 | 11 | 9:0 | [illegible] | [illegible] |
| :1 | e | 12 | :1 | GTO | 44 | :1 | 4 | 04 | :1 | 5 | 05 | :1 | [illegible] | [illegible] |
| :2 | UP | 27 | :2 | 9 | 11 | :2 | FMT | 42 | :2 | a | 13 | :2 | [illegible] | [illegible] |
| :3 | CLX | 37 | :3 | 6 | 06 | :3 | GTO | 44 | :3 | XTO | 23 | :3 | [illegible] | [illegible] |
| :4 | X=Y | 50 | :4 | FMT | 42 | :4 | 9 | 11 | :4 | e | 12 | :4 | [illegible] | [illegible] |
| :5 | STP | 41 | :5 | GTO | 44 | :5 | 4 | 04 | :5 | UP | 27 | :5 | [illegible] | [illegible] |
| :6 | STP | 41 | :6 | f | 15 | :6 | FMT | 42 | :6 | CLX | 37 | :6 | [illegible] | [illegible] |
| :7 | CLX | 37 | :7 | XEY | 30 | :7 | GTO | 44 | :7 | X>Y | 53 | :7 | [illegible] | [illegible] |
| :8 | 8 | 10 | :8 | CLX | 37 | :8 | GTO | 44 | :8 | 8 | 10 | :8 | FMT | [illegible] |
| :9 | 1 | 01 | :9 | X=Y | 50 | :9 | 3 | 03 | :9 | 1 | 01 | :9 | GTO | 44 |
| :a | FMT | 42 | :a | 5 | 05 | :a | 2 | 02 | :a | XTO | 23 | :a | GTO | 44 |
| :b | GTO | 44 | :b | b | 14 | :b | UP | 27 | :b | b | 14 | :b | [illegible] | [illegible] |
| :c | 2 | 02 | :c | 6 | 06 | :c | 9 | 11 | :c | GTO | 44 | :c | 0 | 00 |
| :d | 3 | 03 | :d | CHS | 32 | :d | 2 | 02 | :d | 8 | 10 | :d | END | 46 |

Afterwards, manually key in

4
8
RDN
7
0
FMT
GTO
GTO
0
0
CNT

## |48| RELATIVE PREFERRED NOTATION

Prior to running this computation manually key in

7
1
FMT
GTO
GTO
0
0
CNT

and then

4
8
FMT
GTO
GTO
0
0
CNT

## |49| DATA RECORD

This program self-destructs. Read it into 00 and key in GTO 00. At the STP enter one of the addresses 170, 180, 190, 200, 210, 228, 238. Push CNT. Be sure to depress the RECORD button. Finally, check the magnetic card output for the presence of 46 in a0.

| Addr | Key | Code | Addr | Key | Code | Addr | Key | Code | Addr | Key | Code | Addr | Key | Code | Addr | Key | Code |
|---|---|---|---|---|---|---|---|---|---|---|---|---|---|---|---|---|---|
| 0:0: | GTO | 44 | 2:0: | | | 4:0: | XTO | 23 | 6:0: | + | 33 | 8:0: | RCL | 61 | a:0: | END | 46 |
| :1: | 3 | 03 | :1: | | | :1: | e | 12 | :1: | DN | 25 | :1: | 1 | 01 | | | |
| :2: | 2 | 02 | :2: | | | :2: | FMT | 42 | :2: | XTO | 23 | :2: | + | 33 | | | |
| :3: | | | :3: | | | :3: | π | 56 | :3: | e | 12 | :3: | DN | 25 | | | |
| :4: | | | :4: | | | :4: | XTO | 23 | :4: | FMT | 42 | :4: | XTO | 23 | | | |
| :5: | | | :5: | | | :5: | 1 | 01 | :5: | π | 56 | :5: | e | 12 | | | |
| :6: | | | :6: | | | :6: | RCL | 61 | :6: | XTO | 23 | :6: | FMT | 42 | | | |
| :7: | | | :7: | | | :7: | 1 | 01 | :7: | 4 | 04 | :7: | π | 56 | | | |
| :8: | | | :8: | | | :8: | + | 33 | :8: | RCL | 61 | :8: | XTO | 23 | | | |
| :9: | | | :9: | | | :9: | DN | 25 | :9: | 1 | 01 | :9: | 7 | 07 | | | |
| :a: | | | :a: | | | :a: | XTO | 23 | :a: | + | 04 | :a: | RCL | 61 | | | |
| :b: | | | :b: | | | :b: | e | 12 | :b: | DN | 25 | :b: | 1 | 01 | | | |
| :c: | | | :c: | | | :c: | FMT | 42 | :c: | XTO | 23 | :c: | + | 33 | | | |
| :d: | | | :d: | | | :d: | π | 56 | :d: | e | 12 | :d: | DN | 25 | | | |
| 1:0: | | | 3:0: | | | 5:0: | XTO | 23 | 7:0: | FMT | 42 | 9:0: | XTO | 23 | | | |
| :1: | | | :1: | | | :1: | 2 | 02 | :1: | π | 56 | :1: | e | 12 | | | |
| :2: | | | :2: | CLR | 20 | :2: | RCL | 61 | :2: | XTO | 23 | :2: | FMT | 42 | | | |
| :3: | | | :3: | STP | 41 | :3: | 1 | 01 | :3: | 5 | 05 | :3: | π | 56 | | | |
| :4: | | | :4: | XTO | 23 | :4: | + | 33 | :4: | RCL | 61 | :4: | XTO | 23 | | | |
| :5: | | | :5: | e | 12 | :5: | DN | 25 | :5: | 1 | 01 | :5: | 8 | 10 | | | |
| :6: | | | :6: | FMT | 42 | :6: | XTO | 23 | :6: | + | 33 | :6: | RCL | 61 | | | |
| :7: | | | :7: | π | 56 | :7: | e | 12 | :7: | DN | 25 | :7: | 1 | 01 | | | |
| :8: | | | :8: | XTO | 23 | :8: | FMT | 42 | :8: | XTO | 23 | :8: | + | 04 | | | |
| :9: | | | :9: | 0 | 00 | :9: | π | 56 | :9: | e | 12 | :9: | DN | 25 | | | |
| :a: | | | :a: | RCL | 61 | :a: | XTO | 23 | :a: | FMT | 42 | :a: | FMT | 42 | | | |
| :b: | | | :b: | 1 | 01 | :b: | 3 | 03 | :b: | π | 56 | :b: | π | 56 | | | |
| :c: | | | :c: | + | 33 | :c: | RCL | 61 | :c: | XTO | 23 | :c: | XTO | 23 | | | |
| :d: | | | :d: | DN | 25 | :d: | 1 | 01 | :d: | 6 | 06 | :d: | 9 | 11 | | | |

## |70| CONCLUDE

```
0:0: f   15
 :1: XEY 30
 :2: CLX 37
 :3: X<Y 52
 :4: 1   01
 :5: b   14
 :6: DN  25
 :7: 2   02
 :8: 2   02
 :9: 8   10
 :a: FMT 42
 :b: +   33
 :c: CLX 37
 :d: UP  27
1:0: 2   02
 :1: 4   04
 :2: 4   04
 :3: FMT 42
 :4: YTO 40
 :5: 1   01
 :6: 6   06
 :7: 0   00
 :8: FMT 42
 :9: SFL 54
 :a: STP 41
 :b: FMT 42
 :c: END 46
```

## |71| RESET

```
0:0: CLX 37
 :1: UP  27
 :2: 2   02
 :3: 3   03
 :4: 7   07
 :5: FMT 42
 :6: YTO 40
 :7: 2   02
 :8: 3   03
 :9: 6   06
 :a: FMT 42
 :b: YTO 40
 :c: 2   02
 :d: 3   03
1:0: 5   05
 :1: FMT 42
 :2: YTO 40
 :3: 2   02
 :4: 3   03
 :5: 4   04
 :6: FMT 42
 :7: YTO 40
 :8: 2   02
 :9: 3   03
 :a: 3   03
 :b: FMT 42
 :c: YTO 40
 :d: 2   02
2:0: 3   03
 :1: 2   02
 :2: FMT 42
 :3: YTO 40
 :4: 2   02
 :5: 3   03
 :6: 1   01
 :7: FMT 42
 :8: YTO 40
 :9: 2   02
 :a: 3   03
 :b: 0   00
 :c: FMT 42
 :d: YTO 40
3:0: 2   02
 :1: 2   02
 :2: 9   11
 :3: FMT 42
 :4: YTO 40
 :5: 2   02
 :6: 4   04
 :7: 6   06
 :8: FMT 42
 :9: YTO 40
 :a: 1   01
 :b: 7   07
 :c: 0   00
 :d: UP  27
4:0: 2   02
 :1: 4   04
 :2: 7   07
 :3: FMT 42
 :4: YTO 40
 :5: FMT 42
 :6: END 46
```

## |72| TAB

Subroutine 72 adds the number of character widths specified in register 228 to the tab setting in register 245.

```
0:0: 2   02
 :1: 2   02
 :2: 8   10
 :3: FMT 42
 :4: π   56
 :5: UP  27
 :6: 3   03
 :7: 6   06
 :8: X   36
 :9: 2   02
 :a: 4   04
 :b: 5   05
 :c: FMT 42
 :d: YTO 40
1:0: FMT 42
 :1: END 46
```

## |73| WEIGH

```
0:0: CLX 37
 :1: UP  27
 :2: XTO 23
 :3: e   12
 :4: f   15
 :5: UP  27
 :6: 2   02
 :7: DIV 35
 :8: DN  25
 :9: UP  27
 :a: INT 64
 :b: -   34
 :c: AC+ 60
 :d: UP  27
1:0: CLX 37
 :1: X<Y 52
 :2: 0   00
 :3: 6   06
 :4: RCL 61
 :5: 2   02
 :6: X   36
 :7: UP  27
 :8: FMT 42
 :9: END 46
```

## |74| COMPUTE LITERAL

```
0:0: e   12
 :1: UP  27
 :2: 3   03
 :3: UP  27
 :4: 8   10
 :5: 8   10
 :6: FMT 42
 :7: GTO 44
 :8: DN  25
 :9: 3   03
 :a: 0   00
 :b: DIV 35
 :c: CLX 37
 :d: UP  27
1:0: c   16
 :1: X=Y 50
 :2: 2   02
 :3: 3   03
 :4: DN  25
 :5: X>Y 53
 :6: 1   01
 :7: d   17
 :8: 3   03
 :9: -   34
 :a: GTO 44
 :b: 2   02
 :c: 6   06
 :d: 9   11
2:0: GTO 44
 :1: 2   02
 :2: 5   05
 :3: DN  25
 :4: 3   03
 :5: +   33
 :6: YTO 40
 :7: e   12
 :8: d   17
 :9: UP  27
 :a: CLX 37
 :b: UP  27
 :c: c   16
 :d: X=Y 50
3:0: 4   04
 :1: 2   02
 :2: DN  25
 :3: 6   06
 :4: X>Y 53
 :5: 3   03
 :6: b   14
 :7: 9   11
 :8: GTO 44
 :9: 4   04
 :a: 4   04
 :b: 3   03
 :c: +   33
 :d: GTO 44
4:0: 4   04
 :1: 5   05
 :2: DN  25
 :3: 3   03
 :4: -   34
 :5: YTO 40
 :6: d   17
 :7: 7   07
 :8: 6   06
 :9: FMT 42
 :a: GTO 44
 :b: FMT 42
 :c: END 46
```

## |75| ASSEMBLE LITERAL

This subroutine stores the appropriate decimal-coded literal in the f register given an integer n in the Y register and an offset in register b. The three possible values -6, 0, and +6 of this offset relate the answers to the inferior, canonical, and superior levels of preferred notation, respectively (see Fig. 7.5)

```
0:0: b   14
 :1: +   33
 :2: 7   07
 :3: 7   07
 :4: FMT 42
 :5: GTO 44
 :6: f   15
 :7: +   33
 :8: 1   01
 :9: 0   00
 :a: DIV 35
 :b: 1   01
 :c: X>Y 53
 :d: 1   01
1:0: 4   04
 :1: GTO 44
 :2: 0   00
 :3: 8   10
```

## |76| SWITCH

This subroutine is the nucleus of the orthographic synthesis process.

```
0:0: e   12   2:0: 9   11   4:0: CLX 37   6:0: +   33
 :1: UP  27    :1: UP  27    :1: X>Y 53    :1: 7   07
 :2: CLX 37    :2: 1   01    :2: 5   05    :2: 5   05
 :3: XTO 23    :3: 6   06    :3: 3   03    :3: FMT 42
 :4: f   15    :4: +   33    :4: d   17    :4: GTO 44
 :5: X<Y 52    :5: 7   07    :5: X>Y 53    :5: FMT 42
 :6: 3   03    :6: 5   05    :6: 5   05    :6: END 46
 :7: 1   01    :7: FMT 42    :7: 4   04
 :8: d   17    :8: GTO 44    :8: UP  27
 :9: X<Y 52    :9: e   12    :9: 4   04
 :a: 1   01    :a: UP  27    :a: +   33
 :b: 7   07    :b: CLX 37    :b: 7   07
 :c: UP  27    :c: X>Y 53    :c: 5   05
 :d: 4   04    :d: 5   05    :d: FMT 42
1:0: +   33   3:0: 3   03   5:0: GTO 44
 :1: 7   07    :1: d   17    :1: e   12
 :2: 5   05    :2: X<Y 52    :2: UP  27
 :3: FMT 42    :3: 4   04    :3: d   17
 :4: GTO 44    :4: 0   00    :4: X   36
 :5: e   12    :5: UP  27    :5: 2   02
 :6: UP  27    :6: 8   10    :6: 7   07
 :7: CLX 37    :7: -   34    :7: CHS 32
 :8: X<Y 52    :8: 7   07    :8: X<Y 52
 :9: 3   03    :9: 5   05    :9: 6   06
 :a: 1   01    :a: FMT 42    :a: 5   05
 :b: d   17    :b: GTO 44    :b: UP  27
 :c: X>Y 53    :c: e   12    :c: 4   04
 :d: 2   02    :d: UP  27    :d: 0   00
```

## |77| ENCODE LITERAL

This subroutine converts an integer n ranging from -20 to +28 inclusive, which is found in the Y register, to the corresponding decimal-coded literal $\ell$ on the range 1888 to 7999 inclusive, and places the result in the Y register.

```
0:0: 2   02   2:0: a   13   4:0: 5   05
 :1: 1   01    :1: 2   02    :1: 8   10
 :2: X<Y 52    :2: 1   01    :2: -   34
 :3: 4   04    :3: .   21    :3: .   21
 :4: a   13    :4: 8   10    :4: 9   11
 :5: 1   01    :5: 8   10    :5: 9   11
 :6: 4   04    :6: 8   10    :6: +   33
 :7: X<Y 52    :7: GTO 44    :7: GTO 44
 :8: 4   04    :8: 5   05    :8: 5   05
 :9: 2   02    :9: 1   01    :9: 5   05
 :a: 7   07    :a: -   34    :a: -   34
 :b: X<Y 52    :b: .   21    :b: .   21
 :c: 3   03    :c: 8   10    :c: 9   11
 :d: 9   11    :d: 8   10    :d: 9   11
1:0: CLX 37   3:0: GTO 44   5:0: 9   11
 :1: X<Y 52    :1: 4   04    :1: +   33
 :2: 5   05    :2: 6   06    :2: 1   01
 :3: b   14    :3: -   34    :3: 0   00
 :4: 7   07    :4: .   21    :4: X   36
 :5: CHS 32    :5: 8   10    :5: 1   01
 :6: X<Y 52    :6: GTO 44    :6: 0   00
 :7: 3   03    :7: 3   03    :7: X   36
 :8: 3   03    :8: c   16    :8: 1   01
 :9: 1   01    :9: -   34    :9: 0   00
 :a: 4   04    :a: .   21    :a: X   36
 :b: CHS 32    :b: 9   11    :b: FMT 42
 :c: X<Y 52    :c: +   33    :c: END 46
 :D: 2   02    :d: GTO 44
```

## |78| RESURRECT COORDINATES

```
0:0: YE  24
 :1: 2   02
 :2: 2   02
 :3: 4   04
 :4: 0   00
 :5: FMT 42
 :6: π   56
 :7: XEY 30
 :8: 2   02
 :9: 4   04
 :a: 6   06
 :b: FMT 42
 :c: YTO 40
 :d: 2   02
1:0: 4   04
 :1: 1   01
 :2: FMT 42
 :3: π   56
 :4: XEY 30
 :5: 2   02
 :6: 4   04
 :7: 7   07
 :8: FMT 42
 :9: YTO 40
 :a: YE  24
 :b: 2   02
 :c: FMT 42
 :d: END 46
```

## |79| SAVE COORDINATES

```
0:0: 2   02
 :1: 4   04
 :2: 6   06
 :3: FMT 42
 :4: π   56
 :5: UP  27
 :6: 2   02
 :7: 4   04
 :8: 0   00
 :9: FMT 42
 :a: YTO 40
 :b: 2   02
 :c: 4   04
 :d: 7   07
1:0: FMT 42
 :1: π   56
 :2: UP  27
 :3: 2   02
 :4: 4   04
 :5: 1   01
 :6: FMT 42
 :7: YTO 40
 :8: FMT 42
 :9: END 46
```

## |80| WRITE NUMBER

Subroutine 80, which invokes subroutines 90 and 92, first records a signed number and then inserts after it a space of one character width. Using this subroutine the basic calculator can cause the X,Y plotter to print out numerical data at a slow, but usually adequate rate

```
0:0: 9   11
 :1: 0   00
 :2: FMT 42
 :3: GTO 44
 :4: CLX 37
 :5: UP  27
 :6: 9   11
 :7: 2   02
 :8: FMT 42
 :9: GTO 44
 :a: FMT 42
 :b: END 46
```

of about twelve characters per minute, without operator attention. Optional peripheral accessories, however, such as a high-speed plotter, or an electrostatic or impact printer, can be procured at reasonable cost to provide a speedier output of analytic or statistical results in a tabular format.

## |81| COMPUTE HISTORY

Subroutine 81 adds a term to the partial sums representing the x and y components of the composition vector, calculates the tonal impulse assuming a unit mass, updates the historical file, and finishes up by placing the value of $\Theta = \arg z$ in the Y register.

```
0¦0¦  1  01   2¦0¦ FMT 42   4¦0¦  3  03   6¦0¦  1  01
 ¦1¦  9  11    ¦1¦  π  56    ¦1¦ FMT 42    ¦1¦  9  11
 ¦2¦  8  10    ¦2¦  -  34    ¦2¦ YTO 40    ¦2¦  5  05
 ¦3¦ FMT 42    ¦3¦  1  01    ¦3¦ DN  25    ¦3¦ FMT 42
 ¦4¦  π  56    ¦4¦  9  11    ¦4¦  +  33    ¦4¦  π  56
 ¦5¦ RDN 31    ¦5¦  0  00    ¦5¦  1  01    ¦5¦ UP  27
 ¦6¦  1  01    ¦6¦ FMT 42    ¦6¦  9  11    ¦6¦  1  01
 ¦7¦  9  11    ¦7¦ YTO 40    ¦7¦  5  05    ¦7¦  9  11
 ¦8¦  4  04    ¦8¦ DN  25    ¦8¦ FMT 42    ¦8¦  4  04
 ¦9¦ FMT 42    ¦9¦  1  01    ¦9¦ YTO 40    ¦9¦ FMT 42
 ¦a¦  π  56    ¦a¦  9  11    ¦a¦ DN  25    ¦a¦  π  56
 ¦b¦ XEY 30    ¦b¦  6  06    ¦b¦  1  01    ¦b¦ POL 62
 ¦c¦  1  01    ¦c¦ FMT 42    ¦c¦  9  11    ¦c¦ FMT 42
 ¦d¦  9  11    ¦d¦ YTO 40    ¦d¦  7  07    ¦d¦ END 46
1¦0¦  2  02   3¦0¦  1  01   5¦0¦ FMT 42
 ¦1¦ FMT 42    ¦1¦  9  11    ¦1¦  π  56
 ¦2¦ YTO 40    ¦2¦  9  11    ¦2¦  -  34
 ¦3¦ DN  25    ¦3¦ FMT 42    ¦3¦  1  01
 ¦4¦  +  33    ¦4¦  π  56    ¦4¦  9  11
 ¦5¦  1  01    ¦5¦ RDN 31    ¦5¦  1  01
 ¦6¦  9  11    ¦6¦  1  01    ¦6¦ FMT 42
 ¦7¦  4  04    ¦7¦  9  11    ¦7¦ YTO 40
 ¦8¦ FMT 42    ¦8¦  5  05    ¦8¦ DN  25
 ¦9¦ YTO 40    ¦9¦ FMT 42    ¦9¦  1  01
 ¦a¦ DN  25    ¦a¦  π  56    ¦a¦  9  11
 ¦b¦  1  01    ¦b¦ XEY 30    ¦b¦  7  07
 ¦c¦  9  11    ¦c¦  1  01    ¦c¦ FMT 42
 ¦d¦  6  06    ¦d¦  9  11    ¦d¦ YTO 40
```

## |82| DISPLACE

For k ' = 1 this subroutine places the rectangular coordinates x,y of the displacement vector **r** in extended memory registers 238 and 239 respectively.

```
0¦0¦  7  07   2¦0¦ FMT 42   4¦0¦  1  01
 ¦1¦  8  10    ¦1¦ GTO 44    ¦1¦  9  11
 ¦2¦ FMT 42    ¦2¦  d  17    ¦2¦  8  10
 ¦3¦ GTO 44    ¦3¦ UP  27    ¦3¦ FMT 42
 ¦4¦ CLX 37    ¦4¦  b  14    ¦4¦  X  36
 ¦5¦ UP  27    ¦5¦  X  36    ¦5¦  1  01
 ¦6¦  1  01    ¦6¦  3  03    ¦6¦  9  11
 ¦7¦  9  11    ¦7¦  0  00    ¦7¦  9  11
 ¦8¦  8  10    ¦8¦  X  36    ¦8¦ FMT 42
 ¦9¦ FMT 42    ¦9¦  1  01    ¦9¦  X  36
 ¦a¦ YTO 40    ¦a¦ RCT 66    ¦a¦ FMT 42
 ¦b¦  1  01    ¦b¦ UP  27    ¦b¦ END 46
 ¦c¦  9  11    ¦c¦  1  01
 ¦d¦  9  11    ¦d¦  9  11
1¦0¦ FMT 42   3¦0¦  8  10
 ¦1¦ YTO 40    ¦1¦ FMT 42
 ¦2¦  9  11    ¦2¦  +  33
 ¦3¦  6  06    ¦3¦ DN  25
 ¦4¦ FMT 42    ¦4¦  1  01
 ¦5¦ GTO 44    ¦5¦  9  11
 ¦6¦  f  15    ¦6¦  9  11
 ¦7¦ UP  27    ¦7¦ FMT 42
 ¦8¦ CLX 37    ¦8¦  +  33
 ¦9¦ X=Y 50    ¦9¦ GTO 44
 ¦a¦  3  03    ¦a¦  1  01
 ¦b¦  c  16    ¦b¦  2  02
 ¦c¦  8  10    ¦c¦  e  12
 ¦d¦  3  03    ¦d¦ UP  27
```

## |83| EVALUATE

```
0¦0¦  f  15   2¦0¦ UP  27   4¦0¦ X>Y 53
 ¦1¦ UP  27    ¦1¦ GTO 44    ¦1¦  4  04
 ¦2¦  1  01    ¦2¦  0  00    ¦2¦  7  07
 ¦3¦ EEX 26    ¦3¦  9  11    ¦3¦  -  34
 ¦4¦  1  01    ¦4¦  8  10    ¦4¦ GTO 44
 ¦5¦  2  02    ¦5¦ X=Y 50    ¦5¦  4  04
 ¦6¦ DIV 35    ¦6¦  3  03    ¦6¦  0  00
 ¦7¦ YTO 40    ¦7¦  8  10    ¦7¦ YTO 40
 ¦8¦  f  15    ¦8¦  9  11    ¦8¦  d  17
 ¦9¦ CLX 37    ¦9¦ X=Y 50    ¦9¦ GTO 44
 ¦a¦ X=Y 50    ¦a¦  3  03    ¦a¦  1  01
 ¦b¦  4  04    ¦b¦  3  03    ¦b¦  d  17
 ¦c¦  c  16    ¦c¦  1  01    ¦c¦ FMT 42
 ¦d¦  1  01    ¦d¦  -  34    ¦d¦ END 46
1¦0¦  0  00   3¦0¦ GTO 44
 ¦1¦  X  36    ¦1¦  3  03
 ¦2¦ DN  25    ¦2¦  c  16
 ¦3¦ UP  27    ¦3¦  7  07
 ¦4¦ INT 64    ¦4¦ UP  27
 ¦5¦  -  34    ¦5¦ GTO 44
 ¦6¦ YTO 40    ¦6¦  3  03
 ¦7¦  f  15    ¦7¦  a  13
 ¦8¦ UP  27    ¦8¦  5  05
 ¦9¦ CLX 37    ¦9¦ UP  27
 ¦a¦ X<Y 52    ¦a¦  d  17
 ¦b¦  2  02    ¦b¦  +  33
 ¦c¦  4  04    ¦c¦  1  01
 ¦d¦  f  15    ¦d¦  2  02
```

## |84| GET COORDINATES

This subroutine finds both the polar and rectangular coordinates for the tonality vector of a charm specified in the Z register. The answer consists of v in Z, ϕ in Y, x in f, and y in e.

```
0¦0¦ DN  25   2¦0¦ UP  27
 ¦1¦ YTO 40    ¦1¦  3  03
 ¦2¦  c  16    ¦2¦  0  00
 ¦3¦ CLR 20    ¦3¦  +  33
 ¦4¦ XTO 23    ¦4¦ YTO 40
 ¦5¦  d  17    ¦5¦ GTO 44
 ¦6¦  c  16    ¦6¦  0  00
 ¦7¦ UP  27    ¦7¦  5  05
 ¦8¦ CLX 37    ¦8¦ RCL 61
 ¦9¦ X=Y 50    ¦9¦ POL 62
 ¦a¦  2  02    ¦a¦ UP  27
 ¦b¦  8  10    ¦b¦ FMT 42
 ¦c¦  2  02    ¦c¦ END 46
 ¦d¦ DIV 35
1¦0¦ DN  25
 ¦1¦ UP  27
 ¦2¦ INT 64
 ¦3¦ XTO 23
 ¦4¦  c  16
 ¦5¦ X=Y 50
 ¦6¦  1  01
 ¦7¦  d  17
 ¦8¦  d  17
 ¦9¦ UP  27
 ¦a¦  1  01
 ¦b¦ RCT 66
 ¦c¦ AC+ 60
 ¦d¦  d  17
```

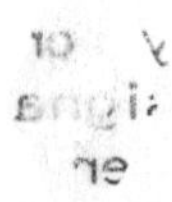

## |85| CALCULATE SPAN

Subroutine 85, which calls upon subroutines 78 and 96, is used to calculate the span of a component expressed in decimal-coded literal notation. The component in question is obtained piecemeal, by invoking subroutine 96 sufficiently many times.

```
0|0| 7   07   2|0| 1   01   4|0| 0   00   6|0| XEY 30
 |1| 8   10    |1| 7   07    |1| DIV 35    |1| a   13
 |2| FMT 42    |2| -   34    |2| XEY 30    |2| X<Y 52
 |3| GTO 44    |3| CLX 37    |3| INT 64    |3| XTO 23
 |4| CLR 20    |4| XEY 30    |4| GTO 44    |4| b   14
 |5| 1   01    |5| X<Y 52    |5| 1   01    |5| YE  24
 |6| 7   07    |6| 4   04    |6| 7   07    |6| 8   10
 |7| XTO 23    |7| c   16    |7| a   13    |7| YTO 40
 |8| b   14    |8| DN  25    |8| XEY 30    |8| 8   10
 |9| CHS 32    |9| 2   02    |9| GTO 44    |9| X>Y 53
 |a| XTO 23    |a| DIV 35    |a| 3   03    |a| XTO 23
 |b| 8   10    |b| DN  25    |b| 8   10    |b| 8   10
 |c| 4   04    |c| UP  27    |c| a   13    |c| GTO 44
 |d| CHS 32    |d| INT 64    |d| XEY 30    |d| 0   00
1|0| XTO 23   3|0| X=Y 50   5|0| 1   01   7|0| c   16
 |1| a   13    |1| 4   04    |1| +   33    |1| YE  24
 |2| 9   11    |2| 7   07    |2| YTO 40    |2| 8   10
 |3| 6   06    |3| a   13    |3| a   13    |3| b   14
 |4| FMT 42    |4| XEY 30    |4| DN  25    |4| UP  27
 |5| GTO 44    |5| 1   01    |5| 1   01    |5| DN  25
 |6| f   15    |6| 4   04    |6| -   34    |6| -   34
 |7| RDN 31    |7| +   33    |7| UP  27    |7| 1   01
 |8| DN  25    |8| 7   07    |8| DN  25    |8| +   33
 |9| CLX 37    |9| -   34    |9| CLX 37    |9| 2   02
 |a| X=Y 50    |a| YTO 40    |a| X<Y 52    |a| UP  27
 |b| 7   07    |b| a   13    |b| 4   04    |b| FMT 42
 |c| 1   01    |c| DN  25    |c| c   16    |c| END 46
 |d| DN  25    |d| 1   01    |d| b   14
```

The answer consists of the span of the given component--a two-digit number, which is placed in the Z register--and the integer 2, which is put in the Y register for convenience in printing. To use this routine as an independent entity, substitute the instructions STP, CNT, CNT, CNT, CNT for the instructions 9, 6, FMT, GTO, f in program steps 12 through 16. Then enter one literal of the component each time the machine stops and push the CNT key. After the final literal enter a zero end marker, push CNT, and read the answer from the Z register.

## |86| CHARACTERIZE

Subroutine 86 computes the sonoral characteristic and level of a designated harmonic of a specified charm. Given the designation or specification in register f, it places the required characteristic in the Z register and level in the Y register.

To activate this subroutine as an independent program, first key the given argument into register f. Then with the control switch in the RUN position, press the END and CONTINUE keys. This procedure will

```
0|0| 4   04   2|0| UP  27   4|0| X<Y 52   6|0| XEY 30
 |1| 0   00    |1| 1   01    |1| 4   04    |1| GTO 44
 |2| 9   11    |2| -   34    |2| b   14    |2| 2   02
 |3| 6   06    |3| YTO 40    |3| GTO 44    |3| b   14
 |4| XTO 23    |4| a   13    |4| 5   05    |4| RCL 61
 |5| a   13    |5| 1   01    |5| 3   03    |5| a   13
 |6| XTO 23    |6| 2   02    |6| a   13    |6| X<Y 52
 |7| c   16    |7| CHS 32    |7| +   33    |7| -   34
 |8| XTO 23    |8| XTO 23    |8| GTO 44    |8| CNT 47
 |9| e   12    |9| b   14    |9| 3   03    |9| FMT 42
 |a| f   15    |a| DN  25    |a| 4   04    |a| END 46
 |b| RDN 31    |b| 2   02    |b| UP  27
 |c| DN  25    |c| X   36    |c| XTO 23
 |d| a   13    |d| a   13    |d| f   15
1|0| DIV 35   3|0| -   34   5|0| c   16
 |1| DN  25    |1| CLX 37    |1| XTO 23
 |2| INT 64    |2| X>Y 53    |2| e   12
 |3| CHS 32    |3| 4   04    |3| b   14
 |4| UP  27    |4| 6   06    |4| UP  27
 |5| a   13    |5| YTO 40    |5| 1   01
 |6| X   36    |6| d   17    |6| +   33
 |7| DN  25    |7| YE  24    |7| YTO 40
 |8| +   33    |8| c   16    |8| b   14
 |9| YTO 40    |9| 2   02    |9| CLX 37
 |a| d   17    |a| DIV 35    |a| X=Y 50
 |b| YTO 40    |b| YE  24    |b| 6   06
 |c| f   15    |c| c   16    |c| 4   04
 |d| a   13    |d| DN  25    |d| d   17
```

result in the answer being put in the Y and Z registers, as indicated.

## |87| SPECIFY

Subroutine 87, which calls upon subroutine 96, encodes a given charm in specific form. It has several instructions in common with subroutine 85, so that some of the remarks made before remain applicable. The answer consists of the charm specification--a twelve-digit decimal number, which is placed in both the Z register and register f--and the integer 12, which is put in the Y register. To use this routine as an independent entity, substitute the instructions STP, CNT, CNT, CNT, CNT for the instructions 9, 6, FMT, GTO, f in program steps 08 through 0c. Then enter one literal of the component each time the machine stops and push the CNT key. After the final literal, enter a zero end marker, push CNT, and read the answer from the Z register.

```
0|0| CLR 20   2|0| DN  25   4|0| XEY 30   6|0| CHS 32   8|0| 4   04
 |1| CLX 37    |1| 2   02    |1| GTO 44    |1| UP  27    |1| 0   00
 |2| XTO 23    |2| DIV 35    |2| 2   02    |2| 4   04    |2| 9   11
 |3| a   13    |3| DN  25    |3| d   17    |3| 0   00    |3| 6   06
 |4| .   21    |4| UP  27    |4| b   14    |4| 9   11    |4| X   36
 |5| 5   05    |5| INT 64    |5| XEY 30    |5| 5   05    |5| GTO 44
 |6| XTO 23    |6| X=Y 50    |6| 2   02    |6| X   36    |6| 6   06
 |7| b   14    |7| 3   03    |7| X   36    |7| b   14    |7| 9   11
 |8| 9   11    |8| d   17    |8| YTO 40    |8| +   33    |8| a   13
 |9| 6   06    |9| b   14    |9| b   14    |9| YTO 40    |9| XEY 30
 |a| FMT 42    |a| XEY 30    |a| DN  25    |a| b   14    |a| b   14
 |b| GTO 44    |b| 4   04    |b| 1   01    |b| a   13    |b| +   33
 |c| f   15    |c| X   36    |c| -   34    |c| XEY 30    |c| YTO 40
 |d| RDN 31    |d| 3   03    |d| UP  27    |d| b   14    |d| a   13
1|0| DN  25   3|0| 2   02   5|0| DN  25   7|0| DIV 35   9|0| GTO 44
 |1| CLX 37    |1| X   36    |1| CLX 37    |1| DN  25    |1| 0   00
 |2| X=Y 50    |2| YTO 40    |2| X<Y 52    |2| INT 64    |2| 4   04
 |3| 9   11    |3| b   14    |3| 4   04    |3| UP  27    |3| a   13
 |4| 3   03    |4| DN  25    |4| 4   04    |4| 2   02    |4| UP  27
 |5| DN  25    |5| 1   01    |5| b   14    |5| DIV 35    |5| YTO 40
 |6| 1   01    |6| 0   00    |6| XEY 30    |6| DN  25    |6| f   15
 |7| 7   07    |7| DIV 35    |7| 4   04    |7| UP  27    |7| 1   01
 |8| -   34    |8| XEY 30    |8| 0   00    |8| INT 64    |8| 2   02
 |9| CLX 37    |9| INT 64    |9| 9   11    |9| X=Y 50    |9| UP  27
 |a| XEY 30    |a| GTO 44    |a| 5   05    |a| 8   10    |a| FMT 42
 |b| X<Y 52    |b| 0   00    |b| DIV 35    |b| 8   10    |b| END 46
 |c| 4   04    |c| d   17    |c| DN  25    |c| b   14
 |d| 4   04    |d| b   14    |d| INT 64    |d| XEY 30
```

## |88| ROUND AND TRUNCATE

Subroutine 88 adds the quantity

$$0.5 \times 10^{-n},$$

where n is an integer such that $0 \leq n \equiv 8$, to the absolute value of the signed decimal number that is given in the Z register. Next it reattaches the original algebraic sign to the sum, discards the digits to the right of the nth decimal place and then puts the result back into the Z register. The integer n must be placed in the Y register prior to entry to this subroutine.

```
0¦0¦ CLX 37   2¦0¦ INT 64
 ¦1¦ RUP 22    ¦1¦ RDN 31
 ¦2¦ X<Y 52    ¦2¦  .  21
 ¦3¦ SFL 54    ¦3¦  9  11
 ¦4¦ CNT 47    ¦4¦  +  33
 ¦5¦ RDN 31    ¦5¦ CLX 37
 ¦6¦  .  21    ¦6¦ X=Y 50
 ¦7¦  9  11    ¦7¦  3  03
 ¦8¦  -  34    ¦8¦  7  07
 ¦9¦ CLX 37    ¦9¦  .  21
 ¦a¦ X>Y 53    ¦a¦  1  01
 ¦b¦  1  01    ¦b¦ RUP 22
 ¦c¦  7  07    ¦c¦  X  36
 ¦d¦  1  01    ¦d¦ XEY 30
1¦0¦  0  00   3¦0¦ RDN 31
 ¦1¦ RUP 22    ¦1¦  .  21
 ¦2¦  X  36    ¦2¦  1  01
 ¦3¦ XEY 30    ¦3¦  -  34
 ¦4¦ GTO 44    ¦4¦ GTO 44
 ¦5¦  0  00    ¦5¦  2  02
 ¦6¦  5  05    ¦6¦  5  05
 ¦7¦  .  21    ¦7¦ RUP 22
 ¦8¦  5  05    ¦8¦ IFG 43
 ¦9¦ RDN 31    ¦9¦ CHS 32
 ¦a¦ ¦Y¦ 55    ¦a¦ CNT 47
 ¦b¦ RDN 31    ¦b¦ RDN 31
 ¦c¦  +  33    ¦c¦ FMT 42
 ¦d¦ DN  25    ¦d¦ END 46
```

## |89| WRITE NUMERAL NOT ONE

```
0¦0¦  9  11   2¦0¦  2  02   4¦0¦ GTO 44   6¦0¦  9  11
 ¦1¦ X=Y 50    ¦1¦ X=Y 50    ¦1¦  7  07    ¦1¦  7  07
 ¦2¦  7  07    ¦2¦  2  02    ¦2¦  9  11    ¦2¦  9  11
 ¦3¦  3  03    ¦3¦  c  16    ¦3¦  7  07    ¦3¦  1  01
 ¦4¦  8  10    ¦4¦  1  01    ¦4¦  4  04    ¦4¦ GTO 44
 ¦5¦ X=Y 50    ¦5¦  3  03    ¦5¦  6  06    ¦5¦  7  07
 ¦6¦  6  06    ¦6¦  9  11    ¦6¦  9  11    ¦6¦  9  11
 ¦7¦  7  07    ¦7¦  7  07    ¦7¦  3  03    ¦7¦  4  04
 ¦8¦  7  07    ¦8¦  1  01    ¦8¦ GTO 44    ¦8¦  6  06
 ¦9¦ X=Y 50    ¦9¦ GTO 44    ¦9¦  7  07    ¦9¦  9  11
 ¦a¦  6  06    ¦a¦  7  07    ¦a¦  9  11    ¦a¦  7  07
 ¦b¦  1  01    ¦b¦  9  11    ¦b¦  9  11    ¦b¦  1  01
 ¦c¦  6  06    ¦c¦  7  07    ¦c¦  7  07    ¦c¦  3  03
 ¦d¦ X=Y 50    ¦d¦  9  11    ¦d¦  4  04    ¦d¦  6  06
1¦0¦  5  05   3¦0¦  6  06   5¦0¦  6  06   7¦0¦ GTO 44
 ¦1¦  6  06    ¦1¦  4  04    ¦1¦  3  03    ¦1¦  7  07
 ¦2¦  5  05    ¦2¦  1  01    ¦2¦  1  01    ¦2¦  9  11
 ¦3¦ X=Y 50    ¦3¦  3  03    ¦3¦ GTO 44    ¦3¦  1  01
 ¦4¦  4  04    ¦4¦ GTO 44    ¦4¦  7  07    ¦4¦  3  03
 ¦5¦  b  14    ¦5¦  7  07    ¦5¦  9  11    ¦5¦  9  11
 ¦6¦  4  04    ¦6¦  9  11    ¦6¦  9  11    ¦6¦  7  07
 ¦7¦ X=Y 50    ¦7¦  7  07    ¦7¦  7  07    ¦7¦  4  04
 ¦8¦  4  04    ¦8¦  9  11    ¦8¦  1  01    ¦8¦  6  06
 ¦9¦  3  03    ¦9¦  6  06    ¦9¦  3  03    ¦9¦ UP  27
 ¦a¦  3  03    ¦a¦  5  05    ¦a¦  6  06    ¦a¦ FMT 42
 ¦b¦ X=Y 50    ¦b¦  6  06    ¦b¦  4  04    ¦b¦ END 46
 ¦c¦  3  03    ¦c¦  3  03    ¦c¦ GTO 44
 ¦d¦  7  07    ¦d¦  1  01    ¦d¦  7  07
```

## |90| WRITE SIGNED NUMBER

Subroutine 90, which calls upon subroutines 89 and 92, is used to control the X,Y plotter and to adapt it for use as a character-displaying device. This subroutine inserts a decimal point where indicated and draws the successive characters of the decimal number, to be recorded, on the plotter paper surface with a fine-line pen. Program steps 45 and 46 must be adjusted to the value obtained by tripling the scale factor inserted in program steps 2 and 3 of subroutine 92.

The signed number that is to be output must be placed in the Z register just prior to entering the subroutines. This number should be of the form

$$Z_{m-1}Z_{m-2}\ldots Z_0.Z_{-1}\ldots Z_{-n},$$

with the $Z_i$ being chosen nonnegative integers less than ten. The parameters m and n, where

$$0 \leq m \leq 12, \quad 0 \leq n \leq 9,$$

$$\text{and } 0 \leq m + n \leq 12,$$

also are to be entered immediately beforehand into the Y register as a single decimal number m.n.

The disadvantage of this method of output, as mentioned previously, is the excessive time required for some printouts. Although the music analysis system described herein operates very well unattended, so that calculations can be run independently, automatic typewriters and matrix printers are available to offer an accelerated means for recording information from today's desk-top computers.

```
0¦0¦ CLX 37   2¦0¦  e  12   4¦0¦ XTO 23   6¦0¦ CLX 37
 ¦1¦ RUP 22    ¦1¦ UP  27    ¦1¦  e  12    ¦1¦ X=Y 50
 ¦2¦ X<Y 52    ¦2¦  1  01    ¦2¦ RUP 22    ¦2¦  7  07
 ¦3¦  4  04    ¦3¦ X=Y 50    ¦3¦ XTO 23    ¦3¦  c  16
 ¦4¦  0  00    ¦4¦  7  07    ¦4¦  f  15    ¦4¦  2  02
 ¦5¦ RDN 31    ¦5¦  6  06    ¦5¦  4  04    ¦5¦ UP  27
 ¦6¦ DN  25    ¦6¦  8  10    ¦6¦  5  05    ¦6¦  9  11
 ¦7¦ XTO 23    ¦7¦  9  11    ¦7¦ UP  27    ¦7¦  2  02
 ¦8¦  f  15    ¦8¦ FMT 42    ¦8¦  2  02    ¦8¦ FMT 42
 ¦9¦  1  01    ¦9¦ GTO 44    ¦9¦  4  04    ¦9¦ GTO 44
 ¦a¦  0  00    ¦a¦  9  11    ¦a¦  5  05    ¦a¦  f  15
 ¦b¦ LN  65    ¦b¦  2  02    ¦b¦ FMT 42    ¦b¦ UP  27
 ¦c¦ XEY 30    ¦c¦ FMT 42    ¦c¦  -  34    ¦c¦  1  01
 ¦d¦  f  15    ¦d¦ GTO 44    ¦d¦  5  05    ¦d¦  0  00
1¦0¦ INT 64   3¦0¦  f  15   5¦0¦  6  06   7¦0¦  X  36
 ¦1¦  X  36    ¦1¦ UP  27    ¦1¦ UP  27    ¦1¦ YTO 40
 ¦2¦ DN  25    ¦2¦  1  01    ¦2¦  9  11    ¦2¦  f  15
 ¦3¦ EXP 74    ¦3¦  -  34    ¦3¦  2  02    ¦3¦ GTO 44
 ¦4¦ INT 64    ¦4¦ YTO 40    ¦4¦ FMT 42    ¦4¦  3  03
 ¦5¦ DIV 35    ¦5¦  f  15    ¦5¦ GTO 44    ¦5¦  a  13
 ¦6¦  1  01    ¦6¦  1  01    ¦6¦ RCL 61    ¦6¦  2  02
 ¦7¦  0  00    ¦7¦ X>Y 53    ¦7¦ ¦Y¦ 55    ¦7¦  8  10
 ¦8¦  X  36    ¦8¦  5  05    ¦8¦ UP  27    ¦8¦ UP  27
 ¦9¦ DN  25    ¦9¦  c  16    ¦9¦ GTO 44    ¦9¦ GTO 44
 ¦a¦ UP  27    ¦a¦ RCL 61    ¦a¦  0  00    ¦a¦  2  02
 ¦b¦ INT 64    ¦b¦ GTO 44    ¦b¦  6  06    ¦b¦  a  13
 ¦c¦  -  34    ¦c¦  1  01    ¦c¦  f  15    ¦c¦ FMT 42
 ¦d¦ YTO 40    ¦d¦  6  06    ¦d¦ UP  27    ¦d¦ END 46
```

## |91| DRAW CHARACTER

Subroutine 91, which serves as the kernel of subroutine 92, commands the plotter to shape various characters with successive preprogrammed strokes of the pen. The term "character" refers to a letter of the alphabet in either upper or lower case, a numerical digit, some other symbol that can be printed (such as an asterisk, a minus sign, or a notational inflection), or a non-printable space character, or blank.

```
0:0: IFG 43    2:0: DN  25    4:0: XEY 30    6:0: 3   03    8:0: 2   02
 :1: 6   06     :1: UP  27     :1: -   34     :1: RCL 61     :1: DIV 35
 :2: 7   07     :2: INT 64     :2: .   21     :2: FMT 42     :2: CLX 37
 :3: d   17     :3: -   34     :3: 6   06     :3: UP  27     :3: XEY 30
 :4: UP  27     :4: YTO 40     :4: 4   04     :4: GTO 44     :4: AC- 63
 :5: CLX 37     :5: d   17     :5: DIV 35     :5: 0   00     :5: DN  25
 :6: X>Y 53     :6: UP  27     :6: b   14     :6: 3   03     :6: GTO 44
 :7: 7   07     :7: YE  24     :7: X   36     :7: UP  27     :7: 0   00
 :8: 9   11     :8: c   16     :8: RUP 22     :8: b   14     :8: 9   11
 :9: 1   01     :9: X=Y 50     :9: X   36     :9: UP  27     :9: FMT 42
 :a: X>Y 53     :a: 6   06     :a: .   21     :a: .   21     :a: END 46
 :b: 1   01     :b: 1   01     :b: 3   03     :b: 1   01
 :c: 7   07     :c: XEY 30     :c: RUP 22     :c: 6   06
 :d: 1   01     :d: 1   01     :d: X   36     :d: DIV 35
1:0: 0   00    3:0: -   34    5:0: RDN 31    7:0: CLX 37
 :1: XTO 23     :1: 3   03     :1: +   33     :1: XTO 23
 :2: c   16     :2: DIV 35     :2: e   12     :2: f   15
 :3: DIV 35     :3: XEY 30     :3: RUP 22     :3: AC- 63
 :4: GTO 44     :4: UP  27     :4: +   33     :4: RDN 31
 :5: 0   00     :5: INT 64     :5: f   15     :5: DN  25
 :6: 9   11     :6: -   34     :6: RUP 22     :6: GTO 44
 :7: CLX 37     :7: RDN 31     :7: +   33     :7: 0   00
 :8: X=Y 50     :8: X   36     :8: CLX 37     :8: 3   03
 :9: 8   10     :9: CLX 37     :9: RDN 31     :9: SFL 54
 :a: 9   11     :a: X>Y 53     :a: FMT 42     :a: UP  27
 :b: 1   01     :b: EEX 26     :b: DN  25     :b: |Y| 55
 :c: 0   00     :c: +   33     :c: GTO 44     :c: b   14
 :d: X   36     :d: RUP 22     :d: 0   00     :d: UP  27
```

## |92| WRITE

This subroutine plots output data in the form of numbers, letters, and other symbols, on the answer sheet.

```
0:0: YTO 40    2:0: 4   04    4:0: 2   02
 :1: d   17     :1: 4   04     :1: 4   04
 :2: 1   01     :2: FMT 42     :2: 4   04
 :3: 5   05     :3: π   56     :3: FMT 42
 :4: XTO 23     :4: XTO 23     :4: YTO 40
 :5: b   14     :5: e   12     :5: f   15
 :6: f   15     :6: 9   11     :6: UP  27
 :7: UP  27     :7: 1   01     :7: 2   02
 :8: 2   02     :8: FMT 42     :8: 4   04
 :9: 4   04     :9: GTO 44     :9: 5   05
 :a: 3   03     :a: 3   03     :a: FMT 42
 :b: FMT 42     :b: UP  27     :b: YTO 40
 :c: YTO 40     :c: CLX 37     :c: 2   02
 :d: e   12     :d: IFG 43     :d: 4   04
1:0: UP  27    3:0: .   21    5:0: 3   03
 :1: 2   02     :1: 5   05     :1: FMT 42
 :2: 4   04     :2: -   34     :2: π   56
 :3: 2   02     :3: b   14     :3: XTO 23
 :4: FMT 42     :4: X   36     :4: f   15
 :5: YTO 40     :5: DN  25     :5: 2   02
 :6: 2   02     :6: AC+ 60     :6: 4   04
 :7: 4   04     :7: RCL 61     :7: 2   02
 :8: 5   05     :8: FMT 42     :8: FMT 42
 :9: FMT 42     :9: UP  27     :9: π   56
 :a: π   56     :a: DN  25     :a: XTO 23
 :b: XTO 23     :b: DN  25     :b: e   12
 :c: f   15     :c: e   12     :c: FMT 42
 :d: 2   02     :d: UP  27     :d: END 46
```

## |93| WRITE INFLECTION

```
0:0: 9   11    2:0: 1   01    4:0: 8   10
 :1: X=Y 50     :1: 5   05     :1: 3   03
 :2: 2   02     :2: 4   04     :2: 3   03
 :3: 9   11     :3: 6   06     :3: 4   04
 :4: f   15     :4: 2   02     :4: 9   11
 :5: UP  27     :5: 8   10     :5: 9   11
 :6: 1   01     :6: GTO 44     :6: 1   01
 :7: 0   00     :7: 5   05     :7: 6   06
 :8: X   36     :8: 2   02     :8: GTO 44
 :9: DN  25     :9: f   15     :9: 5   05
 :a: UP  27     :a: UP  27     :a: 9   11
 :b: INT 64     :b: 1   01     :b: 1   01
 :c: -   34     :c: 0   00     :c: 6   06
 :d: YTO 40     :d: X   36     :d: 6   06
1:0: e   12    3:0: DN  25    5:0: 4   04
 :1: UP  27     :1: UP  27     :1: 3   03
 :2: 8   10     :2: INT 64     :2: UP  27
 :3: X=Y 50     :3: -   34     :3: e   12
 :4: 1   01     :4: YTO 40     :4: XTO 23
 :5: d   17     :5: e   12     :5: f   15
 :6: 7   07     :6: UP  27     :6: GTO 44
 :7: 2   02     :7: 9   11     :7: 5   05
 :8: 6   06     :8: X=Y 50     :8: a   13
 :9: 4   04     :9: 4   04     :9: UP  27
 :a: GTO 44     :a: b   14     :a: FMT 42
 :b: 5   05     :b: 7   07     :b: END 46
 :c: 9   11     :c: 2   02
 :d: 7   07     :d: 2   02
```

## |94| WRITE LITERAL

Subroutine 94 is similar to subroutine 90 except that it is used to produce literals rather than numerals. Used in conjunction with subroutines 92 and 93, it supplies the letters A, B, C, D, E, F, G and the inflections ♭♭, ♭, ♯, and x. In utilizing this subroutine, the user need not specify the characters to be written; this can be accomplished by orthographic synthesis or transliteration.

```
0:0: f   15    2:0: 9   11    4:0: 4   04    6:0: 5   05    8:0: 3   03
 :1: UP  27     :1: 2   02     :1: X=Y 50     :1: 6   06     :1: 1   01
 :2: 1   01     :2: FMT 42     :2: 6   06     :2: 3   03     :2: 4   04
 :3: EEX 26     :3: GTO 44     :3: 9   11     :3: 1   01     :3: 5   05
 :4: 1   01     :4: f   15     :4: 3   03     :4: 7   07     :4: 4   04
 :5: 2   02     :5: UP  27     :5: X=Y 50     :5: 9   11     :5: 7   07
 :6: DIV 35     :6: 1   01     :6: 6   06     :6: GTO 44     :6: 9   11
 :7: YTO 40     :7: 0   00     :7: 0   00     :7: 9   11     :7: GTO 44
 :8: f   15     :8: X   36     :8: 2   02     :8: 4   04     :8: 9   11
 :9: CLX 37     :9: GTO 44     :9: X=Y 50     :9: 7   07     :9: 4   04
 :a: X=Y 50     :a: 0   00     :a: 5   05     :a: 1   01     :a: 1   01
 :b: 9   11     :b: 7   07     :b: 7   07     :b: 2   02     :b: 7   07
 :c: 8   10     :c: CLX 37     :c: 1   01     :c: 6   06     :c: 9   11
 :d: DN  25     :d: X=Y 50     :d: 4   04     :d: 8   10     :d: 5   05
1:0: UP  27    3:0: 2   02    5:0: 5   05    7:0: 7   07    9:0: 4   04
 :1: INT 64     :1: 4   04     :1: 4   04     :1: GTO 44     :1: 6   06
 :2: -   34     :2: 7   07     :2: 7   07     :2: 9   11     :2: 3   03
 :3: YTO 40     :3: X=Y 50     :3: 9   11     :3: 4   04     :3: 1   01
 :4: f   15     :4: 8   10     :4: GTO 44     :4: 1   01     :4: UP  27
 :5: UP  27     :5: a   13     :5: 9   11     :5: 4   04     :5: GTO 44
 :6: 8   10     :6: 6   06     :6: 4   04     :6: 6   06     :6: 2   02
 :7: X>Y 53     :7: X=Y 50     :7: 3   03     :7: 4   04     :7: 0   00
 :8: 2   02     :8: 8   10     :8: 1   01     :8: 7   07     :8: FMT 42
 :9: c   16     :9: 0   00     :9: 7   07     :9: 9   11     :9: END 46
 :a: 9   11     :a: 5   05     :a: 9   11     :a: 3   03
 :b: 3   03     :b: X=Y 50     :b: GTO 44     :b: GTO 44
 :c: FMT 42     :c: 7   07     :c: 9   11     :c: 9   11
 :d: GTO 44     :d: 4   04     :d: 4   04     :d: 4   04
```

## |95| CLEAR AND STORE

Program 95, which calls upon subroutine 99, is the basic routine for loading music data in coded-decimal form. (Once loaded, the data can be recorded on magnetic cards for simple card reinsertion, using program 49.) The calculator extended memory, plotter, and printer should all be turned on, the "print X" key pushed, and the decimal wheel set on six. After loading routines 99 through 70, in that order, starting at extended memory register 0, the data file and working area are to be cleared by a manually keyed 95 FMT GTO, GTO 00, CNT. When the clearing action has been completed, the program execution will stop with a display of the number 3.333 333 333 15 in the X register. This message indicates that the machine is ready for the next assignment.

At this time the operator is to perform a manual GTO 10, CNT; the machine again will stop. This break is accompanied by an audible click of the plotter pen. This click is the signal that the calculator is ready to accept a piece of data. The data are read in, one coded literal at a time, using the keyboard input unit. After each readin, another click will sound.

To conserve limited memory space of the calculator for program steps, only registers 170 to 227 inclusive are devoted to data. After each register is filled its contents are printed electrostatically. Following the readin of the last component, zeros must be entered until there is another print, to assure synchronization. By making minor adjustments to some of the routines, segmenting the data into blocks, and then overlaying these blocks in the data file, any reasonable number of components can be accommodated. If the musical data file is inadvertently over filled, the value π appears in the X register as a diagnostic and the machine comes to an error stop.

```
0:0: CLR 20
 :1:  1  01
 :2:  9  11
 :3:  0  00
 :4: FMT 42
 :5:  X  36
 :6: UP  27
 :7:  1  01
 :8:  +  33
 :9: DN  25
 :a: GTO 44
 :b:  0  00
 :c:  4  04
 :d: PSE 57
1:0:  2  02
 :1:  0  00
 :2:  0  00
 :3: XEY 30
 :4:  2  02
 :5:  4  04
 :6:  7  07
 :7: FMT 42
 :8: YTO 40
 :9:  9  11
 :a:  9  11
 :b: FMT 42
 :c: GTO 44
 :d: END 46
```

## |96| FETCH LITERAL

```
0:0:  9  11    2:0:  +  33    4:0: YTO 40    6:0:  2  02
 :1:  7  07     :1: GTO 44     :1:  e  12     :1:  4  04
 :2: FMT 42     :2:  0  00     :2: GTO 44     :2:  6  06
 :3: GTO 44     :3:  a  13     :3:  6  06     :3: FMT 42
 :4:  c  16     :4: XTO 23     :4:  c  16     :4: YTO 40
 :5: UP  27     :5:  f  15     :5:  2  02     :5:  1  01
 :6: CLX 37     :6:  9  11     :6:  4  04     :6: UP  27
 :7: X=Y 50     :7:  7  07     :7:  6  06     :7:  2  02
 :8:  2  02     :8: FMT 42     :8: FMT 42     :8:  4  04
 :9:  4  04     :9: GTO 44     :9:  π  56     :9:  7  07
 :a: YTO 40     :a:  c  16     :a: UP  27     :a: FMT 42
 :b:  f  15     :b: UP  27     :b: CLX 37     :b:  -  34
 :c:  9  11     :c:  1  01     :c: X=Y 50     :c: FMT 42
 :d:  7  07     :d:  0  00     :d:  5  05     :d: END 46
1:0: FMT 42    3:0:  X  36    5:0:  b  14
 :1: GTO 44     :1: YTO 40     :1:  1  01
 :2:  c  16     :2:  e  12     :2:  -  34
 :3: UP  27     :3:  9  11     :3:  2  02
 :4:  8  10     :4:  7  07     :4:  4  04
 :5: X>Y 53     :5: FMT 42     :5:  6  06
 :6:  4  04     :6: GTO 44     :6: FMT 42
 :7:  5  05     :7:  c  16     :7: YTO 40
 :8:  f  15     :8: UP  27     :8: GTO 44
 :9: UP  27     :9:  e  12     :9:  6  06
 :a:  1  01     :a:  +  33     :a:  c  16
 :b:  0  00     :b:  2  02     :b:  1  01
 :c:  X  36     :c:  4  04     :c:  2  02
 :d:  c  16     :d: DIV 35     :d: UP  27
```

## |97| STEP COORDINATES

This subroutine moves the component index pointer to the position of the next literal in the string.

```
0:0:  2  02    2:0:  d  17    4:0:  2  02
 :1:  4  04     :1:  -  34     :1: X>Y 53
 :2:  6  06     :2:  1  01     :2:  5  05
 :3: FMT 42     :3:  0  00     :3:  4  04
 :4:  π  56     :4:  X  36     :4:  1  01
 :5: UP  27     :5: YTO 40     :5: UP  27
 :6:  1  01     :6:  c  16     :6:  2  02
 :7:  2  02     :7: YE  24     :7:  4  04
 :8:  -  34     :8:  9  11     :8:  7  07
 :9: YTO 40     :9:  1  01     :9: FMT 42
 :a:  9  11     :a:  +  33     :a:  +  33
 :b:  2  02     :b: YTO 40     :b: CLX 37
 :c:  4  04     :c:  9  11     :c: UP  27
 :d:  7  07     :d: CLX 37     :d:  2  02
1:0: FMT 42    3:0: X>Y 53    5:0:  4  04
 :1:  π  56     :1:  1  01     :1:  6  06
 :2: FMT 42     :2:  5  05     :2: FMT 42
 :3:  π  56     :3:  1  01     :3:  X  36
 :4: XTO 23     :4: UP  27     :4: FMT 42
 :5:  d  17     :5:  2  02     :5: END 46
 :6: UP  27     :6:  4  04
 :7:  1  01     :7:  6  06
 :8:  0  00     :8: FMT 42
 :9: DIV 35     :9:  +  33
 :a: DN  25     :a: FMT 42
 :b: UP  27     :b:  π  56
 :c: INT 64     :c: UP  27
 :d: XTO 23     :d:  1  01
```

## |98| PACK DATA

Subroutine 98 serves as the kernel of subroutine 99. Recall that a 0 input followed immediately by a CNT means that the next item of data is to be interpreted as a duration value. The calculator must receive such a value and another CNT before the readin of a new data frame can begin.

```
0:0:  1   01   2:0:  π   56   4:0:  3   03
 :1:  0   00    :1: XEY  30    :1:  8   10
 :2: UP   27    :2:  1   01    :2: X=Y  50
 :3:  2   02    :3:  2   02    :3:  π   56
 :4:  4   04    :4:  -   34    :4: STP  41
 :5:  7   07    :5: CLX  37    :5: CLX  37
 :6: FMT  42    :6: X>Y  53    :6: XEY  30
 :7:  π   56    :7:  4   04    :7:  2   02
 :8: FMT  42    :8:  c   16    :8:  4   04
 :9:  π   56    :9:  2   02    :9:  6   06
 :a:  X   36    :a:  4   04    :a: FMT  42
 :b: DN   25    :b:  7   07    :b: YTO  40
 :c:  +   33    :c: FMT  42    :c: FMT  42
 :d:  2   02    :d:  π   56    :d: END  46
1:0:  4   04   3:0: FMT  42
 :1:  7   07    :1:  π   56
 :2: FMT  42    :2: PNT  45
 :3:  π   56    :3:  1   01
 :4: FMT  42    :4: XEY  30
 :5: YTO  40    :5:  2   02
 :6:  1   01    :6:  4   04.
 :7: XEY  30    :7:  7   07
 :8:  2   02    :8: FMT  42
 :9:  4   04    :9:  +   33
 :a:  6   06    :a: FMT  42
 :b: FMT  42    :b:  π   56
 :c:  +   33    :c: XEY  30
 :d: FMT  42    :d:  2   02
```

## |99| PACK DATA

A convenient internal coding scheme is based upon the following correspondence between duration values and two-digit decimal numbers:

```
0:0: CLX  37   2:0:  d   17   4:0: STP  41   6:0:  0   00
 :1: UP   27    :1: UP   27    :1: XTO  23    :1:  X   36
 :2: FMT  42    :2: CLX  37    :2:  f   15    :2: DN   25
 :3: DN   25    :3: X=Y  50    :3: UP   27    :3:  -   34
 :4: FMT  42    :4:  7   07    :4:  2   02    :4: DN   25
 :5: UP   27    :5:  0   00    :5:  .   21    :5: INT  64
 :6: STP  41    :6:  9   11    :6:  4   04    :6: UP   27
 :7: XTO  23    :7:  8   10    :7:  1   01    :7:  9   11
 :8:  c   16    :8: FMT  42    :8:  X   36    :8:  8   10
 :9: UP   27    :9: GTO  44    :9: DN   25    :9: FMT  42
 :a:  1   01    :a:  b   14    :a: INT  64    :a: GTO  44
 :b: EEX  26    :b: UP   27    :b: XTO  23    :b: GTO  44
 :c:  1   01    :c:  1   01    :c:  e   12    :c:  0   00
 :d:  2   02    :d:  0   00    :d: UP   27    :d:  0   00
1:0: DIV  35   3:0:  X   36   5:0:  9   11   7:0:  b   14
 :1: YTO  40    :1: GTO  44    :1:  8   10    :1: UP   27
 :2:  b   14    :2:  1   01    :2: FMT  42    :2: CLX  37
 :3: CLX  37    :3:  7   07    :3: GTO  44    :3: X=Y  50
 :4: X=Y  50    :4:  9   11    :4:  f   15    :4:  0   00
 :5:  3   03    :5:  8   10    :5: UP   27    :5:  0   00
 :6:  4   04    :6: FMT  42    :6:  2   02    :6: GTO  44
 :7: DN   25    :7: GTO  44    :7:  4   04    :7:  2   02
 :8: UP   27    :8: CLX  37    :8:  .   21    :8:  c   16
 :9: INT  64    :9: UP   27    :9:  1   01    :9: FMT  42
 :a:  -   34    :a: FMT  42    :a:  X   36    :a: END  46
 :b: YTO  40    :b: DN   25    :b:  e   12
 :c:  b   14    :c: FMT  42    :c: UP   27
 :d: XTO  23    :d: UP   27    :d:  1   01
```

| CODE | NOTE |
|---|---|
| 03 | 32nd |
| 06 | 16th |
| 09 | dotted 16th |
| 12 | 8th |
| 18 | dotted 8th |
| 24 | quarter |
| 36 | dotted quarter |
| 48 | half |
| 72 | dotted half |
| 96 | whole. |

## EXERCISES

**9.18** The analytical objective in running subroutine 85 is clear: calculate the span of any given literal notation. After determining how this is accomplished, by drawing a flowchart, find again the spans of the characteristic Busoni scales.

**9.19** Turn to subroutine 94 and trace the digit strings that appear in program steps 4c-53, 57-5a, 60-65, 69-70, 74-7a, 80-86, and 8a-93 on the numerical portion of the keyboard shown in Fig. 9.9 to discover their meaning. Modify this subroutine so that the new version will write lower case rather than upper case letters.

## PRINCIPLE OF SUPERPOSITION

The following plausibility argument can be given for basing a music analysis methodology on vector addition. To some degree, the vectorial approach to tonality is supported by the observation that different sound waves can mingle in the same concert hall without serious mutual disturbance. The possibility of superposing undulations of different frequencies and wavelengths is the result of the linear nature of sound. The principle of superposition is a mathematical property of all physical phenomena governed by what are called **linear differential equations.** The formula for a vibrating string satisfies this principle, which also applies to other mechanical and electrical oscillations and to light waves, as well as to sound vibrations. In essence, the motion $r(t)$ resulting by a combined force

$$F(t) = F_1(t) + F_2(t) + \dots + F_n(t)$$

is the sum

$$r(t) = r_1(t) + r_2(t) + \dots + r_n(t)$$

of the motions $r_i(t)$ that the system would have if each force $F_i(t)$ were to act separately. The summation

$$v = \sum_{i=1}^{n} v_i$$

involves a superposition principle for tonality, which states that the resultant tonality is the vector sum of the individual tonalities produced by the various tones in the chord. This supposition carries within it the implication that the sensations of tonality that pure tones produce can be duplicated by combinations of such sensations.

## EARS VERSUS EYES

It is well known that the subjective response to the color of light depends on the frequency of vibration of the light. Broadly speaking, the information the eye receives from a colored object is contained in a bundle of light rays of different wavelengths. Any light can be considered as being made up of a superposition of pure colors, just as any sound can be considered as a superposition of pure tones. Experiments with rotating color disks show that red and green form yellow, green and violet form blue, and red and violet form green. Two colors are called "complementary" when together they give the sensation of white light. It is natural to wonder why the trained human ear can pick out the component tones of a chord, yet the human eye cannot seem to learn to detect the component colors in a sample mixture. This question is important for a variety of reasons. First, it illustrates how the principle of superposition might be used to simplify the analysis of tonal mixtures. Second, it furnishes a basis for further experimentation seeking evidence to support the claim that ears may have an innate sensitivity to tonal color mixtures, as much as the eyes do, but that this ability is masked because of the ear's superior ability to act as a Fourier analyzer. It is conjectured that this more primitive sensitivity does exist and forms the basis for the sense of key, which is so important for a keen appreciation of tonality and modulation.

## CONCLUSION

In this book, much emphasis has been placed on the use of computers as tools to assist the music analyst. The first goal of the study has been to develop practical, but theoretically supportable, concepts to permit the average music theoretician to make numerical measurements of the properties of those musical compositions that exhibit a high coordination of voices or have well established keys. The second goal has been to build a model, or at least to suggest a mathematical interpretation, for both tonality and modulation, within the framework of these elementary concepts. The third goal has been to relate the harmonic and contrapuntal aspects of part-writing to a geometrical description of the musical composition under consideration in terms of tonal displacement, tonality, and modulation. The fourth goal has been to build a computer methodology to embrace all possible modes of musical expression, whether diatonic or chromatic, that are compatible with the twelve-tone equitempered system. The fifth goal has been to present a detailed listing of the computer subroutines and programs implementing this methodology, in a straight-forward, precise language. For this purpose, reverse Polish notation has proven highly satisfactory.

The preceding chapters have dealt at length with the theory of tonality and questions closely connected with it--musical orthography, enharmonic change, modulation to new keys, and so forth. This treatment has been largely on the basis of a vectorial model, which regards the twelve primitive tones as unit vectors positionally identified with the twelfth roots of unity, and operated with according to the rules of either vector algebra or complex arithmetic.

The objective of this study has been to develop a computer methodology and to derive a means of graphical display for a total composition, exposing its tonal organization in plan view. It is important from the first to recognize some limitations of this treatment. Perhaps the most obvious deficiency is that a musical utterance is by no means completely specified by only a few variables, namely, displacement, tonality, and modulation. In manuscript analysis, no allowance has been made for tone color, or for decay characteristics of instrumental tones. But maybe this is reasonable because tonality and modulation are fairly independent of the choice of performing instruments. It is suggested that any vectorial representation is at best just a reasonable approximation. Even the more complicated approach taken in performance analysis, discussed briefly, but certainly not a central topic of this book, cannot possibly account for all the many aural attributes of sound or for individual listener's responses to them. The degree of approximation, however, can be improved by adding refinements to the model. In summary, there is a great gap between the kinematic description of a musical composition and its complete psychoacoustic characterization.

The firm conclusions that can be drawn from the present study are significant, but relatively limited in view of the restricted range of music material and the small number of examples. The proposed theory should be tested. The vectorial model appears to offer a practical tool for musicians both for learning and writing music. It also may stimulate thinking in the related field of musical psychology.

As an example of a possible experiment, consider the claim that the human ear can judge whether or not two harmonies are of like tonality. This statement is clearly a quantitative prediction that is suitable for experimental verification or refutation by a listening jury using a well designed experiment with proper controls. In essence, the test situation would require many people of various backgrounds to make relative identifications of membership in tonality classes. Each subject could be asked to judge whether a particular sample harmony is closer to a standard harmony with which to make comparisons or to a second standard that is a known distance away from the first in a specific direction in the tonality plane. The results would probably be suitable for reduction using modern techniques for multidimensional scaling.

In a similar way, a variety of questions involving musical parameters might be investigated. Whether the outcomes of such experiments would be useful to musical science will depend, of course, on whether they help to describe the musical listening experience. Certainly much can be accomplished. After all, musical applications of computers are still in their infancy. Without doubt, computer analysis and synthesis of musical forms will become entrenched in the work habits of future society, because of the growing number of college students who are interested in computers and who are being required to use them. But can a computer methodology ever be definitive? Obviously not, since new musical concepts continually arise, as well as new ways of thinking about old concepts.

## REFERENCES

[1] Thorvald Otterström, *A Theory of Modulation* (The University of Chicago Press, Chicago, Illinois, 1935) pp. 46,47.

[2] H.C. Longuet-Higgens and M.J. Steedman, "On Interpreting Bach," *Machine Intelligence* 6 (American Elsevier Publishing Co., New York, 1971)

**NOTE:** The programming language employed for writing the computer software in this book is referred to as **Reverse Polish Notation** (RPN). This language, a variant of Polish-prefix (parenthesis-free) notation in logic, was chosen not only because of its widespread popularity, but also because of its close structural relationship to internal machine language, and its appropriateness for the pedagogical task at hand.

# Index

(con.) C



D



E

S



(con.)S



T